Praise for *Magnifico*

"This portrait of the 'uncrowned ruler of Florence' does great justice to this most intriguing of all Renaissance princes. Unger's diligent scholarship combines with an impelling narrative to give a full-bodied flavor of the splendors as well as the horrors of Lorenzo's remarkable reign."

—Ross King, author of *Brunelleschi's Dome* and *Machiavelli*

"A meticulous and entertaining study of one of the great characters of the Italian Renaissance, who ruled Florence during one of the most fascinating periods of Italy's turbulent history. Packed with incident and incisive research, this work succeeds in being both popular and scholarly."

—Paul Strathern, author of *The Medici: Godfathers of the Renaissance*

"Dazzling. . . . From the first sentence, *Magnifico* transports the reader to 15th-century Florence, a place of matchless splendor, both natural and man-made. Unger mines a rich lode of sources. . . . The result is an indelible personal profile and an enthralling account of both the glories and brutalities of the era."

—David Takami, *The Seattle Times*

"An excellent biography that deftly weaves Lorenzo's story with the wider saga of politics and culture in both Florence and the other Italian city-states. . . . An outstanding chronicle of the man and his time."

—*Booklist*

"This brilliant book is almost as much the biography of a city as of a man; one of its strengths is an ability to convey the cultural, political and sexual ambiance of 15th-century Florence with a rare clarity. . . . This rich, well-written book should be essential reading for anyone who is interested in the golden age of the Florentine renaissance, in Italian history of the period and, of course, in Lorenzo himself."

—Sarah Bradford, *The Spectator* (UK)

"A smart, highly readable and abundantly researched book. . . . Renaissance Florence—where wealthy aristocrats rubbed shoulders with the poor on narrow city streets and whose art and intellectual life dazzled Europe—is itself an intriguing character, proving Unger's mastery over his facts."

—*Publishers Weekly*

ALSO BY MILES J. UNGER

The Watercolors of Winslow Homer

MAGNIFICO

THE BRILLIANT LIFE AND VIOLENT TIMES OF LORENZO DE' MEDICI

Miles J. Unger

Simon & Schuster Paperbacks

NEW YORK   LONDON   TORONTO   SYDNEY

SIMON & SCHUSTER PAPERBACKS
A Division of Simon & Schuster, Inc.
1230 Avenue of the Americas
New York, NY 10020

First Simon & Schuster trade paperbacks edition May 2009

SIMON & SCHUSTER PAPERBACKS and colophon are registered trademarks of
Simon & Schuster, Inc.

For information about special discounts for bulk purchases,
please contact Simon & Schuster Special Sales at
1-800-456-6798 or business@simonandschuster.com.

Designed by Paul Dippolito
Maps by Paul J. Pugliese

Manufactured in the United States of America

5   7   9   10   8   6   4

The Library of Congress has Cataloged the hardcover as follows:

Unger, Miles.
Magnifico : the brilliant life and violent times of Lorenzo de' Medici / Miles J. Unger.
p.   cm.
Includes bibliographical references and index.
1. Medici, Lorenzo de', 1449–1492. 2. Florence (Italy)—History—1421–1737.
3. Statesmen—Italy—Florence—Biography. 4. Intellectuals—Italy—
Florence—Biography. 5. Florence (Italy)—Biography. I. Title.
DG737.9.U54 2008
945'.51105092—dc22
[B]   2007027669
ISBN-13: 978-0-7432-5434-2
ISBN-10:   0-7432-5434-1
ISBN-13: 978-0-7432-5435-9 (pbk)
ISBN-10:   0-7432-5435-X (pbk)

In memory of my mother, Bernate,
whose adventurous spirit lies behind this book

CONTENTS

CONTENTS

LIST OF ILLUSTRATIONS

Italy in the 15th Century

Florence
Milan
Naples
Papal Territory
Venice

FRANCE

DUCHY OF SAVOY

OTTOMAN EMPIRE

•Milan   •Venice

Genoa   Bologna   DUCHY OF FERRARA

Sarzana   Imola   ROMAGNA

Lucca

Pisa   •Florence   •Urbino

Ligurian Sea

Siena   THE PAPAL STATES

Tiber

Adriatic Sea

ITALY

Corsica (Genoa)

•Rome

•Naples

Sardinia (Spain)

Tyrrhenian Sea

Mediterranean Sea

•Palermo

Sicily

AFRICA

N
W   E
S

0   100 miles
0   100 kilometers

MAP BY PAUL J. PUGLIESE

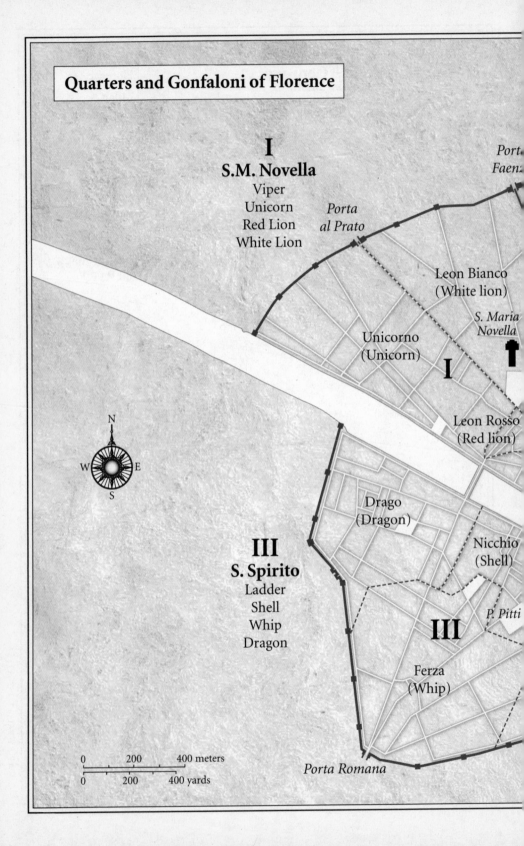

Quarters and Gonfaloni of Florence

I
S.M. Novella
Viper
Unicorn
Red Lion
White Lion

III
S. Spirito
Ladder
Shell
Whip
Dragon

Porta al Prato

Port Faenz

Leon Bianco
(White lion)

S. Maria Novella

I

Unicorno
(Unicorn)

Leon Rosso
(Red lion)

Drago
(Dragon)

Nicchio
(Shell)

P. Pitti

III

Ferza
(Whip)

Porta Romana

N
W E
S

| 0 | 200 | 400 meters |
| 0 | 200 | 400 yards |

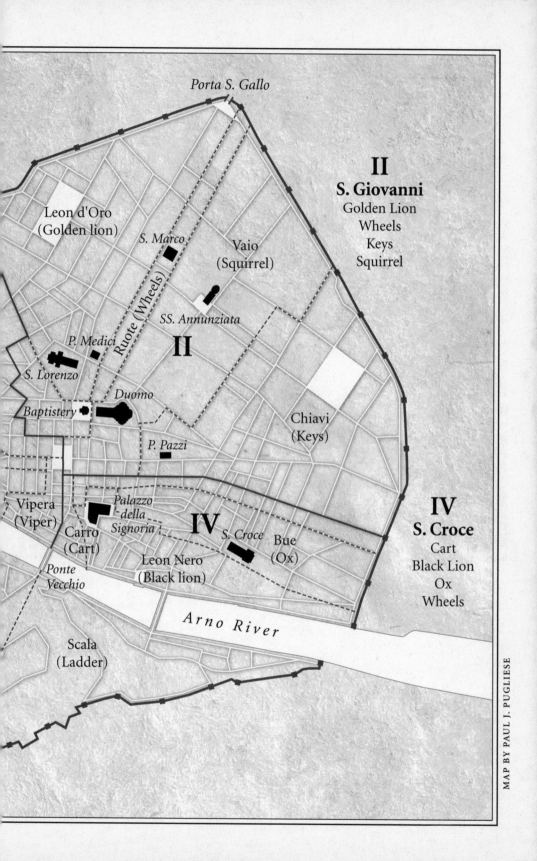

Porta S. Gallo

II
S. Giovanni
Golden Lion
Wheels
Keys
Squirrel

Leon d'Oro
(Golden lion)

S. Marco

Vaio
(Squirrel)

Ruote (Wheels)

SS. Annunziata

II

P. Medici

S. Lorenzo

Duomo

Baptistery

P. Pazzi

Chiavi
(Keys)

Vipera
(Viper)

Palazzo
della
Signoria

IV

S. Croce

Bue
(Ox)

IV
S. Croce
Cart
Black Lion
Ox
Wheels

Carro
(Cart)

Leon Nero
(Black lion)

Ponte
Vecchio

Arno River

Scala
(Ladder)

MAP BY PAUL J. PUGLIESE

The Medici Villa at Careggi (Miles Unger)

I. THE ROAD FROM CAREGGI

"[I]t is necessary now for you to be a man and not a boy; be so in words, deeds and manners."

—PIERO DE' MEDICI TO LORENZO, MAY 11, 1465

LATE ON THE MORNING OF AUGUST 27, 1466, A SMALL group of horsemen left the Medici villa at Careggi and turned onto the road to Florence. It was a journey of three miles from the villa to the city walls along a meandering path that descended through the hills that rise above Florence to the north. Dark cypresses and hedges of fragrant laurel lined the road, providing welcome shade in the summer heat. Through the trees the riders could catch from time to time a glimpse of the Arno River flashing silver in the sun.

On any other day this would have been a relaxing journey of an hour or so, the heavy August air encouraging a leisurely pace, the beauties of the Tuscan countryside inspiring laughter and conversation among the young men. "There is in my opinion no region more sweet or pleasing in Italy or in any other part of Europe than that wherein Florence is placed," wrote a Venetian visitor, "for Florence is situated in a plain surrounded on all sides by hills and mountains. . . . And the hills are fertile, cultivated, pleasant, all bearing beautiful and sumptuous palaces built at great expense and boasting all manner of fine features: gardens, woods, fountains, fish ponds, pools and much else besides, with views that resemble paintings."

But today, the mood was somber. The men peered nervously from side to side, fingering the pommels of their swords. Gnarled olive trees, ancient and silver-leaved, hugged terraces cut into the slopes, and parallel rows of vines glistening with purple grapes gave the hills a tidy geometry worthy of a fresco by Fra Angelico.

Taking the lead was a young man who rode with the easy grace of a born horseman. His appearance was distinctive, though not at first glance

1

particularly attractive. Above an athletic frame, bony and long-limbed, was a rough-hewn face. His nose, which was flattened and turned to the side as if it had once been broken, gave him something of the look of a street brawler, and the prominent jaw that caused his lower lip to jut out pugnaciously did nothing to soften this impression. Beneath heavy brows peered black, piercing eyes more suggestive of animal cunning than refined intelligence. Dark hair, parted in the middle, hung down to his shoulders, providing a stern frame to the irregular features. Even a close friend, Niccolò Valori, was forced to admit that "nature had been a step-mother to him with regard to his personal appearance. [N]onetheless," continued Valori, "when it came to the inner man she truly acted as a kindly mother. . . . [A]lthough his face was not handsome it was full of such dignity as to command respect."*

This homely face belonged to Lorenzo, the seventeen-year-old son and heir of Piero de' Medici. Since the death of Lorenzo's grandfather Cosimo, two years earlier, Piero had taken over the far-flung Medici banking empire, a position that made him one of the richest men in Europe. But it was not wealth alone that made the Medici name famous throughout Europe. The Medici, though they possessed no titles, were regarded by those unfamiliar with the intricacies of local politics as kings in all but name of the independent Florentine Republic, which, though small compared with the great states of Europe, dazzled the civilized world through the brilliance of her art and the vitality of her intellectual life.† Not many generations removed from their peasant origins, the Medici spent lavishly on beautifying their city in the expectation that at least some of its glamour would rub off on its first family.

It was Cosimo who had parlayed his apparently inexhaustible fortune

---

* Lorenzo's homeliness was proverbial among Florentines. When Machiavelli was describing to a friend an encounter with a particularly hideous prostitute, he could think of no better insult than to compare her appearance to that of Lorenzo de' Medici.

† Florence's population reached a peak of nearly 100,000 in the middle of the fourteenth century, but after the Black Death of 1348 was reduced to less than half that. In the fifteenth century, her population probably never reached 50,000. The fields and open spaces that remained inside the city walls throughout Lorenzo's lifetime testify to the fact that it took centuries for the population to recover.

into a position of unprecedented authority in the state. On his tombstone in the family church of San Lorenzo were the words *Pater Patriae* ("Father of His Country"), bestowed on him by a grateful public for his wise stewardship and generous patronage of the city's civic and religious institutions. Cosimo had dominated the councils of government through the force of his personality and his willingness to open his own coffers when the state was short of cash. Florentines, like modern-day Americans, had a healthy respect for money and seemed to feel that those who showed a talent for amassing it must possess other, less visible virtues. Cosimo rarely held high political office, happy to let others enjoy the pomp of life in the *Palazzo della Signoria* as long as important decisions were left in his hands.* For a time the gratitude Florentines felt toward Cosimo earned for his son Piero the allegiance of a majority of the citizens, and, until recent troubles, it had been generally assumed that this crucial position as the leading figure in the *reggimento*—the regime that really ran Florence, whoever temporarily occupied the government palace—would one day pass to the young man now guiding his small band along the road to Florence.

On this August morning, however, the fate of the Medici and their government seemed to teeter on a knife's edge. The ancient constitution of the republic, in which the governing of the state had been shared widely among the city's wealthy and middle-class citizens, had been undermined by this single family's rise to prominence.† The heavy-handed tactics they used to win and to wield power had stirred up resentment as once proud families saw themselves reduced to little more than servants of the Medici court.

---

* This seat of the Florentine government went by many names. The *Palazzo* (Palace) *della Signoria* refers to the capital's role as home to the city's highest governing body, the *Signoria* (lordship), a council of eight men who, along with their leader, the *Gonfaloniere di Giustizia* (Standard-Bearer of Justice), constituted the chief executive of the state. These men, elected on a bimonthly basis, were also referred to as the Priors; hence the capital also went by the name the Palace of the Priors. Florentines also often referred to the building simply as the Palazzo Vecchio, the Old Palace.

† Though Florentine democracy was more restrictive than ours in the sense that it denied the franchise to many of its inhabitants—including the unskilled laborers who made up a majority of the population—in some ways it was more inclusive. Those with full

(*Continued*)

But now a group of rich and influential men saw an opportunity to strike back. The various factions that normally made Florentine politics a lively affair had been secretly arming themselves for months. Rumors of foreign armies on the march—a different one for each side in the contest—increased the general paranoia until it seemed as if the smallest incident might touch off a general conflagration.

On one side were the Medici loyalists, the Party of the Plain (named for the site of the Medici palace on low-lying land on the north bank of the Arno), who favored the current system, which they claimed had brought decades of peace and prosperity. On the other was the Party of the Hill, centered on Luca Pitti's palace on the high ground to the south, who pointed out that Medici ascendance had been purchased at the expense of the people's traditional liberty. The most visible figures in the rebellion were former members of Cosimo's inner circle whose democratic zeal, not much in evidence in recent years, was rekindled by the humiliating prospect of having to take orders from his son. Few of them, in fact, had sterling reformist credentials. Most had connived with Cosimo in his systematic undermining of republican institutions, but now they adopted as their own the slogan *"Popolo e Libertà!"* (the "People and Liberty!").

Discontent with the despotic tendencies of the government was not the only factor precipitating the current crisis. The perceived weakness of the fifty-year-old Piero contributed to a general sense that the regime was not

citizenship, including many artisans and shopkeepers, were actually expected to participate in their own government, sitting on some of the many committees and assemblies that met in the Palace of the Priors. Florentines were not content to vote once every two years and allow their elected representatives to make decisions for them. Even when a citizen was not serving in elected office, he could be certain that among his friends and neighbors were many in a position to affect his life for good or ill. One peculiarity of the political system that had evolved in the Middle Ages was its reliance on election to office by lot. Periodic "scrutinies" were used to determine all those citizens eligible for office. These names were then placed in purses and drawn at random when an office needed to be filled. Terms for the most important offices were made deliberately brief so that no one could accumulate too much power—for the *Signoria*, the chief executive, only two months. It was a system that guaranteed that each citizen would hold many offices during his lifetime. The Medici controlled the system largely by screening the names of those entered into the electoral purses and removing those they deemed untrustworthy. (See Note on the Government of Florence for further discussion, also Chapters V and IX.)

only corrupt but, perhaps even worse, adrift. Even before Cosimo's death in 1464 the influential Agnolo Acciaiuoli, now one of the leaders of the Hill, complained that Cosimo and Piero had become "cold men, whom illness and old age have reduced to such cowardice that they avoid anything that might cause them trouble or worry." The citizens of Florence, said the uncharitable Niccolò Machiavelli some years later, "did not have much confidence in [Cosimo's] son Piero, for notwithstanding that he was a good man, nonetheless, they judged that . . . he was too infirm and new in the state."

Even many of Piero's supporters shared that gloomy assessment. From his youth, Piero (known to history as *il Gottoso*, the Gouty) had been plagued by the family ailment that rendered him for long periods a virtual prisoner in his own house. It was a disease that affected not only his body but his temper. The architect Filarete wrote in his biographical sketch of the Medici leader, "those who have [gout] are usually rather acid and sharp in their manner," but that while "few can bear its pains . . . [Piero] bears it with all the patience he can." Piero also lacked his father's common touch, the earthy humor that endeared Cosimo to the city's humbler elements. (Once when a petitioner, hoping to reform the sagging morals of the city, begged Cosimo to pass a law prohibiting priests from gambling, the practical Cosimo replied, "First stop them from using loaded dice.") Piero, by contrast, was an aesthete and connoisseur who liked nothing better than to retire to his study, where he could gaze at his fine collection of antique busts, ancient manuscripts, and rare gemstones.

Citizens complained that policy was hatched in the privacy of the Medici palace on the Via Larga, rather than in open debate at the Palace of the Priors, as the sickly Piero was often forced to meet with his trusted lieutenants over dinner in his house or in his bedchamber. Such a reserved and quiet man was unlikely to appeal to the pragmatic merchants of Florence, who approached politics in much the same lively spirit as they entered the city's marketplaces, eager to buy and sell, to argue and cajole, to win an advantage if possible but in any case to strike deals and shake hands at the conclusion of a bargain hard driven but mutually beneficial. In both the Palace of the Priors and in the *Mercato Vecchio* (the Old Market in the heart of the city), relations of trust built on face-to-face encounters were more important than abstract ideology. Piero was an intensely private man in a world that valued above all the lively give-and-take of the street corner.

The best contemporary portrait of Piero is the fine marble bust by Mino da Fiesole.* The sculpture reveals a handsome man with the cropped hair of an ancient Roman patrician and alert, thoughtful eyes. But there is something in the pugnacious thrust of his chin, a feature passed down to his oldest son, that suggests an inner strength his contemporaries little suspected.

A more engaging portrait emerges in Piero's private letters that reveal a conscientious man deeply attached to his family and continually fretting over their uncertain future. He was a loving and devoted husband to Lucrezia Tornabuoni, a descendant of one of Florence's most ancient families, and their correspondence reveals an unusually close bond. "[E]very day seems a year until I return for your and my consolation," wrote Lucrezia from Rome to Piero, while Piero confessed that he awaited her arrival "with infinite longing."

Piero was also a devoted, if sometimes overbearing, father, particularly with his oldest son, who could not leave town without being pursued by letters filled with unsolicited advice and constructive criticism. Piero's letters alternately exhibit pride in his son's precocious ability and an almost neurotic need to interfere in the smallest details of his conduct. "You will have received my letter of the 4th," he wrote to Lorenzo in Milan, "telling you what conduct to pursue, all of which remember; in a word, it is necessary now for you to be a man and not a boy; be so in words, deeds and manners." For the most part Lorenzo took his father's nagging in good humor, though occasionally his exasperation shows through, as when he responded to yet another request for information, "I wrote to you two days ago, and for this reason I have little to say."

The leaders of the current revolt were all prominent figures of the *reggimento* who viewed Cosimo's death as an opportunity to satisfy their own ambition. Those like Agnolo Acciaiuoli, who had suffered exile with Cosimo when he ran afoul of the then ruling Albizzi family and shared in

---

* Now in the Bargello Museum in Florence.

his triumphant return in 1434, felt that after thirty years of loyal service to the Medici cause their time had come. "Piero was dismayed when he saw the number and quality of the citizens who were against him," wrote Machiavelli some sixty years after the events in his *Florentine Histories,* "and after consulting with his friends, he decided that he too would make a list of his friends. And having given the care of this enterprise to some of his most trusted men, he found such variety and instability in the minds of the citizens that many of those listed as against him were also listed in his favor."

Machiavelli's account captures something of the confusion of those days as once trusted friends were suspected of secret treachery. Considering the formidable array of figures now agitating for change, a betting man might have thought twice before wagering a few *soldi* on the Medici cause. They included such prominent and respected citizens as Luca Pitti, who, at least in his own mind, was Cosimo's logical successor; the gifted orator Niccolò Soderini; Agnolo Acciaiuoli, a scholar and a friend of Cosimo's whose thoughtful views carried great weight with his fellow citizens; and Dietisalvi Neroni, a shrewd political operator who had been a fixture within the highest circles of the *reggimento.*

In secret nighttime meetings in the city's sacred buildings—the Party of the Plain favoring the monastery La Crocetta, while their adversaries favored the equally pious La Pietà—men began to look to their own defense, each suspecting the other of plotting the overthrow of the constitutional government. In a typically Florentine mixture of the sacred and profane, fervent prayers to the Virgin were often followed by calls to riot and mayhem.

By most measures the Medici were ill prepared for the coming contest. Piero's poor health had thrust Lorenzo into a position of responsibility at an age when his companions were still completing their studies or were apprenticed in the family business. He had already served as his father's envoy on crucial diplomatic missions, including the wedding of a king's son and an audience with the newly elected pope. A few weeks earlier he had returned from a trip abroad to introduce himself to Ferrante, King of Naples, "with whom I spoke," he wrote his father, "and who offered me many fine compliments, which I wait to tell you in person." The importance for the Medici of such contacts with the great lords of Europe is suggested by Piero's hunger for news of the meeting. Lorenzo's tutor and traveling companion, Gentile Becchi, wrote an enthusiastic report of Lorenzo's performance before the king. Referring to this account, Piero confessed, "Three times I read this for my happiness and pleasure." Consorting with royalty provided this family of bankers much-needed prestige, though such social climbing if too vigorously pursued could also arouse the jealousy of their peers who believed that they were thus being left behind.*

The looming crisis would demand of Lorenzo a set of skills different from those he had recently practiced in the courts of great lords. The retiring Piero needed Lorenzo to act as the public face of the regime, the charismatic center of an otherwise colorless bureaucracy. As preparations were made for the coming battle, it was often to Lorenzo, rather than the ailing Piero, that men turned to pledge their loyalty. Marco Parenti, a cloth merchant of moderate means whose memoirs provide an eyewitness account of the events of these months, tells how the countryside was armed in the days leading up to the August crisis. "Thus it was arranged," he wrote,

> that there were 2000 Bolognese horsemen loyal to the duke of Milan. These were secretly ordered to be held in readiness for Piero; the Serristori, lords with a great following in the Val d'Arno, arranged with Lorenzo, son of Piero, a great fishing expedition on the Arno and many great feasts where were gathered peasants and their leaders, who, wishing to show themselves faithful servants of Piero, met amongst themselves and pledged themselves to Lorenzo. These pledges were accepted with much show as if it had not already been planned, though many were kept in the dark, to send them a few days hence in arms to Florence in support of Piero. And so it was

---

* Thus, for instance, the Medici were proud to display the *fleurs de lis*, granted to them by the French king, on their coat of arms, while others jockeyed for knighthoods and foreign titles of nobility. It is typical of Florentine ambivalence toward such feudal titles that while knights were given a special prominence in the city's festivals and ceremonies, anyone stigmatized with the label "magnate" was excluded from participation in the city's government. Suspicion of the hereditary aristocracy stemmed from the centuries of violence committed by the native nobility.

arranged in other places, with other peasants and men who, when called on, would quickly appear in arms.

The fact that those bending their knees were often rude peasants and their lord a banker's son gives to the proceedings a distinctly Florentine flavor, but it is clear that Lorenzo had already begun to take on some of the trappings of a feudal prince.

Lorenzo's prominence, however, was actually a sign of weakness in the Medici camp. Florentines regarded youth as an unfortunate condition, believing that these *giovanni*—a term attached to all young men, including those in their twenties who had yet to assume the steadying yoke of marriage—were, like the entire female sex, essentially irrational and in thrall to their baser instincts. So far Lorenzo had given little indication that he was any better than his peers, having acquired a well-earned reputation for fast living. For the leaders of the Hill a trial of strength now, when the father was crippled and his heir not yet mature, was to their advantage. Jacopo Acciaiuoli, son of Agnolo, who had attended the meeting of King Ferrante and Lorenzo, reported to his father, "And returning to the arrival of Lorenzo, many fathers spend to get their sons known who would do better to spend so that they were not known." Beneath the spiteful jab there is a more substantive message—that neither the ailing father nor his awkward son would put up much of a fight. The next few days would put this judgment to the test.

Indeed there was nothing in the biography of either Piero or Lorenzo to strike fear in an opponent. "[Piero] did not, to be sure, possess the wisdom and virtues of his father," commented the historian Francesco Guicciardini (1483–1540), usually a fair judge of men, "but he was a good-natured and very clement man." A kind heart, however, was not necessarily an advantage in the cutthroat world of Florentine politics; in the centuries of bloody strife that marred the history of the City of the Baptist, men of saintly disposition were notable by their absence.

Despite the rising tension, August 27 dawned in an atmosphere of deceptive calm. Elections for the new *Signoria* were scheduled for the following day, and Florentine citizens, the great majority of whom wished only to go about their daily lives undisturbed by the quarrels of their masters, were cautiously optimistic that the leaders of the opposing factions had pulled back from the precipice. Only the day before, Piero and his family had left Florence for their villa at Careggi, something he would never have contemplated had he believed a confrontation imminent. In a crisis anyone who found himself outside city walls could quickly be marginalized. It was just such a blunder that, thirty years earlier, almost cost Cosimo his life. Taking advantage of his temporary absence from the city, the government, led at the time by the Albizzi family, decided to move against their too-powerful rival. Upon returning to Florence, Cosimo had been arrested, threatened with execution, and ultimately sent into exile. The lesson could hardly have been lost on his son that leaving the city at a time of strife was a recipe for disaster.

Curiously, it was Dietisalvi Neroni, one of the leaders of the Hill, who had persuaded the Medici leader to take this vacation, promising that he, too, would retire to his villa, thus lessening the chances of a violent clash breaking out between their armed supporters. It was an apparently statesmanlike gesture that would allow the democratic process to go forward without interference.

Piero's agreement suggests a misplaced confidence that the situation was moving in his direction, and there were in fact indications that the fortunes of the Medici party, which had reached a low ebb in the winter, were on the rebound. But the decisive factor may simply have been the poor state of his health; a few days earlier a flare-up of gout had confined him to his bed, making it almost impossible to conduct any serious business. Thus when Neroni held out an olive branch, Piero was only too happy grasp it.

Piero had failed to take the measure of Neroni, whose powers of dissimulation were apparently so highly developed that he was able to maintain cordial relations with the man whose destruction he plotted. Piero, not necessarily an astute judge of men at the best of times and now distracted by the pain in his joints, allowed himself to be taken in by Neroni's conciliatory gestures. "[I]n order to better conceal his intent," explains Machiavelli, "[Neroni] visited Piero often, reasoned with him about the unity of the city, and advised him." Though Piero was aware that his one-time colleague had at least flirted with the opposition, Neroni was able to convince him that he was a man of goodwill who could act as a moderating influence on his fellow reformers.

Machiavelli portrays Neroni as an unprincipled schemer who set out to destroy his old friend in order to further his own career, but with him, as with all the leaders of the revolt of 1466, it is difficult to disentangle motives of self-interest from genuine idealism. Neroni does seem to have possessed some republican instincts, though it is uncertain if these were born of principle or sprang from a practical calculation that he could rise further as a champion of the people than as a Medici lackey. As *Gonfaloniere di Giustizia* (the Standard-Bearer of Justice, the head of state) in 1454 he was already an advocate of democratic reform, winning, according to one contemporary source "great goodwill among the people." And in 1465 he had written to the duke of Milan that "the citizenry would like greater liberty and a broader government, as is customary in republican cities like ours."

For the most part, however, Neroni prospered as a loyal servant of the Medici regime. It is unclear when ideological differences combined with frustrated ambition to turn him against his former allies, but as early as 1463 the ambassador from Milan reported to his boss that "Cosimo and his men have no greater or more ambitious enemy than Dietisalvi [Neroni]." In spite of these warnings, at the time of Cosimo's death in 1464 Neroni was still one of Piero's closest advisors.

Neroni's first line of attack, recounts Machiavelli, was to engineer Piero's financial collapse. He describes how Piero had turned to Neroni for advice following Cosimo's death, but "[s]ince his own ambition was more compelling to him than his love for Piero or the old benefits received from Cosimo," Neroni encouraged Piero to pursue policies "under which his ruin was hidden." These policies included calling in many of the loans granted by Cosimo—often on easy terms and made for political rather than financial reasons—a move that caused a string of bankruptcies and added to the growing list of Piero's enemies.

Despite his rival's best efforts, however, Piero weathered the financial crisis, and by 1466 Neroni was growing impatient with half-measures. Guicciardini gives to Neroni the decisive role in the attempted coup: "[It was] caused in large part by the ambition of *messer* Dietisalvi di Nerone. . . . He was very astute, very rich, and highly esteemed; but not content with the great status and reputation he enjoyed, he got together with *messer* Agnolo Acciaiuoli, also a man of great authority, and planned to depose Piero di Cosimo."

While Piero and his family headed to Careggi, Neroni and his confederates prepared to seize the government by force.

For generations, Careggi, with its fields and quiet country lanes, had served the Medici household as a refuge from the cares of the city. Cosimo had purchased for the philosopher Marsilio Ficino a modest farm close by at Montevecchio so that his friend would have the leisure to complete his life's work, the translation of Plato from Greek to Latin. "Yesterday I went to my estate at Careggi," Cosimo once wrote to Ficino, "but for the sake of cultivating my mind and not the estate. Come to us, Marsilio, as soon as possible. Bring with you Plato's book on *The Highest Good.* . . . I want nothing more wholeheartedly than to know which way leads most surely to happiness." Lorenzo, too, enjoyed the philosopher's company, and later in life would convene at Careggi those informal gatherings of scholars and poets that historians dignified with the somewhat misleading label "the Platonic Academy," finding the country air a suitable stimulus to deep thought.

Today, however, the villa at Careggi could provide no escape from the troubles of the city. The family had barely begun to settle in when the peace of the morning was shattered by the arrival of a horseman at the gates.* The messenger, his horse lathered from hours of hard riding, his clothes and skin blackened with dust, announced that he had come from Giovanni Bentivoglio, lord of Bologna, with an urgent message for the master of the house.

The messenger's point of origin was sufficient to set off alarm bells. The ancient university town of Bologna was strategically placed near the passes through the Apennines to keep a watchful eye on anyone coming from the tumultuous Romagna; from here, an army descending on Tuscany from the north would easily be spotted. Bentivoglio was but one of many

---

* Contemporary accounts differ as to when Piero and his family arrived in Careggi; one suggests that they had just arrived that day, though this appears unlikely. It is more probable that they had arrived a day earlier.

trusted allies of the Medici scattered throughout Italy and beyond who kept their eyes and ears open for any scrap of information that might be useful to their friends in Florence.

This morning's letter brought news that Bentivoglio's spies in the village of Fiumalbo had observed eight hundred cavalry and infantry under the banner of Borso d'Este, Duke of Modena and Marquis of Ferrara, setting out in the direction of Florence. To the startled Piero, their objective was clear—to join with the Medici's enemies in the city and topple them from power.

Though Bentivoglio's message has not survived, its contents are summarized by a letter written that same day by Nicodemo Tranchedini, the Milanese ambassador to Florence. In it he informs his master, Galeazzo Maria Sforza, Duke of Milan, that Piero had "received letters from the regime in Bologna, from D. Johane Bentivogli," and that soldiers of the marquis of Ferrara were "already on the move to come here on the invitation of Piero's enemies, with horse and riders of Bartholomeo Colione."

For months the leaders of the Hill had been in close communication with Borso d'Este, a northern Italian lord whose schemes for self-aggrandizement were predicated on a change of government in Florence. In November 1465, the Milanese ambassador had reported to his employer that Borso's agent, *Messer* Jacopo Trotti, "every day meets *M.* Luca, *M.* Angelo [Agnolo Acciaiuoli] and *M.* Dietisalvi [Neroni]." Given the fact that Piero was kept well informed of these machinations by Tranchedini, it is remarkable that he allowed himself to be lured from the city at this critical time.

If the motives of the Florentine rebels were a mixture of idealism and self-interest, those of Borso d'Este were unambiguous. Described by Pope Pius II in his memoirs as a "man of fine physique and more than average height with beautiful hair and a pleasing countenance," Borso d'Este was also "eloquent and garrulous and listened to himself talking as if he pleased himself more than his hearers." In his inflated self-regard he was little different from any number of petty princes who sold their military services to the highest bidder, nor did his taste for costly jewelry, his arrogance, and deceitfulness—other qualities noted by Pius—set him apart from his peers.

Technically a vassal of the pope, Borso was always looking for ways to expand his family's territories at the expense of his neighbors. An important step in his campaign was the removal of the Medici, who were closely linked with his chief rival in the north, the powerful Sforza family of Milan. In June his representative in Florence had contacted Luca Pitti to suggest that "Piero be removed from the city." It took almost two months of negotiation, but by late August the leaders of the Hill had decided to team up with the mercenary adventurer, inviting "the marquis of Ferrara [to] come with his troops toward the city and, when Piero was dead, to come armed in the piazza and make the *Signoria* establish a state in accordance with their will."

Piero had grossly underestimated his enemies' resolve, but he now moved swiftly to correct the situation. First he dashed off an urgent letter to Sforza, asking him to send his troops, some 1,500 of whom were stationed in Imola in Romagna, about fifty miles to the north, to intercept those of d'Este. Desperately seeking friends closer to home, Piero dictated a second letter to the leaders of the neighboring town of Arezzo, pleading that "upon receiving this you send me as many armed men as you can . . . and direct them here to me."

Even more important was the task of mobilizing the pro-Medici forces within the city. Foreign armies could throw their considerable weight behind one faction or another, but victory and defeat would be determined largely inside the city walls. Here the rebels had a great advantage. Piero, in so much pain from gout that he could travel only by litter, would not arrive back in the city for hours, time the rebels could use to prepare the battlefield and set the terms of the engagement.

So it was that Lorenzo found himself this August morning hurrying back to Florence, accompanied only by a few companions as young and inexperienced as himself. It was Lorenzo's mission to ride out ahead of the main party and to raise the Medici banner in Florence, ensuring as well that the gates remained in friendly hands long enough to permit Piero's safe return. As the head of the household made his slow, painful way to Florence, the fate of the Medici regime would rest in the hands of a seventeen-year-old boy.

From the moment he left the fortified compound of Careggi, Lorenzo was on his guard. The countryside through which he passed was as familiar to him as the streets near the family palace in the city, the rolling hills and game-filled copses, destination of many a hunting expedition, a constant source of delight. Today, however, the landscape he loved felt menacing. Every low stone wall and ramshackle farmhouse provided a place of concealment, every patch of shade an opportunity for ambush.

Nothing disturbed the heavy air as the horsemen picked their way cautiously down the winding road. Tiny lizards darted through the underbrush, while hawks circled high overhead. Having completed most of the journey without incident, and with the walls of the city looming before him, Lorenzo brought his small group to a halt. Ahead lay a tiny hamlet known as Sant' Antonio (or Sant'Ambrogio) del Vescovo. Little more than a few buildings shimmering in the summer heat, there was nothing ominous in the rustic scene. But Lorenzo had reason to be wary. The village took its name from the archbishop (*vescovo*) of Florence, whose summer residence was attached to a small chapel there. The reigning archbishop of Florence was Giovanni Neroni, Dietisalvi's brother. (His sacerdotal office could have provided little comfort: a bishop's robes in Renaissance Italy were more often the costume of a political intriguer with a dagger in his belt than those of an unworldly man of God.) With Neroni's recent treachery in mind, Lorenzo knew that to pass through the hamlet, his usual route from the villa to the city, he would have to place himself squarely in the lion's den.

It was at this moment Lorenzo signaled to one of his party to remain some distance behind while he and the rest of his companions spurred their horses into motion and continued along the road to Florence. As the riders passed between the first of the buildings, armed men rushed out from behind walls and doorways, surrounding the riders, the points of their halberds glinting menacingly in the sun. Horses reared as Lorenzo and his companions unsheathed their swords. In the shadows men cocked crossbows. In the commotion apparently no one noticed the lone figure who turned his horse around and sped back along the road in the direction they had come.

The ambush at Sant'Antonio del Vescovo remains one of the more mysterious episodes in the annals of Florentine history. It is a puzzle that must be assembled from bits and pieces, the missing portions filled in with sound conjecture, since no contemporary report gives more than a brief, tantalizing mention. The most detailed account is that of Niccolò Valori, who included it in his biography of Lorenzo, written some thirty years later. But even this narrative raises as many questions as it answers:

[I]t was through the sound judgment of Lorenzo, though still young, that the life of Piero his father was saved; learning that awaiting him as he returned from Careggi were many conspirators who planned to kill him, [Lorenzo] sent word to those who were carrying [Piero] by litter (unable, sick as he was with gout, to travel any other way) not to continue by the usual route, but through a secret and secure way return to the city. [Lorenzo], meanwhile, riding along the usual path, let it be known that his father was right behind him; and having thus deceived the plotters, both were saved.

Francesco Guicciardini supplies some additional information, including the precise spot where the ambush took place. "[W]hen Piero went off to Careggi," he wrote, "his enemies decided to murder him on his return. Armed men were placed in Sant'Ambrogio [sic] del Vescovo, which Piero usually passed on his way back to the city. They could avail themselves of that place because the archbishop of Florence was *messer* Dietisalvi's brother." Interestingly, Guicciardini ignores Lorenzo's role in the drama, attributing their escape simply to "the good fortune of Piero and of the Medici."*

Lorenzo himself never offered a full retelling of the day's events, though it is possible that Valori's version is based on Lorenzo's recollections. References to the ambush must be teased from his own cryptic comments or from the equally oblique remarks of his friends. Lorenzo's silence can be explained by his reluctance to talk about, or even admit the existence of, the many attempts made on his life. In 1477, when his life again appeared under

---

* Despite considerable contemporary evidence, some historians have tended to downplay or contradict the official version of what happened on August 27, 1466. The main disagreement comes over whether, as the Medici contended, the Hill precipitated the crisis by calling on Borso d'Este's troops and attempting to seize Piero at Sant'Antonio del Vescovo, or, as their opponents claimed, the whole event was staged by the partisans of the Plain in order to crush the reform movement. A contemporary account of the plot is given by one Iacopo di Niccolò di Cocco Donati, a member of the *Signoria* that August, who declared that the conspirators "had arranged to assassinate [Piero] at Careggi" (Phillips, p. 246). (It is Donati's account, incidentally, that supplies the crucial detail that Piero had gone to his villa as part of an arrangement with Neroni.) Donati's report offers crucial confirmation of the Medici version. Another contemporary account bolstering the Medici position comes from the diary of the apothecary Luca Landucci, a man whose testimony is all the more credible because he had no political ax to grind (see

threat from invisible assassins, he dismissed a warning from the Milanese ambassador: "and thanks to God, though I have been told by many: 'watch yourself!,' I have found none of these plots to be true, except one, at the time of Niccolò Soderini." Thus the traumatic events of 1466 appear in Lorenzo's correspondence only at the moment when an even more dangerous conspiracy was taking shape, and largely to make light of current threats. From this same period comes another suggestive letter, written by Lorenzo's friend and tutor Gentile Becchi. Urging him to take the rumors of threats on his life seriously, he warns Lorenzo not to heed the counsel of "new Dietisalvis who will advise you to go to your villa like your father."

Given Lorenzo's own reticence, the ambush at Sant'Antonio del Vescovo must forever retain an element of mystery. Even Valori's account contains many puzzling features. Why did those who confronted Lorenzo fail to take him into custody? Why did they accept Lorenzo's assertion that his father was just around the corner, without at least holding him as a hostage? From Lorenzo's few remarks it is clear that he felt his life had been in danger along the road from Careggi to Florence, but Valori's narrative

---

Landucci, *A Florentine Diary*, p. 8). Also significant are the letters of the Milanese ambassador, who confirms the movements of Borso d'Este's army, and Piero's panicky call for troops to his friends and neighbors. The confession of Dietisalvi's brother, Francesco (two versions of which are reproduced in Nicolai Rubinstein's "La Confessione di Francesco Neroni e la congiura anti-Medicea del 1466," Archivio Storico Italiano, 126, 1968), offers important testimony on the coordination between the leaders of the Hill and Borso d'Este. Francesco's confession also confirms the basic outlines of the plot, though it differs on some of the details. The memoirs of Benedetto Dei also tend to support the Medici account (see his *Cronica*, especially 23v and 24r). For the other side see Marco Parenti's *Ricordi Storici*. Parenti, though an ardent adherent of the Hill, had no access to the inner circle that planned the coup. His belief that the accusations against the leaders of his party were false was based on hope rather than fact. Lorenzo's own later recollections are significant, if frustratingly vague. The subsequent behavior of the leaders of the Hill shows the plot to kill Piero to be thoroughly consistent with their characters. It is suggestive that the two great Florentine historians, Machiavelli and Guicciardini, writing within a few decades of the events, largely accepted the Medici version. Rubinstein is no doubt correct when he says, "Fear was probably the decisive element in the final crisis" (*The Government of Florence Under the Medici*, p. 184). Both sides had built up foreign armies just outside Florentine territory, each believing it needed to act to forestall an invasion by the other. Under the circumstances, the pressure to steal the march on one's opponents was great.

does not end in a violent clash. Instead, according to his friend's retelling, Lorenzo manages to confound his enemies not through martial valor but through quick thinking and his powers of persuasion.

One might be tempted to dismiss the tale were it not for the fact that it conforms perfectly with what we know of Lorenzo's character. The confrontation at Sant'Antonio may provide the first instance when Lorenzo was able to deflect the knives of his enemies using only his native wit, but it will not be the last. Time and again he showed a remarkable ability to talk his way out of tight situations. With his back to the wall, and his life hanging in the balance, Lorenzo was at his most convincing. A gift he was to display throughout his life—and one that would be crucial to his statecraft, allowing him to appeal to people from all walks of life—was to suit his language to the moment, effortlessly trading Latin epigrams with scholars or obscenities with laborers in a tavern. This earthier vocabulary would have served him well on this occasion, but his powers of persuasion would have done little good without the confusion and missteps that tend to unravel even the best-laid plans.

From the perspective provided by centuries in which scholars have been able to sift the evidence at leisure, the fact that Lorenzo was allowed to proceed unmolested seems an improbable bit of good fortune. But this view distorts the true situation. Lorenzo's native wit no doubt played a part, but so did the natural perplexity of those who had been instructed to seize his father, the lord of Florence, and now had to make a snap decision with no instructions from their commanders. After a brief conversation, in which Lorenzo no doubt adopted a tone of light banter meant to put them at their ease, they let him go, having been convinced that soon enough the main prize would fall into their laps.

While they waited in vain for Piero to arrive, Lorenzo and the rest of his party made a dash for the city walls. As soon as he passed through the wide arch of the Porta Faenza, Lorenzo could breathe a little easier.* This was

---

* The road from Careggi would have led him to either the Porta San Gallo or the Porta Faenza, just to the west. The Porta Faenza, however, was the natural point of entry for anyone coming from Sant'Antonio del Vescovo. The Porta Faenza has long since been torn down, along with much of the fourteenth-century wall that once girded Florence to the north, but the Porta San Gallo still stands, now forming the centerpiece of a busy traffic circle.

Medici country—the neighborhoods in the northwest corner of the city that in earlier centuries had mustered for war under the ancient banner of the Golden Lion. Familiar faces greeted him at every turn, local wine merchants, grocers, fishmongers, and stonemasons, with a fierce attachment to the few blocks where they were born and an equally fierce loyalty to the powerful family that lived among them. In his poem, "Il Simposio," Lorenzo left a description of this neighborhood and its people that reflects an easy familiarity between the humble folks and the lord of the city:

> I was approaching town along the road
> that leads into the portal of Faenza,
> when I observed such throngs proceeding through
> the streets, that I won't even dare to guess
> how many men made up the retinue.
> The names of many I could easily say:
> I knew a number of them personally . . .
> There's one I saw among those myriads,
> with whom I'd been close friends for many years,
> as I had known him since we'd both been lads . . .

"Above all else stick together with your neighbors and kinsmen," advised the Florentine patrician Gino Capponi, "assist your friends both within and without the city." For decades Lorenzo's forebears had acted upon this Florentine wisdom, knowing that men not masonry form the strongest bulwark in times of civic unrest. From the moment of his birth, seventeen years earlier, Lorenzo's father had been preparing his son for just such a crisis, weaving around him an intricate web of mutual obligation, nurturing those relationships of benefactor and supplicant, patron and client, through which power was wielded in Florentine politics. In moments of upheaval, Lorenzo's ability to draw on those relationships, to command the loyalty of his fellow citizens—above all of neighbors, friends, and kinsmen, bound together both by interest and by affection—would be vital to his family's survival.

The Baptistery of San Giovanni, Florence (Miles Unger)

II. FAMILY PORTRAIT

"Such was our greatness that it used to be said, 'Thou art like one of the Medici,' and every man feared us; even now when a citizen does an injury to another or abuses him, they say, 'If he did thus to a Medici what would happen?' Our family is still powerful in the State by reason of many friends and much riches, please God preserve it all to us. And to-day, thank God, we number about fifty men."

—FILIGNO DI CONTE DE' MEDICI, 1373

LORENZO WAS BORN ON JANUARY 1, 1449,* AT A TIME when the Medici, led by his grandfather Cosimo, stood securely at the summit of Florentine politics. The birth of a male heir to Cosimo's elder son, Piero, the first such birth to the family since their seizure of power fifteen years earlier, opened the prospect, comforting to some and troubling to others, of a true dynastic succession.

His entrance onto the public stage took place on the fifth day following his birth with his baptism in the shrine of San Giovanni. Here in the most ancient and sacred building in the city, into which generations of Florentines had poured their wealth and lavished their artistic talent, Lorenzo made what was, in effect, his political debut. From this moment on he would be in the public eye, a member of the community of Florentine citizens and the wider community of Christian believers, but also set apart, bound to a singular destiny.

Accompanying the proud father from the family home to the Baptistery of San Giovanni on that cold January morning were some of the most distinguished men in Florence. The archbishop of Florence himself, the saintly Antoninus—a close friend of Cosimo's—would stand godfather to

---

* According to the Florentine calendar Lorenzo was born in 1448; Florentines began the new year on March 25, the Feast of the Annunciation.

the child and preside over the ceremony, aided in his sacred duties by Benedetto Schiattesi, prior of the Medicean church of San Lorenzo. This arrangement echoed in ecclesiastical terms the family's political stature in the city; the archbishop represented the entire Christian community of the republic, while the prior of San Lorenzo embodied the Medici's special relationship with the neighborhood in which they resided and that formed the most reliable base of their support.

The attendance of the distinguished clerics honored the family, but it also reminded the citizens how completely Medici money had penetrated the fabric of the city. Both men were Medici clients. Even Antoninus, a man widely revered for his holiness (he was later canonized by the pope), was on the Medici payroll; for many years as the prior of the monastery of San Marco he was the beneficiary of Cosimo's largesse. When he complained that men "are mean in giving alms and prefer to spend on chapels, superfluous ornaments and ecclesiastical pomp rather than on support of the poor," was it a subtle dig at his friend who was filling the city with buildings emblazoned with the Medici arms? As for Schiattesi, his debt to the Medici was even more overt. The church of San Lorenzo, located a block to the west of the Medici palace on the Via Larga, was so dependent on Medici patronage that it often seemed to be little more than an annex of the family residence. Families allied with the Medici—the Martelli, the Ginori, the della Stufa, and, until their disgrace, the Dietisalvi Neroni—all built chapels in San Lorenzo in a typically Florentine synergy of politics and religion. Also typically Florentine was the way the Medici used the church to enhance their own prestige through artistic patronage. By hiring Brunelleschi to design the old sacristy (where Cosimo's father, Giovanni di Bicci, was buried) and Donatello to provide the sculptural decoration, they were transforming their local church into a monument to rival the cathedral itself.

Representing the secular authority on this happy occasion was the entire outgoing *Signoria* (on which Piero had just served) and the *Accoppiatori,* the members of a special commission whose behind-the-scenes meddling with the electoral rolls was vital to maintaining the *reggimento.* Agnolo Acciaiuoli, the outgoing *Gonfaloniere di Giustizia* and still very much one of Cosimo's men, was there to pay his respects, and with him were many leading figures in the regime.

Also standing godfather (by proxy) to young Lorenzo was Federico da

Montefeltro, ruler of Urbino. Years later Federico would play a far more sinister part in Lorenzo's life, but on this occasion the prominence of his representatives at the ceremony was a signal to the Medici's compatriots that the family could boast powerful friends abroad. The prestige gained by the Medici through their association with kings, popes, counts, and other members of the feudal nobility was crucial to enhancing their standing with their own citizens. As an astute political observer later remarked about Lorenzo, "the reputation of the said Mag.co Lorenzo and the esteem that is accorded him from the powers of Italy and the Lords from abroad; not having this, he would not have a reputation in his own land."

Lorenzo's baptism was the first public presentation of the Medici heir to the people of Florence. That there was political calculation involved even in this most sacred rite is indicated by its careful timing: Piero had extended the customary three days between birth and baptism to await a more propitious alignment of the stars, taking advantage of the calendar to associate Lorenzo's baptism with the Feast of the Epiphany. In a clever if fortuitous bit of stagecraft, he managed to tie the ritual to the day on the sacred calendar most closely identified with the family's power and prestige. For generations the Medici had been associated with the celebrations dedicated to the Magi. Every few years magnificent processions, paid for largely from Medici funds, paraded through the city, concluding at the Medicean convent of San Marco, where a holy crèche was housed. Even the usually unostentatious Cosimo felt obliged to participate, marching through the city dressed up in a magnificent cloak of fur or gold brocade.*

It is easy to understand why the Medici were attracted to this particular scriptural tale. The Magi are among the few figures of wealth and power in the Bible who have no difficulty in attaining the heavenly kingdom. No doubt Cosimo and his sons, whose fortune was built on the still suspect business of money-lending, hoped that some of their sanctity would rub off on them. Depictions of the Magi were a staple of Medici iconography. A modest version of the scene by Benozzo Gozzoli adorned Cosimo's private cell in the monastery of San Marco, and a more magnificent version would soon cover the walls of the family's private chapel in the new palace

---

* The Medici palace was situated toward the end of the journey on the Via Larga. In later years viewing stands were set up outside the palace.

on the Via Larga. Lorenzo in particular came to be associated with the glamour of the Magi; many of his earliest portraits are found in paintings of the subject, including masterpieces not only by Gozzoli but by Sandro Botticelli.* As a young man Lorenzo was enrolled in the Confraternity of the Magi, the religious brotherhood that staged the processions that attracted admiring crowds from around Europe and helped give Florence its well-earned reputation for splendid pageantry.

Lorenzo was born to rule. This fact alone set him apart from his grand-father and father, both of whom entered the world at a time when the Medici were a somewhat obscure clan on the margins of Florence's gov-erning oligarchy. Lorenzo's first biographer, Niccolò Valori, wrote of his friend, "Thus, while still only a youth, he merited not only his title of *Mag-nifico* but Magnanimous also." From the beginning Lorenzo possessed the kind of glamour the jealous merchants of Florence were reluctant to con-cede to any fellow citizen. By contrast, at the time of Cosimo's birth in 1389 his father, Giovanni di Bicci de' Medici, had yet to amass the fortune upon which the future greatness of his family would rest. Piero was raised to manhood as merely the elder son of a prosperous banker, and one, moreover, whose family name still carried the stigma of past indiscre-tions.† Lorenzo was the first of the Medici born, so to speak, to the purple, and this awareness of an almost imperial destiny shaped his sense of him-self and the attitudes of those around him.

The house to which the swaddled infant was brought following the bap-tism was an unremarkable building on the Via Larga known as the *casa vec-chia,* or old house. To such unpretentious city dwellings Florentines attached the term *palazzo* (palace), but few possessed the grandeur we associate with the word. A century earlier even immensely wealthy banking clans like the Bardi or Peruzzi had been content to live in modest houses, often knit

---

* Lorenzo is the dark-haired young man on the right of Botticelli's *Adoration of the Magi* (now in the Uffizi Gallery), a row or two in front of the artist himself.

† In fact the Medici had a none-too-savory reputation for violence and political unrelia-bility. A distant relative, Salvestro de' Medici, had been among the leaders of the *Ciompi* uprising, which made all the Medici suspect in the eyes of the ruling oligarchy. See the *Chronicles of the Tumult of the Ciompi* (reprinted in the Monash Publications in History) for further details on Salvestro de' Medici's role in the disturbances.

together haphazardly from pre-existing structures. Then wealth was still suspect (particularly wealth associated with usury) and humility was regarded as the cardinal Christian virtue. The *casa vecchia* was a relic of those earlier times, a sensible burgher's home with few pretensions. It reflected the self-effacing character of its original owner, Giovanni di Bicci, a man who shunned the spotlight and whose reluctance to become embroiled in politics was such that on his deathbed he advised his sons, "Be chary of frequenting the Palace [of the *Signoria*]; rather wait to be summoned, and then be obedient, and not puffed up with pride at receiving many votes"— advice the politically ambitious Cosimo was not inclined to heed.

Cosimo was a far different man. He possessed a much more expansive view of the world and of his place in it, participating as both a patron and gifted amateur scholar in the humanist revival that was making Florence the intellectual capital of Europe, pursuits his father would no doubt have considered a waste of time.

Nowhere was this generational change more evident than in his own home. At the time of Lorenzo's birth, Cosimo was in the midst of building a grand new edifice to accommodate his growing family. Begun five years earlier, it was, according to Giorgio Vasari, "the first palace which was built in [Florence] on modern lines," that is, incorporating the classical architectural forms championed by Brunelleschi. One indication of its ambitious scale is that more than twenty buildings were razed to make room for the new structure, an inconvenience to neighbors justified, as was usual in similar circumstances, on the grounds that the new structure would be an improvement over the squalid tenements it replaced.

As the residence of Florence's most prominent citizen, the new palace rising next door to the *casa vecchia* at the corner of the Via Gori and the Via Larga would set a model for those that followed.* In Cosimo's *palazzo* one can sense the driving ambition that characterized men of the Renaissance. The magnificence that has come to be associated with Florence in

---

* The Medici palace has, over the centuries, come to symbolize the life of the cultured gentleman, a perfect blend of wealth, learning, and art. One can find echoes in the nineteenth-century mansions in Newport and, more surprisingly, in civic buildings like the main branch of the Boston Public Library, where the rich man's home has now been converted into the people's palace. The choice makes sense when one recalls that Cosimo established the first public library in Europe at his favorite monastery of San Marco.

the age of Lorenzo is attributable largely to a moral transformation in which ostentatious display went from being condemned as a vice to being praised as a virtue. A century earlier an anonymous Florentine merchant, more afraid of drawing the unwanted attentions of the tax collector than he was interested in living well, had declared, "Spending a lot and making a big impression are in themselves . . . dangerous." But only a few decades later attitudes had changed when humanist Leonardo Bruni wrote that wealth was not to be despised, for it "affords an opportunity for the exercise of virtue." Money if honestly come by was nothing to be ashamed of. Wisely expended for the common good it could be a creative force, the source of justifiable pride.

Contemporaries used the word *magnificienza* to denote the brilliance and generosity expected of a great man. Nowhere in the world was the thirst for wealth and honor as intense and as productive as in Florence, where families were driven to ever greater displays of wealth and taste by a competitive political and cultural climate. The Florentine expatriate Leon Battista Alberti observed in his book *On the Family,* "everyone [in Florence] seems bred to the cultivation of profit. Every discussion seems to concern economic wisdom, every thought turns to acquisition, and every art is expended to obtain great riches." In contrast to much of the rest of Europe, where feudal hierarchies were fixed by law and hallowed by custom, in Florence social and political status were as fluid as the ups and downs of the business cycle. Nothing did more to secure a precarious perch atop the social heap than building a sumptuous palace on a major thoroughfare.*

By the end of the fifteenth century, every neighborhood boasted at least one imposing residence of a proud, domineering family. Benedetto Dei, writing in the 1470s, noted over thirty fine palaces built over the last half-century. The Palace of the Priors was still the largest secular building in the city (surpassed only by the cathedral), but numerous private residences were nearly as impressive, as if to demonstrate their refusal to be overawed

---

* Often such projects could actually have the opposite of their intended effect. Giovanni Rucellai, for one, spent so much on his building projects, including his famous palace designed by Leon Battista Alberti, that he almost destroyed the family fortune. Still, Rucellai may have gotten his money's worth, since his name is still best known for the palace that bears his name.

by the might of the duly elected government. With their rough-hewn facades and fortresslike appearance, these private residences possessed all the visual authority of civic monuments and suggested a justifiable skepticism in the ability of the elected officials to protect their lives and property. If the Medici led the way, the Pitti, Pazzi, Rucellai, Strozzi, and many others were nipping at their heels.* Nothing so clearly illustrates the weakness of the government of Florence in relation to its principal families as this craggy cityscape bristling with the strongholds of the great and powerful.

For Cosimo, drawing up his plans before the new building boom had gotten fully underway, the construction of the new palace would put some distance between the Medici and their rivals, and give permanent and prominent form to the Medici presence in the district of the Golden Lion in the northwest corner of the city. Other great clans had long been identified with particular districts: the Albizzi with the *gonfalone* of the *Chiavi* (Keys) in the northeast corner of the city; the Bardi concentrated in the Ladder across the river; the Rinuccini in the Ox near Santa Croce; the Strozzi in the *gonfalone* of Red Lion to the west of the New Market.†

The first Medici arrived in Florence among the anonymous crowds of rural folk attracted to the city during the commercial boom that followed in the wake of the Crusades. This violent clash between Christian Europe and the Islamic East had the unanticipated effect of stimulating trade between the two civilizations, much of which flowed into the great Italian seaports and along the highways of the peninsula to markets in western and northern Europe. Florence was but one of many Italian cities to grow prosperous from the trade in spices, rare silks, and other exotic luxuries from the fabled Orient. Many a peasant, hearing tales of easy money,

---

* Many architectural historians trace the origins of the Renaissance *palazzo* to that built by Niccolò da Uzzano (designed by the artist Lorenzo di Bicci) in the 1420s. Though modest by later standards, with its spacious interior courtyard it was an advance over the formless private dwellings of the Middle Ages.

† By the fifteenth century the older divisions of the city—into sixteen *gonfaloni* and, later, into sixths—had been superseded for administrative purposes largely by a division into quarters, each identified with a major shrine: that of San Giovanni (the Baptistery); Sta. Maria Novella; Sta. Croce; and, in the Oltrarno, the district on the south bank of the river, Sto. Spirito. The Medici *gonfalone* of the Golden Lion fell within San Giovanni.

abandoned his plow to seek his fortune in the city, the ancestors of Cosimo, Piero, and Lorenzo among them.*

The obscurity of the branch of the family to which Lorenzo belonged is indicated by its itinerant nature. Originally they had been associated with the more ancient neighborhood near the Old Market and the parish church of San Tommaso, but in making the move a few blocks to the north, outside the circuit of the old, twelfth-century walls, Giovanni di Bicci was venturing into territory already well populated by his kinsmen. Indeed, by the fourteenth century the Medici were among the most prominent families of their quarter, leaders of the popular faction who were battling the magnates for control of the city. One of the earliest mentions of the Medici comes in the fourteenth-century chronicle of Giovanni Villani. "[T]he *popolani* of the quarter of San Giovanni," he records, "having chosen as their leaders the Medici and the Rondinelli and *Messer* Ugo della Stufa, judge, and the *popolani* of the borgo of San Lorenzo, along with the butchers and with the other artisans, assembled without the permission of the Commune in numbers totalling 1000 men . . . saying that the *grandi* were about to launch an attack." This contemporary account reveals not only the Medici's long-standing connection with the parish of San Lorenzo but also their well-earned reputation as populist rabble-rousers.

Giovanni's move may have been motivated by a desire to forge closer links with those more prominent branches of the extended Medici clan. Loyalty to family was the bedrock of social life in Florence; in a corrupt and violent world, consanguinity was the best—though by no means a foolproof—guarantee that one's interests would be looked after. Cosimo's rise to power, for instance, was aided by the efforts not only of his brother Lorenzo but of his cousin Averardo, while Tommaso Soderini's support of Piero in the crisis of 1466 was due in part to the fact that he was married to Dianora, sister of Piero's wife, Lucrezia Tornabuoni.† A distant ancestor of

---

* During their years in power, many a propagandist sought a more distinguished genealogy for the family, but none is convincing. In one colorful history, the red balls of the Medici escutcheon derive from the dents put in the shield of a knightly forebear by a giant he slew in mortal combat.

† Piero's cousin Pierfrancesco de' Medici's ambiguous role in the same conflict could have been predicted by consulting his family tree; he was caught between loyalty to his blood relatives and his father-in-law, Agnolo Acciaiuoli.

Lorenzo, Filigno di Conte de' Medici, captured the tenor of Florentine life when he wrote in his *Ricordi* of 1373: "Such was our greatness that it used to be said, 'Thou art like one of the Medici,' and every man feared us; even now when a citizen does an injury to another or abuses him, they say, 'If he did thus to a Medici what would happen?' Our family is still powerful in the State by reason of many friends and much riches, please God preserve it all to us. And to-day, thank God, we number about fifty men."

One of the simplest explanations for the Medici ascendance was their fertility. The tax roll of 1427 reveals that the Medici, with thirty-one tax-paying households, were among the most prolific, though falling far short of the Strozzi (fifty-four) and the Bardi (sixty). In short, there was strength in numbers. At home the infant Lorenzo was surrounded by a large and growing family. In addition to his mother and father, Lorenzo had two older sisters, Bianca, born in 1445, and Lucrezia (known as Nannina), born in 1447. But in this profoundly patriarchal society it was the male children who guaranteed the survival of the family. As teenagers the girls would be married off to form alliances with other prominent families—Bianca married into the ancient Pazzi clan and Lucrezia into the Rucellai—while the boys were expected to carry on the family name and fortune. Thus, from the start the Medici invested most of their hopes and dreams in young Lorenzo.

To his grown sons, Piero and Giovanni, Cosimo was a formidable figure, but, as their correspondence shows, relations were marked by affection and mutual respect. With his family, as with the republic over which he presided, Cosimo eschewed the harsh methods of the tyrant and was repaid with love and devotion. Piero later recorded that on his deathbed Cosimo told him "he would make no will . . . seeing that we were always united in true love, amity, and esteem." The success of the Medici can be ascribed in large part to the way each member of the family worked toward a common goal, demonstrating a unity of purpose not always present among ruling dynasties, where jealousy and competition are more common than fraternal affection.

As paterfamilias Cosimo presided over a large household, which included siblings, cousins, aunts, and uncles, all under one roof or within a stone's throw of the main residence on the Via Larga. In his tax declaration of 1457 he claimed fourteen dependents, including his nephew Pier-francesco (son of his brother, Lorenzo, who had died in 1440) and his family, and those of his two sons, Piero and Giovanni. In addition he listed four household slaves.* Even if, like most Florentine taxpayers, Cosimo exaggerated the number of his dependents, it is clear that blood relatives were only part of a far larger group that relied on Cosimo's support. "There are fifty mouths to feed in our family, including the villas and Florence," Cosimo reported on his tax return of 1458, "and we also employ forty-one retainers, amounting to more than 400 florins a year."

Among those on Cosimo's payroll were not only simple household servants and humble artisans, but also numerous visiting dignitaries, scholars, philosophers, poets, and artists whose names have since become famous. One of the least appreciative of the Medici houseguests was the painter Filippo Lippi. "So much a slave was he to this [amorous] appetite," wrote Giorgio Vasari of the Carmelite monk turned painter, "that when he was in this humor he gave little or no attention to the works that he had undertaken; wherefore on one occasion Cosimo de' Medici, having commissioned him to paint a picture, shut him up in his own house, in order that he might not go out and waste his time." The strategy backfired, however, when Lippi managed to escape from the palace with a rope he fashioned out of his bedsheets. When Cosimo finally tracked down the restless monk, he agreed to give him the run of the house, concluding that "the virtues of rare minds were celestial beings, not slavish hacks."

The Medici home, particularly before the completion of the new palace, must have been in a constant uproar, with visiting ambassadors passing in the hallways artists in their paint-covered smocks and scholars of genius as well as common workers and peasants begging favors from Florence's most powerful citizen. The noted humanist Francesco Filelfo,

---

* For Cosimo's funeral in 1464, Piero provided mourning clothes for four female slaves, named Chateruccia, Cristina, Catrina, and Zita. Cosimo fathered an illegitimate son, Lorenzo's uncle Carlo, by one of his female slaves; it is not known if she was one of these four. Slaves in Florence were usually women employed as domestic servants—though there are records of slaves being used in the building industries—and a large percentage of babies in foundling hospitals were the children of slaves and (presumably) the master of the house. Many of these children, however, were acknowledged by their fathers, like Lorenzo's uncle Carlo. Most slaves were of Middle Eastern or Slavic origin, shipped from Alexandria or other ports on Venetian ships to serve in the houses of rich Italian merchants. Few in number compared with the tens of thousands of impoverished workers, they remained economically insignificant. Unlike ancient Athens, Renaissance Florence was not built on the labor of slaves.

complaining of Cosimo's favoritism toward the equally distinguished Carlo Marsuppini and Niccolò Niccoli, declared peevishly, "If I do not frequent your house, as they do daily, that is because I am busy."

Much to the chagrin of elected officials, a great deal of the government's business was conducted around the Medici dinner table, where Cosimo met informally with foreign ambassadors and leading men of the regime. The peculiar combination of public and private space in the Medici palace could prove disconcerting to visiting foreign dignitaries. "Cosimo de' Medici," recalled the ambassador from Ferrara,

> was giving an audience to certain ambassadors from the city of Lucca. The audience was taking place at his house, as was customary, and they were deep in conversation when a young boy, his grandson [Lorenzo?], came to him with some reeds and a small knife and begged him to make him a whistle. Cosimo, breaking off the conversation, attended to the boy, fashioning a whistle, and telling him to run off and play. The ambassadors, very indignant, turned to Cosimo saying: "But certainly, *misser* Cosimo, we cannot help but marvel at your behavior, that having come to you on behalf of our communes to treat of such great affairs, you would leave us to attend to a little boy." Cosimo, laughing, embraced them, saying; "O my brothers, are you not also fathers? Do you not know the love one has for one's sons and grandsons. You marveled that I made him the whistle: it is well that he did not ask me to play it, for that I also would have done."

This was an enormously stimulating environment for a young boy. Lorenzo's outlook on life was shaped not only by the luxury of his immediate surroundings but also by the rich, contrasting textures of Florentine life.*

---

* Luxury in the fifteenth century meant something rather different from what it does today. In an age before machine production, items like clothing—even for a family as wealthy as the Medici—were scarce and precious commodities. Garments were sumptuously produced, with intricate patterns picked out in gold and silver thread, fur lining, and colors created from dyes derived from products halfway around the world. But the Medici possessed fewer items than even an average middle-class family today. In 1456 Piero made an inventory of Lucrezia's clothing and listed only thirteen garments. Presumably she possessed additional garments too ordinary and inexpensive to be listed, but this is far from the closetfuls of designer clothing any modern socialite would possess. Clothes were expected to last for years and were mended rather than discarded.

Unlike the aristocracy of other eras, the rich in Florence were not cut off from their less fortunate compatriots. Their shops were located on the same blocks as crowded tenements of rubble and brick. Every day they rubbed shoulders on the narrow streets with lowly wool carders in their soiled rags and wooden shoes; they did business in the same shops and prayed in the same churches. Of course Florence was no paradise in which distinctions between rich and poor had magically disappeared. The contempt of the former for the latter was as great in fifteenth-century Florence as in any other age. But the complex mixture of hostility, misunderstanding, and recrimination, as well as mutual dependence, that marked the relations between the classes was enriched by continual intercourse. Even as a young boy Lorenzo was familiar with the striking contrast between the comfort of his own circumstances and the squalid conditions endured by many of his neighbors, something that aroused his pity however little it affected his sense of his own superiority. The common touch he exhibited throughout his life was a product both of his omnivorous tastes and of the easy familiarity with all types he picked up as a child of the city.

Like many of those city-born and city-bred, the various members of the Medici family all yearned for the tranquillity of the countryside. In this, as in so much else, they were typical Florentines. Every citizen who could afford it owned a farm outside the city walls, and even rich merchants were not too proud to work the land with their own hands. Today in Florence, vineyards and olive groves are still within a few minutes' walk of the city center. In the fifteenth century the margin between town and country was even narrower, with fields and orchards filling out the more sparsely populated neighborhoods within the city walls and, just beyond, hillsides dotted with elegant villas and modest farms.

Lorenzo was from his earliest days shuttled back and forth among the many country residences his family possessed. The descriptions of the labor and planning involved will strike a familiar chord with anyone who has had to pack up a house for a summer vacation. "This evening I received your letter saying you have decided that we are to go to Careggi," Lucrezia wrote to her husband, perhaps betraying some slight irritation with Piero's sudden change of plans. "I must see how we can clean and

scour and do all the needful things, and get in the necessary provisions....
I wanted one of the sheets without hem-stitching from the antechamber,
but you have sent me one from the bed in our room. I am sending you this
back, together with Cosimo's squirrel-lined tunic which you asked for....
The sheet you are sending should be put in the bag in which I am sending
you various things."

Family letters are filled with such homely detail—a missing pair of scis-
sors to be sent to Cosimo or a fur-lined cloak for Piero, who apparently
failed to prepare for the cold and damp of Venice. Lucrezia and her
mother-in-law, Contessina, are kept busy looking after their husbands and
children, sending capons, barrels of oil, wheels of cheese, dried fruit, and
special delicacies after them on their various journeys so that one imag-
ines the roads of Tuscany crowded with mules whose only job is to keep
the bellies of the Medici men well filled. For all their wealth and power, the
Medici women were frugal housekeepers, impatient with waste and anxious to get all they can out of a yard of cloth or barrel of flour. The family's
many farms not only served to stock the larders of the palace in the city
but also were businesses that they hoped to turn to profit. A letter from
Contessina to Giovanni, for example, reminds him to check up on the
manager of their estates at Careggi, who had been commissioned to sell
fifty-three pounds of goat cheese to some local pot-makers. While the men
hobnobbed with dukes and cardinals and attended to affairs of state, the
women continued to display the practical good sense and work ethic of
their industrious and more modest forebears.

Closest to the city was the villa at Careggi, where Cosimo could often
be found puttering about the garden or pruning his vines as he sought
relief from the cares of politics. A day's ride to the north brought the family to the villas of Cafaggiolo or Trebbio in the Medici's ancestral homeland of the Mugello. The estate at Cafaggiolo was so extensive that,
according to Lorenzo's friend the poet Angelo Poliziano there was nothing that Cosimo could see from its high tower that did not belong to
him.* Trebbio was favored as a hunting lodge, and young Lorenzo soon
became addicted to the excitement of the chase, a sport that inspired
some of his best poetry.

---

* By the time Lorenzo sold the estate, in 1486, it comprised sixty-seven separate farms.

Few of these villas could be described as luxurious. They were referred to in the Medici tax returns simply as "fortified houses," and the phrase comes closer to the mark than any notion of a villa based on examples like Hadrian's estate at Tivoli. Contemporary pictures show the high towers and beetling crenellations that reveal their function as refuges in times of unrest, a holdover from the tumultuous Middle Ages.* In one letter, the manager of the estate, Francesco Fronsini, noted that some candles sent from Venice "seem too good for Cafaggiolo," a clear indication that then, as now, the standards for country living were more relaxed than those for the city. All the Medici men, from Cosimo to Lorenzo, followed the advice of such Roman writers on country life as Cato, Cicero, and Virgil, and worked the land with their own hands.

Lorenzo spent many of his happiest hours in the fields and forests of Cafaggiolo and Trebbio. His many letters to the managers of his estates show a detailed and firsthand knowledge of animal husbandry, farming, and, especially, the breeding and care of horses, for which he developed a lifelong passion. He enjoyed fishing as a relaxing pastime, but hunting and hawking stimulated his competitive spirit. Sights and sounds absorbed in the fields and forests fill his poetry, whose evocations of country life are every bit as precise as the landscapes of Gozzoli, Ghirlandaio, and Fra Angelico. This description of a rural sunrise comes from his poem "The Partridge Hunt":

> The wolf retreated to its wilderness.
> The fox retreated to its den,
> For there was now a chance it might be seen,
> Now that the moon had come and gone again.
> The busy peasant woman had already
> Allowed the sheep and pigs to leave their pens.
> Crystalline, clear, and chilly was the air:
> the morning would be fair,
> When I was roused by jingling bells and by
> The calling of the dogs and similar sounds.

---

* See the series of paintings of the Medici villas made in the 1590s by Giusto Utens. They are now housed in Florence's Museo di Firenze Com'Era.

· · ·

But the attractions of the countryside were, ultimately, merely a respite from more serious work that could be done only in the city. As the Florentine statesman and military leader Gino di Neri Capponi wrote in a poetic homily to his sons, "Honor does not reside in the woods . . . / Worthy men are made in the city, nor indeed can he be called a man / whose measure is not taken there."

It was from the heart of the city that Cosimo and his two sons managed the vast and profitable Medici bank. The Medici firm maintained a table on the Via Porta Rossa in the vicinity of the New Market, where businessmen could deposit their coin or redeem bills of exchange. But this business represented only a small portion of a much larger and more varied operation encompassing both small manufacturing establishments (silk and woolen shops in Florence) and international trading cartels. The Medici bank maintained branches in Rome (usually the most profitable because the pope's finances were handled largely by the Medici bank there), Naples, Milan, Venice, Bruges, Avignon, Geneva, London, and other centers of trade and finance.

Management of this vast business empire was conducted largely out of the family home. Four large rooms on the ground floor of the new palace—into which the family moved probably sometime in 1458—served as counting house and office space for scores of secretaries, clerks, and assistants. As in most Florentine *palazzi,* the ground floor was a semi-public space, but in the Medici palace it also included accommodations for both Cosimo and Piero, who had difficulty negotiating the stairs to the main living quarters above.*

The new palace must have been a pleasant change for the nine-year-old boy after the cramped, crowded quarters of the old house. Not least of the attractions were an airy courtyard and a garden, the latter filled with exotic fruit trees. With indulgent, often distracted parents, the spacious and bustling palace offered plenty of opportunities for undiscovered mischief. It was, perhaps, a little too commodious for a family used to living one on top of another. Some years later, after the death of his younger son,

---

* Visitors to the palace report that father and son often traveled about the house in chairs borne aloft by servants.

the aged Cosimo was heard to lament, "Too large a house for too small a family!"

The palace as it exists today differs significantly from the one Lorenzo knew. First of all, it was considerably smaller in the fifteenth century, seven bays of windows having been added in the seventeenth century by the Riccardi family, who evidently found it too cramped for their needs. A loggia opened out onto the busy street, making the building less forbidding than it now seems. During Lorenzo's lifetime this arcade was always crowded with petitioners, visitors, and even tourists armed with letters of introduction. The Milanese envoy Niccolò de' Carissimi da Parma, visiting the master of the house in 1459, complained that he was "obliged to leave because of the multitude who arrived wishing to see the aforesaid magnificent Cosimo."

Even more deceptive is the austere interior we see today. Walking through its largely empty rooms and corridors one gets little hint of its former opulence. It was Piero who took the lead in furnishing the new family home with paintings, sculptures, and decorative objects, a collection to which Lorenzo continued to add after his father's death. Gone is Piero's private study, whose walls were covered floor to ceiling in elaborate patterns of inlaid wood and whose collection of objets d'art so impressed visitors, including the architect Filarete, who has left us a vivid description of the master at his ease:

> He has himself carried into a studio. . . . When he arrives, he looks at his books. They seem like nothing but solid pieces of gold. . . . Sometimes he reads one or the other or has them read. He has so many different kinds that not one day but more than a month would be required to see and understand their dignity. . . . He has effigies and portraits of all the emperors and noble men who have ever lived made in gold, silver, bronze, jewels, marble, or other materials. . . . Another day he looks at his jewels and precious stones. He has a marvelous quantity of them of great value and cut in different ways. He takes pleasure and delight in looking at them and in talking about the virtue and value of those he has. Another day [he looks] at vases of gold, silver, and other materials made nobly and at great

expense and brought from different places. He delights greatly in these, praising their dignity and the mastery of their fabricators. Then another day [he looks at] other noble things that have come from different parts of the world, various strange arms for offense and defense.

It is impossible to overestimate the impact such an environment had on the formation of Lorenzo's tastes and his character. Even among Florentines, accustomed to being surrounded by works of art and architecture of the highest quality, his circumstances were unique. The immense Medici fortune was harnessed to acquire work from the greatest artists and artisans of Europe; from their branches in northern Europe employees were told to be on the lookout for the finest tapestries and the latest works in oil by masters like Jan van Eyck;* agents in Rome and southern Italy sought out antiquities, and scholars on the Medici payroll rummaged through the monastic libraries of Europe seeking lost works by the ancients. Galeazzo Maria Sforza, who as son of the duke of Milan was a youth not easily impressed, was awed by the Medici's fabled treasures. "[T]he aforesaid count," noted his chief counselor,

together with the company, went on a tour of this palace, and especially of its noblest parts, such as some studies, little chapels, living rooms, bedchambers and gardens, all of which are constructed with admirable skill, embellished on every side with gold and fine marbles, with carvings and sculptures in relief, with pictures and inlays done in perspective by the most accomplished and perfect of masters, down to the benches and all the floors of the house; tapestries and household ornaments of gold and silk; silverware and bookcases that are endless and innumerable; then the vaults or rather ceilings of the chambers and salons, which are for the most part

---

* Oil painting, invented in northern Europe, was still a little-known medium in Italy. The importation of masterpieces in oil by van Eyck and Rogier van der Weyden, by the Medici and their employees, stimulated the growth of this new medium in Italy, leading to the masterpieces of Leonardo and Raphael.

done in fine gold with diverse and various forms; then a garden all
created of the most beautiful polished marbles with various plants,
which seems a thing not natural but painted.

Sforza's visit highlights an important function of the palace: it was an
essential tool of Medici statecraft. As private citizens, Cosimo, Piero, and
Lorenzo possessed none of the titles needed to impress those with whom
they negotiated on behalf of the republic. But by building this grand residence and furnishing it with famous works of ancient and modern art
they showed that they belonged in the company of the greatest feudal
lords.* So successful was this strategy that close acquaintance with the
Medici lifestyle could foster a not altogether unintended sense of cultural
inferiority. On a later visit Galeazzo Maria Sforza admitted its collections
far outshone his own, and when his brother, Lodovico, lured Leonardo da
Vinci away from Florence it was partly in an attempt to redress the cultural
deficit.

Ordinary Florentines alternated between feelings of pride and resentment at the opulent lifestyle of their leading family. The treasures of the
palace were celebrated in verse and song, one anonymous poet declaring
"nothing in the world [is] more an earthly paradise than this." But it could
also be a tempting target for those who believed the government had been
hijacked by private interest; during one politically tense moment, the family awoke to find the threshold of the palace smeared with blood.

For the most part, however, the public understood that the honor of
the city was tied to the honor paid to its leading family. Florentines were
painfully aware of their lack of pedigree and took every opportunity to
demonstrate that, despite the absence of hereditary nobility, they were
men of refinement. The pageantry of Florentine life was in large part an
expression of cultural insecurity, and the Medici palace was a key element
in this self-promotion. It is a notable trend in Florentine history—one
that helps explain Medici success in subverting the city's republican

---

* When the Emperor Frederick toured Florence in 1452 he made sure to visit Cosimo's
palace. This was almost certainly the *casa vecchia*, an indication that even before the
move to the new house the Medici collections were renowned throughout Europe.

institutions—that men who otherwise jealously guarded their prerogatives accorded the Medici an almost princely standing if only in order to seem more worthy in the eyes of foreigners.

The one room that still hints at the *palazzo*'s former splendor is the small private chapel on the second floor. In 1459, Benozzo Gozzoli began work on the frescoes that have since made this one of the most beautiful rooms in Florence or, indeed, in all of Europe. Under the close supervision of Piero, Gozzoli depicted the Adoration of the Magi, a theme he had already tackled for the family when, as an assistant to Fra Angelico, he had painted a modest version on the walls of Cosimo's private cell in San Marco. No expense was spared to create a jewel-like effect, including an intricately inlaid floor (designed by Andrea del Verrocchio) and elaborately coffered and gilded ceilings. As for the frescoes themselves, Piero insisted on the finest materials, generous amounts of lapis lazuli (for the deep blues of the sky) and sheets of silver and gold leaf that would cast an otherworldly gleam in the light of flickering candles.

Piero took a strong interest in the painting's day-to-day progress. A series of letters between Piero and the artist suggests that this was a commission particularly close to his heart. "This morning I had a letter from Your Magnificence," wrote Gozzoli to Piero, "and I learnt that it seems to you the seraphs I have done are out of place. On one side I did one among some clouds, and of this you hardly see anything except the tips of the wings. . . . Nevertheless I will do as you command, two little clouds will take them away." This supervision—even micromanagement—of an artist's work was not unusual. Renaissance patrons were often intimately involved in the smallest details of the works they commissioned. In their own eyes they were the true agents of the work of art, and they regarded the craftsmen they employed as, at best, collaborators, and at worst skilled servants whose role was simply to carry out the vision of their employers.

One should not dismiss such attitudes as mere snobbery. Art in Renaissance Florence was the serious business of serious men, inextricably bound up with politics and religion. Later in his career Lorenzo employed the greatest geniuses of the Florentine Renaissance—Botticelli, Michelangelo, and Leonardo—as his own personal emissaries, sending them the length and breadth of Italy in hopes of cementing alliances and maintaining his city's prestige abroad. If Florence was not the most powerful state on the peninsula, it abounded in artists and craftsmen coveted by foreign courts. By exporting Florentine culture, Lorenzo and his predecessors tried to achieve through the dazzle of art what they could not hope to win through strength of arms.

Nor was the role of art connoisseur the effete pursuit of the idle rich. Every Florentine patrician, not least the Medici themselves, spent countless hours serving on the boards (*operaii*) that supervised the great building and artistic projects in the city, making decisions on matters that now would be considered the creative province of the artist. Brunelleschi, himself a member of the ruling class, was exasperated by the constant interference of amateurs who thought they knew more about engineering than he did, but most artists understood that their role was to bring the client's ideas to fruition. Discernment in matters of art was the mark of a true gentleman, as a popular fifteenth-century treatise on education reminds us: "The beauty and grace of objects, both natural ones and those made by man's art, are things it is proper for men of distinction to be able to discuss with each other and appreciate." Cosimo, in a letter to his cousin Averardo, makes an explicit connection between judgment in matters of art and the kinds of judgment demanded of those in positions of political leadership. "Although we do not have the expertise in feats of war of those who practice it continually," he wrote, "nevertheless, seeing what others do, we are able to judge who does it better. I believe that although you are not a great painter, nevertheless you would judge the figures of Giotto to be better than those of Balzanello."

In a very real sense, Piero, as much as Gozzoli, must be regarded as the author of the *Adoration*. The dynastic and political ambitions of its patron are closely woven into the sacred scene. While the fresco ostensibly commemorates the birth of the Savior a millennium and a half earlier, the magnificent procession Gozzoli conjures—in a Tuscan landscape complete with rural castles based on the Medici villas at Trebbio and Cafaggiolo—is couched in terms that would have been familiar to contemporary Florentines. Even the elaborate costumes of the kings and their retinues are based on the gaudy processions that the Medici sponsored every three years on the Feast of the Epiphany.*

Gozzoli's painting is both a sacred narrative and, perhaps more important, a portrait of the Medici regime at the height of its power. Here, in a private setting, Piero could indulge to the full his taste for opulent display, disguising his ambition through an appropriately pious theme. If the political message were not obvious enough, Gozzoli—with Piero supplying the roster of names—painted in the scene all the leading figures associated with the Medici *reggimento*, including, in the entourage of the old king Melchior, many of those who would soon turn against him—Luca Pitti, Niccolò Soderini, and Dietisalvi Neroni.

For centuries the youngest magus, Caspar, was assumed to be a portrait of the ten-year-old Lorenzo. The identification has a certain superficial plausibility. The young king's head is framed by a laurel bush, a plant that was often used as the personal emblem of the Medici heir. Gozzoli, a master of fine detail, has embossed the harness of the king with the Medici *palle* and the family motto, *SEMPER* (always), and the king's entourage includes portraits of Cosimo (riding a donkey), Piero, and important Medici allies like Galeazzo Maria Sforza (riding the white horse to Cosimo's right).

But for all Piero's pride in his son, it is unthinkable that he would have placed him in a position where both he and Cosimo would be seen as supporting players in Lorenzo's triumphal procession. And the fair, angelic face of Caspar bears no resemblance to Lorenzo, who was, in any case, far too young to play the role. Gozzoli has indeed included a portrait of the ten-year-old Lorenzo, but in a far less prominent position. To find Lorenzo we must look further back, in the great crowd of faces following in the young king's wake. There, the swarthy complexion and shrewd, sharp features are immediately recognizable, standing out from amid the sea of less individualized faces, including that of his handsome

---

* Many scholars have seen in the exotic costumes a visual echo of the famous Council of Florence of 1438 in which Cosimo played host to the Byzantine emperor John Paleologus and his entourage. These easterners' opulent garb made a deep impression on Florentines, but Gozzoli's fresco seems more closely modeled on local customs and costumes.

brother, Giuliano, on his left. In this, the earliest known portrait of Lorenzo, the features of the boy are already stamped with the strong personality of the adult.

For Cosimo the new palace served the practical need of accommodating the growing families of two married sons, but it also marked a significant realignment of the larger Medici clan. In the *casa vecchia* the descendants of Giovanni di Bicci had shared a home; they constituted a single lineage sprung from a common ancestor. Now with his own palace, built with his money and according to his tastes, Cosimo set himself up as the pater familias of his own independent dynasty. From this point on the two main branches descended from Giovanni di Bicci will go their separate ways.*

By the time the Medici took possession of their new home the sixty-nine-year-old Cosimo had begun to loosen his hold on the reins of power. Increasingly he deferred to his sons, unloading some of the burden and preparing them for the responsibilities they would assume when he was gone. Given the unofficial nature of Cosimo's position, the continuity of the *reggimento* and of the Medicis' dominant position within it were by no means assured. Working in their favor, however, was Cosimo's longevity, which guaranteed that he would be around long enough to see his children firmly established in the upper echelons of the state. By 1458, Piero was already a leading member of the *reggimento*, having served in important positions, including as a member of the *Signoria* in 1448, while Giovanni also served as one of the priors in 1453 and on the important advisory council known as the Dodici Buonuomini, the Twelve, in 1454.

Even in a city where loyalty to family was paramount, the Medici seem remarkable for their unity of purpose through many generations. The need for collaboration was increased by Piero's poor health. For many years, in fact, it had seemed to most Florentines that the robust and outgoing Giovanni was the more likely successor to Cosimo. In 1455, Giovanni

---

* The descendants of Cosimo's brother, Lorenzo, continued to occupy the *casa vecchia*. The descendants of this older Lorenzo eventually became in the sixteenth century the granddukes of Tuscany.

became director general of the Medici bank, a clear indication of the central role he played in the family's affairs. The mark he left on his nephew is unmistakable; Lorenzo seems to have inherited his gregarious personality and weakness for sensual pleasures from his fun-loving uncle rather than from his dour, humorless father. Giovanni's amiable character is embodied in the delightful villa he had built on the slopes of Fiesole. It was a building of no practical value (in fact its construction on a steep slope was one long series of engineering disasters). After it passed into the possession of Piero and his children it became a favorite haunt of Lorenzo, Giuliano, and their companions, who would spend summer afternoons wandering along its cypress-shaded lanes, heads bent deep in conversation. Unlike Trebbio, Cafaggiolo, and Careggi, working farms that helped to feed the voracious appetite of the *palazzo* in the city, Fiesole's sole function was the pursuit of cultivated idleness; poetry rather than produce was its main export. Lorenzo's friend the poet Angelo Poliziano paints a charming portrait of life at the villa. "When you are made uncomfortable by the heat of the season in your retreat at Careggi," he wrote to Marsilio Ficino,

> you will perhaps think the shelter of Fiesole not undeserving of your notice. Seated between the sloping sides of the mount, here we have water in abundance and, being constantly refreshed with moderate winds, find little inconvenience from the glare of the sun. As you approach the house it seems surrounded by trees, but when you reach it, you find it commands a full prospect of the city. Populous as the vicinity is, I can enjoy here that solitude so gratifying to my disposition.

The villa at Fiesole captures the new ideal of the Renaissance gentleman whose life is spent cultivating his mind and his aesthetic sense—an ideal that will find its fullest expression in the retreat Lorenzo later built for himself at Poggio a Caiano.* The difference between the fortresslike Trebbio and the airy Fiesole is the difference between the medieval and Renaissance mind. For those of Cosimo's generation, the pursuit of pleasure

---

* See Chapter XIX.

unsupported by a steady return on investment was frivolous. For Lorenzo it was exactly those same pursuits that gave savor to life.

Domestic arrangements in the Medici *palazzo* were complicated, with three distinct households and three generations living under one roof, but there is little or no hint of tension or competition. This is largely a tribute to Contessina de' Bardi, Cosimo's wife, a sensible, nurturing woman who was the emotional glue binding the extended family together. Less educated and cultured than her two daughters-in-law, she nevertheless managed multiple households and fussed over the health and well-being of her husband, children, and grandchildren. When Lorenzo was a year old and away with his parents in Trebbio, Contessina included a reminder to Lucrezia "to make him suck well," probably an unnecessary piece of advice for a mother of three.

Lorenzo, for one, was devoted to his grandmother. She lived until 1473, surviving her husband by ten years, and so remained a comforting figure in Lorenzo's life well into his adulthood. Lorenzo, increasingly surrounded by hypocritical flatterers and potential rivals, craved such maternal figures who offered reassurance and unquestioning love without fear of competition.

While his affection for this simple woman was direct and sincere, his feelings for his grandfather were complicated by constant reminders to live up to his example. Even when Cosimo was many years in his grave, Lorenzo found it difficult to emerge from under his shadow. "[A]s God created Cosimo as a model of the universe," the philosopher Marsilio Ficino wrote to Lorenzo, "mold yourself on the model of Cosimo. Indeed you have begun to do so." Lorenzo's own protean achievement as a writer, patron, and statesman may well have been spurred by the desire to make a greater mark in the minds of his countrymen than his illustrious grandfather.

A similar pattern was repeated in his relations with his parents. Piero was a dutiful father, but any expressions of affection were tempered by his belief that it was his role to prepare his son for the difficult position he would inherit. "Be old beyond your years," was the constant refrain in his letters to Lorenzo. In other words, Piero was a typical Florentine father, dispensing stern advice more readily than emotional support.

Piero's affectionate nature becomes apparent only in his letters to his wife, and then often only indirectly. At first their correspondence is marked by a formality dictated by the absolute authority of a husband over his wife. In the first letter we have from Lucrezia (written in 1446), the twenty-one-year-old bride addresses her husband as "My Lord and Master," but after years of marriage their correspondence takes on a tone of mutual respect and deep affection. In 1463, when Giuliano was taken seriously ill while visiting Pisa, Lucrezia hurried to her son's side. Piero, who had remained behind to attend to his work, was evidently distracted with worry. "I write to you several letters on the same day so that," she informed him, "in case one goes astray, you will have another giving you news of Giuliano. . . . I want you to know every little change, so that you may understand better what [the physician] *Maestro* Mariotto writes, and that you may decide, not according to my opinion, but according to what you yourself think best. . . . He is not as cheerful in the day time as I should like, because he is exhausted by the fever. . . . Do not get depressed, however, for Giuliano is strong." When Lucrezia herself fell ill, Piero was equally solicitous. "Have faith and obey the doctors," he urged her, "and do not budge one jot from their orders, and bear and suffer everything, if not for yourself and for us, for the love of God who is helping you."

Piero's devotion to his wife was not misplaced. Not only was she the ideal Florentine housewife, but she was an important political asset, a woman whose kindness and tact more than made up for her husband's shortcomings. Lucrezia's social skills were crucial to maintaining the loyalty of the literally thousands of clients whose support was necessary to maintain the Medici in power. Many petitioners applied directly to Lucrezia rather than dealing with her more forbidding husband. Her correspondents include both the great and the humble. At one extreme is the queen of Bosnia, exiled by the advancing Ottoman Turks, who writes to Lucrezia to implore her to expedite a loan from the Roman branch of the Medici bank; at the other is a letter in which she is asked to intercede on behalf of a humble weaver condemned to death for committing bigamy. (Lucrezia will play a similar role on behalf of Lorenzo, who, while more gregarious than his father, was often simply overwhelmed by the number of demands made on his time.)

Piero relied increasingly on Lucrezia's judgment, sending her on important missions when he was unable to travel and depending on her vivid descriptions of people and places. In addition to being the wife of Florence's leading citizen, she was an important literary patroness and a fine poet in her own right, and participated as much as the limited possibilities available to her permitted in the great artistic and intellectual movements of the day. Lorenzo's tutor, the erudite Gentile Becchi, penned the following tribute to the mistress of the house: "You are well read, your bureau full of books, you have understood how to comment on the epistles of Saint Paul, you have, throughout your life kept company with men of honor." Despite her traditional views on religion, Lucrezia saw nothing incompatible between the new trends in literature, with their almost pagan appetite for the pleasures and flavors of the world, and Christian values.* Her retellings of sacred stories, written for her grandchildren, contain vivid descriptions that owe much to her own life at the palace on the Via Larga. In her "Story of Queen Esther," the feast King Ahasuerus gives for his bride, where "[e]verywhere you could hear instruments playing of every kind," while singers serenaded the guests "with sweet melodies and skillful harmonies," as they supped on "infinite dishes . . . savoring their aromas," recalls similar descriptions of Nannina's or Lorenzo's own wedding feasts.

Impatient with the limited role assigned to her, Lucrezia turned even her physical ailments into opportunities. Like most of the other members of the family, Lucrezia was often in poor health, suffering repeated attacks of fever and eczema (a condition that also plagued Lorenzo) for which she sought some relief by frequenting mineral baths. One of these spas, in Bagno a Morba in the Apennine foothills, she purchased and turned into a thriving business.

Such was Piero's confidence in his wife's good sense that in 1467 he sent her to Rome to consult with the papal curia. It was a remarkably public role for a woman, so contrary to custom that, according to the sour Jacopo Acciaiuoli, it "reduced Florence to the lowest level of repute." That she was equally helpful to her son is revealed in a letter addressed to Lorenzo from Francesco da Castiglione, one of the canons of San Lorenzo, consoling him on the occasion of his mother's death:

---

* Luigi Pulci's ribald and rollicking poem *Morgante,* for instance, is dedicated to "the most noble lady Lucretia di Piero di Cosimo de' Medici."

What part of the state did the wisdom of Lucrezia not see, take care of, or confirm! . . . Sometimes [your mother's] actions, from the political point of view, were more prudent than yours, for you attended only to the great things and forgot the less. . . . She knew how to manage the most important affairs with wise counsel, and to succor the citizens in time of calamity.

Reading between the lines one can sense that Lucrezia softened Lorenzo's harsh edges, soothing the feelings of those who had been brushed aside or ignored by her imperious son.

Benozzo Gozzoli, *Adoration of the Magi* (detail of Lorenzo at center),
Medici Palace, 1459 (Art Resource)

III. MASTER OF CEREMONY

*He for many reasons has great power
Since his family can do much,
Son of Piero and grandson of Cosimo.*

—ANONYMOUS ABOUT LORENZO, APRIL 1459

HUNDREDS OF TORCHES BLAZED FROM SCONCES LINING the Via Larga, their flames shimmering on the fine white sand that had been layered over the paving stones, muffling the sharp clatter of hooves. As the sun sank behind the hills the benches along the palaces began to fill with people. Every window was crowded with men and women craning their necks to get a better view. Bright banners were draped over somber facades of rough stone: the red lily of the Florentine Republic, the gold crescents of the Piccolomini of Siena (now with the added keys and crown showing the elevation to the papal throne of one of their own, Aeneas Silvius, as Pius II), the greyhound stretched beneath a pine tree representing the Sforza of Milan, and, above all, the golden shield emblazoned with the red balls of the Medici.

The torchlight cavalcade and ceremonial clash of arms was to be the crowning event of what had already been a memorable day. The city's guest list on April 29, 1459, included not only Pope Pius II, surrounded by an entourage of scarlet-robed cardinals, but also the lords of Faenza, Forlì, and Rimini. Most important politically for Florence was the gracious attendance of the fifteen-year-old Galeazzo Maria Sforza, count of Pavia and eldest son of the duke of Milan. Hoping to project a mood of confidence and to astonish their visitors with an unparalleled display of wealth and refinement, the *Signoria* had arranged a variety of entertainments. The festivities had begun that morning with a joust at the Piazza Santa Croce, featuring the sons of Florence's best families decked out in full ceremonial armor. This had been followed by a ball at the New Market with "[s]ixty young Florentine gentlemen, who were expert dancers, richly adorned with pearls and jewels, and many pretty maidens and girls." For those who preferred stronger stuff, the priors had arranged what promised to be a gory spectacle in the *Piazza della Signoria*. Here a wooden stockade had been erected and filled with horses, cows, a wild boar, and two young buffalo. As the crowd roared, two lions—symbolizing the martial valor of the Florentine people—were set loose in what was supposed to be a sanguinary spectacle worthy of the Roman Colosseum. Disappointment soon followed as the lions, frightened by the shouting multitude, wandered about in a daze. "The preparations had been great, and the expenses large," grumbled one eyewitness, "but the pleasure given was small." Pope Pius, on whose behalf the show had been staged, was even less impressed. "They spent very little on entertaining the Pope," he complained, "nor did they lay out much on lavish spectacles, though they brought lions into the piazza to fight with horses and other animals and arranged tournaments in which more wine was drunk than blood spilled."

For the Medici family it was important that the evening's events compensate for the afternoon's embarrassment. Not only was the setting, in the heart of the Golden Lion, meant to call attention to the family whose palace would form the backdrop to the nighttime parade, but the star of the whole affair was to be the ten-year-old Medici heir.

It began with the steady rumble of drums and blare of flutes and trumpets from the Piazza San Marco. Thirty musicians soon wheeled into view. Close on their heels were the bannermen, who raised the personal standard of Lorenzo de' Medici depicting a golden falcon caught in a net. Next, riding in formation, came an advance guard, richly dressed and mounted, consisting of twelve youths from the best families—including the sons of Puccio Pucci and Averardo Portinari (both families involved in running the Medici bank), two members of the Pazzi clan, and Lorenzo Neroni, son of Dietisalvi. Each of these brave young knights, dressed in matching uniforms of the lord they served, was attended by an army of pages and servants, again in matching livery bearing the red balls of the Medici crest.*

---

* The splendor of these parades is recalled in Benozzo Gozzoli's *Adoration of the Magi* in which the retinues of the kings, especially that of the young Caspar, are based on contemporary *brigate,* complete with mounted escort and attendants.

"Palle! Palle!" A roar of approval from the crowd announced the arrival of Lorenzo himself, sumptuously attired and mounted proudly atop a snow-white charger. Behind him came the final treat, an elaborately decorated carriage symbolizing—in the best tradition of courtly chivalry—the Triumph of Love.

As the column made its way south along the Via Larga, each adolescent boy preened like a fashion model on a runway. "Every warrior wears a helmet surrounded by a headdress in the form of a garland, beautifully decorated with silver, and with golden feathers rising from it, shining like a star," wrote one bedazzled spectator. They proceeded as far as the baptistery before reversing course and coming to a halt beneath the walls of the Medici palace. Here the assembled dignitaries were treated to a thrilling spectacle as the young men, their armor gleaming in the torchlight, demonstrated their equestrian skill, charging with gold-tipped lances like fierce warriors. At least for this one night, these sons of bankers and merchants were transformed into daring knights who, judging by the splendor of their outfits if not their martial prowess, seemed fit to take their place alongside Charlemagne, Roland, and their brave companions. As always, the Medici had spared no expense, outfitting the entire entourage in the costliest garments and providing the riders with the finest mounts. There was no doubt among the assembled crowd to whom this night belonged: "He for many reasons has great power," wrote one eyewitness,

> *Since his family can do much,*
> *Son of Piero and grandson of Cosimo.*
> *Thus these genteel youths made him* signore *[lord]. . . .*
> *Whence he wanted to show everyone*
> *That they were all subject to one* signore.
> *Now that genuine youth moves*
> *Upon a horse marvelously ornate,*
> *Everyone watches what he does. . . .*
> *His dress surpasses easily that of*
> *All those of whom we've spoken,*
> *And well he shows that he is* signore.

There is something faintly ridiculous about these merchants' sons dressing up as chivalrous knights, but beneath the empty pomp more important business was being transacted. On the most obvious level, those who belonged to Lorenzo's brigade and who wore the livery of his family were declaring their fealty as surely as any knight kneeling before his king. Lorenzo, holding high the baton of the *signore,* accepted their declaration of loyalty with a calm sense of superiority as befitted a feudal lord.

Indeed, the festivities of April 1459 capped a decade-long public relations campaign that had begun with Lorenzo's baptism on the Feast of the Epiphany. From the moment of Lorenzo's birth the Medici were engaged in a continual and delicate process of seduction in which the young boy was presented to the people as both the paragon of the virtuous citizen, a Florentine born and bred of a respectable merchant family, and as a charismatic leader, destined to hold the fate of a nation in his hands. Finding precisely the right balance between the two was difficult, since, as Francesco Guicciardini noted, "In Florence the citizens love equality by nature, and yield unwillingly when they should acknowledge anyone as their superior." To a people steeped in republican traditions, jealous of rank and ready to cut down to size anyone who sought to raise himself too high above his fellow citizens, Lorenzo was something new. He was, to use an anachronistic term, a celebrity, a child star paraded about the city in fine clothes and the center of attention on many public occasions.

Lorenzo was precocious and self-assured from an early age and Cosimo and Piero realized that the boy would be an asset in the general struggle for power and prestige. At the age of five he was dressed up in the latest French fashions and bundled off to the gates of the city to greet the visiting Duke of Anjou "surrounded," we are told, "by a crowd of children and adults." Lisping formal greetings more suited to an adult's mouth, Lorenzo charmed everyone.

Demands to play the part of the young *signore* were constant; not even illness could excuse him from the obligation to promote his family's interests. Recuperating from a bout of eczema at the mineral springs at Macerato in 1455, the six-year-old was elected "Lord of the Baths," a half-humorous title that seemed mostly to involve presiding over parties and picnics in which, sniffed Piero, there were "some gentlemen and more than enough of the other sort." Even in such casual moments Lorenzo learned to play his part as a leader of men.

As Lorenzo matured and began to think for himself he tended to look upon such occasions with an increasingly jaundiced eye. Unlike his father he was naturally sociable, but the hypocrisy and scheming he encountered every day tended to encourage in him a cynical view of men and their motives. He often declared that he wished nothing better than to escape the stench and corruption of the city and lose himself in a simple rustic retreat. "I do not know of riches or honors sweeter than this life of yours— one free of all political intrigue," declared Lorenzo to the country swain in his philosophical poem "The Supreme Good." "Among you happy shepherds and you cowherds no hatred reigns or wicked treachery and in these pastures no ambition grows." Later in life when he was unhappy in love or dispirited by the backstabbing of Florentine politics, Lorenzo would flee to "some solitary and shaded place or the comfort of a green meadow . . . where I could take my ease close by the clear and flowing water or in the shade of a small green tree." In the fields, meadows, and forests of his beloved Tuscany he found an inner peace he could never know in the city.

By the age of eleven Lorenzo was hounded by office-seekers who viewed him as a likely source of patronage. Those who wished to get ahead in Florence knew he had the ear of the most influential men in the city. He was pestered with letters from Medici clients and could hardly leave his house without being mobbed by the petitioners, who crowded around the gates to the palace. Medici power, like that of a Chicago ward boss, rested on an ability to deliver the goods, even for the most humble petitioner. Lorenzo's first extant letter, written in November of 1460, is a plea for special consideration on behalf of one Chalumato of Arezzo, whom he describes as "my most dear friend." In his second, written in September of 1461, he attempts to put in a good word with his father on behalf of *ser* Griso, "who wishes to be named notary of the *Signoria*." For someone in Lorenzo's position, "dear friends" sprouted like mushrooms in the rain.

Travel was one way to escape the constant harrassment he experienced in his native land. Restless by nature, Lorenzo eagerly sought opportunities to escape and Piero often obliged by employing his son as an itinerant goodwill ambassador. Out on the road, surrounded by congenial companions, Lorenzo enjoyed a rare degree of freedom. In July of 1463, Piero arranged for Lorenzo a trip to Pistoia, an important client of Florence's in western Tuscany. There, Lorenzo and his companions were received by the local bishop and presented to the people, all of whom, he recorded in a letter to his father, greeted them very warmly. Never one to allow business to get in the way of pleasure, he then begged his father to allow him a side trip to Lucca and Pisa "to look after our affairs there," but also, he admitted, to try his hand at trout fishing. One can sense that Piero was none too keen on this detour since Lorenzo tried to bribe him by offering him a share of the catch, though in the end, he confessed, "it rained so heavily that few were caught."

Most of these journeys were carefully planned by Piero, but sticking to an itinerary was difficult for someone like Lorenzo, who was always on the lookout for new sensations and experiences. But delays were not always his fault. "You have arrived at Milan later than I thought," Piero complained to his son on one occasion, "and perhaps than you did wish, on account of the delay caused by the honors paid you by the Duke at Ferrara." Poor weather or an outbreak of plague could create long detours, and even in the best of circumstances Lorenzo and his friends were obliged to make frequent stops. Along the way to paying a courtesy call on a provincial bishop or *Signoria* the band would be forced to pause in every hilltop village where the populace would insist they sit down to a dinner of pickled meats, boiled fowl, roast pigeon, and other rustic delicacies, all washed down with ample quantities of sweet trebbiano wine, to name but one menu. "Yesterday after leaving Florence we came as far as San Miniato, singing all the way," wrote the poet Angelo Poliziano of one such journey, "and occasionally talking of holy things so as not to forget Lent. At Lastra we drank *zappolino,* which tasted much better than I had been told. Lorenzo is brilliant and makes the whole company gay."

Not least of the attractions of travel was the opportunity to escape the watchful eyes of his parents, though Piero and Lucrezia were careful to surround him with older men—like his brother-in-law Guglielmo de' Pazzi or his tutor, Gentile Becchi—who acted as both companions and chaperones. Unlike many of those born to privilege, Lorenzo did not surround himself with mediocrities whose dim light would allow him to shine more brightly, but preferred the company of those who could stimulate his appetite for knowledge and against whom he could test his own intellect. Topics were varied, ranging from the typically adolescent subjects of women and sport to religion and the philosophy of Plato and Aristotle. Trading barbs with the likes of Luigi Pulci or Angelo Poliziano was not a pastime for the intellectually bashful, but in such elevated company Lorenzo more than held his own.

Lorenzo's formal education was entrusted to his tutor, Gentile Becchi, a priest as well as an amateur poet of more erudition than talent. His holy orders did not prevent Becchi from covering the entire range of classical literature, much of it deemed indecent by more conservative colleagues.

With Piero's encouragement and Becchi's persistence, Lorenzo was provided with a firm grounding in the classics of ancient literature, as well as in the triumvirate of great "modern" masters, Dante, Petrarch, and Boccaccio. Lorenzo, like most well-born Florentines, was so steeped in the world of the ancients that he would not have felt out of place attending a debate in the Roman Senate or a lecture in Aristotle's Lyceum. "I have the feeling that the days of Cicero and Demosthenes are much closer to me than the sixty years just past," wrote the humanist Leonardo Bruni, sentiments many of his compatriots, Lorenzo included, would have shared. Latin was still the language of scholarship and of the Church, while knowledge of Greek was rapidly taking its place as an essential accomplishment for an educated man. Cosimo's friend, the bookseller Vespesiano da Bisticci, recounts a charming story of the discovery by another young aristocrat, the dandy Piero de' Pazzi, of the joys and practical benefits to be found by thrusting one's nose in musty old tomes:

> One day it happened that Nicolao Nicoli [Niccolò Niccoli], who was as Socrates combined with Cato in temperance and virtue, met *Messer* Piero to whom he had never spoken, and in passing him close to the palace of the Podestà [now the museum of the Bargello], he spoke to him, seeing that he was a very attractive youth. Nicolao was a very distinguished man and Piero at once came to him, whereupon Nicolao asked whose son he was. The youth answered that he was the son of *Messer* Andrea de' Pazzi, and when Nicolao asked him his occupation he answered after the fashion of young men, "I am giving myself a good time." Nicolao said to him, "As you are the son of such a father, and of such good presence, it is a shame that you should not take to the study of Latin, which would make a polished man of you.

If you neglect learning you will win little esteem, and when the flower of your youth has passed you will find yourself a good-for-nothing." *Messer* Piero, when he heard these words, at once understood their meaning, and knew that Nicolao spoke the truth, so he answered that he would set to work as soon as he had found a teacher.

The sudden transformation of the dissolute youth into the diligent scholar after a chance encounter with a wise older man smacks too much of a religious epiphany to be entirely plausible, but Bisticci's narrative captures the climate of an age in which intellectual attainments were as important as social pedigree.

At eleven, Lorenzo was already deep in his studies of Ovid and Justin, Becchi reported to his parents. According to his tutor the future patron of such luminaries as Angelo Poliziano and Pico della Mirandola, guiding light of the Platonic academy, at first found it tough going. "Do not ask how he enjoys his present studies," Becchi reported to Piero. "In all other matters he is obedient, and since you are not here the fear of transgressing makes him more diligent." Lorenzo, for all the praise of his scholarship lavished on him by later biographers, was apparently no prodigy when it came to his studies. Like most active boys he found poring over his books tedious business. Becchi's assertion that he persevered in order not to disappoint his father sheds an interesting light on the psychological roots of his need to excel.

For the men and women of the Renaissance the greatest virtue of classical literature was that it drew on a range of human experience far broader than anything to be found in the writings of the Church Fathers. In the histories of Plutarch or Tacitus or in the sensuous verses of Ovid, Lorenzo could discover a world that mirrored his own experience. Those who populated the histories of Herodotus, Thucydides, Livy, and Plutarch were much like contemporary Florentines, urbane, politically sophisticated people who wrestled with the same questions they faced on a daily basis. The lessons to be learned from the careers of Pisistratus and Pericles, Caesar and Brutus seemed much more relevant than the lives of the holy martyrs.

Small wonder that statesmen like Cosimo de' Medici—no less than his archrival Palla Strozzi—spent a large part of their fortunes on recovering lost manuscripts from the monasteries of Europe. What their agents were disinterring was not simply a vanished body of knowledge but an attitude toward life that embraced the world and man's glorious destiny. "Wonders are many on earth, and the greatest of these is man," wrote Sophocles in *Antigone* . . .

> *He is master of the ageless earth, to his own will bending*
> *The immortal mother of gods . . .*
> *He is lord of all living things . . .*
> *There is nothing beyond his power . . .*

Lorenzo's friend, Giovanni Pico della Mirandola, shared this optimistic creed, writing in his *On the Dignity of Man,* "O great and wonderful happiness of man! It is given to him to have that which he chooses and to be that which he wills."

It is this confident spirit of the ancients, echoed in Hamlet's famous speech, that was the most precious treasure recovered by the scholars of the Renaissance.* Reading about the heroic deeds of those dead for thousands of years, men of the Renaissance craved a similar kind of immortality. Lorenzo was not shy about admitting his own ambition, writing in defense of his own poetry, "The nutriment of every art is honor, and by the desire of glory alone are men's minds spurred to produce admirable works. Thus in Rome we see magnificent triumphal entries, in Greece the famous Olympian games, and both are celebrated by poets and orators with infinite mastery." The electricity of those initial encounters is difficult to recapture and the passion for all things Greek and Roman expressed by fifteenth-century Florentines could often lead to sterile imitation of dead forms. But for those like Lorenzo, driven, ambitious, confident in their own abilities, the ancient texts contained a revelation of man's potential to shape the world, for good or ill, in his own image.

If Lorenzo was often too restless to be a first-rate student, his brother, Giuliano, proved to be more compliant, if less naturally gifted. Part of Becchi's pedagogic method seemed to be to enlist his older pupil to instruct the younger. "Lorenzo is learning the verses his master there gave him and then

---

* "What a piece of work is a man! How noble in reason! how infinite in faculty! in form, in moving, how express and admirable! in action how like an angel! in apprehension how like a god!" (*Hamlet,* II, ii.)

teaches them to Giuliano," Lucrezia wrote to Piero from Cafaggiolo in February of 1457, when Lorenzo had just turned eight and Giuliano was still
three. From the beginning Lorenzo took the lead and Giuliano struggled to
keep pace. The almost five-year age difference and Lorenzo's dominating,
not to say domineering, personality guaranteed that Giuliano would
remain in his brother's shadow. Had Giuliano shared Lorenzo's own competitive fire it is unlikely the two brothers would have remained on such
good terms. Giuliano looked up to his older brother, and Lorenzo rewarded
his loyalty by taking him under his protective wing. To Giuliano, Marsilio
Ficino wrote, Lorenzo was his "other self, both in nature and in will."
Lorenzo's companion Braccio Martelli confirmed their intimacy, noting
that Lorenzo had no better or closer friend in the world than Giuliano.

The protective feelings Lorenzo had for his younger brother kept a
potential rivalry at bay, but in other settings his competitiveness was legendary. Isabella d'Este later wrote of Lorenzo, "he is always wanting to win,
by one means or another," and while in this case she was referring to his
passion for racing horses, it was an observation that held true in most are-
nas. Burdened by high expectations, he strove mightily to live up to them.
It was above all the image of his grandfather Cosimo that was held up to
Lorenzo as a model for his own conduct. Shortly after his own father's
death the ambassador from Milan remarked of the young man that he was
"thinking to achieve more than even Cosimo and Piero had ever done."

No one more often reminded Lorenzo of the high standards he was
expected to meet than Marsilio Ficino, a man whom Lorenzo revered
almost as much as Cosimo himself. "[Cosimo] was just as sharp in discussion as he was wise and strong in government," Ficino wrote to Lorenzo,
perhaps at the very moment when he was called upon to assume the rule
of the city. "Certainly I owe much to our Plato, but I confess I owe no less
to Cosimo. For Plato put before me the concept of the virtues but once;
Cosimo put them into practice every day."

Florence in the fifteenth century was the intellectual capital of Europe,
center of the new humanism and a magnet for scholars of international
renown. Even before the fall of Constantinople to the Turks in 1453, many
of the finest Greek scholars had left their native land to find security and
material comfort in the cities of the Latin West. Some of the most famous,
like Manuel Chrysolaras and John Argyropoulos, made their way to Flor-

ence. They knew that here their abilities would be appreciated and amply rewarded. These men, heirs to an intellectual tradition that reached back to the golden age of Athens, stimulated the growth of a native Florentine school of philosophy led by Marsilio Ficino and carried into the next generation by Lorenzo's friends Angelo Poliziano and Pico della Mirandola.

Lorenzo took advantage of the unparalleled educational resources available to the young men of Florence. In 1458 he attended Cristoforo Landino's course on poetry and eloquence at the Studio, Florence's university, important training for the aspiring gentleman as well as practical preparation for a political career, and studied Greek with Argyropoulos, acquiring at least a passing knowledge of a language that opened up new intellectual vistas.* But for Lorenzo learning was to be a lifelong passion, and he often complained that affairs of state had stolen too much time from pursuing intellectual enlightenment. In this he was typical of his age. Fifteenth-century Florentines did not divide their lives neatly into their school years, to be followed by an adulthood in which all book learning ceased. Education was both less structured and more intense than it is today; no strict program was set out for young men to plow their way through, nor was the possession of particular degrees required for most careers. But middle-aged and elderly men still attended lectures and philosophical discussions both out of a love of learning for its own sake and because such erudition was the mark of a gentleman. A career in business or in politics was facilitated by a proficiency in Latin and familiarity with the standard classical texts, without which it was impossible to earn the respect of your colleagues. Education could be a poor boy's ticket into the ruling class—as it was to be for men like Leon Battista Alberti,[†] Leonardo Bruni, or Bartolomeo Scala—or it could encourage social mobility in the

---

* Lorenzo, though fascinated by ancient Greek culture and literature, was probably not fluent in the language. His love of Hellenic culture is amply demonstrated by his commissioning of numerous beautifully illuminated manuscripts in Greek (over six hundred were recorded in his library), but he probably relied on friends like Angelo Poliziano to reveal their treasures. (See E. B. Fryde's "Lorenzo's Greek Manuscripts, and in Particular His Own Commissions," in *Lorenzo the Magnificent: Culture and Politics*.)

† Alberti came from an aristocratic family but poverty forced him to earn his wages as a secretary in the papal curia.

opposite direction, as it did for Niccolò Niccoli, who pursued his passion for classical literature to the point of bankruptcy. More typical were men like Cosimo, Palla Strozzi, and Giovanni Rucellai, who combined their love of learning with a knack for making money.

While Piero oversaw Lorenzo's intellectual development, Lucrezia nurtured his spiritual growth. Lorenzo's biographers have typically neglected this aspect of his life on the mistaken assumption that Florence in the Renaissance was either indifferent or openly hostile to traditional religious forms and that Lorenzo, as the exemplary figure of his age, was little more than a pagan who concealed his true nature beneath the threadbare cloak of conventional piety. This distorted picture is largely the work of Savonarola, the fanatical Dominican monk who dominated the city in the years following Lorenzo's death and who portrayed the city over which he presided as a latter-day Sodom and Gomorrah. In fact, religion played a profound role in the lives of fifteenth-century Florentines and Lorenzo was typical in his fervent embrace of contradictory worldviews. Despite the new intellectual currents of humanism and a renewed appreciation for the art and literature of the pagan world, Florentines clung to their traditional beliefs, which mixed elevated moral teachings indiscriminately with local legends and pious folktales. Miraculous icons and revered shrines crowded the city. Almost every street corner had its image of the Virgin or some other holy figure and the thick crust of wax from devotional candles attested to their continuing hold on the imagination. Primitive superstition flourished, with pagan astrology added to, but not replacing, Christian belief in the healing power of relics.

Like most Florentines, Lorenzo attended Mass daily and religion always played a vital role in his life, perhaps all the more so because his restless, probing intellect meant that he could never fall back on empty platitudes. Outwardly his observance was diligent and conventional. He was enrolled in many of the religious confraternities, lay brotherhoods in which Florentines came together for worship, pious study, and to devote themselves to charitable work.* Some of them—like that of the Magi—were respon-

---

* The all-male societies could also provide opportunities for homosexual activity. In 1469, for instance, three men were expelled from the flagellant company of San Paolo "because they were condemned by the office of sodomy" (see Michael Rocke's *Forbidden Friendships: Homosexuality and Male Culture in Renaissance Florence*, p. 187).

sible for organizing the religious processions that punctuated the holy calendar; others, the so-called Companies of the Night, were flagellant societies in which men gathered in secret to scourge themselves for their sins. The duty of one, the Black company of Santa Maria della Croce al Tempio (to which Lorenzo belonged), was to comfort the condemned on their way to execution.

Acts of charity were not only a pious obligation but a necessity for any family hoping to wield influence in the city; such acts were a major source of the patronage through which party loyalty was built. "[Lorenzo] was so devoted to religion," wrote Niccolò Valori effusively, "and to the poor and to those in need he was so solicitous, that none seeking help or charity were turned away," habits, no doubt, that owed as much to policy as to any natural sympathy for those less fortunate. By participating in multiple religious brotherhoods, Lorenzo made his presence felt in what were, in effect, secret political clubs. During the crisis of 1465–66, the confraternity of the Magi was an epicenter of pro-Medici activities, while across the city the lay brothers at La Pietà plotted the overthrow of the regime. Ironically it was the official ban on political parties that drove the city's leaders to disguise their activities beneath the cover of religious piety, thus transforming what might have been legitimate political activity into conspiracies hatched by hidden cabals. Not that the government was fooled by the subterfuge: one of the first responses of the *Signoria* to civic unrest was to pass decrees banning their meetings or excluding brothers from holding office. For Florentines, who imbibed both politics and religion along with their mother's milk, it was a natural combination. In nocturnal meetings at the city's holy sites, Florence's leading men met not only to tend to their immortal souls but to plot the destruction of their enemies, apparently finding no discrepancy between the two.

Lorenzo's observance was not merely a case of social conformity (and political expedience) but was guided by a deep, if sometimes unconventional, spirituality. A profound religious anxiety comes through in his writing, which reflects not the certainty of conventional piety but the struggle of a man trying to reconcile his spiritual longing with his skeptical intellect. "The soul is only avid for the good that yields the God we cannot know," he wrote in "The Supreme Good," revealing the kind of doubt that has always plagued rational men who thirst for communion with the divine.

Faith in Lorenzo's case went hand in hand with a streak of anticleri-cism, something he shared with many Florentines who had learned from bitter experience that the Church, and especially the pope in Rome, could be a formidable and unscrupulous adversary. "Do not meddle with priests, who are the scum of the earth," wrote the Florentine patrician Gino di Neri Capponi, "in matters either of money or of the Church. . . . The divided church is good for our commune and for the maintenance of our liberty but it is contrary to the good of the soul."

The fact that the two central Italian powers were neighbors did not make them friends. On the contrary: disarray in the Papal States gave Flor-ence a free hand in central Italy; a united, expansionist papacy, however, meant cramped horizons for the republic, a fact of life that often brought Florentines into conflict with their spiritual father.* Something of this anticlerical attitude can be detected in an anecdote recounted by Angelo Poliziano involving Lorenzo's brother, Giuliano. Once, so the poet recalled with relish, when Giuliano was informed that the pope and his entourage were passing on the street, the six-year-old, apparently unimpressed, replied, "Let him pass, I'm going to shit."

Lorenzo reserved some of his harshest gibes for priests and learned from firsthand experience that those who professed to speak for God were no better, and often a good deal worse, than the run-of-the-mill sinners whose confessions they heard. In his satirical poem "The Symposium," many of the drunks who populate the city are men of the cloth (up to and including the bishop of Fiesole), and in his lecherous tale "Giacoppo" a young man's efforts to cuckold an old Sienese merchant are aided and abetted by a Franciscan monk.

As Lorenzo entered his teenage years he impressed those around him with his talents and driving energy. Described by one family friend as "growing

---

* The most significant conflict between Florence and the pope was the so-called War of the Eight Saints (1375–78). Often the pope's spiritual powers were more devastating than his armies. By excommunicating the citizens and placing their city under interdict, the pope could subject Florentine businessmen throughout Christendom to the threat that their property would be confiscated.

rapidly in all directions at once," Lorenzo continued to excel in all matters of the mind and body. This was an age that prized the well-rounded man more than the specialist: excellence, honor, and virtue were the attributes that marked the noble spirit, and Lorenzo's parents had reason to believe that he possessed those qualities so necessary to inspire loyalty in others. He was, however, still too young to take his place among the sober, elderly gentlemen who ran the government of Florence. And given Piero's health it was unlikely he would attain that age before he was called upon to take up a position of responsibility. His evident abilities and accomplishments would have to compensate for his lack of years, earning him the respect of those who were inclined to doubt the competence of youth. Lorenzo had already made a good start. He was not only conversant with the literary classics—crucial weapons to be deployed in any debate in the *Palazzo della Signoria*—but also in those other skills the mastery of which were so important to a young nobleman: manly arts like riding, the handling of arms, and archery, as well as such gentler pursuits as dancing and playing the lyre.

Lorenzo and Giuliano were both avid sportsmen. Giuliano in particular was a fine athlete, compensating for an intellect that could not match his brother's. With his easy grace, winning personality, and natural athleticism, Giuliano soon won the nickname "The Prince of Youth," a title that Lorenzo, with his growing responsibilities and wide-ranging interests, was all too happy to cede to his younger brother.

Lorenzo's passion for, and knowledge of, all things equestrian was legendary. A number of letters from him survive whose main purpose is to procure for him the finest horses for his stable: "Our Lord the King has ordered two fine horses to be sent to your Magnificent Lorenzo," reported a Neapolitan count, "and says if he wishes for others he is to say so, for finding that he takes pleasure in them, the King intends to keep him supplied." As the lord of Florence, his stable of racehorses became famous, but his affinity for these animals began early. He preferred when he could to care for them himself, though a full-time staff was also always on hand. His chief groom, Apollonio Baldovini, has left a vivid description of Lorenzo exercising his four horses in the cold morning air. It was later said of his most famous racehorse, il Morello, that it would refuse food from any hand but his.

During these years, Lorenzo's rangy frame began to take on muscle, his physical presence to take on a new authority. "Lorenzo was of above average height," Valori records, "broad in the shoulders, his body solid and robust, and so agile that he was never second to anyone." He was not without flaws, which included not only his homely face but his weak eyesight and an almost complete lack of the sense of smell. The latter defect Lorenzo dismissed with a jest, declaring that "for this he was much obliged to nature, since among those odors she offered there were far more that offended than delighted the senses."

His homeliness, however, did not make him less attractive to those of both sexes. His charisma was, perhaps, only enhanced by his famous temper. As generous as he was to his friends, those who opposed him could expect to face the withering blast of his rage. One such storm was witnessed by the Milanese ambassador when, following a diplomatic setback, the young leader of Florence "showed himself in a temper, such as I have never seen in one of his high standing." His was a personality of lights and darks, of fiercely passionate friendships and equally passionate hatreds. He could be loyal to a fault, protecting those who had done little to earn it, while pursuing those who had turned against him with vindictive thoroughness.

Many of the more conservative elements in the city complained that Lorenzo and his circle of friends strutted about the city as if they ruled the roost, raising a ruckus and paying little respect to their elders. Not all of this was the spontaneous exuberance of youth. Indeed there was a conscious attempt by Cosimo and Piero to build around the young Medici heir and his brother something of a cult of youth. Allowing these adolescents a greater role in the affairs of state was one way to counteract the influence of more entrenched elites by creating a class of men loyal to and dependent on Medici favor.

But it is clear that the circles in which Lorenzo traveled were not necessarily of the sort to bring credit to his family. Two of his closest friends, his traveling companions on his trip to Pistoia and fellow members of his *brigata,* were Braccio Martelli (seven years his senior) and Sigismondo della Stufa, sons of Medici neighbors in the *gonfalone* of the Golden Lion. Martelli in particular seems to have been his companion in many a disreputable escapade. "My dear Lorenzo," Braccio wrote to his young friend, who was away in Rome to meet with the pope, "I recommend myself to you, and I encourage you to receive with devotion all those pardons, and beg that you send along a small portion, however much you think would be sufficient penance for the sins we have committed together."

Though Martelli does not elaborate, it is likely that among those sins were those "unnatural" sexual acts for which Florence was notorious throughout Europe. Humanist schools and religious confraternities were often rife with sin, and homosexual encounters, even assaults, were common in the back alleys of Florence.* Lecherous older men arranged trysts with boys who sold their bodies to the highest bidders in the Via tra' Pellicciai (where the furriers had their stalls). Then these youths, with money in their pockets, headed to the taverns and brothels near the Old Market, where they whored and gambled through the night, stumbling home to bed as the sun rose above the Arno. St. Bernardino of Siena paints a portrait of the Florentine upper classes in which parents turned a blind eye to, if they didn't actually encourage, their children's misdeeds: "You don't make your sons work in a shop, nor do they go to school to learn any virtues. Instead you send them out in a *giornea* [a richly appointed tunic] with their long hair and revealing hosiery, and they go around polishing the benches with their falcons and their dogs on leash; they're good for nothing but lusting with sodomites, shameful acts, indecent talk." This effeminate caricature does not exactly fit the young Lorenzo, a robust, athletic and rough-and-tumble boy not likely to be found posing coyly on a bench, but it is also improbable that he remained immune to habits that were common among Florentines of all classes. In fact the names of both Martelli and Luigi Pulci turn up in court records of the Officers of the Night, the officials who attempted, without much success, to curb this "abominable vice." Some of their letters to Lorenzo hint at feelings that were more than platonic.

To conclude from this suggestive evidence, however, that Lorenzo was a covert homosexual who concealed his true nature beneath a more conven-

---

* Antonio Beccadelli's *The Hermaphrodite* is filled with references to well-known scholars who seduced and even raped their students. See especially his screeds against "the pederast Mattia Lupi."

tional lifestyle would be a mistake.* There is ample evidence for Lorenzo's sexual relations with women, both in and out of marriage, including some lurid testimony from Martelli's own letters. But the larger issue is that the term "homosexual" is an anachronism when applied to men of Renaissance Florence. Florentines occasionally celebrated relations between those of the same sex, though more often such acts were condemned as contrary to God and nature, and those apprehended could be brutally dealt with. Antonio Beccadelli's obscene book of verses, *Hermaphroditus*—dedicated, interestingly enough, to Cosimo, who was said to have read it with pleasure—praised in impeccable Latin meters the joys of both heterosexual and homosexual lust. Often homosexuality was considered little more than a youthful indiscretion, a rite of passage like visiting a prostitute or getting drunk and learning moderation from the ensuing hangover. Sodomy—which included homosexual as well as other illicit sexual activity—was a vice produced by unbridled sensuousness, a shameful indulgence like gambling or keeping a mistress. It reflected poorly on the character of those incapable of controlling their sexual impulses, but it did not distinguish the practitioner in any fundamental way, save that of virtue, from his more conventional peers. It was acknowledged that some men became so attached to this particular vice that they refused to take a wife or, if they did, failed to do their duty by her, but these were the exceptions and their sin was not so much that they were of a different, perverse nature but that they failed to avail themselves of the sole licit means society provided to satisfy their appetites.

The probability that at one time or another Braccio Martelli, Luigi Pulci, or Angelo Poliziano was Lorenzo's lover should take its place alongside the better documented liaisons he had throughout his life with women, which included consuming passions and numerous casual encounters. A rounded picture of Lorenzo as a young man reveals that alongside his precocious sociability he pursued his pleasures with almost reckless abandon. Like most males of his class and time, Lorenzo saw no need to confine his sexual activity to the approved bounds of holy matrimony. Nor, indeed, was Lorenzo very different in this respect from either his father or grandfather, both men of sterling reputation in their private

---

* This is the contention of Hugh Ross Williamson in *Lorenzo the Magnificent.* For an illuminating discussion of the larger topic see Rocke, *Forbidden Friendships.*

lives who nonetheless each fathered an illegitimate child with a slave girl. In Lorenzo's story "Giacoppo," he declares, showing a certain familiarity with the subject, that mature women often make the best lovers "because when they are younger they are most often filled with shame and of little spirit; when they are past this age . . . they have cooled to the point that they have no need of lovers."

As both Gentile Becchi and Braccio Martelli attest, Lorenzo was not above frequenting the seedier locales where sex of all variety was for sale, and the names of at least some of his various mistresses seem to have been common knowledge among Florentines. Even when he was older his reputation for licentious behavior sometimes cost him the respect of important men. At one point, when Lorenzo was already a married man and ruler of Florence, Gentile Becchi felt it necessary to reprimand him for "going out at night wenching and engaging in buffoonery that shames those who must have dealings with you the following day."

Emotional if not overtly sexual bonds played a role in the formation of the tight-knit circle of poets, artists, and scholars that grew up around Lorenzo. "If you were with me," Luigi Pulci wrote to Lorenzo while he was away in Venice, "I should produce heaps of sonnets as big as the clubs they make of the cherry-blossoms for May-day. I would recite such things that the sun and the moon would stop in their orbits to hear them, as they did for Joshua. . . . Then I say to myself: 'My Lorenzo is not here—he who is my only hope and refuge.' Only this holds me back." As in ancient Athens, whose combination of democratic institutions and creativity served as a model for many Florentine intellectuals, male bonding was encouraged by educational inequalities between the sexes. Even in progressive Florence there was a pervasive misogyny—shared by Lorenzo himself, despite his evident admiration for his mother and lasting friendships with women of real intellectual attainment—that encouraged friendships among men that were often richer than those they forged with the opposite sex.*

But no matter how intimate, most friendships were marked by the same attention to status and power as all other relationships. There was no

---

* Lorenzo once wrote, "The defect which is so common among women and which makes them insupportable is their affectation of understanding everything" (see Williamson, 92).

one in Florence who could afford to consider himself Lorenzo's equal. Letters from friends like Luigi Pulci and Braccio Martelli express a deep attachment on their part that Lorenzo rarely returned. Lorenzo, glamorous, charming, brilliant, and, above all, powerful, was never the seeker but always the sought.

Sinning together with his friends offered Lorenzo some release from the rigors of his life as the Medici heir. His sense of duty was constantly at war with his natural zest for life, his desire to live up to the expectations of those whose approbation he craved in conflict with his taste for sensual pleasures. In the end he pursued all things to the point of near exhaustion. Machiavelli sensed in him a man divided against himself. "Thus," he concluded in his summation of Lorenzo's life, "considering both his voluptuous life and his grave life, one might see in him two different persons, joined in an almost impossible conjunction." More psychologically perceptive than the political theorists who remained perplexed by Lorenzo's irresponsible side is the playwright William Shakespeare, whose portrait of the young Prince Hal wasting his days in the tavern with Falstaff and Bardolph uncannily resembles Lorenzo and his friends at the baths of Macerato or Bagno a Morba.

Burdened by high expectations and struggling to emerge from the shadow of his famous forebears, Lorenzo's urge to lash out and behave irresponsibly is understandable. Exploring the more sordid neighborhoods of town—the brothel district between the *Mercato Vecchio* and the archbishop's palace, or the Chiasso de' Buoi near the public baths—allowed Lorenzo to escape the formality of palace life and the false flattery of courtiers. But could any friend of Lorenzo ever entirely escape the suspicion of ulterior motives? To be known as a "friend of Lorenzo" was automatically to wield great influence in the city, and much of his time was consumed seeking sinecures for those whose attachment to him was as much a product of ambition as affection. In his poem "On the Supreme Good," Lorenzo despairs of life in the city where "he who lies the best is happiest" and "friendship's measured by expediency."

One of the main constraints on the free play of emotion was that friendship blurred uneasily into clientage, a relationship of unequal partners that could get in the way of genuine affection. Even as a teenager, Lorenzo was a magnet for hungry literati and talented young artists who knew they would get a sympathetic reception. "Our Maeceneas," he was called, referring to the advisor of Augustus and patron of Virgil and Horace. The ambiguities were particularly pronounced in his relations with poets like Angelo Poliziano and Luigi Pulci, who were both literary mentors to Lorenzo and clients of the Medici family. The poet ranked higher on the social scale than those who worked with their hands (a group that included painters and sculptors); literature was even considered a fit avocation for a gentleman. Lorenzo, after all, was a fine poet but one cannot imagine him picking up a brush or chisel, no matter how much he appreciated such skill in others. But for Lorenzo poetry was a passion, not a means of earning a living. The orphaned Poliziano, by contrast, had been rescued from poverty by Cosimo, and the often impecunious Pulci (though a Bardi on his mother's side) was dependent on crumbs from the Medici table. "As I have not had money to spend for some time here [at Pisa] I have spent your reputation," the poet wrote, only half in jest. "Here, as I pass, I am pointed at: 'There goes Lorenzo's great friend,' they say." Pulci's self-deprecating humor cannot conceal the fact, ruefully acknowledged, that he was merely an insignificant satellite in the great man's orbit. In short, no friendship for the Medici heir was free from economic calculation or political consideration.

One client who largely escaped from the bonds of dependence was the philosopher Marsilio Ficino, a man whom Lorenzo revered as a spiritual and intellectual father. As Cosimo's great friend and intellectual mentor he continued to offer guidance to Lorenzo after Cosimo's death. This kindly, mild-mannered man was the foremost philosopher of the age, leader of a movement that sought to reconcile Plato's idealism with Christian notions of the immortality of the soul. "Short in stature, slim, and slightly hunched in both shoulders," of ruddy complexion and his head covered in blond curls, he was a physically unprepossessing figure. In conversation he was little more impressive, hampered as he was by a stammer. Nonetheless he was one of those people whose conviviality makes them the natural center of things.* Lorenzo himself was completely at ease with him, and when

---

* Ficino's natural kindness made him a less than astute judge of character. Two of his regular correspondents, Francesco Salviati and Jacopo Bracciolini, later became involved in a plot to murder Lorenzo. This lapse seems to have led to a temporary chill in their relationship (see later).

they were separated for long periods their letters were frequent and intimate. Chiding the philosopher for his failure to write, Lorenzo teased, "Now if you are not sorry for this—and I seek no other sign of repentance than your letters—know that you will undergo judgment at the court of our mutual love, for it is right that the case should be tried by such a judge. We shall find nobody fairer or more just, or anyone who could be a truer witness to our own soul. This judge gives you only the space of three days to write to me, and if these go by without doing so, he promises you will be condemned." Here we catch a glimpse of the humor that charmed Lorenzo's contemporaries but that is largely absent from the remainder of his extant correspondence. "Who would have believed it?" Lorenzo wrote Ficino in mock despair. "Indeed, I can scarcely believe my own eyes. I sent two letters to you; you sent scarcely one to me, and it was so sparing in words that if you leave out the greetings at the start, the farewell at the end, the date and address, there is almost nothing left. Should a philosopher be talkative, or should he be mute?"

With this man who had been an intimate of his family's household from before his birth, Lorenzo could shed the formalities necessary to maintaining his dignity and authority. Ficino was one of the few people from whom Lorenzo would accept criticism because he was confident in Ficino's love for him. "I was indeed delighted with your letter which reproved me for the waste of past time," Lorenzo wrote, "in such a way that my idleness does not appear to have been entirely useless. For the result of my waste of this brief time is that directions have come from you which are not only for my benefit but for the benefit of all those who suffer from the same disease."

As Lorenzo entered his adolescence he had every reason to believe that his future was secure. The Medici continued to prosper as Cosimo, in the age-old Florentine way, used his considerable political influence to steer business to the family bank. The civil strife that had brought Cosimo to power lay two decades in the past and the republic thrived under his steady leadership.* True, his cavalier disregard for democratic institutions provoked grumbling

---

* This was particularly true after 1454 when Cosimo engineered the Peace of Lodi, which turned Milan from a perennial threat into Florence's most stalwart ally.

that occasionally became serious enough to disrupt the normal functioning of the government (as in 1458 when Girolamo Machiavelli and his followers were arrested and sent into exile for fomenting discontent with the regime), but Cosimo was shrewd enough to use such moments of crisis to strengthen the hand of the *reggimento*.* Medici prospects were also enhanced by a growing family. Giovanni had married late, but his young bride, Ginevra degli Alessandri, had already produced a male heir, named Cosimino (Little Cosimo), after his grandfather. Giovanni, more robust and outgoing than his older brother, was viewed by many as the likely candidate to inherit his father's position. Were Giovanni to outlive Piero by a number of years, as seemed more than likely given Piero's ill health, Cosimino might well have at least shared the leadership role in the family with his older cousin.

But this apparently solid structure was built on shaky foundations. A few years after the move to their new home, the Medici were struck by a series of painful blows that threatened the future of the family and subtly altered Lorenzo's own prospects. The first was the sudden death in 1461 of young Cosimino. The death of a child was not uncommon in fifteenth-century Florence, but coupled with the unexpected death of Giovanni two years later, these tragic events shook the family to its core. "[I]n the last years of his life, [Cosimo] felt very grave sorrow because of the two sons he had, Piero and Giovanni," wrote Niccolò Machiavelli. "The latter, in whom he had more confidence, died; the other was ill and, because of the weakness of his body, hardly fit for public or private affairs." Now the palace that was meant to signal a vigorous and thriving dynasty seemed sadly depopulated; a once proud symbol of a vigorous lineage had become, at least to Cosimo, an empty shell. Among those trying to restore the grieving father to his accustomed vigor was Pope Pius II, who opined, "Mourning accords not with your age; it is contrary to your health, and we ourselves, your native city, and all Italy, require that your life should be as far as possible prolonged." To which Cosimo responded: "I . . . strive to the best of my power, and so far as my weak spirit will permit, to bear this great calamity with calmness."

Cosimo's distress involved more than just the understandable feelings of a father losing a much beloved child. For the aging leader of Florence

---

* The crisis of 1458 never seriously threatened Cosimo's regime but he used the fear of instability to reform the electoral system.

the death of his younger son threatened his dreams for the future of his family. He knew he had not long to live himself; at seventy-four he had already far surpassed the norm, and the family disease of gout had rendered him increasingly feeble. His former allies, once deferential, now circled like vultures around a dying animal. Agnolo Acciaiuoli, Dietisalvi Neroni, and Luca Pitti filled the ears of foreign ambassadors with complaints of Medici weakness and unreliability.

The death of his grandson, followed soon after by that of his son, sent the aging patriarch into a depression from which his aging body and flagging spirit never recovered. When his wife, Contessina, chided him for spending his hours in silent meditation, Cosimo responded, "When we are going to our country-house, you are busy for a fortnight preparing for the move, but since I have to go from this life to another, does it not seem to you that I ought to have something to think about?" In July of 1464 Cosimo left the palace on the Via Larga for the last time. As he was carried by litter through the gates of the city and up the hills to his beloved villa at Careggi, those who watched the procession knew he would never return to the city he had dominated for more than three decades. Among those summoned to the dying man's bedside was Ficino. To ease his pain, Cosimo had his friend read him passages from Plato, whose writing had given him comfort on many trying occasions.

Piero, too, came to his father's bedside, while Lorenzo and Giuliano were sent away to Cafaggiolo, perhaps to keep them from disturbing the dignitaries come to pay their last respects. In a letter to his sons, written during Cosimo's final hours, Piero tried to prepare them for the trying times ahead. "[Cosimo] began to recount all his past life, then touched upon the government of the city and then on its commerce, and at last he spoke of the management of the private possessions of our family and of what concerns you two; taking comfort that you had good wits and bidding me educate you well so that you might be of help to me. Two things he deplored. First, that he had not done as much as he wished or could have accomplished; secondly that he left me in such poor health and with much irksome business." Finally, he urged them to "take example and assume your share of care and trouble as God has ordained, and being boys, make up your minds to be men."

Five days later Cosimo was dead. Not long after, Piero penned the following tribute to his father: "I record that on the 1st August 1464 . . . Cosimo di Giovanni de' Medici passed from this life, having suffered greatly from pains in his joints. . . . He was seventy-seven years old. A tall and handsome man, he was possessed of great wisdom and kindness . . . and for that reason was trusted and loved by the people."

Cosimo's death, though not unexpected, was a blow not only to Piero but to the extended Medici clan and to the *reggimento* that had depended for three decades on his wise counsel and forceful leadership. The exiles of 1434 continued to stir up trouble from abroad, while within the *reggimento* itself many feared that their former colleagues had set out on a path that would lead to the kind of despotism that had long since overtaken most of their neighbors.* As early as 1458, a conspiracy led by Girolamo Machiavelli had sought the overthrow of Cosimo's government. Though quickly discovered, it pointed to a festering discontent within the body politic. One of those approached by Machiavelli was Palla Strozzi, at one time the richest man in Florence.† Strozzi declined to join with the rash Machiavelli, but the reasons he gave could hardly have given comfort to Piero. He had refused, according to the Milanese ambassador (who certainly passed this information along to Piero), only because "these were vain hopes, since while Cosimo was yet living such a thing was impossible, but as soon as he was dead things would of their own accord and in few days turn in their favor." Now that Strozzi's wish had come to pass, many predicted the Medici government would not long outlive its preeminent leader.

---

* Of the republican communes that had arisen in northern and central Italy during the Middle Ages, few now remained. Milan had succumbed first to the Visconti and now to the Sforza; Ferrara and Modena to the Este; Mantua to the Gonzaga; Urbino to the Montefeltro. Only Venice and Florence retained the republican forms of government they had inherited from a more democratic age.

† Palla Strozzi had been a stalwart of the Albizzi regime and was exiled by Cosimo in 1434. He was also a patron of the arts to rival Cosimo himself, commissioning, among other works, the famous Strozzi altarpiece by Gentile da Fabbriano. Interestingly, the subject of the painting (completed in 1423) is the Adoration of the Magi, the same story favored by the Medici themselves. The pageantry of Gentile's work, which now hangs in the Uffizi, served as a model for subsequent versions, including Gozzoli's fresco in the Medici palace.

Workshop of Agnolo Bronzino, *Cosimo de' Medici,*
16th century (Art Resource)

IV. HOPE OF THE CITY

"Lorenzo demonstrated, from his first years, signs of his future greatness and generosity."

—NICCOLÒ VALORI, *VITA DI LORENZO IL MAGNIFICO*

"Lorenzo was endowed by nature, education and training with such great genius and foresight that he was in no way inferior to his grandfather Cosimo, certainly a most able man; and he was of such a subtle and versatile mind that every youthful endeavor he tried his hand at he perfected so that he surpassed all others. From the age of five he learned to dance, shoot arrows, sing, ride, play any number of games, perform on numerous musical instruments, and to do many other things that graced his youthful years."

—ALAMANNO RINUCCINI, *HISTORICAL MEMOIRS*

AMONG THE PAPERS COLLECTED AT THE STATE ARCHIVES of Florence is a document in Piero's hand setting down the costs associated with his father's funeral: twenty-five *braccie** of cloth in mourning black for Lorenzo and Giuliano; another thirty for Contessina, while his wife, Lucrezia, required only fourteen, along with two veils. Nothing was too insignificant to be set down, including the ten *braccie* of black woolen cloth for each of Cosimo's four slave girls (one of them, perhaps, the mother of Cosimo's illegitimate son, Carlo). It details such trivial expenditures as 43½ lire for wax candles and additional outlays to pay for thirteen small torches to be carried by priests attending the body. The neat columns in which expenses were parsed to the last soldo offer a revealing glimpse into the mind of the man who would now lead the

---

* A *braccia* was a Florentine unit of measure. Literally meaning "arm," it measured something under a yard.

government of Florence. Piero was a Florentine merchant through and through, and the frugal, orderly habits of the species showed even in moments of great emotional turmoil. These qualities could prove to be a virtue, as they were during his father's lifetime, when his organizational skills were placed in the service of a regime that had at its head a shrewd and charismatic leader. But in times of crisis simple competence was not sufficient.

After three decades of Cosimo's rule there was a restlessness among the populace, a desire for change that was held in check only by fear of the chaos change might bring. Cosimo had ruled the city well but at the expense of the people's cherished liberties. The always well-informed Alessandra Strozzi noted that "this death has given many of the citizens some new ideas about how the land should be governed," innovations that could come only at the expense of the Medici and their cronies.*

Whatever their political affiliation, all Florentines could agree that one age had come to an end and another was about to begin. Some found this prospect disconcerting, while others saw in Cosimo's passing a golden opportunity to restore republican institutions that had long been supressed. A typical representative of this latter group was Marco Parenti, who, after admitting that his native city was rarely more peaceful or more prosperous than it had been under Cosimo, concluded that "despite this, upon his death there was universal rejoicing, such is the love and desire for liberty, because it seemed to them that they were under subjugation and servitude in government and that his death would set them free."

It was not, however, from modest merchants like Parenti that Piero had most to fear. These small-time merchants and artisans could not hope to wrest the government from the grasp of the narrow directorate that had grown up around Cosimo. The ranks of the disenchanted had recently been swelled by a general economic downturn brought about largely by Turkish advances in the Mediterranean and the subsequent disruption in international trade. Many businesses went under; prosperous merchants saw their capital vanish, while their employees, barely scraping by in the

---

* Alessandra Strozzi was the wife of Matteo Strozzi, who was exiled by Cosimo after his defeat of the Albizzi faction in 1434. Her letters provide a portrait of Florence under Medici rule.

best of times, were forced to beg or to starve. That the causes of the economic downturn were beyond the control of anyone in Florence was beside the point. The ruined and the hungry are never the most dispassionate judges of their circumstances, and in their suffering they turned against those in power. Piero was the most obvious target of the people's wrath; protestations that he, too, was hurting were met with derision, and when he announced (possibly on the advice of Dietisalvi Neroni) that his own losses would force him to call in many of the loans his father had made, that laughter turned to outrage.

The greatest threat to the Medici, however, came from among those *principali* whom Cosimo had lifted from obscurity to the heights of power, but who, forgetting what they owed the family, now hoped to supplant them. Only an alliance between the disenfranchised many and the discontented few would be sufficiently powerful to drive the Medici from their perch—though, once this was accomplished, it was not at all clear whether men like Marco Parenti and Luca Pitti could agree on anything else. It was in an attempt to effect just such an alignment that the city's religious confraternities became the rallying point of secret cabals. In interludes between prayer and the singing of hymns, men plotted strategy and debated the future of the republic.

Piero was hard pressed to halt the momentum for change. His first task as the presumptive head of the *reggimento* was to lay to rest its former leader. The manner in which he orchestrated Cosimo's funeral reveals not only his cautious nature but an understanding of the public mood. Now was not the time to offend his fellow oligarchs by a lavish public display; modesty and understatement would soothe bruised egos and win him much needed friends. It had been his father's dying wish, he announced to the world, "to be buried without pomp or show" in the family's private crypt in San Lorenzo, wishing "neither more nor less wax torches than were used at an ordinary funeral." He airily declined any special consideration from the government, since, for all his services to the republic, his father was merely a private citizen. Though Machiavelli later claimed that all the citizens of Florence poured out onto the streets to follow Cosimo's coffin, eyewitnesses describe a much more modest affair. On the second day of August 1464, accompanied only by the priests and friars from the churches and monasteries he had patronized and a few close relatives and friends, Cosimo was lowered into his unpretentious tomb beneath the tribune of San Lorenzo.

No native-born Florentine would have viewed this understated affair as a sign of weakness, any more than he would have regarded a grander spectacle as a guarantee of strength; Medici power was often most effective when least visible. "[Cosimo] refused to make a will and forbade all pomp at his funeral," Lorenzo later recalled. "Nevertheless all the Italian princes sent to do him honor and to condole with us on his death; among others H. M. the King of France commanded that he should be honored with his banner, but out of respect for his wishes our father would not allow it."

Piero could expect to ride the swell of sympathy for a short while, but it was clear that the struggle for power could not be long delayed. Thus it was more important than ever that Lorenzo be ready to take up his role as First Citizen of the Republic. Among Medici partisans Lorenzo was now referred to openly as "the hope of the city," suggesting both the promise they saw in the boy and their less than sanguine expectations for the sickly Piero.

While Piero was referred to as "the absent senator," a man rarely seen but whose opinion needed to be canvassed on any important matter, his son was increasingly the public face of the regime. Lorenzo took responsibility for many of the ceremonial functions that were critical to maintaining the family's prestige. In 1465, while Lorenzo was out of town on an important diplomatic mission, Piero wrote to him, "I have consulted with the citizens here, and they all agree I must receive the princes in our house on their return, and the *Signoria* has commanded me to do so: I obey willingly, but it would have taken much trouble off my hands had you and Guglielmo [de' Pazzi] been here; however, we will do the best we can." Lorenzo had the gift for social occasions that his father lacked; throughout his life he would be a master at staging brilliant spectacles that enhanced his reputation for magnificence and added luster to the Medici name.

Increasingly, Lorenzo and Giuliano became the center of a society of boisterous adolescents who imparted to the regime a youthful tone, much to the chagrin of the conservative elite, who thought they brought shame to the city. All those who wished to be close to the center of the action flocked to the Medici heir. To be a member of Lorenzo's *brigata* was to enjoy a privileged place in the city; to be seen in his company was as good as credit in the bank. The various Medici villas were the site of frequent gatherings of young men brought together to hunt or to indulge in less strenuous pastimes. Braccio Martelli records a visit in the spring of 1465 to the villa of Lorenzo's reputed mistress, the beautiful Lucrezia Donati, where she and the young men of his *brigata* passed the time listening to the music of the famous lutenist known as "the Spaniard" and dancing the *gioiosa*, the *chirintana*, and the *moresca*. It is a scene straight out of Boccaccio, filled with good cheer, good food, and ripe sensuality. On this occasion a certain decorum was maintained until one unnamed youth, undoubtedly under the influence of too much wine, emerged from Lucrezia's chambers dressed *al travestito* in one of her gowns, a performance that sparked much juvenile hilarity.

Even after he had succeeded his father as head of the family and of the republic, Lorenzo's youth and inexperience were a cause for concern. "Lorenzo was young," wrote a visiting French diplomat disapprovingly, "and he was governed by young men." The loyal Marsilio Ficino hinted that Lorenzo had perhaps come too far too fast, suggesting at one point that the opposition he faced was due to the envy always aroused by any display of "youthful virtue."

It was not, however, an excess of virtue that troubled the elderly men who usually ran things in Florence. "[H]e delighted in facetious and pungent men and in childish games, more than would appear fitting in such a man," scolded Machiavelli. Wild behavior that would hardly have been noticed in his companions generated gossip and reflected poorly on the regime. At one point Alessandra Strozzi complained that while her own exiled son could not return to the city, despite a good word put in on his behalf by the king of Naples, Niccolò Ardinghelli, cuckolded husband of "Lorenzo's lady," Lucrezia Donati, magically gained approval on short notice from the *Signoria*. "Perhaps," she concluded bitterly, "it is better to have a pretty wife than the prayers of a king." Such blatant favoritism tended to confirm suspicions that the Medici were beginning to see themselves as royalty rather than as citizens.

While the Medici's enemies played up Lorenzo's faults, their friends praised him as a prodigy of wisdom and virtue. Encomiums from Medici partisans, like Nicolò Valori, who concluded that Lorenzo "was worthy of being included among those rare miracles of nature," must be taken with a grain of salt, but these words found a curious echo even among those with no reason to love him or his family. "No one even of his enemies and critics denied that he had a brilliant and outstanding mind," declared Francesco Guicciardini.

Intriguing evidence of Lorenzo's growing reputation comes from Alamanno Rinuccini, a man who outwardly acquiesced in the Medici ascendancy but prayed in secret for their destruction in the belief that the family had usurped the government of his beloved republic.* Like Marco Parenti, Rinuccini idealized a past that was never as democratic as he believed while exaggerating the despotic tendencies of the age in which he lived. Rinuccini denounced Lorenzo because he believed a republic simply could not contain a man of such stature and vaunting ambition. "Lorenzo was endowed by nature, education and training with such great genius and foresight that he was in no way inferior to his grandfather Cosimo, certainly a most able man," Rinuccini wrote in his secret memoirs. These are words that could have come from the pen of Valori himself. But Rinuccini goes on to form a very different conclusion from the same facts:

> [H]e was of such a subtle and versatile mind that every youthful endeavor he tried his hand at he perfected so that he surpassed all others. From the age of five he learned to dance, shoot arrows, sing, ride, play any number of games, perform on numerous musical instruments, and to do many other things that graced his youthful years. And I believe that possessing such great abilities, and finding the citizens of our city already so reduced by the imperiousness of his father to timid and servile ways, he resolved, like those most haughty and ambitious, to gather unto himself all dignity, power and public authority, and in the end, like Julius Caesar, make himself lord of the republic.

To be named a Caesar in a culture filled with would-be Brutuses was disconcerting, even if the accusation was only whispered in private. Learned

---

* Rinuccini's distrust of the Medici seems never to have led him into active resistance against the regime. He always kept his criticisms private while seeking advancement in Medicean Florence (see Chapter XIX). It is difficult to know if his views represent those of a "silent majority" or merely a small, if articulate, group of malcontents.

Florentines had long meditated on the career of the Roman general while drawing opposing lessons from the tale of his meteoric rise to the height of imperial power and his catastrophic fall. A millennium and a half after his death the story of his triumph and violent death at the hands of Brutus and his co-conspirators still aroused passions. Dante, for one, had placed Brutus in the lowest circle of hell reserved for betrayers, but other humanists continued to revere the tyrannicide as a political martyr. As an old-style republican, Rinuccini clearly belonged to this latter school of thought, and events would show he was not above advocating violence against those he regarded as betrayers of the people's liberty. That he, and at least some of his bookish colleagues, should already be comparing the young Florentine to the Roman dictator foretold disaster.

In Rinuccini's eyes Lorenzo's native abilities combined with his hereditary position to make him doubly dangerous. These suspicions were only strengthened by the manner of Lorenzo's upbringing in which Rinuccini detected a concerted effort to invest the young man with a prestige unsuitable to a simple citizen of a republic. He and other Medici critics were alarmed by the transformation, slow but inexorable, of the citizen-ruler, first among equals, into the uncrowned prince of the land.

There was, in fact, a conscious strategy on the part of Medici partisans to place before the public an image of a man whose unique status was justified by his native genius. In Medici propaganda he was the paragon of the virtuous citizen. If he could not be king he could at least be *il Magnifico,* a man who used his immense wealth for the greater good and who embodied all the virtues and talents of the ideal gentleman. It was a point picked up by Savonarola, the Dominican monk who in later years became the Medici's most relentless opponent. Savonarola certainly had Lorenzo (among others) in mind when he wrote, "[T]he tyrant needs to show himself superior in everything . . . in small things, as in sport, in conversation, in jousting, in horse racing, in doctrine and in all other things . . . he seeks to be first; and whenever he is not able through his own powers he seeks to through fraud and trickery." Lorenzo's gifts were real, but Savonarola had hit upon an important fact of Italian despotism in the fifteenth century and of Medici authority in particular: without legitimacy built on hereditary title enshrined in law, the would-be despot needed to project a self-confident image thoroughly at odds with the insecure underpinnings of his power.

•   •   •

Cosimo's death demanded an acceleration of Lorenzo's political apprenticeship. He was still too young to hold office, a technicality that could
usually be circumvented, and had to battle the prejudices of those in
authority who doubted the judgment and steadiness of anyone much
beneath the age of forty.* In addition he had to overcome his reputation
for loose living and direct his prodigious energies into proper channels.
Not least among the doubters was his own father, a traditional Florentine
patrician whose attitudes toward his eldest son were colored by rigid views
on the irresponsibility of youth and the deference owed to age and experience. Even after Lorenzo had given ample proof of his abilities, Piero tried
to keep him on a tight rein. As late as 1469, when Lorenzo was an experienced politician and diplomat of twenty, Piero tried to micromanage his
affairs. On the eve of one important voyage he instructed Lucrezia to tell
Lorenzo that he "is not to exceed his orders in any way . . . not being
ambassador, for I am determined that the gosling shall not lead the goose
to drink." He was well aware of Lorenzo's abilities, but equally certain that
the young man thought too highly of himself and failed to heed the advice
of those older and wiser than he. For his part, Lorenzo chafed under his
father's close supervision. Like many adolescents, Lorenzo was impatient
with those who tried to impose limits on him while at the same time he
worked hard to impress them with his ability.

    His first opportunity to demonstrate what he was capable of came in
April of 1465 when he represented his family at the wedding of Ippolita
Maria Sforza, daughter of the duke of Milan, to Alfonso, the eldest son of
King Ferrante of Naples. Lorenzo, now sixteen, accompanied by his sister
Bianca's husband, Guglielmo de' Pazzi, and a small host of servants and
retainers, headed north through the rugged mountain passes of the Apen-
nines, stopping in Bologna (seat of the friendly Bentivoglio), Ferrara, and
Venice, before arriving in Milan. The marriage was, in fact, a vindication
of Medici diplomacy that, since the signing of the Peace of Lodi in 1454,

---

* Florentines divided young men into different categories; *fanciulli* (boys) and *giovanni*
(young men), usually defined as those who had yet to marry. The average age of marriage for men in Florence was about thirty-four (contrast this with girls, who usually
married in their mid- to late teens). Young men were not considered fit for responsible
life until they had reached their thirties; before then, these shiftless youths were a constant source of tension and potential dissension in Florence.

had hitched the Florentine wagon to the Milanese star. With Naples now literally wedded to the alliance through its connection with the powerful northern duchy, an axis was created along the length of the peninsula that would bring stability to the normally fractious region and discourage foreign powers that might exploit Italian disunity to stake their own dynastic claims.

In the current uncertain political climate such an occasion would also involve much behind-the-scenes maneuvering as each side in the Florentine power struggle sought to position itself for the upcoming confrontation. Even before Lorenzo and his traveling companions arrived in the northern Italian capital, the Florentine ambassador to Milan, Dietisalvi Neroni, was using his position to undermine the Medici standing at court. Piero, who was kept abreast of these intrigues by his agents in Milan, was relying on his son to overcome any doubts the ambassador had sown.

It was a proud moment for the adolescent who itched to show his detractors what he was capable of. For the first time Lorenzo could regard himself as a player in the strategic chess match of European diplomacy. It was a role in which he would ultimately show himself a consummate master, but even in taking his first tentative steps he exhibited some of the nimbleness that would later make him the arbiter of war and peace in Italy.

No friendship was more important to the Medici family than that with the ruling dynasty of Milan, though the policy was not without its critics back home, particularly after the death of Cosimo, principal architect of the alliance.* The fissures that had begun to appear among leaders of the *reggimento* in the months since Cosimo's death made it all the more

---

* Some of the opposition came from those old enough to remember the bitter wars with the northern giant that time and again had brought the republic to the brink of disaster; they could not forget, nor forgive, the dark days of 1402 when Duke Gian Galeazzo Visconti sat with his vast army on the hills overlooking Florence, ready to starve the city into submission and unite the entire peninsula in his iron grasp. That Florence was miraculously delivered by Visconti's sudden death of the plague—an apparent instance of divine intervention on behalf of the City of the Baptist—did little to soften Florentine hearts toward this bully to the north. Many Florentines preferred an alliance with their sister republic of Venice, whose oligarchic form of government was widely admired as preferable to the more democratic, but more chaotic, Florentine system. (See Felix Gilbert, "The Venetian Constitution in Florentine Political Thought," in Rubinstein, *Florentine Studies: Politics and Society in Renaissance Florence,* 463–500). Many, however, opposed the Milan alliance simply to undermine the Medici position.

urgent that the Medici make sure of the Duke's friendship. Above all, duke Francesco Sforza wanted a reliable partner to the south and looked on the emerging disunity in the government of Florence with displeasure. It was not beyond the realm of possibility that Sforza would abandon his old friends if they seemed likely to lose out in the power struggle now underway. Piero's opponents, for their part, were hoping to undermine his position at home by throwing his alliances abroad into confusion. Neroni in particular was engaged in a whispering campaign aimed at shaking Duke Sforza's confidence in his Florentine client. Piero was weak, he claimed, unable to promote the duke's interests in Florence.* It was a difficult argument to refute since every complaint on Piero's part as to the perfidy of his former colleagues merely strengthened the impression that he had lost control of the situation.

Sending Lorenzo on such an important mission was a vote of confidence on Piero's part, but it did not stop him from barraging his son with missives filled with detailed instructions on how he should comport himself. Piero informed him that he was to be guided by the advice and instructions of Pigello Portinari, director of the Medici bank in Milan. With his betters, Piero reminded him, he was to behave with becoming modesty, especially with the duke and his family, noting, "you should regard yourself as a servant and familiar of the household of his Illustrious Lordship." But modesty should be combined with a proper sense of the dignity of his family; there were few social deficits that could not be overcome by a handful of gold florins wisely spent. After urging Lorenzo to invite don Federigo, younger son of the King of Naples, to dine with him, he added the rather unnecessary reminder, "do not spare any expense to do yourself honor."

His honor was something Lorenzo knew well how to promote, particularly when that meant spending freely on himself and his friends. Don Federigo was apparently well pleased with his reception and even more pleased with his host, striking up an instant friendship with the young

---

* See, for example, Agnolo Acciaiuoli's letter to Francesco Sforza, April 23, 1465, in which he declares that while "Piero is as honored in this city as he was before," nonetheless "because of his illness he cannot handle such burdens and cares" (Rubinstein, *The Government of Florence Under the Medici*, 157).

Florentine. A second friendship forged at this time that later proved to be of vital importance to Lorenzo was with Ippolita Sforza, a woman as devoted to art and literature as he was. Their relationship would prove enduring and mutually beneficial. While at the chronically underfunded Neapolitan court, Ippolita was often forced to call upon her Florentine friend to advance her the funds necessary for the upkeep of a future queen, and it is not an overstatement to say that Lorenzo would owe his life, or at the very least his position in Florence, to her advocacy and affection.

Lorenzo found time between the various wedding festivities to meet several times in private with the duke and his twenty-year-old son and heir, Galeazzo Maria. In these discussions it was not simply Lorenzo's persuasiveness that helped the Medici cause, though the young man evidently made a good impression. In weighing the competing claims of the Medici and their opponents, the duke had good reason to be suspicious of the latter, particularly after being informed by his agent in Florence, Nicodemo Tranchedini (who was fed the damaging information by Piero himself), that the Medici's opponents had been involved in secret talks with Venice, Milan's chief rival in the north of Italy.* Despite the best efforts of Neroni to downplay such rumors, the duke concluded that future good relations between Florence and Milan were best guaranteed by the continued success of the Medici.

Francesco Sforza's decision to back his old friends may also have been influenced by his sober assessment of the belt-tightening that would be required if the bank withdrew the easy credit it was in the habit of extending to the Milanese court, and Lorenzo's extravagance while visiting the city helped remind the duke of the apparently inexhaustible wells of Medici largesse. Thus while Neroni was fobbed off with the empty honor of a knighthood, Lorenzo met secretly with Galeazzo Maria, who told him that he and his father continued to be "very well-disposed towards our city and very much your partisans." In the upcoming struggle in Florence the Sforza would remain true to their word.

---

* Tranchedini wrote to Francesco Sforza, September 14, 1465, "Being today with the Magnificent Piero, he told me . . . that he has it on good authority that his adversaries wish to stir up anger against your Highness that will put you in low repute here, and then to propose a pact of friendship with the Venetians." (See Rubinstein, *The Government of Florence Under the Medici*, 176.)

As Lorenzo turned toward home, then, he could be well satisfied with all he had accomplished. He also had time to reflect on the difference between his own family's position in Florence and that of the various despots at whose courts he had been elaborately feted. On the one hand he must have envied the stability and certainty that hereditary titles brought. The Sforza of Milan and the Este of Ferrara wielded power not through subterfuge and indirection but openly and without apology, and upon his father's death, Galeazzo Maria could count on a seamless transition.* Lorenzo, on the other hand, was guaranteed nothing on his father's death. The situation was sufficiently volatile—and the history of Florence gave little encouragement in this regard—that even as he made his way back to his native city he could not be certain that the gates would not be barred against him. The rumblings of discontent with his father's regime—which he had observed firsthand at the Sforza court—were a reminder of his family's uneasy position. Even in the best of circumstances the lack of legitimate authority led the Medici into thickets of political ambiguity in which disaster was avoided only through constant vigilance.

Being the duke had other advantages that did not accrue to the unofficial rulers of Florence, including the right to indulge in a public display of power and magnificence that would have seemed an intolerable pretension on the part of private citizens. The Sforza's principal residence in the city was the Castle of the Porta Giovia (now known as the Castello Sforzesco), a massive fortress meant to overawe the populace and discourage any hope of a return to republican government. Here the duke, duchess, and their children lived surrounded by elaborate and stultifying etiquette, attended by graded ranks of courtiers, chamberlains, and personal servants whose duties and obligations—down to the details of their

---

* This is something of an oversimplification. Francesco's title came through his wife, illegitimate daughter of the last of the ruling Visconti clan. After Visconti's death the people of Milan had risen up and briefly established a republic, which Francesco overthrew with an army funded largely by Cosimo's money. His son's accession would not be without drama (he was away campaigning in France when word reached him of his father's death; he was forced to sneak back to Milan through hostile Savoy in disguise), but in the end it went off with no serious opposition. The Sforza title was never officially acknowledged by the Holy Roman Emperor, their ostensible feudal overlords, but this was a mere formality and was no real threat to their legitimacy.

wardrobe and the way they were to address their lord and master—were spelled out in a special handbook. Such a life was unthinkable in republican Florence.*

For all the complaints about his tyrannical disposition and for all the extravagance of his tastes, Lorenzo never showed the least inclination to imitate the feudal splendor of his northern colleagues. In fact he had internalized the republican values of his country. True, he took a boyish delight in elaborate martial display but was realistic about his own shortcomings as a potential warrior. Galeazzo Maria, by contrast, always aspired to the status of a great general, a role he knew would enhance his ducal prestige. Similar ambitions were discouraged in Florence, where it was assumed that any aspiring tyrant would first seek to dazzle the masses through easy victories on the battlefield.

The most tangible evidence of Lorenzo's diplomatic triumph came some months later in the form of a magnificent tunic embroidered with the Sforza crest, a gift from the ducal family to their most devoted servant. The letter of thanks Lorenzo penned to the duke and duchess offers eloquent testimony as to the nature of the Sforza-Medici alliance: "I do not know how I can begin to thank Your Most Illustrious and Excellent Lordships for this most noble and gracious gift. . . . For as long as I live, my family and I shall carry the device of Your Excellencies, not so much upon our shoulders as in our hearts where it shall be forever fixed." With its somewhat servile tone, the letter reveals a relationship not of equals but of master and protégé. The timing of the gift, which arrived in June of 1466, is significant: the embroidered surcoat, sent posthaste on horseback, came just at the moment when the Medici were in greatest need of friends in high places. Wearing the embroidered coat on the occasion of his sister Nannina's wedding to Bernardo Rucellai, Lorenzo was reminding his fellow citizens that the Medici enjoyed the protection of powerful men.

---

* This was especially the case during the reign of Galeazzo Maria. Francesco, an old soldier, was unaccustomed to and uncomfortable with the ways of the court. His son, however, had a taste for luxury and an inability to deny himself any indulgence that eventually contributed to his downfall. The Fortezza da Basso in Florence, which somewhat resembles the Sforza residence for sheer intimidating mass, was built by the Medici grand dukes in the sixteenth century and symbolized the city's loss of its ancient liberties.

Mino da Fiesole, *Bust of Piero de' Medici,* 1453 (Art Resource)

V. DEVIL'S PARADISE

"[A] paradise inhabited by devils."

—AGNOLO ACCIAIUOLI'S DESCRIPTION OF FLORENCE

"In Florence men naturally love equality and are therefore very unwilling to accept and recognize others as their superiors. We are by temperament full of strong passions and restlessness, and it is this which is the cause of discord and disunity among the ruling elite. Through their desire to dominate each other, they pull this person here and that one there. . . . The fact that others dislike anyone being superior to themselves ensures that whenever this happens, these men are destroyed."

—FRANCESCO GUICCIARDINI, *DIALOGUE ON THE GOVERNMENT OF FLORENCE*

LORENZO WAS BACK IN FLORENCE BY EARLY JUNE 1465, just in time to arrange a splendid reception for Ippolita Sforza and don Federigo, who were wending their way back to Naples. There the young bride would take up her new role as the queen-in-waiting of the southern kingdom. For Lorenzo the festivities provided only a temporary distraction from the deteriorating political situation; divisions among the leading men had only grown during his two-month absence. Indeed Lorenzo's mission to Milan may have exacerbated those tensions as his success in cementing the friendship between his family and the Sforza was countered by their rivals' renewed attempt to resurrect the old alliance with Venice.

On the domestic front, Cosimo's former lieutenants had begun a full-scale assault on the edifice of Medicean power. An early sign of trouble was the defeat of a bill Piero had sponsored to extend the special judicial powers granted five years earlier to the Eight, the all-important committee in charge of state security. Agnolo Acciaiuoli was particularly vehement in his opposition, claiming that to renew their power to arrest and imprison those suspected of sedition would "be the death of the city." Without these extraordinary powers, which were intended to be employed only in moments of crisis, the regime's ability to intimidate its opponents was considerably diminished.

Even more distressing was a successful drive on the part of the reformers to close the electoral purses. One of the most powerful weapons in the regime's arsenal had been the ability to select by hand (*a mano*) those whose names were placed in the bags from which officeholders were drawn. The special committee in charge of handpicking candidates, known as the *Accoppiatori*, was a vital cog in the Medici political machine because it allowed the Medici to screen out those whose loyalties were suspect.* In September, reformers, led by Agnolo Acciaiuoli, Dietisalvi Neroni, and, especially, Luca Pitti, succeeded in abolishing the *Accoppiatori* and restoring the earlier methods of filling the purses with the names of *all* eligible citizens. So strong was the momentum for reform that Piero himself felt compelled to support the measure in order to avoid an embarrassing defeat.

October of 1465 saw the high-water mark of the reform movement when Niccolò Soderini's name was drawn from the newly closed purses as Gonfaloniere di Giustizia. Such was the public jubilation that "a great crowd not only of honored citizens but of all people accompanied him to the palace, and on the route a wreath of olive was placed on his head to show that on him both the safety and the liberty of his fatherland must depend." Buoyed by this popular support, Soderini was determined to

---

* The creation of the *Accoppiatori* was typical of the methods the Medici employed to manipulate the republican government to their own ends without eradicating democratic forms and practices. Even Cosimo could resort to such tactics only on the understanding that such departures from constitutional practice were merely temporary responses to emergencies. Though most histories seem to work on the assumption that it was the *Accoppiatori* who actually picked the government, the truth is that they only picked the names—inscribed on little paper tickets—of the candidates, who continued to be drawn, as before, at random from the purses. When the government no longer felt itself threatened by foreign powers or domestic enemies, there were many who naturally clamored for a restoration of traditional methods. Those chosen to serve as *Accoppiatori* included the most powerful and trusted members of the regime. Among those serving on the committee in these years were Piero, Dietisalvi Neroni, and Agnolo Acciaiuoli. (See Rubinstein, *The Government of Florence Under the Medici*, Appendix I for a complete list.)

pursue a bold agenda. "Not without cause did our ancestors ordain that high offices be filled by lot, and not handed over," he proclaimed to the assembled dignitaries, calling on them to dismantle the last vestiges of Medici control.

Initially, Soderini's initiatives met with widespread approval, but with each success his program became more ambitious and with each new proposal he lost a few of his supporters, who now began to suspect that the long arm of reform might reach out to pick their own pockets. Throughout the next days and weeks Soderini proposed steps that would not only curb the abuses and excesses of the Medicean regime but, if enacted, would transform the government of Florence in profound ways. It was a platform so radical that many of those who had initially welcomed his election now began desperately to look for ways to rein in the beast they had unleashed.*

Niccolò Soderini was the most impressive and charismatic of the anti-Medici leaders of the Hill. Bold to the point of rashness, he was also quick to anger and prone to violence. Some saw him as the one true visionary of the bunch, a Tiberius Gracchus standing for the people against the forces of corruption and oligarchy. Parenti described him as "a man both proud and bold, of forceful speech," but to others he was a hypocrite and a demagogue, a populist rabble-rouser who used his talents to grab power and to line his own pockets.

Niccolò Soderini's debut on the public stage more than three decades earlier was of a kind to leave an indelible impression on his fellow citizens. It came in 1429 when Soderini, then an obscure young man of twenty-seven, was charged with plotting the murder of Niccolò da Uzzano, one of Florence's most distinguished citizens and a pillar of the reigning Albizzi regime.† Twenty years earlier, Uzzano had played a prominent role in the prosecution and hanging of Niccolò Soderini's father, Lorenzo, who had

---

* Nicodemo Tranchedini was among those who believed that "the leading citizens will regret closing the bags, and do not understand the good and well-being of the state" (see Rubinstein, *The Government of Florence Under the Medici*, p. 164, note 2).

† There is a wonderful portrait bust of Niccolò da Uzzano by Donatello. The terra-cotta bust in the Bargello depicts him in the guise of a Roman senator, very much the image every Florentine patrician cultivated, but despite its rhetorical formulas it is a portrait full of lively character.

been involved in a scheme to defraud his relatives.* Niccolò, his rage at this affront to the family honor undimmed by the passage of time, had hired a bunch of thugs to murder Uzzano in the street, but after inflicting only minor injuries on their intended victim, the men were captured. Brutally tortured, as was the Florentine custom in such matters, they led the authorities back to Niccolò.

Niccolò was in danger of meeting the same fate as his father when the Medici stepped in like guardian angels to stay the executioner's hand. Their intervention had nothing to do with the merits of the case; it was simply a cynical attempt to exploit what had begun as a sordid criminal act for their own ends. The rising Medici faction was then engaged in a life-and-death struggle with the ruling Albizzi regime, and they saw in Niccolò's trial an opportunity to embarrass their rivals. Spreading rumors that Uzzano had fabricated the evidence against Niccolò, they managed to confuse the issue to such an extent that in the end the *Signoria* was forced to drop the charges.

Thus Niccolò and his younger brother Tommaso were recruited to the Medici cause. The decades of Cosimo's ascendance saw the brothers rise to prominence within the *reggimento,* but political and financial success did not mellow the prickly Niccolò. When he was not employed in running errands for his Medici patrons or attending to his many business ventures—which, now that he was in the good graces of the masters of the city, tended to prosper as never before—he was often embroiled in legal battles. As early as 1432 Soderini had alienated his own brother, quarreling with him over a division of property, and in 1453 Soderini was involved in another lawsuit with his sister-in-law Alessandra Strozzi to seize control of a farm she had inherited. Even among the normally litigious Florentines, Niccolò Soderini stands out for the number and bitterness of his legal disputes.

The origins of his disillusionment with the Medici date to 1453 when, as ambassador to Genoa, he managed to interject himself into a local

---

* Lorenzo Soderini was the illegitimate child of the prominent merchant Tommaso Soderini and a French woman of lowly status. Though Tommaso raised his bastard son, Lorenzo did not inherit his father's wealth or position. In order to redress the wrongs done to him because of his illegitimacy, Lorenzo forged a document purporting to show that his father had actually married his mother, thus entitling him to a substantial portion of the Soderini inheritance. The forgery was discovered, however, leading to Lorenzo's eventual hanging (see Clarke, *The Soderini and the Medici,* pp. 16–17).

political feud, much to the consternation of Duke Francesco Sforza, who resented the Florentine ambassador stirring up the pot in a city that Milan considered within its sphere of influence. After considerable pressure from the duke, Cosimo agreed to find "some honorable excuse" to bring back his hotheaded emissary. Thereafter, Soderini's career declined. A series of minor appointments, including ambassadorships to Rimini and Pesaro, suggest that Cosimo no longer trusted him. Niccolò's conviction grew that he could never prosper as long as the Medici remained in power. During the last years of Cosimo's life, as popular discontent with the *reggimento* began to grow, Soderini became a natural focus of the emerging opposition. With his election in October of 1465 as *Gonfaloniere di Giustizia,* Soderini finally had the opportunity to turn the tables on those he believed responsible for stunting his career.

There is no doubt that Soderini was a gifted and opportunistic politician. One of his first acts upon being named *Gonfaloniere* was to reduce the tax on wine, for which, according to a contemporary diarist, "the people called down blessings on his head." It was during his two-month reign that Parenti was convinced that Piero's star was on the wane. "Piero di Cosimo, at the beginning of [Soderini's] term, feared him and went along with his proposals, because never had a *Gonfaloniere* entered office with such support among the people and with such expectations of the benefits they would receive from him."

But while Soderini's rise had been dramatic, his fall from grace was even more spectacular. As Soderini's reputation soared, his most ardent supporters—including oligarchs like Agnolo Acciaiuoli, Dietisalvi Neroni, and Luca Pitti, who initially thought that Soderini would be useful in helping to trim Piero's sails—now feared they might be swept away by the indiscriminate tide. They had no desire to rid themselves of the overbearing Piero only to replace him with the domineering and reckless Soderini. The scope of Soderini's reforms threatened not only the Medici themselves but all who had risen to prominence on their coattails. Perhaps his most controversial proposal was for a new scrutiny—the periodic canvassing of Florentines to determine those eligible for political office—that was to be more democratic and wide-open than any held in recent times.* By including in the purses many names previously left out, the *Gonfaloniere* threatened to

---

* See "Note on the Government of Florence."

undercut the power base of the leading families by diluting the dominant position they had built up in the electoral rolls.* The head of the Medici household now shrewdly played on those fears. "Piero," Nicodemo Tranchedini reported to Francesco Sforza, "has well demonstrated to these others not to go along, because many of them will fall from power."

By December 1465, it was clear Soderini had overplayed his hand. Many now took a sharper look at the man they had championed just months before, and Soderini's shady past could not withstand the renewed attention. Even Parenti admitted that Soderini's noble goals were sabotaged by questionable business dealings that opened him to charges he was using his position for personal gain. "Niccolò went in boldly, but then he lost heart," his sister-in-law noted with evident relish, "and his brother [Tommaso] said to Giovanni Bonsi, 'he went in like a lion and will leave like a lamb,' and so it happened. As soon as he saw the beans† were not in his favor he began to humble himself, and since he left office he goes around with sometimes five and sometimes six armed men nearby."

While Soderini's fall from grace heartened the Medici and their supporters, Piero, too, had emerged from the contest gravely wounded. The diminished authority of the Eight and the closing of the electoral bags deprived him of the controls that Cosimo had built up over the years. Soderini's overreaching allowed Piero to recoup some of his lost prestige, but it did not alter the fact that the head of the Medici could no longer have things his way in the *Palazzo della Signoria*.

The government of Florence was now effectively shared by more hands

---

* The exact nature of the reforms Soderini was proposing have been hotly debated by historians. His proposal to combine the closing of the bags with new criteria for holding high office would have widened the franchise but also permanently fixed the number of eligible families. Some insist that the effect would have been to make the government more democratic; others insist his reforms would have created a closed oligarchic caste, modeled on that of Venice, that would have killed off the kind of social mobility that Florentines believed was an important part of their political system. (See Rubinstein, *The Government of FlorenceUnder the Medici,* especially pp. 167–86 and Pampaloni, "Fermenti di Riforme Democratiche nella Firenze Medicea del Quattrocento," in Archivio Storico Italiano 119 (1961): 11–62. It is impossible to judge Florentine politics by modern standards, since often reformers were those who actually favored a return to a more oligarchic form of government.

† Votes in the *palazzo* were counted by means of black and white beans.

than it had been in more than a generation. But far from bringing about reconciliation, the new disposition simply added to the mood of suspicion and fear. It was during the summer and fall of 1465 that the emergence of the two factions of Hill and Plain began to push the city toward civil war as the fluid alliances and rivalries typical of Florentine politics hardened during the battle over the closing of the electoral bags and preparations for a new scrutiny. "[I]n this bill one begins to see the emergence of the dissension among the leaders of the city," recalled Alamanno Rinuccini, "because *Messer* Luca Pitti was its author and supporter, and this displeased Piero di Cosimo and his followers." Since Florentine political theory made no allowance for rival parties—assuming instead that men of goodwill naturally agree on what constitutes the common good—differences of opinion led to bitter recrimination as each side accused the other of sacrificing the interests of the republic for private gain.* The tendency to transform small disagreements into epochal battles was increased by ill-conceived regulations that, in a futile effort to abolish the formation of political parties, banned private gatherings of like-minded citizens, forcing men to meet in secret—an outcome that no doubt contributed to the conspiratorial atmosphere. As Agnolo Acciaiuoli described Florence in a colorful turn of phrase, the city had now become "a paradise inhabited by devils."

One unintended consequence of the political reforms was that it led to Lorenzo's first position of real responsibility in the government. At the age of sixteen he was chosen to sit on the controversial and contentious committee tasked with supervising the new scrutiny.† The following year

---

* In an earlier crisis, one Florentine declared, "He who creates party, sells his liberty" (see Dale Kent, *The Rise of the Medici Faction*, p. 22). This fear of faction reflects the violent history of the city in which Guelfs and Ghibellines, and later Black and White Guelfs, murdered each other with abandon in the streets. There is an interesting parallel to the early days of the American republic. The almost universal support for George Washington initially masked the quarrels between the followers of Thomas Jefferson and those of Alexander Hamilton. Each side accused the other of "faction" and disloyalty. But, unlike fifteenth-century Florence, the American system quickly adapted, leading to the formation of political parties that pursued their aims openly.

† Lorenzo was qualified to replace a deceased relative. Replacements were supposed to be at least twenty-five, but exceptions were made in a few cases, including not only Lorenzo but Piero de' Pazzi's son Renato. The following year Lorenzo was appointed to the board of trade (*Mercanzia*).

Lorenzo, substituting for his ailing father, participated in his first major public art commission, serving on the board that chose Andrea del Verrocchio to sculpt *Christ and St. Thomas* for the niche belonging to the *Mercanzia* (the board of trade) in the facade of the church of Orsanmichele.* The two appointments, one political, the other cultural, indicate the accelerated pace at which the teenager was being groomed to take his place at the apex of Florentine society.

More noteworthy to contemporary observers was the sudden rise of the fabulously wealthy Luca Pitti as the leading opponent to Piero. (While initially supporting Niccolò Soderini's reforms, he had been among those who had balked at the more extreme proposals of the *Gonfaloniere.*) His growing stature was signaled by the splendid new residence, designed by the great Brunelleschi, he was now building for himself on the high ground on the south bank of the Arno River. Its massive scale was "greater than any other that had been built by a private citizen until that day." Unlike the palace on the Via Larga, Pitti's monument to himself stood in haughty isolation on the highest land within the city walls, more like a princely castle than a merchant's home.† During the winter of 1465–66,

---

* A replica of this masterpiece can still be seen in its original location on the facade of Orsanmichele. This church, which also served as a public granary, was one of the major civic monuments of Florence. Its medieval facade was punctuated by numerous niches, each one belonging to one of the major trade guilds, who were expected to fill them with sculptures of their patron saints. Among the famous works adorning the church are Donatello's *Saint George* (for the armorers' guild), Nanni di Banco's *Four Crowned Saints* for the guild of wood- and stone-workers, and Lorenzo Ghiberti's *St. Matthew* for the bankers. The sculptures now in place are mostly replicas of the originals, most of which are in the Bargello. Orsanmichele, with its singular blend of religion, business, and art, is a perfect symbol of the spirit of Renaissance Florence.

† The palace we see today, which still dominates the neighborhood of the Oltrarno, has been expanded since Pitti's day. In an ironic twist, the Pitti palace was enlarged when it became home to the Medici grand dukes in the sixteenth century. It now houses one of the world's premier art museums. The story is told in Vasari's *Lives of the Painters, Sculptors and Architects* how Cosimo had originally asked Brunelleschi to design his own palace. But upon seeing "the very beautiful model" he rejected it, "thinking it too sumptuous. . . . [He] refrained from putting it into execution, more to avoid envy than

Pitti's half-completed residence had become the meeting place for those disenchanted with the Medici regime. Marco Parenti's description of the scene at Pitti's residence in March of 1466* shows that he had now surpassed his onetime ally as the leading citizen of Florence:

> [Piero's] reputation was much diminished at this time. And *messer* Luca Pitti held court at his house, where the greater part of the citizenry went to deliberate on matters concerning the state. *Messer* Agnolo Acciaiuoli and *messer* Dietisalvi di Neroni, most prominent among the other citizens, though they were thought superior in prudence to *messer* Luca, nonetheless allowed him to rise in esteem, and that it might rise even further they too attended him at his house. All this they did to obstruct Piero di Cosimo, to whose house men were once accustomed to go to discuss matters public and private, and to deny him the authority he once possessed, which had now become burdensome to everyone. In this way they had brought him down to such an extent that few, and these few of little prestige, frequented his house, and so thought that in little time they would bring him down completely.

Luca Pitti's emergence as the leading exponent of reform must have come as a surprise to any Florentine who had followed his career. Only seven years earlier he had been vilified for the harsh methods he had used to push through legislation that strengthened the controls of the Medici regime. Like most of those now in opposition to Piero, Pitti had been willing to do Cosimo's bidding, but his pride would not allow him to place himself under the authority of his son. This was a generational as much as an ideological conflict, pitting those who felt that they had earned the right to succession through their long years of loyal service to Cosimo against Cosimo's natural heirs.

---

by reason of the cost." Luca Pitti apparently had no such compunctions, allowing the offended genius to fashion him a home of "such grandeur and magnificence that nothing more rare or more magnificent has yet been seen in the Tuscan manner."

* Parenti uses the date 1465, following the Florentine usage of beginning the New Year on the Feast of the Annunciation in March.

For all his sudden celebrity, however, Pitti could not command the affection of his followers or inspire trust in his compatriots. His main attribute, embodied in his ostentatious palace, was a vanity ill suited to one who claimed to speak for the rights of the ordinary citizen. Cosimo summed up the difference between the two men during the last years of his life, when the two former allies had begun to grow apart. "You raise your ladder to the heavens," he observed, "while I rest mine upon earth lest I should mount so high that I may fall. Now it seems to me only just and honest that I should prefer the good name and honor of my house to you: that I should work for my own interest rather than for yours. So you and I will act like two big dogs who, when they meet, smell one another and then, because they both have teeth, go their ways."

Now in his seventies, with hollow cheeks and the sharp profile of a bird of prey, Pitti had been one of Cosimo's most effective lieutenants, though, according to Guicciardini, he prospered in Medici Florence only because "he had not sufficient brains that Cosimo need fear him." In the summer of 1458, when the government was besieged by reformers who wished to abolish the electoral controls that ensured the dominance of the regime, it was Pitti, then serving his two-month term as *Gonfaloniere di Giustizia,* who led the pro-Medici reaction. At the time, according to Parenti, he was "a man entirely devoted to Cosimo."

Since Cosimo's death, however, Pitti had been angling for the top position in the *reggimento,* and those electoral controls that had appeared to him so necessary only a few years back were viewed in a different light now that they favored Piero at Pitti's expense. Pitti's leadership of the anti-Medici faction was confirmed in May when his signature appeared prominently atop an oath signed by four hundred of his fellow citizens pledging to work toward democratic reforms. One of its stated goals was to ensure that "[a]ll the affairs of the commune should be conducted in the Palace of the Priors," an attack directed at the sickly Piero, who, even more than his father, was accustomed to doing the government's business in his private chambers.*

---

* The practice of undermining the legally constituted government by conducting business in the private houses of the leading citizens did not begin with the Medici. During the Albizzi regime, Giovanni Cavalcanti complained that the state "was governed more from the dinner-table and the study than from the Palace" (Dale Kent, *The Rise of the Medici Faction,* p. 19).

Both Neroni and Acciaiuoli were content to let Pitti serve as the public face of the rebellion precisely because, as Guicciardini noted, he posed no long-term threat to their own ambitions: "Thinking that *Messer* Luca Pitti, with his strong following, would be a useful instrument, they entered into negotiations and convinced him that they would make him head of the city—though they are said to have agreed among themselves that as soon as they had deposed Piero they would also get rid of *Messer* Luca. That much, they thought, would be easy, since he was not a very capable man." Marco Parenti, who knew him well, shared their low opinion of Pitti, judging both Acciaiuoli and Neroni "superior in prudence."

Agnolo Acciaiuoli, like the other leaders of the Hill, was driven to oppose Piero out of motives that were at least as much personal as ideological. At one time Cosimo had counted him among his closest friends. Their affection was based on a mutual passion for classical literature and philosophy that they had both discovered while young men attending learned discussions in the garden of Santa Maria degli Angeli conducted by the great humanist scholar Ambrogio Traversari. Acciaiuoli's attachment to Cosimo was genuine and cost him dearly when the Albizzi government banished them both in 1433. Having demonstrated his loyalty in this most trying time, Acciaiuoli soon reaped his reward. The following year he returned to Florence in triumph with Cosimo, quickly rising to a place of prominence within the highest circles of the regime.

For all his skill and erudition, there seems to have been a streak of naïveté in Acciaiuoli that allowed his passions to overrule his better judgment. This naïveté was compounded by the fact that over the years he spent much of his time abroad on important missions for the government, and was therefore ill equipped to engage in the sort of intrigues that were a perpetual feature of Florentine political life. "Now Agnolo had been absent from Florence for a long time," Vespesiano da Bisticci explained, and "he did not realize the treachery of the democracy of the city so, being strongly importuned, he cast in his lot with *Messer* Luca."

But Acciaiuoli was not just the dupe of shrewder and more violent men; he had his own reasons for wishing to rid the city of the Medici. Vespesiano da Bisticci traces his estrangement from his old friend to Cosimo's attempts to block the appointment of Agnolo's son Lorenzo as archbishop of Pisa in order that he might promote his own kinsman, Filippo de' Medici, for the job. Though Lorenzo was given as consolation the less prestigious bishopric of Arezzo, Agnolo resented Cosimo's behind-the-scenes maneuvering.

It was a second betrayal, however, that turned the friends into bitter enemies. When the young Alessandra de' Bardi wed Acciaiuoli's son Raffaello, she brought with her the prestige of the ancient Bardi name (Cosimo himself was married to Contessina de' Bardi) as well as a substantial dowry. Marriages between leading merchant families carried important political and financial ramifications, and though love rarely entered into the equation, this marriage proved more than usually unhappy. Shortly after the wedding Alessandra began complaining to her relatives of abuse at the hands of Raffaello. The complaints grew so persistent that the Bardi dispatched a band of armed men, who showed up at the Acciaiuoli palace in the dead of night to rescue the long-suffering bride. Agnolo, if not Raffaello, might have reconciled himself to the loss of the Bardi girl, but to return the dowry would entail not only financial loss but would constitute a permanent stain on the family escutcheon. Cosimo, whether out of a sense of fair play or out of political calculation, ultimately intervened in favor of the Bardi. Agnolo, already less than pleased by Cosimo's neglect of his family's interests, saw this as an unforgivable breach of friendship, and from that moment he worked to take his revenge against the family that had wronged him.

Though all the leaders of the Hill were motivated in part by personal grievances, it would be a mistake to dismiss the revolt as simply the work of a few disgruntled men driven by greed and ambition. Whatever motivated the break, they had tapped into a genuine current of discontent. Few would deny that Cosimo had led the city wisely, but even his loyal supporters acknowledged that his unprecedented power had come at the expense of the traditional prerogatives of the Florentine upper classes. To concede the same authority to his son would be to admit that republican government had been replaced by dynastic rule. With Cosimo in the grave, Piero laid low by illness, and Lorenzo not yet grown, the traditional ruling class saw this moment as perhaps the final opportunity to reclaim its ancient status.

Among those now frequenting Luca Pitti's doorstep was Niccolò Soderini. From the moment his government left office—to the accompaniment of celebratory bonfires in the Piazza della *Signoria* and graffiti on the *Palazzo* declaring "Nine fools out"—Soderini redoubled his efforts to bring about a change of regime, his hatred for Piero sharpened by the Medici's behind-the-scenes role in his recent disgrace. To accomplish his goal he would need to mend fences with his former allies. Soderini's task was made considerably easier by the fact that since his disastrous tenure as *Gonfaloniere* Piero had once again emerged as the chief threat to their collective ambitions. Sometime between December of 1465 and May of 1466, Soderini and the other dissidents ironed out past differences and forged an alliance powerful enough to bring about Piero's downfall.

By the winter of 1465–66, Florence was a city divided and all signs indicated that a violent confrontation was imminent. Both Hill and Plain were hurriedly organizing militias in the countryside around Florence and urging foreign powers to intervene on their behalf as soon as the fighting broke out.* These preparations generated their own momentum as an escalation on one side was met by an equal or greater response by the other. Each faction could plausibly claim, and probably sincerely believed, that in calling their partisans to arms they were merely responding to the provocations of their opponents.

The mood of the city was not improved by a disastrous January flood that left the entire quarter of Santa Croce under six feet of water or by the lingering effects of the economic downturn that had begun in the months following Cosimo's death. In February of 1466, in an atmosphere of growing crisis, Lorenzo set out on another vital diplomatic mission, this time to meet with the two great leaders of southern Italy—the pope and the king of Naples. Piero's willingness to be without Lorenzo at this critical juncture is one more indication of the decisive role that foreign powers were expected to play in the looming political contest. Marco Parenti reported to Filippo Strozzi in Naples, "everyone knows that Florence has turned towards Venice," citing "a secret agreement among Luca Pitti, Agnolo Acciaiuoli, and Dietisalvi Neroni . . . intended to counter Piero de' Medici."

Under the circumstances it was important to bring on board or at least

---

* On the side of the Hill were the Venetians, acting largely through their proxies, Borso d'Este and the mercenary leader Bartolomeo Colleoni, a general in the Venetian employ. Backing the Medici were the forces of Milan, also gathering in the vicinity of Bologna.

neutralize the two southern powers, neither of whom had firmly committed to either side. In each case the Medici had cause for concern. The current pope, Paul II, was Venetian-born and was inclined to favor his hometown as long as its interests did not clash with those of the Holy See. His suspicions of Florence had been aroused when it signed the tripartite treaty with Milan and Naples, which he believed, not without reason, was aimed in part at containing papal ambitions in central Italy. As for Naples, Ferrante had proven himself an unreliable and unpredictable ally. His treacherous murder the year before of the mercenary captain Iacopo Piccinino, Francesco Sforza's son-in-law, had thrown the whole structure of alliances into doubt.* An additional cause of concern was that Ferrante's finances were largely in the hands of the Acciaiuoli family, which had ancient ties to the southern realm. Agnolo's son, Jacopo, had long enjoyed the confidence of the king, a position he was now using to undermine his Florentine rivals.

The gravity of the mission can be gauged by the company Lorenzo kept, which included not only his tutor, Gentile Becchi, who could be expected to keep his young charge focused, but the battle-tested *condottiere* Roberto Malatesta. Absent were the boisterous companions who so often accompanied Lorenzo on his voyages. Among those left behind was Luigi Pulci, who complained, "So you intend, finally, to leave me in these snow-bound woods, alone and unhappy, while you go to Rome. When shall I join you? when I am old? . . . How many times have we thought of Rome, and how I should be at your side."

Another purpose of this southern journey was to round out Lorenzo's education as a budding merchant prince and statesman. While the trip to Milan had taken him to the source of Medici political power, the Roman journey brought him to the heart of his family's business empire. Since the days of Giovanni di Bicci, Lorenzo's great-grandfather, the Medici bank's

---

* Many, according to Marco Parenti, believed that Sforza had connived in his son-in-law's assassination, but Parenti concluded "that the duke of Milan had no fault in this" (see *Ricordi Storici,* p. 80). Francesco Sforza's anger, demonstrated by his delaying Ippolita's journey to Naples to consummate the marriage to Alfonso, had less to do with the murder itself than with the false accusations that were rained down upon him by this rash act of his kinsman. Eventually the incident was papered over, but relations between Naples and Milan remained tumultuous. One of the principal goals of Florentine diplomacy was to keep these two natural competitors at peace.

most lucrative business had been managing the finances of the papal curia. Nurturing good relations with whoever occupied the throne of St. Peter was thus of vital importance to maintaining a sound fiscal footing. While in Rome, the most pressing task for Lorenzo was to obtain the pope's signature on a contract naming the Medici bank sole distributors of alum from the papal mines at Tolfa, a deal Piero hoped would pump much needed cash into the Medici coffers.* Pope Paul had agreed in principle to hand over the concession in return for a portion of the proceeds, and Lorenzo was entrusted with finalizing the terms. Paul II's willingness to expand his already substantial financial arrangements with the Medici bank was welcomed not only for the profits it would generate but as a public affirmation of his continued confidence. With the pope himself consigning his treasure to the Medici bank, who would not feel reassured doing business under the sign of the *palle*?

Lorenzo and his entourage arrived in the ancient capital at the beginning of March, taking up residence at the Medici headquarters just across the Tiber from the Castel Sant' Angelo, where his uncle, the corpulent, sour-faced Giovanni Tornabuoni, served as host and guide to the mysteries of the Roman branch.† Under his uncle's tutelage Lorenzo could study the intricacies of double-entry bookkeeping and delve into the *libro segreto,* the secret accounts, where the real assets and liabilities of the bank

---

* This mineral was used in the manufacture of glass, in the tanning of leather, and, most vitally as far as the Medici were concerned, as a cleanser and in the cloth-dying industry that was the major employer of Florentine workers. Before its discovery in the Papal States in 1460, this valuable mineral had to be imported from the Far East at much expense and peril. Gaining the concessions on these mines had important financial rewards as well as political implications. "I give you a great victory over the Turks," Giovanni di Castro wrote to the pope when he discovered the deposits in Tolfa. This mineral would play a role in Lorenzo's life out of all proportion to its apparent humbleness.

† Giovanni had just been recently made managing partner of the bank after a long dispute with his colleague Leonardo Vernacci. Vernacci implied that there was nepotism involved, claiming that "[w]hile advancement was based on merit, everyone was satisfied," implying that things now ran differently (see de Roover, *The Rise and Decline of the Medici Bank,* p. 219). The timid, fretful Giovanni turned out to be a plodding, but honest, manager, loyally serving his nephew to the best of his abilities until the expulsion of the Medici from Florence in 1494. The bank was located on the Canale di Ponte, now called the Via del Banco di Santo Spirito, in the main financial district of the city, near the Vatican.

were set down out of sight of the prying eyes of the tax inspectors.* Such a tour was long past due. Business was a neglected aspect of Lorenzo's education that required immediate remedial attention. Both Cosimo and Piero had been bankers first and politicians second, but Lorenzo, by contrast, seemed to have more talent in spending than in making money. Dipping into his purse to put on lavish entertainments for the cardinals and nobility of Rome, he demonstrated that he had learned the alchemical trick of transmuting gold florins into political capital, but where those florins came from or how to turn one into two or ten into twenty were subjects in which he had shown little interest or aptitude.

Among other things, Giovanni explained that while profits from the Roman branch were vast, dealing with constantly changing popes and a venal College of Cardinals brought with it peculiar difficulties.† Tornabuoni was a cautious man and the risks inherent in doing business with the

---

* Florentine bankers usually kept two sets of accounts, the public books where profits were minimized and liabilities were exaggerated, and a "secret book," where the real accounting took place. Naturally it is to these latter that historians refer in reconstructing the economic history of the period. The existence of these secret books should make us skeptical of taking the *catasti,* or public tax statements, too literally.

The importance of Rome to the Medici can be seen in a comparison of profits from various branches for the years 1420–35 (in de Roover, table 11, p. 55). Over those fifteen years the Roman branch made a profit of 117,037 florins, representing almost 63 percent of the total. By contrast the Florentine branch brought in less than 10 percent. The second most profitable branch was in Venice, followed closely by Geneva, but neither approached that of Rome. Over the course of the fifteenth century, as more branches were added in cities like Avignon, Pisa, Milan, and London, Rome declined in relative importance, but it still remained the critical piece of the Medici financial empire. From 1435 to 1450, profits from the Roman branch, 88,511 florins, still constituted 30 percent of the total (de Roover, table 17, p. 69). Unlike most branches, where much of the capital was supplied by the partners of the bank, the Roman branch drew its funds from deposits by individual clerics and the papal treasury. In 1427, the deposits amounted to almost 100,000 florins, four times the amount in all the other branches combined (see de Roover, *The Rise and Decline of the Medici Bank* p. 106).

† Throughout much of the fifteenth century the Medici bank acted, in effect, as the pope's treasury department. Under Popes John XXIII (later declared an antipope), Martin V Nicholas V, Eugenius IV, and Calixtus III, comprising the years 1410–58, the Medici bank in Rome had served as the Depository General of the Apostolic Chamber, the place where the Vatican kept and distributed its funds. From 1458 to 1471, under Popes Pius II and Paul II, the accounts were placed elsewhere. Sixtus IV reinstated the Medici to this important role upon his accession in 1471 (see Chapter XII).

profligate and dishonest men of the papal curia caused him no end of worry. Money and power, rather than prayer and charity, were the twin pillars propping up the Renaissance version of Christ's holy edifice; the College of Cardinals and the less than saintly men who sat on St. Peter's throne were acquainted from firsthand experience with the seven deadly sins. A savvy banker could exploit such weakness, but he could also be bankrupted by accepting unsecured pledges from men whose spiritual authority inoculated them against the obligation of most mortals to repay their debts.

Paul II, by no means the worst of his breed, was particularly susceptible to the blandishments of those with ready cash since he was a man less noted for his piety than for his love of jewelry, objets d'art, and fine clothes. His friendliness toward the Medici, as Lorenzo's uncle pointed out, was directly proportional to his financial need. One benefit the Medici discovered of doing business on the pope's behalf was that it allowed them to threaten excommunication against those who failed to pay their bills, a spiritual weapon any modern collection agency would be glad to have. "Pope Paul's head is empty," wrote an anonymous poet after the pope had himself crowned with a tiara ostentatious enough to throw the papal finances into immediate disarray. "It is then right that it be loaded with jewels and gold."

On his journey to Rome, Lorenzo had a chance to observe the corrupt heart of the Renaissance church in all its sordid splendor, and the unsavory impression it left only grew over the years. In a famous letter he wrote late in life to his son Giovanni (who had just taken up residence in Rome as a newly minted cardinal), Lorenzo referred to the capital of Christendom as "that sink of all iniquities." Other aspects of life in the ancient imperial capital he found more to his taste. As Pulci's letter suggests, the Eternal City loomed large in the collective imagination of Lorenzo and his circle, as it did for all who drew inspiration from the classical past. While contemporary Romans showed little interest in their own history, turning ancient buildings into rubble to be burned in their lime kilns, it furnished more constructive material to the humanists of Florence. Ever since Brunelleschi and Donatello had come here more than a generation earlier to sketch and measure the Forum, the Colosseum, and the Pantheon, Rome had been a site of pilgrimage for those passionate, as Lorenzo surely was, about the vanished classical civilization.

The Eternal City offered a spectacle at once melancholy and sublime. Its greatness was hinted at in the massive, crumbling monuments that still rose above the sheep pastures and orchards that over the centuries had encroached upon the neighborhoods of the ancient city. As great as it once had been, in its ruined state it seemed to offer a profound message about the transience of worldly glory. "You may turn all the pages of history," wrote Lorenzo's compatriot the humanist Poggio Bracciolini, "but you will find that fortune offers no more striking example of her own mutability than the city of Rome, the most beautiful and magnificent of all those that either have been or shall be. . . . How much the more marvelous to relate and bitter to behold, how the cruelty of fortune has so transformed its appearance and shape, that, stripped of all beauty, it now lies prostrate like a giant corpse, decayed and everywhere eaten away."

It was a brief encounter with a young girl, however, that would ultimately have a more serious impact on the course of Lorenzo's life. He left no account of his meeting with Clarice Orsini, the thirteen-year-old niece of the formidable Cardinal Latino Orsini, but, as his mother later confirmed, his first glimpse of his future bride was sufficient to leave, if not an indelible memory, at least pleasant associations.

Lorenzo, in fact, was unlikely to have had more than passing thoughts of this tall, redheaded girl. True, she belonged to one of the most ancient and influential families in Rome, but her shyness and modesty, perfectly appropriate to her age and situation, would not have captured the imagination or excited the passions of a worldly young man. That he should have remembered her at all two years hence suggests a mild attraction, if nothing else.

In any case more urgent issues soon claimed his attention. Lorenzo's mission was made more difficult by news, arriving ominously on the Ides of March, that instantly transformed the calculus of Florentine politics and sent shockwaves along the length and breadth of the peninsula. It was on the anniversary of Caesar's murder that Lorenzo learned of the sudden death of Duke Francesco Sforza, an event that at the best of times would have tested the Medici's strength. In the current troubled atmosphere, the duke's demise deepened the sense of impending crisis by depriving the Medici of their most reliable protector and threatening to throw into disarray the system of alliances that Cosimo had built and that had kept Italy relatively peaceful for the past decade.*

---

* Despite having made his fortune as a mercenary general and having seized the ducal thrown by force, once in power, Francesco, with the backing of Cosimo, labored hard for peace.

"I am in such affliction and sorrow for the sad and untimely death of the Illustrious Duke of Milan that I know not where I am," Piero wrote to Lorenzo upon hearing the news. (The situation was made worse by the fact that at the time of his death the duke's heir, Galeazzo Maria, was earning his spurs as an aide in the armies of the king of France. On his return journey he was forced to travel through the hostile territory of Savoy in disguise and arrived in his native city only on March 20). Evidently shaken, Piero urged Lorenzo to meet with the pope once more, to impress upon him the need for statesmanship in these perilous hours and to remind him once again of the devotion of the Medici family. Knowing his son's inclinations, he also reminded him to "put an end to all playing on instruments, or singing or dancing," adding "be old beyond your years, for the times require it." He even contemplated bringing Lorenzo back to Florence to help combat the growing civic unrest. Ultimately, however, he decided that Lorenzo should proceed to Naples in the hope of bringing the king on board and countering the harmful influence of the Acciaiuoli.

Lorenzo left Rome on April 8, arriving four days later in Nola, where the king interrupted his hunting trip to receive him. Gentile Becchi's report on the meeting was ecstatic. He informed Piero that with all gathered in the room "the King took Lorenzo by the arm and, alone with the Secretary, exited into the antechamber. There I think that Lorenzo satisfactorily discharged your commission to him, spending with His Majesty more than a half hour." Lorenzo was equally pleased with his reception, telling his father, "I spoke with him, and he replied with many kind words, which I wait to tell you in person." Even Jacopo Acciaiuoli, who thought his performance awkward at best, was forced to admit that the king had shown him much kindness.* According to Ferrante, his kind reception of Lorenzo was due to "love which we bear towards his Magnificence, your father, to you, and to your house which merits even greater demonstra-

---

* One factor in Lorenzo's favor was the king's desire to see the decree of exile lifted on his friend Filippo Strozzi, something that could happen only with the blessing of Piero. The bulk of Marco Parenti's correspondence, so helpful in reconstructing the events of these years, was addressed to his brother-in-law Filippo in Naples and concerns his efforts to revoke the exile imposed on the Strozzi for their father, Matteo's, support of the Albizzi faction in the struggles of 1433–34.

tions," adding, in words that may have irked the proud adolescent, the paternal advice that he should "strive to follow the example of the revered Magnificent Cosimo and of your father."

Important testimony on the diplomatic maneuverings in the southern kingdom comes from Sacramoro da Rimini, Milan's new ambassador to Naples (he was soon to hold a similar position in Florence), who assured Lorenzo that, despite the "crowing" of their opponents, the king was "well-disposed towards his state and opposed to those who are the enemies of your magnificent father," adding, significantly, that "here you will be received with the same favor as in Milan itself." As on his earlier trip to Milan, by the time Lorenzo departed from his hosts he had convinced them to stand behind the Medici in the upcoming contest. Ferrante's tacit support, if not his active involvement, was a welcome boost to Florence's ruling family, now more than ever in need of powerful friends.

By the end of April, Lorenzo was back in Tuscany. But before returning to Florence he made one final stop in Arezzo, an important client city some twenty miles to the south, where he was honored with a magnificent reception hosted by the city elders. Of all the stops on his journey, it was this one that would pay the most immediate practical dividends. Luca Pitti had long-standing ties to Arezzo, but Lorenzo was able to win the backing of leading citizens so that during the height of the crisis, in late August, the government of Arezzo pledged one hundred troops to the Medici cause.

Passing through the Porta Romana on May 6, Lorenzo and his companions found Florence on the brink of civil war. Two days earlier the *Signoria* had tried to head off a violent confrontation by demanding that all members of the ruling class twenty years and older sign an oath forswearing violence. The oath also banned all private political associations, a commitment broken so often and so openly that it served merely to demonstrate the impotence of the elected officials. Strong anti-Medici sentiment in the government was confirmed the following week by the defeat of a bill to deliver a promised loan of 60,000 florins to Bianca Maria, widow of Francesco Sforza, a rejection that mortified Piero, who had hoped to demonstrate his loyalty to the ruling house of Milan.

As tensions rose throughout the summer, Lorenzo was called upon to rally the Medici forces. In the countryside around Careggi and in the hills of the Mugello he met with local leaders loyal to the Medici and drilled their militias, while Piero sought to overawe his opponents by inviting infantry and cavalry under the banner of Milan to march to the very borders of Tuscany. Thankfully for the Medici, while Galeazzo Maria got his bearings, the day-to-day running of the government of Milan lay in the hands of Bianca and her capable minister Cicco Simonetta, who made it clear that the powerful Milanese army—even without the promised 60,000 florins—would come to the aid of their friends in Florence.

While Piero met with his supporters behind closed doors, Lorenzo was out among the people. He was, if not yet an equal partner with his father, someone to whom Medici partisans could look for guidance and inspiration. There was no doubt that Lorenzo could now play the part. He had returned to Florence more confident than when he had left it, having proven to himself and those around him that he could hold his own in the world of high-stakes diplomacy. In the space of a year he had held discussions with some of the most powerful men of the age, including a pope, two dukes, a king, and a doge, effectively representing both his country and his family.

Thus when, after a long, tense summer, Dietisalvi Neroni and his fellow conspirators sprang the trap while the family was vacationing at Careggi, Lorenzo was no longer a callow youth more interested in frivolous pleasures than in taking up his responsibilities as the future leader of Florence. But if it was clear to Medici partisans how important Lorenzo had become to the regime, his transformation had largely escaped the notice of their opponents. Perhaps on the morning of August 27, 1466, his reputation for immaturity actually worked in his favor because, despite ample evidence of the central role he had come to play, the leaders of the Hill apparently made no provision for his capture, allowing him to warn his father of the ambush that awaited at Sant'Antonio del Vescovo and to return to Florence, where he could launch the Medici counterattack.

Filippo Brunelleschi and Bartolomeo Ammanati, Palazzo Pitti
(Garden View), early 15th and late 16th centuries (Art Resource)

VI. GAMES OF FORTUNE

"I am laughing at the games of fortune and at how it makes friends become enemies and enemies become friends as it suits it."

—AGNOLO ACCIAIUOLI IN NAPLES TO
PIERO DE' MEDICI IN FLORENCE

"Your laughing over there is the cause that I do not weep, because if you were laughing in Florence, I would be weeping in Naples."

—*PIERO DE' MEDICI IN FLORENCE TO
AGNOLO ACCIAIUOLI IN NAPLES*

AROUND MIDDAY ON AUGUST 27, 1466, WHILE LORENZO was completing his perilous journey from Careggi to the city, the leaders of the Hill gathered in Luca Pitti's half-completed *palazzo* on the slopes of San Giorgio, just south of the Ponte Vecchio. Here, amid the sounds of hammering and the clattering of masons' carts, Pitti, along with Agnolo Acciaiuoli and Dietisalvi Neroni, anxiously awaited word of Piero's capture.

In fact, though they did not yet know it, Piero and his men had already slipped through the net. Warned by the horseman sent back by Lorenzo of the trap awaiting him at Sant'Antonio del Vescovo, they had turned off the main road and were somewhere unseen and unheard among the back country lanes. As minutes lengthened to hours with still no word, tensions rose in the cavernous rooms. The bid by leaders of the Hill to seize power had been predicated largely on the assumption that Piero was weak and incapable—a "vile rabbit" Agnolo Acciaiuoli had called him, a man unwilling or unable to take decisive action—but failure to seize the Medici patriarch would turn what was meant to be a swift and decisive coup into a long, drawn-out struggle for which they had not adequately planned.

The assessment of Piero as an unworthy opponent helps to explain why the leaders of the Hill were so unprepared for the coming fight. Also greatly hampering their effort was the lack of a clear chain of command. "There were three chiefs," says Marco Parenti, "and each one waited for the others to act." The Party of the Hill was, in fact, nothing more than a temporary coalition of men "unified more by a common hatred than a common ideal." Even in these early hours the alliance was beginning to show signs of cracking under the pressure of events.

By contrast, across the city Lorenzo's arrival at the Medici palace had sparked a flurry of purposeful activity. The one guest whose presence is recorded that day was Nicodemo Tranchedini, the Milanese ambassador to Florence, and it was this battle-tested veteran who girded the residents for the expected onslaught. "Nicodemo [Tranchedini], well schooled in these arts, set about defending Piero's house," wrote Parenti, "erecting scaffolding above the windows to serve as battlements, with many stones and other arms of war, and occupying the streets around the house with armed troops, he seized as well the gate of San Gallo in order to allow the entrance of his own men, who were expected to arrive, while the others were closed to ensure that their enemies would not be able to enter the city."*

To those dithering across the river at Luca Pitti's home, confidence soon gave way to concern. Only when couriers brought word of growing crowds outside the *Palazzo Medici* did they begin, belatedly, to prepare their own defenses. Soon cries of "Popolo e Liberta!" rang out in the neighborhoods of the Oltrarno, the *gonfaloni* of the Dragon and the Ladder, while anyone of known Medici sympathies was forced to beat a strategic retreat across town. "And thus," records Marco Parenti, "there arose two fortresses, each guarded by its own men."

Marco Parenti says that Piero returned "around the 22nd hour [that is, around four in the afternoon] in great fright with many armed men," while Machiavelli confirms that he arrived "in the midst of a great multitude of armed men." At least some of these must have been with him when

---

* The seizure was clearly a violation of law. "The keys to the gates of the city of Florence must be kept under the power and the custody [of the *Gonfaloniere*] . . ." read the applicable statute: "these keys every night must be brought to the said palace and placed under the control of the notaries of said officials." According to one critic, this act alone made Piero a tyrant of the city.

he left Careggi, while others may have joined the cavalcade along the way. Once inside the city walls Piero's entourage was joined by additional partisans, who escorted him to the Via Larga. That the neighborhoods closest to the Medici palace remained solidly behind their cause is revealed by the fact that Neroni, whose palace was only a few doors down from theirs, was unable to return to his own house for fear the enraged mob would tear him limb from limb.

As soon as he was safely home Piero assembled his closest advisors. In addition to Lorenzo and Nicodemo Tranchedini, they included Francesco Sassetti, manager of the Medici bank in Florence, and Tommaso Soderini, Niccolò's younger brother, whose loyalty to the Medici was cemented by his recent marriage to Dianora Tornabuoni, Lucrezia's sister.*

For Piero and his advisors, survival would depend as much on the skillfull manipulation of popular sentiment as on the application of brute force. In times of political crisis the greatest danger was that quarrels among the city's rulers would lead to violent social revolution. With their masters at each other's throats, the downtrodden workers might grasp the opportunity to throw off their yoke as they had in the summer of 1378 during the violent upheaval known as the revolt of the *Ciompi*.† Visions of the hungry masses pouring out from their squalid hovels in San Frediano and rampaging through the streets was enough to send chills down the spines of the burghers who ran things in Florence.

For the Medici faction, maintaining discipline among the armed mobs now gathering to defend their palace was vital; as representatives of the status quo they had the most to lose should the situation descend into general anarchy. Here Lorenzo played a pivotal role, as Niccolò Valori writes: "The plebs, thirsting after novelty, thought of nothing but riot, and as happens in similar cases, with suspicion growing and without hope of receiving pardon, every day their sedition and mischief increased. And if to these dangers Lorenzo, along with those citizens who loved him and counseled

---

* This made Tommaso Lorenzo's uncle, but the familial connection did not always lead to harmonious relations. (See especially Chapter IX for an account of the often stormy history between uncle and nephew.)

† The *Ciompi* was the name given to salaried workers of the city's textile industries. The origin of the word is uncertain.

him, did not find remedy, without doubt the city with the greater part of the noblemen would have been endangered."

But while Piero and his advisors kept a tight rein on their supporters, the leaders of the Hill could ill afford to be so fastidious. They had already stirred up the masses with cries of "Popolo e Liberta!" and it was on their strong backs that they hoped to ride to victory. But in exploiting the discontent of the city's underclass, potentially their most effective weapon, they risked being destroyed by forces they themselves had unleashed. This points out a fatal contradition at the heart of the reform movement. The leaders of the Hill were not radicals but social conservatives who believed that the removal of the Medici would lead to a return to the good old days when the city's wealthy merchants took collective responsibility for government. However much they resented Piero and his cronies, the nightmare that kept them awake at night was the specter of destitute workers rising up to slit the throats of their masters.

With signs that the tide in the city was beginning to flow against them, the leaders of the Hill did in fact briefly contemplate tapping into that undercurrent of poverty and despair among the weavers and dyers and using it against the *reggimento*. "While things were in such a state," records Marco Parenti, "Niccolò Soderini, a spirited man as we have said, reached the house of *messer* Luca armed and on horseback, accompanied by many companions." Already present as we have seen were Neroni, Acciaiuoli, "and other honorable citizens" engaged with their host in lengthy but fruitless discussions. Soderini, frustrated that there was much discussion but little action, proposed that

> all those who were armed should follow him, and go to the houses of their friends who were hidden out of doubt and timidity and rouse them to join with them, and those who did not would be treated as enemies, and having gathered together many in this way, as it seemed to him would surely happen, he would gallop through the city shouting "Liberty!" . . . and proceed to Piero's house with every promise of victory. . . . It seemed to everyone that this was sure to succeed, but doubt crept in: this was caused by the fear that the little people, all in arms and having sacked Piero's house, would be so aroused that, having tasted the sweetness of such destruction, would

turn against other magnates, thinking in this way to relieve their poverty and becoming themselves among the well-to-do, and then perhaps, turn against the government and take it for themselves as they did in 1378.

In the end their fear of the mob proved greater than their fear of Piero. The three other leaders vetoed Soderini's proposal, a decision Parenti describes as "very cowardly, since their situation had become so precarious that they had no other means to preserve their own safety."

Throughout the evening of August 27, while Pitti, Neroni, Acciaiuoli, and Soderini quarreled over basic elements of strategy and even ideology, the Medici seized the initiative. Confronting his cousin Pierfrancesco, whose palace was next door to his on the Via Larga, Piero extracted an emergency loan of 10,000 florins, demonstrating that the rabbit had now become the wolf. Pierfrancesco had been one of the signatories to the oath of May 4 aimed at undermining Medici authority, and Piero must have relished the opportunity to settle the score. The sight of heavily armed men outside his window proved sufficient inducement for Pierfrancesco to rediscover the virtue of the family solidarity he had so recently forgotten.

While the leaders of the Hill, showing themselves to be frugal as well as indecisive, were reluctant to dip into their own pockets, Piero put his coins to immediate use. "With this money he showed great liberality in spending on what was required. First he emptied the bakeries in Florence of bread and sent it to his house, a double blow since it supplied his men while denying sustenance to his adversaries. He emptied the shops of their arms and the piazza of wine." The Party of the Hill, which earlier in the day seemed to hold all the cards, suddenly showed itself to be outmatched by the sickly and reputedly weak-willed Piero. "*Messer* Luca, *messer* Dietisalvi and *messer* Agnolo, seeing fall so great and sudden a blow, stupefied and without provision, seemed almost lost."

As the sun set over the city, Florence was divided into two hostile camps. Men and women flocked to the churches to pray for a peace that seemed ever more improbable, then returned home and locked their doors against the coming conflagration. In the courtyards of the Pitti and

Medici palaces torches crackled and sparked while armed guards kept up a tense vigil. In the *gran sala* of the Medici palace, surrounded by suitably warlike scenes painted by Antonio del Pollaiuolo depicting the labors of Hercules,* Piero, Lorenzo, and their trusted lieutenants prepared for the decisive confrontation, which was sure to come the next day. A comical scene played out at the Medici palace captures the eerie mood of the long night:

> *Messer* Antonio Ridolfi, one of Piero's friends, wishing to go that night to his house to talk over events, reached the door of the house with a company of armed men and, knocking, the armed guards inside, wishing to know who had come and why, as was only reasonable, raised some small ruckus with their weapons and loud voices. From this came a rumor among some of the armed men inside that their enemies had come to attack them. Thus was born such a great fright that many sought out hiding places while others threw down their arms hoping to flee; soon, seeing their error, order was restored. From this one can judge how Piero's defenses would have held had he actually been attacked.

In spite of this fiasco, by the time the sun rose above the Arno valley Piero had taken up a commanding position. As the mists parted, the roads from the north could be seen filling with armed men streaming toward the city walls. Some came from the hills near Mugello, the Medici's ancestral home, others from nearby Arezzo and Pistoia. Luca Pitti was also bringing reinforcements toward the city, but they were of little use to him since Medici partisans had already shut the gates. Now Piero's foresight in buying up all the bread and wine was revealed; while his supporters, camped outside the Porta San Gallo, were well provisioned, Pitti's men across the river were forced to scrounge for whatever scraps they could find.

Had Piero so desired, it is almost certain that he could have taken the government by force, storming the Palace of the Priors, arresting his

---

* The monumental originals of Pollaiuolo's canvases are now lost, but the smaller studies for them were rediscovered following the Second World War. Two of these studies, *Hercules and Antaeus* and *Hercules and the Hydra,* are now in the Uffizi Gallery.

opponents, and establishing a despotism of the kind already common throughout the Italian peninsula. (Cosimo himself had famously quipped, "Better a city ruined than a city lost.") But with absolute power within his grasp, Piero chose a different course. Rather than seizing the government and abolishing the constitution and the civic traditions to which Florentines were so deeply attached, he preferred to rely, as his father had before him, on those very instruments to legitimize and perpetuate his personal authority.

Here the calendar came to his aid. August 28 was election day, and in spite of the crisis the citizens were determined to press ahead with the cumbersome ceremony that to a Florentine was the essential ingredient of his cherished liberty. Piero, in fact, had much to gain from a change in the executive. Though under the timid leadership of Bernardo Lotti the current *Signoria* had been unable to impose its will on either faction, most of its members were known to be in sympathy with the Hill. The election of a new government—the eight priors plus the *Gonfaloniere di Giustizia* who comprised the *Signoria*, the chief executive body of the land—could well tip the balance of power in his favor.

With bells ringing out from dozens of churches all across the city, the attention of the citizens was drawn to the great basilica of Santa Croce, where the leather purses containing the names of those eligible for office were stored in large chests under the watchful eyes of the Franciscan brothers. Even as armed bands converged on the city, officials of the government, accompanied by a mounted escort and led by heralds and trumpeters, arrived at the sacristy to remove the purses and carry them in solemn procession to the Palace of the Priors, where the drawing of the names would take place.

Once inside the palace, the nine purses—one for each of the priors and another for the *Gonfaloniere*—were brought to the great hall and placed in full view of the current government and the assembled citizenry. As the *podestà*, the chief judicial official of the state, proceeded to draw a name ticket from each of the purses, tension in the hall mounted. The bags contained scores of names: scoundrels and sages, rabid partisans of one faction or another and those with no known political affiliation, all jumbled together. In this strange procedure lay the heart of Florentine democracy. By choosing their officials at random from a large pool of eligible citizens—

and by reducing the term of service for the most important offices to a mere two months—Florentines believed they had perfected a democratic system that would best represent the community as a whole and, as important, would prevent a single man or clique from monopolizing power. It was a process that guaranteed inefficiency because the corrupt and incompetent were as likely to serve as those of proven ability. Over the years Florentines had devised ingenious methods for mitigating the most baleful consequences—by weeding out undesirables from the purses or by instituting various councils of wise men who could steer the government in the desired direction—but there remained an element of unpredictability that to a true Florentine was synonymous with liberty itself.

The results of the current election would be all the more unpredictable because only months earlier the reformers had pushed through—against Piero's will—a measure to close the electoral purses, that is, to prevent members of the *reggimento* from removing from the bags the names of those they deemed unreliable. Thus today's election would be one of the freest in recent memory. Again, Marco Parenti is an eyewitness: "That same morning, at the usual hour, with high expectations from every corner, a new *Signoria* was drawn. The lottery went to friends of Piero, demonstrating the truth of Virgil's verses—*Audaces fortuna iuvat, timidosque repellit*—Fortune rewards the bold and repels the meek."

Some partisans of the Hill cried foul, claiming that Piero had tampered with the purses to ensure a friendly majority in the *Signoria*. According to one contemporary observer, "before the drawing for the *Signoria*, the bags had been gone through, and all those Piero suspected were removed."* But the charge is implausible. Not only does Parenti—a man usually willing to

---

* This quotation comes from the secret memoirs of Alamanno Rinuccini (*Ricordi Storici*). Rinuccini's memoirs provide invaluable eyewitness testimony to the political struggles of the era. Rinuccini was not a dispassionate observer but a man with a political agenda. While making a political career as a Medici insider, he frequently found himself on the outs with the *reggimento* and with Lorenzo in particular. He represents the viewpoint of the old-line republicans who believed that the Medici had established a tyranny in Florence. The most thorough exposition of his political philosophy comes in his "Dialogue on Liberty," written in 1479. This essay is included in Renée Neu Watkins's *Humanism and Liberty: Writings on Freedom from Fifteenth Century Florence.* The introduction to this essay contains a revealing biographical sketch.

believe the worst of Piero—make no mention of such nefarious doings, but for the Medici to tamper with the bags stored in the sacred precinct of Santa Croce would have almost certainly provoked a violent backlash. However much the Medici and their cronies were accustomed to interfering in the electoral process, they were careful to do so by scrupulously legal means. Such a blatant subversion of the process would have risked alienating the very people whose support they now needed.

Even more telling is the fact that while Parenti declared in hindsight that all were "friends of Piero," at the time he made no such claim. In fact the new *Gonfaloniere di Giustizia,* Roberto Lioni, was initially described by Parenti as "a sensible man and a good man of the people who, had he followed his own inclinations, would have been in favor of the commune and of liberty." Parenti attributes his change of heart to ambition, which is another way of saying that both Lioni and his colleagues (who quickly followed the new *Gonfaloniere's* lead) knew a winner when they saw one and had concluded that the Medici were more likely to be in a position to reward their followers than their feckless opponents. It is not surprising that the newly elected government bent to the prevailing wind that now blew strongly in the Medici's direction.

Piero, still in bed at his palace on the Via Larga, received word of the election with satisfaction, but he realized that the successful election brought new dangers as well as opportunities. With superior forces at his disposal and a friendly government scheduled to be seated on the first of September, time was on Piero's side. But if this was obvious to Piero, so it was to his opponents; the looming deadline might well provoke them to desperate acts. Tensions continued to run high in the *Palazzo della Signoria* as the newly elected priors, now openly committed to Piero, refused to leave the premises as required by law, fearing the old *Signoria* had no intention of relinquishing power when their term of office expired in three days. A confrontation was avoided only when Piero persuaded his newfound allies to return peaceably to their homes.

Still unwilling to concede defeat, the rebels sought to erase the advantage Piero had gained by the morning's election. Piero's worst fears seemed to be realized when a courier arrived with a demand from the *Signoria* that he immediately appear before them at the Palace of the Priors. This placed him in a difficult position. He had gained the moral high ground by adhering to the strict letter of the law, but in obeying the government's summons he knew he would be venturing onto unfriendly turf. Earlier in the day Neroni had appeared before the *Signoria* to plead his case, and the sympathetic hearing he had received could have left Piero in little doubt as to what his own reception might be. Piero was acutely aware that after obeying a similar summons his father had been arrested and imprisoned in the palace tower by the Albizzi. Rather than leave his well-guarded home, then, Piero "excused himself because of his illness . . . and instead sent Lorenzo and Giuliano his sons."

Awaiting Lorenzo and Giuliano at the *Palazzo della Signoria* were the assembled Priors and *Gonfaloniere,* seated on a dais and dressed in their scarlet robes of office. The atmosphere was decidedly chilly. The *Signoria,* which compensated for a lack of effective power by an inflated sense of their own dignity, made it clear that they believed the substitution of the Medici boys for their father was a calculated snub. "In not coming, [Piero] showed his arrogance and lack of civility, sending instead his sons Lorenzo and Giuliano," complained Alamanno Rinuccini. The moment was made all the more awkward by the presence of Luca Pitti, who, like his rival, had been called before the government to account for his actions. In the end the *Signoria* issued a stern message to both Lorenzo and Pitti, demanding that each party "expel from Florence all the soldiers stationed at his house . . . and that all the citizens who had taken up arms by that same hour be disarmed."

Significantly, the implementation of this decree depended entirely on the goodwill of the parties involved since the government lacked the power to compel obedience. And, in fact, when Lorenzo returned home to inform his father of the *Signoria*'s demand, Piero dismissed it out of hand. Piero's refusal to disband his forces, a departure from the path of strict legality he had so far adhered to, was viewed by his critics as a sign that he possessed "the soul of a tyrant rather than that of a good citizen." But from Piero's point of view, the demand, eminently evenhanded on its surface, was altogether unacceptable, since as matters currently stood his forces in the city and the surrounding countryside were clearly superior to those of his opponents. In insisting on the disarmament of both sides, the *Signoria* was in fact adopting a policy Neroni had urged upon them in his earlier visit to the palace.

In any case, Piero now had another option, one that might allow him to achieve his objectives without forcing him to rely on the honor and good intentions of his enemies. Returning from the *Palazzo della Signoria*, Lorenzo carried not only the government's public pronouncement but also a private message. It was this second message that would ultimately provide the key to a peaceful resolution of the crisis.

The secret communication came, perhaps surprisingly, from Luca Pitti. Shortly after their joint appearance before the *Signoria*, Pitti and Lorenzo held a private meeting in which Lorenzo dangled the prospect of political rehabilitation for the old man were he to turn his back on his fellow conspirators and throw in his lot with the resurgent Medici. "In part through persuasive words and entreaties, and in part with promises of bonds of family," wrote Niccolò Valori, "[he] began to pacify the leading rebels among whom the chief was Luca Pitti, such was the genius and art of Lorenzo, who could turn the most implacable foe into a friend." In fact, Pitti's sudden change of heart probably had less to do with Lorenzo's eloquence than with his desperation to turn back from the brink of the precipice he now saw yawning before him.

Shortly after this meeting negotiations between *Messer* Luca and Piero's agents began in earnest. The cagey Francesco Sassetti, general manager of the Medici bank, took charge of the delicate proceedings, crossing hostile lines for a meeting with Pitti in his palace. The agreement as it was finally hammered out between the two men captures Florentine political scheming at its cynical worst; Pitti's loyalty was purchased through the promise of material benefits and, since loyalty in his case was an apparently mercurial substance, fixed more permanently through the extension of bonds of kinship. In return for abandoning both friends and principles, Luca's brother Luigi was to be named one of the Eight of the Watch (the *Otto*), the city's feared secret police commission, while Luca himself would be assured a permanent place in the upper echelons of the government as one of the *Accoppiatori,* the officials whose job it was to go through the electoral purses and remove the names of anyone unfriendly to the regime.*

---

* Piero must have been confident indeed that he would have things his own way in the palace since the *Accoppiatori* had only recently been abolished. He might well have relished the irony that it was Pitti himself who led the fight to abolish the committee on which he now so desperately wished to serve.

With a place in both these critical bodies, Luca Pitti's position in Florence would be assured. As for those marriage ties that were the glue of party affiliation: "*Messer* Luca had a daughter of tender age whom he wished to see married, and Piero had his son Lorenzo, who was eighteen [sic]. It was *messer* Luca's understanding that these two were to be wed, but out of delicacy he was not explicit. With these arrangements he believed himself secure and as exalted in the state as he had been previously."

On this last point Francesco Sassetti was deliberately vague, and Pitti apparently did not press him, perhaps fearing that to insist on Lorenzo as a son-in-law might jeopardize a deal he was ever more desperate to conclude. Whatever Lorenzo's virtues as a prospective son-in-law, they were not, apparently, worth risking his life for. (Ultimately, Piero fulfilled the letter of his promise to Pitti by arranging a marriage between his brother-in-law, Giovanni Tornabuoni, and Pitti's daughter.)

The following morning the pact was sealed when Pitti rode to the Via Larga and embraced his former rival, "declaring himself," said Piero, "ready to live or die with me."

With Pitti's abject surrender the rebellion effectively crumbled. Those who had opposed Piero now scrambled to salvage what they could from the wreckage. Soon a procession of men with frightened faces could be seen snaking its way along the Via Larga as those of suspect loyalty came to pay homage to the man they recently judged a "vile rabbit." Among those seeking absolution was Agnolo Acciaiuoli, who, according to Tranchedini, pledged his obedience using "very submissive words." Neroni and his brothers also came to beg forgiveness, receiving for their pains a tongue-lashing from Piero, who "rebuked them with grave words full of indignation." Such was the mood among the Medici's supporters that, according to Machiavelli, "if Piero had not held them back, they would have handled them with arms."

Luca Pitti, compensating for past indescretions, worked harder than anyone to ensure the triumph of the man he had recently sought to destroy. It was he who in a meeting of leading citizens on September 2— one that took place, significantly enough, not in the *Palazzo della Signoria* but in the Medici palace—put the final seal on Piero's victory by calling for a *parlamento*, an assembly of all citizens held in the great piazza before the

palace, that would call on the government to enact sweeping reforms.*
Any lingering doubts as to who was now in charge were put to rest by the
official account of the assembly, which could have been written by Piero
himself: "To establish the peace of the city there gathered in the house of
Piero di Cosimo, who, being impeded, could not attend, in which it was
decided to ask the *Signoria* to quell the disturbances in the city by means
of a *parlamento* quickly, and do it today, so that the city gets rid of its arms
as quickly as possible."

On September 2, with three thousand armed men, all Medici loyalists,
stationed at the narrow streets leading into the piazza, the citizens of Florence assembled. The Sienese ambassador, Cione de' Ravi, claimed he had
never seen "so many soldiers in one place" and that their "shouts of victory"
helped sway the crowd in their favor. Towering above them, resplendent in
full armor, rode Lorenzo, the glamourous, glittering symbol of Medici
power. Under the circumstances the results were a foregone conclusion.
With the *Signoria* and other high officials lining the podium in front of the
palazzo, heralds read a petition put forward by one of the priors, Bernardo
di Francesco Paganelli, to request that a special committee (known as a
Balìa) be nominated with full powers to reform the government. According
to Parenti, who witnessed the scene with a sinking heart, "it was approved
with excited and loud voices by the great multitude of people who were in
the piazza, both those armed and those unarmed, and having been
accepted by two thirds of the people the reforms were thus ratified."

The triumphant Lorenzo then dismounted and greeted the *Signoria*,
accepting on behalf of his father the congratulations of the duly elected
government. While the crowds dispersed, Lorenzo rode back to his palace
surrounded by cheering supporters. Few could have missed the signifi-
cance of the scene. The day had been a demonstration of raw power on the
part of the Medici, an affirmation, were any needed, that a single family

---

* A holdover from the first days of the commune when government truly rested in the
hands of all the citizens, a *parlamento* was called only in moments of greatest crisis and,
though ostensibly the purest expression of Florentine democracy, every citizen knew it
was an instrument of tyranny. Such an unwieldy mob was easily manipulated by those in
power to achieve their ends.

now dominated the city. While the constitution was not suspended, and in fact the whole charade had been conducted with scrupulous observance of Florentine law, no one doubted that the Medici and their supporters were now in complete control of the levers of government.

Over the next days and weeks the victorious party meted out punishment not only to the ringleaders but to many others whom the government suspected of having been sympathetic to the rebels.* Typical of this latter group was one Carlo Gondi, who was stripped of his rights as a citizen, though he protested he had done nothing more than affix his signature to the oath of May 4. "I knew that in an instant I had lost honor, wealth, friends and relatives," he wrote despairingly, "and not only me but also Marriotto [my brother] and his and my sons."

Despite Gondi's bitter recriminations, the reprisals were moderate by the standards of the day. One eyewitness, the apothecary Luca Landucci, reveals that "after the failure of the plot, many citizens connected with it were exiled, about twenty-seven of them being restricted within certain boundaries and made ineligible for office." Benedetto Dei's chronicle contains the names of twenty-six among the banished or disenfranchised, starting with Agnolo Acciaiuoli, Dietisalvi Neroni, and Niccolò Soderini and concluding with Carlo Gondi. It is true that Piero's treatment of his foes would certainly not pass muster in a modern courtroom—he himself admitted that Francesco Neroni's confession, upon which much of our knowledge of the rebellion is based, was extracted after "little torture, or hardly any"—but what struck contemporaries was the mildness of his response. "Unlike his father Cosimo," concludes Guicciardini, "Piero proved most clement, for he allowed no one to be punished except for those whom it would have been too dangerous not to punish." Having been ruthless in pursuit of victory, Piero could afford to be generous. His clemency reassured a jittery public and reconciled the majority to whatever loss of liberty his triumph entailed. Having lived in fear of wholesale retribution and feeling relief when the response proved milder than anticipated, the citizens had little to complain of when the electoral bags were again held open to the prying hands of the *Accoppiatori*.

---

* For a complete list of those punished and their sentences see Parenti, *Ricordi Storici*, pp. 136–37.

Chief beneficiary of Piero's clemency was Luca Pitti. Having been the public face of the rebellion, Pitti was now one of the regime's most ardent supporters. But Pitti's last-minute conversion brought him little happiness in the end. Alamanno Rinuccini sums up the attitude of the reformers toward their fickle friend: "From vileness or because he had been corrupted with money or with promises from the other party, he brutally betrayed his allies and himself." Nor was he fully trusted by those whose cause he now espoused. Abandoned by those who felt betrayed and excluded from the inner circle of the regime, he was now a broken man. "He remained cold and alone at home," Parenti remarks, believing he got nothing better than he deserved, "and no one visited him to confer on matters of state, where once his house was filled with every kind of person." This was a kind of living death for a Florentine, shut out from the lively give-and-take that was part of every citizen's daily life.

For their parts in the rebellion, Dietisalvi Neroni and Niccolò Soderini were banished from Florence, the usual fate of those on the losing side in the periodic struggle for political control; after the two continued to conspire against their homeland from their places of exile death sentences were imposed in absentia. Agnolo Acciaiuoli was also banished from Florence but, unlike his colleagues, he still hoped for a reconciliation, something that, according to Machiavelli, he had almost achieved when Piero's untimely death intervened. The State Archives of Florence contain a moving exchange of letters between the two former friends that reveals feelings embittered but not entirely extinguished by the events of that summer. First Agnolo, writing to Piero from Naples:

I am laughing at the games of fortune and at how it makes friends become enemies and enemies become friends as it suits it. You can remember when in your father's exile I considered his injury more than my own dangers, I lost my fatherland and nearly lost my life; nor, while I lived under Cosimo, did I ever fail to honor and support your house; nor after his death had I any intent of offending you. It is true that your bad constitution and the tender age of your children dismayed me, so that I judged it better to give such a form to the state that after your death our fatherland would not be ruined. From this arose things that were done, not against you but for the

benefit of my fatherland—which, even if it was an error, deserves to
be canceled because of my meaning well and my past deeds. Nor can
I believe, since your house found such faith in me for so long a time,
that I cannot now find compassion in you and that my many merits
will be destroyed by one single mistake.

To which Piero replied:

Your laughing over there is the cause that I do not weep, because if
you were laughing in Florence, I would be weeping in Naples. I confess that you wished my father well and you will confess that you
received well from him; so much more was your obligation than
ours, as deeds must be valued higher than words. Thus, since you
have been well recompensed for your good, you ought not now to
marvel if your evil brings you just rewards. Nor does love of the
fatherland excuse you, because there will never be anyone who will
believe that this city has been loved and increased less by the Medici
than by the Acciaiuoli. So live there in dishonor, since you did not
know how to live here in honor.

With the successful *parlamento* and the banishing of his principal enemies, Piero's position as the preeminent citizen of Florence was assured.
But even now he was by no means the tyrant of Florence. His own verdict
is reflected in the inscription he had placed on the statue by Donatello of
Judith slaying the tyrant Holofernes that stood in the garden of his palace:
"Pietro de' Medici, son of Cosimo, dedicated the statue of this woman to
the strength and liberty that the citizens, through their constant and invin-
cible spirit, restored to the republic." While certainly biased, the inscription reflects his own view of himself as the champion of Florentine liberty,
not the uncrowned king of the city.

As he reasserted his control over the government, Piero came to rely
more than ever on his son, who now acted as his eyes and ears in the Palace
of the Priors. At his request the *Balìa* granted that Piero's "most honorable
and famous young son Lorenzo—notwithstanding the fact he is under
age, since his outstanding probity and virtue supply his defect in age—to
represent his father in the Council of One Hundred." Here, then, is official

recognition of the new role Lorenzo had begun to assume. Though still only a teenager, he was now a fixture in the inner circle of the *reggimento*.

In addition to playing an ever more visible role on the domestic scene, the events of August and September 1466 raised Lorenzo's stature in the eyes of the world. He was no longer the awkward son of Florence's first citizen but a leader in his own right, his father's right-hand man and the ruler-in-waiting of one of the richest and most powerful states in Italy. The transformation is most clearly marked in a letter to Lorenzo from King Ferrante, dated September 28. "Already," he wrote, "we loved you on account of your excellent qualities and the services done by your grandfather and father. But as we have lately heard with what prudence and manly courage you behaved in the late revolutions, and how courageously you placed yourself in the foremost ranks, our affection to you has grown remarkably." At the tender age of seventeen, Lorenzo had marched boldly onto the world stage and grabbed the spotlight. It was a starring role he would not relinquish for the remainder of his years.

School of Giorgio Vasari, *Joust in Santa Croce,* 16th century (Art Resource)

VII. LORD OF THE JOUST

"To do as others do I held a joust in the Piazza S. Croce at great expense and with great pomp. I find we spent about 10,000 ducats."

—LORENZO DE' MEDICI, *MEMOIRS*

"[H]aving in my youth been much persecuted by men and by fortune, some little solace ought not to be denied me, and this I have only found in loving ardently and in composing and commenting upon my verses. . . . Such terrible persecutions as I have undergone are very well known because they are public knowledge."

—LORENZO DE' MEDICI, *COMMENTARY ON MY SONNETS*

THE DEFEAT OF THE HILL AND THE EXILE OF THE MOST prominent exponents of reform left the Medici and their friends in undisputed control of the machinery of government. But perhaps Piero's greatest success lay in securing the acquiescence of the majority of Florentines to the new state of affairs. Over the coming months and years any lingering wounds were healed by a concerted effort to broker marriages between families on either side of the political divide.

Though Piero was more than ever confined to his own bed, this did not mean that he was out of the loop. "[Piero] was crippled with gout like his father," recalled Marco Parenti, "to such an extent that he could no longer get out of bed. Because of this all those who had need of him went to his chambers, including the magistrates who would take no decision in serious matters without his approval; similarly foreigners, ambassadors and lords, who had any business with our city were forced to seek him there, so that his rooms were always crowded with men on diverse errands and it was often difficult to speak with him."

The job of keeping Piero abreast of what went on in the *Palazzo della Signoria* fell largely to Lorenzo. A letter written in March 1468 reveals the nature of his role. "Magnificent Lord," Lorenzo wrote to Cipriano Seregni, then *Gonfaloniere di Giustizia*, "In obedience to the *Signoria* I spoke with Piero. He declared himself, in respect to creating a new *Dieci* [council of war], to be wholly in favor." Dividing his time between the halls of the *Signoria* and his father's private chambers, Lorenzo was the vital link between the elected officials and the effective boss of the city.

Aiding Piero in his efforts to direct the city's foreign policy were the vast resources of the Medici bank, which maintained, in effect, its own intelligence service; agents in foreign capitals had access to information vital to political decision-making, and well-placed friends in strategic locations reported to Piero directly, rather than through official channels. Much of this correspondence now passed through Lorenzo's hands. "I have received your letters, both thick and thin," the nineteen-year-old Lorenzo wrote to Cristofano di Valsvignone, Piero's private secretary, "filled with news of Flanders, England and of [the castle of] Marradi, of the plague, of the [clerical] benefices, and every other thing."

Lorenzo's able performance during the recent crisis had dramatically increased his influence and prestige. Foreign leaders paid him tribute, while his compatriots began to treat him with newfound respect. As his father's closest aide and confidant he spent much time conferring with the *principali*. Veterans of the political scene like Tommaso Soderini, Otto Niccolini, Carlo Pandolfini, and Luigi Guicciardini had a chance to observe him on a daily basis and judge his character, and as Piero's health continued to deteriorate, the question uppermost in the minds of all those concerned about the future of the republic was whether the ship of state could be entrusted to the captaincy of one so young and untested.

Reviews of Lorenzo's character in this period reveal a young man whose gifts exceed his wisdom. The Milanese ambassador wrote what is probably the most balanced judgment: "[Lorenzo] is of such a nature as I have written previously: astute and possessing great insight he surely is; but he thinks too highly of himself and he sets his sails too high for comfort." This observation on the part of a friend is similar to the conclusion reached by his bitter critic Alamanno Rinuccini—that Lorenzo was immensely able but dangerously arrogant. Piero himself noted similar qualities in his son and often seemed to think that paternal duty required him to knock Lorenzo down a peg or two.

Indeed, relations between father and son were not without difficulties. Lorenzo was too much the dutiful son for the natural tension that existed between them to lead to an open breach, but as Piero struggled with his infirmities, Lorenzo, bursting with youthful energy, grew increasingly impatient with his father's efforts to hold him back. Their relations mirrored in miniature the perennial rivalry between generations, which in fifteenth-century Florence had traditionally been heavily slanted toward age and experience and had only partially succumbed to the cult of youth built up around Lorenzo and Giuliano. Complaints that the government had been handed over to unruly adolescents were surely exaggerated, but they were common enough to have contained at least a grain of truth. Lorenzo's government would be distinguished by its youth, vitality, and dynamism, qualities that stirred up resentment among the city's entrenched elites.

Tensions between father and son, however, were as much a matter of temperament as of age. While Lorenzo was outgoing and socially skilled, Piero was reserved with strangers and uncomfortable with the ceremonial aspects of government. Piero knew that Lorenzo was blessed with skills he did not possess, confessing during one of his absences that without him, "I shall be as a man without hands." Particularly after the death of his gregarious uncle, Giovanni, in 1462, Lorenzo became the social coordinator and principal spokesman for the Medici regime.

During his adolescent years Lorenzo was busy building up his own personal authority, a process that fostered a growing belief in his own abilities and encouraged a sense of independence. Those in Florence wishing to advance their careers, or who found themselves on the wrong side of the law, appealed to Lorenzo, who thus developed a following of clients dependent on his favor.* The way in which Lorenzo wielded patronage in these years is suggested by a letter he wrote to the leaders of the commune

---

* Lorenzo was not always successful in seeking favors for his clients, belying any notion that his writ was law in Florence. For instance, one man imprisoned for debt found little benefit from Lorenzo's intervention. (See "The Young Lorenzo," in *Lorenzo the Magnificent: Culture and Politics,* especially p. 19.)

of Arezzo: "The enduring and intimate good will that has always existed between your community and our house, particularly owing to the revered memory of my grandfather Cosimo and now with Piero my father, encourages me to appeal to Your Lordships with great confidence in every case. *Ser* Carlo di Piero di Berto da Firenzuola, notary, a noble youth and my great friend . . . would like to obtain from your community the position of notary of the office of the Civil Court, at the first vacancy, or whenever possible."

After 1466, Lorenzo's day-to-day role became more prominent and that of his father receded somewhat into the background. Lorenzo was no longer merely the "hope of the city" but a practicing and practical political operative. As his confidence grew and as he became more familiar with the intricacies of statecraft, Lorenzo began to criticize his father's ways of doing business. "Lorenzo demonstrates that he has thought things out for himself," reported the Milanese ambassador to Galeazzo Maria Sforza, "and he complains that he was unable to remedy the many ways of his father, which were more apt to lose him every friend within the city than to increase them abroad by even one."

It is a tribute to Lorenzo's prodigious energy that the growing list of official duties did nothing to dampen his appetite for more frivolous pursuits. Far from trimming his sails, Lorenzo seemed more determined than ever to enjoy himself at every opportunity. One incident in particular shows how Lorenzo chafed under the burdens imposed by his newfound responsibilities. It came in the fall of 1467, during a period of unrest stirred up by the continuing machinations of the exiled leaders of the Hill,* and the streak of recklessness that Lorenzo exhibited at the time caused friends and family once again to question his judgment.

In mid-September, with the countryside plagued by marauding bands of mercenary soldiers, many of them in the pay of the exiles, Lorenzo set aside his duties in the city and headed for the spa at Bagno a Morba, an

---

* The exiles had even managed to foment a small-scale war, persuading the mercenary captain Bartolomeo Colleoni, secretly backed by Venetian money, to invade Florentine territory. The so-called Colleonic War amounted to little in the end, but Colleoni's failure meant that for years to come the Medici regime would have little to fear from foreign intervention.

isolated hamlet located in the rugged hills near Volterra.* There was nothing unusual about such a trip. Lorenzo, like all the Medici, was plagued by
eczema as well as gout and arthritic pains, and throughout his life he
would seek relief in the various mineral spas that dotted the countryside.
An additional motivation was that his mother had stopped by the baths
on her return from Rome to recover from a bout of fever, and Lorenzo was
anxious to see her and to catch up on the news from the great capital.

But spas like Bagno a Morba were not only prized for their medicinal
effects: something about the sulfurous vapors seemed to loosen morals as
well as muscles, and there is no doubt that Lorenzo left the city in order to
pursue some sort of sexual liaison. "[He] who want[s] a son," went an old
Tuscan saying, "leaves his wife at the baths, where she'll have fun."

No sooner had Lorenzo and his companions set out than word began
to spread that bandits in the pay of the exiles were planning to descend on
the village to kidnap or murder him. Alerted to the danger, Piero hurried
messengers to the baths and urged his family to seek safety, though he concluded that the threats "are all dreams." The rumors, though unsubstanti-
ated, brought forth one letter that provides a telling glimpse into the
character of the young Lorenzo. It was Gentile Becchi, Lorenzo's tutor,
who was given the task of coaxing the young man back to Florence. "There
[at the baths] you risk unnecessary peril," he scolded Lorenzo. "It seems to
your friends that you should return. And they wish that, having returned,
you looked after yourself better, valuing those who value you, and not
putting us off with one of your 'leave-it to-me's,' and that *in re venere* [i.e.,
in matters of love] you avoid those places where you are in danger."

The *re venere* that enticed Lorenzo to the baths are not spelled out by
Becchi, but gossip about Lorenzo's mistresses, as well as the ribald banter
of letters from his friend Braccio Martelli, confirm that young Lorenzo
was not leading a life of monkish denial. Becchi's missive had the desired

---

* Lorenzo usually made these journeys with a large entourage. On a trip to Bagno a Morba
in 1485 Lorenzo's company included thirty-three people, berthed in fifteen beds. Among
those accompanying him were the sculptor Bertoldo di Giovanni and the composer
Antonio Squarcialupi, two singers, two secretaries, two waiters, a sommelier, five
archers, a stable master, two cooks, a wagoner, and assorted grooms and servants (see
Draper, *Bertoldo di Giovanni*, p. 15).

result of bringing an early end to Lorenzo's tryst. More important from the historian's point of view, his admonishment reveals a headstrong young man unwilling to forgo his pleasures and liable to respond to criticism or advice with a dismissive "leave-it-to me." Such self-assurance was to be both a source of strength and significant weakness throughout Lorenzo's life, allowing him to take decisive action while others hesitated, but also leading him into perilous waters when he failed to heed the council of more experienced men.

The incident, though amounting to little in the end, is significant for the light it sheds on that perennial conflict within Lorenzo between duty and pleasure. Such conflicts are, of course, a natural part of growing up, but the violent backdrop to this inner struggle, and the potential for disaster should any of the choices he made turn out badly, added to the normal stresses of adolescence.

The incident also highlights the contrasting roles played by town and country in Lorenzo's mind, a contrast that imparted a certain predictable rhythm to his life. While it was largely in the city that important business was conducted, the countryside provided a much needed release whenever the pressures of city life grew too great. Lorenzo drew sustenance from the hard physical labor of the fields and the practical hands-on management of his various estates; in his library ancient and modern texts on agronomy and animal husbandry shared the shelves with beautifully illuminated manuscripts and rare volumes of Plutarch, Homer, and Plato. Like his grandfather before him, he found in the workaday chores of pruning and planting the perfect means to clear his head after the intrigues and petty squabbles of political life. He was invigorated by the pungent smell of the stable (where he preferred to groom his horses himself) and rejuvenated by the feel of the hot Tuscan sun on his neck.

But the family's many villas in the Tuscan hills offered more than simple rustic pursuits. Those close to the city, like Fiesole and Careggi, were the preferred venues for the philosophical discussions to which Lorenzo and his circle of friends were addicted. Music and dance were also part of the daily fare, with Lorenzo an enthusiastic participant in both, performing with particular skill on the lyre. The more distant villas, like Trebbio and Cafaggiolo in the Apennine foothills, served as hunting lodges from which to set out in pursuit of a stag or to watch the soaring flight of a well-trained hawk. These pastimes, too, were not entirely without intellectual content since they provided the inspiration for much of his best poetry.

Lorenzo's need to find a refuge from the cares of the city grew with his political responsibilities. "Let search who will for pomp and honors high" he wrote in one of his sonnets,

> the plazas, the temples and the great buildings,
> the pleasures, the treasures, that accompany
> a thousand hard thoughts, a thousand pains.
>   A green meadow filled with lovely flowers,
> a little brook that bathes the grass around,
> a little bird pining for his love,
> better stills our ardor . . .

It is not surprising that Lorenzo longed to put the stone and brick of Florence far behind him. In the city he could not avoid the crowds clamoring for his attention. Down the Via Larga flowed an endless stream of citizens, rich and poor, begging a little more of his time to plead their case. In the piazza and even in the privacy of his chambers men and women tugged at his sleeve. Just a word from him and all could be arranged! A letter to the proper official and the petitioner or his son would be set for life; a nod from Lorenzo and a debtor might be set free or a judge persuaded to change his verdict. Even the most intimate matters were the business of the Medici heir. Marriages were as much a political as a personal affair, and soon Lorenzo found himself the city's matchmaker, with the power to determine whose daughter would share a bed with whose son.* The role of *mezzano* (intermediary) gave him a wide, if somewhat jaundiced, view of the human condition. As thousands of trivial and sordid details were whispered in his ear he came to know more about the private lives of his fellow citizens than any priest hearing confession.

It was during his teenage years that he began to write poetry. Lorenzo spent many of his happiest hours among artists and poets, and under the

---

* Lorenzo's role as Florence's most important marriage-broker stirred up much resentment. But while many families decried this humiliating loss of freedom, there were at least as many who pestered Lorenzo to find a good match for their sons and daughters.

influence of Luigi Pulci he now tried his hand composing his own verses, a pursuit that cleared his head as effectively as the country air and provided an outlet for his creative energies. His admiration for Pulci's talents did not prevent Lorenzo from poking fun at his absentminded ways in his own verses. These lines from his "Partridge Hunt" evoke pleasant days spent hunting in the woods where poetic inspiration was pursued as vigorously as bird or beast:

> *And where is Pulci, that he can't be heard?*
> *A while ago he went into that spread*
> *Of trees, perhaps he wants to spin a sonnet—*
> *He's sure to have some notion in his head.*

Breaking with tradition, Lorenzo wrote in his native Tuscan dialect, rather than the more elevated Latin, "to prove the dignity of our language" by demonstrating that it can "easily express any concept of our minds."* His preferred idiom was the sonnet, a form perfected more than a century earlier by his illustrious compatriot Petrarch, because, Lorenzo explained, "honor, according to the philosophers, is attached to that which is difficult." There was nothing he liked better than a challenge, and the rigid structure of the sonnet constituted a formidable literary bastion whose conquest could only impart added luster to he who conquered it.

Once he began to write in earnest, poetry was not simply a pastime to fill up the dull hours but an integral part of Lorenzo's self-conception and self-presentation. Sometime around 1467 or 1468, he sent to don Federigo—the younger son of King Ferrante, whom he'd befriended during the wedding of Ippolita Sforza to his older brother Alfonso—a compilation of poems by famous Tuscans, along with a spirited defense of the vernacular in which they were written. "At the end of the volume (as seemed

---

* Lorenzo was not the first Florentine to write in the vernacular. Dante more than a century earlier had written his masterpiece, *The Divine Comedy*, in Italian. More recent, Leon Battista Alberti had championed use of the vernacular. Lorenzo's contributions, however, confirmed the value of the native dialect and put him at odds with more prissy poets who believed that elevated thoughts could only be expressed in the language of Virgil. The brilliant contributions of these Florentines meant that the Tuscan dialect would become the foundation of modern Italian.

to be your request)," wrote Lorenzo to the prince, "we have copied a few of our own sonnets and songs, so that when reading them you can remember my loyalty and affection. . . . Receive, therefore, Illustrious Lord, this volume and myself, not only in your house, but in your heart and soul, as you have a blithe and enduring abode in ours."

Poetry was a calling card Lorenzo could use to gain entry to the great courts of Europe. Throughout his life he deployed the cultural assets of Florence as kings and princes deployed their armies, marshaling a glittering array of talent to impress outsiders with the glory and majesty of the republic. For the Medici, as for other Florentine patricians, art and literature were the great equalizers in the competition for honor and prestige. A mere banker's son he may have been, but his literary flair, his erudition, and his cultivation were the factors that, along with his fabled wealth, allowed him to treat with kings and princes on a level playing field. It is difficult to imagine the Neapolitan prince writing in a similar vein; while Lorenzo strove by every means to show himself worthy of a place among the great don Federigo, secure in his titles, was encouraged in a life of intellectual laziness.

This letter reflects the two most significant elements of Lorenzo's contribution to the culture of the Florentine Renaissance—his role as patron and as a creative figure in his own right. Lorenzo's closeness to and active collaboration with some of the most creative spirits of the age—artists like Botticelli, Verrocchio, Leonardo, and Michelangelo and writers like Luigi Pulci, Angelo Poliziano, and Pico della Mirandola, who regarded him as a colleague as well as a patron—gave to the Lorenzan age its aura of a golden moment for the arts, and his role as arbiter of taste on all matters artistic increased with each passing year. His influence grew to the point where no major artistic project went forward in Tuscany without at least his tacit approval. When the city of Pistoia commissioned an important tomb for its cathedral in 1477, the city fathers sent the competing models to Lorenzo for adjudication "because you have a quite complete understanding of such things, and of everything else." Angelo Poliziano, who had experienced Lorenzo's generosity firsthand, penned numerous tributes to his friend and patron:

> Whilst Arno, winding through the mild domain,
> Leads in repeated folds his lengthen'd train;

Nor thou thy poet's grateful strain refuse,
Lorenzo! sure resource of every muse;
Whose praise, so thou his leisure hour prolong,
Shall claim the tribute of a nobler song.

In assuming the role of artistic arbiter, Lorenzo was following in the footsteps of Piero and Cosimo (though his fame as a man of sound aesthetic judgment ultimately exceeded theirs). But by plunging into the literary fray, and staking his reputation on his talent, Lorenzo was departing from the time-tested path of the Florentine patrician whose dignity permitted him to pay for creativity in others but not to have more intimate intercourse with the muses. The explanation for this transformation from patron to artist is complex, involving factors that were both personal and political. In writing poetry, Lorenzo not only gave vent to his most private thoughts but also constructed his public persona; however much his poetry seems to offer an intimate autobiography of a private man, it was also an important factor in shaping his public image.

In its apparently confessional tone, Lorenzo's poetry marks a profound shift from the more reticent generation of his father. In fact Lorenzo may well have been motivated in part by a fear of repeating his father's mistakes; if Piero was cold and aloof, Lorenzo would be warmly human and accessible. His verses collapsed the psychological distance between the ruler and the ruled, giving the Florentine people the sense, real or illusory, that they knew the man who held their fate in his hands.* His sonnets include numerous admissions of weakness and personal torment almost without precedent for a public figure:

O sleep most tranquil, still you do not come
to this troubled heart that desires you!
Seal the perennial spring of my tears,
O sweet oblivion, that pain me so!
    Come, peace, that alone can stanch

---

* Lorenzo's verses gained wider circulation through the songs he wrote for popular festivals like Carnival or the Feast of St. John the Baptist, but these songs tended to reveal less of the man than the sonnets. They were part of a more consciously propagandistic program.

the course of my desire! And to
my sweet lady's company guide me,
she with eyes so filled with kindness and serene.

Such apparently heartfelt verses softened the harsh edges of his rule, help-ing to perpetuate the myth that he was merely a private citizen rather than the de facto tyrant of the city.

Lorenzo was defensive about his literary endeavors. He tried to forestall criticism that writing poetry about affairs of the heart was a trivial occu-pation for someone engaged in affairs of state: "I could easily be thought to possess poor judgment, having consumed so much time in composing verses and commenting upon them, the material and subject of which are in large part an amorous passion; and this being much more reprehensible given the constant affairs, both public and private, which ought rather to turn me away from such thoughts, thoughts that, according to some, are not only frivolous and of little weight, but are even pernicious and as prej-udicial to our souls as to our worldly honor."

Indeed it would be a mistake to view Lorenzo's poetry—or his artistic patronage, for that matter—simply as an extension of his statecraft, wholly calculated and cynical in its motives. Writing seemed to fill for Lorenzo a deep psychological need and it is certainly more than mere coincidence that his initial plunge into poetry corresponded with a time of political turmoil. "[H]aving in my youth been much persecuted by men and by fortune," he wrote, "some little comfort ought not to be denied me, and this I have found only in loving fervently and in composing and com-menting upon my verses."* Creative work was a response to stress; he found emotional release from the pressure of his position through his amorous pursuits, while love, in turn, repaid him by providing the mater-ial he needed for his poetry.

The self-pitying tone of the passage reveals another aspect of both the man and the artist—his tendency to succumb to melancholy. "He seemed to be two men, not one," wrote one of his servants during a particularly

---

* The compilation of poems and commentaries now known as *A Commentary on My Sonnets* first began to take shape sometime in the early 1470s. Lorenzo tinkered with the poems and commentaries throughout the remainder of his life.

difficult moment of his life. "During the day he appeared perfectly easy, restful, cheerful, and confident. But at night he grieved bitterly about his own ill fortune and that of Florence." This observation from one who knew him well finds an eerie echo in Machiavelli's famous judgment that "one might see in him two different persons, joined in an almost impossible conjunction." Of course Machiavelli was referring not to his moods but to the mix of high-minded purpose and irresponsibility he exhibited throughout his life, but the two are closely related. His tendency to engage in "childish games" and to take delight in "facetious and pungent men" was a form of self-medication, a means of fending off the darker demons of his soul through a frenetic plunge into wine, women, and song. Francesco Guicciardini, writing in the decades following his death when tales of his exploits were still fresh in people's minds, concluded: "He was libidinous, amorous and faithful in his loves, which would last for a number of years. In the opinion of many he was so weakened by his amorous excesses that he died relatively young."

Making love and writing poetry both helped to alleviate his natural moodiness. Often these two passions were combined in bawdy verses that more prudish generations tried to expunge from the record. Typical of this genre is his "Song of the Village Lasses," an extended double entrendre in which a chorus of neglected wives have found substitutes for their absent husbands in their own gardens:

> We also have some beanpods, long
> And tender, morsels for a pig.
> We have still others of this kind,
> But they're well cooked, quite firm, and big,
> And each will make a foolish clown
> If you first take the tail in hand
> Then rub it gently up and down.

It is hard to think of anything less becoming to a traditional head of state than such sophomoric jests, but with Lorenzo the political is never far removed from the personal, and even the most apparently trivial verses could be exploited for propogandistic effect. Like most of Lorenzo's earthier productions, these lines were meant to be sung in Carnival celebrations. Belted out by raucous celebrants parading through the streets of the city, they formed yet another link between the leader and his people, most of whom no doubt preferred this rude humor to his more philosophical digressions.

If Lorenzo seemed like a young man intent on getting as much out of life as possible, his irresponsible behavior could be excused—or so he told himself—by the knowledge that he would soon enough be forced to shoulder the burdens of adulthood. The hedonism of his poetry is always given a desperate edge by the sense of life's fleeting passage:

> *Soon autumn comes and the ripe, ruddy freight*
> *Is gathered: the glad season will not stay;*
> *Flowers, fruit and leaves are now all desolate.*
> *Pluck the rose, therefore, maiden, while 'tis May!*

If old age quickly consumed the young maid's carefree life, how much sooner would adult responsibilities descend upon the Medici heir? Later in life Lorenzo felt he had been robbed of part of his childhood and looked back on these years with nostalgia and regret.

The most obvious sign that he would soon be forced to put aside childish things were the plans now underway to find him a suitable bride. Florentine men tended not to marry before the age of about thirty, but Piero's ill health made it urgent that Lorenzo be wed as soon as possible. It was a matter upon which Piero and Lucrezia had already devoted much deep thought. There was so much riding on the outcome, not only for the Medici themselves but for all their peers, that it became a matter for much public speculation. Popular gossip linked Lorenzo to the beautiful Lucrezia Donati, but among her other deficits as a potential mate was the inconvenient fact that she was already married to Niccolò Ardinghelli.

In fact whatever hopes those Florentine families with eligible daughters may have cherished, Piero and Lucrezia were already looking in another direction for Lorenzo's bride. With the family preeminent in its native land following the crisis of 1466, Florence began to seem too small a pond in which to fish. Rome offered richer prizes. Here in the capital of Christendom the Medici had vital business interests, and in forging an alliance with one of Rome's powerful feudal clans they would go a long way to securing permanent access to that lucrative market.

In seeking a foreign bride for his son, Piero was breaking with Florentine custom and with the methods that had brought his family to prominence. Cosimo and Piero, as well as their brothers, had all married into distinguished Florentine families—Cosimo into the ancient Bardi clan, Piero into the equally distinguished Tornabuoni (formerly the Tornaquinci).* These alliances promoted collegial feeling among the *principali*; it was gratifying to their fellow citizens to see that for all their wealth and international renown the Medici continued to view themselves merely as members of the Florentine ruling class. Piero had conformed to those time-honored customs in seeking husbands for his daughters: the illegitimate Maria was given to the Rossi; Bianca to the Pazzi; and Nannina, just a year earlier, to the Rucellai. But with no serious internal rivals, Piero concluded that he could no longer advance his family's fortunes by wedding his son to a daughter of Florence.

By the spring of 1467, Piero and Lucrezia had made their choice. Lorenzo would marry a girl from one of the preeminent Roman families, the fifteen-year-old Clarice, daughter of Jacopo Orsini, lord of Monte Rotondo, and niece of the powerful Cardinal Latino Orsini. So powerful were great Roman clans like the Orsini (and their chief rivals, the Colonna) that the Medici bank refused to lend them money because, as a virtual law unto themselves, no power in heaven or earth could force them to repay what had been borrowed.

In the early months of 1467, Lucrezia traveled to Rome in order to conduct some minor diplomatic business for her husband and, more important, to pass her observant eye over the girl.† Her sharp, unsentimental observations were not initially of the kind to set a young man's heart

---

* Giovanni di Bicci was married to Piccarda Bueri, born in Verona but of Florentine parentage.

† Of her diplomatic mission we have the usual sour observations of Jacopo Acciaiuoli who, with a combination of male chauvinism and anti-Medici prejudice, claimed her behavior "reduced Florence to the lowest level of repute" (*Lucrezia Tornabuoni's Sacred Narratives*, Introduction, note on p. 35). Filippo Martelli had a different view, reporting

aflame. "On the way to S. Peter on Thursday morning I met Madonna Maddalena Orsini, sister to the Cardinal [Latino Orsini], with her daughter, who is about fifteen or sixteen years old," she wrote to Piero. "She was dressed in the Roman fashion with a *lenzuolo* [long loose shawl or cloak]. In this dress she seemed to me handsome, fair, and tall, but being covered up I could not see her to my satisfaction." A second meeting at the cardinal's house was arranged so that Lucrezia might make a closer inspection of her prospective daughter-in-law:

> We talked for some good time and I looked closely at the girl. As I said she is of good height and has a nice complexion, her manners are gentle, though not so winning as those of our girls, but she is very modest and would soon learn our customs. She has not fair hair, because here there are no fair women; her hair is reddish and abundant, her face rather round, but it does not displease me. Her throat is fairly elegant, but it seems to me a little meager, or to speak better, slight. Her bosom I could not see, as here the women are entirely covered up, but it appeared to me of good proportions. She does not carry her head proudly like our girls, but pokes it a little forward; I think she was shy, indeed I see no fault in her save shyness. Her hands are long and delicate. In short I think the girl is much above the common, though she cannot compare with Maria, Lucrezia, and Bianca.

Lucrezia's businesslike tone was appropriate for a transaction that resembled nothing so much as the merger of two corporations. For Piero and Lucrezia the political and financial standing of the bride's family counted for more than charm or grace. Clarice's malleability was an asset, as Lucrezia pointed out, since it meant she would more easily adapt herself

---

to Lorenzo, "Her visit has been most valuable, for she has not only fulfilled her vow, but she has acquired high favor with all this Court, and especially with these gentlemen, in such a way that even if she had no more than her presence, her conversation and her appearance, it would show that she was greater than her reputation. I know that the Cardinals have talked about her, and have decided that no finer lady ever came to Rome." (Maguire, *The Women of the Medici*, p. 77.)

to Florentine ways. Perhaps Lucrezia overplayed the role of dispassionate observer; in one letter she was forced to defend herself against Piero's accusation that she was less than enthusiastic. "You say I write coldly about her," Lucrezia wrote. "I do it not to raise your hopes too high: there is no handsomer girl at present unmarried in Florence." Even her detailed descriptions of Clarice's face and figure, which have all the precision of someone in the market for a prize cow, speak less to her sexual allure than to the wife's principal function, which was to bear her husband many healthy heirs.

It is telling that in the selection of his future wife Lorenzo never showed the least inclination to defy his parents' wishes. This was a decision that not only affected him personally but one that was vital to the future of the entire family. For someone in his position, marrying rashly for love was unthinkable. Compensating for this rather impersonal arrangement was the expectation that he would continue to find emotional and sexual fulfillment outside the matrimonial bed. When Lorenzo, composing verses for his lady love, lamented, "O that the marriage bond had joined our fate, / Nor I been born too soon, nor thou too late!" few were shocked by the reference to amorous passion outside the bonds of matrimony. For Florentine men marriage was but one of many outlets for their sexual energies, though the only one that served the interests of the family through the production of legitimate heirs. Lorenzo's own laconic note, written years later in a brief autobiographical sketch, suggests how little a part his feelings played in the selection of his future wife. "I, Lorenzo, took to wife Clarice, daughter of the Lord Jacopo Orsini, or rather she was given to me."

The announcement of Lorenzo's future bride came as a blow to Florentine families hoping to snare a Medici bridegroom for themselves, but even those without eligible daughters were dismayed since it suggested that the Medici thought themselves too good to associate with their compatriots. The connection with the Orsini would ultimately prove a classic case of overreaching. Machiavelli is perhaps exaggerating the case when he declares that Piero, in seeking a foreign bride for Lorenzo, had concluded "the city no longer included him as a citizen and that therefore he was preparing to seize a principate: for he who does not want citizens as relatives wants them as slaves." But it is clear that the engagement with one of the great feudal clans of Italy marked a new stage in the aggrandizement of the Medici. In seeking a wife for Lorenzo abroad, Piero was following in the footsteps of royalty, that exotic breed whose superiority to their countrymen was such that they could find mates only in distant lands.

Given the potential for stirring up the animosity of the Florentine people, why did Piero and Lucrezia pursue an alliance with the Orsini? Domestically, the connection would put some distance between the Medici and their rivals. Marrying into a family that had already produced two popes—Celestine III (1191–98) and Nicholas III (1277–80), as well as a host of cardinals and powerful mercenary generals—would solidify the Medici's place among the great clans of Europe. To the lilies of the king of France, already proudly displayed on their escutcheon, and the Sforza hound, they could now add the protection of the Orsini bear. Piero and Lucrezia expected this union would shore up the fortunes of the most important branch of the Medici bank. No family wielded more power in the halls of the Vatican than the Orsini, and with their blood flowing through Medici veins, the next generation would have easy access to the curia from whence much of the family wealth derived.

To the extent that Lorenzo himself was involved in the decision, his betrothal to Clarice Orsini marks the beginning of his personal obsession with Rome. While three generations of Medici had handled the papal finances, none staked so much there as Lorenzo, and both his greatest triumphs and tragedies were to be intimately bound up with that most spellbinding and devious of cities.

As for the Orsini, the advantages were more straightforward. According to Filippo de' Medici, the archbishop of Pisa, who conducted the negotiations on behalf of his cousin, "their pleasure is not to be described." The agreed-upon 6,000 florin dowry—to be paid out not only in gold but in jewels and richly embroidered dresses—was a small price for being able to dip their hands into the bottomless Medici coffers. The family business of soldiering (second only among the Orsini to a career in the church) also stood to gain by the connection to the ruling family of a state always in dire need of mercenary generals.

Negotiations, which involved both the archbishop of Pisa and Lorenzo's uncle, Giovanni Tornabuoni, were completed by November 1468. With the hard bargaining behind them, all those involved now showed their softer side. Clarice's uncle, Cardinal Latino, warmly embraced his new relations, calling Lorenzo "our nephew" and jocularly referring to Piero and himself as a couple of old men who could contemplate the blooming of young love with a benign twinkle. Lorenzo's uncle, having dickered over every florin, now tried to sell his nephew on his bride's charms in terms that the hard-nosed Lucrezia would have spurned. "Not a day passes that I do not see your Madonna Clarice, who has bewitched me," Giovanni wrote Lorenzo in January of 1469. "[S]he improves every day. She is beautiful, she has the sweetest of manners and an admirable intelligence." Admittedly, much was required before Clarice could equal Florentine girls in the quality of her mind and cultural attainments, but Giovanni makes it clear that she was hard at work improving herself. One detects in the letters of both Giovanni and Lucrezia a somewhat patronizing attitude toward this simple Roman girl: given her foreign birth, she could hardly be expected to meet the higher standards of Florence, cultural center of the universe, but with hard work those deficits might yet be remedied.

Lorenzo adopted a similar attitude toward his bride-to-be. Though Clarice was the daughter of one of the most illustrious families of the most fabled city of Europe, she was provincial by the standards of sophisticated Florentines. Over the years a genuine affection grew up between husband and wife, but there was never any question of a union of kindred spirits. Lorenzo, whose chauvinism was both sexual and nationalistic, never thought of his wife as his equal, and Clarice stood in awe of her accomplished and powerful husband. A pious, somewhat narrow-minded girl, she found the livelier atmosphere of Florence uncongenial, and the vibrant culture of the city largely passed her by.

At no time during the long engagement did Lorenzo make an effort to woo Clarice. He was too busy with his duties in Florence to go to Rome and showed little inclination to rearrange his life to conform to his new status. For all intents and purposes, Lorenzo and Clarice continued to be strangers to each other, and repeated requests by Clarice and her family for him to make the journey south were met with evasions and delays.

The months between her betrothal and her departure for a strange city, and equally unfamiliar husband, must have been a time of cruel anxiety for Clarice. If Lorenzo had but a vague memory of her, Clarice's recollec-

tion of Lorenzo was equally ill-formed. She may not have heard of his reputation for fast living, but even without specific knowledge of his pecca-
dilloes Florence's reputation as a city of luxury and vice would have given
the shy, sheltered maiden reason to worry. Nor was the process itself con-
ducive to peace of mind. The close inspection she endured beneath the
penetrating gaze of Lorenzo's formidable mother was an ordeal calculated
to make even a more experienced woman tremble.

   To break the tension of the months between the promise and the consummation, Clarice took up a correspondence with her future husband. It
was no doubt a daunting task and her language betrays a certain hesitancy.
The terms of their relationship were set early, with Lorenzo forced to
excuse himself for neglecting her and Clarice expressing her delight when
he showed the least bit of attention: "Magnificent consort, greetings, &
c.,—I have received a letter from you and have understood all you write.
That you liked my letter rejoices me, as I am always desirous to do what
pleases you. Then you say that you write but little; I am content with whatever is your pleasure, living always in hope for the future." The letter to
which she refers is now lost, but others written shortly after their wedding
are matter-of-fact, with little of the lighthearted banter that characterized
his correspondence with his friends. Lorenzo gives the impression of a
young man having too good a time to consider the feelings of his bride.
There is little indication that Lorenzo understood or sympathized with the
plight of a girl taken from her home and forced to live in a foreign land
among strangers.

   The truth is that during the months of their betrothal Lorenzo's
thoughts were less focused on his future bride than with the magnificent
tournament he was now planning. Not only was Clarice not invited to this
spectacle, calculated to outshine any held in the City of the Baptist for generations, but Lorenzo was to enter the lists as a champion of another
woman—his reputed mistress, Lucrezia Donati. One can almost hear the
petulance in Clarice's voice when, despite the urging of Lorenzo's uncle
Francesco Tornabuoni, she refused to write to him because, as Tornabuoni
reported, "she told me you were evidently extremely occupied with this
tournament; and then arrived Donnino who brought no letter from you."
To assuage her hurt feelings, Francesco advised Lorenzo to "write to her
often, it would give her great pleasure." It was advice to which Lorenzo,

as usual, paid little attention. While all of Florence turned out to celebrate Lorenzo's feats of arms and gossiped while his ladylove presented
him with a garland of violets, Clarice was left in Rome to work on her
trousseau.

To be fair to Lorenzo the tournament was not simply a childish indulgence, though with its make-believe combat and elaborate costumes it
resembled a boy's fantasy grown to gargantuan proportions. The magnificent spectacle—which lived in the collective consciousness of Florentines
long after those who had witnessed it were in their graves, primarily
through Luigi Pulci's epic poem *Stanzas on the Joust of Lorenzo*—was held
in February of 1469. Occurring shortly before Lorenzo's accession to
power, this event was as close as the republic could come to the pageantry
of a coronation.* Its official purpose was to celebrate the peace following
the Colleonic War, but it also marked in a very real sense the passing of the
torch from father to son. Lorenzo's wedding a few months hence would
mark his proper entry into the responsibilities of adulthood, but the tournament in which he played the leading role gave the people of Florence an
opportunity to take stock of and to cheer on their future leader.

On the morning of February 7, most of the population of Florence
could be found in the grandstands set up around the Piazza Santa Croce
or leaning from the windows of the four- and five-story buildings that
bounded the square. Forming the eastern end of the great rectangle was
the great Franciscan church of Santa Croce, its facade a grim expanse of
unadorned brick casting its shadow across much of the field of battle.† On
the steps leading up to the basilica were tiers of seats where the red-robed
judges and important dignitaries could sit in comfort. Among them were

---

* Jousts were not an infrequent occurrence in Renaissance Florence, and most of the
larger ones were held, like this one, in the Piazza Santa Croce. Some were staged by private families, but many were under the aegis of the aristocratic Guelf Party and were, to
some degree, a challenge by the city's most prominent families to Florence's republican
institutions.

† Florentine architects had a difficult time completing the facades of their churches. Most
of the ornate marble facades currently visible date from the nineteenth century, including that of Santa Croce and the cathedral. The best example of a completed Renaissance
facade is the church of Santa Maria Novella, designed by Leon Battista Alberti and paid
for by Giovanni Rucellai. Today, San Lorenzo, with its simple, rusticated front, gives the
best notion of what most Florentine churches looked like in Lorenzo's day.

Lorenzo's parents, along with the queen of the tournament, Lucrezia Donati, crowned with flowers and basking in the admiration of the assembled populace.

The piazza itself was admirably suited to the clash of arms. Covered inches deep in fine white sand and divided lengthwise with wooden rails, it provided ample space for the galloping horsemen to throw themselves at each other with furious abandon. When Clarice prayed for Lorenzo's safekeeping, and later wrote to him to tell of her relief that he had made it through the day in one piece, she was expressing more than a conventional wifely sentiment. Though lances were blunted and armor thick, serious injuries—and rarely, death—were a real possibility. Lorenzo was unhorsed more than once, and after one particularly brutal clash his horse was unable to lift itself from the turf.*

Lorenzo's joust is one of the best-documented events in his life. Numerous contemporary poets provided a blow-by-blow account and some—including Luigi Pulci—include a detailed portrait of Lorenzo at a particularly happy point in his life, when he was at the height of his physical powers and when the future seemed filled with endless possibilities. But despite copious firsthand testimony, Lorenzo's joust presents many a puzzle to the modern mind, unaccustomed as we are to the conventions of chivalry and to the complex motives that lay behind both the spectacle and the many narratives it inspired.

Above all it is difficult for us to comprehend how the recently betrothed Lorenzo could enter the lists as the champion of another lady. Here is how Luigi Pulci describes the scene as Lorenzo, a lighthearted Achilles, prepares for battle:

> Lorenzo, laughing, donned his helm,
> crowned already with a garland of flowers,
> then all of a sudden a nymph [Lucrezia] laughed
> when at her feet he kneeled . . .

---

* Pulci in describing this incident dwells at length on the heroism of Lorenzo's horse, Falsamico, a gift of the king of Naples: "And on the ground the youth was thrown, / and all in the field ran to help him; / but that horse through its great nobility / strove to do what it could not; / now he rises, and now he falls / causing those who admired him to sigh." (Pulci, *La Giostra di Lorenzo de' Medici,* cxiv.)

What is one to make of this charming vignette, played out before the multitudes, involving a married woman and a man just recently engaged to someone else? If Lucrezia was really Lorenzo's mistress, as many later historians have supposed, this public declaration of affection would have been entirely inappropriate. But to take Pulci's verses at face value and use them to pry open Lorenzo's elusive private life is to misunderstand both the poetry and the event. Lorenzo's tournament was, in fact, little more than a clever charade in which both the battles and the passions that sent men careening toward each other at breakneck speed were equally artificial. By the 1460s chivalry was primarily a nostalgic literary genre, particularly in Florence, which, much to the chagrin of its social-climbing rulers, had no real tradition of a warrior caste and where notions of knightly courtesy were formed by reading books and listening to the songs that accompanied drowsy feasts.

It is not surprising, then, that Pulci adopts a gently ironic tone. On one level his verses celebrate Lorenzo and his valiant companions as heroes worthy of being seen in the company of Hector and Agamemnon, but at the same time they acknowledge with every allegorical allusion a certain distance between the poetic fiction and the prosaic reality. This deliberate artfulness characterizes not only Pulci's description of the clash of arms but also his account of Lorenzo and Lucrezia's passion. In truth there was much in Lorenzo's private life, especially those hours spent in the seedier parts of town, of such a nature that not even the finest poet could make them fit for public consumption. Cosimo's protégé Antonio Beccadelli might celebrate the charms of "the blond Elena and the sweet Matilda, both adept at wiggling their behinds," but it would have tested even his courage to place Lorenzo in their company. Lorenzo's upcoming nuptials were equally unfit for poetic apotheosis; marriage was a sacred but rather prosaic affair, meant for the production of children and hopefully free of dramatic incident. In his epic poem, Luigi Pulci dismissed Clarice in a couple of lines, while dedicating whole paragraphs to the beautiful Lucrezia.*

Less easily dismissed is the testimony of Lorenzo's friends, who seem

---

* The pertinent lines are "and had there been then Clarice, /never would a city have been so happy"—all in all a rather tepid tribute (Pulci, *La Giostra di Lorenzo de' Medici*, xxvi–xxvii).

only too happy to dwell on the more salacious details of his supposed affair with the beautiful daughter of the distinguished Donati family. Shortly after Lucrezia's marriage, Braccio Martelli, with his usual coarseness, taunted Lorenzo: "and as you know, Niccolò [Ardinghelli] has a cock like the horn of a bull." If this was not sufficient to goad Lorenzo to action, another friend, Giovanfrancesco Ventura, gave him a further nudge. "I do not believe that your relations with the noble L[ucrezia] are at the same point as when I left," he wrote in mock scorn to Lorenzo in the spring of 1468. "Each seeks the health of his soul; it is time now to see to the pleasure of the body . . . you are too reserved and too contained . . . the time has come to seek the sweet goal and not to lose time. . . . I have learned that her N[iccolò] will be absent for some time: it would be a pity to leave unplowed such sweet terrain."

But even these apparently spontaneous utterances play off the conceit already established in Pulci's literary production. The vulgar humor of Lorenzo's friends, far from providing confirmation of an illicit love, pokes fun at a chivalric convention that by now had worn a bit thin. Beccadelli strikes a similarly cynical pose in his *Hermaphroditus*: "The Graces and Venus chose Alda's beautiful eyes as a dwelling place and Cupid in person smiles on her lips. She does not piss, or, if she does piss, she pisses fragrant balsam; she does not shit, or, if she does shit, she shits violets." You could dress a Florentine banker in a knight's armor, but the pungent vocabulary and hardheaded realism of the marketplace, where men were accustomed to sifting truth from fiction, would quickly pierce the disguise. If Lorenzo was ever tempted to fly too high, to see his own life in terms of heroic feats performed at the behest of lovely damsels, he was sure to be brought down to earth by friends like Martelli and Ventura who mocked all that courtly nonsense.

While the presence of the beautiful Lucrezia gave Lorenzo's tournament a fairy-tale quality, far more prosaic things were actually at stake. For those crowded into the Piazza Santa Croce that day the twin pillars of Florentine life, money and politics, were clearly visible behind the artful spectacle and classical references. The real competition began long before the first blows were struck as each champion tried to outdo his rivals in the extravagance of his furnishings and size of his retinue. More fashion-conscious than divas on a red carpet, the young men from the best families of the land—Medici, Salutati, Pazzi, Pitti, Pucci, and Vespucci, among others—cantered into the square with their armor all but invisible beneath yards of silk, velvet, and ermine, their family crests or personal devices picked out in silver and gold thread. Even the horses, covered head to hoof in silk and jewels, carried a king's ransom on their backs. Few could forget Benedetto Salutati's entrance, his horse so splendidly attired that, according to one breathless eyewitness, the bridle alone required 168 pounds of silver. Others were decked out with equal sumptuousness, the point being to project a splendid image that the citizens were quick to tabulate in terms of florins or ducats.*

The joust, while borrowing its form from medieval traditions, reflected the worldly ethos of the Renaissance. Gone were the frugal habits of former generations, replaced by a culture in which attention-grabbing splendor was a requirement for anyone wishing to make his way in the city. The modest man was no longer praised for his Christian virtue but condemned as stingy and small. He who cut the most splendid figure was greeted with the loudest applause. But before one condemns too harshly this conspicuous consumption, it should be noted that events like these contributed to the most sublime achievements in the arts by offering steady employment to Florence's greatest painters and sculptors. The account books of artists like the Pollaiuolo brothers, Verrocchio, and Botticelli record the income derived from the floats, banners, and armor they designed for the jousts and festivals that filled the yearly calendar. Little of this ephemeral matter has survived, but as much skill and artistry were lavished on the cuirass of a jouster as on the most ornate altarpiece.

Lorenzo's own feelings about his joust convey a mixture of pride and cynicism. In his memoirs, he evinces little real taste for such occasions, writing, "To do as others do I held a joust in the Piazza S. Croce at great expense and with great pomp. I find we spent about 10,000 ducats." But his anxiety to acquire the best horses from around Italy betrays a passion

---

* Florentines were obsessed with the cost of everything, from ladies' gowns to altarpieces, and contemporary chronicles are chock-full of price tags for even the most sacred objects. Piero had inscribed on the tabernacle he built for the miraculous image of the Virgin in Santissima Annunziata the boast, "The marble alone cost 4000 florins." This obsession with money did not strike Florentines as crass. This was a mercantile society in which the simplest, most understandable way to fix the value of anything was in terms of its monetary cost.

for such spectacles not admitted in these laconic remarks. No doubt he enjoyed the trappings and vigorous physical activity of the tournament, but he also understood that it was a necessary exercise in public relations. He was on the verge of assuming the leadership of the republic, and his tournament was calculated to win over hearts and minds. Who, after all, would not prefer to be led by a young lord resplendent in ermine and gleaming helm rather than a college of nattering old men in somber robes?

Lorenzo did not fail to remind the people on this martial occasion of his contributions to the gentler arts of peace. His banner, designed by Andrea del Verrocchio (with possible contributions by Leonardo da Vinci, who had recently entered his studio), depicted a sun and a rainbow in which were inscribed in golden letters the words *"Le tems revient"* (The time returns). Lorenzo's famous motto—rendered, significantly, in the archaic French of chivalric tradition—is a play on his father's *"Semper"* (Always), and reflects the perennial Medici obsession with time.* Perhaps the message was a bit obscure, since Pulci felt the need to explain the words to posterity, writing that "one can interpret them as meaning, the time returns and the century renews itself." For spectators not conversant in French, the theme of rebirth was elaborated in the vests of Lorenzo's twelve-member honor guard, showing roses both withered and in full bloom, as if the Medici heir had breathed new life into a dying world. The phrase, ultimately derived from the *Fourth Ecologue* in which Virgil prophesied the return of a golden age under Augustus, demonstrates how assiduously Lorenzo cultivated his image as a patron of the city's vital culture. Indeed, as his banner makes clear, the myth of a golden age under Lorenzo was not the invention of later generations but part of a deliberate strategy to identify the reigning family with the city's splendid achievements in the realms of art and literature.

For the vulgar masses, on whom much of the symbolism was lost, the sheer extravagance of Lorenzo's costume conveyed a similar message. From his velvet beret encrusted with pearls, diamonds, and rubies, to the silver harness sculpted by Antonio del Pollaiuolo, to his shield, sporting at its center the famous Medici diamond known as *il Libro* (said to be worth

---

* The diamond ring, an emblem employed by both Piero and Lorenzo that can be seen on the facade of their palace, as well as in paintings like Botticelli's *Pallas Athena and the Centaur* and Gozzoli's *Adoration of the Magi*, also stands for eternity.

at least 8,000 ducats),* Lorenzo was a walking—or riding—advertisement for his family's magnificence.

Political messages were conveyed as well by the roster of those who rode with him into the piazza. He was accompanied by two illustrious men-at-arms, Giovani Ubaldini, lieutenant of Federico da Montefeltro, and Carlo da Forme, representing the *condottiere* Roberto di Sanseverino—an impressive display of military muscle. The fact that he rode five different horses for the tournament had less to do with the fury of the combat than the opportunity thus afforded to pay and receive homage: three came from King Ferrante, one from Cesare Sforza, and one from Borso d'Este, who hoped through his generosity to redeem his reputation after his indiscreet attempts on Piero's life.

While Pulci tries to turn the joust into a ferocious battle of Iliadic proportions, most of the participants managed to escape with little more than bumps, bruises. As the sun began to set, individual battles gave way to a confused melee in which Lorenzo was thrown from his horse:

> *Seeing this his famous father*
> *commanded that his helm be removed [thus ending the fight];*
> *and so prayed his pious mother,*
> *and willingly would it have been done,*
> *but to his lord he [Lorenzo] answered with fine words:*
> *"This was not the promise and the pact"*
> *then adding that in any case the day would die happy.*

Artfully, Pulci turns what could have been an embarrassing moment into an occasion for Lorenzo to display his gallantry. He describes how Lorenzo quickly remounted and charged back into the fray until "the sun bathed his golden rays in the ocean." With most of the field lost in shadow so that only the tops of the helmets caught the last glint of sunlight, the heralds finally signaled the end of the contest.

---

* Gold ducats were minted by the Venetian Republic, florins by Florence, and were roughly equivalent in value. In the time of Lorenzo, a skilled artisan might earn about 50 florins, or ducats, a year. One florin could purchase about thirty chickens. By contrast, income from Pietro Riario's benefices totalled 60,000 florins per year.

It was a glorious end to a glorious day. To no one's surprise, and despite the fact that he had been twice unhorsed, "to the youth [Lorenzo] with great celebration/ was given Mars' highest honor."*

As the crowd dispersed, how many grumbled at the outcome and how many argued that it had been fairly won? Wine flowed freely in the taverns and bonfires lit up the streets and squares as the day's festivities continued long into the moonlit hours and knightly etiquette gave way to drunken revelry. In the days and weeks that followed congratulations flowed in from across Europe filled with flattering allusions to Lorenzo's martial prowess. All sang the praises of the youth who "carried on his helm both honor and victory, and raised to new heights the emblem of the illustrious Medici." From Rome came letters from his soon-to-be kinsman: "A few days ago I heard, but not by any letter of yours, of the tournament and the honor done to you," wrote Clarice's brother, Rinaldo Orsini. "God be praised for all, and especially that you emerged safe and unhurt; in which I think you were aided by the prayers of your Clarice." Clarice wrote in a typically self-effacing vein: "Most magnificent consort, greetings. I have received a letter from you which was most pleasing to me, telling me of the tournament wherein you gained much honor. I am most glad that you have been satisfied in a thing which gives you pleasure; and if my prayers have been granted in this, I, as a person who desires to do something to give you pleasure, am well satisfied."

Lorenzo himself was realistic about the day's events. "[A]nd although I was not highly versed in the use of weapons and the delivery of blows," he later recalled, "the first prize was given to me; a helmet fashioned of silver, with Mars as the crest." As a warrior he had acquitted himself passably. More important, he had supplied the Florentine people with an entertainment they would not soon forget. While some may have complained that the event was rigged, most went away with a greater appreciation of Medici wealth and of their willingness to spend it on behalf of the city. On this day, at least, Lorenzo had earned much goodwill that he might soon be forced to draw upon.

---

* Among the judges were Tommaso Soderini, Lorenzo's uncle, the *condottiere* Roberto di Sanseverino, and such important members of the *reggimento* as Carlo Pandolfini and Bongianni Gianfigliazzi: a distinguished but not necessarily unbiased panel.

Andrea del Verrocchio, *Tomb of Giovanni and Piero de' Medici*,
c. 1470 (Art Resource)

VIII. A WEDDING
AND A FUNERAL

"The second day after [my father's] death, although I, Lorenzo, was very young, being twenty years of age, the principal men of the city and of the State came to us in our house to condole with us on our loss and to encourage me to take charge of the city and of the State, as my grandfather and my father had done. This I did, though on account of my youth and the great responsibility and perils arising therefrom, with great reluctance, solely for the safety of our friends and of our possessions. For it is ill living in Florence for the rich unless they rule the state. Till now we have succeeded with honor and renown, which I attribute not to prudence but to the grace of God and the good conduct of my predecessors."

—LORENZO DE' MEDICI, *RICORDI*

LORENZO'S JOUST MARKED A SYMBOLIC END TO HIS youth. Along with his armor and the silver helmet shaped in the image of the war god Mars, he put away the last vestiges of a life of irresponsibility and donned instead the plain robes denoting a man of substance in the republic. His grandfather had once remarked that a few yards of scarlet cloth were all it took to make a citizen, and Lorenzo now usually appeared in public in that quintessential uniform of the Florentine burgher. The part of romantic hero, the Prince of Youth, now fell exclusively to his brother, Giuliano, who could act the part with effortless grace.

A revealing, if obviously exaggerated, portrait of the two brothers and their very different personalities comes in Angelo Poliziano's *Stanzas on the Joust of Giuliano*. Poliziano describes Lorenzo as a lovesick wretch whose pain can only be assuaged by writing verses to his cruel mistress: "For in starkest winter I have seen / him, his hair, shoulders, and face full of frost, / complain to the stars and moon of her, of us, of / his cruel fortune." "Handsome Julio," by contrast, is a natural hunter and an athlete, powerful on horseback and so "ferocious in the hunt that the woods seem afraid of him." It is only with difficulty that Cupid turns him from these violent exertions to more tender passions. Of course these are romanticized portraits, but there is no doubt that Poliziano based his mythological fantasy on the real characters of two men he knew and loved, particularly since the contrast is confirmed by countless other contemporary sources. Unlike the introspective, melancholic, and cynical Lorenzo, Giuliano was an extrovert who played the role of the glamorous prince without ambivalence.

That Lorenzo regretted the passing of his youth is clear from his own poetry in which he revels in sensual pleasures even as he mourns their passing. "How beautiful is youth," he wrote in his most famous Carnival song, "that quickly flies away. / He who would be happy, let him, / Since of tomorrow none can say." Written after many years in which he was burdened by having to care for both his family and the state, these lines record his resentment at time stolen from him, at the devouring of irresponsible youth by the demands of adulthood. The hedonism of his nature was always clouded by mortal thoughts, as if he knew that the enjoyment of life's carnal delights came at a cost.

For Piero, Lorenzo's entry into adulthood could not come quickly enough. At twenty Lorenzo might have anticipated many more years of carefree bachelorhood, but this was not a luxury permitted the Medici heir. With the survival of the entire clan resting on his procreative powers and its fortune dependent on his political and financial skills, it was vital that Lorenzo establish himself immediately as a full-fledged member of the community.* Not only would the upcoming union with the Orsini secure the Medici's position among Europe's ruling elite, but it was hoped married life would also serve as a steadying influence. A man with a family to care for was a man focused on the important things of life. It was marriage, above all, that marked the passage from youth to manhood, and though few expected the married man to completely discard the vices of his irresponsible adolescence, he was permitted to indulge in them only as

---

* It is not clear whether Piero and Lucrezia contemplated an ecclesiastical career for Giuliano. This would have made it all the more important that Lorenzo quickly produce heirs of his own to carry on the family name.

long as doing so did not interfere with the crucial task of producing heirs
and providing for their future.

It was Archbishop Filippo de' Medici who broke the welcome news
from Rome. "I know not where I shall begin in order to inform your Magnificence that I have today espoused the noble and illustrious Madonna
Clarice degli Orsini in your name," he wrote to Piero: "according to my
opinion, a maiden of such physical gifts, appearance, and manners, that
she deserves no other bridegroom than him whom, I believe, heaven has
destined for her." While it might seem strange that Lorenzo was not present at his own wedding, this was not unusual in cases where the bride and
groom came from different cities. The espousal was a formal contract with
the bride's family, not to be confused with the wedding feast, which would
be celebrated in the groom's hometown. When Galeazzo Maria Sforza
married Bona of Savoy, the wedding was "consummated" by Galeazzo's
half-brother Tristano, who ceremonially kissed the bride and climbed into
her bed where they "touched one another's bare leg . . . according to the
custom." A similarly quaint ceremony, with Filippo doing the honors,
probably also solemnized Lorenzo's marriage.

The legal niceties observed, Lorenzo's new mother-in-law wrote to
him: "How glad I should be to see you before sending my daughter, I cannot express, but I am sure the Magnificent Piero knows best. . . . At all
events I hope you have the wish to know me and all your relations here."
But despite repeated pleas, Piero decided he could not afford to be without
Lorenzo for any extended period. Instead, in May 1469, he sent a distinguished delegation of fifty citizens—led by Giuliano, along with his cousin
Pierfrancesco de' Medici, brothers-in-law Bernardo Rucellai and
Guglielmo de' Pazzi, and the faithful Gentile Becchi—to Rome to fetch
Clarice and escort her back to her new home. By the beginning of June she
had arrived in Florence, where she was lodged at the house of the mer-
chant Benedetto degli' Alessandri.

If Clarice had any concerns that this less-than-triumphal entry was a
signal of Lorenzo's continued indifference, the next few days allayed her
fears. However tepid his feelings for his bride-to-be, neither he nor his
parents would let such an important occasion pass without extracting the
maximum propaganda benefit. A few days before the festivities were set to
begin, the streets were crowded with columns of mules and carts bearing

gifts from the principal towns, villas, and castles of Tuscany. "Calves 150," recorded one anonymous chronicler. "More than 2000 couples of capons, geese, and fowls. Sea fish and trout in large quantities. I do not yet know how many. Sweet things in abundance; sugar plums as big as artubus berries, almonds, pine-seeds, sweetmeats." This bounty from the cities and territories subject to Florentine rule was an impressive display of the power of the Medici name.

On Sunday morning, June 4, Clarice, dressed in a white, hooded gown sparkling with gold thread and riding Lorenzo's horse Falsamico, proceeded from the Alessandri palace to the Via Larga, accompanied by trumpeters and fifers along with thirty matrons representing the leading families of Florence. As she dismounted before the palace, decorated with tapestries and awnings displaying the Medici and Orsini crests, a live olive tree was hoisted into the palace through a second-story window to serve during the feast as a symbol of abundance and fertility.

The marriage festivities, though not officially a public occasion, managed nonetheless to embrace the entire city. During the three days of banqueting more than a thousand people passed through the doors of the palace, though there were limits to the Medici's hospitality: "In the house here, where the marriage feast was, every respectable person who came in was at once taken to the ground-floor hall. . . . The common folk were not invited."

For those not fortunate enough to be allowed inside, there was plenty to see on the streets surrounding the palace. The eating, drinking, and dancing spilled out onto the Via Larga, where a platform had been set up to accommodate the overflow guests. For the most part the weather cooperated, allowing the family to seat the crowds in the open air, though a sudden downpour on Monday turned expensive silk and brocade gowns, worked on for months, into damp, unsightly rags—much to the delight of those censorious moralists who felt that Florentine women spent too much money on their clothes and far too much time before the mirror.

Most Florentines of the better sort clamored to be included on the guest list, but the honor could also have its drawbacks. Alessandra Strozzi recounted how her daughter-in-law, the attractive Fiametta, had been repeatedly importuned by Lucrezia Tornabuoni to attend, but had tried to excuse herself on the grounds that she had recently given birth. "She doesn't want to go," Alessandra wrote to her son Filippo, "first because you're not here and also because if she does go we'll have to spend several hundred florins. I must tell you that they are having a lot of brocade gowns and robes made, and we'd have to have them made for her as well, and she doesn't have much jewelry."

Others, however, were only too happy to make it inside the palace where they could gawk at the damask-covered tables piled high with roasts, trays of sweetmeats, marzipan, jellies, and sugared pine nuts. Donatello's bronze *David* served as the centerpiece of an elaborate refreshment stand with four huge copper vessels filled with iced water and wine ladled out by a team of liveried attendants. In the adjacent garden, where Donatello's *Judith* stood as a model of female virtue, Clarice dined with fifty maidens chosen for their beauty and grace. Older matrons, less able to withstand the June sun, dined in the loggia above at tables presided over by Lucrezia.

Much of the information on Lorenzo's wedding comes from an anonymous chronicler who heard it, he tells us, from "Cosimo Bartoli, one of the principal Directors of the Festival, particularly as regards Sweetmeats and sugar-plums, and also what I saw myself."* Despite the five banquets spread over three days, served up on gleaming silver and glittering crystal and staffed by an army of servants, musicians, and entertainers, Lorenzo's wedding was in fact deliberately understated. "[T]here was never more than one roast," the chronicler noted approvingly. "I think it was done . . . as an example to others not to exceed the modesty and simplicity suitable to marriages." Given the opulence he describes, such a comment might strike one as facetious until one considers other fifteenth-century banquets that rivaled the worst excesses of pagan Rome.† In fact, Lorenzo's wedding was a relatively low-key affair. Particularly when foreigners were present, Florentines went out of their

---

* The author has been tentatively identified as Piero Parenti, the nineteen-year-old son of Marco.

† For example, see Chapter XII for a description of Cardinal Pietro Riario's banquet.

way to demonstrate their republican austerity. When Galeazzo Maria
Sforza stayed at the Medici villa at Careggi in 1459, for instance, he was
particularly struck by the fact that Giovanni, Cosimo's younger son, did
not dine with him but waited on tables, and that after dinner Lucrezia
herself joined some local peasant girls to perform a charming rustic
dance. Foreigners often misunderstood the Florentine taste for simplicity. Years later, when Lorenzo's son-in-law Franceschetto Cibo paid a
visit, he was insulted by the frugality of the repast; Lorenzo was forced to
explain that far from being an insult, this meant he was to think of himself as a member of the family.

The Medici were always most successful when they maintained the
proper balance between ostentation and simplicity. Everyone knew they
could have done more, and appreciated the reserve that paid homage to
their communal traditions. The wedding was elegant but not excessive; in
distributing alms they were generous, but never to the point that their
generosity could be construed as a demagogic attempt to purchase the loyalty of the masses.

But if none could fault them in the way they conducted the ceremonies,
there were many who grumbled that they had erred in their choice of a
bride. On Tuesday morning, as Clarice brought the festivities to a close by
attending Mass in San Lorenzo, the populace awoke to the uncomfortable
fact of a foreign bride in the *Palazzo Medici*. Her simplicity of manner and
modesty of demeanor could not conceal the fact that she was the daughter
of a haughty, aristocratic, and, most damning of all, *foreign* family; the
Orsini name would be a constant reminder of the Medici's dynastic ambitions. Years later, when considering a match for one of his own children,
Lorenzo remarked, "It would be a burden and a danger to me if I were to
contract a marriage, so contrary to custom, with great lords and men, whose
condition in life is quite different from mine." Guicciardini later attributed
the arrogance of Lorenzo's firstborn son to his "bastardized" blood that
made him "too insolent and haughty for our way of life." Who among the
prominent families attending the banquets at the Via Larga could have failed
to conclude that none had been judged good enough to furnish a bride for
the Medici son? To even the most loyal of followers, the snub must have left
a bitter taste that no amount of sweet wine could wash down.

• • •

At the time, however, Piero and Lucrezia appeared well pleased with the match. Of more immediate concern was Piero's steadily declining health. Wracked by pain in his joints, he was now barely able to lift himself from his bed. Foreign ambassadors and leaders of the *reggimento* who shuttled back and forth between the *Palazzo della Signoria* and the *Palazzo Medici* now openly prepared themselves for a future without Piero.

Foremost among the supporters of the regime, and a man who over the years had built a following second only to Piero himself in the government, was the sixty-five-year-old Tommaso Soderini, whose loyalty in the crisis of 1466 had earned him a place at the Medici leader's right hand. Known as a man of ability, but also disliked by many for the ruthlessness with which he exploited his position for personal gain, his voice would carry enormous weight in the period of transition.* Would he stick by the Medici as he had done in the past or would he follow the example of men like Luca Pitti, Dietisalvi Neroni—or even his own brother, Niccolò—whose pent-up ambition had burst forth after the death of their leader?

As the torpor of the Tuscan summer gave way to the bustle of fall, time for the harvest of the grape and olive, Piero's hold on the affairs of state began to slip. The "absent senator," once consulted on every important matter, was largely sidelined as the more vigorous members of the *reggimento* jockeyed for position or tried to squeeze out one last florin of profit before Piero's death threw everything into confusion.

Instead of a peaceful interlude in which to prepare his soul for its final journey, Piero's last days were troubled by dissensions within and the rumblings of war without. In Machiavelli's account of Piero's final days, the dying leader brought together his most powerful associates and chided them for their pursuit of selfish ends:

---

* Tommaso had used his positions on important financial committees, including as director of the state-funded debt, the *Monte,* and as one of the twelve officers of the *Pratiche et Banchi,* to boost his own private fortunes. This was not an unusual practice in a system where the wall between public and private finance was so porous, but Tommaso seems to have been more than usually diligent in using public office to line his own pockets.

I would never have believed that the time would come when the modes and customs of my friends would make me bitter and desire enemies, and victory make me desire defeat; for I thought I had in my company men who had some limit or measure to their cupidity and for whom it would be enough to live safe and honored in their fatherland and, besides that, to have had revenge on their enemies. But I know now how greatly I have deceived myself as one who knew little of the natural ambition of all men and less yours. . . . You despoil your neighbor of his goods, you sell justice, you escape civil judgments, you oppress peaceful men and exalt the insolent. . . . I promise you, by the faith that ought to be given and received by good men, that if you continue to carry on in a mode that makes me repent having won, I too shall carry on in a manner that will make you repent having ill used the victory.

This speech is largely Machiavelli's invention, but it reflects the very real divisions between the leader of the party and his various lieutenants who took advantage of his debility to pursue their own agendas. The very thoroughness of the victory of the Plain in 1466 had fostered corruption. In the time-honored fashion of Florentine politics, one faction, having swept all opposition before it, used its authority to tax and spend to enrich friends and ruin enemies, thereby consolidating its hold on power. So distraught was Piero over dissension and mismanagement among his associates that he contemplated allowing the return of some of the exiles—particularly Agnolo Acciaiuoli, with whom he was said to have met secretly at his villa in Cafaggiolo—to act as a counterweight to the more arrogant and ambitious members of the *reggimento*.

But Piero was ultimately too crippled in mind and body to effect the necessary reforms, and the threat to recall the exiles was too weak a club, and too uncertainly wielded, to frighten those grown fat on the spoils of victory. Adding to his dismay was the fact that dissension within the *reggimento* came at a particularly inopportune moment. Even as Piero tried to rein in his unruly lieutenants, ominous clouds had begun to gather in the ever tempestuous Romagna.

The Romagna, a region bordering Tuscany to the north and east, made up part of the territory under the nominal rule of the leader of the

Church known as the Papal States.* Here in central Italy the decay of the
Holy Roman Empire in the Middle Ages had left a patchwork quilt of
petty states and competing jurisdictions; the removal of the papacy to
Avignon in the fourteenth century had further eroded centralized
authority. But with the restoration of the popes to their traditional capital in Rome at the beginning of the fifteenth century, successive occupants of the throne of St. Peter sought to reassert their authority over
vassals accustomed to treating their territories as hereditary possessions.
Each successful extension of papal authority, however, threatened the
fragile balance of power within Italy, which was predicated in part on
depriving Rome of her traditional role as the mistress of Italy. This was
particularly problematic for Florence, surrounded as she was by territories claimed by the pope.

The current crisis originated in Rimini, a city on the Adriatic coast
some sixty miles east of Florence. The despot of Rimini, Sigismondo Pan-
dolfo Malatesta, had died in October of the previous year, leaving behind
him his widow, Isotta, and an illegitimate son, Roberto. In theory the
Malatesta ruled Rimini only as the vicars of the Holy Father, but like many
of their colleagues they treated the city as their private domain, leading
lives of violence and dissipation and virtually ignoring their titular overlord.[†] Paul II's predecessor, Pius II, had been so fed up with his vassal's
wayward behavior that he took the unusual step of burning him in effigy
and condemning him to the deepest pits of hell: "Until now, no mortal has
been solemnly canonized in Hell. Sigismondo will be the first man worthy
of this honor. By edict of the Pope, he will be condemned to the infernal

---

* The Papal States comprised much of central Italy, bounding Florentine-controlled Tuscany on the north, south, and east. The pope's temporal realm derived from multiple
sources, including grants from the Carolingian and Byzantine empires. In the Middle
Ages a document known as "The Donation of Constantine" was fabricated to establish a
more ancient and holy title to these territories. The fraud was exposed by the Renaissance humanist Lorenzo Valla, though not acknowledged until much later.

† Like many of the Renaissance's most unpleasant characters, Sigismondo was a refined
patron of the arts. He filled his time between murderous rampages commissioning
refined works of art and architecture. The Temple of San Francesco he had built in Rimini by Leon Battista Alberti is one of the masterpieces of Renaissance architecture. Its
serene sense of order belies the violence of the man who conceived it.

city where he will join the damned and other devils. He is hereby condemned, while still alive, to Orcus and eternal fire."

Following Sigismondo's death, Paul went in search of a more pliant servant. He found just such a candidate in Isotta, Sigismondo's widow, and stiffened her resolve by installing at her side a Venetian commissioner. Not surprising, Sigismondo's bastard son, Roberto, who had inherited his father's temper if not his title, reacted to this attempt to disinherit him with vehemence. With the secret backing of the duke of Urbino, he raised an army and proceeded to march toward Rimini with the intention of reclaiming his patrimony by force. On October 20 he entered the city and proclaimed himself *signore*.

This petty squabble would hardly have been worth notice except for the fact that, as in the Balkans on the eve of the First World War, the slightest tremor in this fractured corner of the globe threatened to drag the regional powers into the maelstrom. The Venetian-born Paul naturally turned to his native city to help him assert his feudal rights, while Naples, Florence, and Milan, wishing to chastise the arrogant Venetians and fearing the pope's ambition, came in on the side of Roberto Malatesta. (It didn't hurt Malatesta's prospects that he was currently employed as a general in the pay of the triple alliance).*

For Lorenzo, the pressures of war added to the uncertainties of his succession. An already difficult situation was made infinitely more complex when disagreements broke out among the allies over the war's prosecution and ultimate aims—disagreements that soon split the Florentine *reggimento* into quarreling factions. At a time when Piero needed the government to come together, its leaders were too busy attacking each other to think about rallying behind his chosen successor.

With his mind thus troubled and his body wracked with pain, Piero, like his father before him, had himself carried to his villa at Careggi. Outside his window the bare branches rasped in the chill autumn breeze, and as the nights grew long and bitter, Piero tried to free his mind of earthly cares. Stories of the blessed saints and of the equally stoic philosophers provided more comfort than the potions of doctors. Friends and family

---

* The alliance among Milan, Florence, and Naples had been the chief diplomatic triumph of Lorenzo's grandfather Cosimo, cemented by the Peace of Lodi in 1454.

kept a constant vigil at his bedside. Here, far from the noise and distractions of the city, he would compose his soul for its final journey, trusting in God, if not his feckless colleagues, to care for his wife and children.

Lorenzo, however, was trusting his fate to powers nearer at hand. Grieved by his father's suffering and oppressed by the difficulties he faced, he turned to those who had been his family's most stalwart patrons in times of trouble—the Sforza of Milan.* Unfortunately for Lorenzo, now desperately in need of friends abroad, he could no longer count on their automatic support. Differences arising over the prosecution of the Rimini War between Naples and Milan left Florence caught awkwardly in the middle and the Florentine government seriously divided.

In August, allied forces under Federico da Montefeltro and King Ferrante's son, Alfonso, duke of Calabria, routed the combined armies of Venice and the pope and succeeded in lifting the siege they had placed on Rimini. But no sooner had this victory been won than the divergent aims of the allies became apparent: Galeazzo Maria Sforza, harrassed by his northern neighbor Savoy, hoped to conclude a quick peace with the pope so he could attend to business closer to home; Ferrante, by contrast, wished to use the recent momentum to achieve a more decisive victory, believing that a weakened papacy would permit Neapolitan expansion in the south. Milan needed a strong ally in the *Palazzo della Signoria*, but it was just this kind of forceful leadership that the ailing Medici patriarch was unable to provide. Trying to steer a middle course between the two quarreling parties, Piero managed to displease both. The extent to which Piero's authority had slipped is revealed by an exchange between the *Signoria* and Luigi Guicciardini, the republic's ambassador in Milan. Guicciardini was instructed to abandon Milan should the duke persist in pursuing a policy of appeasement, a policy that placed Piero, who wished to maintain amicable ties with the Sforza, in an untenable position. Filippo Sacramoro, the Milanese ambassador to Florence, spoke ominously of secret meetings "of the enemies of Piero and . . . those who favor Venice."

---

* Galeazzo Maria did not acquire his full authority until January 1469, when he turned twenty-five. Before that the government was in the hands of his mother, Bianca Maria, and her minister Cicco Simonetta, who continued to serve in a similar capacity with the young duke.

The rifts were so pronounced that Agnolo Acciaiuoli, Dietisalvi Neroni, and the rest of the exiles of 1466 seemed ready to pack their bags for a triumphal return to the native land. Neroni in particular was full of grandiose plans, writing to his son that upon Piero's death the pope should hurry an ambassador to Florence with an offer of peace as soon as they resolved to mend their wicked ways and "to live in a manner in which they would no longer be the cause of every scandal in Italy, and that their citizens would live freely as citizens, and not as despots."

In October, the Milanese ambassador confided to the duke that he feared the ailing Piero was losing his grip. Given this crisis of confidence in his leadership there was a real danger that Milan would look for a more reliable ally within the city. It was up to Lorenzo to prove to the duke and his ambassador that the Medici could still be counted on,* a strategy that required him to distance himself from his father's policies and to demonstrate that, whatever Piero's failings, he was still fully behind the Milanese alliance. It must have been painful for Lorenzo to so openly question his father's judgment, particularly when Piero could do little to defend himself. But the strategy apparently worked, for Sacramoro shortly wrote to the duke predicting that Lorenzo "will show himself to be of a different nature from his father."

By early December it was clear that Piero's illness had entered its final phase. A flurry of letters back and forth between Florence and Milan records Lorenzo's anxiety for his own future. Over the course of three days, from December 1 to 4, 1469, Lorenzo wrote three letters to Galeazzo Maria Sforza (the final one signed as well by Giuliano), each one more fawning than the last. "I would like to declare myself as the devoted servant of Your Excellency, and to recall the ancient devotion of our house and myself in particular toward Your Illustrious Lordship," he wrote on

---

* Lorenzo's second trip to Milan that summer, where he stood godfather to Galeazzo's firstborn son, was in part an attempt to rebuild the Duke's shaken confidence in the Medici. While there, Lorenzo reminded his guests of the benefits of Medici friendship by presenting the Duchess a necklace of gold and diamond valued at 2,000 ducats. He in turn was received "with much honor, more so than the others who came for the same purpose" (see Ross, p. 154).

December 1. This reminder of past friendship became all the more urgent the following day when Piero's health took a sudden turn for the worse: "My Most Illustrious Lord. Yesterday I wrote to Your Excellency of the illness of my father. Subsequently he deteriorated to such an extent that I have little hope for his recovery, and again assure Your Illustrious Lordship that all my hope resides in you, and that I pray you know, as I already said, that my preservation derives from Your Excellency alone, to whom I humbly recommend myself."

At the same time as he was stroking the vanity of the duke, Lorenzo was trying to shore up domestic support. "[W]hile certain of having here the support of many good friends," he explained to Galeazzo, "it seems to me it would do little good without the favor and aid of Your Illustrious Lordship." Fortunately, the Milanese ambassador was now fully behind Lorenzo. "I can report," wrote Sacramoro to the duke on December 1, "that [Lorenzo] has so arranged and secured his affairs in the city in regard to the leading citizens, that he seems to be squarely in the saddle."

But was Lorenzo as fully in control of the situation as both he and Sacramoro implied? Despite their bold predictions, the situation was still volatile. Niccolò Roberti, the Ferrarese ambassador to Florence, was far less certain of Lorenzo's success, predicting that after Piero's death the old oligarchy would reassert control and that "all business will once again return to the palazzo [Publico]." In truth, the government was split, the normal divisions exacerbated by the lack of a strong leader and by the growing dissension between Florence's two principal allies over the conduct of the Rimini War. Both Naples and Milan had their adherents in the *reggimento,* while others hoped to overthrow the triple league altogether in favor of a rapprochement with Venice.

Much would depend on Tommaso Soderini, now the most powerful man in the state. Despite Soderini's long service both to the Medici and in promoting the interests of Milan, Sacramoro distrusted the wily Tommaso, whose relations with the duke had been strained in recent months by the marriage of his son Piero to the daughter of a nobleman who was a rival of the Sforza. Among other things, this marriage into foreign nobility bespoke vaunting ambition; perhaps Soderini hoped through this connection to outshine the Medici themselves. Also troubling was the fact that at the very same time Soderini was protesting his loyalty to the ruling dynasty of Milan he was expressing admiration for their Venetian rivals.

On the morning of December 2, Soderini—who had been following the course of Piero's illness so closely that he seems to have been as well informed as Lorenzo himself—called for a meeting of 150 of the leading friends of the *reggimento*. Even before they had a chance to assemble in the small hall they had reserved near the butchers' guild, news reached Soderini that Piero was only hours from death. Given the gravity of the situation Soderini thought it prudent to transfer proceedings to the more commodious convent of Sant'Antonio, conveniently located a few blocks west of the *Palazzo Medici,* so that all those "well respected but of varying views" might attend the extraordinary nighttime meeting.*

Even before the citizens had assembled, the news came from Careggi that Piero had died. "At the twenty-third-and-a-half hour [about 4:30 in the afternoon] there came upon him a sudden fit of pain in his limbs and seizures that the Magnificent Piero passed from this life," reported Sacramoro to Duke Galeazzo; "he showed with gestures and squeezings of the hand, since he could no longer speak—so impetuous was the onset of this catarrh—that he wished to place his sons in the care of Your Highness; he died with a great show of contrition and, like his father, ordered a funeral without pomp."

It was thus with a heavy heart and fears for the future that the leading men of Florence made their way through darkened streets to the monastery close by the Porta Piacenza.†

"*Messer* Tommaso Soderini took the word as eldest, and explained how Piero had left his sons already grown up and gifted with good judgment and intellect," Niccolò Roberti reported the dramatic scene:

> Out of regard for their predecessors, and especially Cosimo and Piero, who had always been friends, protectors, and preservers of the commonwealth and benefactors of the State, for which reason they

---

* According to Sacramoro, seven hundred attended the meeting, while Marco Parenti claims that there were only five hundred, though they were "citizens of every sort" (see Parenti, *Lettere,* no. 75). Another participant counted only four hundred.

† In his *Florentine Histories* (vii, 25), Machiavelli places Lorenzo and Giuliano at the meeting, but contemporary accounts don't seem to support this.

had taken the first rank and borne the whole weight of government wisely and with dignity, always displaying courage and mature judgment, it seemed to him that they should leave to Piero's family and sons, notwithstanding their youth, the honorable position which he himself and Cosimo had enjoyed. He added that he saw the two no less considerate and desirous of winning the good opinion of the commune, and of all the Florentine citizens, than their grandfather and father. This was confirmed by three or four of those present, by *Messer* Manno [Temperani], son-in-law of *Messer* Luca Pitti, who was not himself present, by *Messer* Giannozzo Pitti, and Domenico Martelli. The last two remarked that a master and a head was needed to give the casting-vote in public affairs.

With Soderini's statesmanlike speech and its endorsement by other powerful members of the regime, most in the hall quickly rallied behind the Medici until, according to Sacramoro's report, a consensus quickly emerged that all would "work together for the good of the state and the preservation of the house of the Medici and the maintenance of the league."

While many historians, including Machiavelli, have assumed that the outcome of this meeting was a foregone conclusion, subsequent events reveal that Soderini had at least considered briefly taking the opposite course. Indeed, in supporting Lorenzo's claim, he had not renounced his personal ambition. As late as December 1, Sacramoro was fretting about the possibility that Soderini would betray the cause, concluding, however, that he lacked the popular following to strike out on his own: "The common people don't believe he is so good as he is clever, and therefore I don't think that he can expect all the spices to be sold at his house." The colorful turn of phrase captures the shrewd calculation behind Soderini's decision, which was based less on personal loyalty than on a clear-eyed assessment of his market value. He was smart enough to know that without a popular following he could never rally the leadership behind him, much less the city as a whole. Like the leaders of the Hill in 1466, he could only unseat the Medici by posing as the champion of democratic reform, a role to which his past history made him singularly unsuited and that might unleash forces he would be hard pressed to control. By standing before the assembled leaders of the state and urging them to throw their support behind Lorenzo and Giuliano he hoped to retain, and even to strengthen, his role as the éminence grise of the regime. It was a role to which he was eminently suited and, as subsequent events were to reveal, it is clear he now thought of himself as, in effect, the regent to the young and inexperienced Medici heir.

Thus it was that the following morning a delegation of "leaders, knights and citizens," led again by Tommaso Soderini, called upon Lorenzo and Giuliano at the Via Larga, to pay their respects and to place control of the state into their hands.* Lorenzo, though outwardly unchanged from the youth of yesterday, would have grown enormously in their eyes. From the dutiful son ably helping his father he had become overnight the pater familias, the lord of his household with almost unlimited powers beneath his own roof. The palace through which these distinguished gentlemen walked—the most magnificent in all of Florence and filled to the rafters with works of art and antiques that would turn many a king green with envy—was now his personal property. Though only a youth of twenty, the riches at his disposal, the vast estates and far-flung business enterprises that he now commanded, gave him a gravitas that yesterday he lacked.

Lorenzo received the delegation dressed in mourning black in the great hall beneath the enormous canvases by Pollaiuolo representing the labors of Hercules, a hero to whom another great artist would one day compare him.† He responded to the delegation's offer with words of admirable humility. Unworthy as he was of the honor, and aware of how much he would still have to rely on the wisdom of those older and wiser than he, he would, for the sake of his family and his country, accept what was so generously proffered:

> The second day after [my father's] death, [he wrote many years later] although I, Lorenzo, was very young, being twenty years of age, the principal men of the city and of the State came to us in our

---

* The extent of Giuliano's power and influence in the government has been much debated. In the beginning, at least, Lorenzo was the dominant figure while his brother was a valuable assistant.

† Michelangelo's now lost *Hercules* was a posthumous tribute to his friend and patron.

house to condole with us on our loss and to encourage me to take charge of the city and of the State, as my grandfather and my father had done. This I did, though on account of my youth and the great responsibility and perils arising therefrom, with great reluctance, solely for the safety of our friends and of our possessions. For it is ill living in Florence for the rich unless they rule the state. Till now we have succeeded with honor and renown, which I attribute not to prudence but to the grace of God and the good conduct of my predecessors.

The picture of the reluctant prince taking up the burden of rule with a heavy heart strikes many as disingenuous at best. His critics point out that days, and even years, before, Lorenzo had been preparing himself for this moment. His letters to the duke of Milan do not show someone taking up the scepter only grudgingly but, on the contrary, reveal someone who desperately sought power. It is also certain that Lorenzo was deeply involved in the behind-the-scenes maneuvering that culminated in the mass meeting at Sant'Antonio; his agents were heavily represented in the crowd and, like party bosses at a convention, labored diligently to ensure a successful outcome. Even before the crowd had dispersed Lorenzo knew he had prevailed.

But for all the hard work that had gone into assuring his succession, his reluctance to take up the burden was very real. To don the mantle once worn by Cosimo, *Pater Patriae,* and just lately slipped from the shoulders of his father, was the culmination of his ambitions, but he was under no illusions as to the difficulties he would face or the onerous daily pressures under which he would stagger. Already adult responsibilities had begun to squeeze out youthful pastimes; now those burdens would be infinitely multiplied.

The truth was that Lorenzo had no choice but to accept what was offered to him. His explanation that he did so "solely for the safety of our friends and of our possessions" is disarmingly candid. At the tender age of twenty, Lorenzo was now both the patriarch of his extended family and the father of his nation. From the peasants employed on their many estates to the workers in the various factories floating on capital from the Medici bank, there were literally thousands of souls counting on his wise and benevolent leadership. He was sufficiently versed in the ways of Florentine government to understand that he could hardly meet his obligations without a controlling hand on the spigots through which patronage flowed. "For it is ill living in Florence for the rich unless they rule the state," he wrote, as pithy a critique of the political system as ever penned. But if he recognized the corruption inherent in this system of government, he had no thought of reforming practices hallowed by long usage. His Medici forebears were as adept as any in making sure their friends profited and their enemies suffered, and Lorenzo felt that duty demanded he do no less.

Similar factors motivated those who called on him that December morning. These were men who had prospered both politically and financially under Cosimo and his son and who stood to lose in the uncertainty accompanying a change of regime. Along with, perhaps, genuine sorrow at the loss of a trusted colleague and admiration for Lorenzo, one can sense their hard calculation. Lorenzo, while no doubt moved by their expressions of sympathy, was sufficiently realistic to understand that and self-interest, rather than bonds of affection, was what led these men to his door that day.

Piero's funeral, like his father's before him, was an understated affair, the coffin traveling the few blocks from the palace to the church draped in the simple black cloth of an ordinary citizen and escorted by a contingent of priests and monks of institutions blessed by Medici patronage. Ambassadors of both the king of Naples and the duke of Milan formed part of the procession, as did the *condottiere* Roberto di Sanseverino, but few other dignitaries accompanied Lorenzo, Giuliano, and their family to San Lorenzo. Once inside the church the few guttering candles dimly illuminating the great basilica added to the somber mood of the funeral mass. With the last echo of the concluding *Agnus Dei,* Piero was laid to rest beside his brother, Giovanni, in the family sacristy.*

Donato Acciaiuoli, who had delivered the eulogy on the occasion of

---

* The magnificent tomb that Lorenzo and Giuliano commissioned to hold the remains of Giovanni and Piero was created by Verrocchio with help from his assistant Leonardo da Vinci. Work on the tomb was begun shortly after Piero's death.

Cosimo's death, was one of countless distinguished gentlemen who wrote Lorenzo consoling him on his loss: "When shall we find another so reasonable in council, so just, true, mild in character, so loving towards home, relations, friends, so worthy of respect, as your excellent father, who has been taken from us to our great sorrow." Lorenzo's comments on his father's death are unrevealing; the letters he wrote in the following days are filled with conventional expressions of sorrow and a recognition of the heavy responsibilities under which he labored, but they are formal exercises and convey little of the emotional turmoil of the moment. A more vivid testament to Lorenzo's feelings comes in a letter by Marco Parenti, who witnessed the funeral. Catching a glimpse of the new ruler in a rare moment of vulnerability, he reported that Lorenzo wept openly on his way back from church.

Domenico Ghirlandaio, *Annunciation to Zachariah* (detail), showing Marsilio Ficino, Cristoforo Landino, Angelo Poliziano, and Gentile Becchi, 1483–86, Sta. Trinita (Art Resource)

IX. MASTER OF THE SHOP

"They are agreed that the private affairs of the Signoria shall pass through Lorenzo's hands in the same manner as previously through those of his father."

—NICCOLÒ ROBERTI, FERRARESE AMBASSADOR

IN HIS PHILOSOPHICAL DIALOGUE, *DISPUTATIONES Camaldulenses,* the humanist Cristoforo Landino includes an idealized portrait of Lorenzo shortly before his assumption of power. The setting is the cloister of the Camaldoli, an isolated monastery on the wooded slopes of the Apennine foothills; the time is the autumn of 1468; and the conversation revolves around the rights and responsibilities of a citizen in a free republic.* The conversation, which involves many of Florence's leading intellectuals—including both Lorenzo and Giuliano, the expatriate Leon Battista Alberti, Marsilio Ficino, Donato Acciaiuoli, and, intriguingly, Lorenzo's secret enemy Alamanno Rinuccini—takes place in the kind of rural setting Lorenzo loved and often wrote about himself, a fragrant meadow shaded by a beech tree overhanging a clear spring. The idyllic surroundings provide a perfect foil for the ensuing debate over the relative merits of the active and contemplative life, though the attractions of this rustic spot might seem to tip the balance in favor of the latter.

Landino's narrative does not pretend to provide a realistic portrayal of the young Lorenzo. His presence in this gathering is plausible enough since he often enjoyed such learned discourses and preferred to engage in

---

* Though set in 1468, the work was probably written in 1472, shortly after the death of the main protagonist, Leon Battista Alberti. (See the introduction to the *Disputationes Camaldulenses* by Peter Lohe, especially xxx–xxxiii, for a full discussion of the controversies surrounding the dating of the manuscript.) Published in 1480, the work was dedicated to Federico da Montefeltro.

them in the midst of natural beauty. But the real reason for his inclusion is to provide dramatic context for what might otherwise seem to be an abstruse philosophical debate. For someone about to take over the government of a powerful city-state, the question Landino raises is of more than academic interest. Should one retire from the hustle and bustle of civic life, with its perpetual quarrels and inevitable compromises, in order to attain true wisdom, as Alberti urges? Or, in the words Landino puts in Lorenzo's mouth, is it one's obligation to use the wisdom thus acquired for the benefit of one's compatriots? For no one were these questions as pressing as they were for the young man on the verge of taking his place as the first citizen of the republic.

While Landino gives to Lorenzo the role of advocate for the active life, it is Alberti who strikes a balance between the two worlds more in keeping with Lorenzo's own sense of himself:

But if [philosophy] be an occupation suitable for all men of learning, it is more particularly so for you, on whom the direction of the affairs of the republic is likely, from the increasing infirmities of your father, soon to devolve. For although, Lorenzo, you have given proof of such virtues as would induce us to think them rather of divine than human origin; although there seems to be no undertaking so momentous as not to be accomplished by that prudence and courage which you have displayed, even in your early years; and although the impulse of youthful ambition, and the full enjoyment of those gifts of fortune which have often intoxicated men of high expectation and great virtue, have never yet been able to impel you beyond the just bounds of moderation; yet, both you and that republic which you are shortly to direct, or rather which now in a great measure reposes in your care, will derive important advantages from those hours of leisure, which you may pass either in solitary meditation, or social discussion, on the origin and nature of the human mind. For it is impossible that any person should rightly direct the affairs of the public, unless he had previously established in himself virtuous habits, and enlightened his understanding with that knowledge, which will enable him clearly to discern why he is called into existence, what is due to others, and what to himself.

In practice Lorenzo found it far more difficult to find the leisure necessary for intellectual growth in his increasingly hectic schedule. His long philosophical poem *The Supreme Good*, whose title echoes the second part of Landino's dialogue, includes a passage in which his old friend and mentor, Marsilio Ficino, scolds him for frittering away the afternoon in the countryside when he should be in Florence attending to his duties. "It does amaze me greatly, though, to find you, Lauro, on this wooded mountain slope," the philosopher gently chides his pupil,

> *"not that your presence doesn't bring me joy.*
> *Who counseled you to leave your native city?*
> *You know the burdens your familial*
> *and civic duties put upon your shoulders."*

To which Lorenzo responds:

> *"The things of which you speak*
> *bring on such agony that the mere thought*
> *of them enfeebles me and makes me grieve.*
> *I've fled, a while, those vexing public cares*
> *in order to refresh my soul by pondering*
> *the pastoral way of life, a life I envy."*

In part Lorenzo is simply poking fun at himself. Despite his frenetic work pace, he liked to portray himself as a man addicted to indolence and only reluctantly shouldering the cares of state. But Lorenzo would never have exchanged his life of privilege for that of a simple shepherd, nor did he really expect his audience to believe him. Nonetheless, the poem reflects a genuine distress at the endless drudgery of his official duties. To exercise power was his birthright but not his passion. He still took his greatest pleasure in vigorous outdoor activities, composing verses on his favorite themes, and in pleasant conversation with his learned and witty friends. The oceans of official correspondence he was now required to wade through with the aid of only a few secretaries, the constant demands made on his time by foreign ambassadors, government officials, and humble petitioners, the obligation to entertain lavishly every visiting dignitary, all stole from him precious seconds that could be better spent on the things he loved. He must often have wondered if the glory of being his father's son was worth the price.

As Lorenzo prepared to receive the distinguished delegation of leading Florentines the day after his father's death, he was under no illusions as to the burdens he was assuming. But what, after all, were Tommaso Soderini and his colleagues offering him that December morning? He received no official title from their hands; after their departure he was, as he had been before, a simple citizen of Florence—a particularly rich and prominent one, but one whose name would not appear in the roll of any of the key positions of the government. If asked to name the current head of state, Florentines would have pointed not to Lorenzo but to Piero di Lutozzo Nasi, who, dressed in his ceremonial robes and living in pampered isolation in the *palazzo* as *Gonfaloniere di Giustizia,* presided over the deliberations of the *Signoria* for his two-month term of office.

In fact, as Marco Parenti pointed out, neither the assembly at Sant'Antonio, nor the delegation of *principali* who conveyed their decision to offer Lorenzo the preeminent role in the governing of the state, had any official standing. "It was merely a ceremony, of little weight." But it was crucial nonetheless, for it provided Lorenzo a legitimacy his father had lacked. The absence of a similar consensus at the time of Cosimo's death led directly to the crisis two years later, and it was in order to avoid such confusion that Tommaso Soderini and his fellow magnates had convened the meeting at Sant'Antonio. It was a clever move, for it bound Lorenzo to them even as it raised him to a position of authority. The agreement among the leading members of the regime to defer to Lorenzo was practically the sole basis of his power, and it imposed strict limitations on his freedom of action. Dependent as he was on their continued goodwill, his policies were likely to reflect the combined wisdom of the men who had eased his way to power.

Some observers even asserted that the city was returning to the kind of collective rule that had characterized Florentine government before Cosimo's day. Six months after Lorenzo took power, Bartolomeo Bonatto reported to his boss, Ludovico Gonzaga, Marquis of Mantua: "Some say that this city is taking a republican path, acknowledging the authority of the *Signoria* in the *Palazzo Vecchio.* Not a soul goes to Lorenzo's house, and he stays there behind locked doors, seemingly interested only in mercantile affairs, and he goes to the palace only when invited." Bonatto's comment recalls Marco Parenti's description of Piero in 1465, but now, as then, the writer underestimated the resilience and resourcefulness of the Medici. Lorenzo knew that at this early stage of his career an appearance of humility was likely to succeed where a brazen display of power would merely offend. Like Cosimo, he was shrewd enough to know that authority was often most effectively wielded when least visible. Deferring to the duly elected authorities reassured those who had initially feared placing their fates in the hands of one so young and inexperienced.

How was it that a mere handful of men controlled a government that was almost without precedent in the thoroughness of its democratic impulse?* Though by the standards of modern democracies the franchise was restrictive—open only to those male citizens enrolled in one of the major or minor guilds—those eligible citizens were expected not only to vote but to participate actively in their own government. In theory the political class consisted of the entire citizen body, but by the time of the Medici ascendance the reality was far different. While small-scale merchants like Marco Parenti continued to participate in the political system, real power was closely held by the inner circle of the *reggimento*. According to Benedetto Dei, whose detailed survey of Florence in the year 1472 is an invaluable resource on issues of political, economic, and cultural concern, the effective government rested in the hands of thirty-four men, with Lorenzo's and Tommaso Soderini's names topping the list.[†]

---

* According to Giovanni Cavalcanti, a contemporary of Cosimo's, during the Albizzi oligarchy the government was in the hands of some seventy or so *principali* who rotated through the various *pratiche* (committees) where policy was debated and legislation proposed. Within this group, certain key figures like Maso degli Albizzi or Niccolò da Uzzano dominated through their prestige and force of personality. In the Medici era, various attempts to enshrine a reliable inner core in such councils as the One Hundred, the Seventy, and the Forty give some idea of the small number of men whose loyalty and prestige entitled them to a permanent place in the inner circle. By contrast, those constitutionally eligible for high office—and who, if the constitution were followed to the letter, could expect to serve at numerous times in their lives—numbered in the thousands. In theory anyone matriculated in one of the Major Guilds or Minor Guilds should have played his part in the government of the city. In reality, most found themselves on the outside looking in.

[†] He lists twelve whom he calls "principals" of the government. Another group, which includes, interestingly, Jacopo de' Pazzi, a man regarded as Lorenzo's enemy, he refers to as belonging to the "second tier of the state" (see Dei, *Cronica*, 35v).

Some sense of the way a small number of leading citizens worked behind the scenes to run things in Medicean Florence is revealed in a letter written by the Ferrarese ambassador, Niccolò Roberti, a couple of days after Piero's death: "They are agreed that the private affairs of the *Signoria* shall pass through Lorenzo's hands in the same manner as previously through those of his father, for which purposes his friends will take care to procure him credit and reputation from the beginning. They can easily do so, for they have the government in their hands, and the ballot-boxes at their disposal." Though this letter reflects the foreigner's tendency to underestimate the difficulty of imposing order on the notoriously fractious Florentines, it accurately describes the manipulation of the electoral process by which the Medici and their partisans controlled the machinery of government.

Though nowhere officially acknowledged, the *reggimento* was a palpable reality to Florentines. They knew that real power resided within this somewhat ill-defined group whose function was to steer the ship of state that so often in the past had followed an erratic course. They accomplished this, in part, by agreeing amongst themselves upon a single captain, a position that from Cosimo's day had been unofficially reserved for the head of the Medici household. While there was nothing inevitable about this choice—which, as we have seen, was often challenged by prominent men who felt they had a better claim—history would prove that only the magic of the Medici name could rally sufficient support. As Roberti reported, the consensus reached at Sant'Antonio was to acknowledge "one lord and superior" in the person of Lorenzo, a decision made more palatable to the ambitious because it was assumed that this inexperienced youth would place himself in their capable hands.

When describing Lorenzo's rise to power it is always important to keep in mind that the alternative to Medici rule was not democracy as we understand it today, but rather a form of oligarchy in which the self-appointed "worthiest" citizens controlled the great mass of the disenfranchised. Many so-called republicans agreed with Giovanni Cavalcanti's description of the common people as either "the stupid, crazy mob" or "the brutish masses," and one of the complaints most frequently leveled at the Medici regime was that they tried to dilute the ranks of the aristocracy with common artisans and new men. In Guicciardini's *Dialogue on the Government of Florence*, written a few decades after Lorenzo's death, Piero Capponi states the case for the opposition: "Our intention was to remove the city from the power of one man and restore liberty, as has been done. It is true that we wanted to avoid giving the government absolutely to the people, but rather to place it in the hands of the leading and worthiest citizens, to make it a government of men of worth rather than a totally popular regime. We did not, however, want to restrict it to so few that it would not be free, nor to slacken the bridle so much that it came into the hands of the masses, with no distinction made between one person and another."

In fact there is plenty of evidence that Medici rule actually encouraged social mobility as the *reggimento* co-opted members of the artisan class to serve as a counterweight to the older families who were their most intractable enemies. Bernardo del Nero, another speaker in Guicciardini's *Dialogue,* makes the case for Medici rule: "I have enjoyed a very long friendship with the Medici and I am infinitely indebted to that family. Not being of noble birth nor surrounded by relations like you three, I have received favors from them and have been elevated and made equal to all those who would normally have preceded me in being awarded political offices and honors in the city."* Piero Guicciardini, the historian's father, analyzing the scrutiny of 1484, wrote that the most humble, having once made a respectable showing in one election, "in another gain something better, according to their ability, or their wealth, and in a short time . . . they ascend from the lowest level and proceed to the next, always rising, and in their place are succeeded by even newer men to fill up the lowest ranks, and thus continually new men make the grade, and in order to give them a place in the governing class it is necessary to eliminate from it long-established citizens; and that is what is actually done." Indeed it is just this kind of social mobility that Medici critics found so distasteful, believing that under the current regime the social order had been stood on its head.

Preserving the delicate balance between old and new families, great merchants and simple shopkeepers, required all of Lorenzo's tact. A few days after his accession to power the Milanese ambassador offered Lorenzo these words of advice: "Among other things [he reported to Duke Galeazzo] I told Lorenzo that he must be able to show the leading citizens that he is of a different nature than his father, who wanted always to show his superior-

---

* Medici opponents like Alamanno Rinuccini feared this social mobility. He described del Nero as "a base rag dealer . . . most iniquitous, most rapacious, bearing enmity toward all upstanding citizens" (see Rinuccini, *Ricordi Storici,* cxxxvii).

ity . . . and to do it in such a way that others will not feel he has his foot on their throats." Lorenzo had already expressed similar reservations about Piero's methods, and announced his intention to "follow his grandfather's example and use, as much as possible, constitutional methods." But it was more a matter of style than substance. In the intimate world of Florentine politics success depended on one's ability to cultivate friendships and soothe easily bruised egos. Piero, a man of many virtues, fell short in those vital interpersonal skills. Lorenzo's future would depend on his ability to cajole, persuade, mollify, and sometimes play off one ambitious ego against another; it was a role that required an ability to judge the strengths and weaknesses of his rivals, qualities that Lorenzo had learned above all from his grandfather. His long apprenticeship as his father's right-hand man had given him a keen appreciation of the subtleties of politics in Florence, and throughout that period, *principali* like Manno Temperani, Rodolfo Pandolfini, and Tommaso Soderini had an opportunity to take their measure of the youth and had determined he was someone they could work with.

Perhaps equally important, they had concluded they could not work with each other, preferring to give supreme power to an untested youth than to one of their rivals. Lorenzo was the beneficiary of the mutual jealousies and suspicions that divided the magnates. It was an inherently unstable situation in which coalitions, quickly formed and quickly broken, constantly threatened the fragile consensus that had lifted Lorenzo to power.

There is no single word to describe Lorenzo's status. Fifteenth-century Florentines sometimes likened him to a "master of the shop," a familiar term in a city of craftsmen and merchants. The phrase conveys something of the intimate, informal nature of a relationship between a paternalistic boss and his employees. Like any good master, Lorenzo was expected to run the city for the benefit of all and to know each of his underlings by name. Florentines expected to have a personal relationship with their leaders, and even the man at the top could not avoid being collared on the street by the least of his subjects and forced to listen while they filled his ears with a long list of complaints.

Some modern historians have likened the various heads of the Medici household to Mafia dons,* ruling the city through terror and intimidation while pocketing profits from their corrupt enterprises. Others eulogize the

---

* Public television recently ran a series titled *The Medici: Godfathers of the Renaissance.*

Medici as altruistic statesmen and patrons of the arts, reluctantly shouldering the burdens of government for the sake of their country—less
interested in power than in nurturing masterpieces of art and literature.*
Those seduced by the glories of Renaissance Florence often paint too
uncritical a picture of the family whose name has become synonymous
with enlightened artistic patronage (and even here their behavior was
hardly disinterested), but the first analogy is clearly inadequate. Unlike the
fictional Don Corleone or Tony Soprano, and resembling even less real-
life thugs like John Gotti, the Medici were not bosses of a parasitic organization that leeched off the otherwise healthy body politic. Unofficial
parties of the kind they set up were essential to the proper functioning of
the government. Without the sinew provided by the Medici and their
allies—or by the Albizzi and theirs before them—the government lacked
the strength to enforce its legitimate will.

The origins of Florence's weak constitutional government are to be
found in the medieval city. The merchants who had established the commune in the twelfth and thirteenth centuries had been so concerned about
the potential for tyranny that they weakened government institutions to
the point of debility—making it easy prey for exactly those would-be
tyrants they had feared. Rotating men in and out of office before they had
a chance to familiarize themselves with their duties made it difficult for
them to seize power, but it also made it next to impossible to develop consistent policies or strategies. Foreign ambassadors and heads of state were
driven to despair by a government that could not seem to make up its
mind or follow through on a policy once adopted. Sacramoro was only
one of many ambassadors who complained about the difficulties of dealing with the Florentine government. In the midst of the Rimini War, when
the seriousness of the situation demanded swift action, the proposal to

---

* To some extent these differences can be ascribed to the different disciplines of the scholars who study the Medici: political historians tend to focus on the way they undermined
the republican institutions of earlier centuries; art historians who focus on their role as
patrons tend to be more forgiving of the stratagems they used to maintain themselves in
power. While in earlier centuries historians dazzled by the achievements of the Florentine Renaissance were often too uncritical of the family that presided over its golden age,
contemporary scholars have gone too far in the other direction by underestimating the
role Cosimo, Piero, and Lorenzo played in fostering the artistic achievements of these
years.

renew the contract of the *condottiere* Roberto di Sanseverino made its leisurely round from committee to committee with no one apparently willing or able to take responsibility. "Today the proposal went before the *Signoria* and the Colleges according to their constitution and the council of Twenty," wrote Sacramoro in frustration, "then it was put before the Council of 100 . . . tomorrow it will be attempted to place it before the Council of the People."

Exasperating as all this was, Lorenzo, like his father and grandfather before him, could not extinguish these myriad bodies that allowed a majority of citizens at least a nominal role in their own government, and he resisted the advice of foreigners (including Sacramoro himself) to abolish them and set himself up as despot. To the citizens of Florence, inefficiency was the very essence of their liberty and they resisted any changes to the letter of their constitution, preferring instead the evasions and obfuscations that characterized the Medici regime.*

Lorenzo's political honeymoon was brief. The sense of common purpose that had been so impressive on the night of December 2 quickly disintegrated under the pressure of events. Florence's two key allies, Naples and Milan, continued to bicker and, like children in a messy divorce, the Florentines were pulled this way and that in a bitter contest of wills. By late December 1469, the rift was so serious that a conference of the three allies was hastily organized in Florence to try to resolve their differences. But far from bringing the two rivals closer together the conference merely served as a platform from which the ambassadors could hurl accusations at each other at closer range. The critical rupture came in late March. Responding to rumors that Ferrante was involved in secret negotiations with Venice, Galeazzo Maria Sforza, much to the consternation of Lorenzo and most Florentines, suddenly withdrew his delegates from the conference. It was for many Florentines merely the latest act of bad faith on the part of an ally

---

* Strange as the Florentine system might seem, contemporary Americans should feel a certain twinge of recognition. It was the same suspicion of too much power concentrated in too few hands that led to the American system of a government by "checks and balances." Though Florentines singularly failed to strike the right balance, their goals were essentially the same as those of James Madison and the other Founding Fathers.

who always showed himself ready to sacrifice his friends to expedience. (In the Colleonic War, for instance, Sforza had practically extorted money from the republic in return for his services, which were in any case so incompetently rendered that they would have been too expensive had they been given for free.) On April 11, 1470, the Neapolitans followed suit. Florentines formed themselves into two distinct and hostile political camps: war "hawks" favored the Neapolitans, who wished to pursue the Rimini War with vigor, and the "doves" favored Milan's demands for an early peace. Lorenzo, who would have preferred to be guided by the collective wisdom of the *reggimento*, now found the leading men divided against themselves.

New to his position and still unsure of himself, he leaned heavily on his uncle Tommaso. While Sacramoro warned him that Soderini's interests were not necessarily his own, Lorenzo had a hard time convincing himself that his uncle would pursue any policy at odds with the interests of the Medici family. Soderini had backed Lorenzo at the most critical moment and had earned his gratitude. From the beginning he was Lorenzo's most trusted advisor and, according to many, the real power behind the throne. The consummate political insider, Soderini thrived in the chaos that resulted from the collapse of the triple alliance, using the atmosphere of crisis to shore up his own influence with Lorenzo and increase his leverage within the inner circle.* But as he consolidated his position he aroused resentment among the other magnates, who were put off by his conspiratorial ways and tendency to gorge himself at the public trough.

Respected and even feared, Soderini was not well liked. Alessandra Strozzi once declared that Soderini walked about the city with "honey in his mouth and a knife in his belt," and there is no evidence that the years had mellowed his passion for political skullduggery. Colleagues who had recently helped him smooth the way for Lorenzo, particularly Luigi Guicciardini and Antonio Ridolfi, now felt they had been shunted aside. Jealous of his unique standing with the new ruler of Florence, they now sought every means to bring him down. It did not take them long to find an oppor-

---

* According to Sacramoro's analysis, the course Soderini chose over the coming months (initially portraying himself as a partisan of Milan while moving inexorably into the camp of the king of Naples) was determined by his belief that in times of war "the offices and affairs . . . must be entrusted to a smaller number in order to be kept more secret" (see Clarke, 185).

tunity. Soderini's propensity to mingle private affairs with public funds, a practice common to all Florentine politicians but one in which Soderini was known to be particularly adept, opened him to the charge of corruption. In an effort to embarrass him in the eyes of Lorenzo and the wider public, his rivals in the government exposed some of the shady practices by which the republic's treasure had found its way into his pockets. It was a scandal that might have finished the career of a lesser man, but Soderini was too shrewd a player to allow himself to be so easily sidelined. Returning the disputed money, he now struck back, pushing an ordinance through the *Otto di Guardia* (Florence's security apparatus, which he had filled with his own partisans), banishing his chief opponents from Florence.

Having outmaneuvered his enemies, Soderini now set his sights on Lorenzo, the one man in Florence whose prestige rivaled his own. The confrontation between the two marks not only an important moment in the education of the young ruler of Florence, but is an episode that sheds much light on the backstairs intrigue that Florentine politicians had long ago mastered.* Its resolution in Lorenzo's favor, surprising to many who noted the wide discrepancy in the two combatants' experience, reveals a natural instinct for the political game.

The confrontation came over the Florentine response to the rift that had opened up between Naples and Milan. After months of prevaricating in which no one, including the Milanese ambassador, could say which side Tommaso Soderini was on, he tipped his hand at a meeting held April 11, 1470, the very day the Neapolitan delegation was set to leave Florence. Arguing that Milan was to blame, he now proposed a new system of alliances built around the axis of Naples and Venice. In tilting toward Naples, Soderini was reflecting the general mood of Florentines, who were heartily sick of the duke's high-handed ways. Even Lorenzo and Luigi Guicciardini, both strong adherents of Milan, concluded that Naples must be placated to prevent them from bolting the alliance.

But while Lorenzo was willing to feint in the direction of Naples in order to pressure the duke to return to the fold, he could not abandon his chief foreign ally. Only a few months earlier the duke had put his prestige on the

---

* It is no surprise that this same city gave birth a generation hence to Niccolò Machiavelli, the first modern political scientist and a man whose name has become, rather unjustly, synonymous with the cynical scheming for power.

line for Lorenzo and Giuliano, writing to the *Signoria* that he cherished them as brothers. For almost two decades the houses of the Medici and the Sforza had been intimately linked in the minds of Florentines and however much Lorenzo was irritated by the Galeazzo Maria's feckless policies, he could not abandon him without undercutting one of the strongest props of his regime. In other words, while Soderini could afford to adapt to circumstances, Lorenzo was wedded, for good or ill, to the Milanese cause.

At first it seemed as if Soderini would be successful in shepherding Florence into the Neapolitan camp, particularly after the appointment his close friend, the staunchly partisan Otto Niccolini, as ambassador to the southern kingdom. Immediately upon taking up his appointment, Niccolini began writing a series of letters calculated to frighten the Florentine government into precipitous action. In a private letter to Soderini, dated April 25, the ambassador indicated (prematurely as it turned out) that Naples had already concluded a treaty with Venice. (It was a sign of Soderini's growing influence that most of Niccolini's correspondence now went directly to him, rather than to Lorenzo or through official channels.) With the geopolitical realignment already an accomplished fact, he said, Florence must jump on board to avoid being left out in the cold.

King Ferrante's threat to leave Florence in the lurch for an understanding with Venice presented the government with an uncomfortable dilemma. While many wished to maintain the old triple league that had kept Italy relatively peaceful, they could not afford to be shut out of the new system of alliances. With Otto's letters in hand, Soderini now called a *Pratica* for May 5.* It was a typical bit of partisan sleight-of-hand of the kind so often practiced in Florentine politics: organized in haste and secrecy, most of the duke's supporters were unaware it was taking place until after it was already over. It was a sign of how confident Soderini felt that Lorenzo was not informed of the meeting and almost missed it. By the time he arrived, Lorenzo confessed to Sforza, he "found the letter [with instructions for the ambassador] already completed, so that it was not possible to fix it, so hastily was it written and sent off by horse." In public Soderini continued to claim that he was taking Ferrante's side merely to save the triple alliance, but his private correspondence with Otto Niccolini reveals him to be very much the king's man. "Let us abide by [the

---

* A *Pratica* was a special committee convened to resolve particularly weighty issues.

king's] advice," he wrote, "and follow where ever his Majesty shall lead us."

Sforza must have been deeply disappointed that the man for whom he had done so much now proved himself unable or unwilling to fight for his interests. The *Pratica* of May 5 was a grave embarrassment for Lorenzo, who had been outflanked by an old hand at the political game. It also proved to be his wake-up call. When Sacramoro relayed the duke's displeasure at the course Florence was taking, Lorenzo and Luigi Guicciardini became "upset and desperate, feeling that they have been reduced to an extremity, as they see their reputation has been placed in serious danger."

The first sign that Lorenzo had found his stride came late in May of 1470. Ferrante, hoping to prod Florence into committing to the Neapolitan side, demanded that she openly declare her intentions without consulting her northern ally. Not wishing to offend Ferrante, still one of the pillars of the triple alliance, but now certain that he must defend the duke's interests at any cost, Lorenzo deftly played for time. Without dismissing the king's offer, he convinced the government of Florence that it should accept no deal from Naples until *after* it had heard from the duke. This was a critical step since the king and his Florentine supporters—among whom Soderini was now a leading exponent—hoped they could commit Florence to the Neapolitan side before Milan could respond, thus placing Sforza in the difficult position of reentering the alliance on their terms or risk being left out altogether.

The delay was a tactical victory for Lorenzo and the duke, one that halted the momentum that had been building in favor of Naples. The critical showdown came the following month. By this time Soderini had publicly committed himself to the king. Indeed rumors were rife that his newfound allegiance to Ferrante had been helped along by generous donations to Soderini's bank account.

But Sacramoro had been busy as well, urging his usually tight-fisted boss to match the king bribe for bribe. If ducats in the pockets of his partisans was the carrot, the Milanese ambassador also wielded a heavy stick, threatening that the duke would withdraw his ambassador should Florence cut a separate deal with Naples. In this charged atmosphere another *Pratica* was called for June 27. Lorenzo now showed that he had learned a thing or two since the council held the previous month. This time Lorenzo made sure that the meeting was dominated by *his* men, who now succeeded in shouting down their rivals. The demonstration of vigor and purpose by the newly minted Medici patriarch was enough to convince many fence-sitters to leap into the fray on Lorenzo's side. By the end of the tempestuous meeting Soderini and his followers, seeing that the winds had suddenly shifted, reluctantly agreed to instruct Otto Niccolini not to conclude a separate treaty with Naples. The pro-Naples faction was dealt another blow when it was discovered that Venice had rejected King Ferrante's terms for an alliance, paving the way for an eventual restoration of the league on its original terms. Lorenzo could thus plausibly declare that through delay he had salvaged the triple alliance and secured the peace of Italy. In Sacramoro's account, Soderini and the pro-Naples faction were "white" with shock over the sudden turn of events.

On the twelfth of July Lorenzo reported the happy news that Naples had agreed to rejoin the league. So overjoyed were Florentines at the restoration of the old league, Lorenzo reported to his ambassador in Milan, that church bells pealed throughout the city and at night the streets were illuminated by dozens of bonfires. Much of the credit went to Lorenzo himself, who now emerged from the shadow of the men who had raised him to power. Soderini, by contrast, had been knocked down a peg or two. He had faltered because he forgot the lesson he seemed to have absorbed in December—that is, how difficult it was to go toe-to-toe against a Medici, even one as inexperienced as Lorenzo, because however much the ruling family was resented, most of the *principali* preferred to take their business to the Via Larga rather than to try their luck on someone else's doorstep. Now properly chastened, Soderini returned to the fold. Throughout the remainder of his political career he would serve as a diligent, if by no means uncritical, servant of the Medici regime.

Lorenzo's triumph was marked by a visit in March 1471 by the duke and duchess of Milan, accompanied by 1,500 mounts and four hundred footmen, "all lords and worthy persons and . . . all in courtly style, with pomp and without arms." The official reason given for the trip was to visit the church of Santissima Annunziata, whose miracle-working image of the Virgin was the destination of many a pilgrim, but it was also a public affirmation of the ties of friendship binding the two cities and the two leaders. As on his earlier trip to Florence, Galeazzo Maria Sforza was put up in Lorenzo's palace on the Via Larga. Florentines were both fascinated and scandalized by the splendor of the Milanese: there were men to tend the hawks, others to keep the hounds, liveried grooms and liveried servants, trumpeters and fife players, along with assorted courtiers, cooks, jesters, and bodyguards—not to mention a separate suite to attend to the needs of the duchess. It was said that the cost of furnishing them all with mounts and wardrobes of silk and gold amounted to no less than 200,000 florins. For Lorenzo the visit provided both an opportunity to bask in the reflected glory of his princely friend and to demonstrate, by way of contrast, the relative sobriety of his own lifestyle.

In the end, the carefully orchestrated visit was less than a resounding success. Many Florentines resented the burden of putting up such a vast and hungry horde and were offended by their self-indulgent guests, who would not even forgo eating meat during Lent. It was as punishment for such impiety that, according to popular opinion, the church of Santo Spirito caught fire during a spectacle staged in honor of the duke. While Sforza offered to pay for repairs, for many Florentines, including no doubt Lorenzo himself, the visit could not end soon enough.

Though Lorenzo had won a decisive victory over his domestic rivals, the divisions and political infighting that marked his first months as leader illustrated the inadequacy of the ad hoc electoral controls that served as the basis of Medici power. The council of One Hundred (il Cento)—a body created in 1458 that had co-opted much of the authority of the older, more democratic councils of the people and of the commune—had become a club of powerful and ambitious men who were as likely to oppose as to support the head of the Medici household. Most of the opposition to Lorenzo came, in fact, from those who served on this elite council, just as it was members of the inner circle who almost succeeded in overthrowing Piero's regime in 1466. According to Francesco Guicciardini, whose grandfather and great-uncle were both frequent members, it was not uncommon for the One Hundred to reject a slate of candidates proposed by Lorenzo and his friends.

How could Lorenzo guarantee that the vast majority of the *reggimento* would consist of Medici loyalists?—something that neither he nor his predecessors had been able to achieve with any consistency. The *Gonfaloniere di Giustizia* himself, Carlo Pandolfini, had been among those who conspired with Tommaso in the *Pratica* of March to ensure that Lorenzo and his partisans were shut out. The key was the committee of the *Accoppia-*

tori, usually five in number, whose job it was to screen the names that were to fill the various electoral bags used when selecting men for the *Tre Maggiori*, that is, the three highest offices of the land (the *Signoria*, which included at its head the *Gonfaloniere di Giustizia*, the *Dodici Buonuomini*, and the *Sedici Gonfalonieri*).* "If I understand matters correctly," wrote the somewhat befuddled ambassador from Milan, "whether or not Lorenzo will preserve his ascendancy depends on the reforms of the *Accoppiatori*." The *Accoppiatori* effectively managed the electoral process but the system was only as reliable as the men who comprised it.

Over the next months Lorenzo employed all his diplomatic skills and powers of persuasion, as well as the usual arm-twisting and bribery, to reform the *Accoppiatori*. His opportunity finally came when, with his staunch ally Agnolo della Stufa occupying the *Gonfaloniere*'s seat, he rammed through a bill that went a long way toward removing the One Hundred from the electoral process. Prospects for victory were greatly enhanced when the *Signoria*, following della Stufa's lead, declared that the reforms need only be passed by a bare majority in the One Hundred, rather than the usual two-thirds. Even so, the new legislation was approved by a margin of only two votes.

In the new system the *Accoppiatori* were to be selected each year by the outgoing members and the current *Signoria*. Since the *Accoppiatori* were in turn responsible for electing the *Signoria*, the whole electoral system became a kind of closed loop from which the majority of Florentine citizens was effectively excluded. As the Milanese ambassador commented,

---

* The role of the *Accoppiatori* is generally misunderstood. Even when elections were held *a mano* (by hand) as they were for much of the Medici reign, the *Accoppiatori* could not actually hand pick the candidates for office. Rather they culled from the *scrutinio*, the five-year census of Florentine citizens, those believed to be politically reliable and placed only these into the bags. Whose name was ultimately drawn from the bag remained a matter of chance so that the *Accoppiatori* could not completely control the makeup of the government at any particular moment. Given the fact that any individual was barred from holding the same office for five years and that there were restrictions placed on the number of family members holding office at the same time, the *Accoppiatori* were still obliged to place a large number of names into each bag. This ensured a wider, more representative, and more unpredictable cross section of the Florentine citizen body continued to rotate through the *Tre Maggiori*. It represented a compromise between the evident need to place some controls on the system while at the same time retaining the element of randomness that Florentines believed was essential to the functioning of their democracy.

"In this way the *Signoria* will always be that which [Lorenzo] wishes."

Having achieved a greater degree of control over the electoral process than either Cosimo or Piero, Lorenzo used the momentum to push through other initiatives. The close vote within the One Hundred over the reform of the *Accoppiatori* revealed the extent of opposition to his rule. In July 1471, with a friendly *Signoria* again seated, he called a special council (a *Balìa*) to enact a series of new measures to "arrange and correct many things in the city, where are born continuously many harmful sentiments."*

The oligarchic nature of the One Hundred was diluted by opening up membership to those from outside the ruling clique, a liberalization that allowed Lorenzo to bring in men who were personally dependent on his favor.† But the most important reform to emerge from the *Balìa* of 1471 was the creation of a permanent steering committee within the council of the One Hundred. The newly minted council of the Forty, as it was called—a permanent core within the One Hundred, largely made up of Lorenzo's closest friends and supporters and given the critical responsibility of co-opting the others—became the most effective instrument for imposing his will on the direction and composition of the government.

After little more than a year and a half in power Lorenzo had succeeded where both Cosimo and Piero had failed, providing the Medici regime an efficient and streamlined structure without destroying the republican framework that Florentines cherished. By December of 1471, Sacramoro

---

* A *Balìa* was an extraordinary council called in times of emergency authorized to reform the government. It was distinct from the *pratiche*, which were largely advisory. The most extreme option was to call a *parlamento*, an assembly of the entire citizen body in the *Piazza della Signoria*, convened only in moments of gravest danger, as in September of 1466.

† Originally the One Hundred were chosen from among a group known as the *veduti*, or "the seen." By a curious Florentine process, those whose names were selected for the office of *Gonfaloniere*—that is whose presence in the electoral bags was confirmed by having their names read out at the bimonthly election but who had not necessarily served in that capacity—constituted a privileged political caste. Even those not eligible to serve—either because they were too young, or owed taxes, or had other family members serving in important positions—still reaped the benefits of having been named. Lorenzo never reached the age where he was eligible for the office of *Gonfaloniere*, but he was frequently among the *veduti*. To be "seen" was the surest sign that one had made it in Florentine society.

could write, not without some concern, that "things have come to such a pass in this city that nothing is decided without Lorenzo's approval, and it is thought that no one else is worth a zero."

To what extent, then, had the republic under Lorenzo become a despotism in all but name? While old-line republicans like Marco Parenti and Alamanno Rinuccini—not to mention the exiles of 1466—certainly felt that the ancient institutions had become so corrupted as to reduce Florentines to the status of slaves, Lorenzo and his partisans regarded the changes as necessary modifications to a constitution that was woefully deficient. The truth, as usual, lies somewhere in between. After 1471 the government was in the hands of a narrow directorate that Lorenzo had fashioned into an efficient instrument of his will. But because the outward forms of a republic endured and the ancient councils continued to meet and to debate, much of the lively civic atmosphere of earlier decades was preserved. Indeed, criticism of Lorenzo and his methods was common enough to dispel any notion that Florentines had grown too fearful to speak their minds. Lorenzo also continued to live the life of a private citizen, conducting business from his home and mingling with the people in the streets and squares of the city. All of this fostered a climate that was far different from the absolutist states elsewhere in Italy and beyond. It should be remembered as well that what people like Parenti and Rinuccini were advocating as an alternative to Lorenzo's despotism was not anything we would now recognize as democracy. The genius of Lorenzo's system, inherited from his forebears and refined over time, was to balance oligarchical elements with democratic forms, to pay homage to time-honored customs while pruning their worst excesses. There is no doubt that, as many of his contemporaries recognized and some bitterly decried, the vast majority of citizens no longer had a say in the daily operations of their own government. But it is also difficult to imagine, given the limitations of bureaucratic structures and the rudimentary understanding of political philosophy at the time, that a better alternative could have been found. It is striking that when Florentines finally rose up against Medici "tyranny" and attempted to institute a more democratic system, they quickly reverted to form and placed in the hands of a single man powers Lorenzo never sought.

Piero della Francesca, *Federico da Montefeltro*, c. 1465 (Art Resource)

X. FAT VICTORY

"Better a lean peace than a fat victory."

—TOMMASO SODERINI QUOTING
AN OLD TUSCAN PROVERB

*"'What say you now that Volterra has been acquired?' To which
Messer Tommaso replied, 'To me it appears lost; for if you had
received it by accord, you would have had advantage and security
from it; but since you have to hold it by force, in adverse times it will
bring you weakness and trouble and in peaceful times, loss and
expense.'"*

—MACHIAVELLI, *FLORENTINE HISTORIES*

FROM THE BEGINNING, LORENZO'S RULE WAS ALMOST
as vulnerable to foreign threats as to domestic cabals. One of the lessons
of 1466 was that events unfolding within the walls of Florence were
exquisitely attuned, as if in sympathetic vibration, to those playing out
often miles distant from the protective girdle of brick and stone. The
most sensitive area, as far as the government was concerned, lay within
Florence's Tuscan empire, where among the vineyards and the olive
trees rose dozens of walled cities that had fallen under the rule of the
City of the Baptist. It was possession of these once proudly independent
communes that made this mid-sized, landlocked city a player on the
world stage, and the Florentine people were sure to punish severely a
politician who allowed any of them to slip from his grasp. The fierce
local patriotism that burned in these subject cities—the same parochial-
ism that turned the Italian peninsula into a patchwork of competing

political entities—was a constant threat to Florentine prosperity and peace of mind.*

Most worrisome was the possibility that local separatists would ally themselves with malcontents within Florence proper to make common cause against the regime. The normal fractiousness of the ruling elites created myriad opportunities for mischief. In the Middle Ages divisions between Guelfs and Ghibellines, and later among the victorious Guelfs, who quickly split into warring Black and White factions, leapt like a contagion from town to town.† Though the fifteenth century witnessed a significant diminution in factional violence, age-old rivalries continued to fester beneath the surface, awaiting a propitious moment to flare up with renewed virulence. A combination of rebellion abroad and discontent at home was a toxic brew potent enough to bring even the healthiest body politic to its knees.

Lorenzo had been in power for barely four months when the first such crisis erupted, so close to the city gates that it seemed as if the cries of "Popolo!" and "Liberta!" could be heard echoing in *Piazza del Duomo*. The difficulties arose in the city of Prato, a bustling commercial town north of Florence that had long since fallen under the thumb of her larger neighbor.‡ It was here that the Nardi family had landed after being exiled for their role in the uprising of 1466. At that time it was Salvestro who had been the chief troublemaker. Now it was his younger brother Bernardo, a "ready and a spirited young man . . . [u]nable to bear exile because of his poverty and seeing no mode for his return because of the peace that had

---

* The Italian word for such parochial loyalty is *campanilismo*. It derives from the word for bell tower, *campanile*, and describes the fierce attachment Italians feel toward that patch of territory from which the tolling of the cathedral bell can be heard.

† The splitting of the Guelfs into the two rival camps of Whites and Blacks, for example, which was to have such a profound impact on Dante's life (he belonged to the defeated Whites and was forced into exile), began in the neighboring city of Pistoia, where the terms were used to denote two branches of the ruling Cancellieri family. In 1296, Florence took over the divided town, only to find that it had thereby contracted the sickness that now set the leading families at each other's throats.

‡ Though long dominated by Florence, Prato was officially purchased by the commune in 1350.

been made," who led the charge against the regime that had ruined him. With a handful of supporters, largely recruited from Pistoia, another Florentine dependency that dreamed of reclaiming past glories, he and his companions stormed the communal palace, capturing the Florentine representative, Cesare Petrucci. Meanwhile the rest of the rebels were hurrying through the city shouting "long live the people of Florence and liberty!" in an effort to provoke a general uprising.

It did not take long for word of the rebellion to reach Florence and send the *principali* scurrying to the *palazzo* in a panic. The rebels assumed that the government of Florence was too divided following the disintegration of the triple alliance to put up effective resistance. Unfortunately for them, few things were better calculated to bury, if only temporarily, the hard feelings among members of the ruling party than the threat of insurrection in one of Florence's dependencies. Men who could normally agree on nothing were unanimous that any move toward independence on the part of one of her subject cities should be mercilessly crushed.

It was an irony often pointed out by those who resented being lectured on the virtues of their republican system of government that Florentines could be so ruthless in imposing their will on others. Cherishing liberty themselves, Florentines assumed that others would be as quick as they in seizing an opportunity to throw off the shackles of slavery. This empathy for the rebels' cause, unaccompanied by any sympathy for their plight, probably made Florentines overestimate the danger. Even as the rebellion was beginning to lose steam in Prato itself, the leading men of Florence worked themselves into a frenzy by imagining mobs of angry peasants and tradesmen descending upon the city walls. To head off such a calamity they instructed the *condottiere* Roberto di Sanseverino to gather an army and lead it against the rebellious city. It was only after Sanseverino had assembled and equipped his small force that it became clear their fears had been exaggerated. The mercenary captain had barely set his troops in motion when a messenger arrived from Prato bearing good tidings: the people of Prato had turned against their would-be liberators; Cesare Petrucci had been freed; Bernardo and his companions were now the prisoners of the restored government.

In the end, Bernardo Nardi's ill-fated rebellion did little more than provide a few sleepless nights for the leaders of the regime, an inconvenience more than compensated for by the satisfying spectacle of mass executions in the squares of Florence and Prato. Lorenzo's role in the affair is unclear, though he must have been deeply involved in the frantic discussions in the *palazzo,* particularly after it was learned that among those egging on Bernardo were his old enemies Dietisalvi Neroni and Bartolomeo Colleoni. Lorenzo's low profile suggests that he was still finding his way and willing to be guided by more experienced hands.

The most important legacy of the ill-fated rebellion was that it increased Lorenzo's sense of insecurity. The return of the rebels of 1466 was a reminder of how deep the enmity toward the Medici family ran. The Prato incident reinforced Lorenzo's belief that any move toward independence on the part of one of Florence's subject cities was merely a pretext for a coup against him, and it bolstered his belief that only by showing firmness could he avert disaster.

Perhaps Lorenzo should have learned a different lesson from the episode. Florence was spared not by a show of force but by the people of Prato themselves, who apparently preferred security under the Florentine umbrella to the desperate chance of freedom under a bunch of adventurers. Fear alone could not keep in subjection cities with their own proud history of independence. Instead, fostering a sense of common purpose and interest might win friends where harsh methods would only cause the republic's enemies to multiply.

When a far more serious rebellion began to bubble up in Volterra the following year, Lorenzo and other leaders of the regime were tempted to repeat the strategy they believed had been so successful against Prato—a prompt show of force that would cause the revolt to collapse without the unpleasant and dangerous necessity of actual fighting. But Volterra was not Prato. Volterra, some twenty-five miles to the southwest, was an ancient town, more ancient, in fact, than Florence, and her antiquity and impressive history as an independent commune fostered in her people a stubborn pride. While Florence boasted of its founding by Roman legions—either in the late republic or early imperial period; Florentines could not decide which legacy provided the nobler pedigree—Volterra had been one of the twelve cities of the powerful Etruscan League that rose to heights of wealth and power while Rome was still an obscure village hugging the hills above the Tiber River. From the brow of a steep hill,

Etruscan Volterra, then called Felathri, was a formidable citadel commanding a valley known for its rich mineral deposits of copper and silver. Lorenzo himself was well acquainted with the region's geologic treasures because it was to the nearby mineral baths at Bagno a Morba he and his family so often retired to restore their health.

Like Florence, Volterra had emerged as an independent commune during the eleventh and twelfth centuries, taking advantage of the vacuum created by rivalry between the Holy Roman Emperor and the pope to establish a government outside the prevailing feudal structure.* Unfortunately, Volterra resembled Florence in her vices as well as her virtues. By the fourteenth century she had been rendered so weak through civil strife that she fell easy prey to Florentine imperialism. Volterra was now fully under the thumb of her bigger, more prosperous cousin to the north, forced to pay taxes into Florentine coffers and suffer the intimidating presence of Florentine representatives in her midst.

Volterra's story was typical of the mid-sized Tuscan communes that had grown up in the High Middle Ages. Wracked by internal dissensions, these fiercely independent city-states had been gobbled up one by one and added to the growing Florentine empire.† Once a city was subjected to Florentine rule, however, these divisions did not cease but rather mutated into a new, pernicious form. Now instability was positively encouraged by rival factions within Florence who took advantage of these ancient enmities for their own purposes. When the Medici began to dominate Florentine politics they sought allies within each subject city; their rivals naturally did the same, creating in each dependency two hostile camps, one loyal to Florence's leading family, the other violently opposed. Thus outbreaks of separatist violence were often spurred as much by a desire to

---

* Volterra's *Palazzo dei Priori* is contemporary with the Bargello in Florence, the first seat of the city's communal government. Volterra's capital was built by 1239. The Bargello, completed in 1261, was quickly outgrown by the burgeoning republic, which set about building more suitable headquarters. The *Palazzo della Signoria* was ready for use by 1299.

† Within Tuscany the most significant holdouts against Florentine expansion were Siena, not conquered until the sixteenth century, and the ancient imperial capital of Lucca. Pisa, Florence's greatest rival throughout the Middle Ages, had finally succumbed in 1406. The conquest of Pisa provided landlocked Florence with an outlet to the sea.

see the *palle* trampled in the dirt as they were by local patriotism. It is safe to assume that behind many of the rebellions that threatened Florence's Tuscan empire was a cabal of treasonous Florentines who hoped to use the crisis to seize power in the capital.

It is only in this wider context that one can understand how an apparently trifling incident could have precipitated a war that inflicted terrible suffering on the citizens of Volterra and blackened the reputation of Lorenzo for centuries to come. That Lorenzo felt personally threatened by the rebellion of Volterra is beyond question. What is more difficult to assess is whether his feelings of insecurity were justified by either the domestic or international situation and, more important, whether the harsh measures he advocated were the best means of achieving his ends. For a man who came to be regarded as the greatest statesman of the age, one who achieved his goals primarily by persuasion and the delicate balancing of opposing interests, the manner in which he dealt with the current crisis seems at the very least clumsy, and at worst almost criminal. Late in his life Lorenzo confessed that the war with Volterra was his greatest blunder, a judgment that posterity has largely confirmed.

The precipitating event was a dispute over a contract to exploit an alum mine in Castelnuovo, a territory under the control of the still nominally independent Volterran commune.* The mineral was indispensable as a fixative in Florence's vital textile industry and so valuable that six years earlier Lorenzo himself had gone to Rome to obtain the pope's signature on a contract awarding the Medici bank a monopoly on the sale of alum from the mines at Tolfa. The Castelnuovo contract was initially awarded to a consortium of investors from Florence, Siena, and Volterra, led by one Paolo Inghirami. Inghirami and his colleagues were Medici clients, and had they been successful in making good on their claim they would certainly have managed their affairs to the benefit of their Florentine patron. It was also true that in the normal course of things money found its way from clients' hands to patrons' pockets. Lorenzo thus stood to gain, directly or indirectly, from the success of his friends.

---

* The fact that the mine in Castelnuovo never yielded significant profits is irrelevant to the state of mind of those involved. In 1471 the newly discovered deposits seemed to promise lucrative rewards.

If greed played some small role in Lorenzo's thinking, it played an equal part in the behavior of the communal government of Volterra. On June 8, 1471, the priors of Volterra voided the contract, asserting it had been improperly awarded to Inghirami and his fellow investors. There was much more at stake, however, than financial considerations. Inghirami was not only Lorenzo's friend but his chief supporter in Volterra. In voiding the contract the leaders of the commune were striking a blow for Volterran independence by embarrassing Lorenzo's agents and, thus, undermining the prestige of Lorenzo himself.

Both sides saw the dispute over the mine as a test of strength between the pro- and anti-Medici factions within the city. Even more important, Lorenzo regarded it as a test of his strength within Florence. Inghirami and his fellow investors formed part of Lorenzo's personal empire, that vast system of clients dependent on the Medici patronage, and in attacking his servants, the priors of Volterra were effectively attacking the basis of his power. By neglecting this crucial aspect of the contest, historians have misinterpreted the calamitous course of events as the product of an immature politician who misunderstood what was at stake and who believed that an easy military victory would enhance his popularity at home. It is clear, however, that Lorenzo knew exactly how much was at stake and that the hard line he took, while not perhaps the most effective course, was justified by the gravity of the situation.

Indeed there is little doubt that the priors of Volterra were working in concert with Lorenzo's domestic rivals. They voided the alum concession in June 1471, at the very moment when Lorenzo's power seemed to have reached a low point. (The *Signoria* seated in May had just demonstrated its independence by openly opposing Lorenzo's wishes in the matter of a loan to the king of Naples.) But if the priors of Volterra hoped that Lorenzo had been permanently marginalized they were quickly disappointed. Even as they paraded their defiance before an appreciative populace, Lorenzo was routing his domestic opposition. The *Signoria* that followed the unreliable government of May–June 1471 was more favorable to Medici interests, and Lorenzo was able to ram through new legislation that greatly enhanced his control over the machinery of government.

When Inghirami and his associates came to Florence in November 1471, they received a warm reception from a government now dominated by Lorenzo's men. Having rushed precipitously toward the brink, the priors of Volterra now seemed anxious to find a face-saving way out of the crisis. On January 4, 1472, the apparently chastened priors voted to give Lorenzo full power to arbitrate the dispute.

Thus far a diplomatic solution still seemed within reach. No blood had been shed and both sides appeared willing to resolve their differences in a peaceable manner. But while in public a spirit of compromise reigned, in private there were those who saw profit in a more violent outcome. It is not clear if the ruling body of Volterra deliberately set out to deceive Lorenzo or, as seems more likely, its erratic course was the result of an internal power struggle. What is certain, however, is that at least some members of the priorate were determined to push events past the point where a peaceful resolution was possible. The new and more dangerous phase of the crisis came on February 23, 1472, when Paolo Inghirami, surrounded by an armed escort provided by the Florentine government, attempted to return to Volterra. Awaiting Inghirami as he entered the city gates was a mob of armed peasants who quickly overwhelmed his bodyguards and chased him into the *palazzo*, where he and his father-in-law were murdered.

The peasants who hacked Inghirami to death were not simply a spontaneous mob of Volterran patriots but a well-organized vigilante squad assembled on orders from at least some members of the government. Their complicity was confirmed over the next few days when the priors appointed an extraordinary committee (a *Balìa* selected, as in similar emergencies in Florence, by hand), deliberately excluding all Lorenzo's supporters. While Lorenzo was seeking a negotiated settlement, the city of Volterra was girding for war.

Most disturbing to Lorenzo, this act of rebellion was abetted by members of his own government. According to Sacramoro, the treacherous behavior of the Volterrans was encouraged by certain "malcontents who do not wish to be governed by [Lorenzo]," and who "tolerate and perhaps even secretly favor those things that create difficulties." Among those who secretly wished to embarrass Lorenzo was Antonio Ridolfi, a man who had been among Lorenzo's staunchest allies in the crisis over the triple alliance. A contemporary poem celebrating the life of Federico da Montefeltro, lord of Urbino, contains a passage that reveals the dangerous synergy between the Volterran rebels and malcontents within Florence:

De Medici Lorenzo, his spirit
troubled unless Volterra were repaid for her iniquity,
since, if many pursued this war, it served him more than others,
having in this undertaking many enemies in his own land,
and because in the new government there was kindled
much envy against him, as always happens
among those in a state of lesser stature.
It is certain that to him exile and many other troubles
were being planned, and the ruin of his fortune, which, as you know,
in that city, or in others was the greatest of our time

Adding to this catalogue of woes was the fact, soon uncovered, that Dietisalvi Neroni and Jacopo and Neri Acciaiuoli had once again jumped into the fray and were proposing a secret pact with the Volterrans to bring about "the destruction of the house of Medici." Nor could the irrepressible Bartolomeo Colleoni be kept on the sidelines; in April, Sacramoro learned that the *condottiere* was preparing to cross the mountains once again in yet another attempt to topple Lorenzo's government.

The story of the war of Volterra is usually framed as a cautionary tale about an impetuous young politician in over his head, resisting the counsel of older and wiser men in a desperate desire to prove his mettle. Tommaso Soderini in particular is credited for giving a sage speech in the months leading up to the war in which he quoted the old Tuscan proverb, "Better a lean peace than a fat victory." But the details tell a somewhat different tale, one in which Lorenzo appears rather less hotheaded than is usually presumed and in which he had the backing of many of those older men whose counsel he is supposed to have rejected.

By April the Florentine government had responded to Inghirami's murder and the treachery of the Volterran government by appointing its own extraordinary committee, the Ten of War, on which Lorenzo was assigned a prominent place. But even now he hoped to avoid all-out confrontation. Sacramoro reported to Duke Galeazzo Maria Sforza in March that Lorenzo hoped that by exploiting the rivalries that usually beset the Volterran regime he might yet achieve his goals without war. In the meantime, backed by the rest of the Ten of War, he prepared for the worst.

The Volterrans, though overmatched, hoped that the mutual jealousies among the leading powers of Italy would persuade at least some of them to leap to her aid. To encourage them they hastily dispatched emissaries to all the major courts, including Milan, Naples, and Rome, pleading their case and inviting them to intercede on their behalf. Lorenzo had reason to be concerned: Colleoni, as we have seen, was itching to renew his Tuscan adventures and behind him stood the wealth and power of the Venetian empire; the pope, the newly elected Sixtus IV, might also be tempted to discomfit the Florentines, whose expansion always came at the expense of the Papal States. Most worrisome to Lorenzo was the stance of King Ferrante, who had revived his dreams of a peninsula-wide empire. He had just disembarked 1,500 of his own men in the Tuscan coastal city of Piombino, who could as easily be employed against Florentine interests as on her behalf. Even Duke Sforza, Lorenzo's most reliable ally, equivocated. According to the secret correspondence of Sacramoro, Milan had decided to let Lorenzo twist in the wind for a while. (The duke was worried that if Lorenzo grew too powerful in Florence he would lose his dependence on the court of Milan.)

War was officially declared by the Ten on April 26, 1472, and 100,000 ducats raised to hire and equip an army. Lorenzo scored a great coup when he persuaded Federico da Montefeltro, the most distinguished *condottiere* of the day, to spearhead the assault.

Facing Federico's well-equipped troops, five thousand foot soldiers and five hundred cavalry, the Volterrans, disappointed in their efforts to create an anti-Florentine coalition, could muster barely one thousand men. Only Siena, governed, according the Florentine diarist Benedetto Dei, "by a crowd of mad adventurers," came to her aid. The other major powers, including the pope, Naples, and, tardily, Milan, decided to back Florence, now in a commanding position and capable of punishing those who had deserted her in her hour of need.

Realizing the precariousness of their position, the priors of Volterra sent an emissary to plead for mercy with the government of Florence. He was met by Tommaso Soderini, who told the ambassador that the crisis was the fault of the Volterrans, who were "not observing their agreements, because of which the people of Florence were constrained to defend their honor and dignity." He threatened that unless the city were given up freely to Florentine troops they would impose their will "so as to conform to their obligations and to preserve honor."

Federico's army, strengthened by troops from Milan, the Papal States, and Naples, was encamped before the walls of Volterra by late April, having met little or no resistance on its approach to the city. Throughout the course of the twenty-five-day siege soldiers hurled insults back and forth across the walls of the city. During the night cries could be heard rising from around the twinkling campfires that encircled the town: "*Marzocho, Marzocho!*" for the Florentine lion,* and "*Palle! Palle!*" for the Medici. Cries also went out from the camps of the troops of the duke, the king, and the pope, a constant reminder to the besieged townspeople of the formidable coalition arrayed against them. Inside the city the troops were demoralized and restive. Ill-fed and ill-paid, they were almost as much a threat to the people as the armies on the plains below. The inevitable outcome was clear to even the most patriotic Volterran. On June 4, the government of Florence invited the Volterrans to offer their city "freely" into the hands of Federico's army in return for guarantees that life and property would be protected. The offer was immediately accepted and on June 17, 1472, the gates of Volterra were opened to the victorious army.

Had the crisis ended there Lorenzo would have achieved an unadulterated triumph. In reasserting his authority in Volterra with a minimum of bloodshed he had boosted his popularity at home and his prestige abroad. But once the hounds of war are unleashed they are difficult to call back. The disaster was sparked when one of the priors, upon returning from the *palazzo,* was accosted by a soldier from Federico's army. What had begun as a peaceful occupation quickly turned violent as the mercenaries who were supposed to be defending Volterra—but who had gone without pay and with little food and who now saw little prospect of profit from their long ordeal—started shouting "Sack it! Sack it!" Rampaging through the city streets they were quickly joined by allied forces. So sudden and violent was this outburst that Federico was caught completely off guard. Apparently this bibliophile general was so enraptured by a rare polyglot Bible he had discovered that the sack went on for hours before it was called to his attention.

By the time Federico had captured and hanged the ringleaders, much

---

* The most famous version of this shield-wielding mascot, symbol of Florentine martial prowess, is by Donatello. For many years it stood outside the *Palazzo della Signoria*. It is now in the Bargello Museum.

of the city lay in ruins and many citizens lay dead in the streets. Upon hearing of the calamity, Lorenzo himself lamented that the victory was much diminished by "the cruelty of the sack." A kinsman of the murdered Inghirami begged for Lorenzo's help, noting that the violent rampage made no distinctions between rebels and loyalists. "You have seen the afflicted and faithful friends and servants of Your Magnificence," he wrote to Lorenzo in March of 1473, "naked, despoiled of all their goods, robbed without mercy, for everything was taken during the sack of the city; and I doubt not that Your Magnificence with your kindly nature was moved to great compassion. Your arrival and seeing with your own eyes has been the sole hope of this people and has consoled and comforted them greatly." And indeed, after touring the ruined city, Lorenzo was sufficiently moved that he pledged 2,000 florins of his own money toward its rebuilding.

But despite his evident distress, the war had been completely justified from his point of view and the sack merely an unfortunate consequence of the Volterrans' own intransigence. Nor, at least in the short run, did the sack greatly tarnish Lorenzo's reputation at home. Florentines appreciated firm leadership, particularly when it came to asserting their dominion over weaker neighbors. No one was more bellicose than a Florentine when victories were cheaply won, nor as quick to turn upon his leaders when things turned sour.* When Federico returned to Florence, the victorious general was awarded a banner, two basins, two silver ewers, 180 lire, and a silver helmet, as well as honorary citizenship, by a public apparently well satisfied with his services.

The most enduring legacy of the war was the huge fortress Lorenzo ordered built on the site of the ruined bishop's palace. It still dominates the Volterran skyline, a permanent reminder of the gamble her leaders took and lost. If the Volterrans for centuries afterward blamed Lorenzo for their miseries, there is no doubt that in Florence his popularity increased. The victory, coming as it did on the heels of his successful reforms—which placed unprecedented powers in the hands of a single man—provided ample proof that the youth at the helm had grown into a vigorous and decisive leader. But there were some—including Lorenzo himself—

---

* Rinaldo degli Albizzi's fall from grace in 1434 came not when he urged his countrymen to wage war against Lucca but only when the war began to go badly.

concerned with the long-term consequences of the war and its violent aftermath. Machiavelli, writing with the value of hindsight, records the following encounter on the streets of Florence, which took place shortly after the war:

> The news of the victory was received with very great joy by the Florentines, and because it had been altogether Lorenzo's campaign, he rose to very great reputation from it. When one of *Messer* Tommaso Soderini's most intimate friends reproached him for his advice, saying to him: "What say you now that Volterra has been acquired?" To which *Messer* Tommaso replied, "To me it appears lost; for if you had received it by accord, you would have had advantage and security from it; but since you have to hold it by force, in adverse times it will bring you weakness and trouble and in peaceful times, loss and expense."

Like most of the speeches Machiavelli puts into his protagonists' mouths, this one is intended not so much as a literal record of what was said but as a foreshadowing of future events. What Machiavelli knew, and what many Florentines probably suspected even at the time, was that the seeds of war, so hopefully planted that spring, might well bear bitter fruit a few years hence.

Giusto Utens, *Medici Villa at Trebbio* (Art Resource)

XI. DOMESTIC TRANQUILLITY

And you, well-born Laurel, under whose shelter
happy Florence rests in peace . . .

—ANGELO POLIZIANO, "THE JOUST
OF GIULIANO," IV

"There is nothing new here, except that in the neighborhood of
Pisa, where the illustrious Lorenzo is hawking with King Ferrante's
men, two of the ten falcons sent by His Majesty, and those the best,
are lost. Your excellence must not wonder that I speak of such
things, for I only follow the example of others. Idleness has so
gained the upper hand in Italy that, if nothing new happens, we
shall have more to say about the slaughter of fowls and dogs than
about armies and deeds of war. For the rest, I am of the opinion that
those who have to govern Italy in peace will not reap less fame than
those who kept her at war. For the object of war is, after all, peace,
and the only consideration is that it should be a permanent peace."

—THE AMBASSADOR OF FERRARA TO ERCOLE D'ESTE

IN THE SHORT TERM THE VICTORY OVER VOLTERRA
helped Lorenzo cement his position as the leader of the *reggimento*. Florentines liked nothing better than to put their uppity neighbors in their place, as long as this could be accomplished with a minimum of Florentine blood and treasure. Dino Compagni described his native city as "proud and combative, and rich with unlawful profits, distrusted and feared for its greatness by the nearby cities, rather than loved." And while Compagni was probably more reflective than most, his fellow citizens would have agreed that there was nothing like good old-fashioned terror to suppress any thoughts of rebellion.

Crowned with the victor's laurels, Lorenzo's popularity forced potential rivals underground and persuaded the ambitious that their best hope
for advancement was to hitch their wagon to the rising star of Florentine
politics. It was around this time that Lorenzo first came to be named in
documents as "the first citizen of the republic," while the Milanese ambassador noted that he was "thinking to achieve more than even Cosimo and
Piero had ever done, so far as I understand him."

But despite his success in the political arena, Lorenzo remained
ambivalent about his role as a statesman. Politics took time away not only
from more pleasurable pursuits but from areas of life he could ill afford to
neglect. For both Cosimo and Piero, political power had been a natural
outgrowth of their business activities. Wealth was the key to power in Florence and, conversely, political power was wielded largely in order to protect one's fortune. Giovanni Rucellai, whose son Bernardo was married to
Lorenzo's sister Nannina, wrote in a revealing passage of his memoirs,
"and it seems to me very helpful to remember that in our city of Florence
one doesn't hold on to one's riches with little difficulty but with very great
difficulty. And this because of the many wars of the commune, which
requires them to make great expenditures which cause them to demand
from her citizens much by way of taxation and frequent loans. . . . I have
found no other way to defend myself than not to make any enemies,
because a single enemy can do more harm than four friends can do good;
thus, to be on good terms with one's relatives and in-laws and neighbors
and the rest of the citizens of your *gonfalone*."

Lorenzo was candid about his own motives for accepting the role of
first citizen, for, as he explained in his memoirs, "it is ill living in Florence
for the rich unless they rule the state." The cost of public service could
prove ruinous. Looking back over his father's and grandfather's account
books, Lorenzo was astonished to learn that they had expended over
650,000 florins on charitable donations, building projects, and in taxes. It
was money well spent, since it contributed to the family's popularity in the
city, but such expenditures could be sustained only as long as the bank
upon which the family fortune was built continued to thrive.

The health of the bank, however, was something Lorenzo found difficult to maintain, since the more deeply he delved into politics the less time
he had to attend to the minutiae of the family business. Though Lorenzo
has long been criticized for his poor management, the bank's declining

fortunes during the years he was at the helm were not entirely his fault. Each local branch—in Rome, Bruges, Venice, London, Lyons, Geneva, Florence, and Naples—was a separate enterprise under the control of a manager whose honesty and ability were essential to success but difficult to judge from the central office in the Via Larga. Communication was slow and incomplete, and Lorenzo was too preoccupied to micromanage his scattered enterprises. In 1470, Lorenzo complained to Tommaso Portinari, manager of the Medici bank in the commercial center of Bruges:

> If I have been later in responding [to your letter] as you or I would have liked, you must excuse me since the continual business in the *Palazzo [della Signoria]* leaves me no time to attend to my own affairs, as is probably required. I find myself at this time with heavy burdens, both public and private, upon my shoulders, and yet I hope through God's grace and the help of my friends that soon they will lighten and to be able to arrange things properly, seeing as I have the spirit and the desire to strive to increase the dignity of our house, a subject on which, I find, all citizens are agreed and well disposed.

His concerns turned out to be well founded. Left largely to his own devices, Portinari would eventually cost the bank huge losses through his ill-conceived loans.*

Part of the problem was that, unlike his grandfather, Lorenzo was reluctant to fire those who had proved themselves inept or dishonest. His patience with subordinates was due both to a misplaced sense of loyalty and simple inattentiveness. While the Lyons branch was teetering on the brink of bankruptcy in the 1480s, Lorenzo dragged his feet for years before calling to account its manager, his brother-in-law Lionetto Rossi, a delay that shook public confidence in the firm. The sureness of touch and ability to judge character in political matters seemed to desert Lorenzo when it came to business. One on one his ability to bully, cajole, or simply to charm a potential opponent into seeing things his way was a powerful

---

* Despite his lack of business acumen, Tommaso Portinari was an important patron of the arts. The magnificent *Adoration of the Shepherds* by Hugo van der Goes and the fine portraits of him and his wife by Hans Memling are among the Flemish masterpieces that found their way to Florence and helped influence the course of painting in his native city.

weapon, but he had far less success when forced to operate at a distance as he was compelled to do in managing his far-flung business empire. Junior partners in the various branches, knowing his reluctance to pore through the details of the secret account books, took advantage of him, running up huge debts that they concealed in an avalanche of spurious numbers.

Lorenzo was in many ways less modern in his economic views than his forebears; while Giovanni di Bicci, Cosimo, and even Piero had understood that wealth could be created by manipulating numbers on a piece of paper, Lorenzo possessed an old-fashioned prejudice in favor of tangible wealth in the form of real estate. After four generations of prosperity the Medici under Lorenzo were slowly transforming themselves from merchants to landed gentry. Even as his profit margins sank and his debts rose, he continued to purchase additional properties throughout Tuscany. And having become one of the greatest landholders in Italy, he devoted increasing amounts of time to managing his estates. In fact he much preferred the science of agronomy and animal husbandry to the abstract world of accounting. He could size up the quality of a racehorse in an instant—a talent more typical of a feudal knight than an urban merchant—but even hours spent poring over an account book yielded little useful information. He had a depth of feeling for the natural world, conveyed in the vivid descriptions of fields and forests that cause his poems to pulse with life, but little understanding of market conditions. He was rarely bold in seizing a business opportunity and, even more critical, was slow to cut his losses in adverse conditions. In short, the most famous banker in Europe was not much of a businessman.

It must be said in Lorenzo's defense that the business climate in Florence was less favorable in the second half of the fifteenth century than in the first half. The Medici bank was but one of many struggling to keep its head above water during a period of slow economic decline. By 1495, banking had reached such a low ebb in Florence that the guild of money changers (*l'Arte del Cambio*), once an economic engine of the city, was forced to close its doors due to dwindling membership. Perhaps most important, Lorenzo was in an impossible bind, forced to neglect his financial affairs in order to hold on to the political power that offered the only real means to protect his fortune.

•   •   •

Despite his recent political successes, Lorenzo was always on guard against a reemergence of potential rivals. Francesco Guicciardini spells out some of the "divide and conquer" methods Lorenzo used to ensure that no organized opposition to his rule arose:

> As he grew stronger, Lorenzo decided to become master of the city, and not have anyone control him. He wanted to make sure that *messer* Tommaso [Soderini], and others who enjoyed esteem and the backing of relatives, did not grow too strong. He would allow them to be represented in the legations and in all the high offices and magistracies of the city; but at the same time he held them back, sometimes not letting them finish the business they had begun. He showed favor to men from whom he had nothing to fear, men who were then devoid of connections and standing, such as *messer* Bernardo Buongirolami and Antonio di Puccio; and, a year or so later, to such men as *messer* Agnolo Niccolini, Bernardo del Nero, and Pierfilippo Pandolfini. He used to say that if his father had done likewise, and put a little pressure on *messer* Luca, *messer* Dietisalvi, *messer* Agnolo Acciaiuoli, and others like them, he would not have come so close to losing his power in '66.

This shrewd political operator was a far cry from the young man who, only three years earlier, had ridden into power on the shoulders of the *principali*. Then, these commanding figures were confident they could master the inexperienced youth for their own ends. Now, most had reconciled themselves to a secondary role and faithfully served the young man they thought would serve them.

Lorenzo had matured in other ways, too. In August 1470, Clarice gave birth to their first child, Lucrezia, a happy event that gave Lorenzo a certain gravitas in the eyes of his fellow citizens. For Florentines, nothing defined a man of substance as surely as fathering a child in wedlock. The responsibilities of citizenship were inextricably bound up in the role of fatherhood, the two linked by a shared impulse to make one's mark in the civic arena. "There are two principal things that men do in this world," Giovanni Rucellai declared in his memoirs. "The first is to procreate, the second is to build." In the first of these roles Lorenzo was precocious by

Florentine standards; in the second, while never equaling the achievements of his grandfather, he would eventually come into his own, leaving
a permanent mark on the city.

By the end of 1473, still a young man of twenty-four, Lorenzo had
fathered five children. In addition to Lucrezia, Clarice had delivered twin
boys in 1471; born prematurely, they lived only long enough to be baptized. Fortune was kinder when on February 15, 1472, Clarice delivered a
healthy boy, Piero, who would ultimately succeed his father as first citizen
of Florence. Piero was followed in July of 1473 by a second healthy daughter, Maddalena.

Clarice, clearly, was fulfulling the role assigned to her by nature and
by the Medici. It was assumed that after this initial—and admittedly
essential—biological contribution, however, she would play only a secondary role in shaping her children's development. In this patriarchal
society the moral and intellectual education of the young was largely left
to the head of the household. This was especially true in the case of sons,
who were molded by their fathers for the parts they would play in the
civic arena. Leon Battista Alberti in his book *On the Family* relegates a
mother's contribution to the first years of life. In reality, busy men like
Lorenzo relied heavily on the good sense and nurturing instincts of their
wives, while reserving for themselves the right to make all important
decisions in shaping their sons' futures. Fortunately, Clarice was both a
loving wife and mother, and Lorenzo knew he could safely entrust the
children to her care.

Indeed he had little choice in the matter. Even while he was preoccupied by affairs of state, he insisted on being kept informed of the daily routine he could rarely share. The numerous letters that provide an intimate
portrait of Lorenzo's household were prompted by his frequent absences.
They attest to his deep affection for his children, and to his regret at not
being able to spend as much time with them as he wished. Among the topics that appear most frequently in these letters—after the necessary reas-
surances as to everyone's health—are those that concern the children's
education. Lorenzo was not far removed from his own days of wrestling
with Greek and Latin grammars and he insisted that his own children
receive an equally solid grounding in the classics. All of his children, but
especially Piero, were anxious to impress their father with what they had

learned. In 1478, the six-year-old Piero sent the following report to his father: "I write this letter to tell you that we are well. Although I do not yet know how to write well, I will do my best for the present. I will try and do better in future. I have already learnt many verses of Virgil, and I know nearly all the first book of Theodoro [a book of Greek grammar by Theodoro of Faza] by heart, and I think I understand it. The Master makes me decline and examines me every day. Giovanni sometimes comes to Mass with the Master."

Frequent and prolonged absences did not prevent Lorenzo from making the most of his time with Clarice. By the end of 1479 he had conceived seven healthy children: following Maddalena came his second son, Giovanni, born in 1475; Luigia and Contessina, both in 1478; and, finally, Giuliano in 1479. An engaging family portrait from the year of Giuliano's birth is provided in a letter from Piero's hand, written from the rustic retreat at Cafaggiolo:

> MAGNIFICENT FATHER MINE. . . . We are all well and studying. Giovanni is beginning to spell. By this letter you can judge where I am in writing; as for Greek I keep myself rather in exercise by the help of Martino than make any progress. Giuliano laughs and thinks of nothing else; Lucrezia sews, sings, and reads; Maddalena knocks her head against the wall, but without doing herself any harm; Luisa begins to say a few little words; Contessina fills the house with her noise. All others attend to their duties, and nothing is wanting to us save your presence.

It is tempting to read into these juvenile scribblings hints of the men and women Lorenzo's children will become. "Please send me some figs," the five-year-old Piero wrote to his grandmother from Trebbio, "for I like them. I mean those red ones, and some peaches with stones, and other things you know I like, sweets and cakes and other little things, as you think best." Piero's nagging for various gifts seems to portend the future leader who will alienate his fellow citizens by his ostentatious lifestyle and high-handed ways. When, years later, Piero insulted Michelangelo with the demeaning request that he sculpt him a snowman for the family court-yard, it was only the latest in a long string of demands from one who was used to having his every whim indulged.* And when Lorenzo's daughter Lucrezia passes along a request by four-year-old Giovanni for "some sugar-plums, and says that last time you sent very few," can we detect the first signs of the appetite that will turn the future Pope Leo X into the glutton whose massive girth fills out the famous portrait by Raphael?

Family life, while often chaotic, was marked by warmth and genuine affection. Lorenzo valued Clarice for her maternal instincts, all the more because he could rarely spend as much time at home as he would have liked. A household intimate recounts one happy occasion when Clarice, having been away for a few weeks, was reunited at long last with her children:

> Then near the Certosa we met paradise full of festive and joyous angels, that is to say, *Messer* Giovanni and Piero, Giuliano and Giulio on pillions, with all their attendants. As soon as they saw their mother they threw themselves from their horses, some without help, others aided by their people, and they ran forward and were lifted into the arms of Madonna Clarice, with such joy and kisses and delight that a hundred letters could not describe it. Even I could not restrain myself but got off my horse, and ere they remounted I embraced them all twice; once for myself and once for Lorenzo. Darling little Giuliano said, with a long O, O, O, "Where is Lorenzo?" We said, "He has gone to Poggio to find you." Then he: "O no, never," almost in tears. You never beheld so touching a sight.

Not surprising, Lorenzo's daughters have come down to us as less fully realized personalities than his sons, all of whom played prominent public roles later in life. But Lorenzo's love for them emerges even more clearly than for his sons, where a fatherly affection was mingled with concerns lest they not live up to his expectations for them.[†] In this he was repeating his

---

* "While [Michelangelo] was working on this statue [of Hercules], a great quantity of snow fell in Florence, and Piero de' Medici, Lorenzo's eldest son, who had taken his father's place but lacked the grace of his father, being young, wanted a statue of snow made in the middle of his courtyard." (Condivi, *The Life of Michelangelo*, p. 15.)

† Lorenzo was reputed to have said, "I have three sons: one dumb [Piero], one smart [Giovanni], one sweet [Giuliano]" (Parks, 243), a description that accurately reflects their later careers.

relations with his own parents and grandparents: relations among the men were always complicated by their heavy responsibilities and by a streak of competitiveness; only the women could give their love unstintingly, without fear that an overt display of affection would encourage weakness. Indeed one of the reasons that mothers were not more deeply involved in their sons' education was the fear that the female influence would make them soft and unfit for the world.

As for Clarice, she—along with Lorenzo's grandmother Contessina (until her death in 1474) and the always competent, energetic Lucrezia—continued faithfully to tend to hearth and home during Lorenzo's frequent absences. Though not unhappy with the role assigned to her, an occasional note of reproach creeps in: "We are sending you by the bearer seventeen partridges, which your falconer took today," she wrote to Lorenzo from Cafaggiolo, where she had been anxiously awaiting his arrival:

> I should have been glad if you had come and enjoyed them with us here. We have expected you for the last three evenings up to the third hour, and were very surprised you did not come. I am afraid something out of the ordinary must have detained you. If there is anything new, please let me know, for in any case it would be better to be together, rather than one in Florence and the other in Lombardy [sic]. We expect you tomorrow in any case, so please do not let us wait in vain. The children are all well, and so are all the rest.

For all Lorenzo's desire to spend more time with his family, he was not willing to sacrifice those recreations that were vital to his sense of well-being. Any journey was certain to be interrupted by side trips to particularly well-stocked hunting grounds, and even when Lorenzo was attending to important business he managed to find time for his favorite sports. It is perhaps telling that Clarice usually received reports of these expeditions not from Lorenzo himself but through one of his companions who was given the task of keeping her abreast of his activities. "Yesterday," wrote Angelo Poliziano in 1475 during Lorenzo's extended sojourn in Pisa, "though there was little wind, he went hawking, but their luck was not good, as they lost Pilato's nice falcon, the one called *Il Mantovano*. This morning we also went into the country, but the wind again spoilt the sport. We saw some fine flights, however, and Maestro Giorgio made his peregrine falcon fly, and it returned most obediently to the lure. Lorenzo has fallen completely in love with it."

Though Clarice would never openly accuse her husband of neglect, it is difficult to imagine she read these vivid reports without some twinge of jealousy. This letter may have been particularly hard to bear since at the very moment Lorenzo was galloping across the countryside she was confined to bed, about to deliver their fifth child. But one should not assume that Clarice was fundamentally discontented with her lot: a fifteenth-century wife knew it was her fate to remain at home while her husband pursued his many interests, and the expectation of narrow horizons made them more tolerable, if no less diminishing to the women who thus found little scope for their talents. Lorenzo, while busier than most husbands, was not untypical in his attitudes, and Clarice accepted her role with few complaints.

Only on rare occasions would she stand up to her formidable husband, though in the end it was always Lorenzo who prevailed in important matters. Their most famous quarrel came, not surprisingly, over the education of their children. Their disagreement is interesting not only for the light it sheds on their personal relationship but on the clash of cultures between the pious Roman matron and the liberal-minded Florentine. The confrontation was precipitated by a young man who would ultimately come to be regarded as the greatest poet of the age, a talented writer and scholar whom Lorenzo had discovered and invited into his home to serve as tutor to his children—Angelo Poliziano.*

Lorenzo's friendship with Poliziano, perhaps the most profound and enduring of his life, had all the complexity and difficulty that comes from affection between two men of equal talent and ambition but of unequal status and power. Poliziano first came to Lorenzo's attention in 1470 when the sixteen-year-old student, orphaned and impoverished, boldly

---

* Angelo Poliziano's real name was Angelo Ambrogini. The name Poliziano comes from his hometown, Montepulciano, *Mons Politanus* in Latin, of which Poliziano is the Italianized version. Born in 1454, his father, a local adherent of the Medici party, had been killed in a local political quarrel, leaving the precocious ten-year-old to fend for himself. He made his way to Florence where he impressed Cristoforo Landino with his intelligence and literary gifts.

introduced himself to the first citizen of Florence. "Magnificent Lorenzo," he wrote,

> to whom heaven has given charge of the city and the State, first citizen of Florence, doubly crowned with bays lately for war in S. Croce amid the acclamations of the people and for poetry on account of the sweetness of your verses, give ear to me who drinking at Greek sources am striving to set Homer into Latin meter. This second book which I have translated . . . comes to you and timidly crosses your threshold. If you welcome it I propose to offer to you all the *Iliad*. It rests with you, who can, to help the poet. I desire no other muse or other Gods but only you; by your help I can do that of which the ancients would not have been ashamed.

This was an ambitious calling card for someone who had yet to establish his reputation, but Poliziano could count on Lorenzo's love of ancient poetry and his appreciation of literary talent, particularly when combined with youthful enthusiasm, to gain him entrée into his glittering circle of artists and intellectuals. Poliziano clearly hit the mark, and within three years he had become an intimate member of Lorenzo's household.

For the brilliant poet and scholar there was no better place on earth than the Medici household, with its unparalleled collections of ancient manuscripts and objets d'arts collected over three generations by men of learning and discernment and with the vast resources to indulge their passions. "Almost all other rich men support servants of pleasure, but you support priests of the muses," Ficino wrote to Lorenzo on hearing that he had taken the young poet under his wing. "It was due to you that Homer, the high priest of the Muses, came into Italy, and someone who was till now a wanderer and a beggar has at last found with you sweet hospitality. You are supporting in your home that young Homeric scholar, Angelo Poliziano, so that he may put the Greek face of Homer into Latin colors." Under Lorenzo's aegis, Poliziano would come to prominence as both a scholar and a poet. The friendly literary competition he engaged in with his boss would prove fruitful for both men, each of whom pushed the other to new heights of poetic invention. In his *Silvae*, Poliziano described himself as both Lorenzo's "client and pupil."

Poliziano's initial service to Lorenzo was to act as his children's tutor; the master to whom Piero refers to in his letter watching over his shoulder as he plows through his lessons is none other than the great poet himself, who often must have thought his talents wasted in trying to cram Greek and Latin grammar into the head of his less than diligent pupil.* He also served as Lorenzo's unofficial secretary; it was he who took up the burden of writing to Clarice when Lorenzo was too busy or preoccupied.

For the most part Poliziano accepted his role, largely because it came with the friendship of a man he genuinely loved and admired. No one can read his poetry—including the heartbreaking verses he wrote upon his master's death—or note his many acts of devotion without concluding that theirs was a friendship cemented by deep and abiding affection. There were times, however, when Angelo's pride was stung by his lowly status, as in the summer of 1479 when he felt himself in exile in Cafaggiolo while Lorenzo was in Florence caught up in great affairs of state: "The children play about more than usual, and are quite restored in health," he wrote, concluding mournfully, "I would have liked to serve you in some greater thing, but since this has fallen to my lot, I will do it gladly."

Like Clarice, Angelo was forced to adjust to Lorenzo's needs. Staring out the windows of the isolated villa into the rain of a Tuscan winter, he sorely felt his exile from the great events happening elsewhere. Adding to his gloom was the constant fear for Lorenzo's safety. "I am anxiously await-ing news that the plague has ceased," he wrote to Lorenzo, "both because I fear for you, and because I want to return to serve you. I had hoped and wished to stay with you, but since you, or rather my bad luck, has given me this position in your service, I will endure it."

With Lorenzo tied up with pressing business and with the family shut-tling from one distant villa to another, a quarrel between the lady of the house and her husband's closest friend became almost inevitable. The breach came early in 1479 when Clarice decided to replace the materials

---

* One of the best contemporary portraits of Poliziano shows him in just this role. It appears in the series of frescoes Ghirlandaio painted for the Sassetti family in Santa Trinità. Here the swarthy, hawk-nosed poet is seen, book in hand, with two of his charges, Giuliano and Piero. Lorenzo himself is depicted standing next to the painting's donor, Francesco Sassetti, general manager of the Medici bank.

that Poliziano was using to instruct the children in Latin. In keeping with own his humanist education, these texts were primarily drawn from the great pagan authors of antiquity, a choice that distressed the conventional Clarice, who, without her husband's consent, substituted the morally uplifting (but to Angelo's point of view grammatically barbarous and inelegant) Book of Psalms for Seneca and Cicero. Clarice was particularly worried about the effect pagan literature would have on the precocious and impressionable Giovanni, already being groomed by his parents for a life in the Church. In a letter of April 6, Poliziano warned Lorenzo: "As to Giovanni, you will see. His mother has changed his reading to the Psalter, of which I do not approve, and has taken him away from us. When she was away it is incredible what progress he made. . . . I have no other daily prayer to God than that I may some day be able to show you my fidelity, diligence, and patience, which I would gladly do, even at the expense of death."

The quarrel was due to mutual jealousy, but there were larger issues at stake that reflected wider rifts within Renaissance culture between traditional Christian values and the new vogue for ancient learning of which Florence under Lorenzo was the leading center. When Poliziano declares that Clarice "has taken [Giovanni] away from us," he knows he can count on Lorenzo as his ally in a struggle pitting an enlightened humanism against a narrow-minded piety. While most historians have sympathized with Poliziano, history has oddly vindicated Clarice's more conservative views. The young Giovanni would grow up to become Pope Leo X, a cleric more noted for his cultivation than for his piety. It was this learned aesthete who sat on the throne of St. Peter when Martin Luther, railing against the corrupt, pagan idolaters in Rome, split Christendom in two. Had Clarice convinced her husband to let Giovanni spend more time studying scripture and less time on the profane delights of Ovid, might he have been more sympathetic, or at least more sensitive, to the concerns of the German reformer?

For the moment, however, the stakes seemed rather smaller, though in the context of Lorenzo's family the contest of wills was fierce enough. Asserting her authority as mistress of the house, Clarice banished the offending poet. A few days later Poliziano wrote to Lorenzo defending his position: "I am here at Careggi, having left Cafaggiuolo by order of Madonna Clarice. I beg you allow me to tell you the reason and the way of my departure by word of mouth, for it is a long story. I think that when you have heard my tale you will agree that I was not wholly in the wrong." But though Lorenzo sympathized with Angelo's aims, he had no desire to antagonize his wife. In the end he tried to defuse the situation by installing his exiled friend in his villa in Fiesole, a far more congenial spot for the worldly poet than the wilds of Cafaggiolo, while he made other arrangements for the education of his sons.

But Clarice was not so easily mollified. Instead of being disgraced, Angelo appeared to have been rewarded by Lorenzo for his insults to her. This only increased her sense that she was becoming a stranger in her own home. She already felt out of place among the brilliant and witty circle of men around Lorenzo and knew how vicious they could be when jockeying for position. Their cruel wit spared no one, and she feared she would now become the butt of their jokes. "I should be glad not to be turned into ridicule by [Matteo] Franco* in the same way as Luigi Pulci," she wrote to her husband, "nor to hear that *Messer* Angelo can say that he will stay in your house against my will, and that you have given him your own room at Fiesole. You know that I said that if you wished him to remain I would be content, and though he has called me a thousand names, if it is with your approval, I will endure it, but I cannot believe that it is true."

Lorenzo hurried to Cafaggiolo to try to smooth things over with his wife, but apparently Clarice continued to wage a long-distance battle, for some days later he scolded her for her petty attempts to get back at her rival: "Monna Clarice. I have been much annoyed that the books have not been handed to *Messer* Agnolo, as I requested you through *Ser* Niccolò, and that *Messer* Bernardo has not come here to bring them."

With this final jab the feud between Lorenzo's wife and best friend came to an end. While Lorenzo bowed to Clarice's wishes and relieved Angelo as tutor to their children, he made it clear that he would not banish his dear friend from his presence. Angelo himself was no doubt happier with the current state of affairs, which left him free to pursue his own interests in between his stints on important diplomatic missions for Lorenzo. Clarice, having technically won the battle, felt humiliated, realiz-

---

* Matteo Franco, one of Lorenzo's new favorites, had taken over the role of court buffoon from Luigi Pulci. In a bitter contest for Lorenzo's favor, Franco had bested the companion of his earlier days.

ing she had lost the war. Her children would grow into true Florentines, steeped in the liberal classical culture that fundamentalists like Savonarola would conceive as their life's mission to destroy.

The longest of Lorenzo's extended absences from Florence during these years was occasioned by a project close to his heart—the reopening of the University of Pisa, an institution that, much to the chagrin of many of his fellow citizens, would soon rival and even surpass that of his own home-town.* For months at a time between 1471 and 1473, Lorenzo and Giuliano—sometimes accompanied by Lorenzo's family, sometimes by their mother—lived at one of their many properties in or around the ancient seaport, meeting with learned men and *principali* of the city to discuss the plans to turn Pisa into a center of scholarship. Here Lorenzo was able to exercise his authority in an area where he was truly passionate. But even while conversing with philosophers, scientists, and scholars, Lorenzo was always sensitive to political nuance. In order to minimize competition with the Florentine university he proposed a division of the curriculum: to the *Studio* in Florence went the faculty of philosophy and philology; to Pisa the more practical studies of law, medicine, and theology.

One of the earliest and most prominent students at the reinvigorated university was Lorenzo's brother. A letter of May 1474 reveals that, like many a student before and since, Giuliano did not let his books get in the way of more obvious delights. "We have arrived safely and are all well," he reported to his mother. "Today we dance, and tomorrow we joust, which, as is the custom of this country, should be very fine."

Though Giuliano gracefully fulfilled the role of Prince of Youth that Medici propaganda had assigned to him, he was no empty-headed play-boy. Like his older brother he had a passion not only for sport but for phi-losophy and letters, as his correspondence with the philosopher Marsilio Ficino reveals. Lorenzo helped direct Giuliano's studies, employing the ever helpful Poliziano, a year younger but more studious than his pupil, for the task. "I rejoice most heartily to find our Giuliano so devoted him-

---

* The university, which probably dates to the fourteenth century, had fallen into decay after the conquest of the city in 1405 by Florence and the economic stagnation that fol-lowed. Lorenzo revived what was, in effect, a moribund institution.

self to letters," Lorenzo wrote to Angelo. "I congratulate him thereupon, and thank you for the zeal you have shown in guiding him the right way." The best description of the young man in the prime of his life, one confirmed in the many contemporary portraits, comes from the pen of his friend and teacher:

> He was tall and sturdy, with a large chest. His arms were rounded and muscular, his joints strong and big, his stomach flat, his thighs powerful, his calves rather full. He had bright lively eyes, with excellent vision, and his face was rather dark, with thick, rich black hair worn long and combed straight back from the forehead. He was skilled at riding and at throwing, jumping and wrestling, and prodigiously fond of hunting. Of great courage and steadfastness, he fostered piety and good morals. He was accomplished in painting and music and every sort of refinement. He had some talent for poetry, and wrote some Tuscan verses which were wonderfully serious and edifying. And he always enjoyed reading amatory verse. He was both eloquent and prudent, but not at all showy; he loved wit and was himself witty. He hated liars and men who hold grudges. Moderate in his grooming, he was nonetheless amazingly elegant and attractive.

The project to restore a functioning institution of higher learning in Pisa devoured large portions of Lorenzo's personal fortune. More was involved than Lorenzo's love of learning, though this was certainly a major factor in his willingness to sacrifice both time and treasure. Pisa was once a proudly independent state whose mercantile empire, like that of her rivals, Genoa and Venice, spread throughout the Mediterranean. She still resented her subservience to the upstart inland community, and Lorenzo's generosity was in part meant to assuage her wounded vanity. It was the opposite tactic he had employed in Volterra, the two approaches combining to demonstrate the advantages of being a friend to the Medici and the tribulations that awaited their enemies.

These were happy times for Lorenzo and his growing family, and for the city over which he ruled. Italy was enjoying a rare interlude of peace, something noted by the ambassador of Ercole d'Este, Duke of Ferrara, though not without a twinge of regret:

There is nothing new here, except that in the neighborhood of Pisa, where the illustrious Lorenzo is hawking with King Ferrante's men, two of the ten falcons sent by His Majesty, and those the best, are lost. Your excellence must not wonder that I speak of such things, for I only follow the example of others. Idleness has so gained the upper hand in Italy that, if nothing new happens, we shall have more to say about the slaughter of fowls and dogs than about armies and deeds of war. For the rest, I am of the opinion that those who have to govern Italy in peace will not reap less fame than those who kept her at war. For the object of war is, after all, peace, and the only consideration is that it should be a permanent peace.

One can almost here him yawn as he tracks Lorenzo's court from Florence to Pisa and out to one of his many villas. Peace abroad and prosperity at home left little for the ambassador to do but pass along the latest gossip. On the domestic front opposition to Lorenzo's rule had turned strangely silent, though no one presumed it had vanished entirely. The reasons for this rare quiescence were twofold. On the one hand there was no doubt of Lorenzo's personal popularity after his recent chastisement of the upstart Volterrans. But it is also true that under the watchful eyes of the *Otto*, the security police whose informers kept them abreast of any seditious talk, Florentines, while not exactly living under a reign of terror, knew the peril of loose tongues. Vocal opponents could expect to see their tax burdens mysteriously rise, while those found guilty of plotting against the government could expect no mercy from the courts. An incident recorded by the diarist Luca Landucci vividly illustrates the dangers awaiting those who threatened bodily harm to the leading citizens of the regime:

27th September [1481]. A certain hermit came to the house of Lorenzo de' Medici at the Poggio a Caiano; and the servants declared that he intended to murder Lorenzo, so they took him and sent him to the Bargello, and he was put to the rack.

15th October. This hermit died at Santa Maria Novella, having been tortured in various ways. It was said that they skinned the soles of his feet, and then burnt them by holding them in the fire till the fat dripped off them; after which they set him upright and made him walk across the hall; and these things caused his death. Opinions were divided as to whether he were guilty or innocent.

Even the staunch Medici partisan Benedetto Dei acknowledges that the regime's methods for ensuring loyalty could be heavy-handed: "He who doesn't turn to the cross cannot be saved, and likewise, I say, I have said, and I will say: He who doesn't throw in his lot with the *palle,* will have both his head and his shoulders broken."

Under the circumstances it is not surprising that people were reluctant to express their views in public. It was only in a private letter that the Florentine merchant Francesco Bandini felt free to describe the mood of his compatriots in 1476: "if one considers how life in this one place is rendered difficult from the unheard of vexations, the ruin of fortunes, the incessant extortions, the favors of corruption, the instability of the state, the rancor, the cruelties, the hatreds, the pilagings, the continual disquiet and the uncertainty each has of his own goods, one would assuredly estimate that it is a paradise inhabited by perverse and horrible spirits."

Though Bandini did not speak for a majority of Florentines, his complaints dispel the propagandists' claims that the current regime enjoyed universal support. Newly streamlined by Lorenzo's reforms, the *reggimento* was accepted by the majority as long as its policies seemed to be successful, but an influential minority continued to nurse a persistent and increasingly bitter hatred.

One factor working in Lorenzo's favor was the vibrant cultural life of the city that made Florence a magnet for men and women of taste and refinement. This cultural flowering, comparable to Athens in the age of Pericles, rested on a solid economic foundation. In 1472, Benedetto Dei wrote a description of his native city meant to put a boastful Venetian in his place. With a merchant's eye for the bottom line, his tour of the city gives equal time to butchers' shops and artists' studios. "Our beautiful Florence," he wrote to the "envious" Venetian,

contains . . . two hundred seventy shops belonging to the wool merchants' guild, from whence their wares are sent to Rome and the Marches, Naples and Sicily, Constantinople and Pera, Adrianople,

Broussa, and the whole of Turkey. It contains also eighty-three rich and splendid warehouses of the silk merchants' guild, and furnishes gold and silver stuffs, velvet, brocade, damask, taffeta, and satin to Rome, Naples, Catalonia, and the whole of Spain, especially Seville, and to Turkey and Barbary. . . . The number of banks amounts to thirty-three; the shops of the cabinet-makers, whose business is carving and inlaid work, to eighty-four; and the workshops of the stonecutters and marble workers in the city and its immediate neighborhood, to fifty-four. There are forty-four goldsmiths' and jewelers' shops, thirty goldbeaters, silver-wire-drawers, and a wax-figure maker. . . . Go through all the cities of the world, nowhere will you ever be able to find artists in wax equal to those we now have in Florence, and to whom the figures in the Nunziata [Santissima Annunziata] can bear witness. Another flourishing industry is the making of light and elegant gold and silver wreaths and garlands, which are worn by young maidens of high degree, and which have given their names to the artist family of Ghirlandajo.

It was during these years that a young apprentice in Verrocchio's studio first enrolled in the Fraternity of St. Luke, signaling his matriculation as an independent master in painting. Leonardo, the illegitimate son of a notary from the Tuscan village of Vinci, was already his master's most important assistant. He was also currently hard at work for Lorenzo, contributing to the elaborate tomb he and Giuliano had commissioned to receive their father's remains in San Lorenzo.

At one time or another Lorenzo employed most of the finest painters in the city to decorate his villas. Botticelli, Filippino Lippi, Perugino, and Domenico Ghirlandaio were all engaged in painting frescoes at his villa at Spedaleto, unfortunately now destroyed. But unlike a royal court, which, through its monopoly on prestige, tends to suck all the oxygen out of the cultural atmosphere, Lorenzo's "court" encouraged imitation and competition. It was not in his interest to monopolize all the best artists, if only because this would create the impression that he believed himself superior to his fellow magnates. To be the first citizen of the land, rather than its king, meant that he had to exemplify those civic virtues of patronage without depriving others of their opportunities. Whether or not Lorenzo commissioned a particular work, it is clear that he strived to foster a climate in which architecture, painting, sculpture, literature, scholarship, and music all flourished. It was not only his friend Poliziano who saw Florence under Lorenzo as a second Athens. "Men of intellect and ability were contented [wrote Guicciardini], for all letters, all arts, all talents were welcomed and recognized."

Nor was it only the richest citizens and the most famous artists who participated in the cultural ferment. While artists like Verrocchio, Ghirlandaio, and Botticelli commanded the highest prices, there were dozens of more modest shops in the narrow streets behind the Duomo churning out small devotional Madonnas and bust-length portraits. In these latter works, especially, one can see the pride and individuality of the humble Florentine tradesman who thought enough of himself to have his features, warts and all, recorded for posterity. In fact large shops like Verrocchio's or Ghirlandaio's, with their dozens of apprentices and assistants, were something like art factories, turning out works of varying quality. Only the most important and most finicky clients would insert into the contract the phrase "all from his own [the master's] hand, and particularly the figures," as the Strozzi demanded of Filippino Lippi for their family chapel in Santa Maria Novella.

It was part of Lorenzo's conscious strategy to foster the development of the arts in his native city and his compatriots responded to his call with enthusiasm. They took pride in the beauty of the city, which raised their status in the eyes of their rivals. Even states with larger armies and populations were compelled to acknowledge the preeminence of the City of the Baptist when it came to cultural matters. Art had far greater propaganda value in the fifteenth century than it does today, and Lorenzo was always willing to lend his favorite artists as a peace offering or when he wished to strengthen diplomatic ties. Following his conflict with Pope Sixtus IV, for instance, he signaled his newfound devotion to the Holy Father by sending along Botticelli, Perugino, and Ghirlandaio to help decorate the just constructed Sistine Chapel.

But it was not simply for reasons of state that Lorenzo encouraged artists and writers to come and work in the city. As a poet and well-known authority on all matters artistic, he fostered a climate of intellectual ferment and artistic creativity almost unparalleled in the history of civilization. Of course Lorenzo did not initiate the great age of artistic achievement that has come to be known as the Renaissance—Florence had been a leading center of art and literature since the age of Dante and Giotto a century and a half earlier—but he stamped his personality and his taste on the art of his own times.

One of the artists whose work most directly reflects Lorenzo's influence—whether or not he actually commissioned a given painting—is Sandro Botticelli, who was painting some of his greatest masterpieces during these years, including the *Primavera* which is said to include a portrait of Giuliano's mistress Simonetta Vespucci as the goddess Flora. Lorenzo employed Botticelli directly on many occasions, and the artist's debt to the Medici family is indisputable. In return for paying the artist's wages, the Medici men are often depicted in his work: Lorenzo's portrait, along with that of his father and grandfather, is contained within the famous *Adoration of the Magi,* while the athletic Giuliano is likely the model for the war god who slumbers next to the goddess of love in the allegorical *Venus and Mars.** More important, Botticelli's *Primavera* and *Birth of Venus,* while no longer ascribed to Lorenzo's direct agency, drew inspiration from the circle of poets and philosophers who gathered at his villas to sup at his table and engage in arcane metaphysical discussions. Among the most immediate sources for Botticelli's mysterious allegories are the poems of Angelo Poliziano. The following passage from his "Rusticus," a poem of springtime composed while he was staying at Lorenzo's villa in Fiesole, finds its visual equivalent in Botticelli's masterpiece:

> *Nourishing Venus comes, companion to her*
> *sister, and is followed by the little loves; Flora*
> *offers welcome kisses to her eager husband*
> *(Zephyr); and in their midst with hair unbound*
> *and bared breasts dances Grace, tapping the*
> *ground with rhythmic step.*

Leaving its indelible imprint on both the poem and the painting—each poised vertiginously between rigorous intellectuality and ripe sensuousness—is the restless and contradictory spirit of the man who ruled the state.

---

* Lorenzo is probably the caped figure just below and to the left of Cosimo who kneels next to the Christ child. Directly below are the kneeling figures of his sons, Piero and Giovanni, while Giuliano stands with bowed head just to the right. Botticelli has included his self-portrait in the figure on the far right, staring confidently back at the viewer.

Melozzo da Forli, *Pope Sixtus IV Appointing Platina*, 1477 (Art Resource)

XII. THE SHADOW OF ROME

"She who was once mistress of the world is now, by the injustice of fortune, which overturns all things, not only despoiled of her empire and majesty, but delivered over to the basest servitude, misshapen and degraded, her ruins alone showing forth her former dignity and greatness."

—POGGIO BRACCIOLINI "ON THE RUINS OF ROME"

JUST BEFORE DAWN ON JULY 26, 1471, POPE PAUL II, THE grasping, quarrelsome Venetian who had headed the Church of Rome for the past seven years, departed this life. It took almost two weeks of hard bargaining to elect his successor, the fifty-seven-year-old Cardinal Francesco della Rovere, who ascended the papal throne as Sixtus IV.

Despite the usual chicanery employed to lift della Rovere to the very summit of the Church hierarchy—including the funneling of gold ducats into the pockets of the eighteen cardinals in the conclave—the choice struck a hopeful note for an institution that for the past few years seemed more a slave to Mammon than a servant of Christ.* Indeed, the contrast with his aristocratic predecessor, could not have been greater. Unlike the well-born Venetian, della Rovere was a self-made man who during his previous four years as cardinal had led an existence of unusual frugality. He was so poor, in fact, that when he was elected cardinal he could not afford to restore the dilapidated palace attached to the church of San Pietro in Vincoli (St. Peter in Chains) that served as his official residence.

Sixtus had been born the son of a poor fisherman from Savona, near Genoa, and had achieved his lofty position by dint of his own drive and

---

* Corrupt political bargaining was nothing new in the election of popes. Aeneas Silvius Piccolomini (Pius II) recalls in his memoirs being accosted in the privy by cardinals demanding his vote.

intelligence. His one discernible fault was an excessive fondness for his numerous relatives, who, with their strange accents and boorish manners, had descended upon the city like barbarians of old. This shrewd, toothless peasant with the pugnacious face of a snapping turtle promised to reinvigorate a papacy sapped by petty squabbles with other Italian states and an unbecoming taste for ostentation.

Florentines, whose own sphere of influence abutted that of the heir of St. Peter at many sensitive points, looked on with a mixture of hope and apprehension. For Lorenzo in particular, the transition offered opportunities as well as potential dangers. Despite the official condemnation of usurious practices, cardinals and noblemen continued to deposit their coin in Medici coffers at interest and to borrow against their assets, much to the profit of each. Rome was more than ever the financial as well as spiritual capital of Europe, with money from the sale of indulgences and priestly offices flowing to the Vatican from the furthest reaches of Christendom. The Medici bankers knelt beside this bountiful stream and drank their fill.*

There was reason to believe that the new occupant of St. Peter's throne would be particularly well disposed toward the ruling family of Florence. Upon hearing of Cardinal della Rovere's election, Lorenzo's kinsman Filippo de' Medici, archbishop of Pisa, wrote that it "would be very acceptable to Your Magnificence." Lorenzo, who through his Orsini in-laws had acquired a good deal of influence in the Vatican, had championed della Rovere during the elections. Shortly after his elevation the new pope sent a fulsome letter to Lorenzo expressing his gratitude toward the house of Medici for the "infinite blessings received, which redound to its honor and exaltation." What exactly these blessings were is unclear, but in della Rovere, Lorenzo believed he had a friend on the papal throne.

Also contributing to the general optimism was the belief that this Franciscan would avoid the imbroglios that had marred the tenure of his predecessor. "This pope evidently intends to be on good terms with every

---

* The Roman branch of the Medici bank continued to be the most important, but under the direction of Giovanni Tornabuoni it, too, began to suffer reverses. Maintaining good relations with the reigning pontiff required generous loans that were easier to make than to collect on. The accumulation of bad debts troubled the Roman branch no less than the others.

one," the ambassador from the marquis of Mantua reported.* Promoting the cause of harmony was the fact that Sixtus found himself so deeply in debt from the excesses of his predecessor, and from the bribes that ensured his election, that his scope for an aggressive policy in Italy was severely circumscribed. This fiscal irresponsibility was not all bad as far as Lorenzo was concerned since it encouraged Sixtus to remain on friendly terms with the Medici, the most experienced and well connected of the papal bankers. In order to equip the fleet readying itself to set out against the Turks, for instance, Sixtus was forced to sell a large part of the jewels amassed by Paul II—including fifty-four silver shells filled with pearls valued at 30,000 ducats and a diamond valued at 7,000 ducats—which the Medici bank snapped up for the bargain-basement price of 23,170 florins.†

Lorenzo was one of the six distinguished citizens—all of them men at the core of the *reggimento*—who set out from Florence on September 23, laden with gifts—including four hundred pounds of silver plates, vases, and saucers—for the new pontiff. The warm reception they received reinforced their conviction that Sixtus was eager to be a good neighbor. Lorenzo was treated with special favor by the pope, who was impressed by the poise and cultivation of his young guest. In a particularly gracious gesture, Sixtus, having learned of Lorenzo's passion for antiquities, presented him with two fine marble busts of Agrippa and Augustus. Lorenzo also purchased at discounted prices numerous cameos, vases, and carved gemstones from the papal treasury to add to his own collection. On a more practical note, Sixtus reappointed Lorenzo's uncle Giovanni Tornabuoni depositor general of the Apostolic Chamber, restoring the Medici bank to the same privileged position it had enjoyed under previous popes, and

---

* Apparently the pope's benevolence did not extend to the Turks, an inconsistency that bothered few Christian rulers. In fact the zeal with which the newly crowned pope set about organizing a Crusade against the Ottomans was seen as further evidence of his integrity. As infidels, the Turks were fair game for even the most irenic of popes. Given the Turkish advances in the eastern Mediterranean—including, most ominous, the conquest of the Venetian colony of Negroponte in 1470—that were now threatening the Italian mainland, Sixtus's initial belligerence on this front seemed amply justified.

† Like most recent campaigns against the infidels, this one ended in disappointment. The expedition that went out with high hopes in 1471–72 under Cardinal Caraffa achieved little. Quarrels between Venetian and Neapolitan factions contributed to the futility.

extended the Medici monopoly on the sale and distribution of alum from the papal mines at Tolfa.*

In addition to ensuring the continued solvency of the Roman bank, Lorenzo had another vital issue to raise with the pontiff: the long-standing desire of the Florentine people for a native-born cardinal. Lorenzo reminded Sixtus of the Holy Father's traditional deference to the Florentine *Signoria* when it came to filling major ecclesiastical positions within their territory, and Sixtus, grateful for Lorenzo's help in easing his way onto the papal throne, seemed happy to oblige, promising he would appoint someone "close to the hearts of all the citizens of the state."[†] This was not only a point of pride for Florence but a mark of independence. Without the capacity to control, or at least guide, the selection of church officials within its own borders, no state could feel itself to be truly sovereign. It was even more critical for Lorenzo, whose ability to find sinecures for his favorites was an important part of the patronage system upon which his personal authority depended.

With these important matters satisfactorily settled, Lorenzo now took the opportunity to tour the city's ancient ruins with Leon Battista Alberti, the foremost architect and architectural historian of his generation. Clambering among the shattered vaults and broken columns of the imperial capital like Donatello and Brunelleschi a generation earlier, Lorenzo sharpened his own architectural ideas, ones he would later put into practice in both public and private commissions.

Like other fifteenth-century Florentines, Lorenzo felt himself the heir of the civilization that had emerged two thousand years earlier along the banks of the Tiber.[‡] But Rome in the fifteenth century was a sorry specta-

---

* Tornabuoni took up the position of depositor general reluctantly, believing it would lead to no end of difficulties. The pope was financially overextended and Tornabuoni feared that he would borrow money he could not repay. Lorenzo's willingness to accept the deal may have been based on political rather than financial considerations.

† There is no doubt that Lorenzo felt he had assurances from Sixtus on this point, though it is not certain that these date from the initial meetings.

‡ Florence was in fact founded by Roman imperial legions, though Florentines made rather more of this birth than is warranted by the archaeological record, which suggests that in classical times it was little more than an obscure military outpost.

cle in which past grandeur served to highlight present decadence. Sheep grazed in pastures where ancient temples once stood; wolves hunted rabbits and deer among the broken columns that Caesar and Augustus had first raised. Open sewers had replaced the aqueducts that once had supplied the city with fresh water, causing a stench to rise from crooked streets overhung by ramshackle tenements. Through the squalor and the rubble, cardinals with their vast retinues of liveried servants daintily picked their way from sumptuous palaces to the Vatican, where they conferred with their master about the fate of millions of souls. "Surely this city is to be mourned," Lorenzo's compatriot Poggio Bracciolini had written earlier in the century,

> which once produced so many illustrious men and emperors . . . the mother of so many good arts, the city from which flowed military discipline, purity of morals and life, the decrees of the law, the models of all the virtues, and the knowledge of right living. She who was once mistress of the world is now, by the injustice of fortune, which overturns all things, not only despoiled of her empire and majesty, but delivered over to the basest servitude.

Lorenzo returned to Florence after a twelve-day sojourn in the Eternal City, his aesthetic ambition stimulated by his exposure to its splendid monuments, his saddle bags filled with treasures to adorn the already crowded rooms of his palace, his spirits lifted by the tokens of friendship he'd received from the head of Christendom. Though his attention was soon diverted by other pressing matters—including the war with Volterra that was reaching its sorry climax—he had not forgotten the promise Sixtus had made to appoint a Florentine cardinal. In fact, the more he thought about it, the more it seemed to him that the pope's apparent agreeableness provided the perfect opportunity to advance not only the prestige of the city but the fortunes of his family. During his conversations with Sixtus he had been content with the vague formulation of a candidate "close to the hearts of all the citizens of the state"; now he had in mind a particular name. The identity of this candidate is suggested in a letter he wrote to Pope Sixtus in November 1472: "In order not to trouble Your Blessedness," he began, "I write to Giovanni

Tornabuoni, who will speak of the longstanding wish of our house to have a cardinal; and such is the faith that I place in Your Holiness, that I am certain I need no other assurances than those already freely promised in this matter, nevertheless, hearing the news that soon more cardinals will be named, I wish to place once again in the mind of Your Blessedness a reminder of this our ancient desire."

There is little doubt that when Giovanni Tornabuoni met with Sixtus it was to lobby on behalf of Giuliano, Lorenzo's eighteen-year-old brother. If Lorenzo had his way—and he had little reason to doubt that the pope would oblige him in this matter—the carefree, high-living teenager would exchange his doublet and hose for the scarlet robes and skullcap of a cardinal. This would mark the final transformation of this family of bankers into one of the great noble houses of Europe, making the Medici a force to be reckoned with in both the secular and spiritual realms. In a matter of such importance Lorenzo was unwilling to leave things to chance. Shortly after instructing Tornabuoni to broach the subject with the pope, he dispatched another emissary to Rome—his devoted friend and manager of the Medici bank in Florence, Francesco Nori. Even before Nori arrived Lorenzo had softened up potential opposition by unleashing a barrage of letters to all the leading prelates, including the pope's nephew, the newly minted cardinal Pietro Riario.

Why had Giuliano's career suddenly become a matter of such urgent concern to Lorenzo? A clue can be found in a report by the Milanese ambassador in April of 1472. It concerns a disagreement between the two brothers, one of the few on record, over a trip Giuliano had planned to Venice. This was to be his first journey to an important foreign state on his own. Conferring with the Doge and senators of the Most Serene Republic he would show the world that he was not merely Lorenzo's younger brother but a man of substance in his own right. "Such is the desire of Giuliano to make the journey to Venice," wrote the Milanese ambassador, "that it has caused some quarrel to arise between Lorenzo and him." It is not clear why Lorenzo objected to the trip—perhaps he felt that his brother was still too immature, or perhaps there was important business to attend to in Florence—but whatever the reason, Giuliano felt he had been publicly humiliated, complaining, according to Sacramoro's report, that "he [Lorenzo] does not wish him to make his way in the world, or to enjoy any reputation whatsoever." Ironically, Giuliano was now in the same position Lorenzo had once been in, anxious to prove himself and chafing under the heavy-handed supervision of his elders. In the end Lorenzo relented. Giuliano's journey to Venice turned out to be both a personal and diplomatic success, but the incident was a reminder that now was the time to think seriously about his future.

The quarrel over the Venetian junket was a symptom of a larger problem. Contemporary sources all attest to the genuine affection that united the two brothers—Marsilio Ficino, writing to Giuliano, refers to Lorenzo as "your other self, both in nature and in will"—but beneath the surface there were signs of strain that grew out of Lorenzo's unique and uniquely complex position as the first citizen of Florence. So far Giuliano's role had caused few difficulties. He ably assisted his brother with affairs of state, filling in for Lorenzo while he was away and serving as his most trusted advisor when they were together. His charm and easygoing personality served Lorenzo well on those many occasions when Giuliano was called upon to entertain visiting dignitaries or to deputize for his older brother at state functions, much as Lorenzo himself had once done for their father. When Lorenzo was detained in Pisa overseeing the reopening of the university, he informed the Milanese ambassador, "I wrote to Giuliano, my brother, that you would confer with him in everything and that you would make sure that all went according to the wishes of Our Lord [the Duke]."

But by the spring of 1472 it was becoming clear to Lorenzo that the teenager had begun to bridle at his junior status. Giuliano's friend Piero Vespucci wrote some years later, "Many times he told me that he was the most unhappy youth, not only of Florence but of all Italy." These lines paint a picture at odds with the usual one of the carefree youth who cared for nothing but hunting, drinking, and making love to the prettiest girls of Florence.

The pain this struggle caused Lorenzo may be gauged indirectly by verses he wrote many years later. They are found in his play *The Martyrdom of Saints John and Paul*, a drama that has clear parallels to his own situation. The play is set in the court of the Constantine, riven by a deadly struggle for power among the emperor's sons, that surely contains some echo, however faint, of the palace on the Via Larga. Perhaps it was only through the camouflage of his art that Lorenzo could give voice to the fear that jealousy and ambition would ultimately poison the relationship he cherished most:

Sometimes discord can spread
Even in brothers bound by love most deep.

Personal feelings no doubt contributed to the sudden urgency with which Lorenzo pursued the matter of his brother's career, but settling Giuliano in the Church was also part of a strategy to forge stronger links between the Medici family and the inner circle of the papal curia, building on those already established through the Orsini family. True, Giuliano had not yet shown the least aptitude for or interest in a life in the Church, his appreciation for scripture a less notable feature of his character than his appreciation for fast horses, but he would not be the first worldly young man to make the leap from man of the world to man of the cloth. Giuliano, in fact, fit the profile of a typical Renaissance cardinal. The Renaissance Church was a wealthy and worldly institution run by wealthy and worldly men. Sixtus, who had risen from obscurity based on his talents rather than his connections, was the exception rather than the rule. As a young cardinal from a rich and powerful family, Giuliano would be following in the footsteps of his Orsini relatives. Son of the even more famous Medici, he would have the prestige and cash on hand necessary to uphold the reputation and authority of the Sacred College.

For all Sixtus's bland assurances, however, the pope seemed to be in no hurry to name a Florentine, let alone a Medici, to the highest dignity of the Church. His first slate of nominees, published in December 1471, included only two names: that of his nephews, Pietro Riario and Giuliano della Rovere. As new lists were compiled with equally disappointing results, Lorenzo began to suspect he had been deceived. Cardinal Ammanati, who along with Giovanni Tornabuoni had been entrusted by Lorenzo to pursue this matter, remained hopeful: "I see no difficulty, if his Holiness lives, to his attaining the highest honor, for I can promise for more than one [vote]. Have no uneasiness about the cardinals who have just been made, as it will be necessary soon to create others for the Emperor and King Ferrante, for Rome and for you Florentines, if you desire it."

As new appointments were announced, however, a clear pattern began to emerge: the Sacred College was to be a tightly controlled instrument of Sixtus's foreign policy whose chief aim was to place the della Rovere and Riario names among the great clans of Europe.* It was not only Pietro Riario and Giuliano della Rovere who profited from their uncle's generosity: in 1477, Sixtus elevated his sixteen-year-old great-nephew Raffaele Sansoni Riario—a youth in whom spiritual qualities were no more apparent than in Giuliano de' Medici—to the cardinalate, showing once again a tendency to treat the Holy Church like a family-run business.

Sixtus was neither the first nor the last pope to engage in nepotism. Relatives of a reigning pontiff were automatically vaulted into the first rank of European nobility, feudal titles and lucrative benefices dropping into their laps like manna from heaven, but the obscurity of the della Rovere family, coupled with the burning ambition of the man at its head, combined in a particularly virulent strain of what was a chronic papal disease. The fisherman's son, having reached the pinnacle of power, was determined to use his high office to compensate for an oversight of history that had left his family impoverished while less deserving clans lorded over vast feudal estates and surrounded themselves in unimaginable luxury. Membership in the College of Cardinals would be reserved for blood relations or, failing

---

* Della Rovere was Sixtus's own family name; Riario was the married name of his sister, whose children were among those whose fortunes were advanced by their uncle. From Sixtus's own day, rumors have circulated that his many nephews were in fact his own children, but no firm evidence has ever been uncovered to support this contention. The only supporting evidence is his obvious affection for the boys and the assiduousness with which he advanced their careers, but this might well have been simply the transferal of the paternal instinct to the closest object. Savonarola, who lived during the reign of Alexander VI who openly acknowledged his children, wrote: "The priests used to call their sons nephews; now they are not nephews, but sons, sons plain and simple!" (Roeder, *Man of the Renaissance,* p. 77.) Sixtus's brother-in-law, Paolo Riario, had supported him early in career, inviting him to tutor his sons. Sixtus later wrote to him, "I well know that to you, after God, I owe it that I have become what I am; I will show myself grateful; let me have your son Pietro for my son: I will give him the best possible education, and make a notable man of him." (Pastor p. 234.) Sixtus's vices, unlike those of his successor and many other Renaissance popes, did not seem to include excesses of the flesh. In addition to Pietro Riario, Giuliano della Rovere, and Raffaele Sansoni Riario, two other papal nephews were elevated to the Sacred College—Cristoforo and Girolamo Basso della Rovere.

this, for those from whom immediate material benefits could be expected. Clearly there was no room in such company for the name of Medici.

In pursuing such blatantly selfish aims Sixtus disappointed those idealists who saw his election as an opportunity to reform a corrupt institution. But even hardheaded diplomats worried about the deleterious effects of the pope's fondness for his relatives, fearing that efforts on their behalf would upset the delicate balance of power in Italy. Nowhere was that nervousness more apparent than among the occupants of the Palace of Priors, who knew that the realization of papal ambition could only come at Florence's expense.

The first and most favored recipient of Sixtus's largesse was his nephew Pietro Riario, whose deftness at filling the pockets of the cardinals with gold had been instrumental in his uncle's success. Sixtus was determined to refashion his nephew into a prince of the Church by showering him with lucrative appointments. In the space of a few short months the young Franciscan monk had emerged from obscurity to become one of the wealthiest and most powerful men in Europe.

Pietro Riario's meteoric career is emblematic of the corruption of the Renaissance Church. Among its greatest abuses—and one that was to be a particular target of reformers like Martin Luther—was the practice of allowing a single prelate to acquire multiple titles, each of which paid a hefty salary while demanding nothing of its holder. One man might serve simultaneously as an archbishop in Scotland and an abbot in Bavaria, drawing income from each while setting foot in neither. The accumulation of these so-called benefices allowed a well-connected Church officer to live like a prince in Rome while his nominal parishioners were left to fend for themselves. In addition to receiving a cardinal's hat, Pietro received bishoprics in Split, Seville, and Valencia, benefices that netted an income of 1,000 ducats a year. After his uncle conferred upon him the patriarchate of Constantinople and the abbey of Sant'Ambrogio, Pietro's income swelled to 60,000 ducats. With the death in 1473 of Giovanni Neroni—brother of Dietisalvi, who had been living in exile since the failed conspiracy of 1466—Sixtus added to Pietro's already impressive portfolio by bestowing on him the crucial archbishopric of Florence.

Cardinal Riario was an energetic and capable advocate for papal interests, at least as Sixtus defined them. Even more intelligent and capable was

Cardinal Giuliano della Rovere, the future Pope Julius II, under whose aggressive rule the Renaissance Church would reach the pinnacle of its military, if not spiritual, power. A man of aggressive and martial temperament, Giuliano would work for most of his adult life to extend the authority and reach of the Church, donning armor and leading his troops into battle for the sake of God's glory. Whatever one thought of the militant Giuliano, no one could describe him as a nonentity.

The same could not be said for Girolamo Riario, Pietro's younger brother. Before his uncle's elevation, Girolamo had served as a part-time customs clerk in a small Ligurian town, a station in life that suited the abilities if not the aspirations of this temperamental and somewhat dim young man. Brought to Rome by the newly anointed Sixtus, the twenty-eight-year-old Girolamo shared the family ambition but possessed little of the ability that marked most of the Riario–della Rovere clan.

So far Sixtus had used his position to advance his relatives within the ecclesiastical hierarchy of which he was the titular head, but a career in the Church had its drawbacks for anyone with long-term ambitions. Most inconvenient was the fact that celibate priests could not pass on their titles and lands to legitimate children. Thus if the Riario and della Rovere were to insinuate themselves into the landed aristocracy, at least one of their members would have to remain a layman, to marry and to father children upon whom he could bestow the honors and estates he had acquired in his lifetime. This was the role that fell to Girolamo. Sixtus, showing an equal zeal in pursuing secular titles as he had in securing ecclesiastical preferments for his other nephews, strained body and soul to provide the lands and titles that would transform him into a great feudal lord.

Sixtus's ambition for his family did not make a clash with Lorenzo inevitable. In fact his policy was in many ways the mirror image of Lorenzo's own. For Lorenzo, whose family leveraged business success into political power, the prestige of high Church office would offer a legitimacy not available within the republican framework of their native city. For Sixtus, by contrast, the trick was to turn his meteoric rise in the Church hierarchy into something permanent by trading spiritual capital for the more tangible asset of feudal titles and the real estate that went along with them. In some ways their aims were complementary and, had Lorenzo been willing to play the game, they might well have come to an arrangement whereby both families prospered by allowing the other to pursue their ambitions unhindered. In this scenario Lorenzo would have given Sixtus a free hand to pursue a fiefdom for his nephew in central Italy, and in return the pope would settle Giuliano handsomely in the Church. That their relations instead deteriorated into murder and mayhem reveals the complexity of Lorenzo's position as both a private citizen and effective head of state, and offers a rare insight into the character of the two men soon to be locked in a life and death struggle.

The Riario–della Rovere clan is immortalized in one of the most remarkable group portraits of the Renaissance, a fresco painted by Melozzo da Forli to commemorate Sixtus's reopening of the Vatican Library and his appointment of the humanist Bartolomeo Platina as its chief librarian.* The fresco is less remarkable for its artistic merit than for the psychological insight it offers into these men of disparate talents and temperaments, united only by a common desire to grasp all they can while there's still time. In a magnificent architectural setting whose coffered ceiling and gilded columns recall the grandeur of imperial Rome, the family gathers, looking strangely ill at ease and out of place. The pope himself, gripping the arms of his throne like a bird of prey, scowls unpleasantly, not so much looking at the kneeling Platina as through him.† At his side stands young Cardinal Riario, his beak-nosed profile deliberately echoing Sixtus's own—perhaps a covert recognition of a closer relationship between the two than could be admitted officially. Before him stands the formidable Giuliano, the monk's tonsure revealing his membership in the peace-loving Franciscan order but his massive frame and authoritative posture suggesting more the fighting spirit of a warrior-king.

---

* This fresco, with its magnificent architectural setting, also suggests a more constructive aspect of Pope Sixtus's reign. Sixtus was one of the great builder popes of the Renaissance, who helped transform the decaying ciy into the glorious capital of Christendom it would become in the following centuries.

† Platina had every reason to be grateful to Sixtus. He had been imprisoned and tortured by Paul II, who suspected him and his fellow humanists of plotting against his authority. Sixtus had restored Platina to his former position and then appointed him to head his new library. Platina was also a great admirer of Lorenzo, dedicating his book *On the Best Citizen* to him.

And then there's Girolamo. Facing away from his uncle, he seems no part of the gathering at all. His artfully tousled hair and heavy gold chain of office over a blue satin robe suggest a fragile vanity.* His pose mirrors that of his cousin Giuliano, but this only serves to contrast their characters—the cardinal's strength and Girolamo's weakness; the gravity of the former, his jaw thrust forward determinedly, the petulant sulk of the latter whose expression resembles that of a child who has just been punished for misbehaving.

The first step in Sixtus's ambitious plan to elevate the Riario–della Rovere clan into the ranks of the landed aristocracy was to acquire a title for Girolamo, purchasing in his name the hamlet of Bosco d'Alessandria for the price of 14,000 gold florins. This rustic village in northern Romagna was hardly worth the price but for the fact that the former grocer's clerk could now style himself *Count* Girolamo. Having thus bought his way (on credit) into the feudal nobility, Count Girolamo now set about finding a bride to match his newly won eminence. His agent in this delicate matter of the heart was his brother, the wily Cardinal Pietro, who, with an instinct for the main chance, set his sights on one of the most powerful families in Italy—the Sforza of Milan. Though not the most ancient lineage of Europe—their association with Milan dated only to the time of the current duke's father—the Sforza ranked above all but a few of the greatest monarchs in Europe. Critically, as the ruling dynasty of the greatest city-state in Italy, the Sforza could offer powerful protection for the fledgling entity that Sixtus and Pietro were stitching together for Girolamo from the independent communes of the Romagna.

At first the plan was to wed Girolamo to the duke's twelve-year-old niece, Costanza, but the deal fell through when, after months of delay, the impatient count insisted that he be allowed to consummate the marriage then and there, mortally offending the girl's mother, Gabriella Gonzaga.† Anxious to avoid giving offense to the pope, Duke Galeazzo offered in her place his illegitimate daughter, the ten-year-old Caterina. The ceremony

---

* In 1477, the year of this painting, Sixtus appointed Girolamo burgher of the city of Rome and a member of the Roman nobility; the medal probably signifies his new rank.

† Gabriella Gonzaga angrily rejected the suggestion by her father, Lodovico, Marquis of Mantua, that the two "lie together without intercourse."

took place January 17, 1473, in the Pavia Castle with the duke himself presiding. The modesty of the affair, which was attended only by the duke, a
few officials, and the two principals, can be explained only by the fact that
Caterina was illegitimate. Even so, Pietro and his uncle were well pleased
with the fruit of their efforts: the daughter of a duke, even an illegitimate
one, opened up breathtaking vistas. Galeazzo's own father, the *condottiere*
Francesco, had parlayed a similar match with Duke Filippo Maria Visconti's illegitimate daughter into a dukedom for himself. Perhaps equally
glorious opportunities awaited young Girolamo.*

Though both sides hoped to profit from the connection, Sixtus was
quicker to exploit the situation. Having used the little town of Bosco
d'Alessandria to bait the Sforza, he now used the Sforza connection to
land a bigger fish. Casting about in the grab bag of jumbled principalities
of the Romagna for a feudal property that would add luster to the Riario
name, his greedy eyes lighted upon a likely piece of real estate.

Imola was a mid-sized city of some seven thousand souls strategically
located on the ancient Roman Via Emilia, which led through the rugged
Apennines before descending into the vineyard- and olive-carpeted Tuscan valley below. Though nominally part of the Papal States, this town,
some fifty miles due north of Florence, had for generations been under the
effective control of the Manfredi family. The *Signoria* of Florence had long
kept a watchful eye on Imola, hoping someday to add it to their Tuscan
empire or at the very least to ensure that it remained out of unfriendly

---

* The match proved just the beginning of an eventful career for Caterina, whose sudden
turns of fortune offer a fascinating glimpse into the violence and chaos of Renaissance
Italy. Caterina would in time prove herself one of the truly remarkable women of the
century, a survivor who negotiated the treacherous waters of Italian politics with skill
and courage. To those who assumed that being a woman she was naturally weak and
incapable, she declared, "I am not Duke Galeazzo's daughter for nothing: I have his
brains in my head." (Pastor, 301) She was married at a tender age to a violent and
insignificant man but managed to outlive her spouse and fight for her own rights and
those of her children against powerful lords, even facing down the ferocious Cesare Borgia, an act of defiance that earned her the admiration of Machiavelli. When her sons had
been taken hostage by an army besieging her fortress and the soldiers threatened to kill
them before her eyes, she pulled up her skirt and taunted them, "Don't you think, you
fools, that I have the stuff to make others?" (Breisach, 104) The siege was soon lifted and
her sons released.

hands.* This second goal was jeopardized by the current lord of Imola, Taddeo Manfredi, a feckless ruler who had forfeited the people's trust by embroiling himself in family squabbles and generally mismanaging his affairs. Faced with open insurrection, in May of 1473 he secretly ceded his patrimony to the duke of Milan, exchanging the troublesome possession for the smaller but more secure Castelnuovo di Tortona.

The transfer caused much consternation among the leaders of Florence. Possession of Imola would place Milan directly astride Florence's major trade routes to northern Europe and enable the duke to dominate his southern ally. Now, if ever, was the time for Lorenzo to put his friendship with Galeazzo Maria Sforza to the test. Appealing to both personal sentiment and to greed, Lorenzo soon managed to work out a suitable arrangement. Under its terms, kept secret until Florence could secure its new territory, the duke would part with his new acquisition in return for a hefty monetary consideration, ultimately fixed at 100,000 ducats.† It was an arrangement that suited both parties. Sforza, always hard up for cash, was happy to oblige his old friend as long as he was adequately compensated for his troubles, while the government of Florence was pleased to add another jewel to the imperial crown with so little effort.

But Lorenzo had little time to celebrate his diplomatic triumph. The moment Sixtus got wind of the proposed sale he flew into a rage, for this was exactly the town that he hoped to offer his nephew as a wedding present. "O my son!" wrote the aggrieved pontiff to the duke, "listen to your father's counsel; depart not from the Church, for it is written: 'Whoever separates himself from thee, must perish.'" This was no idle threat. Wielding the power of excommunication, the pope could place in jeopardy not only the duke's immortal soul but those of his subjects, who would be denied the holy sacraments unless and until their leader saw the light. Salaries as well as souls were threatened: excommunication, by rendering

---

* On January 26, 1472, the Florentine emissary declared that the rulers of Florence "would spare neither expense nor any effort in making themselves lord of that state." (See *Lettere di Lorenzo de' Medici*, i, 443.)

† The documents actually call the transfer a "gift" of the duke to the Florentine people; 50,000 ducats, however, went to defray the costs Sforza had supposedly incurred, while another 50,000 was to cover expenses associated with the transfer itself.

invalid all contracts and treaties signed by citizens of the wayward state, could quickly lead to economic collapse. Faced with such dire consequences, the duke beat a prudent retreat, tearing up the agreement. Then, much to the consternation of Lorenzo and his fellow countrymen, he offered the contested city to Pietro Riario for the discounted price of 40,000 ducats.*

Up to this point, relations between Florence and Sixtus had been friendly. Lorenzo in particular, despite continued frustration over his inability to obtain a cardinal's hat for his brother, strived to remain in the pope's good graces. But Sixtus's interference in the sale of Imola strained the relationship to the breaking point. Most troubling, it threatened to drive a wedge between Lorenzo and the people of Florence, since it was clear that on this critical issue the interests of family and state clashed. As if to make the choice even more painful, the pope now turned to the Medici bank to advance him the funds he lacked to make the purchase. Whether or not Sixtus intended in this way to test Lorenzo's loyalty, it was soon apparent that Sixtus regarded Lorrenzo's willingness to assist him in this matter as a crucial measure of their future relations.

But on this vital matter Lorenzo would also be judged by the people of Florence. There was no doubt where his own self-interest lay: both for the sake of the family business and for his brother's future, the wisest course would be to accede to the pope's demand. Good relations with the Vatican were critical to the Medici bank, since the bulk of their funds were tied up in one way or another in business with the papal curia. But he could not please Sixtus without provoking the wrath of his fellow citizens, whose suspicion of the papacy had ancient roots. Not surprising, Lorenzo agonized over the decision. Though he would have preferred to remain on friendly terms with Sixtus, his patriotism recoiled at the prospect of a powerful papal enclave on Florence's northern border. Reluctantly, he concluded he had no choice but to refuse the pope's request, for he could not claim to speak for his people while at the same time putting self-interest above country.

---

* Lorenzo did not immediately give up hope of buying off the pope. Indeed, his uncle Giovanni Tornabuoni assured him that with a few thousand ducats strategically scattered all could be arranged to Lorenzo's satisfaction. He was also assured by those close to the duke that all would eventually be resolved in Florence's favor (see *Lettere*, i, pp. 443–46).

Having made the painful decision, however, Lorenzo thought he could evade its consequences, enlisting Sforza to plead his case. Curiously, the duke seemed more than happy to oblige. He told Lorenzo he would write to Cardinal Riario explaining Lorenzo's actions in the matter, blithely assuring him that a good word from the duke of Milan was sufficient to restore the Medici's reputation in Rome. In fact, Sforza had been secretly encouraging Lorenzo to refuse the pope's request for a loan, despite the fact that the 40,000 ducats would presumably find their way into his pocket. This bizarre scenario illustrates a streak of deviousness in the duke's character. The truth is that while Sforza could not afford to alienate the pope, he still hoped the deal would fall through, thereby opening the way for the more lucrative and geopolitically advantageous transfer of Imola to Florentine rule.

It was a strategy too subtle and convoluted to succeed. In the end Cardinal Riario found another party willing to lend him the 40,000 ducats and the sale of Imola went through in the winter of 1473 without help from the Medici. This was the worst possible outcome for Lorenzo. Not only had he failed to block Girolamo's acquisition of the strategic town, but he now had to face the wrath of a pope who viewed the young Florentine as the chief obstacle to his family's advancement. Vanished was the paternal benevolence Sixtus expressed at their meeting two short years ago, replaced instead by feelings whose bitterness can only be explained by a sense of betrayal. In years to come, when relations between Lorenzo and the pope had descended to murderous depths, the sin Sixtus would most often attribute to him was that of ingratitude, an indication that his fury had less to do with politics—though the issues at stake were very real—than with his outrage over an affection he believed had been treacherously abused.

Imola marks the point on the geopolitical map where the interests of Lorenzo's family and his country most sharply diverged. Lorenzo's critics have never given him any credit for apparently putting country above family, arguing that he had no real choice in the matter. To have agreed to the pope's request would have meant forfeiting the confidence of the people without which he would have lost all status in the republic. But far from proving that Lorenzo cynically manipulated the government of Florence for his own ends, the episode reveals the extent to which his primacy was dependent on the goodwill of the people. This point is succinctly made in Guicciardini's *Dialogue on the Government of Florence* in which Bernardo del Nero, one of Lorenzo's staunchest supporters, explains the relationship between the Medici family and the state they ruled: "For the Medici did not enjoy a lordship or a separate state to give them greatness; everything they had depended on the power of the Florentine state. Their prosperity and growth lay in its prosperity and growth, for the greater and more powerful the city became, the more powerful they became too."

While Guicciardini may have overstated the extent to which the fortunes of the Medici bank depended on the fortunes of the state as a whole— sometimes, as in the crisis over Imola, they were in fact diametrically opposed—the general premise is accurate: over three generations the Medici became so closely identified with Florence that they were compelled to pursue policies that benefited the state, even to the detriment of short-term profits. Though nominally a private family, they could not afford to pursue interests that ran counter to those of the republic they served.

Of course this was not simply a matter of altruistic patriotism, nor were Lorenzo and his forebears above using the instruments of government for their own private gain.* But the insecurity and irregularity of Lorenzo's position meant that he was more sensitive to changes in public opinion than a monarch whose right to rule was sanctioned by God and tradition. The peculiar nature of Medici power, and the difficulty Florentines had in distinguishing between private interest and the public good, caused no end of perplexities for Lorenzo. Political power, originally built on the foundation of financial power and pursued in order to protect those inter-ests, had gradually taken on a life of its own until the current head of the family was often forced to neglect the very thing that first brought his ancestors to prominence. Robbing Peter to pay Paul, that is, investing ever

---

* Critics rightly point out that the Medici, and Lorenzo in particular, illegally appropri-ated public money for their own use, but it is not at all certain that they took more than they spent. As private citizens, without salaries and without access to an efficient bureau-cracy, they were often forced to dip into their personal fortune to further the interests of the republic. Lorenzo was by no means selfless in his pursuit of power, but neither was he the crook portrayed by his enemies. Lorenzo's increasingly precarious financial position reveals that being the uncrowned ruler of Florence was no guarantee of prosperity.

larger portions of his capital to the cause of shoring up his political fortunes, was a strategy that could not long be sustained and one that gives
Lorenzo's later career the desperate quality of an acrobat juggling too
many balls. As the Imola crisis well illustrates, reconciling the needs of the
state with those of the bank was a puzzle not even a man as resourceful as
Lorenzo could solve.

Thus far the dispute over Imola remained a little more than a minor irri-
tant. Few could have imagined—least of all Lorenzo—that this obscure
international incident would touch off a crisis serious enough to threaten
not only his regime but his life. Just as the crisis of Volterra fed off internal
divisions in Florence, the crisis of Imola would expose deep wounds
within the body politic. The rivalries that characterized Florentine society,
sometimes suppressed but never completely eradicated, awaited such
moments of stress to reassert themselves, often with shocking ferocity, so
it is not surprising that there were among the citizens at least a few willing
to exploit Lorenzo's difficulties for their own ends. As Lorenzo flailed this
way and that in an attempt to defend the interests of the republic while
protecting the assets of the bank, his policy was undercut by another Florentine family, one whose name was even more prominently featured in
the storied annals of the republic. This was the ancient and noble family of
the Pazzi, a proud and vigorous lineage who saw in Lorenzo's quarrel with
Sixtus the opportunity they had long been seeking to profit from their
rival's troubles and to place themselves once again in their rightful place at
the pinnacle of Florentine society.

Workshop of Luca della Robbia, *Pazzi Arms*, 16th century (Art Resource)

XIII. UNDER THE SIGN
OF MARS

"... that noble city, in the province of Tuscany, built under the sign of Mars..."

—DINO COMPAGNI, *CHRONICLE OF FLORENCE*, BOOK I

"And so it is clear that this life-destroying enmity comes from no other source than the sin of the pagan Florentines themselves who in ancient times worshiped the idol of Mars, since at his feet they committed the murder from which so much evil followed."

—GIOVANNI VILLANI, *CHRONICLE*, VI, XXXVIII

WHEN FLORENTINES LOOKED BACK ON THEIR TROUBLED history they located the source of their suffering in an ancient act of betrayal. According to legend, the city had been founded in the century before Christ by the legions of Caesar's army. At the very heart of the new city, built to guard a narrow crossing of the Arno River, these soldiers raised a temple dedicated to the terrible deity to whom they owed their allegiance—Mars, the Roman god of war. When Christianity displaced the old forms of worship the shrine was not destroyed but simply reconsecrated, this time to that most gentle of men, the desert preacher John the Baptist.*

---

* The best account of Florentines' traditional beliefs about her ancient history comes in Giovanni Villani's fourteenth-century *Cronica Nuova*, Book I, where he recounts the story of Caesar's destruction of Fiesole and the establishment of Florence in the valley below. Modern archaeologists have traced the city's founding to soldiers of the imperial age. The oldest parts of the Baptistery of San Giovanni, though erected on Roman foundations, date to the fourth century A.D. The present octagonal building, with its distinctive exterior paneling of green and white marble, dates largely to the twelfth century. The statue of Mars remained at the foot of the Ponte Vecchio until it washed away during a particularly violent flood in 1333.

Like most legends, however, this is not a simple story of a triumphal march from barbarism to enlightenment, but rather a cautionary tale about the dangers of courting and then abandoning the vengeful spirits that inhabit the dark corners of the world. Neglected but not entirely forgotten, the angry god who had been present at the city's birth still exerted his malevolent influence over future generations. It was he who for centuries set Florentine against Florentine, who saw to it that the streets ran red with blood and that such madness filled the minds of men that whole neighborhoods were put to the torch. Even that most pious of Christians, Dante Alighieri, testified to the ineradicable power of the bloodthirsty deity: "I was of the city that changed for the Baptist its first patron," he wrote in *Inferno*, "who for this will always afflict it with his art; and were it not that at the passage of the Arno there yet remains some semblance of him, those citizens who afterwards rebuilt it on the ashes left by Attila would have labored in vain."

The "semblance" Dante spoke of was the statue of Mars that the citizens, hedging their bets, had moved to the foot of the Ponte Vecchio when the ancient temple was rededicated. From here his doleful countenance witnessed with grim satisfaction one of the most famous murders in Florence's bloody history:

on Easter morning [wrote Giovanni Villani in his *Chronicle*], day of our Lord's Resurrection, the conspirators gathered in the house of the Amidei of Santo Stefano, while approaching from the Oltrarno was *messer* Buondelmonte, nobly attired in a mantle of spotless white, his palfrey also covered in snow-white cloth, until he reached the foot of the Ponte Vecchio on the near bank, just beside the pillar where stood the statue of Mars. Here, *messer* Buondelmonte was pulled from his horse by Schiatta delgi Uberti, and set upon by Mosca Lamberti and Lambertuccio degli Amidei who wounded him grievously, and by Oderigo Fifanti who along with one of the counts of Gangalandi cut open his veins and made an end of him. Hearing of the deed, there arose in the city a great commotion and the citizens gathered up their arms. The slaying of *messer* Buondelmonte was the cause and the beginning of the accursed parties of Guelf and Ghibelline, the sects that divided the noble citizens one against the other, and the cause of the quarrels between those who favored the Church and those who swore allegiance to the Emperor; because of the death of *messer* Buondelmonte all the noble lineages and other citizens were drawn into the fray, and of those who called themselves Guelfs the Buondelmonti were their leaders, while the Uberti commanded the Ghibellines; from which dissensions our city derived great evil and ruin, as will be shown, evils that will endure forever unless God himself makes an end of it. And so it is clear that this life-destroying enmity comes from no other source than the sin of the pagan Florentines themselves who in ancient times worshipped the idol of Mars, since at his feet they committed the murder from which so much evil followed.

Mars's baleful influence, however, did not end with the triumph of the Guelfs, who, having defeated their Ghibelline rivals, immediately split into two warring factions whose hatred for each other was every bit as lively as that for their vanquished foes.

Among the most prominent of the lawless feudal clans who turned the streets of Florence into a perpetual battlefield was the ancient and noble Pazzi.* In 1099, Pazzo de' Pazzi had been the first knight to scale the walls of Jerusalem when Godfrey of Bouillon's crusading army wrested the holy city from the infidels. As a reward for his bravery Godfrey presented him with a flint chipped from the tomb of Christ in the Church of the Holy Sepulcher, a precious relic that Pazzo brought back to his native land as a souvenir of his adventures. It was through a spark struck from this stone that every Easter evening a new flame was kindled on the high altar of the cathedral, a ritual that is still commemorated in Florence with the great fireworks display known as the *Carro de' Pazzi*.

Over the centuries, the Pazzi continued to render distinguished service to their city. Pazzo's descendant Jacopo de' Pazzi carried the banner of the republic at the disastrous battle of Montaperti (1260), when the Florentine army was overwhelmed by their ancient rival, Ghibelline Siena; such was his courage that even after the traitorous Bocca degli Abati lopped off his hands, Jacopo continued to hold high the banner of the red lily with his stumps, loosening his grasp only in death. When a few years later the

---

* Their name has the unfortunate meaning in Italian of "madmen," not altogether inappropriate given their history of violence and irrationality.

Black Guelfs reclaimed the city, Jacopo's son Pazzino rose to the first ranks as a leader of the Blacks.*

But Pazzino, while belonging to the faction that would ultimately emerge victorious in Florence, had no better luck than his father. Dino Compagni's *Chronicle* provides a compelling account of Pazzino's demise, and a chilling glimpse into the ghastly carnival of death staged daily in the streets of the medieval city:

> *Messer* Pazzino de' Pazzi [wrote the fourteenth-century chronicler], one of the four principal leaders of the city, sought peace with the Donati on his own behalf and that of messer Pino de' Rossi—even though messer Pino bore little guilt for the death of messer Corso, because he had been messer Corso's good friend and had cared for little else. But the Cavalcanti, who were a powerful family and had about sixty men who could bear arms, nursed a great hatred for these six leading knights who had constrained Folcieri the *Podesta* to decapitate Masino Cavalcanti. They bore this without any open display.
>
> One day Paffiera Cavalcanti, a very spirited young man, heard that *messer* Pazzino had gone to the banks of the Arno near Santa Croce with a falcon and just one servant. He mounted his horse with some companions and they went to find him. When *messer* Pazzino saw them coming, he began to flee towards the Arno. Paffiera, pursuing him, struck him in the kidneys with a lance. He fell in the water, and they cut his veins and then fled towards the Val di Sieve. And so he died miserably.
>
> The Pazzi and Donati armed themselves and ran to the palace of the Priors. They rushed to the Cavalcanti houses in the New Market with the standard of justice and with part of the *popolo*, and with kindling they set fire to three of the Cavalcanti palaces. Then they turned towards the house of *messer* Brunetto, believing that he had instigated this deed.

While the Pazzi were inscribing their names in blood on the pages of Florentine history, the first of the Medici began to trickle into the city from

---

* The White and Black Guelfs were distinguished not by any ideological differences but by family rivalries. The Cerchi family led the Whites, the Donati the Blacks. Dante, an adherent of the Whites, was exiled when the Blacks took over.

their homeland in the Mugello, hoping to take advantage of the booming economy to lift themselves up from their peasant origins. As families like the Medici clambered up the social and economic ladder by engaging in trade and money-lending, the older landed gentry, represented by families like the Pazzi, were rudely shoved aside. It was "new men" like the Medici, with no pedigree but plenty of cash, to whom the future of the city belonged. With a growing sense of their own power and a growing disdain for their social betters, these citizens of middling rank seized the reins of government in the second half of the thirteenth century. Under the so-called *Primo Popolo,* the First Government of the People (1250), and even more dramatically with the Ordinances of Justice (1293), all power in Florence devolved upon the tradesmen and professionals organized into the trade associations known as *arte,* or guilds.

Empty honors continued to come to the older magnate families, but they no longer controlled the city as they had in the past. Self-interest might argue in favor of an outward conformity to the new social order, but around the dinner table, in the privacy of their own homes, aristocrats like the Pazzi continued to vent bitterly against a topsy-turvy world in which they were forced to grovel before money-changers and shopkeepers. The Pazzi made themselves particularly obnoxious through their obvious disdain for democratic forces. Such was their reputation for arrogance that in the revolutionary period of 1378 angry mobs sought out the family palace and burned it to the ground.

Throughout their rise to prominence and power the Medici were most closely identified with "the little people," the artisans and shopkeepers who vied with the great magnates for control of the government. A distant relative of Lorenzo's, Salvestro de' Medici, had been one of the leaders of the rebellion of the *Ciompi* (when the city's working poor had seized power in the late fourteenth century) and a contemporary noted that Cosimo had triumphed "because the masses had chosen him as their champion and looked on him as a god." Even after they had been in power for many years, the Medici could not shake the faint whiff of their disreputable past.

It is one of the ironic twists of Florentine history, then, that among the beneficiaries of Medici rule were the aristocratic Pazzi. In 1458, during a period of political tension, Cosimo arranged to have the magnate stigma removed from the Pazzi and other families, thereby allowing them to participate fully for the first time in over a century in the electoral process.* But while the Pazzi and their peers could now serve in office, the political landscape had changed drastically in the intervening years. The polity they rejoined was one in which a single family, supported by a motley assortment of collaborators and hangers-on, some well-born, others plucked by Medici hands from the mass of the great unwashed, held sway in the city. For the Pazzi to take advantage of their newly won privileges they would have to swallow their pride, roll up their sleeves, and get down to the business of making money, a far more useful commodity in Renaissance Florence than an ancient name.

It was Andrea de' Pazzi who first began to restore the family's fortunes. As early as 1422 Andrea was actively lobbying the government to have the magnate label removed, assuring his fellow citizens that "since childhood he has been continually involved in mercantile activities and in honest affairs, and he has tried always to imitate the life and the mores of the people." This was a far cry from his forebears, who prided themselves on their disdain for business. Like the Medici, the Pazzi would make their money primarily as bankers, following them to Rome where they, too, tapped the lucrative market associated with the papal court. The two families did a good deal of business together. In fact Andrea's principal partner in the Roman branch of the Pazzi bank was none other than Averardo de' Medici, Cosimo's cousin. Andrea de' Pazzi further consolidated his position in Florence's ruling class by marrying Caterina Salviati, from a respectable family living close-by in the neighborhood of Santa Croce.†

To advertise their restored standing in the city, Andrea's son Jacopo

---

* From the 1450s through the 1470s the Pazzi had ten members among the "Three Majors," the top offices of Florentine government. This was a marked improvement over the previous century. From 1300 to 1420 only one Pazzi had been so honored. In the 1440s, their name appears four times, a sign that even before Cosimo made it official in 1458, the Pazzi were well on their way to respectability. But compared with the Medici the yield was still meager. From 1280 to 1470 various Medici held high office 158 times, while over the fifty years from 1430 to 1480 the name Medici crops up forty-two times (see the online *Tratte of Office Holders*). Thus even during the high-water mark of Pazzi political influence, they could not compete with the reigning family. Serving in one of the so-called Three Majors was not the same as wielding real political power, but it was a fairly accurate measure of a family's social and political prominence.

† The Salviati palace can still be seen in Florence on Via Vigna Vecchia, around the corner from the Pazzi Palace and a couple of blocks from Santa Croce.

began construction in 1462 of a palace that would rival that of the Medici on the Via Larga. Located in their traditional neighborhood in San Giovanni, the *gonfalone* of the Keys, the Pazzi palace was every bit as elegant as the Medici's. Today one can still see the palace with its distinctive family crest sporting two savage-looking dolphins whose bellicose appearance mars the otherwise serene and harmonious classical facade.

An even more telling sign of the Pazzi's growing prominence was the erection of a family chapel in the Franciscan basilica of Santa Croce. It was in the family chapel that the aspirations of Florence's great clans were most fully realized. Here wealth, culture, and piety came together. Here a man served his immortal soul, providing a focus for prayer and place of burial that would ease his passage into heavenly realms, but here, also, he expressed in fullest his civic pride and worldly ambition. The church in which the family chapel was situated became the focus of patronage and a source of identity. Particular families and particular churches would be forever linked in the minds of Florentines: the Medici with San Lorenzo, the Sassetti with Santa Trinità, the Tornabuoni with Santa Maria Novella, and now the Pazzi with Santa Croce.

The family chapel also served as the most visible expression of a patron's cultivation. In this, as in many other things, Andrea and his children seemed deliberately to be following the lead of the masters of the city, perhaps even trying to do them one better. It was in Andrea de' Pazzi's chapel that the architect Brunelleschi created perhaps the finest expression of the Renaissance ideal of measure and harmonious proportion, employing the classical language he had derived from his study of Roman monuments and that he had already used to fine effect in the Medici chapel in San Lorenzo. Delicate arches and vaults traced in the gray stone known to Florentines as *pietra serena* play off surfaces of pristine white, with bright accents provided at strategic points through terra-cotta reliefs modeled by Luca della Robbia. It is a space that encourages a serenity at odds with the ferocious reputation of the family that built it.*

The kind of competition embodied in the two chapels, the Medici's at San Lorenzo and the Pazzi's at Santa Croce, demonstrates that the rivalry

---

* The building, completed in 1461, well after both Andrea de' Pazzi's and Brunelleschi's deaths, may well have been completed by Giuliano da Maiano, the architect credited as well with the Pazzi palace.

among the great clans of Florence could be a creative as well as a destructive force.* The Medici encouraged such expressions of family pride, particularly among their followers, perhaps to serve as an outlet for ambitions that might otherwise turn violent. Renaissance Florence, like ancient Athens, was a society in which clans and individuals fought over the scarce commodity they called honor. "Life without honor is a living death," wrote the Florentine Piero di Giovanni Capponi, and most of his compatriots would have agreed. Fifteenth-century Florentines would have recognized themselves in Aristotle's famous description in the *Nicomachean Ethics* of the motivation for participating in civic life: "People of superior refinement and of active disposition identify happiness with honor: for this is, roughly speaking, the goal of political life." And, as in that ancient city that many held up as a model for their own, honor could be obtained not only through political office but through attaching one's name to some worthy public project. The Parthenon and the Duomo are both expressions of a fiercely competitive ethos in which men vied with each other for the right to spend for the greater glory of the community.

The new palace and chapel at Santa Croce raised the Pazzi profile in the city, and there were many other signs as well that the family was adapting to new circumstances. It was Piero de' Pazzi's friendship with the equally cultivated Piero de' Medici that truly signaled the Pazzi's embrace by the city's elite. Friendship became kinship in 1460 with the marriage of Piero de' Pazzi's great-nephew, Guglielmo, to Piero de' Medici's daughter Bianca. "Had it not been for this friendship between the two Pieros," notes Vespesiano da Bisticci, "this kinship would never have come to pass; now, by means of it, the Pazzi recovered their position, and were able to meet their taxation, as they would never have done, but for this marriage. It may be said that this alliance restored their house to prosperity." By means of this match, the Pazzi, who not long before had been excluded from participating in the government, were now familiars in the Via Larga.

But for all Andrea's pragmatism and Piero de' Pazzi's fine manners, one cannot help but feel that something was yet amiss with this family that had once stood at the forefront of the nobility but that now had to play second fiddle to the parvenu Medici. Francesco Guicciardini certainly detected

---

* Benedetto Dei's *Cronica* lists both the Pazzi chapel and the Medici tombs as among the few sites that made Florence "a new Rome" (see Dei, *Cronica*, 33r).

what he considered their fatal flaw: "But although the Pazzi were Florentine nobles with many family connections," he wrote, "and although the
men of that family were magnificent and generous, they nevertheless had
never enjoyed much political power, for they were considered too high
and mighty—something which men in a republic will not tolerate."

Even more intriguing than the historian's retrospective analysis are
Alessandra Strozzi's contemporaneous comments. A letter she wrote to
her son in 1461 includes one of her typically astute observations: "Yesterday Piero de' Pazzi entered the city in great triumph and magnificence,
more than any other knight in recent times. You shouldn't place much
stock in this, however; for in Florence they always show one thing and then
do another." Near the end of the letter she made this startlingly prescient
dig: "Remember, according to what I have observed, that he who sticks
with the Medici has always done well, while with the Pazzi it is always the
opposite—they are let down."

Hints of an incipient rivalry between the two families are tantalizing,
though one has to sift the evidence carefully to discover traces of a bitterness that remained deliberately hidden from view. Later accounts, like that
of Niccolò Valori, give events the quality of a Greek tragedy: "There was in
Florence in those days a family, the Pazzi, who had grown most powerful,
both because of their incomparable riches and because they were related
through ties of blood and marriage to most of the city's nobility. And as
often happens among the great, they, wishing to alter the state of things,
set themselves against the house and family of the Medici; they thought of
nothing but of how to diminish the authority and supremacy of Lorenzo."

But at the time the antipathy of the two great families was harder to discern. As a teenager Lorenzo was close with his brother-in-law Guglielmo,
but he seems to have regarded the family with suspicion, particularly old
Jacopo, who had succeeded his father, Andrea, as the family patriarch.
According to Machiavelli, Jacopo and his relatives felt insufficiently honored by the regime, though, at least in the case of Jacopo, it was as much a
matter of perception as reality. In 1468, after serving as *Gonfaloniere di
Giustizia*, Jacopo was knighted by Tommaso Soderini for services rendered
to the republic. But despite this mark of official favor there are indications
that Lorenzo made sure that Jacopo never rose to a position from which he
could pose a real threat. During the attempted reforms of 1471, Lorenzo's
friends had advised him to exclude Jacopo and his followers from the new

Balìa, treating them as if they were "*mezo amoniti,*" that is, half excluded from office. But the Pazzi were already so prominent that they could not be completely cut off without stirring up the resentment of other aristocratic clans. Lorenzo's advisors proposed replacing Jacopo's name with another, more pliant member of the family. "[T]hey will put in his place his relative Guglielmo instead of the said Jacomo [sic] to his greater discomfiture," reported Sacramoro. Ultimately, however, Lorenzo decided not to oppose Jacopo's nomination to the all-important council, explaining to the Milanese ambassador that one man could do him little harm.

In other words, Lorenzo would do as he so often did with families with the wealth and prestige to offer a legitimate alternative to Medici rule: he would draw their fangs by heaping them with meaningless honors while at the same time restricting their access to real power. Benedetto Dei lists Jacopo as one of the leading men of the government but relegates him to the "second tier."

Aiding Lorenzo in this difficult juggling act was the fact that each of the prominent families of the regime was as jealous of each other as they were of the Medici themselves. Lorenzo pursued a cautious course with Jacopo de' Pazzi, allowing him to serve on occasion in honorable positions but never giving him a central role in the government to which he felt his wealth and status entitled him.* Unlike their peers, however, the Pazzi chafed against the invisible yoke that kept them in their place. Jacopo was so frustrated that he considered abandoning the city for Avignon, a threat made but never carried out.

The competitive world of business offered more opportunities for conflict. In the 1440s, the Pazzi bank had been one of the few sufficiently trusted by the Medici to be extended unlimited credit, but in more recent decades the Pazzi had become competitors rather than collaborators. As the Pazzi bank continued to prosper in Rome, it became the principal rival to the Medici; managers of the two banks vied for accounts and for favors from the papal court. The Pazzi made significant inroads into the Medici's once unassailable position at the Vatican, and in the mercantile towns of Bruges and Lyons the Pazzi threatened to overtake the more established bank.

---

* In 1473 and 1474 Jacopo served as one of the twelve Good Men (*Buonuomini*), one of the so-called Three Majors, a sign that whatever Lorenzo's reservations, he was still included within the inner circle of the regime.

The rivalry only sharpened when Guglielmo's younger brother Francesco left Florence to take over management of the Roman branch. Francesco's departure, like his grandfather's threatened departure for Avignon, was a form of self-imposed exile prompted by the daily humiliation of living in Florence under the Medici. "He was incredibly angry that the Medici outshone him," wrote Angelo Poliziano, who knew him well. "He spent some years at the Pazzi bank in Rome, for he felt that in Florence he had no standing compared to the Medici brothers."

Though one should take Poliziano's description of Francesco de' Pazzi with a pinch of salt because when Poliziano wrote he had good reason to hate him, his is still the most vivid contemporary portrait of the man who was to bring the Medici family and regime to the brink of disaster. "His stature was short, his body slender, and his color pale," he recalled. "He had blond hair, which he was overly concerned to keep well groomed. The mannerisms of his face and body revealed his prodigious insolence, and his great efforts, especially in first encounters, to cover this up were not very successful. He was a bloodthirsty person, besides, and the sort who, once he desired something in his heart, would go after it undeterred by considerations like honor, piety, fame, or reputation."

According to Lorenzo's friend, Francesco de' Pazzi was also "naturally stubborn" and had "grown fixed in his passion and his arrogance." He was, in other words, a typical representative of the family, sharing "the peculiar Pazzi irascibility to a surprising extent." Biased as his account surely is, it has the ring of truth, particularly since it conforms with the few known facts of his short, violent career. Guicciardini's more measured description of Francesco—"a very restless, spirited, and ambitious man" he called him—still suggests someone seething with barely suppressed rage.

An intriguing insight into Francesco's character comes from the pen of another poet, Luigi Pulci. His references to Francesco's role in the joust of 1468, while more oblique than Poliziano's since they are disguised by the conventions of chivalry, are all the more suggestive for having been written at a time when the Pazzi and Medici were still closely allied. Pulci's epic poem reveals that years before his open breach with Lorenzo the two had met on the field of battle. Even Pulci's flowery language cannot conceal the ferocious spirit that drove the diminutive "little Francesco" to deeds beyond his physical abilities. It was he who dealt Lorenzo such a blow during his joust that he not only unhorsed him but caused his friends such concern that they almost called off the tournament. And, if Pulci is to be believed, of all the competitors that day it was only Francesco who felt cheated, "believing that Fortune did him a thousand wrongs." It must have been galling to a Pazzi that while he received little recognition for his feat, the man he sent sprawling into the dust walked away with the trophy.

It was not just Lorenzo's undeserved victory that stuck in Francesco de' Pazzi's craw. Ceremonial events like this were intended to make visible through glorious pageantry the pecking order in the city, and it was clear to those who watched from the grandstands that the Pazzi were but one of many minor satellites in the great family's orbit. Thus it would always be in Florence, Francesco concluded, as long as the Medici lived. Even Francesco's older brother had allowed himself to be drawn inside the magic circle, until Guglielmo could be seen tagging along in Lorenzo's train like any other servant or bootlick. Francesco was made of different stuff; he was no toady born to bow and scrape. In Rome, whence he now fled, the Medici writ was no longer law. In the Eternal City he no longer had to hold his tongue while the Medici and their hangers-on strode about the streets like young princelings. In Rome he would not be reminded at every turn of how his once proud family had to scrounge for crumbs from the Medici table. And, not least of all, in Rome, he was in a position to hurt his rivals where it counted.

At first Pazzi's rivalry expressed itself in perfectly legitimate ways. Despite his volatile temper, he was a shrewd businessman and through his efforts the Pazzi bank in Rome prospered. In boldness and energy he proved more than a match for the cautious and cantankerous Giovanni Tornabuoni. While Tornabuoni fretted over the growing debt run up by the pope, Pazzi was ingratiating himself with the papal family. Soon he could be seen in the company of Girolamo Riario, a man whose star was on the rise and whose influence over his uncle was growing. To what extent Pazzi's profits were made at the Medici's expense is unclear, but it is perhaps no coincidence that in the very years that the Medici branch began its steep decline the Pazzi branch was moving in the opposite direction.

If the rivalry between the two banks went beyond the usual competition of two firms vying for a single market, Lorenzo himself showed no signs of apprehension. Indeed the Medici bank's troubles, which grew increasingly apparent throughout the 1470s, took a back seat in his mind to political matters. Many decisions Lorenzo made regarding the bank were in fact driven by political necessity, a complicating factor that never bothered the Pazzi. Consider, for instance, the Medici bank in Milan, which seemed to have little purpose except to supply luxuries to the ducal court. Even as the debts run up by the duke and his entourage threatened to swamp the bank, Lorenzo felt he could not shut it down for fear of alienating his friend and political ally. He faced a similar predicament in regard to the pope's account in Rome.* By the time of the Imola crisis, Lorenzo found himself pulled so hard in opposite directions by political and financial imperatives that the entire Medici empire threatened to burst at the seams.

The Pazzi were well aware of the precariousness of Lorenzo's position. In fact, Francesco de Pazzi's cousin Renato claimed that they need only wait a few years for Lorenzo's financial troubles to lead to the collapse of the bank, which, inevitably, would be followed by a loss of power in Florence. In cozying up to the pope and his relatives, Pazzi was doing his best to hasten that happy day.

It was the crisis over Imola that brought the rivalry between the two families out into the open. Up to this point Lorenzo had treated the Pazzi like any other potential rival, permitting them to accumulate minor honors while denying them any real share in power. On the business front, his policy of containment was far less successful. Lorenzo's defiance of the pope provided Francesco de' Pazzi and the Pazzi bank the opportunity they had been looking for to reverse the course of history. "Lorenzo asked [the Pazzi] not [to] supply the money," wrote Francesco Guicciardini, "for if the pope could not buy it, Imola would come into our hands. But soon afterward, they provided the pope with 30,000 [sic] ducats for the purchase, and they revealed to him and to Count Girolamo the request Lorenzo had made." By this single move Pazzi not only earned Pope Sixtus's gratitude, but, equally important, exposed the extent to which Lorenzo had been working against the Holy Father. In Rome, Francesco de' Pazzi's stock soared, while Lorenzo's plummeted.

---

* See *The Rise and Decline of the Medizi Bank*, de Roover, pp. 261–275. In 1467, the duke's personal debt to the Medici bank was 179,000 ducats. In 1472, right before their final rift, Sixtus's debt to the Medici bank stood at 107,000 florins. Allowing such reckless borrowing could only be justified on political grounds.

After Andrea del Verrocchio, *Bust of Lorenzo il Magnifico*, 1478
(National Gallery of Art)

XIV. CONSPIRACY

"But after the victory of '66, the whole state had been so restricted to the Medici, who took so much authority, that it was required for those who were malcontent at it either to endure that mode of living with patience or, if indeed they wanted to eliminate it, attempt to do so by way of conspiracy and secretly."

—NICCOLÒ MACHIAVELLI, *FLORENTINE HISTORIES* VIII, 1

"The Count [Girolamo], who regarded Lorenzo as his great and secret enemy, was at the time on the most intimate terms with Francesco de' Pazzi; wherefore he explained to him what he had in mind, and the two conferred with Francesco Salviati, who was likewise ill disposed towards Lorenzo whom he blamed for denying him the archbishopric of Pisa."

—NICCOLÒ VALORI, *LIFE OF LORENZO IL MAGNIFICO*

GIROLAMO RIARIO AND FRANCESCO DE' PAZZI WERE NOT the kind of men one would expect to strike up an intimate friendship. Both were wealthy and powerful, but they had come to prominence following very different paths, and in a society attuned to every nuance of culture, breeding, and pedigree, the gulf between them might in normal circumstances have proved unbridgeable. Girolamo carried himself with all the ostentation of someone only recently vaulted into the first ranks of society—the epitome of the parvenu. His clothes were of the finest silk brocade, his manicured fingers sparkled with gold and gemstones. Francesco, small, pale, and filled with a nervous energy, dressed with the understated elegance of one with nothing to prove. One had been born into an obscure family from a provincial fishing village, a former customs clerk who owed his high position to the talents and energy of his uncle;

when he spoke it was in the harsh, untutored syllables of the Ligurian coast where he was born. The other was the bluest of blue bloods, an aristocrat intensely conscious of his family's contribution to the glorious history of Europe's most glittering and cultured metropolis.

Despite the difference in upbringing, they did share one distinctive trait—a prickly sense of their own honor that made them quick to anger and incapable of forgetting an insult. They both were ambitious and intemperate men who tended to view political rivals as mortal enemies. This natural affinity was greatly enhanced by the fact that each felt he had been wronged by the same man—Lorenzo de' Medici, the tyrant of Florence. A common hatred proved a strong inducement to overlook other differences.

Precisely when their anger, rising with each new sign of Lorenzo's deviousness, crystallized into a more definite plan of action is not known. The Imola affair was certainly the prime catalyst, focusing their anger and drawing them closer together, but it is likely that their thinking evolved slowly over the course of months or even years. As outrage followed outrage, the two reached a critical point where it seemed to them that the only solution to their troubles lay in the murder of the Medici brothers and the overthrow of their regime. Niccolò Valori, writing a few decades after the events, claimed it was Riario who first hit upon assassination as the method most likely to achieve their ends, while Guicciardini credited Pazzi.* Most plausibly, Machiavelli gives them both an equal share in the conception of the plot: "And since he [Francesco] was very friendly with

---

* "The Count [Girolamo], who regarded Lorenzo as his great and secret enemy, was at the time on the most intimate terms with Francesco de' Pazzi," Valori wrote (*Vita di Lorenzo de' Medici*, p. 48), "wherefore he explained to him what he had in mind." Guicciardini's account of the origins of the conspiracy is as follows: "Francesco, who resided in Rome almost permanently (and who was called Franceschino because of his small stature), began to plot with Girolamo ways of removing Lorenzo from power. He reminded the count that Lorenzo was his arch enemy, and that as soon as Pope Sixtus died, Lorenzo would hound him until he deprived him of the Romagna" (*The History of Florence*, IV). It is important to note that most of the contemporary or near contemporary accounts tended for diplomatic reasons to minimize the involvement of various heads of state— of the king of Naples, the duke of Urbino, and the pope himself. This, in turn, created the distorted impression that a small cabal was responsible for the entire conspiracy. Whatever the origins of the plot, it soon grew into a large-scale undertaking involving many of the most powerful statesmen in Italy.

Count Girolamo, they often complained to one another of the Medici: so after many complaints they came to the reasoning that it was necessary, if one of them was to live in his states and the other in his city securely, to change the state of Florence—which they thought could not be done without the deaths of Giuliano and Lorenzo."

For Riario the elimination of the Medici brothers was a pressing, practical matter. As long as they reigned in Florence, Riario's fledgling state in the Romagna would be threatened with extinction, squeezed as if between two millstones by the powerful states of Milan and Florence. Riario was haunted by the specter of his elderly uncle's death, at which time, as he confessed to one of his co-conspirators, "his state would not be worth a bean, because Lorenzo de' Medici wished him ill, nor did he believe that there was a man in the world who wished him greater ill; and that after the death of the Pope he would not seek anything less than to rob from him his state and finish him off because he felt he had received many injuries from his hands."

Pazzi's motives were at once more personal and more abstract. It enraged him to see the Medici receive princes and emperors at their palace on the Via Larga while his more ancient family was left in the shadows. As long as Lorenzo lived, Pazzi would be forced to grovel at his feet or endure the ghostly existence of a rootless exile. Like many frustrated politicians, he transformed his personal disappointment into an ideological crusade.

Though the unfolding plot has long been referred to as the Pazzi conspiracy, suggesting it was Francesco who took the lead, neither could have done without the other: Riario, one of the most powerful figures at the papal court, had connections and access to money and military muscle, while Francesco de' Pazzi possessed an insider's knowledge of Florentine government and, vitally, personal access to the Medici brothers. Pazzi's hatred of Lorenzo, like his pedigree, was of older vintage—one might say it predated his birth since the chip on the collective Pazzi shoulder went back generations—but Riario's feelings were no less virulent for their recent origin. Ultimately, Riario comes across as the more calculating of the two, spinning his web from the comfort and safety of Rome, while Pazzi, driven by fantasies of vengeance and of a hero's martyrdom, would prove himself both more courageous and more reckless.

From the beginning the conspirators were faced with a major structural difficulty—the lack of meaningful Florentine involvement. The contrast with 1466 is telling: while in that earlier coup the main instigators were Florentines at the highest level of government, men whose faces, characters, and reputations were familiar to the citizens of the city, none of the original Pazzi conspirators was well known or well liked in the community. Francesco, though native-born and from a prominent family, had lived abroad for so many years that he was practically a stranger in his own hometown. Worse still, his recent involvement in the Imola affair had angered his compatriots. Even those ideologically opposed to Medici rule would have a hard time accepting "liberty" from the likes of Francesco de' Pazzi. Riario was even less acceptable to a Florentine public that bridled at the slightest hint of outside interference in their affairs. However distorted their notions of Florentine opinion, Riario and Pazzi knew that a more respectable, more Florentine, face must be put on the undertaking.

Thus it was that as their plans ripened they brought a new figure into their confidence. In some ways this new addition to the inner circle appeared ideally suited to the task. Not only was he a Florentine from a distinguished family but, as a powerful figure in the curia, aide to Cardinal Pietro Riario and cousin of Francesco de' Pazzi, his loyalty was never in doubt. In addition to his ties with both of the principal plotters, he had his own reasons to hate Lorenzo. It is a measure of how out-of-touch they were with public opinion in Florence that the second native son drawn into the web was almost as unpopular in his native land as Francesco de' Pazzi himself.

Born in 1425, Francesco Salviati was older than his fellow conspirators. He was already well into middle age and with a distinguished ecclesiastical career behind him by the time he joined with Girolamo Riario and Francesco de' Pazzi in their perilous undertaking. (Girolamo, born in 1438, was thirteen years his junior, while Francesco, born in 1445, was twenty years younger.) Like his partners, Salviati was unhappy with the current state of affairs, believing he had been denied the ecclesiastical appointments he coveted most through the malicious interference of the First Citizen of Florence. But while he certainly had good reason to resent Lorenzo, it seems curious that a man of his mature years, with everything to lose and perhaps little time to enjoy the fruits of his victory, should have allowed himself to become involved with a couple of young hotheads with a taste for mayhem.

It is unclear how far back Francesco Salviati's hatred for Lorenzo and his family went. The Salviati were an old and respected Florentine clan, but during Francesco's lifetime they had seen a decline in their fortunes.* The Salviati palace still stands, around the corner from that of the Pazzi, with whom they were allied by ties of marriage, but in Francesco's day it was one of the few remaining assets of a family that had fallen on hard times. The worst blow to the Salviati came in the economic depression of 1466, a disaster for which many people still blamed Lorenzo's father. Francesco Salviati had particular reason to be bitter. Piero's retrenchment following the death of his father, in which he tightened the liberal credit extended by Cosimo, contributed to the failure of a wool shop in Pisa owned by the Salviati family.

But if Salviati harbored resentment toward those responsible for his family's descent into poverty it was not immediately apparent. Indeed it was in Cosimo's Florence that, as an ambitious young man, Salviati first distinguished himself, aided in his efforts by many within the ruling elite. He belonged to the circle gathered around the philosopher Marsilio Ficino, an impressive group that included not only Angelo Poliziano but also Giuliano and Lorenzo. Poliziano later wrote that Salviati was "devoid of knowledge of and also respect for the law, divine as well as human . . . lost in sensuality and disgraceful intrigues." He also attributed to him the sins of gambling at dice, flattery, and vanity, though this standard catalogue of vices was compiled only after his treachery was revealed. In fact at one time the two had been on friendly terms. As a young man Poliziano had written Salviati some flattering letters in hopes of obtaining a position.

Like many a youth with more education than money Salviati pursued a career in the Church. It was his cousin Jacopo de' Pazzi (Jacopo's mother, Caterina Salviati, was Francesco's aunt) who bankrolled Salviati's fine humanist education, a necessity for one seeking employment in the papal courts. After completing his schooling he proceeded to Rome, where he joined such intellectual luminaries as Bartolomeo Platina and Leon Bat-

---

* Their solidly middle-class status is revealed by the number of times a member of the family held a position in one of the Three Major offices of government. From 1282 to 1500 the Salviati name appears 154 times, a record bettered by only a few families. By comparison, the noble Pazzi only appear twenty times over the same period, while the Medici name appears 173 times (see online *Tratte of Office Holders*).

tista Alberti, who were determined to place the latest humanist scholarship at the service of a modernized Church. With his Pazzi connections,
his drive to succeed, and his Florentine education, Salviati rose through
the hierarchy, becoming in time the indispensable right-hand man of Cardinal Pietro Riario.

That Salviati was more than the list of vices attributed to him by
Poliziano is revealed in his correspondence with Marsilio Ficino, though
the latter was clearly a better philosopher in the abstract than he was a
judge of humanity in the flesh.* The philosopher's affection for Salviati is
attested to by the fatherly advice he was wont to bestow on his fellow
humanist when, as often seemed to be the case, Salviati felt thwarted in his
ambitions. "I wanted something important in your affairs to happen,
which would prompt me to write a congratulatory letter to you, and I
expected it every day," Ficino wrote. "I see that nothing has yet happened
worthy of my desire and your deserts. Trust in God, Salviati. I know you
were not born for small or commonplace purposes. So be of good heart
and, as is usual to you, strong in spirit. You will achieve great things if you
are strong in spirit." Urging patience on Salviati, however, was a futile
effort. For all their kindly advice, Ficino's letters betray the frustration of
their recipient, who already seemed to feel he had been cheated of the stel-
lar career to which his abilities entitled him.

Salviati's great break came in December of 1473 when his boss, Cardinal Pietro Riario, died suddenly in Rome. As always occurs with the unexpected deaths of powerful men there were the inevitable rumors of
poisoning. A more likely explanation is that Cardinal Riario was a victim
of his own excesses. Debauchery is never the most healthy of lifestyles, and
Riario was the epitome of the dissolute Renaissance prelate. "Our delightful feasts all came to an end, and everyone lamented the death of Riario,"
went one contemporary's facetious obituary.†

Cardinal Riario's passing had many consequences beyond the losses
suffered by the procureresses, vintners, and pastry chefs of Rome, not least

---

* Ficino also befriended another of the plotters, Jacopo Bracciolini, son of the distinguished humanist Poggio Bracciolini.

† Despite the income from his many benefices, Pietro Riario died leaving a debt of 60,000
  gold florins.

of which was that it unhinged his uncle, who seems to have lost what little sense of proportion he once possessed. Indeed Sixtus was so grief-stricken that many feared for his sanity. Nothing could replace the indispensable Pietro, either in the pope's heart or in the more practical role as his chief financial and political advisor, but the void was eventually filled to the best of his somewhat limited abilities by his younger brother, Count Girolamo. The contrast between the two was striking. Both, it is true, possessed the burning ambition common to all the Riario, but Pietro had been a man whose intelligence was placed at the service of an expansive vision of papal power. Girolamo, by contrast, could hardly see beyond the narrow horizons of his own immediate advantage. After Pietro's death papal policy grew increasingly violent and erratic as Girolamo lunged first this way and then that in a desperate attempt to secure his uncertain future.

As for Salviati, the death of his patron cleared the path to greater things. Of all the titles held by the deceased cardinal, the one Salviati coveted most was that of archbishop of Florence. In the end his bid to become the chief prelate of his native land was unsuccessful, but somewhere in the obscure negotiations that led to the appointment of Lorenzo's brother-in-law Rinaldo Orsini to the vacancy, the pope seems to have promised Salviati that he would be named to the next available position. The opportunity to make good on this pledge came later that year. On October 7, 1474, Filippo de' Medici, archbishop of Pisa, died. Seven days later the pope issued a bull announcing Salviati as his replacement.

The nomination of Francesco Salviati as archbishop of Pisa touched off a new crisis in the already strained relations between Lorenzo and the pope. It also put Sixtus on a collision course with the Florentine *Signoria,* which had not been consulted in the matter as tradition dictated and as the pope had earlier promised. Even before Filippo de' Medici's death the *Signoria* had placed before the pope a list of acceptable successors. Salviati's name was, pointedly, not among them.* It is understandable, then, that when the government of Florence learned of Salviati's appointment they reacted with outrage and indignation. Not only had the pope

---

* The list included Gentile Becchi, Lorenzo's old tutor, on whose behalf Lorenzo lobbied unsuccessfully. The *Signoria* also recommended either Donato de' Medici or Antonio Agli, bishops respectively of Pistoia and Volterra.

failed to consult them, but he had chosen a candidate whose activities on behalf of the pope and his family made him obnoxious to all patriotic Florentines.* Worse still, it was clear that the pope was grooming Salviati for the cardinalship, filling that vital office with the one native son unacceptable to his own people. On October 18 a special committee of leading members of the *reggimento* resolved to oppose this insult to the dignity of the republic with all the means at their disposal. Noting that the Holy Father was entitled by law to select whomever he chose to be his bishop, they also pointed out that only the government of Florence had the right to determine who could set foot on their territory. Thus while they could not stop Salviati's appointment, they could effectively bar him from claiming his prize by preventing him from crossing the border into Tuscany.

It has often been claimed that Lorenzo was wholly responsible for his government's defiance of the pope. This was certainly the assumption of Sixtus, who denounced Lorenzo's "depraved and malignant spirit," calling him a "usurping tyrant." It was a charge Lorenzo vehemently denied, explaining that he was merely carrying out the wishes of the *Signoria* whose honor had been besmirched by the pope's high-handed refusal to consider its wishes. He set out his defense in a letter written to Duke Galeazzo on December 14, 1474. "The matter is of utmost importance," Lorenzo began,

> and it seems to me that I have been done a grave injustice and wrong, because His Holiness cannot complain of anything of me, nor ... should offense be taken over *messer* Francesco Salviati's being denied possession of the archbishopric of Pisa; and this offense, if offense there be, comes from the entire city, yet he wishes to avenge himself on me alone. It is true that for the grace of God and the warmth and favor of Your Excellency, I believed that I would have control of the said archbishopric, but it did not seem to me right to acquiesce in such a humiliation of the entire public for the sake of my own interests, which the city does not deserve from me.

---

* Salviati had made himself unpopular in Florence by his role in the sale of Imola to the Riario, having been entrusted with conveying the money borrowed from the Pazzi to Duke Galeazzo Maria Sforza.

Panorama of Florence looking north with *Palazzo della Signoria* (left) and *Duomo* (right): The center of Florence looks much as it did in Lorenzo's day: a sea of terra-cotta rooftops dominated by the centers of secular and religious power, the *Palazzo della Signoria* and the *Duomo*. (Miles Unger)

Palazzo della Signoria: Built as the seat of government, the *Palazzo della Signoria* (also known as the Palace of the Priors and *Palazzo Vecchio* or "Old Palace") was a symbol of Florentine might. Its fortresslike appearance reflects the pervasive fear of civil unrest. (Miles Unger)

Palazzo Medici-Riccardi: Cosimo built the new family palace on the widest street in Florence, the Via Larga, as a symbol of his wealth, taste, and power. Designed by Michelozzo di Bartolomeo and with sculptures by Donatello, decorations by artists like Antonio del Pollaiulo and Paolo Ucello, and an unparalleled collection of antiques and rare manuscripts, the building was as much a museum as a residence. (Miles Unger)

Benozzo Gozzoli, *Adoration of the Magi*, Palazzo Medici-Riccardi, c. 1459: This fresco in the chapel of the Medici Palace, ostensibly a biblical scene, contains numerous portraits of the family—including Cosimo, riding a donkey, flanked by Piero on a white horse—along with their chief allies. The ten-year-old Lorenzo is depicted in the retinue of the youngest Magus, Caspar (see detail on page 48). (Art Resource)

Duomo, Interior: The center of religious life in Florence was also the scene of its most famous act of violence, the attack on Giuliano and Lorenzo, April 26, 1478. In the distance is the high altar, beneath Brunelleschi's famous dome, near where Giuliano was struck down. (Art Resource)

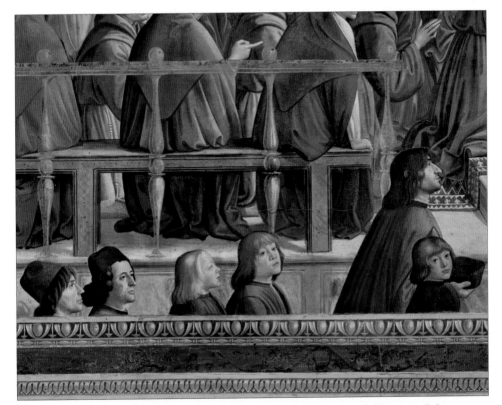

Domenico Ghirlandaio, "Angelo Poliziano with the Sons of Lorenzo," from *The Confirmation of the Rule of the Order of St. Francis by Pope Honorius III*, the Sassetti Chapel, Santa Trinita, c. 1483–86: This fresco was commissioned by Francesco Sassetti, general manager of the Medici bank. In homage to his boss he included portaits not only of Lorenzo but also of his children. Here Angelo Poliziano is shown with Lorenzo's three sons, from left to right, Giuliano, Piero, and Giovanni. (Art Resource)

Medici Villa at Fiesole, 1450s: Unlike the medieval villas of Trebbio and Caffagi-olo with their towers and crenellations, Fiesole, designed by Michelozzo di Bar-tolomeo, was neither a working farm nor a fortress. It was a favored haunt of poets and intellectuals like Poliziano and Pico della Mirandola. (Miles Unger)

Pazzi Chapel, Santa Croce, 1440–61: This family chapel at Santa Croce was commissioned by Andrea de' Pazzi, a friend of Piero's who restored the fortunes of the ancient clan. Designed by Brunelleschi and decorated with terracotta reliefs by Luca della Robbia, the chapel was built both to emulate and rival the Medici Chapel at San Lorenzo. (Miles Unger)

The Villa Ambra at Poggio a Caiano, 1480s: Lorenzo's favorite villa, Ambra was designed by his favorite architect, Giuliano da Sangallo. Lorenzo was himself heavily involved in planning both the building and the landscaping, which reflect his vision of the villa as an ideal place of retreat. This villa was a model for generations of country houses, from those of Palladio to Thomas Jefferson's Monticello. (Miles Unger)

Sandro Botticelli, *Primavera*, c. 1480: This masterpiece of the Florentine Renaissance is thought to have been commissioned by Lorenzo's cousin Lorenzo di Pierfrancesco de' Medici. The erudite classicism and sensuality reflect the ideas of the philosophers and poets who gathered around Lorenzo, and the painting's allegorical theme appears to be largely based on the poetry of Lorenzo and Poliziano. (Art Resource)

To some extent Lorenzo's letter is disingenuous, since the *Signoria* would surely follow his lead in this matter. But it was true as Lorenzo said that the appointment of Salviati against the express wishes of the Florentine government set a dangerous precedent. Salviati did not make matters easier by loudly trumpeting his own status as a client of the papal family, signing his correspondence *d. Franciscus Salviati de Riario.**

The appointment was all the more disturbing because Pisa was a particularly tender spot in the Florentine empire. As recently as 1405, Pisa had been an independent republic, and many of its citizens still yearned to reclaim their lost autonomy. Lorenzo, as we have seen, worked hard to reconcile its citizens to Florentine rule, spending lavishly on its university and much of his free time in the vicinity. Lorenzo voiced his concerns to Duke Galeazzo:

> And while in the letter of the said Count [Girolamo] he wrote that His Holiness had received letters from many citizens in favor of Salviati, it seems to me all the more reason to prevent him taking possession of his see; since the *Signoria* and leading citizens are not well disposed towards him, those who are reveal themselves to be men who do not wish the government well, and it would seem all the stranger that in a city as unreliable and sensitive as Pisa that this man should be acceptable to some who is so objectionable to the government. Does Your Excellency think that you would easily accept having in Pavia or another one of your lands a man who had gained his place through the good offices of your enemies?

---

* Not everyone immediately grasped the implications of Salviati's appointment. Of those close to Lorenzo, Giovanni Tornabuoni and Marsilio Ficino showed themselves to be the most naive. Shortly after learning of the appointment—in fact it may well have been through his uncle's letter that Lorenzo first heard of it—Tornabuoni wrote to his nephew, "I cannot tell you how much the Archbishop is disposed to be your servant ... and though I know that my writing is superfluous, I did not want to remain silent knowing how great is the desire of the Archbishop to be all yours, hoping in this and in everything to do as you would wish" (see *Lettere,* ii, p. 56). Marsilio Ficino congratulated his protégé on his success, writing, "It is still pleasant and right for me to prophesy like this, for when divine providence created you Archbishop of Pisa, it proclaimed me a prophet.... I wish you good fortune, and pray you take the greatest care of your health, for through you I see that the priesthood in Florence, long since dead, will shortly be renewed to life." (Ficino, *Letters,* 87, p. 109.)

Those "men who do not wish the government well" were the Pazzi and their clients, who had orchestrated a letter-writing campaign to convince the pope that there was a groundswell of support in Florence for his nominee. Not only was the pope challenging Lorenzo's authority on an important matter of international diplomacy, but he was doing so by exploiting divisions within the Florentine ruling class.

Despite the growing rift with the pope, Lorenzo continued to downplay the seriousness of the situation. His enemies in the Vatican could cause him a good deal of trouble but he dismissed any thought that they might pose a threat to his life. This was not for lack of warning. Though the conspirators tried to maintain strict secrecy, the courts of Italy were abuzz with rumors. Galeazzo Maria Sforza, perhaps catching some faint whiff of what is afoot through his connection to the Riario family, had urged Lorenzo to "keep himself safe and his eyes on what is happening inside [the city]." Lorenzo's response to repeated admonitions to protect himself was, typically, to dismiss most of the rumors as "fantasies" cooked up by a group of malcontents with little standing in the community.* He assured Sacramoro that "those who wish to engage in machinations are weak and few in number." His attitude, as in 1466, reflects the overconfidence of youth. The frequent complaints he made to Sforza show a concern for his pocketbook but none for his life. In his letter to the duke, written in September of 1475, he belittles his opponents, even as he begs him to intervene on his behalf in Rome:

> I find that all of this comes from the same source, that is these Pazzi, my relatives, who because of their nature and because they have been put up to it by His Majesty the King and the duke of Urbino, seek to wrong me in every way possible; and in this they forget their debt, because as perhaps Your Excellency has been informed, everything they have achieved in this city they owe to our house, towards which they show themselves ungrateful. I shall arrange it so that they can do little to harm me and will keep my eyes open, though I believe it is all a fantasy since they have little prestige and are

---

* It was not only the duke of Milan who was concerned. Gentile Becchi also expressed concern, warning him of "new Dietisalvis" who wish to do him harm.

despised by everyone. . . . I think with little effort all will work out. . . . [T]he new Archbishop of Pisa belongs very much to them, bound to those Pazzi by ties of marriage and of friendship. I am more than ever harassed in Rome to force me to allow him to take possession of Pisa, which, it seems to me, would give the Pazzi great prestige and me the reverse. . . . I pray that Your Excellency would speak with such heat to count Girolamo, in such a manner as to make it clear to him that you object to my being humiliated in this way, as much as if it were done to you yourself, I being a faithful servant of yours. This should have two effects: one, that it will perhaps cause him to stop harassing me; the other, that in Rome all will know that I am truly loved by Your Excellency, which, as I have written at other times, is enough to lift me up and draw the malice from the minds of every man.

This letter reveals that Lorenzo continually underestimated both the determination and the imagination of his opponents, lulled into a false sense of security by his belief in his own powers and his faith in the loyalty of his people.

In the end neither Lorenzo nor the *Signoria* could defy a pope determined to have his way. Francesco Salviati formally took possession of his bishopric on October 30, 1475, though only after a humiliating one-year exile in Rome during which his hatred for Lorenzo had ample opportunity to ripen. Once again Lorenzo had publicly defied the pope and emerged with little to show for it. To a friend he confided, "if it could be done without scandal, it would be better to have three or four popes rather than one."

As for the one pope who actually sat on the throne of St. Peter, Lorenzo's difficulties with him were just beginning. Even as the two tussled over the appointment of Salviati, a new diplomatic quarrel was brewing. It concerned a small city on the border between Tuscany and the pope's domain known as Città di Castello. Città di Castello was one of those innumerable dependencies, like Imola, Urbino, Rimini, Bologna, and Perugia, to name a few, that made up the territory that went under the hopeful heading of the Papal States. It had long been Vatican policy to bring order and obedience to this fractious territory. As part of this wider program, and in order to find employment for his bellicose nephew, Cardinal Giuliano della Rovere, Sixtus had already sent him at the head of an army to reassert papal authority in the towns of Spoleto and Forlì. Città di Castello, nominally within papal territories but usually regarded by the government of Florence as within its sphere of interest, was next on his list of conquests.

Sixtus was aided in his purpose by internal divisions within the town. For decades rule over Città di Castello had been contested by the Giustini and Vitelli families, a matter that seemed to have been settled in 1440 when Pope Eugenius IV made Vitelozzo Vitelli his vice-regent. But nothing is ever settled as long as the aggrieved party is still around to argue his case. While Vitelozzo's son, Niccolò Vitelli, placed himself under the protection of the Medici and the Florentine government, becoming in effect a client of the *Signoria,* Lorenzo Giustini made his way to the Vatican, where he filled the pope's ears with complaints about Vitelli and his Florentine patrons.* Dubious though Giustini's claims were, Sixtus used them as an excuse to tighten his control over the strategic town that he hoped to use as "an example to all the lands of the Church."

Thus it was that on June 24, 1474, troops under Giuliano della Rovere arrived before the walls of Città di Castello and began laying siege to the town. Girolamo Riario wrote to Lorenzo in the mildest of tones urging his cooperation in the matter: "If you would have me see that I am loved by you, and that my friendship is agreeable to you, and would also have our Master perceive that you are towards his Holiness all that I have ever declared you to be, then deal with me in this matter as you wish me to deal with you and your affairs." Lorenzo was not moved by these friendly words. Though it was clear he was risking further reprisals from Sixtus, he refused to abandon his longtime ally, knowing that to do so would be to guarantee the creation of a formidable papal enclave on the very borders of Tuscany.

---

* Giustini had become an intimate of Girolamo Riario and was among those who accompanied him to Milan to solemnize his wedding to Caterina Sforza. He was also involved in the negotiations over Imola (see *Lettere,* ii, p. 476). Meanwhile, Vitelli, as a signatory of the triple alliance, had placed himself under the protection of the great powers of Italy.

Under the circumstances it was natural for Lorenzo to turn to his allies in the triple alliance, all of whom had obligations to Vitelli because he had a contract to serve as a mercenary captain on their behalf. Unfortunately the alliance, already strained by the rivalry between Sforza and King Ferrante of Naples, splintered further under the pressure of events. While Lorenzo and the government of Florence advocated a bold response, Sforza not wishing to offend the pope, equivocated as he was prone to do when faced with a difficult choice. The duke's vacillation was all the more disappointing since Florence could expect no help from Naples. Since the beginning of his reign Sixtus had been courting the king of Naples in hopes of detaching him from the tripartite alliance, a task rendered simpler by his rivalry with Duke Sforza. Now the pope's policy of reconciliation with his southern neighbor paid its first dividends. Not only did Ferrante refuse to act in concert with Florence and Milan, but he committed his forces alongside those of Sixtus in the siege. Diplomatically and militarily isolated, Lorenzo and the Republic of Florence could do little more than nip at the heels of the mighty host that had descended upon the small town.*

Even though Lorenzo's military efforts on behalf of his "great friend" Vitelli amounted to little in the end, this did not shield him from the pope's fury. Lorenzo tried to deflect criticism by employing the now familiar excuse that he could not defy the will of the people. Much as he would like to stand with the pope, he explained, "all the Commune wished to go to the aid of Castello, and had he tried to oppose it, all the state would revolt." Halfhearted Florentine efforts on behalf of Vitelli could not long stem the tide. When the celebrated *condottiere* Federico da Montefeltro appeared with his army before the walls of Città di Castello, adding his might to that of Cardinal Giuliano and the king of Naples, its ruler quickly sued for peace.

On July 16, 1474, Sixtus initiated a series of reprisals against Lorenzo and the Medici bank. The papal accounts were withdrawn immediately and some months later the Medici were removed as the pope's agent in the alum trade. Adding insult to injury was the news, not long in coming, that

---

* Florence hurried six thousand troops to nearby Borgo San Sepolcro, from which point they could cause the papal forces some concern but do little real damage.

both prizes were to be offered to the Pazzi bank as a reward for their role in the Imola purchase and their willingness to put the pope's interests ahead of those of their native country.* To further harass the already beleaguered firm, Girolamo Riario, in his capacity as his uncle's chief financial officer, launched a series of inquiries into the Medici bank's dealings, uncovering irregularities dating back to the reign of Paul II. As so often in the past Lorenzo turned to the duke of Milan, complaining, as Sacramoro reported, that Riario had "initiated new policies in Rome, reviewing the accounts, and depriving them of the assignments and many other peculiar things; and now he warned that the Count is threatening him greatly . . . and instead is directing all business towards the company of the Pazzi." The duke, perhaps hoping to make Lorenzo forget his recent duplicity in the Imola affair and his even more recent cowardice in regard to Città di Castello, responded by sending a forceful letter to his new son-in-law, reminding him that upon his uncle's death he would lose papal protection and that to secure his newborn state he would require good relations with his neighbors, especially Florence. Sforza went on to warn him against "the stratagems, which he used in favor of the Pazzi and against Lorenzo de Medici," and that "all the good or bad that is done towards him [Lorenzo], we will treat as if it was done to ourselves."

The Imola affair, combined with Lorenzo's defiance over Salviati's appointment and the siege of Città di Castello, had transformed Sixtus from a friend to an implacable enemy, and no amount of scolding from the duke could change that basic equation. Indeed, Lorenzo was neither the first nor the last Florentine leader to cross swords with the pope. As head of the Medici bank it behooved him to remain on good terms with the reigning pontiff, but as the First Citizen of Florence he was the natural foe of papal expansion. Lorenzo twisted this way and that in the hope of clinging to two ropes that were pulling in opposite directions, but in the

---

* The Pazzi were not immediately given the papal accounts. For a brief period they were transferred to Bartolomeo Maraschi, the pope's majordomo, and to the Genoese banker Meliaduce Cigala. But the transfer to the Pazzi was only a matter of time, since, as Sacramoro noted, they "have always aspired to the office of the Depository" (*Lettere*, ii, 18). The alum concession went to the Pazzi only in 1476 at the expiration of the Medici contract. If the delay was supposed to conceal the Pazzi role as the pope's errand runners, it fooled no one.

end he was forced to let one or the other slip from his grasp. Which he would cling to and which let go was never really in doubt. Lorenzo was too much a patriotic Florentine and too dependent on the goodwill of his people to pursue short-term financial gain at the expense of his beloved republic.

The crisis over Città di Castello hastened the disintegration of the already fragile system of alliances that had kept Italy relatively tranquil for two decades. The Peace of Lodi, masterminded by Cosimo in 1454, had substituted the republic's traditional allegiance to Venice for one with Milan, her traditional enemy. Once the kingdom of Naples was added, this triple alliance largely succeeded in preventing those vast conflagrations that had disturbed the peninsula throughout the early decades of the century. By the time Lorenzo succeeded his father this system of alliances had already begun to fray due to the mutual distrust between the duke of Milan and the king of Naples. For a time Lorenzo was able to paper over the disagreements between his two principal allies, but he could not ultimately bridge their differences.* The fact that this breakup was taking place at the very moment a dynamic new pope was ascending the throne was particularly inauspicious, since one of the main advantages of the triple alliance, at least as far as Florence was concerned, was that it served to contain the ambitions of the papacy. The collapse of the triple alliance allowed Sixtus to wriggle out of the diplomatic box into which he had been placed.

To exploit this opening, Sixtus needed to overcome an additional hurdle: the traditional rivalry between the pope and his neighbor to the south, the Aragonese kingdom of Naples. Papal relations with the kingdom of Naples had long suffered from the same kinds of irritations that plagued his relations with his neighbors to the north. Sixtus knew that his ambitions in central Italy required the acquiescence, if not the cooperation, of the southern kingdom, and so from the moment of his election he had

---

* One of the chief sticking points was Milan's and Florence's close ties to the royal family of France, the Anjou, which had dynastic claims on the throne of Naples. More trivial matters also continued to keep the pot boiling, like Duke Sforza's habit of luring the best singers in the king's choir to Milan.

worked hard to repair the damage caused by centuries of mistrust. Early in his reign he had shown his friendly disposition to the Aragonese kingdom by treating Ferrante's daughter, Leonora, to such lavish entertainment during her stay in Rome that the festivities, presided over by Pietro Riario, scandalized the more sober-minded of the clergy. As Ferrante's relations with Duke Sforza went from bad to worse, Sixtus sensed an opportunity to rearrange the diplomatic map of Italy more to his liking.

The other state pushing for a major realignment was that most mercurial of the peninsular powers, the Most Serene Republic of Venice. For many centuries the Venetians had remained proudly aloof from the chaotic affairs on terra firma, growing fabulously wealthy through trade and devoting their energies to protecting the republic's extensive possessions in the Aegean and Mediterranean. But as Ottoman advances in the eastern Mediterranean threatened her maritime empire, Venice had begun to make good her losses by expanding her holdings in northern Italy. This inevitably involved her in conflicts with Milan, the other great regional power, and then with Milan's ally Florence. But after meddling unsuccessfully in Florentine affairs during Piero's reign—primarily through her secret backing of the *condottiere* Bartolomeo Colleoni—the Most Serene Republic decided to reverse course. The royal treatment given Giuliano during his visit in May of 1472 was one of the first signs of a softening of attitude toward Florence and to the Medici family in particular. Soon the Venetian ambassador was signaling a desire to come to a more formal understanding, an offer that grew more appealing to Lorenzo as the old alliances disintegrated.

The war of Città di Castello exposed the stark truth that the triple alliance had run its course. Florence, which had the greatest stake in preventing an expansion of papal power on her doorstep, felt understandably let down; most Florentines had concluded that King Ferrante was treacherous and Duke Sforza unreliable. Under the circumstances it was natural that Lorenzo should lend a receptive ear to the blandishments of the Venetian ambassador, who now proposed a defensive treaty between the two great republics of Italy. Rumors of an impending agreement soon reached Sforza, who tried to discourage Lorenzo from taking such a momentous step, reminding him of the "faithlessness" of the Venetians. But in the aftermath of the Città di Castello fiasco, the duke's influence over his former protégé had waned. Lorenzo was particularly critical of Sforza's incoherent diplomacy that one day favored Venice, the next Naples, and the following week sought to renew a general league that included the pope. He decided that the time had come to act, assuming that once his determination to bind himself with Venice was known, the duke would be forced to come on board. With this in mind he asked Tommaso Soderini, then the Florentine ambassador in residence at Milan, to make his way to Venice, where he was to finalize an agreement with the Senate, even over the objections of the duke. Lorenzo's hunch proved correct; once the Venice-Florence alliance became a virtual fait accompli, Sforza made up his mind to join. On November 2, 1474, a new triple alliance among Venice, Florence, and Milan was announced.

The new pact, celebrated with bonfires and fireworks in the piazzas of Florence, appeared to provide Lorenzo with a much needed diplomatic success. He had replaced the crumbling alliance of 1454 with a new system of accords that included the three greatest states of the north. He was hopeful that faced with such a formidable array, Sixtus would curb his appetite for adventures in central Italy. But Lorenzo overestimated the strength of his hand. The pact he believed would tame the pope merely strengthened Sixtus's determination to oppose the new confederation with every means at his disposal. The king of Naples was equally suspicious of Florentine motives. According to a Milanese observer, Ferrante predicted that "should Lorenzo pursue this league [with Venice and Milan], within a year he will have reason to repent," adding ominously, "it will provide much stimulus to exiles who want to come to live in Naples, with the intention and promise of stirring up trouble for him."

Thus instead of guaranteeing the peace of Italy, the new system led halfway down the path to war. Machiavelli sums up the situation succinctly: "Italy . . . was divided into two factions: pope and king on one side; Venetians, duke, and Florentines on the other. And although war had not yet been ignited between them, nonetheless every day gave them new causes for igniting one; and the pontiff, especially, in whatever his enterprise, strove to offend the state of Florence."

With the major states of the peninsula now arrayed in two mutually hostile camps, attention turned to those small city-states that often supplied both the generals and the fighting men employed by the great powers.

Federico da Montefeltro, Count of Urbino, was the most accomplished warrior of his day.* This mercenary captain, ruler of the minor power in the Apennines that had long been a nursery of doughty warriors, had already distinguished himself in the service of the Florentine state, though Lorenzo might well have wondered if he had been well served by his conduct in the war with Volterra. (It was Montefeltro's troops who were largely responsible for the sack of that town that earned Lorenzo so much ill will among its citizens.) The shifting of loyalties that followed the disintegration of the first triple alliance meant not only that this professional warrior was free to choose a new master but that the services he supplied would be in even greater demand. It was with satisfaction, then, that from his splendid hilltop palace he contemplated the shifting map of Italy. The fact that this learned gentleman, whose home would serve as the setting for Baldassare Castiglione's *The Courtier*, was Lorenzo's godfather did not seem to weigh too heavily on his conscience as he considered his options.

Sixtus was determined to win over the *condottiere*, deploying in the process of seduction such charms as only a pope had at his disposal.† First he arranged a marriage between Giovanni della Rovere, brother of Cardinal Giuliano, and Montefeltro's daughter Giovanna. In May 1474, while attending Mass in Rome, Montefeltro was seated in the papal chapel on the benches of the Sacred College just below the last cardinal, "an honor hitherto reserved for the eldest sons of Kings." Finally, acting in his role as Montefeltro's feudal overlord, Sixtus offered to the lord of Urbino and his descendants the exalted title of duke. For Montefeltro, no less enamored of

---

* Castiglione praised him as "the light of Italy," attributing to him the virtues of "prudence, humanity, justice, generosity and unconquerable spirit." He praised his military prowess, "which was brilliantly attested by his many victories, his ability to capture impregnable places, his swift and decisive expeditions, his having routed many times with few troops great and formidable armies, and his never having lost a single battle." (Castiglione, *The Book of the Courtier*, p. 40). Federico's involvement in the Pazzi plot, while always assumed, was confirmed by a newly deciphered message (see Marcello Simonetta, "Federico da Montefeltro contro Firenze. Retroscena Inediti della Congiura dei Pazzi," in *Archivio Storico Italiano*, n. 596, a. CLXI, 2003 II). The decoding of the letter led to the overstated headline in the *New York Times* (March 6, 2004): "1478 Assassination Solved. The Humanist Did It."

† It helped that as the ruler of Urbino in the Romagna, Montefeltro was technically Sixtus's vassal.

gold and titles than most soldiers of fortune, these honors proved sufficient to win him to the papal cause. The courtship paid immediate dividends when the mere appearance of Montefeltro's army at the gates of Città di Castello led to the capitulation of Vitelli.

The new Italian order was confirmed when, in January 1475, King Ferrante, accompanied by hundreds of retainers, made his triumphal entry into Rome.* The pernicious nature of the papal-Aragonese alliance, at least as far as Lorenzo was concerned, was quickly revealed when Ferrante offered to Antonio de' Pazzi, Francesco's cousin, the bishopric of Sarno. It was a slap in the face of the Florentine leader, whom not so long ago he had praised to the skies for his "prudence and manly courage." But it was more than simply a public rebuke: in raising up a Pazzi against Lorenzo's known wishes, the king was reminding Florentines that while Lorenzo's favorites saw their careers grind to a halt, those who threw in their lot with the pope prospered. Invidious comparisons were inevitably drawn between Giuliano, whose ecclesiastical ambitions had come to nothing, and Francesco Salviati, now comfortably ensconced in his Pisan see.

If one also considers the precarious state of Lorenzo's finances, it must have seemed likely that his days as ruler of Florence were numbered; the cabal that had formed in Rome had simply to play out its apparently winning hand. But it is a testament to the passions that drove them, the impatience that clouded their judgment, and the arrogance that caused them to believe their own propaganda, that instead of pursuing a successful strategy to its logical conclusion, they rushed heedlessly down a path that would lead to the ruin of so many.

Despite signs of impending trouble, Lorenzo did not seem entirely displeased with the new state of affairs. From the rubble of the old triple alliance had emerged a new confederation, as formidable (at least on paper) as the one it had replaced. With the military might of Milan and the economic might of Venice solidly behind the Florentine Republic, Lorenzo felt confident he could weather the storm of papal disapproval. Even Sixtus's sanctions against the Roman branch of the Medici bank did

---

* So many falconers accompanied the king that, according to one eyewitness, the birds exterminated the entire owl population of Rome.

not dampen his spirits. He still had plenty of pocket money and intended to use it as he always did, to burnish his own and his family's image. To this end Lorenzo arranged a splendid joust in which Giuliano was to play the starring role, just as he himself had done six years earlier. Officially the joust was held to celebrate the recently concluded treaty with Venice and Milan, but it was simultaneously a coming-out party for Giuliano, recalling Lorenzo's own debut on the public stage made under similar circumstances.* Like that earlier event, this one would be staged in the Piazza Santa Croce, whose squat, workaday buildings would be transformed into faerie castles by banners, pennants, and rich brocades such as only the workshops of Florence could supply. The greatest artists, artisans, goldsmiths, armorers, poets, and musicians of the age were once again assembled to display the magnificence and sing the praises of the Medici family.

Lorenzo spared no expense to ensure that this festival was even more magnificent than his had been.† Giuliano himself was deeply involved with the preparations, conferring with artists on the details of his outfit and scouring the country for the finest mounts. The one sour note came when Giuliano wrote to the duke of Urbino asking him to loan him a particularly fine jousting horse. The answer he received was brusque to the point of rudeness. "I sent it to Renato de' Pazzi," replied Lorenzo's godfather, "who requested it from me."

The twenty-one-year-old Giuliano could shrug off this snub in the general excitement of the moment. The prince of Florentine youth was in his element, orchestrating the elaborate program and relishing the chance to show off his athletic prowess. If Lorenzo tended to have mixed feelings about such pomp and empty display, Giuliano not only knew the value of projecting a splendid image but could show off with unself-conscious enthusiasm.

---

* Though this fact is largely forgotten, Lorenzo's joust marked the end of hostilities with Colleoni after the attempted coup of 1466.

† Giuliano's joust was dedicated to the beautiful Simonetta Cattaneo, wife of Marco Vespucci, cousin of the explorer who gave his name to the New World. Modern audiences can still judge whether Florentines were right to celebrate her beauty; her long, golden tresses, pale complexion, and delicate features are familiar through the many famous paintings that contain her image. Simonetta's face is said to be the model for Flora in Botticelli's *Primavera* and the goddess Venus in his *Venus and Mars* (with Giuliano said to be the model for the sleeping god of war). She may also be the model for Piero di Cosimo's portrait of a young woman in the guise of Cleopatra.

As the populace streamed into the stands around the square on the morning of January 29, 1475, it appeared to many that the city had never been more prosperous nor the Medici family more firmly in control. Even those who resented the Medici and their high-handed ways could not deny that they knew how to put on a show. Statecraft in Florence was as much about spectacle as policy and Lorenzo was a master impresario. Giuliano rode into the square resplendent in armor designed by the famous Milanese armorer Antonio Missaglia, holding aloft a banner painted by Botticelli, and a shield with an image of the head of Medusa picked out in pearls. His entourage, comprised of the flower of Florentine youth, was almost equally sumptuously attired in silk brocades of a richness that only a city made up of bankers and merchants could afford.

The task of immortalizing his special day was given to Giuliano's good friend Angelo Poliziano. While on the occasion of Lorenzo's joust, Luigi Pulci stuck fairly close to the day's events, thinly disguising the more prosaic elements in an epic language that made all merchants' sons appear like chivalric knights, Angelo Poliziano kept to his reportorial task only long enough to launch into a dreamlike allegory that transported readers far from the narrow streets of Florence. It is a testament to the new cultural era that was coming into being under Lorenzo's aegis that Poliziano's epic poem, *Stanzas Begun for the Joust of the Magnificent Giuliano de Medici,* bears so little resemblance to its predecessor. The poet himself acknowledges his debt. Beginning his verses by praising the city "that bridles and gives rein to the magnanimous Tuscans," he then pays tribute to his patron, "well-born Laurel,* under whose shelter / happy Florence resting in peace, fearing neither / winds nor threat of heaven." A more significant measure of Lorenzo's influence than the flattery, typical for an artist who wished to please the man who paid his bills, is the poetry itself, which is steeped in the imagery that Poliziano had absorbed in the stimulating atmosphere of the Via Larga. Unlike Pulci's poem, which follows the courtly conventions of northern Europe, Poliziano's is a truly Renaissance creation that shows the fruits of the classical revival then in full force in the city on the Arno. Giuliano's joust is recounted as a magical tale filled with the gods, goddesses,

---

* The laurel bush (*lauro* in Italian), sacred to the god Apollo, was often used as a pun on Lorenzo's name. Paintings of the time often refer obliquely to the ruler of the city through the use of its distinctive foliage.

and supernatural creatures of pagan mythology, couched in a language whose allegorical richness reflects the sophisticated philosophical conversation that was the daily fare of those who supped at Lorenzo's table.

In Poliziano's tale, one in which the day's events are but the thinnest excuse for a flight into realms of fantasy, Lorenzo is cast as the lover, still pining for his cruel mistress Lucrezia and pouring his heart out in verse, while "handsome Julio" cares for nothing but feats of arms and of the hunt. "And you know," Cupid himself tells the assembled gods,

> what his arms and shoulders
> are, how powerful he is on horseback: even now
> I saw him so ferocious in the hunt that the
> woods seemed afraid of him; his comely face
> had become all harsh, irate, and fiery. Such were
> you, Mars, when I saw you riding along the
> Thermodon, not as you are now.

Though the tournament took place on a chill January morning, the poem floats on the breath of Arcadian groves filled with fragrant blossoms and populated by wood nymphs. Poliziano's narrative bears little resemblance to contemporary Florence but seems to have been conjured while dreaming in Lorenzo's library surrounded by the works of Ovid. It is the same gossamer world evoked by Botticelli's most famous paintings, *Primavera* and the *Birth of Venus*, both of which drew at least some of their inspiration from lines in the poem.* Both poem and paintings, in turn, owe their inception to the learned conversations held by Lorenzo in Careggi or his city home, led by the mystical philosopher Marsilio Ficino and with the bust of Plato, their spiritual and intellectual father, looking down approvingly.

With Giuliano's tournament, at least as it has come down to us through Poliziano's verses, the classical strain within the Florentine Renaissance is sung most sweetly. Rarely does the God of Jews and Christians intrude

---

* Octaves 99–101 (Book One) could almost serve as a blueprint for *The Birth of Venus*: "a young woman with nonhuman countenance, is carried on a conch shell, wafted to shore by playful zephyrs; and it seems that heaven rejoices in her birth." For *Primavera*, octave 68 offers the closest parallel: "to the realm where every Grace delights, where Beauty weaves a garland of flowers about her hair, where lascivious Zephyr flies behind Flora and decks the green grass with flowers."

upon this idyll, much less any Christian piety. Lorenzo and those brilliant poets, scholars, and artists with whom he liked to surround himself had not rejected Christianity for paganism—the emotional meditations on Christ's passions and the Virgin Mary that have come down to us from the various confraternities attended devotedly by Lorenzo and his circle belie this simplistic notion. But their infatuation with the art and literature of the pagan world and admiration for its breadth of intellectual inquiry and joyous sensuality led them to reject a narrow version of Christianity in favor of one that was expansive, inclusive, and, frankly, replete with contradictions.* In retrospect, this seems like a golden moment before the tragic events of the following years, as unreal a time as it was inspired, as beautiful as it was fragile. But intruding on this idyll is the first premonition of darker days to come. "The air seems to turn dark and the depths of the abyss to tremble," Poliziano writes near the end of the unfinished poem:

> the heavens and the moon
> seemed to turn bloody, and the stars seemed to
> fall into the deep. Then he [Giuliano] sees his nymph rise
> again, happy in the form of Fortune and the
> world grows beautiful again: he sees her govern
> his life, and make them both eternal through fame.†
>
> In these confused signs the youth was shown
> the changing course of his fate: too happy, if
> early death were not placing its cruel bit on his
> delight. But what can be gainsaid to Fortune
> who slackens and pulls the reins of our affairs?

---

* For example, this sermon preached by the humanist Cristoforo Landino at the company of the Magi, the confraternity most closely associated with Medici patronage, could have come from the mouth of Savonarola himself: "And we, vilest men, stooped and filthy in the mire of all vices in such measure that each may say of himself 'Vermis sum et non homo' . . . do not deign to show the slightest bit of gratitude; we do not deign, most ungrateful men—nay, beasts—for his love (and not for his but for our own benefit) to cast away a couple of sighs and shed four teardrops so that they may be the wind and water to put out the fire prepared for the punishment of our sins" (quoted in Hatfield, "The Compangia dé Magi," p. 130).

† These lines were written after Simonetta Cattaneo's untimely death in 1476.

Antonio and Piero del Pollaiuolo, *Galeazzo Maria Sforza*, 1471
(Art Resource)

XV. MURDER IN THE CATHEDRAL

*The air seems to turn dark and the depths of
the abyss to tremble; the heavens and the moon
seemed to turn bloody, and the stars seemed to
fall into the deep.*

—ANGELO POLIZIANO, *STANZAS ON THE
JOUST OF GIULIANO*, II, XXXIV

*"It was a worthy, laudable, manly deed, which should be imitated
by all who live under a tyrant or anything similar. But the cowardice and depravity of the men were to blame, that the example
bore little or no fruit, and those who had acted well must suffer
death. Nevertheless, they freed the earth from the most worthless
monster, who was stained with more shameful sins than any in his
time and long before."*

—ALAMANNO RINUCCINI, *RICORDI STORICI*, CXXV

ON THE MORNING OF DECEMBER 26, 1476, GALEAZZO
Maria Sforza awoke from a troubled sleep in the forbidding castle of Porte
Giova. Shaking off the effects of a tormented night, he called to his stew-
ards of the wardrobe, who helped him into an ornate doublet of crimson
and white (the Sforza heraldic colors) that he was to wear while attending
Mass at the Church of Santo Stefano.* On this day, whether by design or
through carelessness, the duke neglected to put on the armored breast-
plate he usually wore beneath his tunic. It was a rare lapse in a man for

---

* December 26 is the Feast of St. Stephen, dedicated to the life and violent death of the first
Christian martyr.

291

whom personal safety was something of an obsession. Perhaps he had succumbed to a fatalistic streak. Duke Sforza, like most Renaissance princes,
was as likely to place his fate in the hands of his astrologers as to depend on
the practical benefits of hard steel. Unlike Lorenzo, whose carelessness for
his own safety bordered on irresponsibility, Sforza's usual behavior might
be described as paranoid but for the fact that it reflected the real circumstances under which he lived: he insisted that any well from which he
might drink be kept locked at all times, and on his travels he was accompanied by a bodyguard of fifty mounted crossbowmen and fifty foot soldiers. The atmosphere of the ducal court was always thick with rumor and
intrigue; many of his ancestors had met violent deaths within the walls of
their castles, and the current duke had no wish to uphold this particular
family tradition. Even his own flesh and blood was suspect. Some whispered that he had poisoned his own mother, and less than a month earlier
Sforza had sent two of his brothers, Lodovico and Sforza Maria, on some
obscure mission to France, in part because he feared they might be plotting against him.

Thus it was surprising that on this particular morning he went out
unprotected and with only a small contingent of armed guards. His retinue
this cold December morning contained mostly foreign ambassadors and a
handful of courtiers, most of whom grumbled at the long cross-town journey to the church in the biting wind. Whether one is inclined to believe the
reports of various gloomy portents, the duke had every reason to be out of
sorts. The generally unhealthy atmosphere of the ducal court had recently
grown even more toxic, a situation for which Sforza had only himself to
blame. In addition to the cloud of suspicion that normally hung over his
intimates, he had alienated many of his friends by seducing their wives,
daughters, and sisters. Sforza's uncontrolled libido managed to offend even
in an age not easily shocked. It was not that he kept a mistress, the Countess
Lucia—for whom Sforza had begged of Lorenzo a gift of a famous ruby in
his possession—a situation that most would have regarded as normal. Less
easy to dismiss were the sexual escapades Sforza was in the habit of
indulging in, up to and including rape. The incessant preying on
respectable girls and women—and, it was rumored, handsome young
men—offended even the most jaded sensibilities. He himself confessed to a
friend that his greatest sin was "lust—and that one I have in full perfection,

for I have employed it in all the fashions and forms that one can do." But if Sforza regarded his own vices with amused tolerance, others were less forgiving. One father went so far as to accuse the duke publicly of turning his daughters into common whores. To make matters worse, his taste for luxuries he could not afford, much of it provided on credit from the Medici bank in Milan, had thrown the state finances into turmoil. Nor was this fiscal irresponsibility balanced by any notable successes in war or diplomacy. In short, Galeazzo Maria Sforza had done little to win the loyalty of his people while managing to antagonize those who were closest to him.

It was a sorry decline for a young man who had begun with such promise. When Pope Pius II had first met him, the "handsome youth was not yet sixteen, but his character, eloquence, and ability were such that he exhibited a wisdom greater than that of a grown man." Lorenzo's roving spy and troubleshooter Benedetto Dei thought that as a boy he appeared to be "the most handsome creature ever seen in our day ... so that he seemed the son of the god Mars newly descended." But by 1476, though Sforza was then still only thirty-two, this same observer was so disillusioned that he concluded, "his misdeeds were such that he deserved to be assassinated by his own people." Many of the duke's compatriots agreed, a fact that he seemed dimly aware of—all of which, combined with the general gloom of the season, was certainly sufficient to cause him sleepless nights.

When Sforza arrived at Santo Stefano he found the ancient church already crowded with worshippers. Also present in the church were three young noblemen: Andrea Lampugnani, Gerolamo Olgiati, and Carlo Visconti, part of that vast body of companions, servants, advisors, petitioners, favor-seekers, and hangers-on that swarmed about the duke like flies.

Making his way toward the Point of the Innocents, a large stone at the center of the church stained, it was said, with blood shed during the Massacre of the Innocents, Sforza recognized the three familiar faces. As he approached, Lampugnani threw himself on one knee as if in supplication. The crowd watched as Sforza made an impatient gesture of dismissal. A few sharp words were exchanged. Suddenly Lampugnani pulled a dagger from his belt and, still kneeling, plunged it into Sforza's groin. As the duke fell, crying "I am dead!," Lampugnani struck again, this time joined by Olgiati and Visconti, who continued to hack away at the duke as his blood mingled with that of the innocents shed centuries before.

A shocked silence hung in the air for an instant before pandemonium broke out. Few came to the duke's assistance; most were too busy saving their own skins to tend to their fallen lord. It was, in any case, too late. With the name of the Blessed Virgin on his lips, Galeazzo Maria Sforza breathed his last.*

Olgiati and Visconti took advantage of the confusion to make good their escape. (Some said they were assisted by those in the crowd who had been in on the plot.) Lampugnani was less nimble, getting tangled up in the skirts of the women in the crowd, where he was caught by one of the duke's guardsmen, who dispatched him with his sword.

Fear paralyzed the city in the immediate aftermath of the assassination. The surviving conspirators waited anxiously from their hiding places for signs of the revolution they anticipated would arise spontaneously after their heroic deed. But to their despair, instead of "liberta! liberta!" all they heard were the shouts, "Duca! Duca!" The truth is that while the duke was unpopular, the conspirators had done nothing to foster a larger political movement. Only one of them, Gerolamo Olgiati, was motivated by anything resembling a coherent political agenda. A student of the humanist Cola Montano, he had become inspired by the great tyrannicides of the ancient world and hoped by this murder to emulate them.[†] He dreamed of a return to the days of the Ambrosian republic when, following the death of Duke Filippo Maria Visconti in 1447, the people of Milan had proclaimed their own self-government and held out for three years against Francesco Sforza's attempts to seize the vacant throne. Both Visconti and Lampugnani had more mundane motives: Visconti sought to avenge the duke's seduction of his sister, while Lampugnani was enraged over the duke's failure to intervene on his behalf in a property dispute.

In the end, the citizens of Milan were too complacent or simply too cowed to throw off their shackles. Many a Florentine republican echoed, in

---

* His widow, Bona, was deeply concerned, since her husband had died before receiving last rites. She knew, she said, that he had been guilty of numerous sins but she hoped the pope would pray for his soul to shorten his stay in Purgatory.

† After the assassination, Cola Montano fled Milan. In 1482 he was captured while traveling through Florentine territory. Papers were found on him implicating him in a plot against Lorenzo and he was hanged from a window in the Bargello.

private at least, the sour verdict of Alamanno Rinuccini, who was happy to advocate the shedding of blood in the cause of liberty as long as he himself was not at risk.* "It was a worthy, laudable, manly deed, [he wrote] which should be imitated by all who live under a tyrant or anything similar. But the cowardice and depravity of the men were to blame, that the example bore little or no fruit, and those who had acted well must suffer death. Nevertheless, they freed the earth from the most worthless monster, who was stained with more shameful sins than any in his time and long before."

Once the threat of revolution had passed, the conspirators were hunted down. Olgiati was captured after his hiding place was revealed by his own father, who later reminded the duchess that he had offered to kill his traitorous son "a thousand times" with his own hands. Visconti and Lampugnani's servant, who had joined his master in the mayhem, were likewise rooted out and executed in the castle on December 30, strapped to a wheel that slowly tore them in half. Galeazzo Maria's son, the seven-year-old GianGaleazzo, was proclaimed duke, while Bona, Galeazzo's widow— joined by his minister Cicco Simonetta—was named regent. In a sign of trouble to come, the deceased duke's brothers now hurried back to Milan to see how they might profit from the new situation.

Among those who stood to lose the most by Duke Sforza's assassination was Lorenzo. In 1466 the sudden death of Francesco Sforza had emboldened the Medici's enemies in Florence, and the situation a decade later was even more precarious. On December 29, the *Signoria* was called into an emergency session, where they voted to send to Milan two of Florence's most able and respected citizens, Tommaso Soderini and Luigi Guicciardini, to proclaim the republic's unwavering support in these perilous times. A few days later Lorenzo wrote to the duchess in his own hand, vowing to stand by Milan "as long as he had life in his body, and if that failed, [to] leave instructions in his will for his sons to do the same."

In Milan a power struggle soon emerged, pitting the seven-year-old duke, his regent mother, and Simonetta against Galeazzo's ambitious

---

* Rinuccini no doubt would have agreed with Thomas Jefferson that "the tree of liberty must be refreshed from time to time with the blood of patriots and tyrants."

brothers.* The contest would absorb the attention and the resources of Milan for the foreseeable future. As the diplomatic situation in Italy continued to deteriorate, Lorenzo could anticipate little help from his most stalwart ally.

The most important consequence of Sforza's assassination was that it temporarily shifted the balance of power in Italy, weakening the northern alliance and emboldening Sixtus and his allies, who, now more than ever, were determined to rid themselves of the troublesome lord of Florence. But as the conspirators in Rome elaborated their plans, Lorenzo and Giuliano remained strangely oblivious. In the spring of 1476 their attention was riveted by an event that, at the remove of five hundred years, might seem of little consequence—the life-threatening illness of the beautiful Simonetta Vespucci. So consumed were both brothers by news of her failing health that Lorenzo, then residing in Pisa, insisted on receiving daily updates on her condition. As she continued to decline, Lorenzo even sent his own personal physician to her bedside. In the end his ministrations proved fruitless and the young woman died on April 26, much to the grief of the entire city that seems to have adopted her as a kind of minor deity.† A clue that Giuliano's affection for Simonetta was more than just a poetic fiction is suggested by the fact that after her death her father-in-law sent him some of her dresses as a keepsake. Lorenzo's own feelings are recorded in his *Commento,* where Simonetta's untimely death provided the material for many a mournful sonnet. As always with Lorenzo's poetry, so much artifice and intellectual straining lies between the event and the verse as to give it secondhand quality: "As she was thus dead, then, all the Florentine wits, as is fitting for such a public loss, variously mourned, some in verses and some in prose, for the bitterness of this

---

* Galeazzo Maria had five brothers: Filippo Maria, Sforza Maria, Ascanio Maria, Ottaviano Maria, and Lodovico Maria. The last of these, Lodovico—still only twenty-four at the time of his brother's assassination—was the most formidable. We will hear much of him in the following chapters.

† It is impossible to mention this incident without remarking on the coincidence of the date and the tragic events that took place on the same day two years later. If astrologers had determined April 26 to be a particularly inauspicious day for the Medici, they apparently failed to bring it to the attention of either Lorenzo or Giuliano.

death, and each one felt compelled to praise her according to his ability and talent. Among these, I also set about doing it and about joining my tears with theirs in the sonnets written below, the first of which begins thus . . ." No doubt Lorenzo's dismay at the death of the beautiful young lady, so intimately associated with his brother, was real, but by the time he sat down to compose his verses, sufficient time had passed to transform genuine sorrow into literary conceit.

On the international front, renewed quarreling among the Italian powers was sparked by the march of a mercenary army under the *condottiere* Carlo Fortebraccio, who, after spending time in the employ of Venice, had decided to strike out on his own and help himself to Perugia, a city upon which his family had a dubious ancestral claim. The depredations of this aptly named freebooter (Fortebraccio literally means "Strongarm"), whose wild beard and aversion to bathing gave him something of the aspect of a barbarian king, stirred up the pot but did not fundamentally tip the diplomatic or military balance. When this ragtag band turned away from Perugia—a town that, though nominally part of the Papal States, the Florentines considered within their sphere of influence—and began to lay waste to the territory of Siena, many concluded that he was acting with Lorenzo's knowledge and approval. But Lorenzo remained studiously neutral in the matter, declaring that "having decided not to get involved in this affair, in which we have absolutely no interest at stake, and having maintained this position up until now, we do not see any reason for changing our minds at present." He proved true to his word, standing on the sidelines while the forces of the pope and the king of Naples laid siege to Fortebraccio's castle of Montone, forcing his surrender on September 27, 1477. The only significant result of this minor flare-up was to further alienate the Sienese, who now entered into formal alliance with the pope and Naples, thus providing a useful jumping-off point for any future invasion of Florentine territory.

Despite these petty squabbles, to most observers the Italian landscape seemed surprisingly untroubled. The Ferrarese ambassador wrote, "Idleness has so gained the upper hand in Italy that, if nothing new happens, we shall have more to say about the slaughter of fowls and dogs than about armies and deeds of war." A chronicler in the city of Viterbo, while noting the same lack of news, was less sanguine, as if the drowsy scene was but the lull before the storm. "It seemed as if men were weary of the long peace and took the field for little money."

In fact the writer from Viterbo proved the more astute observer. The serenity of the political scene obscured much behind-the-scenes maneuvering as Lorenzo's enemies continued to plot his destruction. In January of 1478 Girolamo Riario wrote Lorenzo a conciliatory note with the hope of luring him to Rome, where he could more easily be dispatched:

> [I]t would please me much for the State and on account of your personal position if your Magnificence would resolve to come to Rome and present yourself to the Pope for the removal of all misunderstanding and doubts. I do not in the least doubt that the Holy Father would receive you with joy; while I, with the affection which I owe you from our mutual friendly relations, would behave so as fully to satisfy your Magnificence, and all considerations of grievance which may have arisen from the afore-named events would vanish.

Lorenzo was wary enough to refuse Riario's hospitality, but despite his suspicions of the pope and his kin he assumed he was safe as long as he remained in Florence. In fact the whole series of events leading up to the tragic day in April 1478 shows a decided lack of symmetry. On one side there is much purposeful activity—ciphered messages hurrying back and forth across the length and breadth of the peninsula, supplies being stockpiled, and armies assembling in secret locations—while on the other, life proceeds much as it always has, untroubled by any presentiment of what's to come.

The one offensive action Lorenzo did take demonstrated his misunderstanding of the nature of the threat he was facing. In this incident, which provided the people of Florence with gossip enough to last them a year or more, there is no question that Lorenzo was the instigator, but the matter was so trivial that it served only to increase the irritability of his rivals without doing them any real harm. While Lorenzo continued to think of his battle with the Pazzi in terms of ducats and florins, his enemies were playing for higher stakes.

In 1477, the wealthy Giovanni Borromeo died without male heirs, and Florentine law dictated that in such circumstances the surviving daughter would inherit her father's estate. Borromeo's daughter, Beatrice, was married to Francesco de' Pazzi's brother Giovanni, who thus stood to profit handsomely at his father-in-law's passing. But Beatrice's cousins, who were well connected within the *reggimento*, petitioned Lorenzo to change the law in their favor. After a few behind-the-scenes meetings with members of the Eight, Florence's chief judicial body, a new statute was passed giving priority to surviving male relatives, thus depriving Giovanni Borromeo's daughter and her Pazzi in-laws a large windfall. Even Giuliano balked at this underhanded maneuver, "saying that he feared that by wanting too many things, all of them might be lost."

Not surprising, Francesco de' Pazzi was beside himself with rage, but since he was already contemplating murder it is hard to make the case, as some have tried to do, that the Borromeo affair had a decisive impact on the evolving plot. Generations of historians have expressed outrage at Lorenzo's bald-faced abuse of power, but Lorenzo was acting in the best tradition of Florentine government, where the opportunity to help friends and discomfit rivals was one of the few inducements to holding high office. When Lorenzo declared that he had agreed to succeed his father "solely for the safety of our friends and of our possessions," this was exactly this kind of situation that he had in mind. Is there any doubt that had the Pazzi been in power they would have done exactly the same thing?

In any case, the tussle over the Borromeo inheritance did nothing to slow down preparations for the coup. With Lorenzo Giustini, Niccolò Vitelozzo's rival for power in Città di Castello, acting as go-between, Riario drew Federico da Montefeltro into the heart of the plot. Despite later denials, it is certain that the duke of Urbino was intimately acquainted with the details of the coup for which he agreed to furnish men and logistical support. By the beginning of 1478 the duke had contracted to lend six hundred troops to assist the conspirators in toppling Lorenzo's government.

Relations between Lorenzo and Ferrante were equally poisonous. Montefeltro, not without some relish, revealed the king's private thoughts in a letter in which he declared "his majesty would never consent to meet with a lowly merchant and citizen like Lorenzo, who is the greatest and most determined enemy he has, but he would, as has many times been noted, expel him from Florence or tear him to pieces, which he says would be easy to do since Lorenzo is hated in Florence as a tyrant by the majority of citizens."

With most of the military pieces now in place, the conspirators turned their attention to Lorenzo and Giuliano. After Lorenzo rebuffed Riario's invitation that he come to Rome, the conspirators concluded that the assassinations would have to be carried out in Florence. Making their task more difficult was the fact that the brothers rarely appeared in public together, one of the few concessions Lorenzo made to his friends' pleas that he protect himself. Hoping to add muscle and military know-how to this most difficult aspect of the plot the conspirators approached a battle-tested soldier in Riario's employ, Giovanni Battista, Count of Montesecco, captain of the Apostolic Palace Guard, and commandant of the Castel St. Angelo. A career military man from Abruzzo, this no-nonsense soldier could be expected to bring professionalism to an undertaking that was led by men with little or no military experience.*

Montesecco's eyewitness account of the meetings leading up to the attempted coup reveals the feverish excitement that now gripped the conspirators. Over the past months they had worked themselves into such a state that the old soldier's practical objections could do little to stop or even slow the momentum. Luxuriating in the comfort and splendor of their Roman apartments, fortified by wine and good food, it seemed such a simple thing to move men and armies about like so many pieces on a board until, at last, victory seemed not only likely but inevitable.

The first meeting between Montesecco and the leaders of the plot took place in the archbishop's residence in Rome. It began badly. From the beginning, Montesecco was skeptical, demonstrating a better understanding of the realities on the ground than those who had planned the coup. Hoping to overcome the *condotteiere*'s objections, a second meeting was held the following day in Riario's apartments in the papal palace. After enduring a harangue in which Riario recounted the many injuries he had suffered at Lorenzo's hands and those he would be forced to endure in future, Montesecco asked him to spell out precisely what it was that they were asking of him.

---

* Much of our knowledge of the plot comes from Montesecco's confession. This invaluable document, dated May 4, 1478, has both the virtues and drawbacks of firsthand testimony. It provides an essential eyewitness account of the conspiracy from the inside, but it is also subject to distortions and omissions. Frustratingly, though Montesecco provides much telling detail, he fails to provide crucial dates for various conversations and events. The conversations he reports likely took place in the summer of 1477.

Salviati, apparently irritated by the general's lack of enthusiasm, cut in: "Haven't I told you that we wish to change the government of Florence?"*

Montesecco: "Yes, you have told me, but you have not told me the means, and not knowing the means I can give you no answer."

Montesecco continued to press until, at last, the conspirators put their cards on the table, declaring "there was no other way but to tear to pieces both Lorenzo and Giuliano, and to have armed men ready to go to Florence, and to gather those soldiers beforehand in such a way that no one would suspect anything." But far from being impressed by their strategic brilliance, Montesecco scolded them: "Lord, watch what it is you do. . . . I do not know how it can succeed because Florence is a great undertaking, and the Magnificent Lorenzo is well loved, according to all I know."

Count Girolamo disagreed. "They tell me the opposite: that he has little favor, and is greatly loathed, and that upon his death everyone will raise his hands to the sky."

Salviati was equally dismissive: "Giovanbatista [Montesecco], you have never been to Florence: how things really are there and how Lorenzo is regarded we know better than you."

"Our Lord [the pope] how will this please him?" Montesecco asked, hoping that once the Holy Father was apprised of what was going on he would put a stop to the madness. Their response was discouraging: "Our Lord will do always as we wish, since His Holiness is ill disposed towards Lorenzo."

Still unconvinced, Montesecco insisted on speaking with the pope in person. This third meeting, held a few days later in the pope's private apartments, is the most controversial and difficult moment in the entire Pazzi conspiracy. Here amid the pomp and splendor of the papal residence, surrounded by the antiquities and treasures accumulated by generations of learned and worldly men, the gruff general met with the pope to hear from his mouth whether he would sanction the murderous plot against the Medici brothers. For all he knew, Girolamo Riario had been acting without his uncle's knowledge or approval, but Montesecco's account of this meeting in the Vatican leaves no doubt that Sixtus was at the very least an accessory, and most likely an active participant, in the plot to assassinate the Medici brothers.

---

* Most of what follows is the dialogue as reported by Montesecco himself in his confession.

The meeting began with a diatribe by the pope enumerating Lorenzo's many offenses agains his person and expressing his fervent desire that he be removed from power. Montesecco, as impatient with evasions and half answers as he had been in the earlier meetings, probed deeper. "Holy Father," he said, "it is difficult to execute such an intention without the death of Lorenzo and Giuliano, and several others perhaps." To which Sixtus responded, "In no case will I have the death of anyone; it is not my office to cause the death of a man. Lorenzo has behaved unworthily and badly towards us, but I will not hear of his death, though I wish for a revolution in the State."

"We will do our best that no one fall a victim," Riario said: "should it, however, be unavoidable, your Holiness will pardon him through whom it happens."

At this, Sixtus turned angrily to his nephew: "You are a villain; I tell you I will have no one die, but only the government overthrown. And to you, Giovan Batista, I say that I wish the revolution to proceed in Florence and the government to be taken out of the hand of Lorenzo, for he is a violent and bad man, who pays no regard to us. If he were expelled, we could do with the Republic as it seemed best, and that would be very pleasing to us."

"Your Holiness speaks the truth," Riario replied. "Be then satisfied that we shall do all in our power to attain this end."

As the audience drew to a close, Sixtus repeated his earlier objection: "I say again, I will not. Go and do what you will, but no lives shall be lost."

Salviati responded, "Holy Father, be satisfied that we guide the bark; we will steer safely."

"I am content," Sixtus answered, "but give heed to the honor of the Holy See and the Count." With this final word of warning Montesecco and his companions took their leave.

What is one to make of this conversation in which the pope gives his blessing to the plot while insisting that no one be hurt?—a paradox on the order of Portia's injunction to Shylock that he take his pound of flesh but without spilling even one drop of blood. The impracticality of this scheme was immediately apparent to everyone, if not to the pope himself. "[We] retired to the apartment of the Count," Montesecco continued, "and it was soon concluded that the thing could not be achieved without the death of both, that is the Magnificent Lorenzo and his brother."

What had occurred during his meeting with the pope that caused Montesecco to change his mind, agreeing to throw in his lot with those whom he had recently dismissed as madmen? According to Montesecco's testimony, the pontiff had explicitly forbidden the spilling of blood in his name— which was exactly what he and his colleagues were now proposing to do. It is possible that Sixtus was hopelessly naive, a man whose trust was abused by corrupt and violent men, but it seems far more likely that Montesecco understood that the pope's vehement denials were accompanied by a wink and a nod; no pope could admit that he was sanctioning murder, but everyone in the room knew what he meant.* Indeed, subsequent events hardly show Sixtus to be a man with a deep aversion to the shedding of blood.

By the first months of 1478 the plot had built up such momentum that it threatened to slip from the control of those who had set it in motion. As more and more people were drawn in, and as troops were assembled at various strategic points,† it became urgent to strike before word of the

---

* Another plausible explanation is that in his confession Montesecco was simply lying to protect his lord and master from the universal condemnation that would follow were it known that he had conspired to kill his rivals. Another possibility, for which there is some supporting evidence in contemporary documents, is that between the time Montesecco—under duress and facing certain execution—spilled his heart out and the time his words saw the light of day, the Florentine magistrates made certain alterations in the text to tailor it to the diplomatic exigencies of the moment. Not only did the authorities delete all references to the roles played by Ferrante and Montefeltro (see Simonetta, "Federico da Montefeltro contro Firenze," *Archivio Storico Italiano,* p. 275), but they deliberately minimized the role played by the pope. Why would Lorenzo wish to conceal the fact that his archenemy had tried to have him killed? His motive is revealed in a letter by Cicco Simonetta written a couple of weeks after the attempted assassination. In it he urged Lorenzo to "keep silent and maintain the greatest secrecy possible and to wait before revealing the part played by the Pope so as not to make him desperate, rather counting on his cowardice" (Simonetta, p. 275). In the dark, uncertain days following the attempt on his life, Lorenzo still believed that there was a chance to avoid all-out war by omitting most of the references to the vital part played by outside powers. By slanting the evidence so that it exaggerated the importance of his domestic rivals and minimized that of the formidable coalition of the pope, the king of Naples, and the duke of Urbino, he hoped to contain a dangerous situation.

† One method used to mask their intentions was to incorporate the troops into the ongoing siege of Montone, but as Montesecco himself noted, it was difficult to conceal their presence for long.

conspiracy leaked out. The most difficult aspect of the planning was to insert enough people into Florence to carry out the coup. One of those whom the conspirators managed to slip beneath the watchful eyes of the Eight was Jacopo di Poggio Bracciolini. It must have amused Riario to use Lorenzo himself for the purpose, writing to request that this "man of letters, virtuous and of substance," be allowed to return to Florentine territory as the secretary of the young Cardinal Raffaele Sansoni Riario.* Lorenzo's personal intervention may have been required since Jacopo, son of the famous humanist Poggio Bracciolini, had been implicated in the 1466 plot to overthrow Piero.

Montesecco himself made two trips to Florence. On both he met with Lorenzo, using the pretext that he had been sent by Riario to explore the possibility of a reconciliation with the pope. The first meeting took place in Lorenzo's palace in the city. On this occasion, and against his better judgment, Montesecco was favorably impressed with the First Citizen of Florence, dazzled by his wealth and cultivation and captivated by his charming manner. Much to his surprise he found Lorenzo "so well disposed towards the Count, that verily he could not have spoken of a brother more affectionately, telling me: 'Go to Imola, and you will see how things stand . . . that all will proceed so that nothing shall be lacking to satisfy his Lordship the Count.'"

On his second visit, this time to Cafaggiolo, Montesecco was even more impressed by the man he had been hired to kill. Lorenzo was a most attentive host, showing him about the estate like any country squire proud of the improvements he had made to his land. A highlight of the tour was the stables, among the finest in all of Europe, where Lorenzo discoursed at length about the animals he loved and about his preference for life in the country. Among the qualities Montesecco found most attractive was Lorenzo's unassuming manner with the grooms and servants, with whom he joked and carried on as if he was among friends. As a further gesture of goodwill, Lorenzo insisted on accompanying Montesecco back to Florence. If Lorenzo had charmed the old general, Montesecco had made a

---

* The nineteen-year-old Cardinal Riario was the son of Girolamo's sister Violante. His recent appointment as cardinal was but the latest example of Sixtus's irrepressible nepotism.

favorable impression as well. After his two official visits he could come and go across Florentine territory without arousing suspicion.

The real goal of Montesecco's visits to Florence was to try to persuade the Pazzi patriarch, old Jacopo, to join the conspiracy. Their first meeting, held secretly at an inn on the outskirts of Florence, proved difficult. Francesco de' Pazzi had already reported that his uncle was "cold as ice" and Montesecco found that the intervening months had not thawed him.

> *Messer* Jacomo [sic] came to the Inn of the Campana, where he and I secretly retired to a room, and on behalf of Our Lord I offered his blessing, and greeted him in the name of his Lord Count Jerolamo [sic] and the Archbishop of Pisa from whom I had a letter of reference which I presented; he read it and having read it said: "What do we have to say to each other, Giovanbattista? Are we speaking of changing the State?" I told him yes. He responded that he wished in no way to be involved because those two, who wished to make themselves lords of Florence, would end up breaking their skulls, which I understand better than they.

Apprised of the old man's continued resistance, the conspirators determined to make a second attempt to win over the Pazzi patriarch. When, some weeks later, Montesecco returned to Florence, he was accompanied by Francesco dé Pazzi. The three men met in the Pazzi palace, where they talked long into the night. The passionate pleading of Francesco finally wore down his uncle. Perhaps the decisive factor in Jacopo's change of heart was his realization that he was now so deeply implicated that whether or not he actually participated the authorities would hold him responsible. In the event the coup failed, what chance would there be that his life and fortune would be spared?

Though Jacopo was the most reluctant participant in the plot, once he made up his mind he strained every nerve to bring about a successful outcome. As the only conspirator intimately acquainted with local conditions he immediately saw the glaring weakness of the plan—the dearth of prominent Florentines willing to risk their necks to overthrow the Medici. After eight years as the unofficial head of state Lorenzo had achieved unprecedented control over the levers of power; the opposition that had been so prominent in the time of his father was all but invisible, having either been bought off through patronage or bullied into submission. Knowing his fellow citizens' disdain for foreigners, Jacopo insisted that Salviati (who would have preferred to watch events unfold from the safety of his Roman apartments) be on the scene to present a Florentine face to the public. This was the one major contribution that Jacopo made to the planning of the coup, but it was to have profound consequences not only for Salviati himself but for the course of the conflict that followed.

The cathedral of Florence rises from the crowded alleyways of the quarter of San Giovanni in muscular ripples like a great and gentle beast.* Crowned by Brunelleschi's soaring dome, the Duomo was the most potent symbol of the independent republic, a testament to the pride, wealth, and piety of her people. On the morning of April 26, 1478, the crowd streaming toward the cathedral for the celebration of High Mass—urged on by the happy chiming from Giotto's bell tower—was larger than usual. It was the tail end of the holy Easter season, the week before the Feast of the Ascension, and many had been drawn to the city by the festivities and the fine April weather. In addition to the usual crowd of pious Florentines there were others who had come to catch a glimpse of the newest cardinal, the pope's nephew, Raffaele Sansoni Riario, who was attending by special invitation of Lorenzo.

It was also the kind of vast, milling throng perfect for anyone who wished to conceal himself in plain sight. In fact for the past few weeks and days men had been trickling into Florence who had good reason for wishing to remain inconspicuous. Taken one at a time their presence in the city was not alarming, but had anyone in authority possessed the imagination to sift out patterns from the ambient noise he might have discerned suggestions of trouble. There were, for instance, more than the usual number of rough-looking men about, burly types bearing weapons that seemed more functional than decorative. Some were Perugians, some from Imola, and others from scattered mountain hamlets in Tuscany and the Papal States, where the vendetta and blood feud were the local sports. All had

---

* The cathedral, or Duomo, was often referred to by native Florentines as Santa Reparata or Santa Liperata, a reference to the obscure martyr to whom a church on that same site was originally dedicated.

legitimate reasons for being here and, presumably, their presence had been noted and approved of by the Eight: the Perugians had come in the train of the Francesco Salviati, while a nattily attired contingent consisting of thirty mounted crossbowmen and fifty on foot had accompanied the count of Montesecco, who had been hired to escort Cardinal Raffaele back to Rome.

The presence of both Salviati and Cardinal Riario was a welcome sign of the recent thaw in relations between Lorenzo and the Holy See. Montesecco had played a role in the easing of tensions, delivering the message to Lorenzo that Count Girolamo was anxious to put past differences behind them. Reciprocating the gesture, Lorenzo had invited to Florence both Francesco Salviati and the young cardinal, who for the past few months had been studying canon law at the University of Pisa. By extending the hand of friendship Lorenzo hoped to win his way back into the good graces of the pope at little cost to himself.

Given the general direction of Lorenzo's policy at this time it was no surprise that another of his old enemies was also present in the city that day. Francesco de' Pazzi, long estranged from his native land, was staying at the family villa in Montughi and was giving every indication that he, too, wished to put aside old grudges. With him were numerous friends and Pazzi clients, like the scholar Jacopo Bracciolini and the ne'er-do-well gambler Bernardo Bandini. The climax of these diplomatic efforts had come the day before (April 25) as Lorenzo hosted a magnificent luncheon in his villa in Fiesole. Held in honor of seventeen-year-old Cardinal Raffaele, the feast was attended by both Francesco Salviati and Francesco de' Pazzi. The ambassadors from Milan, Ferrara, and Naples were also present, happy to put their seal of approval on this feast of reconciliation.

It was, as usual when Lorenzo wanted to charm his guests, a delightful affair. While the guests wandered about the terraced gardens sampling the various delicacies set out on silver plate, musicians sent their lilting strains floating in the limpid springtime air. Adding to the enjoyment of the plentiful food and drink were the magnificent views of Florence below, framed by cypress trees and laurel hedges. The villa had been built by Lorenzo's pleasure-loving uncle Giovanni and it continued to be a favored haunt of many of his friends, including Marsilio Ficino, Pico della Mirandola, and Angelo Poliziano, all of whom found the shaded groves and magnificent views a stimulant to poetic and philosophical musings.

But the pleasant surroundings and rich food were wasted on the arch-bishop and Francesco de' Pazzi, who passed the afternoon in a state of almost unbearable anxiety. When Lorenzo had first announced his inten-tion to invite the cardinal to his villa, the conspirators realized that the luncheon would provide them with the perfect opportunity to do away with both of the Medici brothers. In his eagerness to please the pope's friends and relations Lorenzo neglected even the most basic precautions. He was so indifferent to his own security that Montesecco had managed to insinuate a number of armed men into the crowd (members of the cardi-nal's personal retinue), more than sufficient to do the job. But with all the pieces in place, the plan had to be called off when the one guest whose presence was vital to its success failed to make an appearance: at the last minute Giuliano sent his regrets, declaring that an infection of his eye pre-vented him from attending.*

Giuliano's sudden change of plans might have proved fatal to the con-spirators. With so many now in on the plot and with armies poised to march, how much longer would they be able to conceal their preparations from Lorenzo and his spies? As soon as the luncheon ended the conspira-tors reassembled at the Pazzi villa of La Loggia in nearby Montughi, where they scrambled to come up with an alternate plan. It was clear to them that they would have to act the next day if the whole elaborate scheme were not to unravel, particularly since the signal had already been given for their armies to begin their descent on Florence and could not now easily be called back.

With time running out, Archbishop Salviati devised a stratagem to get the two brothers together in the presence of enough armed men to finish them off. In his chronicle of the conspiracy, Poliziano recalled how Lorenzo and Giuliano proceeded like two sleepwalkers, blissfully unaware of the precipice opening up under their feet: "Again, [the conspirators] sent a servant to say that the cardinal would also like to be invited for din-ner to the house in Florence—he wished to see the way the house was dec-orated, the draperies, the tapestries, the jewels and silver and elegant

---

* The belief that Giuliano feigned illness as part of a deliberate policy on the brothers' part to avoid being seen in public together for fear of assassination appears to be contra-dicted by the ease with which the two were brought together on the following day.

furniture." It was a favor that Lorenzo, justly proud of his possessions and eager to show his friendliness toward any relative of the pope's, would be sure to grant. "The fine young men did not suspect a trap," Poliziano wrote: "they got their home ready, exhibited their beautiful things, laid out the linens, set out the metal and leather work and jewels in cases, and had a magnificent banquet ready."

While preparations were under way for the next day's feast, Lorenzo proposed that his guests join him Sunday morning for High Mass in the cathedral.* This new invitation caused the conspirators to revise their plans once more. "They did not think there would be time to do it [that is, kill the brothers] at Lorenzo's house," Guicciardini explains, "and besides, they doubted that Giuliano would be eating there. So they decided to do it that morning in Santa Reparata, where a solemn high Mass was to be sung. Lorenzo and Giuliano would surely be present."

But this adjustment touched off another crisis. Upon hearing of the change, Count Montesecco seems to have been overcome by a pang of conscience, refusing to commit murder "where," as he put it, "God would see him." Salviati and Francesco de' Pazzi insisted that the anonymity of the crowd would provide them with the perfect cover, but Montesecco would not budge. Not averse to murder under the proper circumstances, he refused to add sacrilege to the crime. From the beginning he had doubted the wisdom of the course his superiors were taking and, in addition, his two meetings with Lorenzo had given him a favorable impression of his intended victim. The demand that he now commit murder in a church provided him with an excuse to avoid something for which he never really had the taste.

The last-minute defection of the one professional military man was a costly setback. Montesecco was to have initiated the attack on Lorenzo, and a single blow from his muscular arm almost certainly would have proved

---

* It has always been assumed that Cardinal Raffaele Riario was an innocent dupe in the affair. His behavior at the time suggested as much and his treatment afterward at the hands of the authorities, while not of the kid-glove variety, seems to indicate that they, too, believed in his innocence. But it is difficult to believe that the cardinal was kept entirely in the dark. The mood at Montughi must have approached something close to desperation that evening, and even the most obtuse young man would have sensed the tension in the air as the conspirators hurriedly revised their plans.

fatal. A substitute had to be found without delay. Fortunately replacements were near at hand. Stepping in to take Montesecco's place were two priests, Antonio Maffei, a Volterran who dreamed of avenging the sack of his native city, and Stefano da Bagnone, a chaplain in the employ of Jacopo de' Pazzi. Though men of the cloth, neither of them seemed to share the soldier's scruples about committing murder in a church.

Early the next morning Cardinal Raffaele and his retinue set out for the city, arriving less than an hour later at Lorenzo's palace, where the cardinal changed from his riding clothes into his scarlet robes. Lorenzo was apparently surprised by this unannounced visit: he was already at the cathedral and had to hurry back to the palace to greet his guest. Then, arm in arm, the two headed back toward the Duomo. Upon arriving, Lorenzo and the cardinal parted company, the latter making his way to the altar, where a seat of honor had been prepared for him, while Lorenzo was quickly surrounded by citizens eager to catch his attention. Among those clustering about Lorenzo were many of his closest friends and associates, including the two Cavalcanti brothers, Francesco Nori, manager of the Medici bank, his neighbor and childhood friend Sigismondo della Stufa, Antonio Ridolfi, and Angelo Poliziano. Swept up in the talkative crowd, more interested in gossip and socializing than in the liturgy, Lorenzo made his way to a point just to the right of the High Altar. Easily lost in the crowd were the would-be assassins, including the two armed priests, who had maneuvered themselves into position a few feet from where Lorenzo stood.

The already intricate choreography of the assassination was made infinitely more difficult by the need to improvise. While armies marched on a prearranged schedule toward the walls of Florence, those inside the city scrambled to adapt to changing circumstances. Salviati, accompanied by Jacopo Bracciolini and his escort of Perugian soldiers, had barely entered the cathedral when he excused himself, ostensibly to pay a visit his mother, who had taken ill. Just as the choir, housed in twin lofts carved in the workshops of Donatello and Luca della Robbia, began to sing, Francesco de' Pazzi and Bernardo Bandini also left the church in a great hurry, realizing that, once again, Giuliano had failed to make his expected appearance. Rushing back up the Via Larga they coaxed the malingerer out of bed. Whatever had been ailing Giuliano, he had recovered sufficiently so that his visitors had little trouble convincing him to leave his chambers and accompany them back to the cathedral. All three appeared in high spirits as they made their way toward the church, even the usually morose Francesco de' Pazzi joining in the levity. At one point he wrapped his arm around Giuliano, remarking, "Your illness seems to have made you fat." This uncharacteristic bit of playfulness was apparently Francesco's attempt to feel whether Guiliano was wearing any armor beneath his doublet. Much to his relief he discovered that Giuliano had come unprotected.

With Giuliano now accounted for, everything was in place. As the priests chanted and the choir filled the air with angelic strains,* Giuliano found a spot before the altar some twenty to thirty yards away from Lorenzo. The crowd was so thick that neither was able to see the other. Francesco de' Pazzi and Bernardo Bandini stood behind Giuliano, while Bagnone and Maffei stood similarly arrayed behind Lorenzo, their hands gripping the hilts of the daggers they had hidden beneath their robes.

It was now 11:00 in the morning. The assassins waited tensely for the agreed-upon signal—the chiming of the bell that preceded the Elevation of the Host.† In anticipation of this most solemn moment the crowd had grown still and silent. The little bell rang clear beneath the wide stone arches and the priest began to intone the formula *accepit panem in sanctas ac venerabiles manus suas* ("he took bread into his holy hands"). An instant later four steel blades flashed in the dim light.

---

* The choir, one of the finest in Europe, was largely the product of Medici patronage. The cathedral's musical director, Antonio Squarcialupi, one of the most famous organists and composers of the age, was Lorenzo's particular friend and frequent collaborator, setting many of Lorenzo's songs to music.

† Eyewitness accounts vary, but the majority recall this as the moment when the assassins struck. The most valuable account, because it seems the most objective, comes from the diary of the apothecary Luca Landucci. Among the other useful accounts are those by Filippo Strozzi, the Milanese ambassador (who believed the attack coincided with the *Agnus Dei*), one by the Medici partisan Giusto Giusti, and that of Angelo Poliziano, though, as has been pointed out, his narrative is marred by its propagandistic function. The memoir of Philippe de Commynes, emissary of the French king in Italy, also provides a useful contemporary account though he himself was not an eyewitness to the day's events. The diary of the apothecary Luca Landucci, while giving no details of the attacks themselves, offers invaluable insight into the reaction of the average Florentine. The narratives of both Machiavelli and Guicciardini, while based in part on eyewitness testimony, add little new information to contemporary accounts.

Sandro Botticelli, *Giuliano de' Medici,* after 1478 (Art Resource)

XVI. THE BLOODSTAINED PAVEMENT

"[A]nd so for the most part ended the great attempt to transform the state, begun by the family of the Pazzi; whom, to tell the truth, showed themselves to have a spirit both manly and generous, and not being able to tolerate the many injuries and indignities at the hands of Lorenzo de' Medici; but although the undertaking to liberate their fatherland was just and honest, nonetheless it amounted to little, but for the ruination in the space of a few days of one of the most noble, richest, and most powerful families."

—ALAMANNO RINUCCINI,
RICORDI STORICI, CXXVIII

BERNARDO BANDINI WAS THE FIRST TO HIT THE MARK, plunging his sword into Giuliano's chest, shouting, "Here traitor!" Staggering backward, Giuliano was struck again, now by Francesco de' Pazzi who continued to slash at him with his dagger even as he fell to the ground. So furious was Francesco's attack that he wounded himself in the thigh with his own blade. Giuliano received nineteen wounds, the majority of them delivered by Francesco.

At the same moment the two priests came up behind Lorenzo. One of them—it is not recorded if it was Maffei or Bagnone—grabbed him by the shoulders as if to steady himself before delivering the blow. This was the kind of amateurish blunder Montesecco would never have made. Lorenzo broke free from his assailant. Wrapping his cloak about his left arm he parried the next blow and, drawing his own sword, quickly beat back the two attackers. Within seconds Lorenzo's friends had closed ranks around him and hurried him in the direction of the New Sacristy, whose heavy bronze doors would provide a means of defense.*

By now all was chaos. The large crowd pushed, shoved, stumbled, and trampled as men and women tried to make their way toward the exits. Few had seen what actually happened but ignorance merely increased the panic. The crowd grew even more frantic when someone began to shout that the dome was collapsing, a rumor easily accepted since to Florentines it seemed that Brunelleschi's structure had been supported more by black magic than sound engineering. Of the assassins, only Bandini kept his wits about him. Seeing that the two priests had bungled their assignment he sprinted across the apse to catch the fleeing Lorenzo. It was Francesco Nori who turned to face the assailant, but he proved to be no match for Bandini, who ran him through the stomach with his sword. In sacrificing himself, Nori delayed Bandini just long enough for Lorenzo and his friends to reach safety. As Nori, mortally wounded, was dragged bleeding into the sacristy, Lorenzo and his friends squeezed inside. Poliziano managed to bolt the bronze doors just ahead of the onrushing Bandini.

Within the space of a few minutes the cathedral was nearly deserted. Cardinal Raffaele had collapsed in a heap by the High Altar, where he remained until he was escorted to the Old Sacristy by two of the cathedral canons who had bravely kept to their posts while everyone else bolted for the doors. There he remained, pale and trembling, until taken into custody by officers of the Eight.

The four assassins had fled with the crowd. Bandini was quickly through the city gates and galloping along the dusty roads as fast as his horse would carry him. Francesco de' Pazzi, bleeding profusely from his thigh, hobbled the few blocks to the Pazzi palace, where he threw himself into bed, paralyzed as much by his despair over the disastrous turn of events as by his injuries. Quickly disappearing into narrow alleys surrounding the cathedral were the two priests, Bagnone and Maffei, whose ineptitude had spared Lorenzo's life.

---

* These doors, completed in 1466, were the work primarily of Luca della Robbia, one of the artists most beloved by the Medici. In fact the room where Lorenzo now took refuge, which was used to house the vestments worn during the Mass, was filled with reminders of his family's past generosity, including an inscription that read "con Piero di Cosimo" (with Piero son of Cosimo), an indication that his father had been prominent among those who had paid for and overseen its decoration.

Inside the sacristy, Lorenzo's friends anxiously tried to determine the extent of his injuries. He had only one visible wound, a wide gash on his throat received when Lorenzo had deflected the initial blow with his arm. Though the cut was only superficial, Antonio Ridolfi, fearing that the priest's blade had been poisoned, sucked out the wound and spat the blood on the pavement. Alternating between fear for the safety of his family and rage at the unprovoked attack, Lorenzo called out repeatedly for any news of Giuliano. Only when the limber Sigismondo della Stufa climbed up to the choir loft was the sad truth discovered. Finding a perch on della Robbia's frieze of dancing cherubs he found the nave deserted but for the crumpled body of Giuliano dead beside the altar.

It was not long before a loud banging on the door and the sound of familiar voices signaled the arrival of friends. The door was unbolted and, surrounded by a protective cordon of armed men who shielded him from the sight of Giuliano's disfigured corpse, Lorenzo made his way from the empty church and out into the equally deserted streets of the city. Poliziano was not spared the gruesome sight of his dead friend: "Going out through the church towards home myself," he recalled, "I did come upon Giuliano lying in wretched state, covered with wounds and hideous with blood. I was so weakened by the sight that I could hardly walk or control myself in my overwhelming grief, but some friends helped me to get home."

Meanwhile, a second drama was playing itself out only a few blocks away. Francesco Salviati, along with Poggio Bracciolini and his escort of about twenty Perugian soldiers, had exited the cathedral only minutes before the attacks, intending, he claimed, to visit his ailing mother. But instead of heading toward the Salviati palace he and his men made straight for the Palace of the Priors, less than a quarter mile from the cathedral along one of the city's main thoroughfares. It was Salviati's job to seize this vital seat of government while his colleagues went about their bloody business in the Duomo.

Upon arriving at the palace, Archbishop Salviati confronted one of the guards and demanded an immediate audience with the *Gonfaloniere di Giustizia*, announcing he was on "very secret business" from the pope. Salviati was told that the head of state was currently dining with the other members of the *Signoria* and would attend him shortly. As Salviati and Bracciolini were led into a second-floor room to await the head of state, their armed escort seemed to melt away into the mazelike warren of rooms behind them. It was during these minutes of agonized waiting that Salviati's nerve failed him completely. Everything about the situation spelled disaster. The building itself, for all its opulence, must have felt like a prison, its thick walls and massive doors meant to foil any attempt at insurrection. The Perugian soldiers who had accompanied him were in fact already trapped inside the chancellery, a room equipped with a lock that could only be opened from the outside—just one of many precautions taken by the building's architects, whose ideas of interior design had been shaped by centuries of civil unrest.

Luck this day seemed to be with Lorenzo rather than the unfortunate archbishop. Lorenzo was singularly fortunate in the man currently serving as the head of state: Cesare Petrucci was not only entirely devoted to the Medici family but had already faced a similar crisis a few years back as the Florentine *Podestà* during the revolt of Prato. (See Chapter IX.) At a critical juncture in that earlier revolt he had faced down the rebels and helped turn the tide in favor of Florence; he was unlikely to lose his cool in the current situation.

When Petrucci entered the room, Salviati's extreme agitation immediately aroused the *Gonfaloniere*'s suspicions. Salviati stammered out something about the pope and his son, but his speech was so garbled that Petrucci could barely make out what he was saying. When Salviati shouted for his men to come and seize the *Gonfaloniere*, Petrucci rushed from the room, running straight into Jacopo Bracciolini, who was waiting in the hallway. Before Bracciolini could unsheathe his sword, Petrucci grabbed him by the hair and threw him to the ground. By now the commotion had alerted the palace guards, who came running to help. They quickly seized both Bracciolini and the archbishop, who was slightly injured in the scuffle. Meanwhile the Perugians had broken through the chancellery doors. Soon the clash of swords could be heard ringing through the hallways as the palace guard did battle with the intruders. Even the servants rushed to help, grabbing spits from the kitchen and any other makeshift weapon they could lay their hands on.

After a few minutes of confusion in which the battle hung in the balance, the palace staff managed to overwhelm the Perugians and secure the building. Still fearing an assault from outside, Petrucci, along with the other Priors and those men not assigned to guarding the prisoners, climbed to the fortified galleries on the top floor, where they barricaded themselves against attack. Petrucci ordered the tolling of the great bell in the tower, alerting the citizens that their government was in danger and that they should assemble in the square below.*

It was not long before those defending the palace heard the clamor of marching men. Friend or foe, they wondered? The answer came quickly as the cry *"Popolo e Liberta!"* rose from the surrounding streets. About sixty armed men poured into the piazza led by old Jacopo de' Pazzi on horseback, who raised the ancient cry of Florentine revolution. Approaching the palace—which they hoped by now was in the hands of Salviati and his Perugians—they found the doors barred against them. They tried to force their way inside, but Jacopo and his men were quickly scrambling for their lives as lances, stones, and other heavy objects rained down on their heads, a pretty good indication that Salviati and his companions had failed to take their objective. For some minutes the Pazzi patriarch kept up a brave show, wheeling about on his horse and calling on the people of Florence to rise up against their oppressors. At first, Jacopo's exhortations were met with stony silence, but then the response came, faintly at first but growing louder with each passing minute: *Palle! Palle!* More joined the chorus as Medici partisans gained their courage and their voice. Soon the cry went from street corner to street corner, drowning out the feeble *Popolo e Liberta!*† Turning his horse back into the narrow streets Jacopo made his way toward home. Here he was met by his brother-in-law Giovanni Serristori, who confirmed his worst fears: all attempts to rouse the people of Florence had been in vain. Realizing all was lost, Jacopo—no doubt cursing his nephew who had gotten him into this fix—fled the city by the gate nearest the church of Santa Croce.

Thus the most concerted effort to topple Lorenzo and his regime was over almost as soon as it began. As Jacopo himself had prophesied, lack of popular support doomed the rebels' cause. Such opposition as there was to Lorenzo and his government was scattered, disorganized, and demoralized. Nor had the conspirators done anything to rally support among old-

---

* Known as *La Vacca* (the cow) for its great mooing sound, the bell was sounded in moments of greatest peril.

† The old Republican Alamanno Rinuccini noted that no one cried out *Marzocco!* the lion that was the traditional emblem of the state. The fact that the citizens declared their loyalty to the Medici family rather than the republic was for him a source of shame, revealing how thoroughly the people of Florence had been corrupted (see *Ricordi Storici*, cxxviii).

line republicans. Men like Alamanno Rinuccini may have secretly prayed for a violent overthrow of the tyranny they believed Lorenzo had imposed on the city, but they would not lift a hand, or endanger their necks, to help. Rinuccini's epitaph on the Pazzi family is revealing: "[A]nd so for the most part ended the great attempt to transform the state, begun by the family of the Pazzi; whom, to tell the truth, showed themselves to have a spirit both manly and generous, and not being able to tolerate the many injuries and indignities at the hands of Lorenzo de' Medici; but although the undertaking to liberate their fatherland was just and honest, nonetheless it amounted to little, but for the ruination in the space of a few days of one of the most noble, richest, and most powerful families." Had the men now facing the hangman's noose learned of Rinuccini's secret admiration they would have derived little comfort from it.*

No matter how compelling the message, the Pazzi were the wrong messengers. They represented no legitimate alternative to Medicean rule in Florence but, as their compatriots well knew, and as even Rinuccini implies, they were proud, disdainful men whose enmity toward the Medici stemmed from personal grievance rather than a love of freedom. Worse, the Pazzi always looked to their own interests first and to the pope's second. Neither cause was one that any Florentine would lay down his life for. Had they managed to kill both brothers, and had Salviati seized the seat of government, it is likely that the coup would have succeeded, at least in the short run; a confused and traumatized people might well have acquiesced for a time in a fait accompli. But even had all gone as planned, Salviati and Francesco de' Pazzi would not have been acclaimed as heroes. The vast majority of their compatriots would revile them as traitors who had handed the state over to foreign occupation. How long would Florentines tolerate papal garrisons on their territory, and how long could those lifted

---

* Rinuccini gives his most cogent critique of Lorenzo's government in his "Dialogue on Liberty," written in secret the year following the Pazzi conspiracy. Among other things he praises the Pazzi for their principled stand: "[F]or to me it is clear than an honorable death is preferable to a life of disgusting shame. This truth did not escape the truly magnanimous mind and noble character of Jacopo and Francesco de' Pazzi and of the various heads of that family. Though they were flourishing, possessed ample wealth, had intimate connections with the most eminent citizens, and enjoyed popularity and the good will of the people as a whole, they scorned all these advantages in the absence of liberty. Thus did they undertake a glorious deed, an action worthy of the highest praise. They tried to restore their own liberty and that of the country."

to power on their shoulders hope to maintain themselves against an angry populace? With Lorenzo still alive and with the resourceful Petrucci showing his mettle, almost all chance of a success was gone. The one glimmer of hope remaining to the conspirators was that the 1,500 or so troops marching toward the city under the banners of Giovan Francesco da Tolentino and Federico da Montefeltro—these latter led in person by Lorenzo Giustini—would be able to storm the city gates before forces loyal to the Medici could organize.

From the Medici's vantage point on the Via Larga, the first hours following the attack in the Duomo were filled with anxiety and confusion. Lorenzo himself had little time to dwell on his loss, busy as he was trying to stave off disaster: "Neither his wound nor his fear nor his great sorrow for his brother's death prevented Lorenzo from overseeing his affairs," wrote Poliziano. Amid the uproar of his household, Lorenzo dashed off a brief note to Bona, Duchess of Milan:*

> My Most Illustrious Lords. My brother has just been killed and my government is in the gravest danger. Thus, My Lords, the time is now that you can come to the aid of your servant Lorenzo. Send as many men as you can with all speed, as you are, always, the shield of my state and the guarantee of her health.
>
> *Florence, XXVI of April*
> *—your servant Lorenzo de' Medici*

Help from that quarter would take days to arrive. In the meantime, Lorenzo prepared for the worst. Poliziano recalled the chaotic scene at the Medici palace: "There, armed men were everywhere and every room resounded with the cries of supporters, the roof rang with the din of weapons and voices. You saw boys, old men, youths, clergy and laymen all arming themselves to defend the Medici house as they would the public welfare."

The palace's well-stocked armories were emptied and, as in 1466, the building quickly became a bristling fortress. Before long the streets of the Golden Lion were filled with men chanting *Palle! Palle!* and waiting for

---

* The letter, dated April 26, 1478, is addressed to "Bona and Gian Galeazzo Maria Sforza, Duke of Milan," but it was Bona and her chief minister, Cicco Simonetta, who were the real power in the state.

the counterattack that never materialized. Typical of those willing to lend a hand was Giusto Giusti:

> I was in Santa Liperata just then, and when I saw Giuliano de' Medici dead, I ran to Lorenzo de' Medici's house to help as much as I could, and I went up to the room for storing arms . . . here too came many of his partisans to take arms. I helped to arm quite a few of them, and I also armed myself with a cuirass, helmet, shield, and a sword, and I stood on guard at the second street exit, along with some of Lorenzo's other supporters. . . . There I stayed on an empty stomach till 21 hours [5:00 P.M.]. Then I disarmed beside the room of the kitchen maid, leaving [the arms] . . . with her, and she gave me back my cloak, hood, and gown, and I went home to eat.

The most dramatic moment came when, pale and with bandaged throat, Lorenzo appeared at a second-floor window.* "I commend myself to you," he told the expectant throng. "Control yourselves and let justice take its course. Do not harm the innocent. My wound is not serious." But despite his statesmanlike pleas for calm, the crowd, emboldened by the knowledge that their leader was not seriously injured, filled the street with menacing cries.

The situation had already spun from Lorenzo's control. Whether he wished it or not, the people of Florence, thoroughly aroused by the threat to their liberty and enraged by the murder of one of their favorites, would not be mollified by prospect of justice patiently and impartially applied.[†] They demanded blood and nothing Lorenzo could say would appease

---

* Vasari, in his "Life of Andrea Verrocchio" confirms the incident, if not the exact words. Friends and relatives commissioned the artist to create effigies of Lorenzo in wax to be set up around the city in thanksgiving for his deliverance from the assassin's dagger. One of these, set up in the nunnery of San Gallo, was described by Vasari as "clothed exactly as Lorenzo was, when, with his wounded throat bandaged, he showed himself at the window of his house before the eyes of the people, who had flocked thither to see whether he were alive, as they hoped, or to avenge him if he were dead" (Vasari, "Lives . . . , I, 556).

† Some have seen Lorenzo's speech as disingenuous, but there is no reason to doubt the sincerity of his calls for calm. His desire to see the guilty punished was real enough, but he had no desire to see an explosion of indiscriminate violence engulf the city. Many times in the coming days he tried to douse the flames his brother's murder had kindled.

them. In fact the reprisals had already begun. The apothecary Luca Landucci describes one of the day's more gruesome incidents: "amongst others a priest of the bishop's was killed [in the piazza], his body being
quartered and the head cut off, and then the head was stuck on the top of
a lance, and carried about Florence the whole day, and one quarter of his
body was carried on a spit all through the city, with the cry of: 'Death to
traitors!'" This act of savagery was not an isolated event; over the next few
days Florence indulged in butchery on a scale not seen in the city for over
a century. Ghastly trophies in the form of assorted body parts began to
appear outside the Medici palace as if it were the home not of the leader of
the most civilized city in the world but the abode of a cannibal king.

Often it was difficult to distinguish between mob passion and official
justice. As violent pro-Medici gangs raged through the streets seeking out
those with ties to the Pazzi and Salviati families, Petrucci and his colleagues, the Priors and the officers of the Eight, meted out summary justice to their prisoners. In the square before the *palazzo* crowds gathered to
watch as one by one the Perugians were hurled from the upper-story windows, their bodies piling up in broken heaps on the platform upon which
the *Signoria* sat to receive foreign dignitaries. Before long armed men
appeared at the Pazzi palace and dragged Francesco from his bed, naked
and weak from loss of blood. Officers of the Eight could barely prevent the
mob from tearing him apart on the short walk to the *Palazzo della Signoria,* where an improvised gibbet had been erected in an upper-story window. Given the certainty of his guilt there was not even the pretense of a
trial. Francesco remained defiant as his hands were bound behind his back
and a noose placed around his neck. To the cheers of the mob in the piazza
below, he was shoved from the window, his naked body left to twitch and
dangle in the air.*

It was not long before the archbishop, still in his clerical vestments,
was dangling alongside his associate. Numerous bodies, including that of
Jacopo Bracciolini and Jacopo Salviati (Francesco's brother), now hung
from windows in the facade like grim Christmas tree ornaments.
Poliziano provides us with a vivid description of Salviati's death that,

---

* Thomas Harris re-creates this gruesome scene in his book *Hannibal* when Francesco's
distant relative, a police inspector, undergoes a similar fate at the hands of Hannibal
Lecter.

MAGNIFICO

more than five centuries later, brings home the violence and terror of that April day:

> The Pisan leader was soon dangling from the same window as Francesco Pazzi, and his body hung above the other's lifeless corpse. When he was lowered, by chance or in mad fury he sank his teeth into the corpse of Francesco Pazzi (a marvel seen, I think, by everyone there and soon reported throughout the city), and even after the rope had choked him he kept his teeth fixed in the other's breast while his eyes stared madly.

That evening, Sacramoro sent a letter to his bosses in Milan in which he noted, "all the signs are in favor of Lorenzo." But the violent reprisals continued even after it was clear that the Medici were no longer in imminent danger. Landucci recorded over three days—April 26 through April 28—more than seventy summary executions and lynchings by angry mobs. Among the victims were some completely innocent as well as many who were only distantly implicated.* The bloodshed, which continued sporadically for weeks, was prompted as much by fear as by rage. On the twenty-ninth, four days after the attacks in the cathedral, the people were, Landucci declares, "still bewildered with terror," though it is not clear whether it was the initial attacks or the violent reprisals that were the more traumatic. Even after the slaughter had ended the usually busy streets were deserted as armed soldiers patrolled the city.

Lorenzo's role in the reprisals is hard to discern. After the few words addressed to the crowd in the hours after the attack he made little attempt to intervene one way or another. Only in the case of his brother-in-law Guglielmo de' Pazzi—who some believed must have had at least some foreknowledge of the plot—did he take a stand on behalf of one of the suspects. After his sister Bianca came to plead for Guglielmo's life, Lorenzo persuaded the authorities to impose a lighter sentence of exile.† For the most part, how-

---

* Among the latter was Renato de' Pazzi, Francesco's cousin, who though not directly implicated, was executed for having failed to inform authorities of the plot.

† Guglielmo was placed in effect under house arrest. He retired to his villa and was required to remain within a zone of from five to twenty miles from Florence (see Landucci, *Florentine Diary,* p. 19).

ever, Lorenzo stood on the sidelines while the executions were carried out in the name of the *Signoria* and the Eight, bodies that while stocked with Medici partisans were fully capable of acting on their own initiative.

Many, both at the time and later, accused Lorenzo of excessive vindictiveness, but the charge isn't entirely fair. Lorenzo was certainly enraged by what he felt was an unprovoked attack and had no inclination to spare the guilty; Poliziano recalls that minutes after the attack Lorenzo "made angry threats and lamented that his life had been endangered by people who had hardly any reason to attack him." Under the circumstances, anger and self-pity, two emotions with which Lorenzo was well acquainted, were perfectly natural. Even in less stressful situations his angry outbursts struck fear into those closest to him, but there is no indication that he was particularly bloodthirsty in this matter. The one area where we can detect Lorenzo's hand in the reprisals was in the government's pursuit of financial and political penalties against the Pazzi. This was the kind of vengeance that Lorenzo understood and pursued with relish. In the months following the attack, the Pazzi family's assets and properties were liquidated and laws passed penalizing anyone who married into the disgraced clan. Even distant relatives were imprisoned at least briefly and questioned by authorities using the none-too-gentle techniques of the era. Such was Lorenzo's rage at the Pazzi that he tried to have the despised name all but obliterated from the public consciousness. Lorenzo never agonized about the violence perpetrated in his name, but in the context of that less squeamish age, when brutal punishments were meted out for minor crimes and where torture was a routine means of interrogation, the mass executions and dismemberments did not seem excessive given the enormity of the crimes.

Less concerned with the tribulations of the guilty than with the survival of his family and his regime, Lorenzo's spirits were buoyed by the demonstrations of loyalty.* Periodically, the crowds camped out below his window would demand he make an appearance, at which they would let out a raucous cheer of *Palle! Palle!* But despite these gratifying indications of public

---

* Sacramoro describes the "demonstrations of love shown by everyone towards Laur.o" in a letter to the duke and duchess of Milan, April 27, 1478 (*Lettere di Lorenzo de' Medici*, iii, 4). Poliziano recorded: "Since the public was anxious about his health, he had to appear often at the windows of the palace. Thereupon the whole people would acclaim him, cheer and wave, rejoice in his safety and revel in their joy." (Poliziano, "The Pazzi Conspiracy" in *Humanism and Liberty*, p. 179.)

support, Lorenzo worried about the rumors of foreign armies on the march. The morning after the murder, Lorenzo held an audience in his palace with many of the leading citizens who wished to extend their condolences for Giuliano's death and to pledge their loyalty to his regime. There he received word that two hundred knights in the pay of Girolamo Riario who had been riding toward Florence had been turned back by angry citizens at the nearby village of Firenzuola. Two days later a force of five hundred soldiers commanded by Lorenzo Giustini was routed by peasants from San Vitale, while an even larger force—three hundred cavalry and one thousand infantry—under the banner of Giovan Francesco da Tolentino retreated when confronted by pro-Medici forces arriving from Bologna.

In the end the military operation organized by Montesecco and Riario proved even more feeble than the efforts within Florence itself. To be fair, the troops, so carefully assembled and cunningly concealed, had never been adequate to take the city by force; they were intended only to prop up an already successful coup. The ease with which these professional armies were beaten back by peasants wielding scythes and pitchforks merely confirmed how little support the conspirators had. Within a day or two these citizen militias were stiffened by troops from Milan, whose response had been so prompt and vigorous that, according to their ambassadors in Rome, the pope and his supporters were thrown into utter confusion.

Even as the city was secured from invasion, authorities continued to tease out the threads of the vast conspiracy and track down the guilty parties. Jacopo was captured on the twenty-ninth by a patriotic farmer in the village of San Godenzo. Knowing the humiliating and painful death that awaited him in Florence, he begged the farmer and his brother to kill him on the spot. When they refused, Jacopo quoted Seneca to the puzzled pair, demonstrating that a Florentine gentleman could face death with the dignity of a Roman senator.* Taken by ox cart to Florence, he, like his nephew, was strung up before the facade of the *palazzo*. The two priests, Bagnone and Antonio, managed to elude authorities for a couple of days before being discovered hiding in the monastery of the Badìa. At first the monks refused to give up the fugitives but changed their minds when the crowd

---

* The line, appropriate to the occasion, was "Fate guides the willing man, and drags the unwilling" (Poliziano, *The Pazzi Conspiracy,* in *Humanism and Liberty,* p. 180).

threatened to storm the building. Having seized them, the crowd showed no mercy, cutting off their noses and ears before dragging them to join their colleagues on the gallows.

Montesecco, who had also gone into hiding, was captured on May 4. Interrogated by the Eight he offered a full confession. Perhaps because he had cooperated with the authorities or because of his status as a soldier in the pope's employ, his death was more dignified: he was beheaded in the courtyard of the Bargello. Of all the principal conspirators— except for those like Girolamo, who never put himself at any risk— Bernardo Bandini managed to evade justice the longest. Eventually he made his way to Constantinople, far enough, he believed, that the long arm of Lorenzo could not reach him. He was mistaken. Writing personally to the sultan, Lorenzo managed to have Bandini shipped back in chains to Florence where, a year after the murders, he was hanged from the *palazzo*.*

The blood that flowed in the wake of the Pazzi conspiracy exposes the sinister undercurrent flowing beneath the civilized crust of this most cultured metropolis, but the worlds of violence and art were not as distinct as one might imagine. In a peculiarly Florentine synergy, Botticelli was commissioned to paint what were in effect glorified mug shots of the condemned men on the walls of the chief magistrate's palace. Lorenzo himself appended suitable verse inscriptions, including one beneath Botticelli's portrait of Bandini that read, "I am Bernardo Bandini, a new Judas / A Traitor and killer in a church was I. / A rebel awaiting a more cruel death."† Lorenzo's two favorite sculptors also commemorated the traumatic events: as an offering of thanksgiving for Lorenzo's miraculous survival, Andrea del Verrocchio modeled a series of lifelike effigies in wax that

---

* One of the eyewitnesses to Bandini's execution was Leonardo da Vinci, who sketched the gruesome scene, including notations on such details as the color of his leggings.

† "Son Bernardo Bandini, un nuovo Giuda / Traditore micidiale a chiesa io fui. / Ribello per aspettare morte piu cruda." When Lorenzo wrote these verses Bandini had yet to be captured. Botticelli depicted him upside down, the traditional mode of depicting a criminal who had yet to be appehended.

were displayed in sacred locations throughout the city, and Bertoldo di Giovanni struck commemorative medals that included on one side portraits of the two brothers and, on the other, scenes of the attack in the cathedral.*

The fiercely competitive atmosphere of the Florentine Republic accounted for both its cruelty and its genius, a fact nowhere more in evidence than in the Pazzi conspiracy and its aftermath. The pride that led Andrea de' Pazzi to build a family chapel to rival that of the Medici themselves was the same pride that led his descendants to commit acts of violence against the leaders of the state. His chapel was also the setting for the macabre scene that closes out this sanguinary chapter in the history of Renaissance Florence. After Jacopo's execution, his body was laid to rest in the family crypt at Santa Croce. Soon, the usually fine May weather turned unseasonably cold and wet, destroying crops in the field and generally making life miserable. The superstitious Florentines claimed that the rain was divine retribution for the sin of burying a traitor in consecrated ground. Thus on May 15, Jacopo's body was dug up and buried near the city wall like a common criminal. Two days later, Landucci recorded,

> some boys disinterred it a second time, and dragged it through Florence by the piece of rope that was still round its neck; and when they came to the door of his house, they tied the rope to the door-bell, saying: "Knock at the door!" and they made great sport all through the town. And when they grew tired and did not know what more to do with it, they went to the Ponte al Rubiconte and threw it into the river. And they sang a song with certain rhymes, amongst others this line: "Messer Jacopo is floating away down the Arno." And it was considered an extraordinary thing, first because children are usually afraid of dead bodies, and secondly because the stench was so bad that it was impossible to go near it.

---

* These medals contain a good deal of valuable information on the attack. One contains a portrait of Lorenzo with the words *"Salus Publicus"* (Salvation of the Public); the other medal has a portrait of Giuliano with the words *"Luctus Publicus"* ("Mourning of the Public"). Both show the moment of the attacks, with Lorenzo parrying the blow and Giuliano falling under the blades of Francesco de' Pazzi and Bernardo Bandini.

On April 30, the Feast of the Ascension, Giuliano was laid to rest in the church of San Lorenzo in a funeral attended by much of the populace of Florence.* Giuliano, the Prince of Youth, had been immensely popular and the outpouring of grief was genuine. His sunny disposition, athleticism, and good looks had appealed even to those who resented the Medici hegemony. Poliziano concludes his account of the Pazzi conspiracy with a tribute to his friend: "He was very mild, very kind, very respectful of his brother, and of great strength and virtue. These virtues and others made him beloved by the people and his own family during his lifetime, and they rendered most painful and bitter to us all the memory of his loss."

Some sense of the shock Lorenzo felt at the death of his beloved brother can be gleaned by an uncharacteristic five-day gap in his correspondence. The heading over two blank pages in his secretary's ledger reads, "Here and on the following page must be recorded the letters written about the tumult, when Giuliano de' Medici was killed in Santa Reparata, may God have mercy on his soul." The fact that they remained empty speaks volumes about Lorenzo's state of mind.

One ray of light pierced these dark days. Shortly after Giuliano's murder, his mother, Lucrezia, received the surprising information that Giuliano had recently fathered an illegitimate son.† Lucrezia sought out the baby and brought him to the Via Larga palace, where Lorenzo happily agreed to raise him as his own. The child, christened Giulio after his father, grew into a clever if somewhat dour man. Following his cousin Giovanni into the Church, he would ultimately ascend St. Peter's throne as Pope Clement VII.

---

* Both Lorenzo's and Giuliano's bodies were ultimately moved to a tomb in the so-called New Sacristy of San Lorenzo (to distinguish it from the Old Sacristy designed by Donatello), designed by Michelangelo. Unfortunately the magnificent tombs sculpted by Michelangelo house the remains of two obscure descendants, one Lorenzo's youngest son, the other a grandson. Both Lorenzo and his brother have to make do with a somewhat unsatisfactory monument tucked into a corner of Michelangelo's architectural masterpiece.

† The mother's name, if known at the time, has never been revealed. The young Giulio's swarthy features suggest that his mother was perhaps a Circassian slave. This was a common occurrence in Florence where men married so late. Even Cosimo had fathered a child with one of his slaves.

Francesco Pagano, *Port of Naples,* 15th century (Art Resource)

XVII. NEAPOLITAN GAMBIT

"For we make war on no one save on that ungrateful, excommunicated, and heretical Lorenzo de' Medici; and we pray to God to punish him for his iniquitous acts, and to you as God's minister deputed to avenge the wrongs he iniquitously and without cause committed against God and His Church, with such ingratitude that the fountain of infinite love has been dried up."

—POPE SIXTUS IV TO FEDERICO DA
MONTEFELTRO, JULY 25, 1478

"It is thus with a good heart that I depart, knowing that perhaps it is God's will that this war that began with the blood of my brother and myself should be brought to an end by my own hand. My greatest wish is that by my life or by my death, by my misfortune or my prosperity, I should make a contribution to the good of the city."

—LORENZO DE' MEDICI TO THE *SIGNORIA*
OF FLORENCE, DECEMBER 7, 1479

LORENZO'S TROUBLES DID NOT END WITH THE GRUESOME spectacle of his enemies dangling from the facade of the *Palazzo Publico* or even with the retreat of the invading armies from the gates of the city. The failure of the Pazzi conspiracy did nothing to resolve the root causes of the conflict or to deter those determined to bring about regime change in Florence.

Foremost among those still striving to redraw the political map of Italy was Pope Sixtus. Upon learning of the plot's failure, the pope flew into a rage, hurling abuse on Lorenzo and threatening the destruction of his state. Count Girolamo Riario's reaction was equally intemperate. Receiving the bad news from Florence, he lashed out at the nearest target, the Florentine ambassador, Donato Acciaiuoli. "The Count went to Donato's house," recorded Vespesiano da Bisticci, "accompanied by more than thirty men-at-arms, each with his halberd on shoulder."* They seized the ambassador and dragged him to the Castel Sant' Angelo, where he was imprisoned against all the customs of diplomacy. Hauled before the pope to answer for Lorenzo's crimes, Acciaiuoli was defiant: "[Acciauoli] addressed the pope and complained bitterly of the insult that had been done to his state and himself, and turning to Count Girolamo, said, 'Sir Count, I am indeed astonished at your rash presumption, that you have ventured to come to my house with an armed band, I being the ambassador of Florence, to carry me off as if I had been a traitor.'" Acciaiuoli might well have lost his life had it not been for the swift intervention of the ambassadors from Milan and Venice, who protested the rough treatment of their colleague and threatened to leave the city unless he were freed.

Sixtus reluctantly complied, but he remained as determined as ever to punish Lorenzo and the Republic of Florence. Since the mere fact that Lorenzo had escaped assassination was not sufficient reason to take up arms against him, Sixtus was forced to cast around for another excuse. He discovered his casus belli in the unlawful execution of Salviati, who, as a member of the clergy, was subject to ecclesiastical rather than secular judgment. Adding to the severity of the crime was the fact that the archbishop had been hanged in his sacerdotal robes, an intolerable affront to the dignity of the Holy Church.

Sixtus's freedom to maneuver was hampered by the fact that his seventeen-year-old great-nephew, Cardinal Raffaele, was now effectively a hostage. Lorenzo hoped to use him as a bargaining chip, assuming that as long as he remained in his custody the pope would not dare move against him. But it soon became apparent that holding Raffaele was doing Lorenzo more harm than good. The one great advantage Lorenzo had over the pope was the aura of martyrdom that had surrounded him ever since the attack. Sympathy for his loss and outrage over what had befallen him filled the letters, both public and private, that issued in a veritable torrent

---

* Riario tried to deny any involvement in the attack on Lorenzo and Giuliano: "That nefarious act that took place in Florence, has caused me such bitterness and displeasure that it practically drove me out of my mind. It is this that has caused me to delay writing until now . . . that I was unaware that anyone was to be killed, this [most Illustrious Lords] you will discover is nothing but the truth." (Quoted in Ilardi, "The Assassination of Galeazzo Maria Sforza," in *Violence and Civil Disorder,* p.102.)

from the courts and capitals of Europe. Raffaele's sojourn as a reluctant guest in Florence was becoming an embarrassment both to Lorenzo and to those who supported him. Early in June, Lorenzo decided to relinquish his hostage, hoping thereby to take some of the sting out of the pope's attack. According to an eyewitness, when Raffaele was finally handed over to papal allies in Siena he appeared "more dead than alive from the terror he had endured, and still feeling as if the rope were about his neck."

If Lorenzo thought this generous act would restore him to the pope's good graces, he quickly learned his mistake. One day after his nephew's release the pope issued a bull of excommunication, referring to Lorenzo as "that son of iniquity and foster-child of perdition, with a heart harder than Pharaoh's." His crime was that "kindled with madness, torn by diabolical suggestions," he had "disgracefully raged against ecclesiastical persons and laid violent hands upon the Archbishop, detained him prisoner for several hours and hanged him on a Sunday from the windows of the *Palazzo*." (Presumably if he'd been hanged on any other day of the week this would have mitigated the offense.) While Sixtus pursued Lorenzo with the grim determination of the Furies he made it clear that he had no quarrel with the people of Florence. From the beginning his strategy had been to wean them from their dependence on Lorenzo, a tactic he had tried before with little success. Late in July he explained his policy to his general, Federico da Montefeltro. "For we make war on no one save on that ungrateful, excommunicated, and heretical Lorenzo de' Medici," he wrote, implying that the Florentine people might escape his wrath at the small price of sacrificing their leader.

But far from rejecting Lorenzo, the bloody assault in the cathedral seemed to have rekindled their devotion. All differences vanished the moment the citizens of Florence found themselves under attack by a cabal of traitors and foreigners. Spontaneous demonstrations of affection were plentiful in the days and weeks that followed as Lorenzo was mobbed by cheering crowds who lined up on the Via Larga anxious to offer their condolences and to pledge their support.

Lorenzo was encouraged by these displays, but knowing that the coming crisis would place unprecedented strains on the social and political fabric of the city he was determined to put this loyalty to the test. On June 12, in a dramatic meeting at the *Palazzo Publico*, Lorenzo stood before the assembled dignitaries and declared himself willing to step aside if it would serve the cause of peace. "All citizens must place the common before the private good," he said, "but I more than anyone else, as one who has received from you and from my country more and greater benefits." Having thus thrown himself on the mercy of the court of public opinion, he sat down to await the verdict. One by one the *principali* rose to assure him of their continued faith in his leadership. As on that December morning nine years earlier, when the leading citizens came to his house to beg him to don the mantle of his deceased father, Lorenzo played the hesitant suitor who would assume the burden of rule only at the behest of his fellow citizens. Of course this was less a true referendum than a piece of political theater of the kind at which Lorenzo excelled, but despite the fact that the outcome was preordained it was a moving and symbolically important display of the common purpose forged in the wake of the assault on the regime.

Armed with the knowledge that the people of Florence would stand behind him—at least in the short run—Lorenzo proceeded to furnish himself with the tools necessary to make the government an efficient instrument of his will. As was usual in times of crisis, a new emergency committee, the Ten of War, was appointed and granted extraordinary powers to govern the city. Since this involved not only organizing and supplying armies in the field but also raising revenue, the Ten possessed almost unlimited authority for the duration of hostilities. Lorenzo himself was given the lead role, and with a supporting cast that included such close allies as Tommaso Soderini, Luigi Guicciardini, and Bongianni Gianfigliazzi, he now possessed almost dictatorial powers. His new status received official sanction when the Priors voted this ostensibly private citizen a twelve-man bodyguard, as clear a signal as this republican government could send that he was more than "first among equals."

Having put the government in fighting trim, Florence prepared to meet the threat posed by the pope and his allies. Before the actual fighting began this was largely a war of words. In response to the barrage of abuse spewing from Rome, Florence counterattacked along two fronts. The *Signoria* replied to the pope's denunciations in an open letter dripping with sarcasm: "Your Holiness says you are only waging war against our State to free it from a tyrant. We are grateful for your paternal love, but we cannot without sorrow behold an army of the Shepherd entering our territories (when the enemy of Christendom, the Turk himself, is on the threshold of

Italy), ravaging its crops, seizing its villages and carrying off its maidens and the treasures of its shrines as booty."

While papal forces laid waste to the countryside, Sixtus placed Florence under interdict, threatening not only the bodies but the immortal souls of her citizens. Preparing to meet the metaphysical challenge was an assembly of priests, monks, and other ecclesiastical officers under the leadership of Lorenzo's old tutor, Gentile Becchi. United in their love for Lorenzo and their devotion to their native land, they declared they owed no obedience to one who had so brazenly abused his holy office:

> We and the people have proved [Lorenzo] to be, and with one voice we acclaim that he is, the defender of our liberties. We are prepared to sacrifice everything for his safety, which is the one undoubted guarantee of the safety and liberty of the State. Your charges move us to laughter, for you wish us to drive out a man who has in no way degenerated from his illustrious forebears, Cosimo and Piero; a man to whom no one in Florence is to be preferred for true religion, worship of God, charity and piety. . . . Had he permitted himself to be slaughtered by your atrocious satellites whom you sent to Florence for that purpose; had we failed to recover our *Palazzo Publico*, the citadel of our liberties, from the hands of your traitors; had we delivered up ourselves, our magistrates and our citizens to you to be assassinated, then there would be no cause of contention between us! . . . Since you have occupied the Chair of Peter, everyone knows how you have used your office. It is too well known who is the enemy of the public good. Put on, then, a better mind. Remember that the Keys were not given you for such uses.

It was a remarkable act of defiance on the part of the city's spiritual leaders and Lorenzo was deeply moved by this show of solidarity. The priesthood of Florence, united in its opposition to the Holy Father, would play a key role in the war effort, since without the consolation of the sacred rites demoralization would quickly have set in.

As news of the murders spread across the continent the reaction from foreign capitals was also heartening. Louis XI, King of France, proved a particularly vocal supporter, penning letters of condolence to Lorenzo and launching a blistering attack on the pope.* Expressions of sympathy for Lorenzo and his family poured in from as far away as Constantinople, as did condemnations of the plotters and of the man now widely believed to have been their secret backer. From the beginning Sixtus's complicity was assumed, even if most were too tactful to voice their suspicions in public. In a report issued by the Milanese ambassador two days after the attempted coup it was revealed that the Venetian Senate "holds for certain, and states in public without any hesitation, that the King Ferdinando along with Count Ienronimo [Riario] has hatched this plot in Florence to kill Lorenzo de' Medici, and that the Pope has agreed to all of it."

By early June the forces of the pope and the king of Naples were poised to launch an all-out attack. Unfortunately for Lorenzo, occupying the moral high ground could not make up for a lack of reliable soldiers on the field of battle. On paper at least the combined armies of Florence, Milan, and Venice outnumbered the attackers three to one, but from the beginning Lorenzo's alliance was rent by local rivalries and undermined by incompetent leadership. Before the fighting began, the triple alliance issued a proclamation declaring itself to be "one body, with one mind, sincere and indissoluble, so that we are determined to share the fortunes of [Florence] and of the Magnificent Lorenzo." But brave words masked a more disturbing reality. Milan had been weakened by the death of Galeazzo Maria Sforza, and after a quick response in the days immediately following the attempt on Lorenzo's life, the government was preoccupied by more pressing problems, including a revolt by Genoa, instigated by agents of King Ferrante, and the ongoing power struggle between the duchess and her brothers-in-law.

The Republic of Venice, famous for its stability, could offer no such excuses for her halfhearted efforts. Having seduced Lorenzo away from his former attachments, she now proved herself a reluctant bride. Galeazzo Maria Sforza's warnings about the faithlessness of the Venetians must have haunted Lorenzo in the early months of the war. In public the Venetians claimed to be fully behind Lorenzo, but behind the scenes they did their

---

* While there was much talk of sending troops across the Alps to aid the war effort (see especially, *Lettere,* iii, pp. 214–26), the allies were reluctant to see foreign armies on Italian soil. Louis's most important diplomatic effort on Lorenzo's behalf was his call to convene a Church council to look into the pope's conduct in office.

best to wriggle out of their obligations. "It is necessary that this Senate bestir itself or that we be clear that they can't or they won't," Lorenzo wrote to Giovanni Lanfredini, his representative in the maritime republic. The Venetian ambassador himself despaired of his government, writing to Lanfredini, "I do not know what hope I can have, when, even such grave injuries as we have suffered, cannot persuade [the Venetians] to move. I see that at Rome they understand the humor of Venice and speak sweet words in order to send to sleep him who sleeps already."

No such indecision plagued their opponents. On July 13 a herald arrived from the king of Naples bearing a formal declaration of war to the *Signoria*. Six days later Sienese forces invaded Florentine territory, spreading panic in the countryside and sending a wave of refugees fleeing toward the capital. Soon Neapolitan troops under the command of Alfonso, Duke of Calabria—Ferrante's oldest son—and Federico da Montefeltro joined the Sienese in laying waste to the Tuscan countryside. Things hardly improved when Florentine forces counterattacked, "pillaging and working great havoc . . . so that everyone left their homes and felt safe nowhere but in Florence." Initial skirmishes were fought in the Val di Chiana south of Florence, a valley of malarial swamps whose foul miasmas Dante recalled as he traversed the bridge that led to the ninth circle of Hell. But while crops were destroyed and houses put to the torch little was achieved on either side. This lack of progress was the inevitable result of employing mercenary armies whose loyalty was to the general who paid them rather than the state they ostensibly served. Luca Landucci sums up the prevailing attitude toward these professional marauders: "The rule for our Italian soldiers seems to be this: 'You pillage there, and we will pillage here; there is no need for us to approach too close to one another.'"

As the leading member of the Ten, and as *the* indispensable man within the regime, responsibility for the war's conduct fell almost exclusively on Lorenzo's shoulders. Like most Florentines, however, Lorenzo had not been schooled in the arts of war, a failing he himself recognized.* Thus he was forced to rely on his commanders, who gladly took his money but seemed to feel this put them under no obligation to consult him or heed his advice.

---

* Florentine law prohibited a native son from commanding her forces, a precaution against the tendency often seen in ancient Rome of using military success to seize political power.

Often the war seemed to proceed of its own accord, while those in the *Palazzo Publico* looked on helplessly as the situation went from bad to worse. From the outset Florentine forces were undisciplined and poorly led. Ercole d'Este, Marquis of Ferrara, whom Lorenzo hoped to name as captain general of allied forces, remained at home for the first months of the war while he haggled over his fee. Even after he made his tardy arrival on the field of battle his presence did little to alter the basic equation. Inspecting the motley array of forces assembled for the defense of Florence, the *condottiere* Gian Jacopo Trivulzio was horrified by what he saw: "The Florentine troops passed in such a wretched state that I was disgusted—without order or connection, the different troops mingled together, so that I could not distinguish them, one squadron half a mile distant from the other." Given the disarray, exacerbated by the traditional rivalries between some of the cities in the coalition, it was not surprising that they offered little resistance to the first concerted enemy advance. On July 23 the main Florentine camp at Rencine, between Siena and Poggibonsi, was overrun, sending the allied forces retreating toward Poggio Imperiale.

If Lorenzo found his peacetime duties onerous, he discovered that the burden of managing the nation's affairs in time of war was almost more than he could bear. To some extent he was the victim of his own success. Having arranged it so that only his loyal followers were elected to office and having packed the councils with his closest friends, there were few now willing or able to take independent responsibility. Lorenzo had achieved unprecedented authority in the state, but at a high cost to his own peace of mind. Never had the responsibilities of office weighed so heavily or provided so little satisfaction. Given the rudimentary nature of the bureaucracy, Lorenzo himself had to handle much of the diplomatic paperwork aided only by a few personal assistants.* At a time when he could most have used the advice and support of his brother he had to face a seemingly endless list of troubles alone. Where once, according to the testimony of Marsilio Ficino, he toiled late into the night over his philosophical studies, now he stayed at his desk in the *Palazzo della Signoria* to attend to official business, often copying out correspondence himself by candlelight as his secretaries stumbled back to bed exhausted. "For the

---

* Niccolò Michelozzi, son of the architect who built the Medici palace, was Lorenzo's most important secretary. Most of Lorenzo's letters from this period are in his hand.

love of God, Girolamo," he implored his ambassador in Milan, "have compassion on the infinite problems that beset me, so many that I marvel that I have not lost what little sense I have left. I have written to you only briefly because I know that with you there is no need of words and because I am so exhausted that I can do no more."

The burden was particularly heavy because this was in a real sense *his* war. Though he had not picked this fight, Florentines knew that it was for his sake that they bore so many hardships. From the beginning the pope believed that the easiest, if not the quickest, path to victory was to force the people of Florence to abandon Lorenzo. This could be achieved by making the cost to each Florentine citizen so high that he began to question whether continued loyalty to Lorenzo was worth the price. Even as Ferrante presented his declaration of war to the Priors he made this policy explicit, his herald "tell[ing] us that the king and the Holy Father were ready to oblige us in every way, if we sent away Lorenzo de' Medici." In fact the entire assault on Lorenzo, beginning with the attack in the cathedral and continuing through the current battles, was predicated on the notion that he was a hated tyrant and that the citizens of Florence were only awaiting the right moment to rise against him. This strategy explains in part why the pope's generals seemed in no hurry to push home their advantage. A war of attrition, they believed, would achieve their ends with minimal dangers to themselves and their troops. "The Duke of Urbino is said to have quipped," Guicciardini related, "that in the first year of the war, Florentines were lively and energetic; in the second, they were mediocre; and in the third, done for. He was waiting for that third year."

By the time the two armies retired to their winter quarters after a season of unproductive mayhem, the war had already settled into a routine of small-scale skirmishes, mutual atrocities, and tactical maneuvers more calculated to avoid a pitched battle with the enemy than to win a decisive victory.* Thrown back on the defensive, however, Lorenzo felt the pressure much more than his opponents. As the days of misery lengthened and with no end

---

* Among the atrocities Landucci chronicles in the opening months of the war was the destruction of the town of Rencine by Sienese forces, the pillaging of the countryside around Siena by Florentines, the sacking of some fortresses by Niccolò Vitelli with "the burning [of] men, women and children, with every cruelty," to which papal forces responded tit for tat (see Landucci, *Florentine Diary*, pp. 21–23).

in sight, the pope's blandishments fell on more receptive ears. "And at this Christmas-time," Luca Landucci records, "what with terror of the war, the plague, and the papal excommunication, the citizens were in a sorry plight. They lived in dread, and no one had any heart to work. The poor creatures could not procure silk or wool, or only very little, so that all classes suffered."

How long would the people stand by Lorenzo while their fortunes dwindled and their families starved? With fighting taking place largely on Florentine territory the people's suffering depended less on whether battles were won or lost than on whether they were fought at all, since victory and defeat alike destroyed the farms, fields, and orchards surrounding the city. In the markets the price of basic foodstuffs rose alarmingly, a particularly dangerous development for Lorenzo whose popularity in the city's poorer neighborhoods was largely due to his efforts to keep the price of bread down. And it was not only the poor who felt the pinch of hunger: The well-to-do could no longer count on their country estates to supply them with fresh fruit and meat as their properties were overrun by marauding bands. The mercenary captain Rodolfo Gonzaga observed in the summer of 1478 that the war destroyed "many fine palaces belonging to citizens, to such an extent that much damage has been and is being done."

For a man accustomed as Lorenzo was to leavening business with pleasure, the daily routine of governing was oppressive. Adding to the pressure he felt, those excursions to the countryside that were crucial to his mental health had to be cut short or abandoned altogether. This disruption to the rhythms he had known since childhood was made all the more painful by prolonged absences from his family. Shortly after Giuliano's murder, Clarice and the children were spirited out of Florence. With the faithful Poliziano in tow, they led an itinerant life in one or the other of the many family villas or under the protection of friendly lords like the Panciatichi of Pistoia. Rumors of assassins, as well as various outbreaks of disease, continued to stalk them, forcing the family to pick up stakes every few weeks and keeping the household in a state of perpetual disarray. Poliziano painted a gloomy picture of their life in exile for Lorenzo's mother, who had stayed behind with her son in Florence: "I remain in the house [at Cafaggiolo] by the fireside in slippers and a greatcoat, were you to see me you would think I was melancholy personified.... Ser Alberto di Malerba mumbles prayers with these children all day long, so I remain alone, and when I am tired of study I ring the changes on plague and war, on grief for the past and fear for the future." In June of 1479 the family was forced to flee to the out-of-the-way villa of Gagliano where, as Clarice complained to her mother-in-law, "there is nothing but bare walls." Lorenzo got away when he could but often his plans had to be scrapped at the last minute. "I thought I would come this evening," Lorenzo wrote to his wife in Cafaggiolo, "and had sent word to put everything in order; in the meantime so much work has piled up that I have been forced to remain here, and I am writing this note so that you won't wait for me."

The constant anxiety took its toll. Clarice was often ill, exhibiting early signs of consumption, a condition that could hardly have been improved by extended stays in drafty villas meant for summer living. Fulfilling her wifely duties also proved exhausting. On those occasions when Lorenzo did manage to get away his time in the matrimonial bed was productive: in 1478 alone Clarice gave birth to two girls, Luisa and Contessina, and in 1479 she gave Lorenzo his third son, Giuliano. Small wonder, then, that Clarice, usually the mildest and most obedient of wives, lost her temper. It was during these trying months that she and Poliziano quarreled, leading to the poet's banishment from her presence.

Bad news from the battlefield was accompanied by bad news on the financial front as Lorenzo's enemies tried to undermine the foundation of his power. "The news I have received from Naples," Lorenzo explained to Girolamo Morelli, "is that the King hopes to destroy my affairs by insisting I be forced to pay without allowing me to collect. I have no doubt that the Pope, as soon as he hears of this attempt to absolve everyone of their obligations towards me, will seek by similar means to move against my business in Rome." Lorenzo's concern was justified: shortly after the beginning of the war, Sixtus repudiated his massive debt and seized the assets of the Roman bank.

Even before April 1478 Lorenzo's finances had been in a parlous state. The bad news contained in his secret ledgers was so well known that during the months leading up to the murders in the Duomo, Renato de' Pazzi had advised his cousin Francesco against the assassination attempt because he believed that they would achieve everything they wanted by simply standing on the sidelines while the Medici bank crumbled of its own accord. In addition to troubles with the two vital branches in southern Italy, heavy losses sustained in London and Bruges, the latter precipitated by the recklessness of Tommaso Portinari, were causing public loss of confidence in the Medici firm. By the first months of the war the situation had become so dire that Lorenzo, usually a creditor to the great courts of Europe, requested an emergency loan of 12,000 ducats from Bona, Duchess of Milan. In March 1479, with depositors again nervous about the safety of their accounts, he tried to borrow from her an additional 30,000 to 40,000 ducats in an effort to restore his faltering credit. A year after the war began, Lorenzo confessed that he was teetering on the brink of bankruptcy.

It was in these desperate circumstances that Lorenzo resorted to the unscrupulous practices that have forever tarnished his reputation. First he dipped into the inheritance of his cousins Giovanni and Lorenzo de' Medici, the children of Pierfrancesco de' Medici, his embezzlement aided by his position as executor of their father's will. This bit of sharp practice ultimately netted him a total of more than 53,000 florins.* The second stratagem he employed to stave off financial ruin opened him up to the charges of corruption that dogged him the rest of his days and caused no end of troubles for his heirs. With the connivance of his cronies, he managed to divert some public funds for his private use, making repeated raids into the *Monte dei Doti,* the state-funded debt used to provide dowries to the daughters of the poor.† Though Medici partisans tried to scrub the records clean, a few pertinent documents escaped their attention. According to one of them, dated three years after Lorenzo's death, the government sought to recoup from his heirs the amount of 74,948 florins that he had taken "without the sanction of any law and without authority, to the damage and prejudice of the Commune."

There is little doubt that Lorenzo illegally took public money to shore up his teetering financial empire, but it was less a matter of expedience than of sheer necessity. Lorenzo was faced with a stark choice between ruin and malfeasance. It is hard not to agree with Bernardo del Nero who, as a character in Guicciardini's *Dialogue on the Government of Florence,* deplored "the money that Lorenzo drew from public funds for himself and to benefit a few friends," but concluded that "the situation was such that his collapse would inevitably have damaged the public interest, so he was advised to do so by all

---

* Lorenzo was ultimately forced to pay back the money he had borrowed illegally. Most painfully, he had to sign over the villa at Cafaggiolo to his cousins to make up the difference.

† Lorenzo placed the "new man" Antonio Dini in charge of the *Monte.* Dini was executed for malfeasance after the expulsion of the Medici in 1494.

the leading citizens." Lorenzo was sufficiently aware of his own value to the nation not to agonize unduly over what must have seemed a necessary evil.

It is also important to remember that the boundaries between public and private were much more porous in Renaissance Florence than they are today. Public officials like Lorenzo received no salary; in fact they absorbed enormous out-of-pocket expenses as they wined and dined visiting dignitaries and staged magnificent spectacles for the greater glory of the republic. Ironically, the ideal of public service encouraged corruption as amateur citizen-politicians tried to recoup some of their losses by using their office for private gain.

As moral purists like Savonarola were quick to point out, peculation was a way of life for Florentines, from evading taxes to using the law as an instrument to profit at a rival's expense. The rich, in turn, atoned for their many sins by expending huge sums on the beautification of their city and for the greater glory of God. Much of the money Lorenzo and his forebears gained through questionable practices was returned to the public in the magnificent buildings and works of art they paid for. And while he was far from saintly in the conduct of his business, one can hardly make the claim that the net effect of Lorenzo's political activity was to enrich himself at the public expense. On the contrary: if politics did not ruin him financially, it was only by dint of the greatest exertion that he avoided disaster.

As roads that had been turned to mud by the winter rains began to firm up in the spring sunshine, the mercenary armies once again unlimbered and prepared to fight it out over the rolling hills of Tuscany. The second season of the war began on a high note with a victory by Florentine forces near Lake Trasimene, where more than 1,500 years earlier Hannibal had decimated the Roman legions. But the army that had barely held together in the first season of the war now threatened to come apart at the seams. Following the successful battle, Mantuan soldiers under Federico Gonzaga and the Ferrarans under Ercole d'Este came to blows over the distribution of booty, creating such bad blood that the Ten was forced to reorganize the two contingents into separate armies. Both of Lorenzo's principal allies remained distracted, Venice by the advance of the Ottomans in the Aegean, Milan by a simmering rebellion in Genoa. Desultory attempts to broker a peace agreement were scuttled by Sixtus, who remained opposed to any deal that would leave Lorenzo in power. Lorenzo even agreed to go to Rome and beg the pope's forgiveness if it would bring a speedy end to hostilities, but this offer led to nothing.

In Florence the situation grew more desperate as summer approached. Rats and other vermin multiplied along the marshy banks of the Arno, spreading plague among the poorer neighborhoods of the city. "I hear the plague is committing more ravages in Florence than usual," wrote a worried Clarice to her husband. "Your wife and children pray with all their might that you will take care of yourself, and if you can, with due precaution, come here [to Trebbio] and see the festival we should be greatly consoled." The threat of epidemic was increased by the fact that many of those accustomed to spending the summer months in their country villas were driven back inside city walls by the fighting, making the overcrowded, overheated streets a breeding ground for pestilence. In the crowded tenements where the wool-workers lived it was the malnourished who were struck down first, but in a city where rich and poor lived and worked in close proximity no one was spared. "To make matters worse, the plague continues to spread," Lorenzo reported to Girolamo Morelli, "and we have all been exposed: this morning a victim was buried in the cemetery of this church, and we, not knowing this, walked around and over the grave for more than an hour. But this is the least of our worries."

In August 1479, Lorenzo fell ill with a high fever that neither of his personal physicians, Moses the Jew and Stefano della Torre, could cure. Fortunately, the illness was not the plague but the less lethal malarial fever. On September 18, when he again wrote to Morelli, he had still not recovered: "I have written you a long discourse and since I still have a little fever, it isn't strange if I talk a little nonsense."

With no end to the war in sight, morale in the city sank ever deeper. The majority of Florentines continued to back Lorenzo, but not without growing murmurs of discontent. "The citizens accused one another freely and without respect," wrote Machiavelli: "they brought out the errors committed in the war; they showed the expenses made in vain, the taxes unjustly imposed. Such things were spoken of not only within the circles of private individuals but spiritedly in the public councils. And there was one so bold as to turn to Lorenzo de' Medici and say to him: 'This city is weary and wants no more war.'"

One event, while throwing the alliance into temporary turmoil, held out some hope for the future. On September 7, 1479, Lodovico Sforza secretly entered Milan to meet with his sister-in-law, the Duchess Bona, and to hammer out an agreement that would end months of near civil war. Bona agreed to step aside as regent in favor of Lodovico in return for a promise that he would ultimately honor his nephew GianGaleazzo's claim to the ducal throne. Both got what they wanted most from the bargain: Bona security for her son, who would now enjoy the protection of his uncle; Lodovico effective rule over the duchy of Milan until his sickly nephew reached the age of maturity. The only one unhappy with the result was Bona's chief minister, Cicco Simonetta, who upon hearing of the bargain his mistress had struck, lamented "You have taken a decision that will take my life from me and your state from you." These words proved prophetic as Lodovico quickly disposed of his rival by chopping off his head.

Shortly after Lodovico—known as il Moro (the Moor) because of his swarthy complexion—took power, Lorenzo wrote an optimistic note to his ambassador in the city: "I cannot believe that the Lord Lodovico being all-powerful and an absolute ruler will consent to our undoing, because it would be against his interest. He is by nature kindly and has never received any injury from us either public or private. . . . Therefore as soon as you can it would be well to see His Lordship and demonstrate to him that on account of ancient friendship we expect nothing but good from him."

In the meantime, however, the military situation had deteriorated. Early in September, Alfonso, the duke of Calabria, routed Florentine forces at Poggio Imperiale, driving them back to San Casciano, only eight miles from Florence. The war might have ended then and there had Alfonso pursued the defeated army to the city gates. Instead he decided to secure his lines by laying siege to the little town of Colle Val d'Elsa. This village, whose loyalty to Florence was directly proportional to her enmity toward her neighbor Siena, mounted a surprisingly stiff resistance. Alfonso finally succeeded in subduing Colle on November 12, but with winter approaching he proposed the usual seasonal truce—an offer the demoralized Florentines quickly accepted.

Taking stock of the situation, Lorenzo and the rest of the Ten could congratulate themselves on having narrowly averted disaster, but myriad and apparently insurmountable problems remained. Not the least of their worries was the prospect of famine, since much of the city's food production had been put out of commission by the fighting. Adding to the threat of hunger was the related threat of the plague, a disease that thrived in circumstances of misery and deprivation. For Lorenzo this was a period of darkest gloom. The attempt to overthrow his government that had apparently miscarried so badly in April of 1478 might now well succeed unless through some bold stroke he could reverse course and instill new hope in his long-suffering people.

On December 7, 1479, a courier arrived at the *Palazzo della Signoria* bearing an urgent message for the Priors.* It came from Lorenzo and contained news that both startled and dismayed the leaders of the city. He had written the letter in the town of San Miniato, halfway along the road to Pisa, where he had gone in secret the day before. Addressing the leading members of the government, Lorenzo revealed his thoughts on the current crisis and laid out the bold steps he now proposed to bring the war to a speedy conclusion. "Most Illustrious My Lords," he began,

> If I have not already informed Your Illustrious Excellencies of the reason for my departure it is not out of presumption but because it seems to me that the troubled state of our city demands deeds, not words. Since it appears to me that the city longs for and demands peace, and seeing no one else willing to undertake it, it seemed better to place myself in some peril than to further endanger the city. And so I have decided that with the blessing of Your Illustrious Lordships I will travel openly to Naples. Because I am the one most persecuted by our enemies, I believe that by placing myself in their hands I can be the means necessary to restore peace to our city. . . . If His Majesty the King intends to take from us our liberties, it seems to me better to know it as soon as possible, and that only one should suffer and not the rest. And I am most glad to take that role myself for two reasons: first because since I am the chief target of our enemies' hatred I can more easily discover the King's intention, since it may well be that they seek nothing but to harm me; the other is that having received more honors and benefits from our city—not only more than I deserve but, perhaps, more than any other citizen in our day—I owe a greater debt

---

* It is perhaps no coincidence that Lorenzo took this high-stakes gamble at a time when his uncle Tommaso Soderini was serving as *Gonfaloniere di Giustizia*. After his earlier rivalry with his nephew, Tommaso had become one of Lorenzo's most reliable allies.

than any other man to my country, even if I should have to sacrifice my life. It is thus with a good heart that I depart, knowing that perhaps it is God's will that this war that began with the blood of my brother and myself should be brought to an end by my own hand. My greatest wish is that by my life or by my death, by my misfortune or my prosperity, I should make a contribution to the good of the city. I shall therefore follow the course I have set out, and if it succeeds as I wish and hope it shall, I shall have served my country and saved myself. Should, on the other hand, evil befall me, I will not mourn if it benefits our city, as it certainly must; for if our adversaries wish nothing but to seize me I shall already be in their hands, and if they want something else we shall soon know it. It is certain that our citizens will unite to protect their liberty, so that by the grace of God they will come to its defense as our fathers always did. I go full of hope, and with no other goal in mind than the good of the city, and I pray God to give me grace to perform what is the duty of every man towards his country. I commend myself humbly to Your Most Excellent Lordships.
—From San Miniato on the 7th day of December 1479.

Your Excellencies' Servant,
Laurentius de Medicis.

From the moment Lorenzo set out, accompanied only by his secretary, Niccolò Michelozzi, and a couple of servants, his journey to Naples entered the realm of mythology. There is no doubt that Lorenzo carefully calibrated his words and choreographed events to create a sense of drama he knew would appeal to his compatriots. By stressing humility, self-sacrifice, and patriotism, he reversed the downward spiral of public opinion in which he was increasingly viewed as the cause of his people's suffering, recasting himself through this single bold stroke as a martyr for Florence.

But in recognizing the calculating and theatrical element in the enterprise one should not lose sight of the courage it took to hazard all on a virtually solitary voyage into enemy territory. Guicciardini conveyed the judgment of many of his contemporaries when he said it was "regarded as too bold and rash a decision, for he put himself in the hands of a king by nature treacherous, unstable and bitterly opposed to him," though, he concludes, "it was justified by his and the city's need for peace." As Lorenzo made his way to the port of Pisa, where he awaited the arrival of a galley from the king of Naples, all eyes were on him alone. His journey seems to belong in one of those mythical tales where two contending armies stand aside to let their champions determine the outcome in single combat. The armies, hunkered down in their winter camps, suddenly became irrelevant; whether the people of Italy would enjoy the fruits of peace or be forced to endure seasons of war without end would be decided in a meeting of two men, each with reason to distrust and resent the other.

What lay behind Lorenzo's bold stroke? Above all it was a daring gambit whose success depended on Lorenzo's understanding of the geopolitical situation and, perhaps more important, on his ability to size up the character of the men involved. By the second winter of the war it was clear to Lorenzo that something had to be done to change the direction of a conflict that was strangling the republic by slow degrees. Peace, he knew, could never come from the hands of Sixtus, whose hatred for him bordered on irrational obsession. And Federico da Montefeltro was merely a servant of the pope and would do his master's bidding. That left Ferrante as the weak link in the alliance.

Perhaps most significantly for Lorenzo it shifted the contest away from areas where he had little experience or aptitude—such as in financial administration or military strategy—and onto ground where he felt more comfortable. Face-to-face with his rival he had every confidence he could persuade the king to see things his way. But Lorenzo was not relying solely on his charm to win the king over. As he contemplated a strategy that would draw the two principal allies apart, two factors were working in his favor. The first was that Naples and the Papal States were natural rivals; the more likely it seemed that Sixtus would prevail in central Italy, the more Ferrante had to fear from papal domination of the peninsula. If Florence became a puppet of Rome, Sixtus would bestride Italy like a colossus, reducing Ferrante to the status of a puny vassal. A second factor was the continuing advance of the Ottomans, who, having overrun the eastern shore of the Adriatic, were now but a few miles from the Italian mainland. Only by bringing the war to a swift conclusion and turning the united forces of the Italian powers against the Turks could the king hope to repel invasion.

Lorenzo had in fact been laying the groundwork for months. Late in November he had sent Filippo Strozzi on a secret mission to Naples.* Filippo recalled the journey in his memoirs:

---

* Filippo Strozzi was the son of Alessandra Strozzi and had been exiled after Cosimo's rise to power in 1434. He had spent most of those years before his restoration in 1466 in Naples where he had established close ties with the king. He was thus an ideal candidate for this delicate mission.

The situation of affairs appeared serious to all, especially to Lorenzo de' Medici, on whose account, as they said, war was made. The aforesaid Lorenzo sent me to Naples. On November 24 I set out, to say to the king's majesty, he threw himself entirely into his arms, and would willingly agree to that which his majesty wished, whether the king should decide on high or low, within or without, provided he restored peace to the city and gave up the places he had taken. I found the king hunting at Arnone [at the mouth of the Volturno]. After I had delivered my message, he answered me that he had later news: Lorenzo would come in person, and so we must wait to see what will result from his visit.

Lorenzo was also being pressured by his allies to seek an end to hostilities. "I have received many friendly words from [Alfonso] the Duke of Calabria for many months," Lorenzo revealed to Girolamo Morelli in September, "and much encouragement to throw myself into the king's arms, he attempting to show me that only in this manner can I save myself and the state. . . . It is good that Lord Lodovico should know these things, and that if he wishes to save us, he must take up the matter with more energy and act with more decision."

On December 11, two Neapolitan galleys arrived at the little port of Vada, just south of Pisa. Awaiting Lorenzo on board were two of the king's chief councilors, Gian Tommaso Caraffa and Prinzivalle di Gennaro, both learned men and old friends. Their company no doubt enlivened the three-hundred-mile journey down the coast, but despite their assurances that he would be welcomed with open arms, Lorenzo had reason to be apprehensive. Ferrante was a mercurial and violent man, his ever-shifting policies marked by grandiose ambitions, treachery, and paranoia. Though lurid tales that he had the bodies of his dead enemies stuffed so that he might contemplate their comeuppance at his leisure were probably exaggerations, his reputation for cruelty was not unwarranted. Lorenzo might well have considered the fate of the *condottiere* Piccinino, who had been lured to the king's castle only to be thrown into prison where he was strangled by one of Ferrante's slaves. Despite the kindness of Caraffa and Gennaro, Lorenzo knew that the king would have no qualms about offering his head on a platter should he deem it in his best interests.

Early in the evening of December 18, Lorenzo's galley sailed into the magnificent, mountain-girdled harbor of Naples. The Milanese ambassadors who were present noted that he was "received and honored with as much dignity as possible." Among the crowd that greeted him as he made his way down the gangplank was his old friend don Federigo, the king's younger son, whom he had wined and dined on his first trip to Milan. Also greeting him were various ambassadors, members of the court, and trumpeters, who sounded a fanfare as he approached.

The king himself, who had gone hunting the day before, was not present, and for the next day or two Lorenzo was kept in suspense. As soon as word arrived that the king and his party were approaching, Lorenzo rode out to greet him a mile outside the city walls. Their reunion, as Lorenzo reported back to the Ten, was a great success: "He greeted me most graciously and with many kind words, showing in many different ways the affection he had for our city and his desire to enter into a true union."

Indeed, Ferrante went out of his way to make his Florentine guest feel welcome. But if he seemed well disposed to Lorenzo, he was also in no particular hurry to give him the honorable peace he so desperately needed. Lorenzo soon grew frustrated by the slow pace of negotiations. His servant recorded his master's moodiness as his hopes were alternately raised and dashed. "He seemed to be two men, not one. During the day he appeared perfectly easy, restful, cheerful, and confident. But at night he grieved bitterly about his own ill fortune and that of Florence." The twists and turns of the negotiations are suggested in a letter from Bartolomeo Scala, the chancellor of Florence: "Your letter of the 18th rejoiced us all, and peace seemed imminent. That of the 22nd altered the outlook and gave rise to grave thought in those who heard it. The reply was debated for several days. You will see what was decided. Only to you would such large powers be given in so important a matter. It is the first time a white sheet has been given, for it amounts to that. But as it is to you that such a commission is sent no one doubts that good will come of it."

Ferrante, it soon became clear, was playing for time, hoping to figure out a way to end hostilities with Florence while not jeopardizing his relations with the pope. By now Sixtus had caught wind of what was up and was voicing his opposition in the most violent terms. Later he grumbled, "We made a virtue of necessity, but to our serious displeasure for we saw how we missed the victory while we were deprived of the satisfaction of liberating Florence from these tyrants, and restoring freedom and quiet to her and peace to all Italy."

While Lorenzo was kept in suspense he made good use of his time, building up goodwill in the city that might tip public opinion in his favor. Upholding his reputation for generosity, he feted the local nobility and spent freely to help out those in need, including digging into his own pocket to purchase the freedom of one hundred Christians enslaved by pirates and dowering the daughters of the poor—perhaps with the very same money he had recently embezzled from the brides of Florence. Throughout these nervous weeks and months, Lorenzo found comfort and stimulation in the company of Ippolita Sforza, with whom he had been on intimate terms since the two had met at her wedding to Alfonso. Over the years in which they maintained a regular correspondence, Lorenzo had helped her out of many a financial embarrassment, in one case providing her an interest-free loan of 2,000 ducats. Now in his time of need, Ippolita returned the favor, using her considerable influence at court on his behalf. So assiduous was she in pursuing his cause that henceforth the king referred to his daughter-in-law as "Lorenzo's confederate."

In addition to the practical benefits of her friendship, they clearly enjoyed each other's company. Though Lorenzo was not free of the sexism typical of the age, some of the most rewarding friendships he maintained were with accomplished and cultivated women. He had before him always the example of his mother, his closest confidant and a woman who was not only an exemplary wife and mother but also a woman of rare literary and intellectual gifts. With Clarice, Lorenzo could never share his interests, but with the cultivated Ippolita—a woman not only conversant with the great Italian poets, but one who could quote Cicero at length and had some knowledge of Greek, having studied with the famous scholar Constantinos Lascaris—he could indulge in his passion for literature and philosophy. They spent many an afternoon deep in conversation at her castle at Capuano, or wandering along the Bay of Naples at the Riviera di Chiaja. Ippolita later recalled the pleasant times they spent together: "The present letter will not be one of those which refer to alliance and State affairs, but will merely bring to your remembrance that we always think of you, although we are by no means certain that you often think of our garden, which is now most beautiful and in full bloom."

But despite the pleasant surroundings and the equally pleasant company, Lorenzo chafed at the long delay. Worried about his family, he demanded almost daily reports from Antonio Pucci, in whose care he had left them. "[Y]our family are all well," begins one letter. "Never a day passes without my seeing Piero and Giovanni. . . . I am enclosing a letter from Piero; he makes good use of his time. Giovanni goes to bed at an early hour, and he says he never moves all night. He is fat and looks well." In addition to anxiety about the safety of his wife and children, Lorenzo worried about the state he had left in the care of others. On this front he had reason to fret, particularly as the negotiations dragged out with few signs of progress. Though some in the regime contended that all went smoothly in Lorenzo's absence, more honest correspondents revealed that the stirrings of rebellion were in the air. In January 1480, Agnolo della Stufa admitted, "the length of these negotiations means that I am constantly worried. I long for your return. I do not know what to do." Much of the dissension was fomented by the Venetian ambassador, who feared that Lorenzo would cut a separate deal with the king that would leave Venice in the lurch. A note of nervousness crept into even the usually optimistic correspondence of the chancellor, Bartolomeo Scala: "We are all hoping against hope for the conclusion of this affair which has delayed so long. . . . For the love of God get us out of this by the good graces of him [the king] on whom we are to depend in future; for his power and authority are such that finally every one will have to do as he pleases. The Ten desire your return either with peace or without, but more with peace. This long delay is grievous to them and to all, especially your friends. . . . If there is peace you will see how the city will flourish."

By the beginning of February, Lorenzo was determined to push the issue, certain that the king had gone too far down the path of peace to turn back now but equally certain that he would not act unless compelled to do so. On the night of February 27, with a deal still not finalized, he slipped away to the port of Gaeta, where a ship was waiting to take him home. After a journey of more than two weeks, in which the galley was so buffeted by storms that many times it threatened to break up on the rocks, Lorenzo arrived in Pisa. Shortly thereafter word came that the king had finally signed the treaty bringing hostilities to an end. Arriving in Florence a few days later Lorenzo was greeted as a conquering hero. More than 150 men, including ambassadors of Venice, Milan, Bologna, and Ferrara, came out to greet him. It was a spectacle, according to Agnolo della Stufa, "so that you never saw in Florence a finer squadron nor a greater honor than this of his Magnificence," while Valori remembered it as a rare moment of unity in the city where "young and old, noble and commoner came together to celebrate his safe return."

As usual, our best source for understanding the mood of the average Florentine citizen is the diary of Luca Landucci. His entry from March 13, 1480, reads: "Lorenzo arrived from Livorno, on his return from Naples. It was considered a marvel that he should have returned, as everyone had doubted the king allowing him to resume his post, and a still greater marvel that he should have been able to arrange everything so diplomatically. God help him!"

The treaty, ratified three days later, ended the war on terms not wholly favorable to the republic. Some Florentines complained that Milan, while doing little, had received more than her share, while those who had suffered the most from the war profited the least from its conclusion. Most humiliating was the loss of the strategic fortress of Sarzana, seized by Genoa while Florence's armies were occupied elsewhere. But for all its shortcomings, Lorenzo had returned bearing the blessings of peace so that despite some grumbling the overall mood was one of relief, even exaltation. "The ratification of the peace arrived in the night, about 7," recorded Luca Landucci. "There were great rejoicings, with bonfires and ringing of bells."

Lorenzo's great gambit had paid off. Not only had he ended a war that had done so much damage to the republic, but he had done so without compromising Florentines' sense of honor. For many Florentines not the least of the pleasures of the situation was watching the pope lash out in helpless fury.* Though Sixtus seemed as determined as ever to chastise the wayward people of Florence, he could do little without the armies of Naples. Lorenzo's personal prestige soared, not only because of the practical results of his mission but because of the spectacular manner in which he had brought it about. From March 1480, when he seemed to pluck the fruits of victory from the jaws of defeat, Lorenzo acquired a reputation for sagacity in all matters diplomatic that would last the remainder of his days and aid him greatly in his efforts to preserve and sustain the peace of Italy.

---

* On March 29, the pope issued another bull of excommunication but this, like its predecessor, was almost universally ignored (see Landucci, *Florentine Diary*, p. 29).

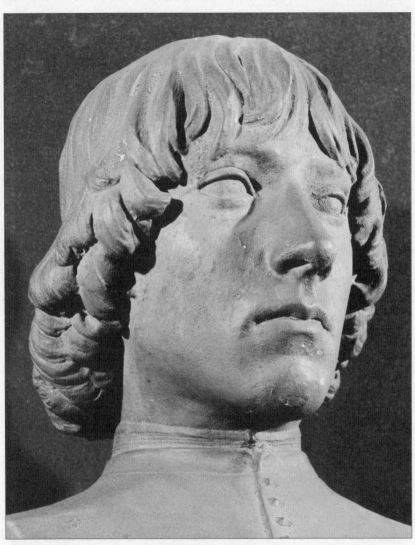

Andrea del Verrocchio, *Bust of Piero de' Medici, the Unfortunate,*
c. 1490 (Art Resource)

XVIII. THE SHADOW LIFTS

Sixtus, at last you're dead: unjust, untrue, you rest now,
you who hated peace so much, in eternal peace.
Sixtus, at last you're dead: and Rome is happy,
for, when you reigned, so did famine, slaughter and sin.
Sixtus, at last you're dead, eternal engine of discord,
even against God Himself, now go to dark Hell.

—ANONYMOUS

One must give praise, my fellow Romans, to Innocent
as his progeny in the tired motherland grew in number.
Eight bastards and eight maidens did he father;
Innocent will be called father of his country.

—ANONYMOUS

FERRANTE'S REVERSAL DEPRIVED SIXTUS THE MEANS
of defeating Florence on the battlefield, but he still had at his disposal enormous, if less tangible, resources. Florence might well have remained indefinitely beneath the shadow of papal interdict had it not been for a catastrophe that made the recent hostilities shrink to insignificance. In July a fleet carrying over 14,000 Ottoman infantry captured the port of Otranto in the heel of Italy. Twelve thousand inhabitants were put to the sword, the rest sold into slavery. The archbishop who had led the resistance was sawn in two to provide a salutary lesson on the zeal of the followers of the Prophet. "In Rome the alarm was as great as if the enemy had been already encamped before her very walls," recalled one contemporary. "Terror had taken such hold of all minds that even the Pope meditated flight."

As Alfonso hurried south to defend his father's kingdom against the armies of the sultan, the pope suddenly found his voice as the leader of the Christian flock: "If the faithful, especially the Italians, wish to preserve

353

their lands, their houses, their wives, their children, their liberty, and their lives, if they wish to maintain that Faith into which we have been baptized and through which we are regenerated, let them at last trust in our word, let them take up their arms and fight." Indulgences were granted to all those who would fight the invaders and the pope's own silver plate was melted down to finance the war effort.

The arrival of the Turks planted terror in the hearts of men from Naples to Milan, but in Florence shock of Muslim armies appearing on Italian soil was mixed with a certain relief since it was clear that under the circumstances the pope could no longer pursue his vendetta against Lorenzo. One Florentine approached sacrilege when he called this deliverance "a great miracle."*

On November 25 an embassy of distinguished Florentines arrived in Rome to receive absolution on behalf of the people of Florence. Sixtus, dressed in purple robes and seated on a high throne before St. Peter's Basilica, received the delegation, which included many of Lorenzo's closest allies, though, significantly, not Lorenzo himself.† Kissing his feet, the ambassadors begged forgiveness for any sins they had committed against his person and his office. After subjecting them to one final tongue-lashing, Sixtus bestowed his blessing and invited them inside to celebrate a Mass of reconciliation.

Thus ended the war between Lorenzo and the pope. After all the blood spilled and treasure squandered, neither could claim a decisive victory. Both of the principals were bruised and battered, but while Lorenzo had

---

* Despite widespread panic, the Turkish invasion ultimately amounted to little. In October, the Ottoman commander, Gedik Ahmed pasha, returned across the straits to his Balkan stronghold, unable to provision his army in the barren lands of the south. By this time Don Alfonso, aided by the pope's call for a Crusade against the invader, had massed his troops to prevent a return landing. The death of Sultan Mehmed II, conqueror of Constantinople, in May 1481 and the accession of his son, the more peaceful Bayezid II, precluded a revival of the Turks' Italian adventure.

† Among them were Luigi Guicciardini, Bongianni Gianfigliazzi, Piero Minerbetti, Guid' Antonio Vespucci, Maso degli Albizzi, Gino Capponi, Jacopo Lanfredini, Domenico Pandolfini, Lorenzo's uncle Giovanni Tornabuoni, Antonio de' Medici, and Antonio Ridolfi—a veritable who's-who of the *reggimento*.

suffered a far greater personal loss than his foe, he emerged from the ordeal far stronger than he had been when the assassins struck. The formidable coalition that the pope had put together to challenge Lorenzo was now in disarray, and while the defection of Ferrante was partially offset by a growing understanding with Venice, the strategic balance had tilted once again in favor of Florence. The greatest reversal in their respective fortunes, however, came not in terms of military or economic assets but in the less concrete area of prestige, a precious commodity that, as Lorenzo would show time and again, could be spent when the coffers were otherwise bare.

In the aftermath of the war, Lorenzo's reputation soared while Sixtus's suffered a precipitous decline. Particularly after his successful mission to Naples, admiration for Lorenzo in the courts of Europe grew by leaps and bounds. No longer was he the inexperienced politician—the junior partner in any alliance, the banker's son who could not treat with the great lords as an equal—but a statesman who almost single-handedly led his nation through its darkest moment and emerged triumphant. Nor was this any ordinary diplomatic coup; the manner of this victory was as important as the victory itself. Having staked his fortune and even his life on a throw of the dice, he was able now to claim the lion's share of the credit. One contemporary chronicler aptly described him as both "Florence's top man and the leading untitled man in Italy."

None of this meant that Lorenzo could rest on his laurels. Though his standing both at home and abroad had never been higher, he returned from Naples with a renewed sense of his own vulnerability. He was determined never again to place himself in such a position. His three-month sojourn in Naples revealed the limitations of the system he had put in place a decade earlier: it was overly dependent on him personally, and those same people who seemed incapable of functioning without him were also prone to disloyalty the minute his back was turned. "When I go more than ten miles out of the city," he complained, "the love and loyalty of friends comes to an end."

To rectify what he felt were glaring deficiencies, a special committee of 240 prominent citizens was appointed for the purpose of reforming the government. The "reforms" Lorenzo pushed through were a typical bit of

Medicean opportunism, taking advantage of a temporary situation in order to make long-term changes that would concentrate power in fewer, more reliable hands. After a week of often acrimonious debate the *Balìa* passed a series of new laws aimed at increasing the efficiency of the various councils that made up the government. The most significant piece of legislation created a new executive committee known as the Council of the Seventy. This body, handpicked from among the leading members of the regime, was given extraordinary powers. Like the Council of Ten, whose job was to guide the state in time of war, the Seventy largely bypassed the Priors, who now were reduced to little more than figureheads. The Seventy would select from their own members two committees responsible for the day-to-day running of the government—the *Otto di Pratica* (the Eight), in charge of foreign policy, and the *Dodici Procuratori* (the Twelve), who would oversee domestic and financial affairs.* Lorenzo's visibility within the government was enhanced by his appointment to both the Seventy and the Eight. Another significant reform, one that gave to the new council even more power, was that the Seventy replaced the *Accoppiatori*, who for most of the Medici ascendancy had selected "by hand" those eligible to serve on the *Signoria*.† This meant in effect that they were a self-replicating elite, not answerable to the wider public and wielding unprecedented power.

Not surprising, the new legislation dismayed many within the traditional governing class who had seen themselves progressively marginalized by the Medici and their associates. Lorenzo tried to soften the blow by limiting membership in the Seventy to those of ancient pedigree, largely excluding the "new men" who had always been central to the Medici's success. But this could not disguise the fact that in the new council Lorenzo had created a pliant instrument of his will. One contempo-

---

* Landucci claimed that the Twelve were "given powers to act for the whole people of Florence" (*Diary*, p. 32). These two committees should not be confused with the older *Dodici Buonuomini*, now largely ceremonial, or the *Otto di Guardia* who ran the state police.

† In 1489 the *Accoppiatori* were once again revived, an indication that the Seventy were not always as submissive as Lorenzo wished.

rary observed, "the members of the new body . . . cared for nothing but to keep their own position and assented to everything," while to Rinuccini the reforms "removed every liberty from the people"—this in spite of the fact that he himself was among those named to the new council. The opposition of men like Rinuccini was to be expected, but even many of Lorenzo's most loyal supporters believed the new council was a dangerous departure from the republican traditions of the past. Viewed from a wider perspective, it merely accelerated the tendency to centralize power that had been underway ever since Cosimo's day, but it appeared to contemporaries as a radical innovation. Even the loyal Medicean Benedetto Dei complained, "they refashioned the government in such a way so that it was based on tyranny rather than on the public good . . . so that it is a shame to see how this state is run."

The reforms did indeed go far beyond those of 1471. The new council, though it contained the usual dissenting voices and independent thinkers, was dominated by Lorenzo's men. It was small enough to be easily controlled from the top, but large enough so that no one member was likely to emerge who could challenge the leadership of the head of the Medici household. By making membership in the Seventy permanent, those named to the council—chosen from among citizens who had held high positions within the government under the Medici ascendancy—were freed from outside pressure while at the same time they were totally dependent on Lorenzo himself.* They became, in effect, Lorenzo's cabinet. With this compact, efficient body in control of the *Palazzo della Signoria,* willing and able to do his bidding, the machinery of the Florentine bureaucracy was placed at Lorenzo's disposal. In fact the reforms went a long way toward creating a professional political class of the kind anathema to the ideals of republican self-government. Increased efficiency was purchased at the expense of that ideal of Florentine democracy in which every citizen felt he had a share in his own government.

The first real test of the newly organized government came in the

---

* The new law claimed the Council of Seventy would last for only five years, but this was, as everybody knew, a fiction meant to make the law seem less of a departure from tradition than it really was.

spring of 1482 and once again it was Girolamo Riario who precipitated the crisis. Sixtus was now a frail man approaching seventy and the window of opportunity for establishing the Riario as a great feudal clan was fast closing. Seeking to shore up his fledgling state in the Romagna, Girolamo traveled to Imola with his bride, Caterina Sforza, from whence he surveyed his neighbors with a covetous eye. An opportunity to add to his holdings soon presented itself in the nearby town of Forli, where feuding among the dysfunctional ruling Ordelaffi dynasty made it a relatively simple matter for Riario, in his role as papal vicar, to step in and claim it as a protectorate of the Holy See.*

With Imola and Forli now firmly in his possession, the next logical candidate for inclusion in the Riario portfolio was Faenza, a town that stood directly between the two halves of his domain. Unfortunately for Riario, all this activity had drawn the attention of Milan, which had no desire to see a powerful papal enclave taking shape on its southern borders. It was exactly this scenario that Riario's marriage to Caterina Sforza was supposed to forestall, but the death of Duke Galeazzo Maria and his replacement by the mistrustful Lodovico meant that the Riario could no longer count on Milan to look benevolently on their territorial expansion. Rebuffed by his wife's family, Girolamo Riario now turned to the other major power in northern Italy—the Most Serene Republic of Venice.

The moment was auspicious. The Venetians, disappointed with the results of their short-lived alliance with Florence that had embroiled them in a costly war and left them with few tangible benefits, were casting about for new partners. As early as the spring of 1480 rumors were swirling about that the pope, abandoned by King Ferrante, had reconstituted the old league with Venice and Siena. With Riario and the Republic of Venice both harboring unrealized ambitions in northern Italy, it was natural that the two should seek an arrangement. Riario saw the opportunity, and in September of 1481 he set out for Venice. When he arrived, the doge himself came down the palace steps to greet him and the Senate conferred

---

* The Ordelaffi's troubles began in the 1460s when a feud erupted between two brothers, Cecco and Pino. It was the kind of tale all too common in the Romagna, involving various stabbings and poisonings. When the sickly youth Sinibaldo Ordelaffi was placed under the protection of papal forces, it was only a matter of time before the city fell into Riario's lap.

upon their title-hungry guest membership in the nobility of Venice, a rare honor for a foreigner, particularly one of such humble origins. The more important work was completed in secret where a bargain was struck by which the Venetians would help Riario acquire Faenza in return for papal recognition of their claims on the duchy of Ferrara.

Lorenzo was kept informed of these dangerous developments by a spy he had planted in Girolamo Riario's court, one Matteo Menghi of Forli, who explained that "to satisfy my debt it seemed best to apprise Your Magnificence of those things that are taking place." This informant was certainly useful when, taking a page from Riario's own playbook, Lorenzo agreed to support followers of the deposed Ordelaffi in an attempt to assassinate their new master. In the end this plot amounted to little; Riario sniffed it out and Lorenzo was forced to try other means to rid himself of the troublesome count. But by now the rest of Italy was growing alarmed at the signs of Venetian and papal aggression and Lorenzo had no problem putting together an alliance to challenge the revived combination. The axis of Milan, Naples, and Florence was taken out of storage and dusted off to deal with old foes, as various smaller states lined up on either side.

War began in the spring of 1482, with Venetian troops advancing on Ferrara while papal forces mobilized in the south. The situation had changed dramatically since the outbreak of the Pazzi war four years earlier, thanks in no small part to Lorenzo, who had weaned Ferrante from his short-lived alliance with the pope. True, Sixtus had replaced Naples with Venice, but this new arrangement proved far less effective than the earlier one. In part this was a matter of simple geography. While Venice was engaged in the north, papal forces were pinned down by the Neapolitans in the south. In one of the bloodiest clashes of the war, the papal army led by Roberto Malatesta smashed the forces of the duke of Calabria on a rare patch of solid ground in the malarial Pontine Marshes south of Rome known as the *Campo Morto* (the field of death). But the pope could not harvest the fruits of his victory.* The battlefield, living up

---

* Machiavelli, who objected to the bloodless wars so often conducted by Italian *condottieri* in which only civilians suffered, approved of the Battle of *Campo Morto*, "fought with more virtue than any other that had been fought for fifty years in Italy, for in it, between one side and the other, more than a thousand men died" (*Florentine Histories*, VIII, 23).

to its name, soon claimed the victorious general, who died of dysentery a month later, while the Florentines, taking advantage of the distraction, equipped Niccolò Vitelli with an army for the purpose of seizing Città di Castello.

Ferrante, meanwhile, was busy stirring up the restless Roman nobility, playing on their bitter rivalries to sow chaos in the pope's own backyard. As followers of the Orsini, the Colonna, and the della Valle clashed in the streets of Rome, Sixtus vented his anger against his nephew, whose selfish policies had placed him in his current predicament. Girolamo Riario was becoming increasingly unpopular with the citizens of Rome, who were suffering under his continued extortions, and their constant complaints were beginning to have an effect on Sixtus. Many war-weary souls across Italy would have agreed with Lodovico Sforza when he remarked bitterly that the latest conflict was begun "for Girolamo's ambitions, without regard for the men who are thrown to the wolves and the people who are ruined." A contemporary reported the unhappy scene in the Eternal City: "In the Pope's antechambers, instead of cassocked priests, armed guards kept watch. Soldiers, equipped for battle, were drawn up before the gates of the Palace. All the Court officials were filled with terror and anguish; the fury of the populace was only restrained by the fear of the soldiers."

Sixtus had finally had enough. Calling the Venetian alliance stupid and ill-conceived, Sixtus turned to Girolamo's cousin Giuliano della Rovere to clean up the mess. No less ambitious than Girolamo, Giuliano's approach to politics could not have been more different. While Riario lurched this way and that in pursuit of every short-term advantage, della Rovere believed that he and his family could prosper only by promoting the long-term interests of the Church. Despite Riario's threat to drive his cousin from the city and set fire to his house, in December, della Rovere persuaded Sixtus to open negotiations in the northern city of Cremona with the aim of bringing the war to a speedy conclusion.

For Lorenzo this sudden about-face was a vindication of the resolute stance he had taken. He was determined to go himself to Cremona to make sure that Florentine interests were not neglected, even over the objections of those in the *reggimento* who reminded him "your presence is very necessary here." This new proof of the fecklessness of his colleagues only confirmed Lorenzo's belief that he could leave such an important mission to no one else.

It was at Cremona that Lorenzo cemented his reputation as a diplomat of unparalleled skill, one who combined an understanding of complex issues with an ability to persuade others of the rightness of his approach. "Various were the opinions, diverse the remedies," wrote Valori, "and the debates were long and ill-tempered. But finally Lorenzo, with great wisdom, laid out the state of affairs in Italy, and spoke with such eloquence and with such seriousness of purpose that all came to share his point of view." Lorenzo was always most effective in face-to-face meetings, where he could deploy his immense learning and considerable charm and where the force of his personality could disguise what was often a weak position. Lacking a significant standing army of its own, Florence could maintain its status as one of the great powers only through a delicate balance of opposing forces and interests, and in the Italian context, with its patchwork of large and small states held together by a common culture but tattered by ancient rivalries, this balance required constant attention.

In this gathering of powerful and titled men, and with the memory of the disastrous Pazzi war still fresh in his mind, Lorenzo first articulated the principles that were to govern his foreign policy for the rest of his life, principles that earned Florence, in Guicciardini's phrase, the title the "fulcrum" of Italy. Over the course of the next decade Lorenzo came to embody the principle of a balance of power, the calm center in a world that threatened at any moment to fall into chaos. The fullest explanation of his policy comes in the opening of Guicciardini's *History of Italy,* in which the historian paints a portrait of his native land in the last decades of Lorenzo's life as a realm of peace and prosperity. It is true that Guicciardini imparts to these years, the years of his own childhood, a certain rosy glow not entirely justified by the facts, but this is understandable given the horrors of the intervening period in which foreign armies used the peninsula to settle their dynastic rivalries. "Italy was preserved in this happy state," he writes

> which had been attained through a variety of causes, by a number of circumstances, but among these by common consent no little credit was due to the industry and virtue of Lorenzo de' Medici, a citizen

so far above the rank of private citizen that all the affairs of the republic were decided by his advice. . . . Knowing that it would be very dangerous to himself and to the Florentine Republic if any of the larger states increased their power, he diligently sought to maintain the affairs of Italy in such a balance that they might not favor one side more than another.

In pursuing this course Lorenzo was greatly aided by the recent governmental reforms. The establishment of the Eight gave the government, for the first time in its history, a permanent body dedicated to the conduct of foreign policy. The council's small size allowed it to deal with delicate matters in secret and Lorenzo's presence gave it enormous clout. It was in concert with the Eight that Lorenzo now began to organize a semiprofessional cadre of diplomats at all the major courts of Europe, a development that made him, perhaps, the best informed of European leaders.

But even with this streamlined organization there was no substitute for Lorenzo's personal involvement in almost every important foreign policy decision. The relationships Lorenzo had built up over time with various world leaders meant that Florentine interests were taken into account even when her military forces were negligible. These relationships, which he had begun to nurture even before his first trip to Milan in 1465 as he played host to visiting dignitaries in the Via Larga or at the villa of Careggi, in turn depended on maintaining a reputation for integrity and good judgment. It is telling that when the king of France wished to test the possibility of marriage between his heir and a daughter of King Ferrante, he went first to Lorenzo. On another occasion, King Louis, hoping to obtain an ecclesiastical appointment for one of his favorites, recruited Lorenzo to plead his case. Lorenzo duly passed along the request to his ambassador in Rome, adding, "not only do I want your prompt assistance in this, but I wish it known that it was through my help that it was accomplished, since it will greatly enhance my reputation and my honor."

Lorenzo cultivated his image assiduously. "I believe I have the reputation of being a man of integrity and good faith," he wrote to his friend Baccio Ugolini, "and I can be believed . . . as much as anyone in the world, both for sincerity and for being without passion." Here Lorenzo was not simply boasting (though it is clear he had a high opinion of his own abilities) but reminding his agent to protect his image, which was one of the few effective weapons Florence had in her arsenal.

Throughout the remaining years of his life, Lorenzo's fame as a mediator continued to grow, but it is at Cremona that he began to stake a claim to being the foremost statesman of the age. Luca Landucci noted with evident satisfaction how at Cremona, Lorenzo was "honorably received as a man of merit," no trivial matter in the eyes of Florentines, who were always conscious of their lowly bourgeois status in settings where dukes, cardinals, and marquises were wont to lord it over their social inferiors. But in spite of the glowing reviews for Lorenzo's performance, he did not achieve everything he had hoped for. The assembled dignitaries were impressed by Lorenzo, but his attempts to restore some of the territory lost in the Pazzi war came to nothing. It was also clear that the negotiations could not bring about an immediate cessation of hostilities, since the Venetians, who felt they were near to achieving military success, refused to cooperate. Still, the main objective of driving a wedge between the pope and the Most Serene Republic was easily accomplished. In this case it was not so much Lorenzo's eloquence that did the trick as fear of growing Venetian power. It was a general rule of Italian politics that when one state seemed poised to dominate the peninsula, the rest forgot their own quarrels to gang up on the pretender. This is what happened at Cremona. Sixtus, showing once again he was not a man for half measures, excommunicated the Venetians when they persisted in their attack on Ferrara and then urged his new friends, Milan, Florence, and Naples, to join him in a Holy League to punish those who had demonstrated their wickedness by ignoring him.

Even with the pope's defection the war dragged on in desultory fashion until the Peace of Bagnolo finally brought an end to the fighting in August of 1484. Though this time Florence had not suffered the worst of the destruction, the news was received in the City of the Baptist with gratitude, because as Landucci lamented, "Many were afflicted and worn out by so many wars." After two years of fighting the situation was pretty much as it had been before, causing many to vent their anger at those who had wasted so much blood and treasure to achieve so little. One of those most responsible for the war was now the least satisfied with the results of peace. Upon hearing the terms agreed to at Bagnolo, Sixtus complained bitterly, "Up to this time we have carried on a dangerous and difficult war, in order, by our victorious arms, to obtain an honorable Peace for the security of the Apostolic See, our own honor, and that of the League. . . . This peace, my beloved sons in Christ, I can neither approve nor sanction." Fortunately for the rest of Italy, by now Sixtus's disapproval was beside the point. These belligerent words, which at other times might have condemned Italy to further years of war, were uttered as the pope lay on his deathbed. Still raging at the perfidy of both friend and foe, the man who had sat on St. Peter's throne for thirteen unlucky years breathed his last on the morning of August 13, 1484. According to a popular couplet it was peace itself that killed Sixtus: "Nothing could daunt the ferocious Sixtus; but as soon as he heard the word of peace, he died."

For Lorenzo the death of Sixtus closed a particularly unhappy chapter in his life during which he had suffered severe financial reverses, years of war and tribulation, and, most painfully, the loss of his beloved brother Giuliano.* But he was not the only one who felt relief at the pope's passing. There were many throughout the length and breadth of the Italian peninsula who shared the feelings of the anonymous poet who rejoiced,

> Sixtus, at last you're dead: unjust, untrue, you rest now,
> you who hated peace so much, in eternal peace.

---

* One of the few who truly mourned the death of the irascible pope was Girolamo Riario. Without his uncle's protection his fledgling possessions in the Romagna were vulnerable to meddling by the more powerful states that surrounded them. Following Sixtus's death Girolamo was forced to lead the life of an impoverished petty nobleman of the Romagna. In order to stave off financial collapse he tried to squeeze more and more money from his long-suffering subjects. In 1487 he murdered one of his creditors rather than pay back a debt. Adding to his unpopularity with the people of Imola and Forlì was his tendency to favor fellow Ligurians at the expense of the natives. All of this eventually caught up with him and on April 14, 1488, four men, with whom he had quarreled over money, stabbed him to death in his palace at Forlì. Though shortly after the murder the assassins wrote to Lorenzo asking for his protection, there is no indication that he knew about the plot in advance. No doubt he took a certain grim satisfaction that the count had gotten just what he deserved, a feeling that may have been enhanced by the fact that he did not have to lift a finger to achieve it. For the view that Lorenzo was in secret correspondence with the conspirators, see Martines, *April Blood,* pp. 9–10. By the time of his death, in any case, Girolamo had ceased to matter on the wider Italian stage.

Sixtus, at last you're dead: and Rome is happy,
for, when you reigned, so did famine, slaughter and sin.
Sixtus, at last you're dead, eternal engine of discord,
even against God Himself, now go to dark Hell.

The crowning of a new pope on September 12, 1484—the Genoa-born Giovanni Battista Cibo, who took the name Innocent VIII—did not resolve the outstanding problems between Florence and Holy See. Florence and Rome remained natural rivals in the struggle to dominate central Italy, and Lorenzo could not single-handedly change the underlying dynamic.* Fortunately for Lorenzo, the fifty-two-year-old Giovanni Battista Cibo was a man of vastly different temperament than his predecessor. When Francesco della Rovere had been elected in 1471, reformers rejoiced that a man of unimpeachable character had ascended the throne of St. Peter. But after more than a decade of turmoil the cardinals may perhaps have felt that they would be better served by someone whose human frailties were more apparent. Innocent, though touchy on matters of papal prerogative, proved far more easygoing than Sixtus—a man more in the mold of Paul II, who cared too much for his own comfort to pursue megalomaniacal schemes of conquest. True, Innocent's moral weaknesses were an embarrassment to a church in need of moral regeneration, but he was a basically kindly man and his vices were garden-variety sins of a kind that threatened his own immortal soul more than the peace of Italy. Worldly, sensual, and corrupt, he had fathered so many illegitimate children that one satirist jested,

One must give praise, my fellow Romans, to Innocent
as his progeny in the tired motherland grew in number.
Eight bastards and eight maidens did he father;
Innocent will be called father of his country.

In other words this was the kind of man with whom Lorenzo might well be able to do business, given a chance. The Medici had shown them-

---

* Lorenzo and the new pope got off on the wrong foot when the leader of Florence decided to attack the Genoese fortress of Pietrasanta in retaliation for the seizure of Sarzana during the Pazzi war, an action to which the Genoa-born pope took exception.

selves adept at turning Paul's passion for jewels and antiquities to their advantage and Innocent appeared equally susceptible to the kinds of enticements the Medici could dangle. Much as he would have liked to take the measure of the man himself, however, Lorenzo was too ill to make the journey to Rome, sending in his stead the thirteen-year-old Piero. This was the first important diplomatic mission for Lorenzo's eldest son and heir, a crucial test for a boy who was already showing signs of the arrogant, self-indulgent man he was soon to become.

Lorenzo's intense desire to restore himself in the good graces of the pope is evident in instructions contained in a letter he sent to his son in Rome. "[Y]ou will inform His Holiness that I am firmly resolved not to transgress his commands," he wrote to Piero, "because besides my natural devotion to the Holy See, my devotion to His Beatitude himself arises from many causes and from obligations which ever since I was a child our house has received from him. Add that I have experienced how hurtful it has been to be out of favor with the late Pontiff although, as it seems to me, I was unjustly persecuted rather for others' sins than for any insult or offense to him of holy memory." Though Lorenzo's friendly words did not immediately thaw the pope's heart, it was the beginning of a campaign that would ultimately bear fruit.

Knowing his son's character, Lorenzo also felt it necessary to remind him, in words reminiscent of his own father's injunctions: "Be careful not to take precedence of those who are your elders, for although you are my son, you are but a citizen of Florence, as they are." It should have come as no surprise that Piero was spoiled. To many Florentines his flaws were carried in his mother's blood. "What could one hope for from Piero?" asked Guicciardini rhetorically. "Not only did he not have the greatest prudence, as you know; he was also not of that good nature and sweet-ness [common to] his father and grandfather, and ordinary in our nation. Nor is this any wonder, for being born of a foreign mother, the Florentine blood in him was bastardized. His external comportment was degener-ate, and [he was] too insolent and haughty for our way of life." It did not help that he was a remarkably handsome youth, vain and anxious, as his father had been at his age, to cut a fine figure as he paraded about the streets of Florence. "Lorenzo declares (and it makes me laugh) that he will not have Piero bothered," wrote Lorenzo's intimate Matteo Franco, "the poor lad cannot go outside the door without all Florence running after him." Such constant adulation would have gone to the head of a more sober boy, and there was no indication that Piero had the moral fiber to resist even lesser temptations.

Rather than instilling in him a greater sense of responsibility, Piero's Roman journey seems instead to have exaggerated his worst traits. This was confirmed on his return when he entered Florence so gaudily outfitted that he ran afoul of the city's sumptuary laws. One contemporary declared disgustedly that Piero's arrogant behavior "made the whole city want to throw up." Lorenzo himself was no more pleased with his son's tactlessness. Such displays of princely hauteur were exactly the wrong note to strike for a family already suspected of harboring dynastic ambitions. Lorenzo's anxiety about his son's character is attested to by the numerous queries he sent to Niccolò Michelozzi (from Bagno a Morba where he was taking the waters). Michelozzi was finally forced to admit, "Piero has not seemed to me the person he was before his departure. He has need of your authority and it is time that you returned to Florence."

Michelozzi's plea to Lorenzo to assert his paternal authority is a reminder of Lorenzo's transformation over the past few years from the brash, irresponsible youth to the sober first citizen of the state—a man who could claim a place alongside his grandfather as not only pater familias but as *Pater Patriae*. The change was partly institutional, codified in the legislation of 1481 that increased his official role within the state, but also emotional and symbolic, expressed through visible signs and gestures that were always carefully scrutinized in the theatrical arena of Florentine politics. The transformation of his public persona also had deeper psychological roots. Lorenzo himself had returned from Naples a changed man. The anxiety and sorrow of that period had aged him both in mind and body. One of his assistants, Francesco di ser Barone, recorded an extended bout of depression in the summer of 1483 during which he could leave his house only through the greatest effort of will. As Lorenzo himself admitted, he never recovered from the trauma of the Pazzi conspiracy. He felt more isolated as even once trusted friends fell under a cloud of suspicion, and his natural enjoyment of life was often consumed in extended periods

in which he preferred to wallow in self-pity.* "We promised in the prologue," he wrote in his *Commento,*

> that when we came to the exposition of this sonnet, we would tell
> how great and wicked was the persecution that I bore at that time
> both from Fortune and from men. But nevertheless I am disposed to
> pass over this very briefly, to avoid being called proud or vainglori-
> ous, since reporting one's own and serious dangers can hardly be
> done without presumption or vainglory. . . . And therefore we shall
> briefly say that the persecution had been very serious, because the
> persecutors were most powerful men of great authority and intelli-
> gence, and they purposed and were firmly disposed to accomplish
> my utter ruin and desolation, as demonstrated by their having
> attempted in every way possible to harm me. I, against whom these
> actions were taken, was a young private person without any counsel
> and with no help except for that which from day to day Divine
> benevolence and clemency administered to me. I was reduced to a
> state that, being at one and the same time afflicted in my soul with
> excommunication, in my mental powers with rapine, in my govern-
> ment with diverse stratagems, in my family and children with new
> treachery and machinations, and in my life with frequent and per-
> sistent plots, death would have been no small grace for me, being
> much less an evil to my taste than any of those other things.

The strain of those years also seemed to have undermined his health. As
an adolescent his robust, athletic physique had been proof against the
family ills, but the physical ailments from which he had always suffered
now threatened to overwhelm him. Gout, which had afflicted Cosimo as
an elderly man and his father in middle age, seemed to be stealing from
Lorenzo the prime of his life. When he returned from Naples in March of
1480, he was still only thirty-one. But already, excruciating pain in his

---

* One of those old friendships interrupted by the Pazzi conspiracy was with Marsilio
  Ficino, who had been close to many of the conspirators, including Francesco Salviati and
  Jacopo Bracciolini.

lower joints forced Lorenzo to curtail the vigorous physical activity he loved, while chronic eczema and asthma added to the daily discomforts of life. When he traveled to the country, instead of rising early for the hunt he sat huddled by the fireplace to ward off the chill that aggravated the aches in his joints; even the palace in the city proved too drafty for comfort. His normal joie de vivre was replaced by stoic endurance, though even when he was laid up he found ways to pass the time. "[T]oday," wrote one well-informed observer, "the Magnificent Lorenzo didn't leave his house, since his gout assaulted him. But he gambled and amused himself in the usual way." Letters from the most famous physicians of Europe attest to his ever more desperate attempts to find some relief. In addition to the conventional remedies—bleeding, purging, the consumption of various mineral waters, and the application of poultices—Lorenzo was willing to try ever more far-fetched solutions. "In order to prevent the return of these pains," advised one physician, "you must get a stone called sapphire, and have it set in gold, so that it should touch the skin. This must be worn on the third finger of the left hand. If this is done the pains in the joints, or gouty pains, will cease, because that stone has occult virtues, and the specific one of preventing evil humors going to the joints."

Apparently such bizarre remedies did little to ease his torment since Lorenzo continued to make more frequent and more extended trips to the medicinal spas that dotted the southern Tuscan countryside. Lorenzo's poor health also had political consequences. His absences meant that legislation was often delayed and diplomatic correspondence left unattended. The government was frequently thrown into confusion while couriers fanned out across the landscape trying to track down the peripatetic lord of the city.* And even when his whereabouts were discovered he usually had little patience for conducting business. In 1485, while recovering at Bagno a Morba from a debilitating flare-up of gout, he chastised his secretary, Michelozzi, explaining "in order to cure himself and to

---

* His new eminence could create logistical problems. In one trip to the spa of San Filippo near Siena in 1490, that republic insisted on accompanying Lorenzo with an honor guard of more than five hundred soldiers (see Trexler, *Public Life in Renaissance Florence*, p. 444).

restore his health he neither could nor would attend to any other matter."

It is not surprising that these assorted ailments affected his mood. Sometimes he responded to these setbacks with self-deprecating humor, as in August 1489 when he wrote to Giovanni Lanfredini, "my having been ill these days with some leg pain means I have not written you; though the feet and tongue are far apart, one can still get in the way of the other." More often, though, pain increased his natural irritability. Accustomed to vigorous exercise to improve his mood, Lorenzo now found himself betrayed by an unreliable and increasingly frail body. After 1480 he more often succumbed to his natural tendency to melancholy; the playfulness that had characterized him as a young man was less apparent while flashes of his always fearsome temper became more frequent. Victims of these withering attacks included not only his household intimates but his colleagues. His impatience with the foolishness of others and assumption that he always knew best meant that he was increasingly surrounded by yes-men who feared making decisions on their own. As Machiavelli noted, even as a young man "he wanted to have a say in everything, and he wanted everybody to acknowledge himself his debtor in almost every particular." This characteristic only grew stronger with time.

His sense of isolation was magnified by the death of his mother in March of 1482. "Still burdened with tears and sorrow," Lorenzo wrote to Duke Ercole d'Este of Ferrara, "I cannot but inform Your Excellency of the grievous death of my most beloved mother, Madonna Lucrezia, who today departed this life. I am more unhappy than I can say, because in addition to losing a mother, the mere thought of which breaks my heart, I have lost someone who lifted from me many a care." Lorenzo had always thrived under the nurturing care of the women in his life, but with Lucrezia gone he lost a vital female presence in his life. Clarice, it was true, was a devoted wife—far more patient with him than he probably deserved—but she lacked the understanding of the ways of the world that could help Lorenzo significantly in his public role.

To both friends and enemies alike Lorenzo appeared a far different person than he had been only a few short years ago. Those who had worried that he was not ready to take over from his father had been reassured by his strong, steady hand at the rudder. Complaints, in fact, were now far more likely to come from those who felt his hand was all too firmly steering the ship of state. His evolving role required changes in the way he presented himself to the people, particularly given the fact that he was still a relatively young man in a society with an inborn mistrust of youth. Shortly after taking over from his father, Gentile Becchi had advised him "to seem older in appearance, in dress, and in habits," and Lorenzo now put this advice into practice every day. He no longer tried to be the center of attention on ceremonial occasions, putting aside the armor, jewels, and silk brocade of his joust and adopting instead the less glamorous *lucco,* the crimson mantle denoting a man of substance.* He also understood that behavior tolerated in an adolescent would not so easily be forgiven in the leading man of the republic, a role that required him to set an example for his fellow citizens.

Some of the change, however, was more apparent than real. As a young man of twenty-two his carousing had become such a scandal that his old tutor rebuked him for "behaving disgracefully with women and engaging in frivolities that shame those who must have dealings with you by day." It is difficult to imagine Becchi or anyone else speaking to him this way after his return from Naples. This is not to say that Lorenzo had decided to deny himself the diversions to which he had grown accustomed, but only that he had learned to be more discreet. In fact he justified his philandering, and the poetry inspired by his sexual adventures, on the grounds that he needed to relieve the tensions brought on by the burdens under which he labored. "Being then placed by Fortune in this darkness, among such great shadows, sometimes the amorous ray, now of the eyes, now of the thought of my lady, brought light," he confessed. That these amorous adventures were more than a literary conceit is suggested by Francesco Guicciardini, who passed along the common gossip of the time: "His last love, which

---

* One of Cosimo's famous quips concerned this uniform of a Florentine patrician: "When warned that it was not prudent to exile so many noblemen, and that through lack of men of quality Florence would be ruined, [Cosimo] responded that so many yards of red cloth (*panni di San Martino*) would make a gentleman; by which he meant that with honors and riches men of low status became noble." (Guicciardini, *The History of Florence*). See also Trexler *Public Life in Renaissance Florence,* note 120, p. 441, for a contemporary's description of Lorenzo's manner of dress.

lasted for many years, was for Bartolomea de' Nasi, wife of Donato Benci. Though she was not beautiful, she was gracious and charming, and he was so obsessed with her that one winter when she was in the country he would leave Florence at the fifth or sixth hour of the night on horseback with several companions to go and see her, and would start back so early that he was in Florence again by morning."

These nocturnal journeys added to his exhaustion, particularly since his daytime duties had not diminished with the return of peace.* Gone was the careless swagger of his youth when a misplaced faith in his own powers caused him to dismiss out of hand rumored plots against his life. Challenges to his authority that would once have been shrugged off were now met with savage force. Some of these fears were well founded: between October of 1481 and March of 1482 alone, three new plots on his life were uncovered with savage efficiency by the vigilant Eight of the Watch, the most serious of which involved two Florentines from well-known families armed with poisoned daggers.† The need for vigilance took its toll. He became wary of colleagues and more guarded in his friendships. The twelve-man bodyguard that now surrounded him as he made his way through the streets of the city was merely the outward manifestation of an inner darkness.

The easy give-and-take with the people of Florence that had been an important element in his charismatic rule was replaced by an increasing distance and formalized ritual. It is significant that at this time even his closest intimates, including Gentile Becchi and his uncle Giovanni Tornabuoni, stopped using the familiar *tu* and started employing the formal *voi* in their correspondence. This transformation, subtle as it was, ran against the grain of Florentine history. The people of the republic demanded that their leaders respect the forms of the city's traditions even

---

* Guicciardini claims that in "the opinion of many he was so weakened by his amorous excesses that he died relatively young" (*The History of Florence* ix). While the claim is perhaps overstated, it is probable that his hectic pace exacerbated his medical conditions.

† The two were Moroto Baldovinetti and Battista Frescobaldi. The latter had helped Lorenzo extradite Bernardo Bandini from Istanbul but felt he had been insufficiently rewarded for his service (see Ross, *Lives of the Early Medici*, pp. 241–44).

when they eviscerated the substance. Cosimo had recognized this and his apparent modesty in dress and habits was an important ingredient in his success. In his youth Lorenzo had been careful to maintain that delicate balance between his role as citizen and as the glamorous prince of the city, but after 1480 the need to avoid offending the sensibilities of his fellow Florentines diminished while his willingness to assert his authority in its rawest form increased.

While he remained attuned to Florentine sensibilities—as his displeasure with Piero's tactlessness demonstrates—he was not shy about the blunt exercise of power. One particularly well-documented event that provides a glimpse into Lorenzo's methods is the general scrutiny of 1484, the latest of those periodic surveys to determine which citizens were eligible for political office. Here Lorenzo's fingerprints are clearly visible in almost every aspect of the complicated procedure. According to Piero Guicciardini (the historian's father, who was a member of the scrutiny council), "the first list was drawn up by Lorenzo and *Ser* Giovanni [Giusti] alone," and Lorenzo continued to pull strings to achieve the desired result at every step along the way. But Guicciardini's account, for all that it reveals about the way Lorenzo was able to interject himself into the electoral process, does not support the claim that he was the tyrant of Florence in all but name. Lorenzo, in fact, had to tread carefully, balancing the claims of ancient, aristocratic families with those of the new men, members of the greater guilds with those of the lesser, even diluting the ranks of his supporters by including known opponents—and all the while keeping in mind the myriad political debts he had to repay. Though Florence was far from a perfect democracy, the constant horse-trading and negotiation involved in the scrutiny reveals the survival of a lively political process.

Contemporaries offers vivid, if sometimes contradictory, glimpses of an influence that was pervasive but never absolute. Florentines employed various imprecise terms to convey the nature of their relationship to the first citizen. They called Lorenzo *maestro della bottega* (master of the shop) and sometimes simply *il padrone,* the boss. Unlike the first term, which emphasizes the benevolent, paternalistic nature of his role, the second conveys a certain toughness appropriate to those less squeamish times. It conjures up gangs of enforcers roaming the streets, of rough justice meted out in dark allies, of secret torture cells in the palace of the *Podestà*, of bruises and broken bones. This is not an entirely inaccurate picture. There is no doubt that Lorenzo, backed by the secretive Eight of the Watch (not to be confused with the *Otto di Pratica,* which conducted foreign affairs), intimidated his opponents. "That office," explained Guicciardini, "had been created long ago and given great authority in criminal affairs. In its judgments, though not in its procedure, it was subject to the laws and statutes of the city; but in crimes concerning the state it had free and absolute powers, beyond all laws. This freedom had been given to it by the men who were in power back at that time, in order to have a stick in their hands with which to strike down those who wanted to criticize or over-throw the government." But Guicciardini, while uneasy about the Eight's unrestrained power, believed they were a necessary evil, concluding: "Although its origin, then, was in violence and tyranny, it turned out to be a most salubrious measure. For, as anyone expert in the affairs of this country knows, nobody could live in Florence if evil minds were not restrained through fear of the Eight—a fear born of their promptness in finding out and punishing crimes."

It is clear that Renaissance Florentines, like Americans today, struggled to find the right balance between security on the one hand and civil liber-ties on the other, and though there were many who applauded the strong-arm tactics of the government, there were perhaps an equal number who feared that their ancient liberties were under assault. Many Florentines noted the chilling effect of Lorenzo's network of spies and informers and waxed nostalgic for an earlier age, only partly imagined, when Florentines were free to speak their minds. But some of the disaffection was less a mat-ter of basic principles than disagreement over who should wield the club and who should receive the blows. Many of those who criticized Lorenzo, for instance, would not have hesitated to use the most brutal means to suppress any impoverished worker who had the temerity to strike for higher wages.

Lorenzo ruled Florence with a firm hand but, as Guicciardini suggests, Florentines, particularly after the revolt of the *Ciompi* in the mid-fourteenth century, generally preferred authoritarian rule to chaos. This was an age when violence, both criminal and state-sponsored, was commonplace. Luca Landucci records the hanging of a man for the crime of removing silver ornaments from a statue of the Virgin and the execution of a Venetian accused of stealing a few florins off a money-changer's table. In a society where torture was routinely practiced in the city jails and where brutal executions were carried out for relatively minor offenses, the tactics Lorenzo used against his political enemies were unremarkable. The ambassador from Ferrara recalled one striking scene in which Lorenzo faced down an angry crowd intent on saving the life of a young man who had killed one of the servants of the Eight. To those who begged for clemency

> [Lorenzo] offered them consoling words, but then saw to it that the man was hanged in the piazza, dangled from the window of the *Podestà's* palazzo. He then commanded that four of those who had been shouting "Escape! Escape!" be seized and each given four strappados, after which they were banished from the city for four years. This was how the mutiny was put down, and at no point did the Magnificent Lorenzo want to leave the scene until he saw that the crowd had calmed down.

Nowhere is there a suggestion that Lorenzo had acted improperly; indeed the ambassador seems to admire his courage in confronting the dangerous mob and defusing their anger. Evidence suggests that if his fellow citizens were inclined to criticize Lorenzo in such matters it was because he was sometimes perceived as being too lenient. Alamanno Rinuccini, for instance, complained that men "condemned by the Committee of the Eight to perpetual imprisonment are removed from jail on the whim of a private person, or rather of a tyrant."

Unlike modern democracies with their anonymous bureaucracies and mass media, Florence was a state in which all politics depended on personal relationships. If his father's authority suffered because of his inability to get along with his fellow oligarchs, Lorenzo owed much of his success to what we today would call "people skills." Without the support of a working majority within the *reggimento,* an inner circle consisting of forty or fifty men from prominent families, Lorenzo could not have dominated the state.* Behind each of these men, in turn, lay a dense but largely invisible web of mutual obligation, of clients and patrons, of debts owed and debts paid, of loyalties going back generations and tied to neighborhoods and to rural homesteads, that formed the basis of his standing in the community. Lorenzo, as the uncrowned head of state, could not stand aloof from politics at this grassroots level. Indeed, as his power increased, more and more of the patronage upon which the Florentine political system floated now streamed through the Via Larga.

In 1465 one of the signs of his father's political jeopardy was the dwindling crowd outside his palace and the growing throng outside Luca Pitti's. Lorenzo never had to worry that the entrance to his house would be deserted. As the preeminent figure in the government he was constantly hounded by office-seekers and petitioners, as well as those in need of advice on business or personal matters. Some of those filling the courtyard and anterooms of the palace came because they genuinely valued Lorenzo's wisdom, but many came out of fear of offending the powerful boss of the city. A vivid account of Lorenzo's modus operandi was left by Tribaldo de' Rossi, a businessman who owned a small copper mine in the countryside. Fearing his isolated property was an easy target for roaming bandits, he wished to place himself under the great man's protection. "It occurred to me to reveal [the existence of the mine] only to Lorenzo de' Medici," he wrote, "and not to trust a single other father's son, and to commend myself freely to him, in his hands only." After collaring Lorenzo's assistant, *Ser* Piero da Bibbiena, in the cathedral one day, he managed to extract an invitation to meet with Lorenzo at his palace.† But when he

---

* Estimates of the number of those whose voices actually mattered in the councils of government varied. It is also not clear that the numbers were a great departure from the Albizzi regime, when power was said to be concentrated in the hands of a few dozen powerful families. At all times Florence was really an oligarchy in which power was held in few hands. Innovations instituted by the Medici systematized and rendered more efficient a form of government already in place. They also gave greater authority to a single man at the top. One aspect that drew the greatest contemporary comment and stirred up the most resentment was that the Medici *reggimento* had a less aristocratic, more populist flavor, even if the number of families wielding power remained the same. The greatest opposition to Medici rule continued to come from the old optimate families that were no longer close to the center of power.

† One wonders if de' Rossi slipped some coins into Bibbiena's hands to arrange the meeting; the narrator never tells us but that was often the way things worked in Florence.

arrived he found "such a large group of citizens waiting to talk to him" that he was forced to return home. His second attempt, six days later, was only slightly more satisfactory. "Lorenzo put on his coat and came down into the courtyard and gave audience," Tribaldo recalled.

> *Ser* Piero told me repeatedly to stay close to him, and that he would tell [Lorenzo] I was there, [we] being at the gate of the courtyard leading out [into the street]. Then *ser* Piero showed me to [Lorenzo]. Lorenzo called to me. I began to tell him: "I gave *ser* Piero the sample of copper . . ." And I had just said a little, and we were going hand in hand together up to the gate of the palace on the street side, when Lorenzo said to me: "Let me give audience to them"—for there were more than forty citizens there—"and then you will come with me." With that I removed myself down the street a few steps.

The situation was clearly frustrating for the petitioner, but how much more taxing for Lorenzo, who could not leave his house without running a gauntlet of needy citizens. His writ extended from the courthouse to the bedchamber. No prominent citizen who hoped to climb the social ladder could think of marrying off his daughter without first consulting Lorenzo. "In making marriages you should incline towards citizens who are in the *reggimento,*" advised Giovanni Morelli in his memoirs. "You should always attach yourself to those who have influence in the halls of government and in the *Signoria.*" While some citizens, like Lorenzo's great-grandfather Giovanni di Bicci, preferred to avoid political entanglements, most took this advice to heart. Thus, for instance, when Averardo Salviati wished to find a husband for his daughter, he first sought out Lorenzo. The father of the bride first suggested the groom—Filippo, son of Bartolomeo Valori, an ally of Lorenzo's—but it was Lorenzo who made the arrangements and set the dowry (at 2,000 florins). The term "father of his country," originally applied to Cosimo, became almost literal with Lorenzo. "No one so much as moves a piece of paper without the consent of the Master," wrote a foreign observer.*

---

* Foreigners typically exaggerated Lorenzo's power partly because they preferred to deal with an individual rather than negotiate the myriad councils and committees of the government, and partly out of genuine confusion about how the system worked.

Politics in Florence, as Lorenzo understood as well as anyone, was not confined to the Palace of the Priors. It shaped every human transaction in the city, from the social networks of neighbors built around the local parish church to more mercenary arrangements involving the exchange of financial or political favors. Neither the great merchants, who kept an anxious watch on the gyrations of tax policy, nor the poorest of the poor, who depended on the charity distributed by religious confraternities that were often political parties in disguise, were above the fray. The authority Lorenzo wielded in the *Palazzo della Signoria* radiated outward into the streets and piazzas of the city, and beyond the walls to the various communes subject to Florentine rule, through the kind of retail politicking that we see in the cases of Tribaldo de' Rossi or Averardo Salviati. There were literally thousands of citizens, both rich and poor, whose livelihoods depended on Lorenzo's ability to find government or ecclesiastical sinecures for them or their relations. The *reggimento* was kept in a constant state of agitation by bitter turf wars because one's standing ultimately rested on how many followers could be provided for. Much of Lorenzo's earliest correspondence concerns matters of patronage—often involving even menial jobs that would seem to be beneath the attention of the Medici heir—and the number of those looking to him for support merely increased with time. These "creatures" of Lorenzo multiplied in the corrupting, hothouse climate of Florence, but they were a hungry breed whose loyalty to their master would continue only as long as they were fed.* Lorenzo regarded the whole process with distaste and viewed many of his most loyal servants as little better than leeches. It is not surprising if there were moments, and more of them every day, when he felt like fleeing the "narrow seas and storms of civic life" for "some clear and running water . . . in the shadow of some lovely tree." It was in one such fit of exasperation that Lorenzo wrote to his secretary, "Get these petitioners off my back, because I have more letters from would-be Priors than there are days in the year and I am resolving not to want everything my way and to live what time I have left as peacefully as possible."

For Lorenzo, power alone could not bring contentment. At best, the

---

* In some ways the political climate was similar to the "spoils system" of nineteenth-century American politics.

successful conclusion of the Pazzi war and elimination of most internal opposition provided the security that allowed him to pursue the things that mattered to him most. "For when the arms of Italy, which had been stayed by Lorenzo's sense and authority, had been put down, he turned his mind to making himself and his city great," wrote Machiavelli. Ultimately Lorenzo could not become the man he wished to be through statesmanship alone, but it is certain that without the blessings of peace and prosperity he worked so hard to achieve, he would not have earned the title by which he is known to history—*il Magnifico*, the Magnificent.

Michelangelo, *Battle of Lapiths and Centaurs*, 1492 (Art Resource)

XIX. THE GARDEN AND THE GROVE

"For when the arms of Italy, which had been stayed by Lorenzo's sense and authority, had been put down, he turned his mind to making himself and his city great."

—NICCOLÒ MACHIAVELLI, *FLORENTINE HISTORIES*

"This is an age of gold, which has brought back to life the almost extinguished liberal disciplines of poetry, eloquence, painting, architecture, sculpture, music, and singing to the Orphic Lyre. And all this at Florence!"

—MARSILIO FICINO

SOMETIME IN THE 1460S OR EARLY 1470S LORENZO PUR-chased a small plot of land adjacent to the monastery of San Marco, a few blocks north of the palace on the Via Larga, for use as a private garden. Though only one of literally hundreds of similar patches of greenery within the encircling walls, Lorenzo's garden was apparently considered by at least one contemporary, the artist Piero del Massaio, to be one of the notable attractions of the city. The image of the garden is contained in his abbreviated view of the city made to illustrate a manuscript of Ptolemy's *Cosmography.* Shown as a walled plot fringed with cypress trees and labeled "Ort[us] L[aurentii] de medicis,"* its prominence demonstrates the importance contemporaries attached to it (which has sometimes eluded modern scholars). It is not, however, the shrubbery that deserves our attention, but the industrious activity of those who spent their time

---

* From the outside, the spot looks remarkably similar today—a wall backed by cypress trees. The garden itself is now a commercial plant store.

learning their craft behind its high stone walls. Among the regular visitors to this oasis was Leonardo da Vinci, who, according to one contemporary account, "stayed as a young man with the Magnifico Lorenzo de' Medici, who, giving him a salary, made him work for him in the garden on the piazza of San Marco, Florence."

While little is known of how Leonardo spent his time in the garden—it may well have been to work alongside his master, Verrocchio, on Piero's tomb—a decade or so later another young artist was a frequent visitor. His exploits here are better chronicled:

> Now that the boy [Michelangelo] was drawing one thing and then another at random [wrote the artist's friend and biographer, Ascanio Condivi], having no fixed place or course of study, it happened that one day he was taken by [his friend] Granacci to the Medici Garden at S. Marco, which Lorenzo the Magnificent ... had adorned with fig-ures and various ancient statues. When Michelangelo saw these works and savored their beauty, he never again went to Domenico [Ghirlandaio]'s workshop or anywhere else, but there he would stay all day, always doing something, as in the best school for such studies.

From this and other similar accounts grew the legend of Lorenzo's sculp-ture garden, a veritable school of the arts under the aegis of *il Magnifico* that served as the nursery of the greatest talents of the Renaissance.* It was here among the cypresses and umbrella pines, under the supervision of

---

* See, for instance, Vasari's "Life of Torrigiano" in his *Lives of the Painters, Sculptors and Architects* (vol. 1, p. 693): "Lorenzo the Magnificent, then, always favored men of genius, and particularly such of the nobles as showed an inclination for these our arts; where it is no marvel that from that school there should have issued some who have amazed the world. And what is more, he not only gave the means to buy food and clothing to those who, being poor, would otherwise not have been able to pursue the studies of design, but also bestowed extraordinary gifts on any one among them who had acquitted him-self in some work better than the others; so that the young students of our arts, compet-ing thus with each other, thereby became very excellent, as I will relate.

"The guardian and master of these young men, at that time, was the Florentine sculp-tor Bertoldo [di Giovanni], an old and practiced craftsman, who had once been a disci-ple of [Donatello]. He taught them, and likewise had charge of the works in the garden, and of many drawings, cartoons and models by the hand of Donat[ello], Pippo [Brunelleschi], Masaccio, Paolo Uccello, Fra Giovanni, Fra Filippo, and other masters, both native and foreign."

Lorenzo's friend the sculptor Bertoldo di Giovanni that talented young men came to learn their craft, aided in their studies not only by the fine examples of ancient sculpture the lord of the city had collected but by drawings of more recent masters.

The ancient statues that served as models for aspiring sculptors were later dispersed, but the memory of Lorenzo's garden has survived in the collective consciousness as one of the high points of civilization. Any site that served as the training ground for both Leonardo and Michelangelo would have a special place in the history of art, but some modern scholars dismiss these stories as largely the figment of Medici propaganda, the fruit of his descendants' efforts to legitimize their rule by depicting Lorenzo's reign as a golden age of art and literature. But while Vasari may certainly be accused of a pro-Medici bias—his chief patron was Grand Duke Cosimo de' Medici, a man whose legitimacy rested largely on the prestige of his family name—there is no reason to doubt the basic narrative, confirmed at key points in other contemporary sources. This scholarly skepticism is part of a larger pattern in which exaggerated claims made for Lorenzo's role in fostering the Florentine Renaissance have led to exaggerated counterclaims in which Lorenzo's contributions have been marginalized or eliminated altogether. The idea that Lorenzo single-handedly brought forth this unparalleled flowering of human creativity, popular among some Enlightenment and nineteenth-century authors, is surely off the mark, but denying the obvious fact that Lorenzo dominated this most fruitful moment in cultural history through the force of his character, the generosity of his patronage, as well as his own creative talents, is equally misleading. Lorenzo's influence in the realm of culture, as in politics, was pervasive and inescapable, and while many of the works once thought to have been directly commissioned by him turn out to have been made for others, his presence was felt everywhere and his spirit is visible in almost every major painting and sculpture to issue from the many workshops of the city in the last two decades of his life.*

---

* For an influential essay minimizing Lorenzo's contribution to art history see E. H. Gombrich's "The Early Medici as Patrons of Art," reprinted in *Norm and Form,* in which Lorenzo's contributions are compared unfavorably with those of his grandfather. For a recent corrective to this view, see F. W. Kent's *Lorenzo de' Medici and the Art of Magnificence.* While Gombrich emphasizes Cosimo's role as a builder and patron and Lorenzo's as a collector of precious antiquities, the Condivi and Vasari passages reveal that the two roles (collector and patron) were mutually reinforcing.

Attempts to belittle Lorenzo's contribution to the culture of the Renaissance Florence are often prompted by uneasiness about his political agenda and by a conviction that he was motivated by selfish, dynastic ambitions rather than by the disinterested pursuit of art for art's sake. It is certainly true that Lorenzo used art as a tool of propaganda, but an art free from worldly taint didn't exist in fifteenth-century Florence. Art was not then the exclusive province of an ultra-rarefied elite but was thoroughly entwined in the religious, economic, and civic life of the community. Florentines were all intensely chauvinistic and took understandable pride in their unparalleled cultural genius. Lorenzo saw it as his mission to promote the city's fame as a center of European culture, knowing that his own prestige was linked to that of Florence. When he fostered such obviously patriotic projects as turning the cathedral into a pantheon of Florentine greats, commissioning a portrait bust of Giotto and seeking to have the remains of Dante returned to his native city, his efforts were applauded by his fellow citizens. Even his own writing can be seen as part of this project. In an age when Latin was the preferred idiom of the cultured man, Lorenzo went out of his way to write in the vernacular in order to show that "this Tuscan tongue" should not be despised but appreciated as "rich and refined." Florentines as a whole, and Lorenzo in particular, were far more effective as cultural than as military or political imperialists.

Even a brief survey of contemporary documents reveals the extent to which Lorenzo took an interest in what was happening in the studios and workshops of his native city. The countless times he was consulted on aesthetic matters, not only by his fellow citizens but by men of taste and learning across Europe, demonstrates that he was universally regarded as an authority on all matters artistic. When Lodovico Sforza wished to find painters to decorate the great monastery of Certosa in Pavia, he asked his agent in Florence to look only at those artists Lorenzo had employed in his villa at Spedaletto because he knew Lorenzo to be an authority in such matters.* Sforza was not alone in his reliance on Lorenzo's judgment. Through queries like this from the courts of Europe, Lorenzo's taste left its

---

* Spedaletto was decorated with frescoes by Botticelli, Filippino Lippi, Perugino, and Ghirlandaio, all of them since destroyed. The notion that Lorenzo was less a connoisseur of painting than of other arts may merely be an accident of history.

imprint far from his native Florence. Lorenzo, for his part, proffered such advice not only because he was genuinely interested in such matters and because it flattered his ego, but because he knew that by these means his influence and fame spread far and wide.

A similar dynamic was at work domestically. Even when Lorenzo was not personally paying for the work, his opinions were usually canvassed on important projects, as in the crucial design of a new facade for the Duomo, where he was asked to pass judgment on the competing proposals because of his "very great architectural expertise." A contract from May 1483 spelling out the terms under which Ghirlandaio was to paint an altarpiece for the chapel of the *Palazzo della Signoria* noted that it should be completed in that "quality and that manner and form as should seem good to, and please, the Magnificent Lorenzo di Piero di Cosimo de' Medici." Similar instances can be multiplied almost indefinitely. Sometimes Lorenzo is literally present in the work, as in the Sassetti chapel frescoes at Santa Trinità or Botticelli's *Adoration of the Magi*, commissioned by the obscure Medici follower Guasparre del Lama, where he and his family are prominently featured in the scene. But even when he did not appear in the company of saints his spirit hovered over the creation.

Lorenzo was unrivaled in Florence and Florence was unrivaled in Europe as the supreme arbiter of taste. Whether at home in his palace on the Via Larga or in one of his many villas, Lorenzo was surrounded by a coterie of talented men. This peripatetic entourage formed a literary and cultural court whose brilliance made it a trendsetter for the rest of society. As the guiding light of this intellectual world, Lorenzo's interests and obsessions seeped into the artisans' workshops crowded near the Duomo and into the scattered classrooms of the Florentine university. The result was that the art of the 1470s and 1480s bears the stamp of his personality—cerebral, sensual, and refined. His weakness for esoteric philosophical allegory (expounded at length in poems like *The Supreme Good*) and love for all things ancient set the prevailing literary and intellectual fashions of the day and influenced artistic practice, not only locally but throughout Europe, where even mediocre Florentine artists were in high demand.

It is not a stretch, then, to speak of an Age of Lorenzo, shaped by the tastes and ambitions of one man. That Lorenzo was well aware of his role in the cultural revival of the age is illustrated by his personal motto, inscribed in pearls on his shield in the joust of 1469—*Le temps revient*, the time returns. In fact it was just this kind of suffocating presence that families like the Pazzi found so demeaning. This was partly a matter of policy, but it was also a product of Lorenzo's fiercely competitive nature, which made him insist on having a say in everything and made it difficult for him to accept that he had been bested in any matter, no matter how trivial. His sometimes overbearing personality comes through in accounts from those courageous enough to match their horses against his in the races to which he was passionately attached. Luca Landucci recalls one race in which his brother's Barbary went head-to-head with Lorenzo's champion: "And when he went to race at Siena, there was a tie between his horse and one belonging to Lorenzo de' Medici, called Firefly, that of Gostanzo [my brother] being in reality one head's length in advance of the other. And the people who were present declared that he had won, and told him to go to the magistrate, and they would bear witness. Gostanzo, however, refused to do this, out of respect for Lorenzo, and as it happened, Lorenzo was proclaimed the winner." It is clear that Florentines were growing ever more accustomed to habits of deference to the lord of the city.

The manner in which Lorenzo left his mark, even when he had no hand in commissioning a particular artwork, can be illustrated in a couple of well-known examples. Two of the most famous works of the period, Botticelli's *Primavera* (1482) and *Birth of Venus* (1485), are no longer believed to have been made for Lorenzo himself but for his cousin Lorenzo di Pierfrancesco de' Medici. But despite attempts to sever the cord linking these works to the first citizen of Florence, they are undeniably products of the cultural and literary environment that grew up around Lorenzo and that found expression in the refined eroticism of his own verse. Of course Lorenzo's cousin was in general terms very much within Lorenzo's orbit but, more significant, the painter seems to have drawn his intricate program from Lorenzo's protégé Angelo Poliziano.*

Some have even attempted to find passages in Lorenzo's own poetry that directly inspired these paintings, but it seems more accurate to say

---

* See Chapter XI.

that a similar spirit, hedonistic and erudite, flows through both, as in these lines from his carnival song "The Triumph of Bacchus and Ariadne":*

> *Those who love these pretty nymphs*
> *Are little satyrs, free of cares,*
> *Who in the grottoes and the glades*
> *Have laid for them a hundred snares.*
> *By Bacchus warmed and now aroused*
> *They skip and dance the time away.*

The Renaissance love affair with ancient literature did not begin with Lorenzo, but through his learning, tastes, and poetic gifts he epitomized the age in which centaurs, nymphs, and dryads were as much a part of the imaginative life of the educated class as holy saints and martyrs. After his death this literary culture, more pagan than Christian in the eyes of its critics, was so closely linked with Lorenzo that reformers like Savonarola waged war with equal fervor on the corrupt political and cultural pillars of his regime.

Lorenzo's contribution was as much practical as inspirational: through his avid collecting of ancient cameos and statues, which he made available to visiting connoisseurs and talented young artists, he provided a treasure trove of models for them to study, while his greed for ancient texts helped build a library filled with volumes by Ovid, Lucretius, and Horace that were mined by writers like Poliziano. One of the criticisms of Lorenzo was that he was a greater collector than patron, an amasser of ancient manuscripts and cameos—like the famous *Farnese Cup*, purchased from Sixtus IV—rather than a commissioner of new art. But, as the tale of the sculpture garden illustrates, the two roles were mutually reinforcing. Lorenzo did not squirrel away his prized possessions but proudly showed them off to anyone who wished to see them, thereby providing an invaluable resource to artists and scholars. (It is telling that the Pazzi conspirators counted on Lorenzo's eagerness to show off his collection to help them

---

* One scholar has made the intriguing suggestion that the dance of the Three Graces in the painting was literally choreographed by Lorenzo (see Emily Jayne's "A Choreography by Lorenzo in Botticelli's Primavera," in *Lorenzo de' Medici: New Perspectives*). Lorenzo's interest in music is well documented; his interest in dance, however, is among the least studied aspects of this *uomo universale*.

plan their ambush.) In May 1490, Lorenzo wrote to his son in Florence: "Piero—Enclosed is a letter from Baccio [Ugolini]; the bearer is the man of whom he writes, who is passing through Florence. He seems to me clever and one who loves to see antique things. I wish you to show him all those in the garden, and also what we have in the study; in short, whatever seems best to you, and thus to give him pleasure."

Lorenzo's passion for small objects, particularly if they were ancient and exquisitely wrought, is well known, perhaps because his near-sightedness made it easier to appreciate things he could hold in his hands. "I have received the cameo I have so long coveted," Lorenzo wrote to one of the many agents he had scouring Europe for antiquities, "which pleases me very much because it is in quite perfect condition." But it was not only precious and exquisite things that caught Lorenzo's covetous eye; among his greatest treasures were the busts of Agrippa and Augustus he had received from Sixtus, objects whose association with the golden age of Rome outweighed their artistic merit. Friends on their travels were instructed to be on the lookout for objects of particular historical value. In one of his greatest coups he obtained from Pistoia a bust of the philosopher Plato, which he installed in a special niche and which became the centerpiece of celebrations held in honor of the philosopher's birthday.

Another attempt to deflate the myth of a Lorenzan golden age involves the so-called Platonic Academy, which in the years after his death grew in the imagination of some propogandists into a school of philosophy founded by Cosimo, directed by Ficino, and coaxed into full bloom by Lorenzo. Recent scholarship has thrown cold water on any notion that there was an institution dedicated to the study of philosophy centered on Ficino's villa in Careggi. Those who created out of the informal gatherings of Ficino, Poliziano, Pico della Mirandola, Lorenzo, Giuliano, and other lesser lights a formal school whose purpose was to revive the philosophy of the Athenian giant were guilty of reading too much into a scanty record. In fact Ficino's "academy" was little more than a loose association of scholars and students who shared an interest in Plato's philosophy and who met from time to time on the occasion of the ancient philosopher's birthday. Many of the "lessons" Ficino taught were in the form of letters filled equally with philosophical tidbits and paternal advice. Ficino described one particu-

larly memorable occasion in the introduction to his book *Plato on Love,*
dedicated to his patron, Lorenzo de' Medici:

> Plato, the father of philosophers, died at the age of eighty-one, on
> November 7, which was his birthday, reclining at a banquet, after
> the feast had been cleared away. This banquet, in which both the
> birthday and the anniversary of Plato are equally contained, all of
> the ancient Platonists down to the times of Plotinus and Porphyry
> used to celebrate every year. But after Porphyry these solemn feasts
> were neglected for twelve hundred years. At last, in our own times,
> the famous Lorenzo de' Medici, wishing to renew the Platonic ban-
> quet, appointed Francesco Bandini master of the feast. Therefore,
> since Bandini had arranged to celebrate the seventh day of Novem-
> ber, he received with regal pomp at Careggi, in the country, nine
> Platonic guests.

There was nothing unusual in this. Casual gatherings of like-minded
scholars had been a feature of Florentine intellectual life for centuries— as
young men Cosimo and Agnolo Acciaiuoli both attended philosophical
discussions in the cell of Ambrogio Traversari—but with the encouragement of Lorenzo, the fatherly Ficino managed to shift the prevailing intellectual mood. Before Ficino, Florentine scholars, building on the medieval
Scholastic tradition, had been concerned primarily to elaborate the philosophy of Aristotle, turning it into a system marked by arid intellectual-
ism and logical hair-splitting. Ficino found Plato's metaphysical flights
much more to his taste. As elaborated by Plato's late classical follower Plot-
inus, and further refined by Ficino, Neoplatonic philosophy taught that
the universe possessed a hierarchical structure in which the material world
as apprehended by the senses existed on the lowest rung. The soul, captivated by beauty, ascends through higher and higher spheres of reality until
it finally approaches the eternal realm of the Divine. Love is the force that
impels the soul upward toward the heavenly realm, starting with sexual
attraction and finding ultimate consummation in the love of God.
Lorenzo himself expounded this doctrine of the soul's ascent to heaven in
a passage that closely follows Ficino's writing. Physical love, he wrote, "is
the first step on the staircase of love, and, naturally, the most imperfect,
since Platonism holds that corporeal beauty is a sort of shadow of true

beauty or the idea of true beauty, which, in the body is seen only under a veil." Lorenzo dwells at length on this theme in his most Platonic, or Plotinian, poem, "The Supreme Good":

> For while the soul is bound in carnal bonds,
> confined within this prison's gloom, it will
> always be governed by desire and doubt.
> The soul is so wrapped up in error when
> it's body-bound, that it won't know itself
> until its liberation is complete.

For Lorenzo, no stranger to the cruder forms of the emotion, it was a philosophy that validated his own appetites; if lust was not the highest form of love, at least it deserved respect as the first step of a journey that ultimately led to God.

Ficino's doctrines had wide-ranging and long-term influence. His philosophy of Platonic love helped reconcile pagan art and literature with Christianity, speeding up the assimilation of ancient texts from which modern philosophy and science sprang. The doctrine of divine love also had profound implications for the visual arts by conceding to physical beauty an element of the spiritual. In the short term, however, the greatest impact of Ficino's ideas may have been on the way Florentines thought of relations between the citizen and the state. Indeed some scholars have detected in these rather esoteric concepts the core of an official ideology intended to excuse a creeping despotism. In this scenario, Ficino and Lorenzo worked hand in glove to craft an intellectual framework for a regime bent on undermining the republican traditions of the city.

In the realm of philosophy, as in art, Lorenzo's critics often find themselves caught between two contradictory theories. There are those who insist that Lorenzo's contribution to the intellectual climate was negligible, his patronage inconsistent, and his own writings derivative. A second line of attack is that he was the guiding light of an intellectual movement that led Florentines away from the civic-minded pragmatism that had characterized the writings of Leonardo Bruni and Coluccio Salutati at the beginning of the century. To these critics, Lorenzo's taste for Platonic allegory appears to be part of a cynical ploy to lead citizens away from politics and into a maze of harmless metaphysics. It is true that Ficino's mysticism was a far cry from Bruni's overtly political writing—and even more out of step with Machiavelli's hardheaded realism in the following generation—but it is implausible to view Lorenzo's philosophical tastes as part of any such consciously "Machiavellian" scheme. Rather, Lorenzo seems to have been genuinely attracted to Ficino's brand of speculative philosophy. Recasting Plato's thought in a form that made it seem the natural precursor of Christian theology, it fulfilled a deep, if rather amorphous, spiritual yearning. The most moving fragment of religious poetry Lorenzo wrote infuses Neoplatonic philosophy with an urgency born of metaphysical anxiety:

> *O' God, O' greatest Good, how is it,*
> *that I seek only you but it is you I never find?*

Like many statesmen before and since, Lorenzo found Plato's thought deeply compelling. Plato's vision of the perfect society, elaborated most fully in *The Republic,* furnishes the would-be ruler with a model of good government unequaled in the history of philosophy not only for its idealism but also its impracticality. There is an indication, particularly during the 1470s when Ficino and Lorenzo were in almost daily contact, that Lorenzo saw himself as something akin to a Platonic philosopher-king, a benign despot who ruled selflessly on behalf of his people. During the early years of Lorenzo's reign the two exchanged frequent letters in which the older Ficino played the role of spiritual advisor to the younger man. "[The ruler] will not, indeed, consider himself a master of the law," Ficino wrote to his eager pupil, "but its faithful interpreter and devoted servant. In administering it he should punish offenses impartially and with even temper. Without envy he should reward virtuous actions according to their worth. He should not give thought to his own interests but rather to those of the community." No doubt the temperamental Lorenzo had difficulty living up to this ideal, but it was a model he strived to emulate. His mentor's words find an echo in his play *The Martyrdom of Saints John and Paul,* where the Emperor Julian sketches an idealized portrait of the enlightened despot that Lorenzo, in his more introspective moments, must have known was a far cry from the realities that confronted him every day:

> *The majesty of our imperial throne*
> *Is built upon the emperor's good name.*
> *He is no private person on his own,*
> *But stands for all his subjects by acclaim.*

There does seem to be an implicit recognition in Ficino's letters to Lorenzo that his correspondent was more than merely the first citizen of the state. He is treated as something resembling a constitutional monarch who through his privileged position incurs certain obligations. But the political implications of Ficino's philosophy went beyond the lessons contained in these overtly political passages. Some have seen his idealism as a key to the political apathy that was a notable element of the Lorenzan age. In the debate between proponents of the active life of the citizen and the contemplative life of the philosopher, explored at length in Cristoforo Landino's *Disputationes Camaldulenses,** Ficino's ethereal flights of fancy seem to support the latter course. Lorenzo's friend Donato Acciaiuoli stated the dilemma of the Florentine intellectual succinctly. "I have gone over in my mind many times the problem of which sort of life is better and more worthy of praise," he wrote to Marco Parenti, "to serve the republic and to fulfill the duties of a good and wise man by taking part actively in it, or to choose a life removed from all public and private activity, a life yet laborious in the diligent pursuit and investigation of the highest things." How Acciaiuoli himself resolved this issue is clear in the long and distinguished career he had as a roving ambassador for the republic, but this was a choice that many Florentines of the intellectual and governing class (peculiarly, the two were one and the same in the Renaissance) felt obligated to make. Judging by Acciaiuoli's own experience, choosing the active life was not always the best option: on his mission to Rome during the Pazzi conspiracy he was roughed up by Girolamo Riario's soldiers, and long after he was entitled to retire he was sent on a mission by the republic, during which he died.

The debate between the merits of the active and the contemplative life were not original to Renaissance Florentines. The same dilemmas had been explored by ancient writers like Cicero, for whom a life of quiet reflection was the consolation for political defeat.[†] A similar dynamic was at work in Renaissance Florence; the more disengaged philosophy that characterized the period of Lorenzo's ascendance reflected a narrowing of

---

* See Chapter IX.

† It found its way into Christianity through the activities of the various monastic movements. While some orders see it as their mission to remove themselves from the world, others believe they are meant to go out into the world. It is no coincidence that the *Disputationes Camaldulenses* is set in a monastery located in the wilds of the Apennines.

political horizons. Clearly a philosophy whose main purpose was to exhort men to participate actively as citizens was inappropriate to an age when power was concentrated in only a few hands. But external events, too, played a role in this philosophical evolution. Salutati and Bruni wrote in a euphoric time, when Florence's ultimately successful contest against the Visconti of Milan, viewed as a biblical contest of David vs. Goliath, encouraged men to reflect on the unique qualities that allowed a small republic to face down a giant and despotic power. Emphasizing the vital democracy of their own city allowed them to draw a more effective contrast with the tyranny they were fighting. A century later, Machiavelli and Guicciardini were both motivated to write about politics out of despair following the trauma of the foreign invasions in the years after Lorenzo's death; as the city-states of their youth crumbled before the nation states of the future, it was only natural to examine the political institutions that had led them down the path to ruin. By contrast, Lorenzo presided over an age of political lethargy. For the most part citizens were willing to give up at least a portion of their ancient rights in return for the stability and peace that Medici rule brought them. It is telling that the greatest crisis of Lorenzo's reign—the Pazzi conspiracy—was overcome not through military might but because the ancient cry of *"Popolo e Liberta!"* no longer stirred the hearts of the citizens.

Even opponents of Lorenzo's regime seemed content for the most part to till their own little plots. One of the most coherent critiques of Medici rule—Alamanno Rinuccini's "Dialogue on Liberty"—was written in secret by someone whose own career was a model of apathy and ineffectualness. Though in private he boldly chastised Lorenzo and his regime, Rinuccini was always happy to pick up whatever political plums were tossed his way.* In fact while Rinuccini and Lorenzo stood on opposite sides of the political fence, the two are not as dissimilar as they might at first appear. Rinuccini's

---

* Rinuccini's opposition to Lorenzo's rule, like that of so many others, can be traced at least in part to his thwarted ambition. He began as a supporter of Lorenzo, having been among those urging the reforms of 1471. His career took a wrong turn in the middle of the decade when, while on a mission to Rome, he reported a papal diatribe against Lorenzo to the *Signoria*. Thereafter, though he continued to hold various offices, he was never trusted by Lorenzo. His "Dialogue on Liberty" was written in 1479, during this period of political exile. For a brief sketch of Rinuccini's life see *Humanism and Liberty* (Watkins, pp. 186–94).

imaginary dialogue concludes with his alter ego, Eleutherius (lover of liberty), issuing something less than a ringing call to arms: "[T]he truth is that I cannot peacefully tolerate our ungrateful citizenry and the usurpers of our liberty. I live, therefore, as you see, content with this little house and farm. I am free from all anxiety. I don't inquire what goes on in the city, and I lead a quiet and free life." Is it any wonder that with friends like Rinuccini the Pazzi revolution never got off the ground?

Rinuccini's dialogue is not too far in spirit from Lorenzo's own writing, which makes no secret of his disdain for the corruption of city life and sings the paeans to the simple virtues of the countryside:

> Lured on, escorted by the sweetest thoughts
> I fled the bitter storms of civic life
> to lead my soul back to a calmer port. . . .
> To free my feeble nature from the load
> that wearies it and stops its flight, I left
> the pretty circle of my native walls.
> And having reached a pleasant, shady glen
> within the shadow of that mountain which
> in its old age preserves the name,
> there, where a verdant laurel cast some shade
> below that lovely peak, I found a seat,
> my heart untrammeled by a single care.

Lorenzo's disillusionment with politics was as profound as Rinuccini's. A speech he places in the mouth of the Emperor Constantine in *The Martyrdom of Saints John and Paul* includes a line that may well have been his own *cri de coeur:* "To rule is wearisome, a bitter feat." Though Rinuccini and Lorenzo disagreed about the cause of the political decline, given their disillusionment with civic life it was only natural for both to turn from an unsatisfactory world of politics toward the consolations of metaphysics. A philosophy that left the storms of daily life far behind and fled to realms eternal best expressed the mood of the times.

For Lorenzo the company of artists and writers had always been one of the antidotes to the poisonous atmosphere of Florentine politics. If no less

mercenary than those seeking political office, artists and writers were usually more entertaining. Among the companions of his later years was the
sculptor Giovanni di Bertoldo. Lorenzo valued Bertoldo not only for his
talent as a bronze caster but for his sarcastic wit.* Bertoldo was constantly
at Lorenzo's house and accompanied him on his travels. Bertoldo's death
in 1491 came while he was staying at Lorenzo's villa at Poggio a Caiano,
much to the grief of his master, who was said to have mourned his passing
as if he had been a member of his own family.

Bertoldo was considerably older than Lorenzo (he was born c. 1430),
but as Lorenzo himself grew into middle age he more often took on the
role of a father figure to a younger generation of brilliant men, reinvigorated by their energy and their wit. Among the young geniuses who came
into Lorenzo's life during these latter years was the teenage Michelangelo.
Condivi relates a charming story of their first encounter in the garden at
San Marco, which the biographer heard from the mouth of the artist
himself:

> One day, [Michelangelo] was examining among these works the
> *Head of a Faun,* already old in appearance, with a long beard and
> laughing countenance, though the mouth, on account of its antiq-
> uity, could hardly be distinguished or recognized for what it was;
> and, as he liked it inordinately, he decided to copy it in marble. . . .
> He set about copying the *Faun* with such care and study that in a few
> days he had perfected it, supplying from his imagination all that was
> lacking in the ancient work, that is, the open mouth as of a man
> laughing, so that the hollow of the mouth and all the teeth could be
> seen. In the midst of this, the Magnificent, coming to see what point
> his works had reached, found the boy engaged in polishing the head
> and, approaching quite near, he was much amazed, considering first
> the excellence and then the boy's age; and although he did praise the
> work, nonetheless he joked with him as with a child and said, "Oh,

---

* There is an undated letter from Bertoldo to Lorenzo so chock-full of obscure puns that
scholars have never been able to convincingly elucidate its meaning, which is a pity
since among the topics it covers is his disdain for Count Girolamo Riario. He concludes
his mocking letter, "I pray him that I may see the Pope, the Count [Girolamo], and
Messer Luca suffocated in a vat full of pepper, and you, beware of their treachery" (see
Ross, p. 176).

you have made this *Faun* old and left him all his teeth. Don't you know that old men of that age are always missing a few?"

To Michelangelo it seemed a thousand years before the Magnificent went away so that he could correct the mistake; and, when he was alone, he removed an upper tooth from his old man, drilling the gum as if it had come out with the root, and the following day he awaited the Magnificent with eager longing. When he had come and noted the boy's goodness and simplicity, he laughed at him very much; but then, when he weighed in his mind the perfection of the thing and the age of the boy, he, who was the father of all *virtù*, resolved to help and encourage such great genius and to take him into his household; and, learning from him whose son he was, he said, "Inform your father that I would like to speak to him."

Thus it was that the fifteen-year-old came to live in the palace of the Via Larga, though even with the lord of the city weighing in on his behalf it took some doing to persuade the elder Buonarroti to allow his son to become an artist, a calling so far beneath him.* Lorenzo, in fact, seems to have had fewer of the prejudices of his class against artisans than Michelangelo's father, a member of the impoverished nobility whose pride was in inverse proportion to the size of his bank account. There was, of course, an element of noblesse oblige in Lorenzo's patronage of talented men he did not consider his social equal. By inviting the artist to stay in his house he was following in the footsteps of his grandfather, who had kept the painter Filippo Lippi on the premises while he was working for him in an effort to keep the lusty monk's mind on the job.

Among the artifacts remaining from Michelangelo's years in Lorenzo's house is a vivid account of the informal atmosphere of the palace he recounted to his biographer:

[Lorenzo] arranged that Michelangelo be given a good room in his house, providing him with all the conveniences he desired and treating him not otherwise than as a son, both in other ways and at his

---

* Among other inducements, Lorenzo offered Michelangelo's father a job as a customs official, a typical example of Medici patronage.

table, at which, as befitted such a man, personages of the highest nobility and of great affairs were seated every day. And as it was the custom that those who were present at the first sat down near the Magnificent, each according to his rank, without changing places no matter who should arrive later, it quite often happened that Michelangelo was seated above Lorenzo's sons and other distinguished people, the constant company in which that house flourished and abounded. By all of them Michelangelo was treated affectionately and encouraged in his honorable pursuit, but above all by the Magnificent, who would send for him many times a day and would show him his jewels, carnelions, medals and similar things of great value, as he knew the boy had high intelligence and judgment.

The casualness of dinner at the palace was confirmed by Franceschetto Cibo, Lorenzo's future son-in-law, who complained at the undignified treatment he had received until it was explained that there was no surer sign that one was thought a part of the family than to be included in such a boisterous, informal gathering.

If Michelangelo felt the need to talk shop he could always rely on Bertoldo, who had a room on the mezzanine near the top of the stairs. Despite the fact that he was a dear friend of Lorenzo's and someone Lorenzo trusted to oversee his collection of valuable objects, Bertoldo's room was listed among those of the household waiters. More influential on the young sculptor's development was another guest of the palace, Angelo Poliziano. "Recognizing in Michelangelo a superior spirit," writes Condivi, "he loved him very much and, although there was no need, he continually urged him on his studies, always explaining to him and providing him with subjects." The fruit of Poliziano's teaching is visible in the relief *The Battle of the Lapiths and the Centaurs,* whose mythological theme was suggested by the poet. In this early work Michelangelo first explores the form of the male nude that will define his work from the *David* to the *Last Judgment* in the Sistine Chapel. Though Poliziano provided the literary background for this seminal work, Michelangelo was also inspired by his surroundings at the palace, where Donatello's *David* stood in the courtyard and Antonio del Pollaiuolo's *Labors of Hercules* hung in the Grand Salon.

Though Michelangelo is the most famous name on the guest list of the

Medici palace, his experience was by no means unique. Three generations of discerning and profligate Medici collecting had turned the palace on the Via Larga into a museum of both ancient and modern art; under the guidance of Poliziano, Lorenzo had amassed one of the greatest collections of manuscripts in the world, turning the two hundred he had inherited to over one thousand at the time of his death. All of which made an invitation to the palace indispensable for anyone wishing to further his visual or literary education. To attract the attention and win the admiration of *il Magnifico* was the goal of any man of talent or ambition; to win his patronage was to be set out on the path to success. Not only was his patronage a good thing in itself, but to be known as a protégé of the lord of Florence was to possess currency that could purchase a place in any court of Europe where learning and cultivation were valued.

Among those drawn to Florence by Lorenzo's reputation for enlightened patronage was the young Count Giovanni Pico della Mirandola, one of the most precociously gifted intellects of the age. With a command of numerous languages, ancient and modern—including those exotic acquisitions for a man of his times, Arabic and Hebrew, which he mastered in order to delve more deeply into the mystical teaching of Cabala—and talent for philosophical disputation, Pico dazzled everyone he met. Admired both for his learning and personal charm, the handsome count was immediately welcomed into Lorenzo's circle, where his formidable erudition added to the liveliness of the discussions. A letter Poliziano wrote to Ficino from the Medici villa at Fiesole paints an idyllic portrait of the life of a scholar under Lorenzo's aegis: "Wandering beyond the limits of his own property, Pico sometimes steals unexpectedly on my retirement, and draws me from the shade to partake of his supper. What kind of supper that is you well know; sparing indeed, but neat, and rendered graceful by the charms of conversation. But be my guest. Your supper shall be as good, and your wine perhaps better, for in the quality of wine I shall contend for superiority even with Pico himself."

For intellectuals, particularly for those of a speculative and daring cast of mind, Lorenzo's favor guaranteed more than just room and board. In 1486 Pico composed his famous 900 Theses, a set of philosophical and theological propositions that were a young man's challenge to the received wisdom of the day. When a committee appointed by Pope Innocent declared seven of them to be unorthodox and a further six questionable, Pico was forced to flee to France. It was only after Lorenzo guaranteed his good behavior and placed him under his protection that Pico was allowed to return to Italy. Even then he was not free from the accusations of heresy, accusations that Lorenzo, always inclined to take the side of freethinkers rather than the clergy, vehemently denied. "The Count della Mirandola is here leading a most saintly life, like a monk," Lorenzo wrote to his ambassador in Rome. "He has been and is now occupied in writing other admirable theological works. . . . He is anxious to be absolved from what little contumacy is still attributed to him by the Holy Father and to have a Brief by which His Holiness accepts him as a son and a good Christian. . . . I greatly desire that this satisfaction should be given to him, for there are few men I love better or esteem more."

Not all of Lorenzo's companions of these years were as high-minded or as erudite as Pico. Lorenzo always had a soft spot for buffoonish types whose pranks and verbal barbs could shake him from his natural tendency to melancholy. As he recast himself as a sober statesman many of the favorites from the days of his wild youth were shunted aside—including Braccio Martelli and Luigi Pulci—but he kept about him at least a couple of men who shared his taste for coarse jokes and ribald tales. When, at the urging of Ficino, Lorenzo distanced himself from Pulci—whom the philosopher regarded as an atheist and sodomite—the role of court jester was taken up by Matteo Franco. Lorenzo described him as "among the first and best-loved creatures of my house," and his presence ensured that Lorenzo's entourage remained lively. A typical example of this impious priest's humor is his witticism at the expense of his disgraced rival as a "louse clinging to the Medici balls" (Pulci in Italian meaning "fleas"). So bold was Franco that not even Lorenzo's wife escaped his sharp wit. "I should be glad not to be turned into ridicule by Franco," Clarice wrote to her husband, "as was Luigi Pulci," a request the not always chivalrous Lorenzo ignored. Despite his coarse humor, Clarice came to love and trust the man. "I will not allow any man to have the spending of my money but Franco," she declared, "and I will eat nothing but what has passed through his hands." Even the prissy Ficino enjoyed Franco's high jinks, admitting that "were it not for Matteo Franco seasoning my dullness with his wit," he would "lose the taste for my own company."

． ． ．

For as long as he could remember, Lorenzo had struggled to emerge from beneath his grandfather's shadow. One acute observer noted that he was driven by a desire "to achieve even more than Cosimo and Piero had ever done," though it was less his own father than Cosimo, *Pater Patriae,* whose example he hoped to emulate and whose place in the hearts of his countrymen he hoped to supplant. Nowhere did Cosimo's achievement loom larger than in his contributions to the urban fabric of Florence. He himself acknowledged that long after his political legacy had crumbled, monuments in brick and stone would be all that was left to remind his compatriots of what he had given to his homeland. In the ecclesiastical realm Cosimo had bettered his prospects in Purgatory by spending lavishly on the reconstruction of San Lorenzo and San Marco; the Franciscan church Santa Croce was provided with a new chapel at his expense, and both San Miniato and Santissima Annunziata received elaborate tabernacles paid for by the profits of his bank.* Nor did he stint when it came to spending on himself; the most notable private building of the era was his palace on the Via Larga. Not only was it a handsome, imposing presence on the street, but through the elegance of its richly appointed interior that he filled with priceless works of art it set a model of gracious living for generations of Florentine patricians.

Lorenzo knew that if he were to rival the achievements of his grandfather he would have to challenge him on this ground, for it was as a builder that a great man's legacy would be measured. As Giovanni Rucellai, no mean builder himself, explained it, "There are two principal things that men do in this world. The first is to procreate, the second is to build." Lorenzo's desire to build on the scale of Cosimo was initially hampered by two factors: the first was that he was simply not as wealthy as his grandfather had been; the second was that after decades of intensive building on the part of public institutions and private citizens there were fewer opportunities to make a mark.

---

* Piero was deeply involved in the latter two projects. It is difficult to apportion responsibility for many Medici commissions, but as head of the family Cosimo had the final say. Another major ecclesiastical project was the monastery known as the Badia in Fiesole, which, like so many of Cosimo's projects, was give to the architect Michelozzi.

And then there was the perennial problem: how to avoid making grandiose gestures that smacked of princely ambition? After the Pazzi war, however, such considerations were less important and Lorenzo was free to pursue his schemes without fear of offending his fellow citizens. As for coming up with the funds to pursue a very expensive hobby, Lorenzo's murky finances were such that he could simultaneously complain to the tax collector that he was near bankruptcy while investing in real estate and pursuing an extensive building program.*

It was a moment for which he had long been planning. Lorenzo was every bit as ambitious as Cosimo and, in addition, he possessed a far wider and more profound understanding of the art, both technically and aesthetically. Indeed the study of architecture had been one of his longstanding passions, pursued with diligence even when he had little prospect of bringing his dreams to fruition. The highlight of his 1471 journey to Rome had been the time he spent in the company of Leon Battista Alberti wandering about the ruins of the ancient city, and the lessons he learned from the master were later put to good use. Among Lorenzo's most prized possessions were three different versions of the *Ten Books on Architecture* by the ancient Roman architectural theorist Vitruvius and a manuscript copy of Alberti's *On Architecture*. When Ercole d'Este wished to borrow Alberti's text from Lorenzo, he agreed only with great reluctance because he "prized it so much and often read it." When Alberti's book was finally put out in printed form, Lorenzo had a servant fetch him the latest chapter straight from the presses so he could have it read aloud to him while he was taking the waters.

Even before the Pazzi conspiracy, Lorenzo had begun to lay the groundwork for his project of urban renewal, purchasing considerable property along the Via dei Servi, a tract that reached from the Medici palace to the Porta San Gallo, which he hoped to turn into rental property. Though little came of the plan during Lorenzo's lifetime, the development of this

---

* The truth is that while Lorenzo was often strapped for ready cash, that never seemed to prevent him from pursuing those things that meant a lot to him. In building, buying up real estate, purchasing rare manuscripts and rare antiques, Lorenzo never appeared to be short of funds. This was no doubt made simpler by having his friends like Antonio di Bernardo Miniati put in control of all the major financial institutions of the state.

neighborhood just inside the northern walls that took place in the early sixteenth century seems to have followed the program first contemplated by Lorenzo.

But it was not until the late 1480s that the stars aligned, allowing Lorenzo to begin an ambitious program of public and private building. By then his position both domestically and abroad was secure, his finances largely recovered from the disaster of the Pazzi war, and Florence itself prospering during a welcome interlude of peace, for which Lorenzo could claim much of the credit. Indeed Lorenzo seemed merely to be riding the crest of a wave that saw an explosion of new building in Florence, spurred on in part by a lenient tax policy that he himself had promoted. His purpose in revising the tax code in 1489, which provided an exemption to those who improved their land in the city, was, "in the manner of his ancestors . . . to make the city larger and more beautiful."

Evidence suggests that had Lorenzo lived even a few years longer his imprint on the city would have surpassed that left by Cosimo. The impression one has of Lorenzo as a less dedicated builder that his grandfather is due in part to the accidents of history and to his own premature death. Many of the structures completed under his supervision—including his villa at Spedaletto and the monastery of San Gallo—have not survived, while plans have been discovered for large-scale projects that he never had time to implement. In the late 1480s, for instance, he began a second major building program near the church of the SS. Annunziata; the so-called Via Laura project was to include a vast palace and gardens for his personal use, the encircling of the Annunziata piazza with colonnades that would complement the famous loggia of the foundling hospital by Brunelleschi, and the construction of two new roads lined with new housing. This "embellishment to the city," as one contemporary called it, was brought to a sudden halt by his death. A drawing for the palace by his favorite architect, Giuliano da San Gallo, gives some idea of Lorenzo's ambitions at this time and reveals the extent to which he now seemed to have felt himself liberated from the restraints of the city's republican traditions. Dwarfing even the Pitti palace, Lorenzo's new home would have been of truly princely dimensions, though it is not certain that it was ever more than a fanciful dream.

At the Porta San Gallo that opened out onto the road that led to Careggi, this same architect was put to work constructing a monastery for the Augustinian friars. "Lorenzo de' Medici [is] paying the lion's share of the expense," wrote Bartolomeo Dei, "and is the inspiration behind the building." It was, in fact, from working on this building that Giuliano Giamberti received the name by which he is known to history:

> For this convent models were made by many architects, and in the end that of Giuliano was put into execution, [wrote Vasari] which was the reason that Lorenzo, from this work, gave him the name of Giuliano da San Gallo. Wherefore Giuliano, who heard himself called by everyone "da San Gallo," said one day in jest to the Magnificent Lorenzo, "By giving me this new name of 'da San Gallo,' you are making me lose the ancient name of my house, so that, in place of going forward in the matter of lineage, as I thought to do, I am going backward." Whereupon Lorenzo answered that he would rather have him become the founder of a new house through his own worth, than depend on others; at which Giuliano was content.

Like most of Lorenzo's urban schemes, the Augustinian convent did not withstand the ravages of time, having been destroyed by anti-Medici forces during a siege early in the following century. Fate has been kinder to those building projects Lorenzo initiated at a distance from the urban center, particularly the villa Ambra at Poggio a Caiano. On no project did he devote more time, money, and energy than to the building of this country retreat on land ten miles to the west of the city center he had earlier purchased from Giovanni Rucellai. On this pleasant hilltop site with a view of his vast estates and of the swiftly flowing river Ombrone, Lorenzo created a model of the ideal country villa, setting a pattern for country living just as Cosimo had earlier set the pattern for the urban palace. It anticipated the future not only in the grace of its architectural forms but by embodying a new ethic, one that emphasized reason over the raw display of power and that celebrated a life dedicated to the cultivation of the muses.

So enamored was Lorenzo of this spot that it inspired one of his most lovely evocations of the Tuscan countryside. The poem "Ambra," the name of both the villa and the nymph who is the object of the river god Ombrone's unwanted attentions, begins with a description of the autumn landscape that is typically Lorenzan in the precision of its observations:

Fled is the time of year that turned the flowers
Into ripe apples, long since gathered in.
The leaves, no longer cleaving to the boughs,
Lie strewn throughout the woods, now much less dense,
And rustle should a hunter pass that way,
A few of whom will sound like many more.
Though the wild beast conceals her wandering tracks,
She cannot cross those brittle leaves unheard.

The stately retreat he worked on almost obsessively in the last years of his life, in close collaboration with Giuliano da San Gallo, would generate a host of imitations through the ages, from the villas of Palladio to the Palladio-inspired country estates of England, and from there to the New World, where at Mount Vernon and Monticello the Founding Fathers would construct their homes very much in the spirit of the First Citizen of Florence.

At Poggio a Caiano, Lorenzo put into practice the ideas he had absorbed from his close study of ancient architecture and his close reading of Alberti's treatise. The villas Lorenzo had grown up in, particularly Trebbio and Cafaggiolo, were medieval fortresses whose bristling battlements bespoke a certain insecurity, if not paranoia. This was hardly the image that Lorenzo wished to project. "I do not approve of turrets and crenellations on the houses of private citizens and the well-ordered state," Alberti had written: "they belong rather to the tyrant, in that they imply the presence of fear or of malicious intent." The man at the head of a well-ordered state should strive to achieve the same qualities of measure and serenity in his own residence. At Poggio a Caiano, Lorenzo was determined that there be no visible means of protection other than the love the people bore him. (His own bodyguards were apparently less sanguine, and remained nervous about the lack of adequate means of defense.) Standing serene and white upon its lofty perch, the villa's elegant classical forms are a monument to reason and harmonious proportion that seem to defy even the possibility of violent passion. As if to emphasize this irenic theme, on the frieze beneath the classical pediment Lorenzo had Bertoldo sculpt a painted terra-cotta frieze evoking Virgil's Golden Age. Depicting scenes of peace and plenty, Bertoldo's relief conveys the message writ large in the neatly arranged landscape as a whole, that under the wise stewardship of Lorenzo Florence had become an earthly paradise.

But for all its sophistication, Ambra was never simply a pleasure palace. It was very much a working farm, and Lorenzo, far from being one of those gentlemen who prefer the idea of rustic life to its grubby reality, took an active role in its management. Lorenzo, in fact, proved himself a much better manager of his estates than he was a banker, no doubt one of the reasons he reinvested so much of his wealth in land. It was also true that Lorenzo shared the prejudices of the age that regarded wealth tied up in land as more aristocratic than wealth acquired through trade or finance. But when it came to real estate Lorenzo exhibited the bottom-line mentality of his mercantile ancestors rather than the feudal sensibilities of the knightly class. Instead of viewing his acreage as primarily a sign of status or as land to be set aside for such princely pursuits as hunting and hawking, Lorenzo actively worked at improving his property, trying to squeeze the maximum amount of profit and efficiency. In 1489, for instance, he told Gentile Becchi that he had planted numerous mulberry trees at Poggio in order to produce silk for Florence's busy looms. In this same letter he also showed off his practical knowledge by declaring, "I have learned that when [the saplings] are tender and young only a stout and thick stake can defend them from the wind."

No doubt Lorenzo put up many of those stakes himself. Like Cosimo, he found physical labor therapeutic and, to the extent his crippled body allowed, worked on his estates alongside the hired hands, sweating in the summer sun and braving the December chill. But for all the time he spent on his favorite project, Poggio a Caiano was but the most prominent of the many building projects Lorenzo was involved in during the last decade of his life. From Spedaletto near Volterra and Agnano near Pisa, Lorenzo showed an insatiable appetite for acquiring new properties and building on them. In real estate, as in politics, he did not necessarily play by the rules. He was not above using his political authority to intimidate those who held property he wanted to add to his own holdings. One cleric whose land abutted Lorenzo's villa at Agnano admitted, "I don't dare contradict him," certain that "one way or another" the Lord of Florence would get his way.

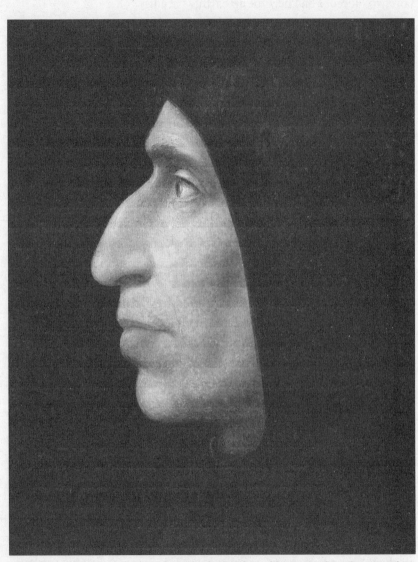

Fra Bartolomeo, *Portrait of Girolamo Savonarola*, c. 1498 (Art Resource)

XX. THE CARDINAL AND THE PREACHER

"Here is a stranger come into my house who will not even deign to visit me."

—LORENZO ON SAVONAROLA

Who from perennial streams shall bring
Of gushing floods a ceaseless spring?
That through the day, in hopeless woe
And through the night my tears may flow. . . .
As the sad nightingale complains,
I pour my anguish and my strains.
Ah, wretched, wretched, past relief;
Oh, grief beyond all other grief!

—ANGELO POLIZIANO ON
LORENZO'S DEATH

"THIS IS AN AGE OF GOLD," WROTE LORENZO'S FRIEND Marsilio Ficino with pride, "which has brought back to life the almost extinguished liberal disciplines of poetry, eloquence, painting, architecture, sculpture, music. . . . And all this at Florence!" Most of his compatriots shared this optimistic vision. Florence in the 1480s was at peace with its neighbors and prosperous at home. The humming silk looms near the Porta San Gallo and the exotic goods piled high in the *Mercato Vecchio* testified to the revitalized economy and, adorned on every street corner and in every parish church by works of genius, the city on the Arno continued to cast its spell on lovers of art and learning

For the man at the center of all this activity, however, these years brought more than their share of troubles and sorrow. Lorenzo would not

407

turn forty until almost the end of the decade, but already he seemed to possess the body of a much older man; his once powerful frame was bent as gout and arthritis spread through his limbs. He knew he would not achieve the ripe old age of Cosimo, who had died at seventy-five; now even his father's fifty-three years seemed out of reach. The death of his uncle Giovanni at forty-two seemed a premonition of his own fate.

Adding to these burdens was the grim spectacle of Clarice's slow wasting from consumption. It is an indication of how much his own ill health had come to dominate his life that when she finally succumbed on July 29, 1487, Lorenzo was away from Florence, attending to his own ailments at the mineral baths at Filetta. He was still in too much pain to return to Florence for her funeral, which took place a few days later in San Lorenzo. Even in this era when men were not expected to treat their wives as equals, many reproached Lorenzo for his apparent callousness. The criticism was so widespread that at least one friend felt the need to defend him against these slanders. "If you should hear Lorenzo blamed for not being at his wife's death, make excuses for him," he wrote to the Florentine ambassador in Rome. "Leoni his physician considered it imperative for his health to go to the baths and no one had any idea that Madonna Clarice's death was so near."

Even granting extenuating circumstances, it is hard to escape the conclusion that Clarice was not, and never had been, the center of his life. In truth, their relationship ended very much as it had begun—with Lorenzo wrapped up in his own affairs and Clarice forced to endure her husband's inattentiveness. In his own way he was devoted to his wife and to his family, but the domestic realm over which she presided could not hold the attention of this restless and ambitious man. Nonetheless her death was a severe blow. Two days later he vented his feelings in a letter to Pope Innocent:

Too often I am obliged to trouble and worry Your Beatitude with accidents sent by fortune and divine interposition, which as they are not to be resisted must be borne with patience. But the death of Clarice, which has just occurred, my most dear and beloved wife, has been and is so prejudicial, so great a loss, and such a grief to me for many reasons, that it has exhausted my patience and my power of enduring anguish, and the persecution of fortune, which I did not think would have made me suffer thus. The deprivation of such habitual and such sweet company has filled my cup and has made me so miserable that I can find no peace. Naught is left but to pray God that He may give me peace, and I have faith that in His infinite love He will alleviate my sorrow and not overwhelm me with so many disasters as I have endured during these last years.

There is no reason to doubt the sincerity of these words. For almost two decades she had shared his bed, if not exclusively, then at least with sufficient regularity that she bore him seven healthy children. The children bound them together in common purpose and the well-being of their children was the main object of Lorenzo and Clarice's collaborative effort. Indeed, securing the future of their children was the one goal to which they both contributed equally and the one thing that could unite two minds that otherwise shared few interests.

Clarice's death had the effect of drawing Lorenzo closer to his children, particularly his daughters. Their mutual affection comes through clearly in a letter Lorenzo wrote to the eleven-year-old Contessina: "My Contessina. I hear that you ask about me every hour, how I am and when I shall return, so I write to tell you that, by the grace of God, I am very well, and I hope, if it pleases God, to return as well as ever I was. I shall come back soon, and in a few days I shall be there to see you. Take care that I find you well and cheerful."

Like many a firstborn son, Lorenzo had grown accustomed to the doting attention of the female members of his family, and now that Clarice was gone this role was taken over by his sister Bianca and by his daughters, particularly Maddalena. Even after Maddalena had been espoused to the pope's bastard son, Lorenzo wished to have her by his side: "I should be glad if you could mention the matter to his Holiness and get it arranged that Maddalena should remain here for the rest of the summer and autumn [1487]. I have not so far had time to see my daughter comfortably, so I earnestly beg His Holiness that of his kindness he will let me have her a few months more."

As his health worsened, Lorenzo was consumed with providing for his children's future. Though his own position in Florence seemed unassailable, the deliberate ambiguity of the Medici role in government made the transition from one generation to the next a perilous undertaking. Lorenzo expected that, initially at least, his oldest son would be accepted by the *reggimento,* but doubts about Piero's character and about the loyalty of the Florentine people continued to haunt him. Of utmost importance was finding a bride for Piero, who turned sixteen at the beginning of 1487. Ready or not, Piero would soon be forced to step into a role of greater responsibility.

Like his father, Lorenzo was determined to look outside the circle of eligible Florentine families. There is no doubt that the selection of Clarice Orsini contributed to the ill will that eventually culminated in the Pazzi conspiracy, but now the Medici were simply too exalted to consider marrying their oldest son to one of the local girls. Piero's bride would come from a powerful foreign family whose aristocratic pedigree could further the Medici's dynastic ambitions.* Lorenzo ultimately settled on Alfonsina Orsini, daughter of the grand constable of Naples, a man whose martial feats of arms earned him the nickname, "The Knight Without Fear."

At first glance the thirteen-year-old seems a curious choice. It was certainly not Alfonsina's personal charms that recommended her (Bernardo Rucellai reported, "She does not seem particularly good or bad"). Nor did strengthening their ties to the Orsini initially appear to offer great advantages. Lorenzo once complained of his in-laws, "The brains of these Orsini citizens are of a strange and peculiar nature . . . they are greedy and ambitious, and if not kept in order by necessity, they are unstable."

Given this track record, why did he seek to bind himself more closely to this great but lawless clan? In part, Lorenzo seems to have believed that the best way to ensure future Medici greatness was through the inclusion of his descendants among the feudal nobility.† Critically, Alfonsina belonged to the Neapolitan branch of the clan, and this connection could prove to be a great help at a time when Lorenzo was seeking to increase his influence in the southern kingdom. Though the Medici could not hope to marry into the royal house itself, they had achieved the next best thing.

---

* The difficulty of making the transition from merchant banker to feudal noble is illustrated by a Florentine who noted that Piero was described in the French court as "the Great Money-Changer, because he did not have any legitimate title of lord in Florence."

† History has vindicated Lorenzo's strategy. While the republic had little future in a Europe soon to be dominated by vast nation states, the Medici "money-changers" endured by marrying into the great noble families, including the royal house of France, where Medici queens became mothers to French kings.

The wedding, carried out by proxy, was held in the royal palace of Naples in February of 1488, with the king and queen and all their court in attendance, gratifying recognition once again of how far this family of bankers had come from their humble origins.

Piero's marriage also confirmed the slant of Lorenzo's foreign policy in the aftermath of the Pazzi war. In 1486 when war broke out between the pope and the kingdom of Naples, Lorenzo remained committed to the Neapolitan side despite the misgivings of his compatriots, who remembered that not so long ago Ferrante's armies had marched almost to the gates of Florence itself. "To me," wrote Giovanni Lanfredini, conveying the mood of mistrust, "it seems the King is arrogant and vile to those he cannot ride." Lorenzo's pro-Aragonese policy in the so-called Barons War* was motivated less by the merits of his cause—no one was more aware of Ferrante's capacity for treachery than Lorenzo himself—but because he knew he could not afford to offend the leader of one of the peninsula's two great military powers, particularly at a time when his relations with Lodovico Sforza were strained. The papacy, by contrast, would always be an unreliable friend, more capable of causing mischief than building constructive, long-term alliances. "[T]his ecclesiastical state has always been the ruin of Italy," Lorenzo grumbled, "because they are ignoramuses and they know nothing of governing states, and so they endanger the entire world."

The wisdom of Lorenzo's pro-Naples policy was quickly demonstrated as Ferrante marched his armies within sight of St. Peter's. Though they were turned back at the last minute by the redoubtable Cardinal Giuliano della Rovere, it was clear that the pope was in no position to challenge the Neapolitan army on the battlefield. In August of 1486 peace was concluded between Ferrante and the pope that narrowly averted a wider European conflagration.

Though Lorenzo appeared to be firmly on the side of Naples, he realized that the security of both the city and of his family could not be achieved without the goodwill of the man who sat on St. Peter's throne. Innocent's incessant squabbling with his southern neighbor made such a rapprochement difficult, but after his recent thumping at the hands of Ferrante's armies he seemed more amenable to a policy of detente. It was,

---

* It was referred to as the Barons War because it began with a rebellion by the feudal barons against King Ferrante and the ruling house of Aragon.

in fact, Innocent who made the first move. In November 1486, Pierfilippo Pandolfini relayed a message from Innocent to Lorenzo. "Lorenzo will know that there was never a pope who so loved his house as I do," he quoted Innocent. "And having seen from experience his faith, integrity, and wisdom, I will govern myself according to his thoughts and wishes." Lorenzo, despite some initial skepticism, was soon convinced that the pope's desire for peace was genuine. He explained his change of course in a letter to his brother-in-law Bernardo Rucellai: "We have been for twelve or perhaps thirteen years always in contumacy with the church, and most of the time in open war. And you know very well how much of a burden I, in particular, have shouldered, because this city inclines naturally towards the church. I believe that had I refused this union, I would have suffered greatly with the people."

Pursuing a policy of rapprochement with the pope, while at the same time keeping the mercurial Ferrante on board, was the kind of diplomatic juggling act Lorenzo had now grown accustomed to and that was well worth the trouble if it kept Italy from plunging once again into war. Never far from Lorenzo's mind, however, were the profits his own family might reap if he could restore the Medici to their old standing in the Vatican. The explanation for the success of this policy, when similar attempts to find a modus vivendi with Sixtus had failed so miserably, can be attributed largely to the character of Innocent himself. Unlike Sixtus, Innocent was a man of fundamentally peaceful instincts. Devoted to his own comfort, Innocent preferred whenever possible to avoid anything that would detract from his enjoyment of the perquisites of his office. Another factor was that, again in stark contrast to Sixtus, he was indecisive and in need of a guide to lead him through a geopolitical landscape whose treacherous terrain he could barely discern. "The Pope seems rather a man in need of advice than one capable of giving it to others," explained one of Lorenzo's agents in Rome. Lorenzo, now acclaimed as the unsurpassed statesman of Italy, seemed just the man to take him by the hand and show him the way.

In his handling of Innocent, Lorenzo demonstrated once again his knack for tailoring his diplomacy to the goal at hand and to the people involved. It helped that Innocent had a taste for the kinds of things that Medici money and connections could easily supply; learning of the pope's fondness for ortolans (small birds prized by epicurean palates), Lorenzo made sure that every courier to Rome was supplied with some for the pope's table, as well as a barrel or two of the local *vernaccia* to wash them down. For Innocent the benefits of friendship with Lorenzo came not only in the form of tasty treats carried in Medici saddlebags, but in access to ready credit. Sixtus's extravagant building projects and even more wasteful foreign adventures had practically bankrupted the Holy See, and the Medici bank, while still not fully recovered from the disasters of recent years, remained among the largest financial concerns in Europe.

Lorenzo was anticipating equally tangible benefits. The Medici bank profited from the restoration of good relations with the pope almost immediately as Innocent ordered the repayment of the papal debts reneged on by Sixtus. Much more was to follow. Perhaps most gratifying was Innocent's restoration in 1488 of the valuable alum concession withdrawn by Sixtus after the Imola affair, a move that returned the Medici bank to the dominant position in Rome it had enjoyed in the reign of Paul II. Giovanni Tornabuoni exulted, "our affairs here, as I have told you, succeed better and better every day because of the love and affection Our Lord feels towards you."*

The pope's new attitude also paid dividends on the military front. Innocent raised no objection when in the spring of 1487 Lorenzo reopened the campaign against the Genoese-held fortress of Sarzana. In fact the pope was now so anxious to retain Lorenzo's good opinion that he put pressure on his compatriots to cede the strategic stronghold to the Florentines. Lorenzo took an active personal interest in the progress of the Florentine troops, riding out to camp when it appeared the siege had stalled. Shortly after his arrival the Genoese capitulated, adding one more feather to Lorenzo's still rather sparse military headdress. "The Magnificent Lorenzo arrived here [Florence] on the vigil of S. Giovanni [June 23]," recorded the Ferrarese ambassador, "and was received with more joy and caresses by the people than I can describe, as they say they owe the taking of Sarzana to him more than to others."

Equally important to Lorenzo was his belief that his improved relations

---

* De Roover's analysis demonstrates that the bank did not in fact prosper during the reign of Innocent as Lorenzo and Giovanni Tornabuoni had hoped. (See *The Rise and Decline of the Medici Bank,* especially pp. 222–24 and 356–375.) Heavy borrowing by the pope and by Lorenzo's Orsini relatives ate away at profits. The main benefits, ultimately, were political and dynastic, but these shouldn't be underestimated.

with the Holy Father might well revive the dream, long deferred, of having a cardinal in the family. It was largely with this goal in mind that he agreed to the betrothal of Maddalena to Franceschetto Cibo, Innocent's fat, hard-drinking, hard-gambling son, in March 1487.* Lorenzo was saddened by the prospect of having to part with his beloved daughter, particularly to someone as unprepossessing as Francesco, but the benefits of such a connection could not be passed up.

Lorenzo had good reason to be concerned for Maddalena's happiness. Most distressing to her father was the fact that the forty-year-old Francesco proved to be an inconsiderate husband to the frail fifteen-year-old girl. "The bad health of Madonna Maddalena and the thoughtless behavior of my Lord [Francesco Cibo] in keeping her up," complained Matteo Franco, who had accompanied her to Rome as her chaplain, "for all this winter he has gambled every night, supping at six or seven and coming to bed at daylight, and she will not, and cannot, eat or sleep without him. Thus she has lost sleep and appetite and has become as thin as a lizard." Adding to Lorenzo's worries was the uncertain future for anyone whose status depended on his relationship with the reigning pope. While Lorenzo had provided for the newlyweds by bestowing on the couple the Pazzi villa at Montughi (where the final plans for the Pazzi conspiracy had been laid) and another at Spedaletto, he had difficulty persuading Franceschetto's father to provide adequately for his son. "It is urgent that his Holiness should once and for all arrange the affairs of *Signor* Francesco so that I should not be daily worried about them," Lorenzo wrote to Innocent in October 1489, "and that we can live in peace and harmony. To speak plainly, *Signor* Francesco has not the position the nephew† of a Pope ought to have, and yet we are now approaching the seventh year of the Pontificate." One wonders if Lorenzo saw the irony in the situation, which exactly reversed the one that prevailed in the previous regime when Sixtus's anxiety to provide for *his* family caused the Medici no end of trouble.

It was impossible to conceal the truth that Maddalena's happiness had

---

* Francesco lost so much gambling at cards to Raffaele Riario, the same young man who had been used as the dupe in the Pazzi conspiracy, that the cardinal used the windfall to build the famous Palazzo della Cancelleria in Rome.

† Though Innocent frankly acknowledged Franceschetto as his own son, Lorenzo apparently felt it necessary to maintain the fiction, at least when putting pen to paper.

been sacrificed for the greater glory of the Medici family. A bit of contemporary doggerel summed up the bargain Lorenzo had struck:

> *To join the Medici girl to his son Franceschetti,*
> *Innocent made a little boy a cardinal.*
> *If it's true that the Holy Spirit*
> *makes the pope superhuman,*
> *in this case the Holy Spirit*
> *made him a matchmaker.*

The little boy in question was Lorenzo's second son, Giovanni, a studious lad who from the beginning had been groomed for a life in the Church. "He is so strictly bred," remarked his tutor, Poliziano, "that never from his mouth comes a lewd or even a light expression. He does not yield to his teachers in learning, nor to old men in gravity of manner." In laying the groundwork for Giovanni's ecclesiastical career, Lorenzo was far more deliberate than he had been in the case of his brother. Giovanni's bookish tastes made him a more suitable candidate, and his early education, despite Poliziano's preference for basing the boy's lessons on pagan authors, had been arranged with an eye to preparing him for a life in the Church. At the tender age of seven he had taken holy orders, and from then on Lorenzo kept up a continual pressure to ensure that local cathedrals held positions open for him. Additional plums for Giovanni were plucked from abroad. As a reward for Lorenzo's helpful role in the Barons War, Ferrante had bestowed on the boy the wealthy Benedictine abbey of Montecassino, while Lodovico Sforza had chipped in with the equally remunerative Miramodo near Milan. Lorenzo also went trawling for likely prospects in French waters where his friendship with the king gave him a leg up on the competition. On one occasion the king proved a little overzealous and was forced to withdraw the particularly rich prize of Aix after discovering that the current occupant was not dead as had been reported.

By 1487, the year of Maddalena's wedding, Giovanni was a plump lad of twelve with a taste for fine food, fine clothes, and classical literature. The twenty-seven benefices he now held provided the adolescent with a handsome yearly income, sufficient even for someone of his expensive habits. Lorenzo left nothing to chance in his campaign to further Giovanni's career, flattering, cajoling, and otherwise tending to the needs of the Holy

Father. He had gained such influence in the Vatican that the Ferrarese ambassador grumbled, "the Pope sleeps with the eyes of the Magnificent Lorenzo," while the Neapolitan ambassador claimed "that the Florentine ambassador . . . governs the policy of Rome."

Lorenzo did not have long to wait for his reward. On March 10, 1489, a large crowd of jubilant citizens began to gather around the Medici palace. "We had heard," wrote the apothecary Luca Landucci, "that the Pope had made six cardinals, who were as follows: two French, one Milanese, two of his nephews [shades of Sixtus], and one Florentine, son of Lorenzo de' Medici. Thank God! It is a great honor to our city in general, and in particular to his father and his house." The spontaneous joy of the Florentine people reveals the extent to which most had come to identify with the ruling family, believing that when a Medici distinguished himself the entire nation could take pride in the achievement. Lorenzo was overjoyed, declaring the news to be "the greatest honor that has ever befallen our house." In naming Giovanni Cardinal Deacon of Santa Maria in Domenica, Innocent had fulfilled the dream of the family that was generations old. Now, surely, the Medici could count themselves among the great families of Europe. In Machiavelli's memorable phrase, Giovanni's elevation "was a ladder enabling [Lorenzo's] house to rise to heaven."

The one sour note was the pope's irritation at Lorenzo for having publicized an appointment that Innocent wished to keep secret. Given the inconvenient fact of Giovanni's extreme youth—at thirteen, he was the youngest cardinal ever appointed—Innocent had instructed Lorenzo to keep quiet for three years until his elevation would appear less of an embarrassment. But Lorenzo had no intention of keeping such spectacular news secret, excusing himself on the grounds "that [the nomination] was a thing of such public notoriety in Rome that people here can hardly be blamed for following the example set there, and I could not refuse to accept the congratulations of all these citizens, down to the very poorest. If it was unseemly it was impossible to prevent." Lorenzo was being disingenuous: while he was correct when he said such matters were difficult to suppress, he never had any intention of forgoing the benefits that would come his way as soon as people learned of Giovanni's elevation. No one could doubt now that the pope was Lorenzo's creature through and through, and anyone who had business with the Holy Father—which was to say pretty much anyone in a position of authority in Europe and beyond—had to take into consideration the feelings and interests of the First Citizen of Florence.

Settling the future of his two oldest sons was the key to putting the family's fortunes on a firm foundation, but his other children had their part to play as well in the dynastic game. In selecting spouses for his remaining children, Lorenzo was motivated largely by the need to heal the wounds that had been opened up in the body politic by the Medici's sudden rise into the aristocracy of Europe. Though he had crushed the Pazzi, who in any case seemed to have little support, Lorenzo understood that among the ancient families of Florence there remained a reservoir of ill feeling that would need to be drained were his family to avoid a repetition of that sorry episode. With this in mind, in 1488 he espoused his oldest daughter, Lucrezia, to Jacopo Salviati (cousin of the infamous archbishop), thus hoping to draw the fangs of those who still sympathized with the Pazzi cause. In an effort to close the rift that had opened up between the branches of the family descended from Giovanni di Bicci's two sons, Luigia, Lorenzo's third daughter, was promised to Giovanni de' Medici, a descendant of Pierfrancesco. (Her untimely death in 1488, when she was only eleven, dashed hopes of an easy reconciliation.) Following a similar pattern of building up local alliances, Contessina was espoused to Piero Ridolfi, from an old and distinguished Florentine family long allied with the Medici, a final effort to demonstrate that they had not risen so high that they had forgotten their neighbors.*

---

* Lorenzo's youngest son, Giuliano, did not marry until 1515 when he took a princess of the French royal house for his bride. The fruits of Lorenzo's matchmaking were to have long-term consequences for the history of Europe. One granddaughter of Piero and Alfonsina was Catherine de' Medici, wife of Henry II, King of France and mother of François II. Cosimo I, the first grand duke of Tuscany, was a grandson of Lucrezia, as well as a Medici through his father, the famous *condottiere* Giovanni of the Black Bands, descended from Pierfrancesco de' Medici. Two of Lorenzo's descendants who are more famous than they deserve are his son Giuliano and his grandson Lorenzo (son of Piero), who are known to history primarily as the occupants of Michelangelo's famous tombs in San Lorenzo. His nephew Giulio, whom Lucrezia had brought to the palace after Giuliano's assassination and who was raised as one of the family, was destined for a life in the Church. Elevated to cardinal by his cousin Giovanni, he also became a pope. As Clement VII he was the reigning pope during the horrific sack of Rome by Hapsburg troops in 1527.

• • •

It was not only through marrying off his children that Lorenzo worked to bridge the gulf that had opened up between the first citizen and the people of Florence, a gulf that only widened with each new Medici triumph and with each new proof that Republican government, and the social compact it implied between the leading families of the city, was failing. The ancient institutions—the *Signoria* in their splendid ermine-lined robes, the bois-terous councils of the People and of the Commune where democratic sen-timent still ran strong—continued to meet in the Palace of the Priors, but they were reduced to little more than a pantomime meant to distract the citizens while the real business of government went on behind closed doors wherever Lorenzo met with his cronies.

Instinctively, and without any well-thought-out plan, Lorenzo was groping toward another kind of leadership, one based on his personal aura, on his achievements and his character—in a word, on his *Magnifi-cence*—rather than on the fickle coalitions and deal-making that charac-terized Florentine politics in the past. This personal style of leadership had been implicit from the beginning as his parents trotted out the lisping infant in full regalia to star in the city's many processions and pageants. It had continued in the cult of youth built around him and his brother, Giu-liano. After his accession to power, and especially after the Pazzi conspir-acy, Lorenzo had eschewed such obvious glamour, but only in order to project an image of himself as a sober statesman, father to his people. To retain a hold on his fellow citizens after he had eviscerated the institutions through which political legitimacy was conferred, he had to create a "charismatic center" without offending his fellow citizens by assuming the trappings of royalty. He did this, above all, by leading the life of an *exem-plary* citizen, doing more and doing better those things that were expected of any man of substance. If charity was the obligation of every Christian, he was a paragon of pious giving; if a gentleman was supposed to be learned, Lorenzo was a scholar beyond compare. In an age that valued the well-rounded person, Lorenzo's mastery of all the noble pursuits of mind and body astounded even those accustomed to talented polymaths. Nor was he shy about trumpeting his accomplishments since he knew that they raised his standing in the eyes of his compatriots. And the men who supped at his table and enjoyed the comforts of his home knew how to repay his generosity by singing his praises: "Blest in your genius," wrote Poliziano of his patron,

> *your capacious mind*
> *Not to one science or one theme confined*
> *By grateful interchange fatigue beguiles*
> *In private studies and in public toils.*

This aura of magnificence was cultivated as well through his material possessions, which betokened not only immense wealth but refinement of mind. The reach of the Medici banking empire through space and time was manifest in his home filled with Flemish tapestries and swords of damascene steel forged in the armories of the Levant, in ancient statues dug from the ground and manuscripts unearthed from dusty libraries. Those lucky enough to receive an invitation spread the word of the dazzling collections of objets d'arts to which he was daily adding, so that the palace on the Via Larga, so austere on the outside, began to seem like the fabled treasury of some Oriental potentate.

To those not easily impressed by such intangibles he had other, more practical, gifts to bestow. Using his own private funds and the unparalleled resources of the Medici bank, he ensured a steady supply of grain to the city that kept the price of bread low. Lorenzo's own coin flowed into the poorest sections of the city where he knew he was purchasing goodwill that he could tap into in times of crisis.* For those who worried about Florence's standing in the world, Lorenzo's personal prestige only added to the credit of the city as a whole. He was a friend of kings, and now of popes, correspondent with all the mighty of Europe, who sought his advice on a wide range of subjects. Even the Ottoman sultan thought so highly of Lorenzo that he sent lions and giraffes to populate his private

---

* Guicciardini's account of Lorenzo's death is revealing. "It was also a great sorrow to the population of the city, especially to the lower classes, always kept by him in abundance, with many pleasures, entertainments, and feasts. It grieved all those in Italy who excelled in letters, painting, sculpture and similar arts, because either they were commissioned by him with lavish salaries or they were held in higher esteem by the other princes who feared that if they did not make much of them they would go off to Lorenzo." (Guicciardini, *The History of Florence*, IX.)

menagerie. In time he was called simply *il Magnifico*, the term of respect used to denote any person of wealth and rank, now clinging to him almost as a title and testifying to his unique claim on the loyalty of his people. His authority had been built over years of careful maneuvering, but in the end it rested on his countrymen's recognition that, in the phrase of one his critics, Lorenzo was the greatest Florentine in history.

Despite this carefully crafted image, Lorenzo's success depended equally on his ability to convince the people that he was one of them. His style of leadership was grand but not aloof. To the end of his life he remained very much the citizen of Florence, greeting supporters and meeting with petitioners in the piazza or in church. According to one account, Lorenzo held daily audiences in the public square "to whomever wanted it." When his portrait is included in contemporary paintings, as in the Sassetti chapel, there is nothing that distinguishes him from his fellow citizens. Indeed, Lorenzo's presence in the lives of his subjects was far more intimate and human-scaled than that of any king. His authority was reinforced through the symbolism of intimacy rather than of awe, a symbolism he projected, particularly in the last five years of his life, through the public ceremonies and festivals that filled the Florentine calendar.

Lorenzo's well-publicized return to the stage of Florentine life, which began a full decade after the murder of his brother, marked the reversal of a long-term trend. After his youth, in which he had been the star attraction on many an occasion, culminating in his own joust of 1469, he had avoided putting himself on public display. The desire to withdraw from the public eye seems to have been at least partly psychological. In his *Commento* Lorenzo recalled being dragged to a festival by his friends "almost against my will . . . for I had been for some time rather alienated from such occasions." But political considerations played a part as well. Even before the Pazzi conspiracy, Lorenzo had sought to diminish the June feast of St. John the Baptist, the traditional celebration of the Florentine commune. His grudging attitude toward this festival is confirmed in a reproachful letter Luigi Pulci wrote him in 1472: "I am a little amazed that you have diminished this *festa* as much as you have. You are after all a citizen and fond of the *patria*, of which the Baptist is protector, and we ought to honor him." But this was exactly the problem: in a city ever more firmly dominated by one family, such a communal festival seemed at odds with the new reality.

This austerity was more pronounced in the wake of his brother's murder as if the entire city had entered an extended period of mourning. But as Lorenzo grew more secure, and as the shock and bitterness of that troubled time wore off, he began to relax this ascetic policy and to interject himself more insistently into the public consciousness. This time, however, instead of putting himself on display, he preferred to play a strictly behind-the-scenes role. In June of 1488, partly to celebrate the marriage of Maddalena and Francesco Cibo, Lorenzo breathed new life into the Feast of St. John by allowing the elaborate floats that had once been the glory of the parade. It was as if Lorenzo sensed that he was in danger of losing the hearts and minds of the people even as he gripped more tightly the levers of power. As Machiavelli notes in his *Histories,* the Medici generally followed "bread and circuses" policy meant to keep the people distracted and entertained. "[I]n these peaceful times," he observed, "[Lorenzo] kept his fatherland always in festivities: there frequent jousts and representations of old deeds and triumphs were to be seen; and his aim was to keep the city in abundance, the people united, and the nobility honored."

But while the traditional communal festivals were revived, it was with a difference. Lorenzo took a particular interest in Carnival, a peculiar choice since this bacchanal was considered by many to be a "feast of the devil." Carnival, as opposed to the more civic-minded feast of St. John, had long been an occasion for aristocratic families to show off their wealth and power, and Lorenzo may well have intended to wrest this popular celebration from oligarchic control. Under Lorenzo's management it shed some of its aristocratic exclusivity and embraced both rich and poor in a symbolic reconciliation of the entire community. The very young and the very poor, groups previously marginalized, were now encouraged to form associations where they gained a sense of pride and common purpose. Lorenzo promoted the formation of new confraternities made up of young boys and of members of the economic underclass, each marching under their own banners, developing their own rituals, and discovering in the process a new sense of identity.

Formation of these new ritual groups eased some of the social tensions that characterized Florentine society. They also provided Lorenzo a means of insinuating himself more directly into people's lives. A confraternity made up of those who had previously been without a voice, organized under Lorenzo's aegis, was much more likely to be loyal to him than an institution like the Guelf Party that had deep roots in the oligarchic past.

One newly founded group was that of the wool-beaters (*battilani*), among the poorest of the urban proletariat, whose charter was approved by the government in 1488, reversing a century-and-a-half prohibition against such working-class associations. In 1489 Lorenzo inserted himself even more blatantly into the picture when he lent his own personal tableware—emblazoned with the red balls of the Medici crest—for the table of the "king" of the Oltrarno wool-workers during their May Day celebrations.

All of this was part of a larger effort to place himself at the imaginative and emotional heart of the republic. While Lorenzo was always something less than a king in terms of his legal authority, in other ways he went beyond the traditional role of a head of state. Perhaps it was because he did not possess a monarch's rigid dignity that he was able to participate personally in the rituals of his fellow citizens, designing the floats, choreographing the festivities, scripting the sacred dramas, and writing the words that were sung by choirs as they marched through the streets. In 1491 he composed his play *The Martyrdom of Saints John and Paul,* for one of these newly formed youth organizations, the Vangelista, a boys confraternity in which his youngest son, Giuliano, was enrolled. The same year the Company of the Star was formed to stage the elaborate symbolic programs that Lorenzo was now orchestrating:

> Lorenzo de' Medici having conceived the idea, he had the Company of the Star construct fifteen *trionfi* [floats] designed by him [recorded Tribaldo de' Rossi]. [They showed] Aemilius Paulus triumphing in Rome on returning from a city with so much treasure that Rome's populace never paid taxes for forty or fifty years, so much treasure had he conquered. . . . As Aemilius Paulus had provided such booty at the time of Caesar Augustus, Lorenzo de' Medici provided it [now]. There were five richly caparisoned squadrons of horses in battle dress alongside the said *trionfi*, and [Lorenzo] had them brought from their stables to take part in this tribute. Forty or fifty pairs of oxen pulled the said *trionfi*. It was considered the worthiest thing that had ever processed on San Giovanni.

The propagandistic intent of such productions is evident, but it would be a mistake to believe that Lorenzo was motivated exclusively by political considerations. "We're going forth to pleasure all," sing the lovely damsels in Lorenzo's "Song of the Cicadas,"

"As is the law of Carnival. . . .
What good will be our loveliness
If as we chatter it grows less.
Long live love and gentle manners!
Death to envy and to slanders!
Talk, then, you who love hearsay
While you prattle, we will play!"

This is not the message of someone who was consumed day and night by affairs of state. One could argue that these simple verses did more to endear him to the people than those more overtly propagandistic efforts, but all attempts to reduce Lorenzo to an exclusively political animal are bound to fail. Clearly this was work that he enjoyed, and these songs were above all an expression of his personality. Earthy and erotic, they convey both his hedonism and the melancholy, never far from the surface, that urged him to flee those darker demons of his soul by throwing himself headlong into sensual pleasures.

In the summer of 1490, word began to spread of a monk recently arrived in Florence from the north. His unblemished character, deep religious passion, and rare oratorical gifts were drawing crowds of admirers to the cloister of San Marco. Florentines, who despite their reputation for paganism always had a taste for fire and brimstone, were clearly entranced. So many showed up that soon he had to move out of the lecture hall and into the cloister's garden. Here in the shade of a rose bower, the monk urged his audience to renounce the ways of the world and return to the purity of the Apostles. "Why do we not follow Jesus and become like little children, simple, trusting, and pure?" he asked rhetorically.

In a city where even the Sunday sermon was larded with classical allusions and priests vied with each other in building elaborate philosophical confections derived from Plato and Aristotle, such simple piety was both shocking and refreshing. The monk's fervor captured the vague sense of unease that hung in the air. Florence was a city where the rich lived in luxury while the poor suffered in unimaginable squalor, where the educated preferred the erotic tales of Ovid to the homely parables of scripture. The priests whose job it was to save men's souls had grown so accustomed to their comforts that they neglected their flocks and set an example of vice that their parishioners were only too happy to emulate. The Dominican's words tore through the veil of complacency to reveal something rotten at the heart of Florentine society. Both Pico and Poliziano attended his harangues and were moved by his sincerity. Soon he was invited to carry his message to a larger audience in the cathedral of Florence.

It was during the Lenten season of 1491 that Girolamo Savonarola first stood on the pulpit in the *Duomo* and aimed a series of jeremiads at a city he likened to a new Sodom or Gomorrah. He prophesied a storm both great and terrifying that would sweep away the wicked and cleanse a land fouled by sin. His first target was the Church itself, a "false proud whore, the whore of Babylon" so corrupted by simony and steeped in every vice that it offered sinners employment rather than redemption. "If there is no change soon," he warned, "the Church of Italy shall be punished for not preaching the pure gospel of salvation."

Then he turned his wrath on his own audience. They thought of nothing but their own pleasure, he railed; they had forgotten Christ's injunction to care for their fellow men. Turning away, if only momentarily, from metaphysics, he demanded social justice. "The poor . . . are oppressed by taxes, and when they pay intolerable sums, the rich cry: Give me the rest. Some, with an income of fifty, pay an impost of a hundred, while the rich pay little because their taxes are levied arbitrarily. When widows come weeping, they are told: Go to bed. When the poor complain, they are told: Pay, Pay!" How could a society that spent so much on adorning churches with gilded altarpieces and jewel-encrusted reliquaries turn a blind eye to human misery? How could men build monuments to their own vanity while their neighbors starved in the gutters outside their palace gates? He attacked banking, that most Florentine of professions and the basis of many a great family's fortune. "No one can persuade you that usury is sinful, you defend it at the peril of your souls," he declared. As he looked about this most beautiful of cities he found little to praise. The glories of art and architecture, music and literature for which the century is remembered held little attraction for him. They were, in fact, mere vanities, false idols meant to distract men and lead them from the path of salvation.

Only a few years earlier this same Savonarola had come to Florence to preach, but at that time his halting speech, foreign accent, and unpolished prose had caused him to be laughed from the pulpit. It may well be that his violent hostility toward the city's ruling class and its culture was fueled in part by that earlier rejection. But now after years honing his rhetorical skills in provincial villages, his words rushed forth in a torrent as if guided by the Holy Spirit; those who had earlier laughed at the uncouth monk with the piercing eyes and gaunt cheeks of a fanatic now trembled at his words and begged forgiveness for their sins. "But already famines and floods, sickness and other signs prefigure afflictions and foretell the Wrath of God," he thundered. "Open, open, O Lord, the waters of the Red Sea and submerge the impious in the waves of Your Wrath!"

There was little, in truth, that was original in Savonarola's thought, but he delivered his message of penitence and divine judgment with an almost frightening intensity that caused the guilty to repent and the righteous to rejoice. As the crowds swelled to hear his sermons so did his faith in his divine mission. "The chief reason I have entered the priesthood is this," he wrote to his father: "the great misery into which the world is plunged, the wickedness of every man, the rapes, adulteries, arrogance, idolatry, the cruel blasphemies, to which this century has succumbed so that it is impossible to find even one of good will."

Less than four years younger than Lorenzo, Savonarola seemed to belong to a different age. Yet something in his preaching captured the spirit of the moment. One can detect in his sermons the beginning of a crisis of confidence that will bring a sudden, violent end to the Lorenzan age. Optimism will soon be replaced by fear, faith in man's nobility by certainty of his sinful nature, intellectual curiosity by fundamentalist rigidity. The embrace by the Florentine people of this man so hostile to everything Lorenzo stood for—the enlightened patronage of art and literature, the uninhibited enjoyment of carnal pleasures, a restless spirituality that questioned received dogma and sought the divine through intellectual inquiry—signals a sea change in the spirit of the Renaissance itself. Savonarola's fiery rhetoric of guilt and repentance was a throwback to the ideology of the Middle Ages, but his reformist zeal also pointed to the future. His uncompromising stance against a corrupt Church marks the beginning of a powerful movement of reformation that will culminate with Martin Luther a generation hence and shatter the unity of Christian Europe.

The legendary battle of wills between Lorenzo and Savonarola, a clash of ideologies as well as a confrontation between two of the truly remarkable men of the age, was in fact somewhat one-sided. While Savonarola took direct aim at the lord of the city as the symbol of all that was decadent, Lorenzo was far more ambivalent about the man who had set himself against him. Like his friends Pico and Poliziano, he found much to praise in the passion and sincerity of the Dominican brother. Even in their views on religion they tread common ground for a while before their paths diverge: both, for instance, did not hide their contempt for a corrupt, worldly clergy and both tended to eschew traditional communal forms of worship in favor of a direct experience of God through the individual conscience. The main difference between the two is that while Savonarola only dealt in certainties, Lorenzo was plagued by doubt. Savonarola drew strength from the belief that he was in direct communication with God, while Lorenzo fell easily into despair as his most fervent prayers were met only by silence. "You have kindled a love for Thee in my breast," wrote Lorenzo to a distant God, "only to vanish, never to be seen."

The result was that while Savonarola hurled abuse upon the world, Lorenzo regarded its defects with ironic detachment. In fact they were a source of amusement; the shortcomings of men became so much grist for the literary mill. It is obvious from works like *The Symposium,* a mock epic in which the heroes are all drunken louts, and his erotic novella "Giacoppo," that Lorenzo's opinion of his fellow man was no higher than Savonarola's, but his response was to poke fun rather than to scold. With his easy tolerance of the vices of men, and his tendency to indulge in many of them himself, he was less virtuous than the preacher but also more humane. His writings show an appreciation for the rich comedy of the human animal and little interest in forcing him to mend his ways. Savonarola, by contrast, believes in human perfectibility while making too little allowance for human frailty. Both approaches had their virtues and their limitations: Savonarola was genuinely concerned with the plight of the poor and labored to address the inequalities that led to so much suffering; Lorenzo, while spending enormous sums on charity, never believed that he or anyone else could make fundamental changes to the way things were. Lorenzo took things pretty much as he found them and was happy to exploit weak men and venal institutions for his own advantage; Savonarola cared too much for his own purity ever to engage in corrupt compromises with the world. When Lorenzo wrote to his son Giovanni, bound for Rome to take up his post, that "at present one sees such a lack of virtue in the College [of

Cardinals]," he echoed the substance, if not the rhetorical style, of Savonarola. But instead of calling for divine retribution on "that sink of iniquities," Lorenzo advised his son merely to make sure "not to slide into the same ditch into which [your colleagues] have fallen."

Lorenzo was inclined to tolerate Savonarola's excesses, and even to express a certain sympathy with his goals if not his means. These benign feelings, however, were not shared by the monk, who was becoming with each passing day more intemperate and more certain of his own infallibility. When Lorenzo stopped by the monastery, Savonarola made it a point to be away from his cell, and when he was named prior of San Marco he did not conceal his scorn for the man whose family had patronized the institution for generations, failing to pay the customary visit of respect to Lorenzo's palace. "Here is a stranger come into my house who will not even deign to visit me," Lorenzo remarked, more in sadness than in anger.

Despite repeated snubs, Lorenzo tried hard to placate the monk, even inviting him to preach in the chapel of his own palace. If Lorenzo hoped that his courtesy would take the sting out of Savonarola he was mistaken. The sermon he preached in Lorenzo's house was, if anything, more insulting to the lord of the city than usual. Surrounded by Gozzoli's opulent frescoes, which embodied everything he loathed, Savonarola delivered a message as notable for its courage as for its tactlessness. "I know a city," he rumbled,

> where the tyrants are incorrigible. They do not walk in light, but in darkness. They are haughty and vain. They listen to flattery. They do not restore their ill-gotten gain to those whom they have despoiled. Arbitrarily they impose heavier taxes on the population. . . . They exploit the peasantry. . . . They buy up votes and are guilty of dishonesty when they debase the coin of the realm.

According to one account, when the friar departed, Lorenzo turned to Poliziano and remarked, "There goes a brave man . . . and an honest one. But he must be broken." The words, like so many of the tales surrounding their confrontation, may well be apocryphal. If Lorenzo had really wanted to break Savonarola he could have done so easily enough. Instead he showed his displeasure indirectly by offering his support to a preacher much more to his taste—the learned Augustinian monk Fra Mariano da

Gennazzano. Poliziano's description of Mariano explains why he appealed to Lorenzo. "I have met Fra Mariano repeatedly," wrote the poet,

> at the villa and entered into confidential talks with him. I never knew a man at once more attractive and more cautious. He neither repels by immoderate severity nor deceives and leads astray by exaggerated indulgence. Many preachers think themselves masters of men's life and death. While they are abusing their power, they always look gloomy and weary men by setting up as judges of morals. But here is a man of moderation. In the pulpit he is a severe censor; but when he descends from it he indulges in winning, friendly discourse.... Lorenzo de' Medici, who understands men so well, shows how highly he esteems him, not only in that he has built him a splendid monastery, but also in that he often visits him, preferring a conversation with him to any other recreation.

This "man of moderation," probably with the encouragement of Lorenzo and his friends, took it upon himself to rebut the apocalyptic visions of Savonarola. In dueling sermons, Fra Mariano's before a packed house at San Gallo and Savonarola's given before 15,000 worshippers in the *Duomo*, they tussled over the souls of the Florentine people. In the building Lorenzo had constructed as a tribute to his learned friend, Fra Mariano chastised the Dominican monk for presuming to know the mind of God, quoting Jesus' reminder, "It is not for you to know the times or the seasons which the Father has placed in his own power." Across town, Savonarola struck back, accusing the Augustinian of hypocrisy and berating him for spouting elegant phrases that meant nothing. "He preaches from Cicero and the poets and not from Holy Writ," scoffed Savonarola.

But in the contest between fanaticism and moderation, fanaticism has certain built-in advantages. While Lorenzo's tolerant worldview could accommodate the fanatical friar, Savonarola's more constricted view could find no place for the worldly, easygoing Lorenzo. It is often forgotten that it was Lorenzo and his cultivated friends who first invited the Dominican friar to come to Florence. And while in retrospect it seems as if Savonarola was determined to destroy the world that Lorenzo and his friends had done so much to build, as long as Lorenzo lived the battle lines were not yet so clearly drawn. The gulf that divided the "Preacher of the Despairing" from the urbane, hedonistic First Citizen was immense, but Lorenzo, now in failing health and focused on family matters, seemed to lack the stomach for an all-out war. The best he could do was to take some of the sting out of the preacher's harangues. Even in his current diminished state Lorenzo's generous spirit continued to exert a moderating effect, ensuring that the city did not fall completely under the spell of the hypnotic friar.

Ultimately the future belonged, if only briefly, to Savonarola. Had Lorenzo lived a few years longer it is possible he would have been able to prevent, or at least temper, some of the worst excesses of the coming age. But the vitality that had characterized the greatest decades of the Florentine Renaissance was already ebbing, in no small part because the man who had ruled the city during some of its most creative years was dying. Savonarola's success was abetted by Lorenzo's debility. By the time the preacher had found his voice, Lorenzo was beginning to withdraw from the public stage he had dominated for so long. His bouts of illness grew more frequent and more intense, and he knew death could not be long delayed. During those rare moments of relief he preferred to pursue his own private interests rather than dwell on matters of state. Much of his time was now spent at home, with friends or alone in his library, where he buried himself in books or pored over his collection of gems and cameos. When he was well enough to travel his greatest satisfaction was to supervise construction on his villas. He more often socialized with his children and with artists and writers than diplomats and politicians; those who came to see him on such matters were often turned away disappointed.

And when he did turn his mind to politics it was not to dwell on large issues of state but rather to reinforce those alliances that would secure his family's future. On this front he had good reason to be pleased. He had been assured by his colleagues in government that, despite reservations about his suitability for the job, Piero would be recognized as his successor. Equally important, Giovanni's elevation to the College of Cardinals meant that the Medici would have a strong presence in the curia to serve as a bulwark against possible discontent at home.

The celebrations marking Giovanni's elevation were among the few bright moments in the gathering darkness of his final days. Giovanni received the cardinal's hat from the pope on March 10, 1492, in the *Badìa* of Fiesole, after spending the night alone in the monastery deep in silent prayer. Lorenzo was too ill to attend, nor was he able to be there the following day when Giovanni celebrated High Mass in the cathedral. Following Mass, the sixteen-year-old cardinal paid a call on the *Signoria*, where he was showered with gifts amounting, according to Luca Landucci, who had difficulty believing it himself, to thirty loads of silver and household items valued at 20,000 florins. Hauling this load back to the Via Larga, Giovanni hosted a splendid feast for foreign dignitaries and leading citizens of the city. Here Lorenzo, stooped and in great pain, received the congratulations of the people, though his appearance was anything but reassuring. His guests were dismayed by his gaunt and ravaged frame, and word spread through the city that *il padrone* was dying. This was, in fact, to be Lorenzo's final public appearance.

The following day Giovanni departed for Rome. Lorenzo, his mind still sharp, composed for his second son a long letter in which he tried to distill the wisdom gained in many years of public service. "*Messer* Giovanni," he wrote,

> You are much beholden to our Lord God, as we all are for your sake, as besides many benefits and honors our house has received from Him it has pleased Him to bestow on you the highest dignity our family has yet enjoyed. . . . It is incumbent on you to try and lighten the burden of the dignity you have obtained by leading a pure life and persevering in the studies suitable to your profession.

Lorenzo had come a long way from the young man whose indiscretions threatened to embarrass his parents. Now he was the one dispensing advice, no doubt comforted by the thought that Giovanni was far more likely to toe the line than he had been at the same age. Warning his son that he was about to enter a "sink of all iniquities," he admonished him to choose his friends wisely and to cultivate habits of modesty and sobriety:

> I advise you on feast-days to be rather below than above moderation, and would rather see a well-appointed stable and a well-ordered and cleanly household than magnificence and pomp. Let your life be regular and reduce your expenses gradually. . . . Jewels and silken stuffs must be used sparingly by one in your position.

Rather have a few good antiques and fine books, and well-bred and learned attendants, than many of them. . . . Eat plain food and take much exercise, for those who wear your habit, if not careful, easily contract maladies. . . . One rule I recommend to you above all others, and that is to get up betimes; besides being good for health, one can meditate over and arrange all the business of the following day.

Some have interpreted this letter as Lorenzo's last will and testament, the summation of the wisdom he accrued in his many years of service to the republic. If so it is a rather disappointing document, filled with practical tidbits but lacking any hint of a larger vision. But Lorenzo's letter is most revealing for what it does not say. Written by a man who knew he was dying, the letter eschews rhetorical flourish. The advice he offers is sensible but conventional, the insights commonplace; the underlying message is one of wariness. He tells his son not to be carried away by the euphoria of the moment, reminding him that even at this moment of apparent triumph he should be on his guard against those who, inevitably, will seek to tear him down. Keep your eyes open, he urges, not only for false friends but for those tendencies in yourself that can do as much harm as the most treacherous enemy. It is a cramped, cautious vision of the world that has often been compared to Polonius's famous speech to his son in *Hamlet.* But if there are no great pearls or flights of eloquence in this letter it is because Lorenzo has seen too much of sorrow and felt the sting of betrayal too often to indulge in grandiose visions. Take this happy event in stride, he seems to say, for the road of life traverses as many valleys as peaks, and only he who accepts this can move forward with a fair chance of success. Lorenzo is more eloquent, if not more uplifting, in a speech he places in the mouth of the dying Emperor Constantine in his play *The Martyrdom of Saints John and Paul:*

> *With endless tribulations I have reigned*
> *And met the dangers offered by each day.*
> *Rest there, my sword, with victories ingrained;*
> *No more I'll challenge Fortune in the fray.*
> *Fickle is she: men lose what they have gained,*
> *And those who seek too much will go astray.*
> *The pain of rule, its anguish, sons, you'll learn*
> *When you control the state for which you yearn.*

Lorenzo's pragmatism is a far cry from Savonarola's Manichaean vision of the world as a battleground between the forces of good and evil. It more closely resembles that of their younger contemporary Niccolò Machiavelli, eschewing grandiose pronouncements in favor of astute observations intended to serve immediate objectives. Neither Lorenzo nor Machiavelli sought to depict men as better or worse than they were, knowing that only by seeing the world as it really was could they hope to achieve anything at all.

Everywhere Lorenzo looked he saw complexity and ambiguity. Even his celebrated hedonism was no mindless surrender to the sensual side of life. Enjoy your youth, he instructed the lads and lasses dancing in the Carnival, not because life is an endless parade of pleasures but because old age and death will quickly rob you of your ability to enjoy them—May blossoms will soon wither in the autumn frost. He was equally skeptical of any vision that predicted heaven on earth or the coming of the Millennium. He filled his poems with detailed observations of both the natural world and of human nature because he believed these solid facts to be worthy of respect and discovered in them an endless source of delight.* He saw no reason to assume that things would not continue, for good or ill, pretty much as they had always done. He was a restless seeker of something finer, but doubtful that he would ever find what he was looking for.

By the time Lorenzo penned this letter he was in almost constant pain. Poliziano describes the near constant fevers that had consumed him, "attacking not only the arteries and veins, but the limbs, intestines, nerves, bones and marrow."†

---

* It can be argued that this delight in material things is inconsistent with Platonic philosophy, which views physical reality as a pale reflection of eternal truths. But logical consistency was never Lorenzo's strong suit. He was, after all, a poet, not a philosopher.

† The exact nature of his final illness is not known, though recent exhumations of some of his relatives confirm that many suffered, like Piero and Lorenzo himself, from severe gout and chronic arthritis. These diseases often confined him to his bed, forcing this once athletic man to lead a life of unhealthful sedentariness. In his final months he suffered from repeated fevers and complained of a swollen neck that prevented him from swallowing. It is likely that the treatment of his physicians, rather than relieving his symptoms, hastened his end. The quality of his medical care may perhaps be suggested by the fact that his personal physician killed himself shortly after his master's death.

"The illustrious Lorenzo suffers so acutely that it is hard to understand how he can hold out," reported the Ferrarese ambassador. On March 18, Lorenzo, though still ailing, felt well enough to travel to Careggi. This modest villa had been the scene of much joy and sorrow. It was here that Cosimo purchased for his friend Ficino a farm so that he could have the pleasure of the philosopher's company while taking a break from business in the city. Careggi was also the starting point for Lorenzo's memorable ride that August morning in 1466 when he barely escaped capture by the conspirators lying in wait for his father. And it was to Careggi that both Cosimo and Piero traveled when it was time to die. There is little doubt that Lorenzo was consciously retracing their final journey. Here among familiar fields and meadows he would end his days, removed from the crowds and commotion of the palace in the city.

Lorenzo was accompanied on this short trip by his sister Bianca. Soon Lucrezia and Piero hurried to their father's side, accompanied by a few of Lorenzo's closest friends. Always in the background in these final days were two or three distinguished physicians who rushed about trying desperately to appear useful. Lorenzo continued to follow their instructions faithfully (which in one case called for him to drink a concoction of pulverized pearls), more to keep up the spirits of his grieving companions than from any belief that they would delay the inevitable.

Calling Piero to his bedside he passed on such words of encouragement as he could, reassuring him that he was to be recognized as his successor but also urging him to "follow that course which appears to be most honorable" in order not to alienate those who put him into power. The ever faithful Poliziano described the final vigil in a letter written little more than a month after the fact, providing the only reliable account of Lorenzo's last days. Most striking, perhaps, is how little thought Lorenzo seemed to give in his final hours to politics. Some months earlier he had told his friend that, should God spare him, he would dedicate the rest of his life to poetry, and it was with poets and scholars that he chose to surround himself in the little time that remained. "Pico came and sat by the bed," Poliziano recalled,

> while I leaned against his knees in order to hear the languid voice of my lord for the last time. With what goodness, with what courtesy, I may say with what caresses, Lorenzo received him. First he asked his pardon for thus disturbing him, begging him to regard it as a sign of

the friendship—the love—he bore him, assuring him that he died more willingly after seeing so dear a friend. Then introducing, as was his wont, pleasant and familiar sayings, he joked also with us. "I wish," he said to Pico, "that death had spared me until your library was complete."

A more surprising visitor to Careggi was Girolamo Savonarola. Arriving shortly after Pico, he had apparently come at Lorenzo's request. Some years later, one of the preacher's followers—Fra Pacifico Cinozzi, who heard the story from Fra Silvestro, who in turn heard it from Savonarola—penned a dramatic narrative of the meeting. In this version, Lorenzo's summons was the result of a guilty conscience:

Thus going to Careggi, where Lorenzo was, he entered and after a few words Lorenzo said he desired to make his confession. Fra Ieronimo [Savonarola] answered he was willing, but before hearing the confession he wished to mention three things, if these were acceded to no doubt whatever his salvation was assured. Lorenzo replied he was willing and would do what was asked. The Father said: "Lorenzo, it is needful for you to have great faith," and he answered: "Father, that I have." Fra Ieronimo then added the second: "Also it is needful that you restore what has wrongfully been taken." After reflecting for a while he answered: "Father, I will do so, or I will cause my heirs to do it if I cannot." The Father then said: "It is needful for you to give back to the Republic the liberty of the city, and to see that she returns to her ancient state." To these words he gave no reply. Thus the said Father departed without further confession.

The story quickly became incorporated into the mythology surrounding the Dominican martyr, but it was apparently an invention, either of Savonarola himself or his disciples. A more plausible, and contemporaneous, account was furnished by Poliziano. According the poet, the viaticum was administered by another priest before Savonarola's arrival:

Towards midnight while he was quietly meditating [Lorenzo] was informed that the priest bearing the Holy Sacrament had arrived.

Rousing himself he exclaimed, "It shall never be said that my Lord who created and saved me shall come to me—in my room—raise me, I beg of you, raise me quickly so that I may go and meet Him." Saying this he raised himself as well as he could and, supported by his servants, advanced to meet the priest in the outer room. There crying he knelt down.

Having just received the sacrament, it is unlikely that Lorenzo sent for Savonarola just so he could repeat the process. It is also highly unlikely that Savonarola, whatever he thought of Lorenzo's policies, would have denied a dying man last rites. Poliziano's less dramatic telling, written only weeks after the fact, no doubt provides a more accurate picture of their final encounter:

> To [Savonarola's] exhortations to remain firm in his faith and to live in future, if God granted him life, free from crime, or if God so willed it to receive death willingly, Lorenzo answered that he was firm in his religion, that his life would always be guided by it, and that nothing could be sweeter to him than death, if such was the divine will. Fra Girolamo then turned to go when Lorenzo said: "Oh Father, before going deign to give me your benediction." Bowing his head, immersed in piety and religion he repeated the words and the prayers of the friar, without paying any attention to the grief now openly shown of his attendants.

In Lorenzo's final hours, evil portents and ominous signs abounded. The gardens of Careggi were populated by strange apparitions that chilled men's hearts with their mournful groans. In the city below, two of the lions on public display that served as the republic's mascots tore each other to death in their cages, while a bolt of lightning struck the Duomo, sending marble blocks crashing to the street below. When Lorenzo heard what had happened, he was reported to have sighed, "Alas! I shall die because [the stones] fell toward my house."

On April 8, Lorenzo descended into his final illness. Still he did his best to keep up the spirits of those around him: "To the last he had such mastery over himself that he joked about his own death," wrote Poliziano.

Thus when given something to eat and asked how he like it he replied: "As well as a dying man can like anything." He embraced us all tenderly and humbly asked pardon if during his illness he had caused annoyance to any one. Then disposing himself to receive extreme unction he commended his soul to God. The Gospel containing the Passion of Christ was then read and he showed that he understood by moving his lips, or raising his languid eyes, or sometimes moving his fingers. Gazing upon a silver crucifix inlaid with precious stones and kissing it from time to time, he expired.

Later that night his body was carried in a solemn torchlight procession along the road to Florence and brought to the monastery of San Marco. The next day the citizens of Florence streamed through the monastery to bid farewell to their leader. On the evening of April 10, his coffin was carried the few blocks to the church of San Lorenzo, where in a quiet ceremony attended only by close friends and relatives he was lowered into the ground beside his brother, Giuliano, in the family chapel. In a mournful reprise of the symbolism that had attended his baptism forty-three years earlier, Lorenzo's coffin was borne on the shoulders of the brothers of the Confraternity of the Magi.

As on those earlier occasions when the deaths of Cosimo and Piero had left the city in a state of uncertainty, Lorenzo's passing meant a period of anxiety for the people of Florence. The uneasiness was all the more pronounced because Lorenzo had dominated the age as no Florentine before him. "This man, in the eyes of the world, was the most illustrious, the richest, the most stately, and the most renowned among men," mourned the apothecary Luca Landucci. "Everyone declared that he ruled Italy; and in very truth he was possessed of great wisdom, and all his undertakings prospered."

Shortly after his death, the *Signoria* of Florence offered the official epitaph in the name of the people of Florence:

Whereas the foremost man of all this city, the lately deceased Lorenzo de' Medici, did, during his whole life, neglect no opportunity of protecting, increasing, adorning and raising this city, but was always ready with counsel, authority, and painstaking in thought and deed; subordinated his personal interest to the advantage and benefit of the community; shrank from neither trouble nor danger for the good of the State and its freedom; and devoted to that object all his thoughts and powers, securing public order by excellent laws; by his presence brought a dangerous war to an end; regained the places lost in battle and took those belonging to the enemies; and whereas he furthermore, after the rare examples furnished by antiquity, for the safety of his fellow citizens and the freedom of his country gave himself up into his enemies' power and, filled with love for his house, averted the general danger by drawing it all on his own head; whereas, finally, he omitted nothing that could tend to raise our reputation and enlarge our borders; it has seemed good to the Senate and the people of Florence, on the motion of the chief magistrate, to establish a public testimonial of gratitude to the memory of such a man, in order that virtue might not be unhonored among the Florentines, and that, in days to come, other citizens may be incited to serve the commonwealth with might and wisdom.

A more moving, and more personal, tribute was penned by the inconsolable Poliziano:

> *Who from perennial streams shall bring*
> *Of gushing floods a ceaseless spring?*
> *That through the day, in hopeless woe*
> *And through the night my tears may flow. . . .*
> *As the sad nightingale complains,*
> *I pour my anguish and my strains.*
> *Ah, wretched, wretched, past relief;*
> *Oh, grief beyond all other grief!*

Raphael, *Pope Leo X, Giovanni de' Medici, with
Cardinals Giulio de' Medici and Luigi de' Rossi*, 1517 (Art Resource)

EPILOGUE: THE SPIRIT IN THE RING

"That man's life has been long enough for his own deathless fame, but too short for Italy. God grant that now he is dead that may not be attempted which was not ventured in his lifetime."

—KING FERRANTE, ON THE DEATH OF LORENZO

IN THE WEEKS FOLLOWING LORENZO'S DEATH, A STRANGE story began circulating among the citizens of Florence. "It was said," a contemporary reported, "when this darkness descended upon Florence, that it was because of Lorenzo di Piero di Cosimo de' Medici who had released a spirit that he had entrapped in a ring; which, it was said, he set free and this was what caused [the stones to fall from the cathedral]. This spirit, it was said, he had kept for many years in that ring; and he liberated it because at that time he was gravely ill." Whether this spirit was malevolent or benign the story does not say, but the supernatural tale testifies to the long shadow cast by the man known as *il Magnifico* and vividly conveys the anxieties that inevitably crowded into the void left by his passing.

As news of his death spread, more prosaic, but equally powerful, eulogies were delivered by the great lords of Europe. "The peace of Italy is at an end!" cried Pope Innocent, and King Ferrante was hardly more sanguine: "That man's life has been long enough for his own deathless fame, but too short for Italy. God grant that now he is dead that may not be attempted which was not ventured in his lifetime."

What Ferrante feared was the long-anticipated invasion of the mighty armies of the French king that hung like Damocles' sword over the collective heads of the Italian city-states. It was largely to avoid such a catastrophe that Lorenzo labored in the last decade of his life to preserve the peace of Italy, hoping thereby to deny an opening that the covetous king might

439

exploit.* But the system of alliances he had cobbled together from proudly independent states could not long survive without him. Lorenzo was a master tactician, but he was unable to reverse centuries of historical development in which each locality jealously guarded its independence and fought its neighbors for supremacy. There were occasional hints in his writing of a grander vision in which an Italy united, at least culturally, under the lead of the city on the Arno would challenge the great nation states arising to the west, but political unification would have to wait until centuries of common oppression by foreigners forged a common sense of national identity. Lorenzo's foreign policy was too dependent on his own personal qualities to lead to enduring peace.

Piero, known to history as "the Unfortunate," inherited his father's position but none of his qualities as a leader. Where Lorenzo had known how to stroke the egos and flatter the vanity of potential opponents, Piero managed to step on every toe and to alienate even his natural allies. It took less than two years for Piero, more interested in horse racing and fine clothes than affairs of state, to squander all the goodwill his father had amassed. Under normal circumstances he might have been granted more time to grow into his job, but under the pressure of events his shortcomings were immediately and cruelly exposed. Lorenzo had not been in his grave many months when the fragile system of alliances that he had put in place began to crumble.

Without the soothing hand of Lorenzo on their shoulders, the tension that always existed between Milan and Naples grew into open antagonism. The immediate cause of the conflict was Lodovico Sforza's refusal to hand over the reins of power to the legitimate duke, his nephew GianGaleazzo, who also happened to be married to Ferrante's granddaughter. Knowing his claim to the ducal throne would never be secure as long as the Neapolitan king continued to agitate on behalf of GianGaleazzo, Lodovico invited the French king to renew his family's claim to the Neapolitan throne. Late in the summer of 1494, Charles VIII, overruling his more cautious advisors, led his sixty-thousand-strong army across the Alps. At first Piero tried to rally a coalition to challenge the French advance, but when this

---

* The current king of France was Charles VIII, who had succeeded his father, Louis XI, in 1483.

massive force, equipped with artillery the likes of which the puny Italian forces had never seen, swept all before it, he panicked and reversed course. In October, with the French bearing down on Florence, Piero rode out to Charles's camp, hoping to forestall a siege of the city by throwing himself on the mercy of the king. Piero's adventure is a classic example of drawing the wrong lessons from history. Hoping to repeat his father's bold gambit of sailing to Naples, Piero made a fatal blunder. Without so much as a shot being fired in anger he conceded to the French all the republic's most important fortresses, including Pietrasanta and Sarzana, which Lorenzo had won with such difficulty. Florence was left defenseless, a fact immediately grasped by the Pisans, who seized the opportunity to declare their own independence. Upon his return to Florence in early November, the entire city, instead of greeting him as a hero, rose up against the arrogant, foolish, and now treasonous Piero. Waiting only long enough for dark of night to cover his flight, Piero, along with his two brothers, Giovanni and Giuliano, snuck through the gates and fled the city.

Thus, ignominiously, ended the reign of the Medici in Florence after six decades in which they had ruled over the city in her years of greatest glory. It was not the end of the association of the Medici with Florence, but it was the end of that special relationship between the family and an independent republic that could count itself as one of the powers of Europe. Humiliated by the capitulation, galled by the loss of Pisa, and furious at the man who had allowed it to happen, the people of Florence plundered the palace on the Via Larga, dispersing the treasures amassed by generations of cultivated men. Some, like the statues of *David* and *Judith* by Donatello, were set up before the Palace of the Priors as symbols of the revived republic, while others were dispersed to the winds. On November 17, 1494, King Charles rode through the gates of the city accompanied by his army, his lance at rest, symbolizing the seizure of a conquered city.

The man to whom Florentines now turned in their moment of crisis was the Dominican friar Girolamo Savonarola. As surely as Lorenzo captured the confident spirit of the Renaissance, Savonarola captured the troubled spirit of this age of anxiety. Someone of Savonarola's messianic outlook could flourish only in unsettled times, and as Italy became the battleground for the great powers of Europe, frightened men and women turned in ever greater numbers to the preacher who seemed to have fore-told their woes. In fact, Savonarola welcomed the humiliation and trauma of the French invasion. It was he who rode out to Charles and negotiated his peaceful entry into the city, and it was he whose calming influence nar-rowly averted a violent confrontation between a nervous population and French troops in the weeks that followed. "O most Christian King," he addressed Charles, "you are an instrument in the hands of the Lord who has sent you to cure the ills of Italy, as I have long predicted."

Once Charles's army departed to pursue dreams of glory in the south of Italy, Florentines set about reconstituting their broken system of govern-ment. Savonarola's moral influence was decisive in the political reforms that followed. In the struggle between the oligarchs and the republicans, he threw his considerable prestige behind the latter, reversing the trend toward an increasingly restrictive franchise that had been underway since the time of the Albizzi. The new government's boldest innovation was the establishment of a Great Council, drawn from a pool of three thousand eligible citizens whose ancestors had held one of three leading offices, which served as the ultimate legislative authority in the state. This was hardly a true democracy in the modern sense, but through this new body more citizens participated in the government than at almost any time in Florentine history.*

Thus Savonarola's name became inextricably bound up with the pro-gressive movement in Florence. But while he became a hero to the little people, he made many enemies among the former ruling elites. The gen-eral disgust with Piero's high-handed ways that led to a wholesale disman-tling of the Medicean system did not translate into social harmony. The loss of Pisa, combined with the instability ushered in by the French inva-sion and years of economic decline, heightened tensions in the city and contributed to bitter political factionalism. Savonarola's followers, known as the *Piagnoni* (weepers), frequently clashed with the *Arrabbiati* (the angry ones) and the *Compagnacci* (the companions), made up largely of aristocrats who agitated for a return to the ancient oligarchy.

---

* The one exception was in the years following the *Ciompi* Revolt of 1348, when the work-ers seized power, but even the most liberal-minded Florentine had no wish to repeat this experiment in democracy.

From the beginning Savonarola was a divisive figure. With the zeal of a visionary, he sought to turn the city from its wicked ways and set it on the path of righteousness, a course that discomfited many who preferred to wallow in their vices rather than adopt the friar's austere virtues. Savonarola's attacks on the decadence of his adopted compatriots, and his even more bitter denunciations of the Church, kept passions boiling and created a climate of perpetual crisis in which his millennial pronouncements gained greater force.

As Italy descended into chaos, the preacher's apocalyptic vision fell on receptive ears. A wholesale dismantling of the previous age began as men and women examined their uneasy consciences and discovered that in pursuing material things they had neglected the word of God. The worst excesses of the prior age were embodied in Lorenzo's Carnival, and Savonarola set about eradicating the memory of those almost pagan bacchanals through a ritual purging. Instead of joining in suggestive songs and revels, Savonarola commanded the citizens of Florence to march into the *Piazza della Signoria*, where huge bonfires had been kindled. Into these "Bonfires of the Vanities" they tossed their jewels and silks in a symbolic rejection of the snares of the world. But Savonarola had more ambitious goals. "My lords of the Eight," Savonarola declared, "I would like to see you make a lovely fire or two or three there in the piazza, of those sodomites male and female—women too pursue that criminal vice. Make, I say, a sacrifice to God, which He will accept as incense [honoring] His life. Make a fire which the whole of Italy will smell." These flaming pyres came to embody the Savonarola era as surely as the great jousts and pageants had symbolized that of Lorenzo—an age of ash to follow an age of gold.

In order to enforce his austere ideal, the Dominican monk organized bands of fanatical youths who roamed the streets seeking out those who had violated the strict sumptuary laws. "Here come the boys of Fra Girolamo!" went the cry when one of these gangs approached, and women covered up their jewels and lace frills. Savonarola's efforts were not all pernicious. He worked hard to feed and clothe the poor and his religious fanaticism was combined with a genuine zeal for democratic reform. "We must . . . conclude," he wrote, "that . . . civil government or democracy is the best government for the city of Florence."

But Savonarola was a man of passionate faith not reason, a man who courted martyrdom and welcomed cataclysm, and a state that took its cues from such a mystic could never know peace. The representative government he established proved unstable, prone to faction, and woefully inefficient. As the years passed, citizens looked back nostalgically on the days when Lorenzo had ruled with such skill and tact.

Savonarola might have averted disaster had he been willing to make the compromises required of a politician. With every passing year, however, he grew more convinced of his divine mission; he welcomed the French army as the instrument of God sent to punish the sinning Italians, only to hurl bitter denunciations at them when they failed to chastise the wicked as he had hoped. His insistence on backing Charles long after the rest of Italy turned against him left Florence diplomatically isolated, and his campaign to reform a corrupt Church—in which the City of the Baptist, now purified under his ascetic rule, was seen as a new Jerusalem—inevitably put him on a collision course with Rome. He began to see himself in messianic terms and to rail ever more bitterly against clergy in the Vatican, now led by the sensual Alexander VI, the epitome of the worldly Renaissance prelate, who openly acknowledged his children, the infamous Lucrezia and Cesare Borgia. For a time the pope tried to seek an accommodation, but when Savonarola defied his order that he cease his preaching, a confrontation was inevitable. In April 1498, the people of Florence, now thoroughly fed up with his histrionics, arrested the friar and many of his followers. On May 23, after enduring weeks of torture, Savonarola and his chief lieutenants, Fra Silvestro and Fra Domenico, were led to a scaffold erected in the *Piazza della Signoria* and hanged before a bloodthirsty crowd. In order to prevent their bodies serving as the focus of a martyrdom cult, their still suspended corpses were consumed by flames in a gruesome reenactment of the bonfires that they themselves had made a symbol of their rule.

Florence's experiment in democracy lasted another fourteen eventful years. Whatever the defects of the Medicean system, the more representative government that replaced it proved incapable of managing the affairs of state. In the chaos that followed the French invasion, the quarreling factions that made up the new Great Council found it impossible to pursue coherent policies. Florence's standing in the world plummeted. In 1502, in order to stabilize the chaotic situation, Piero Soderini—son of Tommaso and Lorenzo's aunt Dianora Tornabuoni—was appointed *Gonfaloniere* for life, the very title that Lorenzo's critics accused him of aspiring to. In ridding themselves of a potential tyrant, Florentines now granted to one man sweeping powers that Lorenzo never possessed.

The troubled times that nurtured Savonarola's unique gifts also gave rise to another remarkable figure, but one whose understanding of the world could not have been more at odds with that of the Dominican friar. No one worked harder on behalf of the republic than Niccolò Machiavelli, who served for much of the period as the secretary for the Ten of War and who struggled, ultimately without success, to make the government work. Years of thankless toil on behalf of weak, corrupt, and vacillating leaders, as well as his exposure to some of the most ferocious tyrants of the age— including, most notably, Cesare Borgia—gave Machiavelli a thoroughly jaundiced view of the human condition. But it was only after the collapse of the republic to which he had dedicated himself heart and soul that, in bitterness and defeat, he wrote his most notorious work, *The Prince,* a treatise for the would-be despot on how to achieve and retain power. It is above all this tract that has made this Florentine civil servant's name synonymous with cynical scheming and deviousness. But this label is largely undeserved. Machiavelli was in fact a disappointed idealist. His unsparing vision of human nature scandalized his own and subsequent generations, but he understood that only by depicting men as they really were could any progress be made toward building a better form of government. Stripping away all pieties to lay bare the darkest recesses of the soul, Machiavelli took the first halting steps toward modern political theory, in which society is viewed as the product of fallible human beings rather than the elaboration of a divine plan.

The republican experiment came to an embarrassing end in 1512 after Piero Soderini had made the unlucky decision to back the French in their struggle against the armies of Spain. The Spaniards, combined with the Holy Roman Empire, Venice, and the pope (now Julius II, formerly Cardinal Giuliano della Rovere), ultimately routed the French forces, and when the victorious army marched on Florence, the government quickly capitulated. After putting up little or no resistance, Piero Soderini, *Gonfaloniere* for life, threw off his ceremonial robes and fled the city. Machiavelli was so disgusted with Soderini's cowardice that he penned this epitaph for his former boss:

> *On the night when Piero Soderini died, his soul descended*
> *to the mouth of hell; at which Pluto snorted: Silly soul, hell is*
> *no place for you; your place is in the limbo of babies.*

On September 14, 1512, Cardinal Giovanni de' Medici returned in triumph to his native city, backed by the might of Spanish arms. Taking up residence at the now desolate palace on the Via Larga, he set about restoring the political machinery that had served his father so well, placing in key positions only those of proven loyalty to his family. Giovanni might have remained the de facto ruler of the city but for the death in February 1513 of Julius II. Hurrying back to Rome for the conclave, Giovanni was elected pope on March 11. Taking the name Leo X, the thirty-seven-year-old finally fulfilled his father's greatest dream, vaulting the once humble family into the stratosphere of European nobility.

As great a coup as this was for the Medici, it seemed equally propitious for the Florentine people, who gave themselves over to delirious celebrations. Leo was the first Florentine to sit on St. Peter's throne and his elevation augured well for City of the Baptist. Rome, her ancient rival, was now bound to Florence by ties of blood and history, and the hope of Florence was that the centuries-old struggle for hegemony would now make way for an era of peaceful and prosperous coexistence.

Unfortunately reality did not meet expectation. Leo was a cultured and intelligent man but his intellectual gifts were not matched by equal energy or commitment to a larger cause. Upon his accession he was reported to have said, "As God has seen fit to give us the Papacy, let us enjoy it," words that sum up his rather negligent approach to his duties as the leader of the Christian flock. In 1517, four years into Leo's reign, the Augustinian monk Martin Luther nailed his Ninety-five Theses to the door of the castle church of the University of Wittenberg, ushering in the Protestant Reformation. But Leo was far more concerned with ensuring that his family retain its hold on his native land than he was with the rantings of an obscure German cleric. For this purpose he installed as his representative in Florence his nephew Lorenzo, son of the unfortunate Piero, who had drowned in 1503 while retreating along with the French army in which he was serving.

The restored Medici rule, carried on after Lorenzo's untimely death by his cousin Cardinal Giulio, did not lead to a renewed era of Florentine greatness. Nor did a second expulsion of the Medici, followed by a second restoration of republican rule in 1527 reverse the inexorable slide of the once great city into oblivion. The truth, from which most Florentines shrank, was that her glory days were behind her. In the dawning age of the nation state, the puny city-states of Italy could no longer count themselves among the great powers. They were prizes to be fought over by their more populous neighbors, and few were more attractive or more defenseless than Florence. The last spasm of that fiercely independent and democratic spirit that had sustained Florence for centuries ended in 1530 when Pope Clement, backed by the Hapsburg Emperor Charles V, reasserted Medici control over the city. In 1532 the republican constitution was officially abolished when Clement named Alessandro, son of Lorenzo (and great-grandson of *il Magnifico*), Duke of Florence. With Alessandro, and with his successor, Grand Duke Cosimo I, the Florentine republic finally became the hereditary possession of the Medici family.

The realm over which these later Medici ruled, while encompassing more territory than the earlier city-state, was a shadow of its former self. After 1494, Italy entered a period of decline from which it never recovered, and Florence declined along with it. That remarkable moment in which a city of under fifty thousand souls sheltered the greatest geniuses of Europe came to an abrupt end once Lorenzo's protective aegis was withdrawn. The poets, philosophers, painters, and sculptors who flocked to the city in the knowledge that *il Magnifico* would reward their genius found other more promising venues in which to ply their trade. Rome, rather than Florence, became the magnet for artistic genius as the great Renaissance popes—Alexander VI, Julius II, and Leo X—spent lavishly in an effort to create a city to match their outsized egos. Michelangelo was one of the many artists who fled Florence for Rome (though only after sculpting a

monumental *Hercules* in tribute to his deceased patron) where he worked
for many unhappy years, carving figures for Julius II's monumental tomb
and painting the Sistine ceiling.* Of those who remained, many succumbed to the new pessimistic spirit of the times. This spirit is easiest to
trace in the work of Sandro Botticelli where the pagan hedonism of his
Birth of Venus and *Primavera* is replaced in his final paintings by the religious mysticism and apocalyptic visions of the Dominican friar under
whose spell he had fallen.

Florence's eclipse was part of a larger transformation. As France, England, and Spain rose to greatness, and as the discovery of the New World
shifted the focus of the great powers away from the Mediterranean and
toward the world's oceans, Italy lost its central role as the economic engine
and cultural beacon of Europe. For centuries, Italy, and Florence in particular, continued to capture the imaginations of cultivated men and
women, but her lingering prestige as a home for the muses was no longer
matched by political or military power.

As the reality of their own impotence slowly dawned on the Italian people, and as each year brought renewed terror and humiliation, men began
to look back on the age of Lorenzo with increasing nostalgia. His genius as
a diplomat, holding together the fractious powers of the peninsula
through the force of his personality, was never more appreciated than in
the following decades when the lack of a comparable statesman doomed
Florentines and Italians generally to suffer the agony of war and chaos.
While some Florentines continued to look on his reign as a period of corruption and tyranny, the subsequent failure to arrive at a workable alternative made these aspects of his rule seem less distasteful. Seen through
the haze of memory, which softens all harsh angles and ugly realities, the
age of Lorenzo appeared suffused in a golden glow. The durable monuments of the age—the unsurpassed works of art and architecture, of

---

* Michelangelo continued to move back and forth between Florence and Rome, quarreling with popes and with whoever was in charge of the Florentine government at the
moment. The greatest work he completed for his native city was the monumental *David*
(in 1504), while, despite his contempt for Lorenzo's son Piero, his services to the Medici
family continued, most notably in the Medici tombs in San Lorenzo. His patriotism was
most directly expressed in the fortress he designed during the years the republic was
struggling to maintain its independence.

music, philosophy, and poetry, all propelled by a fervent belief in man's unmatched power—shone brighter in memory as the gloom of the present deepened. And at the center of this brilliant constellation, a sun encircled by glittering planets, was the uncrowned ruler of Florence, whose effortless command of all the graces of life seemed to sum up a bygone age of unsurpassed magnificence.

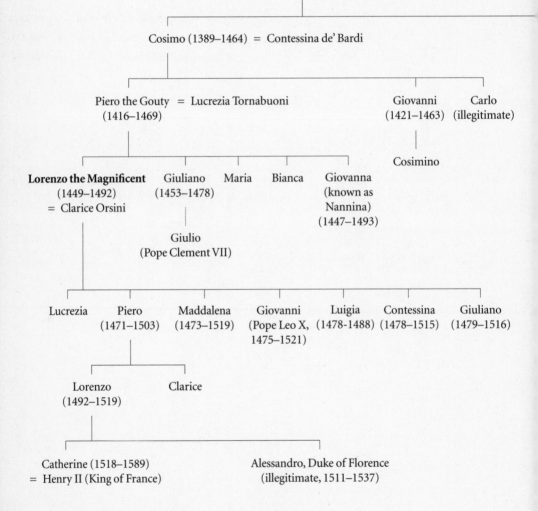

Averardo (Bicci), d. 1363

Giovanni di Bicci (1360–1429) = Piccarda Bueri

Cosimo (1389–1464) = Contessina de' Bardi

Piero the Gouty = Lucrezia Tornabuoni   Giovanni   Carlo
(1416–1469)   (1421–1463)   (illegitimate)

                                               Cosimino

Lorenzo the Magnificent   Giuliano   Maria   Bianca   Giovanna
(1449–1492)   (1453–1478)   (known as
= Clarice Orsini   Nannina)
                                                             (1447–1493)

                              Giulio
                              (Pope Clement VII)

Lucrezia   Piero   Maddalena   Giovanni   Luigia   Contessina   Giuliano
           (1471–1503)   (1473–1519)   (Pope Leo X,   (1478-1488)   (1478–1515)   (1479–1516)
                                         1475–1521)

           Lorenzo   Clarice
           (1492–1519)

Catherine (1518–1589)   Alessandro, Duke of Florence
= Henry II (King of France)   (illegitimate, 1511–1537)

Medici Family Tree

(Showing Relationship to Royal House of France)

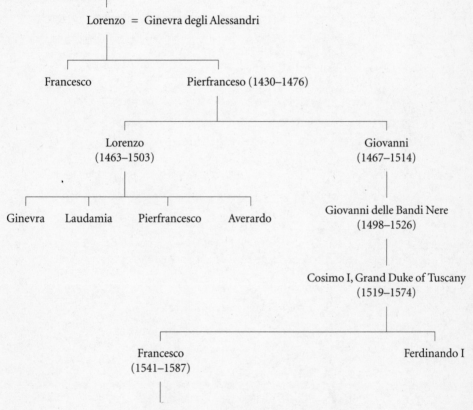

Lorenzo = Ginevra degli Alessandri

Francesco   Pierfranceso (1430–1476)

Lorenzo
(1463–1503)

Giovanni
(1467–1514)

Ginevra   Laudamia   Pierfrancesco   Averardo

Giovanni delle Bandi Nere
(1498–1526)

Cosimo I, Grand Duke of Tuscany
(1519–1574)

Francesco
(1541–1587)

Ferdinando I

Marie (1573–1642) = Henry IV (King of France)

Note on the Government of
Florence in the Age of Lorenzo

The basic form of the Florentine government was established by the Ordinances of Justice in 1293. These laws disenfranchised the feudal aristocracy and gave power to the merchant and artisan classes by making participation in the political process contingent on membership in one of the major or minor guilds. Multiple overlapping councils and committees and rapid rotation in office were intended to ensure that no group monopolized power, but the inefficiencies of the system worked to the benefit of families like the Albizzi and the Medici who were able to create coalitions strong enough to dominate the elected government. The following is a brief summary of the traditional structure of the Florentine government and of Medici innovations.

Tre Maggiori: The "three major" offices of the state, selected on a bimonthly basis. To have one's name drawn from the purses (to be *veduto* or "seen") for one of the *Tre Maggiori* automatically meant inclusion in the political elite. The *Tre Maggiori* included:

> **Signoria** (the Lordship), the chief executive body of the state comprised of eight Priors—two for each of the quarters into which Florence was divided— and the **Gonfaloniere di Giustizia** (the Standard-Bearer of Justice), the official head of state. They in turn were aided by two advisory committees (also known as "colleges"):

> **Dodici Buonuomini** (the Twelve Wise Men) and the

> **Sedici Gonfalonieri** (the Sixteen Standard-Bearers), one for each of the sixteen districts, or *gonfaloni,* that formed the traditional neighborhoods of the city.

Consiglio del Popolo (Council of the People) and the **Consiglio del Commune** (Council of the Commune): the two traditional legislative assemblies of the republic. Their role was to ratify legislation initiated by the *Signoria* and the two colleges. It was in these more democratic, representative bodies that opposition to the regime was most openly expressed. The two councils were slowly marginalized by Medici reforms.

Elections: Florentine elections were designed to spread the burden and the privilege of office holding to a broad cross-section of the citizenry. Elections followed an elaborate three-step process:

1) **Squittino** (the scrutiny)—The periodic canvass to determine those eligible for office. To qualify, a candidate had to be enrolled in one of the city's seven major or nine minor guilds. Nominations for the *Tre Maggiori* were made by the *Gonfalonieri* for each district and vetted by a variety of different councils. Priority was given to members of prominent families whose relatives had already served in high office, thus ensuring the oligarchic nature of the government, but a small percentage of offices was also set aside for shopkeepers and artisans. The *squittino* was always a tumultuous event, since a family's status in the city hierarchy was largely determined by the number of successful candidates.

2) **Sortition**—Names of those selected in the *squittino* were sorted into various bags or purses designating the offices for which they were eligible. Most important were those purses for the *Tre Maggiori,* which included a separate bag for the *Gonfaloniere di Giustizia.* It was at this point that the electoral process was most easily manipulated. Throughout much of the Medici era a body known as the *Accoppiatori* (see below) selected *a mano* (by hand) the name tickets distributed into each bag, giving the regime considerable control over who would ultimately serve in office.

3) **Extraction**—The actual drawing of the names from the purses. For the *Tre Maggiori* the extraction took place every other month in a ceremony at the *Palazzo della Signoria.* It was at this ceremony that Florentines learned who would actually be seated in office. But even those whose names were drawn from the purses but who were ineligible to serve—either because they had already served within the past five years, a close relative was currently serving, they were not old enough, or they owed back taxes, and so forth—gained a great deal. To be seen (*veduto*) even if not actually seated

(*seduto*) conferred considerable prestige. In fact, membership in the important councils and committees was often determined by whether or not one's ancestors and relatives had ever been *veduto* or *seduto* for one of the *Tre Maggiori*.

Balìa: a special committee invested with extraordinary powers in times of crisis. *Balìe* were normally created by means of a **parlamento** (see below) called to give their approval to government reforms. The *parlamento* of September 1466, for instance, approved the *Balìa* dominated by Piero de' Medici that purged most of the opponents of the regime (see below).

The Dieci di Balìa (the Ten of War): a special committee appointed in times of war and given almost dictatorial powers. Lorenzo maneuvered to have himself appointed to this all-important committee during the Pazzi war.

The *Otto di Guardia* (The Eight of Security): the feared committee in charge of state security charged with rooting out treason and political sedition.

Parlamento: assembly of all the citizens of Florence in the Piazza della *Signoria* called in moments of gravest danger to the state.

Medici innovations: The following are the major "reforms" initiated by the Medici that helped strengthen their grip on power:

Accoppiatori—Usually five in number, the *Accoppiatori* had the crucial task of sifting through the names of candidates who had been successful during the *squittino*, selecting only those deemed reliable friends of the regime. Originally convened only in moments of gravest crisis, they became an almost permanent feature of the Medici regime.

The One Hundred—Created by Cosimo de' Medici as part of the reforms of 1458, the One Hundred included the most important members of the regime. Many of the responsibilities previously given to the more democratic councils of the People and the Commune were given to this compact body dominated by Medici allies.

The Seventy—A committee created by Lorenzo in 1480 to streamline the government and place power in fewer, more reliable hands. Important legislation proposed by the *Signoria* now had to be approved by the Seventy. The Seventy also took over from the *Accoppiatori* in selecting candidates for the *Signoria* by hand.

Reggimento (the regime)—the name given by Florentines to the small number of men who wielded real power in the government, regardless of who was actually seated in office. Throughout the era the *reggimento* consisted for the most part of Medici loyalists, though occasionally, as in 1466, the regime itself could split along party lines.

NOTES

CHAPTER I: THE ROAD FROM CAREGGI

PAGE

1   *"There is in my opinion"*: Brucker, *Florence: The Golden Age,* 10–11.

2   *"nature had been a step-mother to him"*: Valori, 30–31.

5   *"cold men"*: Rubinstein, *Government of Florence Under the Medici,* 155.

5   *"did not have much confidence"*: Machiavelli, *Florentine Histories,* VII, 5, 281.

5   *"those who have"*: Filarete, XXV.

5   *"First stop"*: Chamberlin, "Everyday Life in Renaissance Times," p. 71.

5   *rare gemstones:* Filarete, XXV, 319–21.

6   *"[E]very day seems a year"*: Ross, *Lives of the Early Medici* (hereafter *Lives*), 108.

6   *"with infinite longing"*: Ibid., 119.

6   *"You will have received my letter of the 4th"*: Ibid., 94.

6   *"I wrote to you two days ago"*: Lorenzo de' Medici (hereafter Lorenzo), *Lettere,* I, no. 7, 15.

7   *"Piero was dismayed"* Machiavelli, *Florentine Histories,* VII, 13, 291–92.

7   *"with whom I spoke"*: Lorenzo, *Lettere,* I, no. 9, 19.

8   *"Three times I read this"*: Trexler, *Public Life in Renaissance Florence,* 431.

8   *charismatic center:* Ibid., 419ff.

8   *"Thus it was arranged"*: Parenti, *Ricordi Storici,* 123.

9   *"And returning to the arrival of Lorenzo"*: Rochon, 108.

9   *"[Piero] did not, to be sure"*: Francesco Guicciardini, *History of Florence,* 13.

10 *lessening the chances of a violent clash breaking out between their armed supporters:* Phillips, 246.

10 *on the rebound:* Machiavelli, *Florentine Histories,* VII, 15.

10 *"[I]n order to better conceal"*: Ibid.

10 *his onetime colleague had at least flirted with the opposition:* Rubinstein, *Government of Florence Under the Medici,* 163.

11 *"great goodwill among the people"*: Ibid., 107.

11 *"the citizenry would like greater liberty"*: Ibid., 161.

11 *"Cosimo and his men"*: Ibid., 152.

11 *"[s]ince his own ambition"*: Machiavelli, *Florentine Histories,* VII, 11; Rubinstein, *Government of Florence Under the Medici,* 159.

11 *"[It was] caused in large part"*: Francesco Guicciardini, *History of Florence,* 15.

12 *"Yesterday I went to my estate at Careggi"*: Ficino, *Letters,* I, 1.

13 *"received letters from the regime in Bologna"*: Rubinstein, *Government of Florence Under the Medici,* 184–85.

13 *"every day meets* M. *Luca"*: Ibid., 177.

13 *"man of fine physique"*: Pius II, 114.

14 *"Piero be removed from the city."*: Rubinstein, *Government of Florence Under the Medici*, 184.

14 *"the marquis of Ferrara"*: Machiavelli, *Florentine Histories*, VII, 15.

14 *he dashed off an urgent letter to Sforza*: Rubinstein, *Government of Florence Under the Medici*, 184–85.

14 *"upon receiving this"*: Black, "Piero de' Medici and Arezzo," *Piero de' Medici, "il Gottoso,"* (1416–1469), 26.

15 *It is a puzzle*: Andre Rochon is among those who doubt that Lorenzo played a prominent role in saving his father's life (see *La Jeunesse de Laurent des Medicis*, especially 82–84), arguing that Medici propagandists would surely have played it up. Their reticence, however, is understandable, since Lorenzo's glory was won at the expense of his father.

16 *[I]t was through the sound judgment of Lorenzo:* Valori, 31.

16 *"[W]hen Piero went off to Careggi"*: Francesco Guicciardini, *History of Florence*, 17. Marco Parenti, who believed the whole incident was an elaborate deception, confirms that whatever took place occurred at "Sto. Antonio del Vescovo." Phillips, 192.

17 *"and thanks to God"*: Lorenzo, *Lettere*, II, 413.

17 *"new Dietisalvis"*: Ibid., 276.

19 *I was approaching town along the road:* Lorenzo de' Medici, *Selected Poems and Prose*, 43–44.

19 *"Above all else"*: Dale Kent, *The Rise of the Medici Faction*, 17.

CHAPTER II: FAMILY PORTRAIT

PAGE

21 *Accompanying the proud father:* For a complete list of those in attendance, see Trexler, "Lorenzo de' Medici and Savonarola, Martyrs for Florence," *Renaissance Quarterly*, especially Appendix 1.

22 *"are mean in giving alms"*: Lowe, "A Matter of Piety or of Family Tradition and Custom?" *Piero de' Medici, "Il Gottoso,"* (1416–1469), 56.

23 *"the reputation of the said Mag.co Lorenzo"*: Ferrarese ambassador, December 1482, Bullard, 46.

24 *"Thus, while still only a youth"*: Valori, 27.

25 *"Be chary of frequenting the Palace"*: Ross, *Lives*, 6.

25 *"the first palace"*: Vasari, I, 379.

25 *more than twenty buildings were razed:* Goldthwaite, *The Building of Renaissance Florence*, 16.

26 *"Spending a lot and making a big impression"*: Ibid., 77.

26 *"affords an opportunity for the exercise of virtue"*: Gage, 55.

26 *"everyone [in Florence] seems bred to the cultivation of profit"*: Alberti, *The Family in Renaissance Florence*, I, 56–57.

26 *over thirty fine palaces:* Dei, 35r.

28 *"[T]he popolani of the quarter of San Giovanni:"* Villani, *Nuova Cronica*, XIII, xxi.

29 *"Such was our greatness":* Ross, *Lives,* 3.

29 *tax roll of 1427:* Herlihy, Klapisch-Zuber, Litchfield, and Molho, *Online Catasto of 1427.* Version 1.3 (www.stg.brown.edu/projects/catasto/main.php). This database, compiled from information contained in the 1427 tax roll and maintained by Brown University, is an invaluable resource for those interested in fifteenth-century Florence, as is the related *Online Tratte of Office Holders, 1282–1532,* which contains a searchable database of officeholders for those years.

29 *"he would make no will":* Ross, *Lives,* 74.

30 *"There are fifty mouths to feed":* Dale Kent, *Cosimo de' Medici and the Florentine Renaissance,* 319.

30 *"So much a slave was he":* Vasari, I, 437.

31 *"If I do not frequent your house":* Dale Kent, *Cosimo de' Medici and the Florentine Renaissance,* 24.

31 *"Cosimo de' Medici":* Rochon, 48.

32 *"This evening I received your letter":* Maguire, 66–7.

33 *A letter from Contessina to Giovanni:* Ibid., 50.

34 *"seem too good for Cafaggiuolo":* Ibid., 57.

34 The wolf retreated to its wilderness: Lorenzo de' Medici, *Selected Poems and Prose,* "The Partridge Hunt," 31.

35 *"Honor does not reside in the woods":* Dale Kent, *Cosimo de' Medici and the Florentine Renaissance,* 92.

35 *moved probably sometime in 1458:* F. W. Kent, *Lorenzo de' Medici and the Art of Magnificence,* 27.

36 *"Too large a house":* Ross Williamson, 59.

36 *"obliged to leave":* Dale Kent, *Cosimo de' Medici and the Florentine Renaissance,* 306.

36 *He has himself carried into a studio:* Filarete, XXV, 319–21.

37 *"[T]he aforesaid count":* Niccolò de' Carissimi da Parma, in Hatfield, "Some Unknown Descriptions of the *Palazzo Medici*," *Art Bulletin,* Appendix 2, 246.

38 *"nothing in the world":* Dale Kent, *Cosimo de' Medici and the Florentine Renaissance,* 240.

38 *smeared with blood:* Guido Cavalcanti, *Istorie Fiorentine,* in ibid., 223.

39 *"This morning I had a letter":* Chambers, 96.

40 *"The beauty and grace of objects":* Pier Paolo Vergerio, *On Noble Behavior,* 1404, in Baxandall, 34.

40 *"Although we do not have the expertise":* Dale Kent, *Cosimo de' Medici and the Florentine Renaissance,* 279.

41 *Luca Pitti, Niccolò Soderini, and Dietisalvi Neroni:* See Acidini Luchinat, *The Chapel of the Magi: Benozzo Gozzoli's Frescoes in the Palazzo Medici-Riccardi Florence,* for the identification of portraits in the Medici chapel.

42 *the Dodici Buonuomini:* For a searchable database of the offices held by various members of the Medici family, see the *Online Tratte of Office Holders, 1282–1532.*

43 *"When you are made uncomfortable by the heat":* Ackerman, 76–77.

44 *"to make him suck well":* Maguire, 37.

44 *"[A]s God created Cosimo"*: Ficino, *Letters,* 86, 108.

44 *"Be old beyond your years"*: Ross, *Lives,* 103.

45 *"My Lord and Master"*: Maguire, 63.

45 *"I write to you several letters"*: Ibid., 68–69.

45 *"Have faith and obey the doctors"*: Ibid., 82.

46 *"You are well read"*: Rochon, 23–24.

46 *"[e]verywhere you could hear instruments"*: Lucrezia Tornabuoni de' Medici, "The Story of Queen Esther," *Sacred Narratives,* 173.

46 *"reduced Florence to the lowest level of repute"*: Ibid., 35.

47 *What part of the state:* Ibid., 32.

CHAPTER III: MASTER OF CEREMONY

PAGE

50 *"[s]ixty young Florentine gentlemen"*: Ross, *Lives,* 62.

50 *"The preparations had been great"*: Pius II, 109.

50 *"They spent very little"*: Ibid., 109–10.

51 *"Every warrior wears a helmet"*: Luchinat, 126.

51 *"He for many reasons has great power"*: Trexler, *Public Life in Renaissance Florence,* 227.

52 *"In Florence the citizens love equality"*: Reumont, 241.

52 *"surrounded by a crowd of children"*: Gentile Becchi to Piero de' Medici, June 3, 1454, Trexler, *Public Life in Renaissance Florence,* 429.

52 *"Lord of the Baths"*: F. W. Kent, "The Young Lorenzo," in *Lorenzo the Magnificent,* 7.

53 *"I do not know of riches"*: Lorenzo, *Selected Poems and Prose,* "The Supreme Good," lines 45–51.

53 *"some solitary and shaded place"*: Lorenzo de' Medici, *Commento de' Miei Sonetti,* 4.

53 *"my most dear friend"*: Lorenzo, *Lettere,* I, 4.

53 *"who wishes to be named notary"*: Ibid., I, 5.

54 *"to look after our affairs"*: Ibid. I, 7.

54 *"You have arrived at Milan later than I thought"*: Ross, *Lives,* 93.

54 *to name but one menu:* Ibid., 269.

54 *"Yesterday after leaving Florence"*: Poliziano to Clarice de' Medici, April 8, 1476, ibid., 178.

55 *"I have the feeling that the days of Cicero"*: Manchester, *A World Lit only by Fire,* 105.

55 *One day it happened that Nicolao Nicoli:* da Bisticci, 310.

56 *"Do not ask how he enjoys his present studies"*: Maguire, 201.

57 *"Wonders are many on earth"*: Davies, 117.

57 *"O great and wonderful happiness"*: Pico della Mirandola, *On the Dignity of Man,* 5.

57 *"The nutriment of every art is honor"*: Lorenzo to don Federigo, Ross, 88.

58 *"Lorenzo is learning the verses"*: February 1457, ibid., 60.

58 *"other self, both in nature and in will"*: Ficino to Giuliano de' Medici Ficino, *Letters,* no. 61, 80.

58 *no better or closer friend:* Rochon, 28.

58 *"he is always wanting to win":* F. W. Kent, *Lorenzo de' Medici and the Art of Magnificence,* 129–30.

58 *"thinking to achieve more":* Ibid., 62.

58 *"[Cosimo] was just as sharp":* Ficino to Lorenzo, Ficino, *Letters,* no. 86, 108.

61 *"[Lorenzo] was so devoted to religion":* Valori, 25.

61 *"The soul is only avid for the good":* Lorenzo, *Selected Poems and Prose,* "The Supreme Good," lines 79–80.

62 *"Do not meddle with priests":* Holmes, 19.

62 *"Let him pass":* Luchinat, 369.

62 *"growing rapidly in all directions":* Alessandro Martelli to Piero de' Medici, May 4, 1465, Kent, "The Young Lorenzo," *Lorenzo the Magnificent,* 10.

63 *"Our Lord the King":* Ross, *Lives,* 159.

63 *from any hand but his:* Valori, 85.

64 *"Lorenzo was of above average height":* Ibid., 29.

64 *"for this he was much obliged to nature":* Ibid., 30.

64 *"showed himself in a temper":* Lorenzo, *Lettere, I,* 177.

64 *"My dear Lorenzo":* Braccio Martelli to Lorenzo, March 1466, in Rochon, 125.

65 *"You don't make your sons work in a shop":* Rocke, 135.

67 *"because when they are younger":* Rochon, 127.

67 *"going out at night wenching":* Becchi to Lorenzo, January 29, 1471, in Rochon, 128.

67 *"If you were with me":* Luigi Pulci to Lorenzo, April 1465, Pulci, *Lettere,* I.

68 *"Thus, considering both his voluptuous life":* Machiavelli, *Florentine Histories,* viii, 36.

68 *"he who lies the best is happiest":* Lorenzo, *Selected Poems and Prose,* "The Supreme Good," line 64.

69 *"Our Maeceneas":* Benedetto Coluccio, 1468; Kent, "The Young Lorenzo," in *Lorenzo the Magnificent,* 3.

69 *"As I have not had money to spend":* Pulci, *Lettere,* XIV.

69 *"Short in stature":* Giovanni Corsi, in Ficino, *Letters,* no. 26.

70 *"Now if you are not sorry for this":* Lorenzo to Ficino, ibid., no. 23.

70 *"Who would have believed it?":* Lorenzo to Ficino, ibid., no. 28.

70 *"I was indeed delighted with your letter":* Lorenzo to Ficino, ibid., no 84.

71 *"[I]n the last years of his life":* Machiavelli, *Florentine Histories,* VII, 7.

71 *"Mourning accords not with your age":* Ross, *Lives,* 64–65.

72 *"When we are going to our country-house":* Maguire, 56.

72 *"[Cosimo] began to recount all his past life":* Ross, *Lives,* 75.

73 *"I record that on the 1st August 1464":* Archivio di Stato di Firenze, Mediceo Avanti il Principato, filza 163, 2 recto.

73 *"these were vain hopes":* Tranchedini to Francesco Sforza, July 12, 1464, in Rubinstein, *Government of Florence Under the Medici,* 155.

CHAPTER IV: HOPE OF THE CITY

PAGE

75   *twenty-five* braccie *of cloth:* Archivio di Stato di Firenze, Mediceo Avanti il Principato, filza 163, 3 verso.

75   *It details such trivial expenditures:* Ibid., filza 163.

76   *"this death has given many of the citizens":* Alessandra Strozzi, *Selected Letters,* no. 19, September 15, 1464.

76   *"despite this, upon his death":* Parenti, *Ricordi Storici,* 117.

77   *possibly on the advice of Dietisalvi Neroni:* Machiavelli, *Florentine Histories,* VII, 10.

77   *"to be buried without pomp or show":* Ross, *Lives,* 75.

77   *Machiavelli later claimed that all the citizens:* Machiavelli, *Florentine Histories,* VII, 7.

77   *On the second day of August 1464:* Parenti, *Ricordi Storici,* 57.

78   *"[Cosimo] refused to make a will":* Ross, *Lives,* 152–53.

78   *"the hope of the city":* Brown, *Bartolomeo Scala,* 41.

78   *"the absent senator":* Ibid., 48.

78   *"I have consulted with the citizens":* Ross, *Lives,* 94–95. May 11, 1465.

79   *"Lorenzo was young":* Commines, II, 393.

79   *"youthful virtue":* Ficino, *Letters,* no. 29.

79   *"[H]e delighted in facetious and pungent men":* Machiavelli, *Florentine Histories,* VIII, 36.

79   *"Perhaps it is better to have a pretty wife":* Strozzi, *Letters,* no. 44. Alessandra Strozzi to Filippo degli Strozzi, March 29, 1465.

79   *"was worthy of being included":* Valori, 24.

80   *"No one even of his enemies":* Francesco Guicciardini, *History of Florence,* IX.

80   *"Lorenzo was endowed by nature":* Rinuccini, *Ricardi Storici,* cxlvii.

81   *"[T]he tyrant needs to show himself superior":* Davie, *Half-serious Rhymes,* 113.

82   *"is not to exceed his orders in any way":* Lettere, I, 41.

84   *Neroni in particular was engaged:* See Lorenzo, *Lettere,* I, 14–15, for a discussion of Dietisalvi Neroni's intrigues.

84   *"you should regard yourself":* Lorenzo, *Lettere,* I, 15. Piero to Lorenzo, May 11, 1465.

84   *"do not spare any expense":* Ibid.

85   *"very well-disposed towards our city":* Lorenzo, *Lettere,* I, 7.

87   *"I do not know how I can begin to thank":* Lorenzo, *Lettere,* I, no. 10. Lorenzo to Bianca Maria and Galeazzo Maria Sforza.

CHAPTER V: DEVIL'S PARADISE

PAGE

90   *"be the death of the city":* Rubinstein, *Government of Florence Under the Medici,* 160.

90   *So strong was the momentum for reform:* Ibid., 163.

90   *"a great crowd":* Machiavelli, *Florentine Histories,* VII, 14.

91   *"Not without cause":* Rubinstein, *Government of Florence Under the Medici,* 164.

91 *"a man both proud and bold"*: Parenti, *Ricordi Storici*, 89.

93 *"some honorable excuse"*: Clarke, *The Soderini and the Medici*, 49.

93 *"the people called down blessings"*: Landucci, 4.

93 *"Piero di Cosimo"*: Parenti, *Ricordi Storici*, 90.

94 *"Piero has well demonstrated"*: Rubinstein, *Government of Florence Under the Medici*, 168.

94 *questionable business dealings:* Parenti, *Ricordi Storici*, 90.

94 *"Niccolò went in boldly"*: Alessandra Strozzi, *Selected Letters*, 193.

95 *"[I]n this bill"*: Rinuccini, *Ricordi Storici*, xcvi–xcvii.

95 *"a paradise inhabited by devils"*: Rubin and Wright, *Renaissance Florence*. Agnolo Acciaiuoli to Filippo Strozzi.

96 *"greater than any other that had been built"*: Machiavelli, *Florentine Histories*, VII, 5.

97 *[Piero's] reputation was much diminished:* Parenti, *Ricordi Storici*, 122.

97 *Only seven years earlier:* Machiavelli, *Florentine Histories*, VII, 4.

98 *"You raise your ladder to the heavens"*: Bisticci, 225.

98 *"a man entirely devoted to Cosimo"*: Phillips, 93.

98 *"[a]ll the affairs of the commune"*: Rubinstein, *Government of Florence Under the Medici*, 178.

99 *"Thinking that Messer Luca Pitti"*: Francesco Guicciardini, *History of Florence*, 15.

99 *"superior in prudence"*: Phillips, 101.

99 *"Now Agnolo had been absent from Florence"*: Bisticci, 301.

101 *"Nine fools out"*: Clarke, 87.

101 *under six feet of water:* Parenti, *Lettere,* no. 62. Marco Parenti to Filippo Strozzi, January 25, 1466.

101 *"everyone knows that Florence has turned towards Venice"*: Ibid.

102 *"So you intend, finally"*: Pulci, *Lettere di Luigi Pulci*, II. Luigi Pulci to Lorenzo, February 1, 1466.

105 *no end of worry:* Archivio di Stato di Firenze, Mediceo Avanti il Principato, filza 34, no. 147. Giovanni Tornabuoni, May 17, 1477, on the difficulty of making good on bad debts.

105 *"Pope Paul's head is empty"*: Rendina, 421.

105 *"that sink of all iniquities"*: Ross, *Lives,* 332. Lorenzo to Cardinal Giovanni de' Medici, March 1492.

106 *"You may turn all the pages of history"*: Bracciolini, "The Ruins of Rome," in *The Portable Renaissance Reader,* 380.

106 *at least pleasant associations:* Ross, 108–11. See Lucrezia to Piero, March 27 and April 1, 1467.

107 *"I am in such affliction"*: Ross, *Lives,* 102. Piero to Lorenzo March 15, 1466.

107 *"put an end to all playing on instruments"*: Ibid.

107 *"the King took Lorenzo by the arm"*: Rochon, 107. Becchi to Piero, April 14, 1466.

107 *"I spoke with him"*: Lorenzo, *Lettere*, I, no. 9.

107 *"love which we bear"*: Ibid., 20.

108 *"well-disposed towards his state"*: Rochon, 107. Sacramoro da Rimini to Lorenzo, May 6, 1466.

108 *one hundred troops to the Medici cause:* Black, "Piero de' Medici and Arezzo," in *Piero il Gottoso,* 25–27.

108 *Strong anti-Medici sentiment:* Rubinstein, *Government of Florence Under the Medici,* 177–78.

CHAPTER VI: GAMES OF FORTUNE

PAGE

111 *"vile rabbit":* Rubinstein, *Government of Florence Under the Medici,* 155.

112 *"There were three chiefs":* Parenti, *Ricordi Storici,* 125.

112 *"unified more by a common hatred":* Rochon, 80.

112 *"Nicodemo [Tranchedini], well schooled in these arts":* Parenti, *Ricordi Storici,* 125.

112 *"And thus there arose two fortresses":* Parenti, *Ricordi Storici,* 125.

112 *"around the 22nd hour":* Ibid., 124.

112 *"in the midst of a great multitude of armed men":* Machiavelli, *Florentine Histories,* 293.

113 *would tear him limb from limb:* Ibid.

113 *"The plebs, thirsting after novelty":* Valori, 31–32.

114 *"While things were in such a state":* Parenti, *Ricordi Storici,* 126–27.

115 *"very cowardly":* Ibid., 127.

115 *"With this money he showed great liberality":* Ibid., 125.

115 *"Messer Luca,* messer *Dietisalvi* and messer *Agnolo":* Ibid.

116 Messer *Antonio Ridolfi,* one of Piero's friends: Ibid., 127.

116 *Now Piero's foresight:* Ibid., 127–28.

117 *"Better a city":* Machiavelli, *Florentine Histories,* VII, 6.

118 *"That same morning":* Parenti, *Ricordi Storici,* 127–28.

118 *"before the drawing for the Signoria":* Rinuccini, *Ricordi Storici,* CI.

119 *"a sensible man and a good man":* Parenti, *Ricordi Storici,* 128.

119 *Piero persuaded his newfound allies:* Clarke, "A Sienese Note on 1466," in *Florence and Italy: Renaissance Studies in Honor of Nicolai Rubinstein,* 50.

120 *"excused himself because of his illness":* Rinuccini, *Ricordi Storici,* CI.

120 *"In not coming, [Piero] showed his arrogance":* Ibid.

120 *"expel from Florence all the soldiers":* Ibid.

120 *"the soul of a tyrant":* Ibid.

121 *"In part through persuasive words":* Valori, 31–32.

122 *"Messer Luca had a daughter of tender age":* Parenti, *Ricordi Storici,* 130.

122 *"declaring himself ready to live or die with me":* Rubinstein, *Government of Florence Under the Medici,* 186.

122 *"very submissive words":* Ibid., 192.

122 *"if Piero had not held them back":* Machiavelli, *Florentine Histories,* VII, 16.

123 *"To establish the peace of the city":* Brown, "Piero's Infirmity," in *Piero il Gottoso,* 18.

123 *"so many soldiers in one place":* Clarke, "A Sienese Note on 1466," in *Florence and Italy: Renaissance Studies in Honor of Nicolai Rubinstein,* 49.

123 *"it was approved with excited and loud voices":* Parenti, *Ricordi Storici,* 132.

124 *"I knew that in an instant I had lost honor"*: Rubinstein, *Government of Florence Under the Medici*, 188–89.

124 *"after the failure of the plot"*: Landucci, 8.

124 *"little torture"*: Rubinstein, "La Confessione di Francesco Neroni" *Archivio Storico Italiano*, 380.

124 *"Unlike his father Cosimo"*: Francesco Guicciardini, *History of Florence*, 17.

125 *"From vileness or because he had been corrupted"*: Rinuccini, *Ricordi Storici*, CIV.

125 *"He remained cold and alone at home"*: Parenti, *Ricordi Storici*, 141.

125 *"I am laughing at the games of fortune"*: Machiavelli, *Florentine Histories*, VII, 18.

126 *"Pietro de' Medici, son of Cosimo"*: Lucrezia Tornabuoni, *Sacred Narratives*, 47.

126 *"most honorable and famous young son Lorenzo"*: Alison Brown, "Piero's Infirmity," in *Piero il Gottoso*, 14.

127 *"Already we loved you on account of your excellent qualities"*: Reumont, I, 197.

CHAPTER VII: LORD OF THE JOUST

PAGE

129 *"[Piero] was crippled with gout like his father"*: Parenti, *Ricordi Storici*, 58.

130 *"Magnificent Lord"*: Lorenzo, *Lettere*, I, no. 14, March 21, 1468.

130 *"I have received your letters both thick and thin"*: Ibid., no. 16, September 13, 1468.

130 *"[Lorenzo] is of such a nature"*: Alison Brown, *Bartolomeo Scala*, 61. Sacramoro da Rimini to Galcazzo Maria Sforza.

131 *"I shall be as a man without hands"*: Ross, *Lives*, 94. Piero to Lorenzo, May 4, 1465.

132 *"The enduring and intimate good will"*: Lorenzo, *Lettere*, I, no. 13, March 10, 1468.

132 *"Lorenzo demonstrates that he has thought things out"*: Sorzano, "Lorenzo il Magnifico alla Morte del Padre e il Suo Primo Balzo Verso la *Signoria*," *Archivio Storico Italiano*, 42–77. These remarks were made in September 1469, when Milan was unhappy with Piero's policies and looking toward Lorenzo as an alternative.

133 *"[He] who want[s] a son"*: Chambers, "Spas in the Italian Renaissance," in *Reconsidering the Renaissance*, 9.

133 *"are all dreams"*: Ross, *Lives*, 116. Piero to Lucrezia, October 1, 1467.

133 *"There [at the baths] you risk unnecessary peril"*: Archivio di Stato di Firenze, Mediceo Avanti il Principato, filza XX, 339. In Martelli's "Giacoppo" (*Interpres*, 104), the date given is September 26, 1466, but this is almost certainly an error. While the date on the original document is illegible, two letters by Lorenzo to his mother in Bagno a Morba confirm her presence at the baths in the fall of 1467 and his intention of visiting her there. (See letters 11 and 12 in Lorenzo, *Lettere*, I, the first dated September 19, in which he writes, "I had hoped to be there already days ago . . ." and the second, from October 4, in which he says, "I do not think I shall be able, as I had wished, to return to see you there . . .")

135 *"Let search who will for pomp"*: Lorenzo, *il Commento de' Miei Sonetti*, Sonnet 21.

136 And where is Pulci: Lorenzo, "The Partridge Hunt," *Selected Poems and Prose*.

136 *"to prove the dignity of our language"*: Lorenzo, *il Commento de' Miei Sonetti*, 46.

136 *" honor, according to the philosophers"*: Ibid., 51.

136 *"At the end of the volume"*: Ross, *Lives,* 92.

137 *"because you have a quite complete understanding"*: F. W. Kent, *Lorenzo de' Medici and the Art of Magnificence,* 1.

137 Whilst Arno, winding through the mild domain: Roscoe, *Life of Lorenzo de Medici,* 236.

138 O sleep most tranquil: Lorenzo, *Commento de' miei,* sonnet 20.

139 *"I could easily be thought"*: Ibid., 31.

139 *"[H]aving in my youth"*: Ibid., 42.

139 *"He seemed to be two men"*: The Medici: Godfathers of the Renaissance.

140 *"one might see in him"*: Machiavelli, *Florentine Histories,* VIII, 36.

140 *"He was libidinous"*: Francesco Guicciardini, *History of Florence,* ix, 6.

140 We also have some beanpods, long: Lorenzo, *Selected Poems and Prose,* 159.

141 Soon autumn comes: Ross Williamson, 104.

142 *repay what had been borrowed:* See, for example, de Roover, 204.

143 *"On the way to S. Peter"*: Ross, *Lives,* 108–9.

144 *"You say I write coldly about her"*: Ibid., 110.

144 *"O that the marriage bond"*: Roscoe, 232.

144 *"I, Lorenzo, took to wife Clarice"*: Ross, *Lives,* 152.

144 *"the city no longer included him as a citizen"*: Machiavelli, *Florentine Histories,* VII, 2.

145 *"their pleasure is not to be described"*: Ross, *Lives,* 121.

146 *"Not a day passes"*: Ibid., 122.

147 *"Magnificent consort, greetings"*: Ibid., 123

147 *"she told me you were evidently extremely occupied"*: Ibid.

149 Lorenzo, laughing, donned his helm: Pulci, *Stanze sur la Giostra di Lorenzo de' Medici,* c.

150 *"the blond Elena"*: Beccadelli, *The Hermaphrodite,* xxxvii.

151 *"and as you know"*: Martelli, "Il 'Giacoppo' di Lorenzo," 105.

151 *"I do not believe that your relations"*: Rochon, 96.

151 *"The Graces and Venus chose Alda's beautiful eyes"*: Beccadelli, *The Hermaphrodite,* I, xvi

152 *the bridle alone required 168 pounds of silver:* Davie, *Half-Serious Rhymes,* 100.

152 *"To do as others do"*: Ross, 154.

153 *"one can interpret them as meaning"*: Pulci, *Stanze sur la Giostra di Lorenzo de' Medici,* LXV.

154 Seeing this his famous father: Ibid., CXLIII.

155 *"carried on his helm both honor and victory"*: Ibid, CLVIII.

155 *"to be youth"*: Ibid., CLV.

155 *"A few days ago I heard"*: Ross, *Lives,* 126.

155 *"Most magnificent consort"*: Ibid., 125.

155 *"[A]nd although I was not highly versed"*: Ibid., 155.

CHAPTER VIII: A WEDDING AND A FUNERAL

PAGE

157   *"For in starkest winter"*: Poliziano, *Stanze per la hostra di Giuliano di Medici*, II, vii.

157   *"Handsome Julio"*: Ibid., II, x–xi.

158   *"How beautiful is youth"*: *gioventù to uomo fatto*: Trexler, *Public Life in Renaissance Florence*. See especially 387–99 for an illuminating discussion of Florentine attitudes toward the young.

159   *"I know not where I shall begin"*: Reumont, 234.

159   *"touched one another's bare leg"*: Lubkin, 49.

159   *"How glad I should be to see you"*: Maguire, 139.

160   *"Calves 150"*: Ross, *Lives*, 129–34.

160   *"In the house here"*: Ibid., 132.

161   *"She doesn't want to go"*: Alessandra Strozzi, *Selected Letters*, no. 34, May 8, 1469. Fiametta, it turns out, did attend, since her presence among the thirty young matrons accompanying Clarice to the *Palazzo Medici* is recorded by the anonymous chronicler.

161   *"Cosimo Bartoli, one of the principal"*: Ross, *Lives*, 131.

162   *a charming rustic dance*: Ibid., 61.

162   *"It would be a burden"*: Lorenzo, *Lettere*, III, 404.

162   *"too insolent and haughty"*: Trexler, *Public Life in Renassance Florence*, 462.

164   *I would never have believed*: Machiavelli, *Florentine Histories*, VII, 24.

165   *"Until now, no mortal"*: Pernis and Adams, 27.

166   *the secret backing of the duke of Urbino*: Lorenzo, *Lettere*, I, 44.

167   *a policy of appeasement*: Ibid., I, 48.

167   *"of the enemies of Piero"*: Ibid., I, 49.

168   *"to live in a manner"*: Ibid.

168   *Piero was losing his grip*: Ibid. Sacramoro to Galeazzo Maria, October 25, 1469, in which he reports that Piero used "very strange words."

168   *"will show himself to be of a different nature"*: Ibid., I, 50.

168   *"I would like to declare myself"*: Ibid., I, no. 22. Lorenzo to Galeazzo Maria, December 1, 1469.

169   *"My Most Illustrious Lord"*: Ibid., I, no. 23. Lorenzo to Galeazzo Maria, December 2, 1469.

169   *"[W]hile certain of having here"*: Ibid., I, no. 22. Lorenzo to Galeazzo Maria, December 1, 1469.

169   *"I can report"*: Ibid., I, 51.

169   *"all business will once again return"*: Rubinstein, *Government of Florence Under the Medici*, 198. Niccolò Roberti to Borso d'Este, December 4, 1469.

169   *the marriage of his son Piero*: Clarke, *The Soderini and the Medici*, 177–78. The marriage allied the Soderini with Gabriele Malaspina, Marquis of Fosdinovo, whose ambitions in northwest Tuscany often clashed with those of Milan.

170   *"well respected but of varying views"*: Lorenzo, *Lettere*, I, 52.

170   *"At the twenty-third-and-a-half hour"*: Sorzano, "Lorenzo il Magnifico alla morte

del padre e il suo primo balzo verso la *Signoria*," *Archivio Storico Italiano*, 45. Sacramoro to Galeazzo, December 2, 1469.

170 "Messer *Tommaso Soderini took the word as eldest*": Reumont, 246–47. Niccolò Roberti to Borso d'Este, December 4, 1469.

171 "*work together for the good of the state*": Lorenzo, *Lettere*, I, 52.

171 "*The common people don't believe*": Clarke, *The Soderini and the Medici*, 180. Sacramoro to Galeazzo Maria, December 1, 1469.

172 "*leaders, knights and citizens*": Lorenzo, *Lettere*, I, 59.

172 *The second day after [my father's] death:* Ross, *Lives*, 150–56.

175 "*When shall we find another so reasonable*": Reumont, 240.

175 *little of the emotional turmoil of the moment:* See Lorenzo, *Lettere*, I, especially letters no. 25 (to Guglielmo Paleologo) and no. 26 (to Otto Niccolini) for the most timely expressions of his feelings.

175 *wept openly on his way back from church:* Parenti, *Lettere*. The preceding account of Piero's funeral comes largely from Parenti's letter to Filippo Strozzi begun December 3, 1469, but apparently continued over the course of the next few days.

CHAPTER IX: MASTER OF THE SHOP

PAGE

178 *But if [philosophy] be an occupation:* Roscoe, *Life of Lorenzo de Medici*, 99.

179 "*It does amaze me greatly, though*": Lorenzo, *Selected Poems and Prose*, "The Supreme Good," II, lines 40–51.

180 "*It was merely a ceremony*": Parenti, *Lettere*, no. 75. To Filippo Strozzi, December 3, 1469.

180 "*Some say that this city is taking a republican path*": F. W. Kent, *Lorenzo de' Medici and the Art of Magnificence*, 45.

182 "*They are agreed that the private affairs*": Reumont, 248–49. Niccolò Roberti to Borso d'Este, December 4, 1469.

182 "*one lord and superior*": Rubinstein, *Government of Florence Under the Medici*, 200.

182 "*the stupid crazy mob*": Kent, *Rise of the Medici Faction*, 7.

182 "*Our intention was to remove the city*": Francesco Guicciardini, *Dialogue on the Government of Florence*, 18.

183 "*I have enjoyed a very long friendship*": Rochon, 227.

183 "*in another gain something better*": Dale Kent, *Rise of the Medici Faction*, 115.

183 "*Among other things I told Lorenzo*": Sorzano, "Lorenzo il Magnifico alla Morte del Padre e il Suo Primo Balzo Verso la *Signoria*," Archivio Storico Italiano, 45, 50. Sacramoro to Galeazzo Maria, December 15, 1469.

184 "*follow his grandfather's example*": Rubinstein, *Government of Florence Under the Medici*, 204. Sacramoro to Galeazzo Maria, July 3, 1470.

184 "*master of the shop*": See F. W. Kent, "Patron-Client Networks in Renaissance Florence," in *Lorenzo de Medici: New Perspectives,* for a discussion of the sources and limitations of Lorenzo's authority. Benedetto Dei was one of those who employed the phrase "*maestro della bottega*" to describe Lorenzo's role.

186 *"Today the proposal went before the Signoria"*: Sorzano, "Lorenzo il Magnifico alla Morte del Padre e il Suo Primo Balzo Verso la *Signoria,*" *Archivio Storico Italiano,* 49.

186 *withdrew his delegates from the conference:* See Lorenzo to Otto Niccolini, March 24, 1469, in *Lettere,* I, no. 39.

187 *the Neapolitans followed suit:* See ibid., I, 126.

187 *Soderini's interests were not necessarily his own:* Clarke, *The Soderini and the Medici,* 192. Sacramoro to Galeazzo Maria, June 4, 1470.

187 *"honey in his mouth and a knife in his belt":* Alessandra Strozzi, *Selected Letters,* 87.

188 *banishing his chief opponents from Florence:* Clarke, *The Soderini and the Medici,* 186.

188 *including the Milanese ambassador:* Ibid., 184–85.

188 *to prevent them from bolting the alliance:* Ibid., 188–89.

189 *"found the letter already completed":* Lorenzo, *Lettere,* I, 131.

189 *"Let us abide by [the King's] advice":* Ibid.

190 *"upset and desperate":* Clarke, *The Soderini and the Medici,* 192. To the duke, Sacramoro wrote that Tommaso's intention was to "beat Lorenzo over the head and deprive him of the benevolence of Your Highness, in order to be able to manage him in his own way." *Lettere* i, 132.

190 *until* after *it had heard from the Duke:* Lorenzo, *Lettere,* I, no. 46. To Agnolo della Stufa, May 21, 1470.

190 *Soderini's bank account:* See Clarke, *The Soderini and the Medici,* 194.

191 *the streets were illuminated by dozens of bonfires:* Ibid., no. 58.

191 *"all lords and worthy persons":* Lubkin, 99–100.

192 *According to Francesco Guicciardini:* Francesco Guicciardini, *History of Florence,* 24.

192 *Lorenzo and his partisans were shut out:* Clarke, *The Soderini and the Medici,* 191.

193 *"If I understand matters correctly":* Rubinstein, *Government of Florence Under the Medici,* 204. For a complete discussion of electoral reform under Lorenzo see 199–263.

193 *a margin of only two votes:* Ibid., 206–7.

194 *"In this way the Signoria":* Ibid., 207. Sacramoro to Galeazzo Maria, January 9, 1471.

194 *"arrange and correct many things in the city":* Ibid., 208.

195 *"things have come to such a pass":* Alison Brown, *Bartolomeo Scala,* 68.

CHAPTER X: FAT VICTORY

PAGE

198 *"ready and a spirited young man":* Machiavelli, *Florentine Histories,* VII, 25.

199 *"long live the people of Florence and liberty!":* Rinuccini, *Ricordi Storici,* CXII.

200 *mass executions in the squares of Florence and Prato:* Landucci, 9.

200 *frantic discussions in the* palazzo: see Lorenzo, *Lettere,* I, no. 52, for a discussion of Lorenzo's sometimes rocky relations with the city of Prato. Lorenzo's authority increased after the failure of the rebellion.

202 *Inghirami and his colleagues were Medici clients:* On September 1, 1466, for example, the Volterran faction headed by Inghirami received orders from Piero to hurry "with as many soldiers as possible for the salvation of His Magnificence in Florence and of his state" (see Lorenzo, *Lettere,* I, 548).

203 *a loan to the king of Naples:* Rinuccini, *Ricordi Storici,* CXVII.

204 *give Lorenzo full power to arbitrate the dispute:* Lorenzo, *Lettere,* I, 549.

204 *"malcontents who do not wish to be governed by [Lorenzo]":* Ibid., 550.

205 De Medici Lorenzo, his spirit: Simonetta, "Federico da Montefeltro contro Firenze," Archivio Storico Italiano, 262. Giovanni Santi, "The Life and Jest of Federico da Montefeltro."

205 *"the destruction of the house of Medici":* Lorenzo, *Lettere,* I, 551.

205 *"Better a lean peace":* Ross Williamson, 129.

205 *he might yet achieve his goals without war:* Lettere, I, 365. Sacramoro to Galeazzo, March 18, 1472, in which he writes, "Lorenzo hopes shortly to find a way to sow discord among those Volterrans who now govern the city, and told me that he has already begun."

206 *lose his dependence on the court of Milan:* Ibid., I, 552.

206 *"by a crowd of mad adventurers":* Dei, 27 verso.

206 *"not observing their agreements":* Lorenzo, *Lettere,* I, 367.

207 *Cries also went out:* Dei, 28 recto.

207 *the gates of Volterra were opened to the victorious army:* Lorenzo, *Lettere,* I, 386.

207 *accosted by a soldier from Federico's army:* Machiavelli, *Florentine Histories,* VII, 31.

207 *"Sack it! Sack it!":* Landucci, 11.

208 *"the cruelty of the sack":* Rochon, 221.

208 *"You have seen the afflicted and faithful friends":* Ross, *Lives,* 165.

208 *a public apparently well satisfied with his services:* Landucci, 11.

209 *The news of the victory:* Machiavelli, *Florentine Histories,* VII, 30.

CHAPTER XI: DOMESTIC TRANQUILLITY

PAGE

211 *"proud and combative, and rich with unlawful profits":* Compagni, *Chronicle of Florence,* I, i.

212 *"the first citizen of the republic":* F. W. Kent, *Lorenzo de' Medici and the Art of Magnificence,* 62.

212 *"thinking to achieve more than even Cosimo and Piero":* Ibid., 62.

212 *"and it seems to me very helpful to remember":* Rochon, 238.

213 *If I have been later in responding:* Lorenzo, *Lettere,* I, no. 61. Lorenzo to Tommaso Portinari, July 31, 1470.

213 *His patience with subordinates:* See de Roover, 274–75.

215 *As he grew stronger:* Francesco Guicciardini, *History of Florence,* 25.

215 *"There are two principal things that men do":* Dale Kent, *Cosimo de' Medici and the Florentine Renaissance,* 5.

216 *relegates a mother's contributions to the first years of life:* Alberti, *The Family in Renaissance Florence.* See especially 82–84 on the role of the father in his son's education.

217 *"I write this letter to tell you"*: Maguire, 160–61.

217 *MAGNIFICENT FATHER MINE:* Ross, *Lives,* 219–20.

217 *"Please send me some figs"*: Maguire, 100–101.

218 *"some sugar-plums"*: Ibid., 114.

218 *Then near the Certosa:* Ross, *Lives,* 270–71. Matteo Franco to Piero da Bibbiena, May 12, 1485.

219 *"We are sending you by the bearer seventeen partridges"*: Ibid., 152.

219 *"Yesterday, though there was little wind"*: Ibid., 150–51.

221 *"Magnificent Lorenzo"*: Ross, *Lives,* 56–57.

221 *"Almost all other rich men"*: Ficino, *Letters,* no. 17.

221 *"client and pupil"*: F. W. Kent, *Lorenzo de' Medici and the Art of Magnificence,* 55.

222 *"The children play about"*: Maguire, 156. Poliziano to Lorenzo, August 26, 1479.

222 *"I am anxiously awaiting news"*: Ibid., 156.

223 *"As to Giovanni, you will see"*: Ibid., Poliziano to Lorenzo, April 6, 1479.

223 *"I am here at Careggi"*: Ibid., 164.

224 *"I should be glad not to be turned into ridicule"*: Ibid., 165. Clarice to Lorenzo May 28, 1479.

224 *"Monna Clarice. I have been much annoyed"*: Ibid., 165.

225 *"We have arrived safely"*: Ibid., 96.

225 *Like his older brother:* See Ficino, *Letters,* especially the dedication and nos. 18, 60, 61.

225 *"I rejoice most heartily"*: Roscoe, *Life of Lorenzo de Medici,* 407.

226 *He was tall and sturdy:* Poliziano, "The Pazzi Conspiracy," in *Humanism and Liberty,* 183.

227 *There is nothing new here:* Reumont, 288–89. Niccolò Bendedei to Ercole d'Este, January 22, 1475.

227 *27th September [1481]:* Landucci, 31.

228 *"He who doesn't turn to the cross"*: Courtney, 25.

228 *"if one considers how life"*: Rochon, 198.

228 *"Our beautiful Florence"*: Dei, "Letter to a Venetian," in *The Portable Renaissance Reader,* 165–67.

229 *a young apprentice in Verrocchio's studio:* See David Alan Brown, *Leonardo da Vinci: Origins of a Genius* for an in-depth discussion of Leonardo's early relationship with Lorenzo.

229 *Botticelli, Filippino Lippi, Perugino, and Domenico Ghirlandaio:* See Baxandall, 26. This according to a report by the Milanese ambassador to Florence.

230 *"Men of intellect and ability"*: Francesco Guicciardini, *History of Florence,* IX.

230 *"all from his own [the master's] hand"*: Baxandall, 22.

231 Nourishing Venus comes: Cheney, *Botticelli's Neoplatonic Images,* 79.

CHAPTER XII: THE SHADOW OF ROME

PAGE

234 *"would be very acceptable"*: Lorenzo, *Lettere,* I, 317.

234 *"infinite blessings received"*: Ibid., I, 317.

235 *to add to his own collection:* Ross, *Lives,* 155.

236 *a native-born cardinal:* Lorenzo, *Lettere,* I, 398.

236 *"close to the hearts of all the citizens":* Ibid., I, 398.

237 *"Surely this city is to be mourned":* Bracciolini, "The Ruins of Rome," in *The Portable Renaissance Reader,* 379–84.

237 *"In order not to trouble Your Blessedness":* Lorenzo, *Lettere,* I, no. 115. Lorenzo to Sixtus, November 15, 1472.

238 *unleashing a barrage of letters:* Ibid., I, nos. 120–30.

238 *"Such is the desire of Giuliano":* Rochon, 57.

238 *"he [Lorenzo] does not wish him to make his way in the world":* Lorenzo, *Lettere,* I, 399. Sacramoro to Galeazzo Maria, April 9, 1472.

239 *"your other self":* Ficino, *Letters,* no. 61.

239 *"I wrote to Giuliano, my brother":* Lorenzo, *Lettere,* I, no. 147. Lorenzo to Filippo Sacramoro, October 28, 1473. The issue revolved around the possibility of a new league among the papacy, Milan, and Florence, against the erratic ambitions of Ferrante. That Lorenzo entrusted the negotiations to Giuliano is a measure of his faith in him.

239 *"Many times he told me":* Ibid., i. 399. Piero Vespucci to Lucrezia Tornabuoni, January 12, 1480.

240 Sometimes discord can spread: Lorenzo, "The Martyrdom of Saints John and Paul," in *Selected Writings,* 111.

240 *"I see no difficulty":* Ross, *Lives,* 170.

245 *the ten-year-old Caterina:* See Breisach, 269.

247 *"O my son!":* Pastor, 250.

250 *"For the Medici did not enjoy a lordship":* Francesco Guicciardini, *Dialogue on the Government of Florence,* 71.

CHAPTER XIII: UNDER THE SIGN OF MARS

PAGE

254 *"I was of the city that changed for the Baptist":* Dante, *Inferno,* xiii.

254 *on Easter morning:* Villani, VI, xxxviii.

256 Messer *Pazzino de' Pazzi:* Compagni, III, 40.

257 *rebellion of the* Ciompi: For some vivid firsthand accounts of the revolt of the *Ciompi,* see *The Chronicles of the Tumult of the Ciompi* (Monash Publications in History) in which a number of contemporary chronicles have been collected.

257 *"because the masses had chosen him":* Dale Kent, *Rise of the Medici Faction in Florence,* 5.

258 *"since childhood he has been continually involved":* Brucker, *The Civic World of Early Renaissance Florence,* 34–35.

260 *"Life without honor is a living death":* Frick, 77.

260 *"People of superior refinement":* Davies, *Democracy and Classical Greece,* 114.

260 *"Had it not been for this friendship":* Bisticci, 311.

261 *"But although the Pazzi were Florentine nobles":* Francesco Guicciardini, *History of Florence,* 29.

261 *"Yesterday Piero de' Pazzi entered the city":* Strozzi, *Lettere,* no. 26.

261 *"There was in Florence in those days a family"*: Valori, 48.

261 *insufficiently honored by the regime*: Machiavelli, *Florentine Histories*, VIII, 2.

262 "mezo amoniti: See Lorenzo, *Lettere* II, note 3, 123.

262 *"[T]hey will put in his place his relative Guglielmo"*: Rubinstein, *Government of Florence Under the Medici*, 209.

262 *Benedetto Dei lists Jacopo*: Dei, 35v.

262 *the Pazzi bank had been one of the few sufficiently trusted*: See de Roover, 91.

263 *"He was incredibly angry"*: Poliziano, *The Pazzi Conspiracy*, in *Humanism and Liberty*, 171–83.

263 *"His stature was short"*: Ibid., 171.

263 *"a very restless, spirited, and ambitious man"*: Francesco Guicciardini, *History of Florence*, 30.

264 *"believing that Fortune did him a thousand wrongs"*: Pulci, *Stanze sur la Giostra di Lorenzo de' Medici*, CXXXVII and CLV.

265 *"Lorenzo asked [the Pazzi] not [to] supply the money"*: Francesco Guicciardini, *History of Florence*, 30.

CHAPTER XIV: CONSPIRACY

268 *"And since he [Francesco] was very friendly with Count Girolamo"*: Machiavelli, *Florentine Histories*, VIII, 2.

269 *"his state would not be worth a bean"*: "Confession of Giovanni Battista da Montesecco," in Roscoe, Appendix XV.

271 *"devoid of knowledge of and also respect for the law"*: Poliziano, "The Pazzi Conspiracy," in *Humanism and Liberty*, 172.

272 *"I wanted something important in your affairs"*: Ficino, *Letters*, no. 117.

272 *"Our delightful feasts all came to an end"*: Pastor, 254. Stefano Infessura.

274 *"depraved and malignant spirit"*: Lorenzo, *Lettere*, II, 59.

274 *"The matter is of utmost importance"*: Ibid., II, no. 182.

275 *And while in the letter of the said Count*: Ibid.

276 *"keep himself safe"*: Fubini, "La Congiura dei Pazzi," in *Lorenzo de' Medici: New Perspectives*, 230.

276 *"those who wish to engage in machinations"*: Lorenzo, *Lettere*, II, 121. Lorenzo adds, significantly, that his internal enemies are doomed to failure unless they have the support of "the King or others" causing the rebellion of certain dependencies "as happened in the case of Volterra."

276 *I find that all of this comes from the same source*: Ibid., II, no. 201. Lorenzo to Galeazzo, September 7, 1475.

277 *"if it could be done without scandal"*: Ibid., II, no. 240. Lorenzo to Baccio Ugolini, February 1, 1477.

277 *Città di Castello*: See ibid., II, Excursus I, 475–84 for the fullest explanation of the battle for Città di Castello.

278 *"an example to all the lands of the Church"*: Ibid., II, 476.

278 *and began laying siege to the town*: Dei, 71 verso.

278 *"If you would have me see"*: Pastor, 295. Girolamo Riario to Lorenzo, October 26, 1474.

279 *equivocated as he was prone to do:* See Lorenzo, *Lettere,* II, no. 171. Lorenzo to Galeazzo Maria, August 6, 1474.

279 *"all the Commune wished to go to the aid of Castello"*: Ibid., II, 482.

280 *"initiated new policies in Rome"*: Ibid., II, 53. Galeazzo Maria to Sacramoro August 6, 1474.

280 *" the stratagems, which he used in favor of the Pazzi"*: Ibid., II, 53.

282 *a defensive treaty between the two great republics of Italy:* For detailed discussion of the complex negotiations see Lorenzo, *Lettere,* II, especially 5–8, 12–30, and 475–90, as well as Clarke, *The Soderini and the Medici,* 218–29.

282 *the "faithlessness" of the Venetians:* Lorenzo, *Lettere,* II, 487.

283 *even over the objections of the duke:* See Clarke, *The Soderini and the Medici,* 226.

283 *celebrated with bonfires and fireworks in the piazzas:* Rinuccini, *Ricordi Storici,* CXXIII.

283 *"should Lorenzo pursue this league"*: Simonetta, "Federico da Montefeltro contro Firenze," *Archivio Storico Italiano,* 263.

283 *"Italy . . . was divided into two factions"*: Machiavelli, *Florentine Histories,* VIII, 2.

284 *"an honor hitherto reserved"*: Pastor, 261.

285 *"prudence and manly courage"*: Reumont, I, 197. Ferrante to Lorenzo, September 1466.

286 *"I sent it to Renato de' Pazzi"*: Martines, *April Blood,* 103.

287 *head of Medusa picked out in pearls:* See *Le Tems Revient 'L Tempo Si Rinuova: Feste e Spettacoli Nella Firenze di Lorenzo il Magnifico,* 94–100, for a complete description of costumes for Giuliano's joust.

287 *"that bridles and gives rein to the magnanimous Tuscans"*: Poliziano, *Stanze sur la Giostra di Giuliano,* IV.

288 *"And you know"*: Ibid., II, xi.

289 *"The air seems to turn dark"*: Ibid., II, xxxiv–xxxv.

CHAPTER XV: MURDER IN THE CATHEDRAL

PAGE

292 *the practical benefits of hard steel:* See Lubkin, 116–17.

292 *bodyguard of fifty mounted crossbowmen and fifty foot soldiers:* Ibid., 235.

292 *he feared they might be plotting against him:* See Ibid., 239. Whether or not his fears had any basis in reality is debatable. Rumors about his mother are even less plausible.

292 *"lust—and that one I have in full perfection"*: Ibid., 200.

293 *turning his daughters into common whores:* Ibid.

293 *"handsome youth was not yet sixteen"*: Pius II, 105.

293 *"the most handsome creature ever seen"*: Dei, 22 verso and 42 verso.

294 *"Duca! Duca!"*: Ilardi, 75.

295 *"It was a worthy, laudable, manly deed"*: Rinuccini, *Ricordi Storici,* CXXV.

295 *"a thousand times"*: Ilardi, 75.

295 *to proclaim the republic's unwavering support:* See ibid., 97.

295 *"as long as he had life in his body":* Ibid.

296 *"As she was thus dead":* Lorenzo, *Commento,* Argument 1.

297 *"having decided not to get involved in this affair":* Hook, 89.

297 *"Idleness has so gained the upper hand":* Reumont, 308.

298 *"It seemed as if men":* Ibid.

298 *[I]t would please me much for the State:* Ibid., 318.

299 *"saying that he feared":* Machiavelli, *Florentine Histories,* VIII, 2.

299 *for which he agreed to furnish men and logistical support:* Simonetta, "Federico da Montefeltro contro Firenze," in Archivio Storico Italiano, n. 596, a. CLXI, 2003 II.

299 *"his majesty would never consent":* Ibid., 263.

300 *the archbishop's residence in Rome:* See the "Confession of Giovanni Battista da Montesecco," reproduced in Roscoe, *Life of Lorenzo de Medici,* Appendix XV.

304 *before word of the conspiracy leaked out:* See ibid.: "And as I have said, many times it was discussed in the chambers of the Count . . . how things could not long go on as they had . . . the undertaking being on so many tongues."

304 *"man of letters, virtuous and of substance":* Archivio di Stato di Firenze, Mediceo Avanti il Principato, filza 34, no. 275. Girolamo Riario to Lorenzo de' Medici.

304 *implicated in the 1466 plot to overthrow Piero:* See Fubini, "La Congiura dei Pazzi: Radici Politico-Sociali e Ragioni di un Fallimento," in *Lorenzo de' Medici: New Perspectives.* Jacopo di Poggio Bracciolini was the one figure implicated in both the plots of 1466 and 1478.

304 *"so well disposed":* Confession of Giovanni Battista da Montesecco, reproduced in Roscoe, *Life of Lorenzo de Medici,* Appendix XV.

304 *his preference for life in the country:* Hook, 96.

305 *"cold as ice":* Ibid., 96.

307 *fifty on foot had accompanied the count of Montesecco:* Martines, *April Blood,* 114.

308 *"Again [the conspirators] sent a servant":* Poliziano, "The Pazzi Conspiracy," in *Humanism and Liberty,* 175.

309 *"They did not think there would be time":* Francesco Guicciardini, *History of Florence,* IV.

309 *"where God would see him":* Ross, *Lives,* 189.

309 *a favorable impression of his intended victim:* See Valori, 51–52.

311 *"Your illness seems to have made you fat":* Ibid., 52.

CHAPTER XVI: THE BLOODSTAINED PAVEMENT

PAGE

315 *"Going out through the church towards home myself":* Poliziano. "The Pazzi Conspiracy," in *Humanism and Liberty,* 177.

315 *Francesco Salviati, along with Poggio Bracciolini:* See Rinuccini, *Ricordi Storici,* CXXVII.

315 *he and his men made straight for the Palace of the Priors:* See ibid., CXXXVII.

315 *"very secret business":* Ibid., CXXXVII.

317 *the ancient cry of Florentine revolution:* See ibid., CXXVII.

318 "[A]nd so for the most part ended": Rinuccini, *Ricordi Storici,* CXXVIII.

319 "*Neither his wound nor his fear*": Poliziano, "The Pazzi Conspiracy," in *Humanism and Liberty,* 179.

319 *My Most Illustrious Lords:* Lorenzo, *Lettere,* III, no. 272.

319 "*There, armed men were everywhere*": Poliziano, "The Pazzi Conspiracy," in *Humanism and Liberty,* 177.

320 *I was in Santa Liperata just then:* Narratives, *April Blood,* 122.

320 "*I commend myself to you*": Hook, 100.

321 "*amongst others a priest of the bishop's was killed*": Landucci, 16.

321 *the abode of a cannibal king:* Poliziano, "The Pazzi Conspiracy," in *Humanism and Liberty,* 178.

321 *like grim Christmas tree ornaments:* See Rinuccini, *Ricordi Storici,* CXXVII. He says that by the end of the day fifteen bodies were hanging from the palace windows.

322 *The Pisan leader was soon dangling:* Poliziano, "The Pazzi Conspiracy," in *Humanism and Liberty,* 178.

322 "*all the signs are in favor of Lorenzo*": Lorenzo, *Lettere,* III, 4.

322 *The bloodshed, which continued sporadically for weeks:* See Landucci, 17.

322 "*still bewildered with terror*": Ibid.

322 *armed soldiers patrolled the city:* Ibid., 18.

323 "*made angry threats*": Poliziano, "The Pazzi Conspiracy," in *Humanism and Liberty,* 176.

324 *turned back by angry citizens at the nearby village of Firenzuola:* Lorenzo, *Lettere,* III, 4. Sacramoro to the Duke and Duchess, April 27, 1478.

324 *confronted by pro-Medici forces arriving from Bologna:* Ibid., III, 4.

324 *the pope and his supporters were thrown into utter confusion:* Ibid, III, 5.

324 *a patriotic farmer in the village of San Godenzo:* Rinuccini, *Ricordi Storici,* CXXVII.

325 *beheaded in the courtyard of the Bargello:* Landucci, 18.

325 "*I am Bernardo*": Acton, 77.

326 *some boys disinterred it a second time:* Landucci, 19.

327 "*He was very mild, very kind*": Poliziano, "The Pazzi Conspiracy," in *Humanism and Liberty,* 183.

327 "*Here and on the following page*": Hook, 103.

CHAPTER XVII: NEAPOLITAN GAMBIT

PAGE

329 "*The Count went to Donato's house*": Bisticci, 287. For Acciaiuoli's experience in Rome in the aftermath of the Pazzi conspiracy, see also Margery Ganz's "Donato Acciaiuoli and the Medici: A Strategy for Survival in '400 Florence," in *Rinascimento,* 2nd ser., 22 (1982): especially 62–65.

330 "*He addressed the pope and complained bitterly*": Bisticci, 287–88.

331 "*more dead than alive from the terror*": Pastor, 317.

331 "*that son of iniquity and foster-child of perdition*": Ross Williamson, 177.

331 *he had no quarrel with the people of Florence:* Valori, 58.

331 "*For we make war on no one*": Ross, *Lives,* 206.

332 *"All citizens must place the common before the private good"*: Hook, 105.

332 *"Your Holiness says you are only waging war"*: Ross Williamson, 178.

333 *We and the people have proved"*: Ibid., 178–79.

334 *"holds for certain"*: "Assassination of Galeazzo Maria Sforza" in *Violence and Civic Disorder in Italian Cities,* 101.

334 *forces of the pope and the king of Naples were poised:* See Lorenzo, *Lettere,* III, 64–65, and Ross, *Lives,* 194–98.

334 *"one body, with one mind"*: Hook, 107.

334 *instigated by agents of King Ferrante:* See Lorenzo, *Lettere,* III, 131.

335 *"It is necessary that this Senate bestir itself"*: Ibid., III, no. 291. Lorenzo to Giovanni Lanfredini, June 20, 1478.

335 *"I do not know what hope I can have"*: Hook, 110.

335 *a formal declaration of war to the* Signoria: See Lorenzo, *Lettere,* III, 127–32 (especially note 13, 131). Lorenzo to Girolamo Morelli, July 15, 1478.

335 *a wave of refugees fleeing toward the capital:* See Landucci, 21.

335 *"pillaging and working great havoc"*: Ibid., 21.

335 *"The rule for our Italian soldiers seems to be this"*: Ibid., 22.

336 *while he haggled over his fee:* See Lorenzo, *Lettere,* III. Lorenzo to Girolamo Morelli, August 20 and August 21, 1478, 175–85, and to Ercole d'Este, August 27, 1478.

336 *"The Florentine troops passed in such a wretched state"*: Reumont, 367.

336 *he toiled late into the night over his philosophical studies:* See Toscani, "Lorenzo, the Religious Poet," in *Lorenzo de' Medici: New Perspectives,* 86.

337 *"For the love of God, Girolamo"*: Lorenzo, *Lettere,* IV, no. 434.

337 *"tell[ing] us that the king and the Holy Father"*: Landucci, 21.

337 *"The Duke of Urbino is said to have quipped"*: Francesco Guicciardini, *History of Florence,* 43–44.

338 *"And at this Christmas-time"*: Landucci, 26.

338 *"many fine palaces belonging to citizens"*: F. W. Kent, *Lorenzo de' Medici and the Art of Magnificence,* 79.

338 *"I remain in the house [at Cafaggiolo]"*: Ross, *Lives,* 214. Poliziano to Lucrezia Tornabuoni.

339 *"there is nothing but bare walls"*: Maguire, 166.

339 *"I thought I would come this evening"*: Lorenzo, *Lettere,* IV, no. 414.

339 *"The news I have received from Naples"*: Ibid., III, 143–44. Lorenzo to Girolamo Morelli July 25, 1478.

340 *he tried to borrow from her an additional 30,000 to 40,000 ducats:* Ibid., III.

340 *teetering on the brink of bankruptcy:* Hook, 108.

340 *"without the sanction of any law and without authority"*: De Roover, 367.

340 *"the money that Lorenzo drew from public funds"*: Francesco Guicciardini, *Dialogue on the Government of Florence,* 71.

342 *but this offer led to nothing:* See Hook, 110.

342 *"I hear the plague is committing more ravages in Florence"*: Ross, *Lives,* 218. Clarice to Lorenzo May 28, 1479.

342 *"To make matters worse, the plague continues to spread"*: Lorenzo, *Lettere,* IV, no. 407. Lorenzo to Girolamo Morelli, June 23, 1479.

342 *"I have written you a long discourse"*: Ibid., IV, 204.

342 *"The citizens accused one another freely and without respect"*: Machiavelli, *Florentine Histories*, VIII, 17.

343 *"You have taken a decision that will take my life"*: Ibid., VIII, 19.

343 *"I cannot believe that the Lord Lodovico"*: Ross, *Lives*, 227. Lorenzo to Girolamo Morelli, September 11, 1479.

344 *"Most Illustrious My Lords"*: Lorenzo, *Lettere*, IV, no. 444. Lorenzo to the *Signoria* of Florence, December 7, 1479.

345 *"regarded as too bold and rash a decision"*: Francesco Guicciardini, *History of Florence*, IX.

346 *laying the groundwork for months*: See Lorenzo, *Lettere*, IV, 391–400, for a full discussion of the negotiations leading up to his journey.

347 *The situation of affairs appeared serious to all*: Reumont, 397–98.

347 *"I have received many friendly words"*: Ibid., 392.

348 *"received and honored with as much dignity as possible"*: See Lorenzo, *Lettere*, IV, 273.

348 *"He greeted me most graciously"*: Ibid., IV, 274. Lorenzo to the *Dieci di Balìa*, December 22, 1479.

348 *"He seemed to be two men"*: In *The Medici: Godfathers of the Renaissance*.

348 *"Your letter of the 18th rejoiced us all"*: Ross, *Lives*, 232. Bartolomeo Scala to Lorenzo.

348 *while not jeopardizing his relations with the pope*: See Lorenzo, *Lettere*, IV, 275. See also ibid., IV, no. 447, for attempts by Rome to scuttle the peace deal.

348 *"We made a virtue of necessity"*: Reumont, 407–8.

349 *"Lorenzo's confederate"*: Ross, *Lives*, 236.

349 *"The present letter will not be one of those"*: Ibid., 411.

350 *"[Y]our family are all well"*: Hook, 115.

350 *"the length of these negotiations"*: Ibid.

350 *"We are all hoping against hope"*: Ross, *Lives*, 234–35. Bartolomeo Scala to Lorenzo, January 15, 1480.

351 *"so that you never saw"*: Hook, 116.

351 *"young and old, noble and commoner"*: Valori, 68.

351 *"Lorenzo arrived from Livorno"*: Landucci, 29.

351 *"The ratification of the peace arrived in the night"*: Ibid., 29.

CHAPTER XVIII: THE SHADOW LIFTS

PAGE

353 *"In Rome the alarm was as great"*: Pastor, IV, 334–35.

353 *"If the faithful, especially the Italians"*: Ibid., IV, 335–36.

354 *could no longer pursue his vendetta against Lorenzo*: See Ross, *Lives*, 237.

354 *"a great miracle"*: Landucci, 30.

354 *Sixtus bestowed his blessing*: See Machiavelli, *Florentine Histories*, VIII, 21.

355 *"Florence's top man"*: F. W. Kent, *Lorenzo de' Medici and the Art of Magnificence*, 81.

355 *"When I go more than ten miles out of the city"*: Martines, *April Blood*, 245–46.

355 *a special committee of 240 prominent citizens:* See Rinuccini, *Ricordi Storici*, CXXXII.

356 *largely excluding the "new men"*: See Rubinstein, *Government of Florence Under the Medici*, 226–32.

357 *"the members of the new body"*: Hook, 153. Giovanni Cambi.

357 *"removed every liberty from the people"*: Rinuccini, *Ricordi Storici*, CXXXII.

357 *"they refashioned the government in such a way"*: Rubinstein, *Government of Florence Under the Medici*, 231.

358 *had reconstituted the old league with Venice and Siena:* See Landucci, 29.

359 *"to satisfy my debt it seemed best"*: Breisach, 282.

360 *As followers of the Orsini, the Colonna, and the della Valle clashed in the streets of Rome:* See Landucci, 34.

360 *"for Girolamo's ambitions"*: Breisach, 50.

360 *"In the Pope's antechambers"*: Pastor, IV, 356–57. Sigismondo de' Conti.

360 *"your presence is very necessary here"*: Hook, 160. Bartolomeo Scala.

361 *"Various were the opinions"*: Valori, 74.

361 *the "fulcrum" of Italy:* Francesco Guicciardini, *History of Florence*, IX.

361 *to settle their dynastic rivalries:* For a modern corrective to Guicciardini's overstatements, see Mallett, "Diplomacy and War in Later Fifteenth-Century Italy," in *Art and Politics in Renaissance Italy*, 135–58.

361 *"Italy was preserved in this happy state"*: Francesco Guicciardini, *History of Italy*, I, i.

362 *the best informed of European leaders:* See Mallett, "Diplomacy and War in Later Fifteenth-Century Italy," in *Art and Politics in Renaissance Italy*, 135–58.

362 *"not only do I want your prompt assistance in this"*: Bullard, *Lorenzo il Magnifico*, 23.

362 *"I believe I have the reputation"*: Bullard, "Lorenzo and Patterns of Diplomatic Discourse," in *Lorenzo the Magnificent*, 267.

363 *the foremost statesman of the age:* See Francesco Guicciardini, *History of Florence*, IX. See also Machiavelli, *Florentine Histories*, VIII, 36.

363 *"honorably received as a man of merit"*: Landucci, 36.

363 *came to nothing:* See Brown, "Lorenzo and Guicciardini," in *Lorenzo the Magnificent*, 284.

363 *"Many were afflicted"*: Landucci, 39.

363 *"Up to this time we have carried"*: Pastor, IV, 387.

364 *"Nothing could daunt the ferocious Sixtus"*: Francesco Guicciardini, *The History of Florence*, VII.

364 Sixtus, at last you're dead: Rendina, 427.

365 One must give praise, my fellow Romans: Ibid., 429.

366 *"[Y]ou will inform His Holiness"*: Ross, *Lives*, 262.

366 *"Be careful not to take precedence"*: Ibid., 261.

366 *"What could one hope for from Piero?"*: Trexler, *Public Life in Renaissance Florence*, 462.

366 *"Lorenzo declares (and it makes me laugh)"*: Ross, *Lives*, 273.

367 *"made the whole city want to throw up"*: Trexler, *Public Life in Renaissance Florence,* 461.

367 *"Piero has not seemed to me the person"*: Hook, 163.

367 *an extended bout of depression in the summer of 1483:* Brown, "Lorenzo and Guicciardini," in *Lorenzo the Magnificent,* 292.

368 *"We promised in the prologue"*: Lorenzo, *Commento De' Miei Sonetti,* XI.

369 *"[T]oday, the Magnificent Lorenzo didn't leave his house"*: Trexler, *Public Life in Renaissance Florence,* 445.

369 *"In order to prevent the return of these pains"*: Ross, *Lives,* 302. Petrus Bonus Avogarius to Lorenzo, February 11, 1489.

369 *"in order to cure himself and to restore his health"*: Hook, 162.

370 *"my having been ill these days"*: F. W. Kent, *Lorenzo de' Medici and the Art of Magnificence,* 86.

370 *"he wanted to have a say in everything"*: Butters, "Lorenzo and Machiavelli," in *Lorenzo the Magnificent,* 279.

370 *"Still burdened with tears and sorrow"*: Lorenzo, *Lettere,* VI, no. 567. Lorenzo to Ercole d'Este, March 25, 1482.

371 *"to seem older in appearance"*: Trexler, *Public Life in Renaissance Florence,* 439.

371 *"behaving disgracefully with women"*: Brown, "Lorenzo and Guicciardini" in *Lorenzo the Magnificent,* 292.

371 *"Being then placed by Fortune"*: Lorenzo, *Commento De' Miei Sonetti,* XI.

371 *"His last love, which lasted for many years"*: Francesco Guicciardini, *History of Florence,* IX.

372 *three new plots on his life were uncovered:* See Landucci, 31–34.

372 *stopped using the familiar* tu: See de Roover, 220.

373 *"the first list was drawn up by Lorenzo and Ser Giovanni alone"*: See Rubinstein, *Government of Florence Under the Medici,* Appendix XI, where he reproduces Guicciardini's account in full.

373 il padrone, *the boss:* See Brown, "Lorenzo and Guicciardini" in *Lorenzo the Magnificent,* 289. This was a term used by Lorenzo's supporter Bernardo del Nero, according to Guicciardini in his *Dialogue on the Government of Florence.*

374 *"That office had been created long ago"*: Francesco Guicciardini, *History of Florence,* V.

375 *Luca Landucci records the hanging:* See Landucci, 12 and 27.

375 *[Lorenzo] offered them consoling words:* Martines, *April Blood,* 221–22.

375 *"condemned by the Committee of the Eight"*: Rinuccini, "Dialogue on Liberty," in *Humanism and Liberty,* 206.

376 *"It occurred to me to reveal"*: Trexler, *Public Life in Renaissance Florence,* 448.

377 *"In making marriages"*: Dale Kent, *Rise of the Medici Faction in Florence,* 50.

377 *it was Lorenzo who made the arrangements:* See Brown, "Lorenzo and Guicciardini," in *Lorenzo the Magnificent,* 291.

377 *"No one so much as moves"*: Hook, 155.

378 *"narrow seas and storms of civic life"*: Lorenzo, *Commento De' Miei Sonetti,* 73.

378 *"Get these petitioners off my back"*: F. W. Kent, *Lorenzo de' Medici and the Art of Magnificence,* 80.

379 *"For when the arms of Italy"*: Machiavelli, *Florentine Histories,* VIII, 36.

CHAPTER XIX: THE GARDEN AND THE GROVE

PAGE

381 *"Ort[us] L[aurentii] de medicis"*: See Elam, "Lorenzo de' Medici's Sculpture Garden," in *Mitteilungen des Kunsthistorischen Institutes in Florenz* 36 (1992): 41–84, where she marshals copious evidence to prove the existence of Lorenzo's garden.

382 *"stayed as a young man"*: Ibid., 42.

382 *Now that the boy [Michelangelo] was drawing one thing*: Condivi, *The Life of Michelangelo*, 10.

384 *"this Tuscan tongue"*: Ross, *Lives*, 88. Lorenzo to Don Federigo of Naples.

384 *universally regarded as an authority on all matters aesthetic*: See, for instance, F. W. Kent, *Lorenzo de' Medici and the Art of Magnificence*, 1 and 101–4, for his role as artistic arbiter.

385 *"very great architectural expertise"*: Ibid., 102. The story that Lorenzo himself submitted a design is apparently in error.

385 *"quality and that manner and form"*: Ibid., 104.

386 *"And when he went to race at Siena"*: Landucci, 42.

387 Those who love these pretty nymphs: Lorenzo, "The Triumph of Bacchus and Ariadne," in *Selected Poems and Prose*, 162.

387 *mined by writers like Poliziano*: See Cheney, 69–83.

388 *"Piero—Enclosed is a letter from Baccio"*: Ross, *Lives*, 317.

388 *"I have received the cameo"*: F. W. Kent, *Lorenzo de' Medici and the Art of Magnificence*, 34.

388 *celebrations held in honor of the philosopher's birthday*: Ibid., 31.

388 *Recent scholarship has thrown cold water*: See Hankins, "The Myth of the Platonic Academy of Florence," *Renaissance Quarterly* 44 (1991): 429–75. See also Ficino's letter to Jacopo Bracciolini, in Ficino, *Letters*, no. 107.

389 *Plato, the father of philosophers*: Ficino, *Commentary on Plato's Symposium on Love*, Introduction. Some believe this particular scene is an invention since it only appears in the second edition of the book, but it certainly reflects Lorenzo's interest in Plato and the many conversations the two engaged in while neighbors at Careggi.

389 *"is the first step on the staircase of love"*: Hook, 143.

390 For while the soul is bound in carnal bonds: Lorenzo, "The Supreme Good," IV.

391 *O' God, o' greatest Good*: Lorenzo, *Laude*, 1–3, in *Selected Writings*, 155.

391 *"[The ruler] will not, indeed, consider himself"*: Ficino, *Letters*, no. 95.

391 The majesty of our imperial throne: *The Martyrdom of Saints John and Paul*, 133, in *Selected Writings*, 217.

392 *"I have gone over in my mind many times"*: Field, 73.

392 *he was roughed up by Girolamo Riario's soldiers*: See Bisticci, "Life of Donato Acciaiuoli."

394 *"[T]he truth is that I cannot peacefully tolerate"*: Rinuccini, "Dialogue on Liberty," in *Humanism and Liberty*, 222.

394 Lured on, escorted by the sweetest thoughts: Lorenzo, "The Supreme Good," I, lines 1–3, 7–15.

394 *"To rule is wearisome, a bitter feat"*: Lorenzo, *The Martyrdom of Saints John and Paul*, 98, in *Selected Writings*, 237.

395 *as if he had been a member of his own family:* F. W. Kent, *Lorenzo de' Medici and the Art of Magnificence,* 59.

395 *One day, [Michelangelo] was examining:* Condivi, 12.

396 *[Lorenzo] arranged that Michelangelo be given a good room:* Ibid., 13.

397 *no surer sign that one was thought a part of the family:* See Ross, *Lives,* 293.

397 *listed among those of the household waiters:* See Draper, *Bertoldo di Giovanni,* 15.

397 *"Recognizing in Michelangelo a superior spirit":* Condivi, 14–15.

398 *Lorenzo had amassed one of the greatest collections of manuscripts:* Hook, 127.

398 *"Wandering beyond the limits of his own property":* Ackerman, 77.

399 *"The Count della Mirandola is here":* Ross, *Lives,* 310. Lorenzo to Giovanni Lanfredini, June 19, 1489.

399 *"among the first and best-loved creatures of my house":* Ibid., 173.

399 *"louse clinging to the Medici balls":* F. W. Kent, *Lorenzo de' Medici and the Art of Magnificence,* 90.

399 *"I should be glad not to be turned into ridicule":* Ross, 219. Clarice to Lorenzo, May 28, 1479.

399 *"I will not allow any man to have the spending of my money":* Maguire, 183.

399 *"were it not for Matteo Franco":* Ficino, *Letters,* no. 73.

400 *"to achieve even more than Cosimo and Piero":* F. W. Kent, *Lorenzo de' Medici and the Art of Magnificence,* 62.

400 *monuments in brick and stone would be all that was left:* See Bisticci, 223.

401 *grandiose gestures that smacked of princely ambition?:* See F. W. Kent, *Lorenzo de' Medici and the Art of Magnificence,* 48.

401 *"prized it so much":* Ibid. 37.

402 *"in the manner of his ancestors":* Elam, "Lorenzo de' Medici and the Urban Development of Renaissance Florence," in *Art History* i, no. i (March 1978.)

402 *the construction of two new roads lined with new housing:* See ibid. for a full discussion of this little known project.

402 *"embellishment to the city":* Ibid., 44. Giovanni Cambi.

403 *"Lorenzo de' Medici [is] paying the lion's share":* F. W. Kent, *Lorenzo de' Medici and the Art of Magnificence,* 98.

403 *For this convent models were made:* Vasari, "Giuliano and Antonio da San Gallo," *Lives of the Artists,* 700.

404 *Fled is the time of year:* Lorenzo, "Ambra," I, i, in *Selected Poems and Prose.*

404 *"I do not approve of turrets and crenellations":* Alberti, *On the Art of Building in Ten Books,* IX, 4.

404 *remained nervous about the lack of adequate means of defense:* F. W. Kent, *Lorenzo de' Medici and the Art of Magnificence,* 125.

405 *"I have learned that when [the saplings] are tender and young":* Ibid., 117.

405 *"I don't dare contradict him":* Ibid., 131.

CHAPTER XX: THE CARDINAL AND THE PREACHER

PAGE

407 *"This is an age of gold":* Schevill, *History of Florence,* 416.

408 *many reproached Lorenzo for his apparent callousness:* See Ross, *Lives,* 296.

408   *"If you should hear Lorenzo blamed"*: Ross Williamson, 205.

408   *Too often I am obliged to trouble and worry*: Ross, *Lives,* 296–97. Lorenzo to Innocent VIII, July 31, 1488.

409   *"My Contessina"*: Maguire, 177.

409   *"I should be glad if you could mention the matter"*: Ross Williamson, 206.

410   *"The Knight Without Fear"*: Maguire, 186.

410   *"She does not seem particularly good or bad"*: Ibid., 187.

410   *"The brains of these Orsini citizens"*: Ibid., 186.

411   *"To me it seems the King is arrogant and vile"*: Bullard, *Lorenzo il Magnifico,* 67.

411   *"[T]his ecclesiastical state"*: Ibid., 136.

412   *"Lorenzo will know that there was never a pope"*: Ibid., 160.

412   *"We have been for twelve or perhaps thirteen years"*: Ibid., 140.

412   *"The Pope seems rather a man in need of advice"*: Ross, *Lives,* 259. Guidantonio Vespucci to Lorenzo.

413   *"our affairs here"*: Bullard, *Lorenzo il Magnifico,* 145.

413   *"The Magnificent Lorenzo arrived here"*: Ross, *Lives,* 280–81.

414   *"The bad health of Madonna Maddalena"*: Ibid., 328–29.

414   *"It is urgent that his Holiness"*: Ibid., 322.

415   To join the Medici girl to his son Franceschetti: Rendina, 429.

415   *"He is so strictly bred"*: Van Passen, 87.

416   *"the Pope sleeps with the eyes of the Magnificent Lorenzo"*: Hook, 170.

416   *"that the Florentine ambassador"*: Ibid., 170.

416   *"We had heard that the Pope had made six cardinals"*: Landucci, 47.

416   *"the greatest honor that has ever befallen our house"*: Ross, *Lives,* 303. Lorenzo to Piero Alamanni, March 14, 1489.

416   *"was a ladder enabling [Lorenzo's] house to rise to heaven"*: Machiavelli, *Florentine Histories* VIII, 36.

416   *"that [the nomination] was a thing of such public notoriety"*: Ross, *Lives,* 303. Lorenzo to Piero Alamanni, March 14, 1489.

418   *"charismatic center"*: See Trexler, *Public Life in Renaissance Florence,* especially Chapters 13 and 14.

419   *"Blest in your genius"*: Ross Williamson, 224.

419   *the fabled treasury of some Oriental potentate*: See Trexler, *Public Life in Renaissance Florence,* 446.

420   *Lorenzo was the greatest Florentine in history*: See F. W. Kent, *Lorenzo de' Medici and the Art of Magnificence,* 149. This according to Piero Parenti.

420   *"to whomever wanted it"*: Trexler, *Public Life in Renaissance Florence,* 449.

420   *"almost against my will"*: Lorenzo, *Commento,* IV.

420   *"I am a little amazed that you have diminished this* festa*"*: Trexler, *Public Life in Renaissance Florence,* 409.

421   *"[I]n these peaceful times"*: Machiavelli, *Florentine Histories,* VIII, 36.

421   *"feast of the devil"*: Trexler, *Public Life in Renaissance Florence,* 414.

422   *he lent his own personal tableware*: See ibid., 413.

422   *Lorenzo de' Medici having conceived the idea*: Ibid., 451.

422   *"We're going forth to pleasure all"*: Lorenzo, "Song of the Cicadas," in *Selected Poems and Prose,* 160–61.

423 *"Why do we not follow Jesus"*: Van Passen, 52.

424 *"false proud whore"*: Roeder, 10.

424 *"If there is no change soon"*: Van Passen, 89.

424 *"The poor . . . are oppressed by taxes"*: Roeder, *Man of the Renaissance,* 24.

424 *"No one can persuade you that usury is sinful"*: Ibid., 23.

425 *"But already famines and floods"*: Roeder, 5.

425 *"The chief reason I have entered the priesthood"*: Savonarola, *Lettere e Scritti Apologetici,* I. Savonarola to his father, April 25, 1475.

426 *"You have kindled a love for Thee"*: Lorenzo, "Laudi," *Opere Scelte,* 404.

426 *"at present one sees such a lack of virtue"*: Ross, *Lives,* 333. Lorenzo to Giovanni, March 1492.

427 *"Here is a stranger come into my house"*: Hook, 181.

427 *"I know a city"*: Van Passen, 95.

427 *"There goes a brave man"*: Ibid., 96.

428 *"I have met Fra Mariano repeatedly"*: Ross Williamson, 237–39.

428 *"He preaches from Cicero and the poets"*: Van Passen, 69.

430 *household items valued at 20,000 florins:* See Landucci, 52.

430 *You are much beholden to our Lord God:* Ross, *Lives,* 332–5. Lorenzo to Giovanni, March 1492.

431 With endless tribulations I have reigned: Lorenzo, *The Martyrdom of Saints John and Paul,* in *Opere Scelte,* 101.

432 *"attacking not only the arteries and veins"*: Hibbert, *The House of the Medici,* 173.

433 *"The illustrious Lorenzo suffers so acutely"*: Ross Williamson, 262.

433 *"follow that course which appears to be most honorable"*: Hook, 186.

433 *"Pico came and sat by the bed"*: Ross, *Lives,* 338.

434 *Thus going to Careggi:* Ibid., 340.

434 *Towards midnight while he was quietly meditating:* Ibid., 337.

435 *To [Savonarola's] exhortations to remain firm in his faith:* Ibid., 338–39.

435 *"Alas! I shall die"*: Landucci, 52. Landucci adds, "This may not have been so, but it was commonly reported."

435 *"To the last he had such mastery over himself"*: Ross, *Lives,* 339.

436 *"This man, in the eyes of the world"*: Landucci, 54.

436 *Whereas the foremost man of all this city:* Ross Williamson, 269.

437 Who from perennial streams shall bring: Ross Williamson, 111–12.

EPILOGUE: THE SPIRIT IN THE RING

PAGE

439 *"It was said when this darkness descended upon Florence"*: Trexler, *Public Life in Renaissance Florence,* 458.

439 *"The peace of Italy"*: Frieda, 16.

439 *"That man's life has been long enough"*: Ross Williamson, 270.

442 *"O most Christian King"*: Schevill, *History of Florence, from the Founding of the City Through the Renaissance,* 444.

443 *"My lords of the Eight"*: Trexler, *Public Life in Renaissance Florence,* 470.

443   *"Here come the boys of Fra Girolamo!"*: Landucci, 121.

443   *"We must . . . conclude"*: Savonarola, *Liberty and Tyranny in the Government of Men*, 47.

446   On the night when Piero Soderini died: Schevill, *Medieval and Renaissance Florence*, 470.

446   *"As God has seen fit to give us the Papacy"*: Ross Williamson, 178.

BIBLIOGRAPHY

ABBREVIATIONS

AB—Art Bulletin
AH—Art History
ASI—Archivio Storico Italiano
HR—History Review
IS—Italian Studies
JWCI—Journal of the Warburg and Courtauld Institutes
MAP—Mediceo Avanti il Principato, Archivio di Stato di Firenze
MKIF—Mitteilungen des Kunsthistorischen Institutes in Florenz
NYT—New York Times
RQ—*Renaissance Quarterly*

ARCHIVES AND DATABASES

Florence, Archivio di Stato di Firenze, Archivi Digitalizzati, Mediceo Avanti il Principato.
Online Catasto of 1427. Version 1.3. Edited by David Herlihy, Christiane Klapisch-Zuber, R. Burr Litchfield, and Anthony Molho. Machine-readable data file based on D. Herlihy and C. Klapisch-Zuber, *Census and Property Survey of Florentine Domains in the Province of Tuscany, 1427–1480*. Florentine Renaissance Resources/STG: Brown University, Providence, Rhode Island, 2002. www.stg.brown.edu/projects/catasto/main.php.
Online Tratte of Office Holders, 1282–1532. Edited by David Herlihy, R. Burr Litchfield, Anthony Molho, and Roberto Barducci.

PRIMARY SOURCES

Alberti, Leon Battista, *The Family in Renaissance Florence*. Trans. René Neu Watkins. Columbia, 1969.
———. *On Painting and On Sculpture. The Latin Texts of De Pictura and De Statua*. Ed. and trans. Cecil Grayson. London, 1972.
———. *On the Art of Building in Ten Books*. Trans. Joseph Rykwert. Cambridge, 1988.
Albertinus, Prior of S. Martino, to Marchioness Barbara of Mantua. An eyewitness account of the Pazzi conspiracy, in Ludwig Freiherr von Pastor, *History of the Popes*. Appendix 58, 514–15. St. Louis, 1898.
Alighieri, Dante. *The Divine Comedy*. 3 vols. Trans. John D. Sinclair. New York, 1939.
Beccadelli, Antonio, called Panormita. *The Hermaphrodite*. Trans. Michael de Cossart. Liverpool, 1984.

Bisticci, Vespesiano da. *Renaissance Princes, Popes, and Prelates: The Vespesiano Memoirs, Lives of Illustrious Men of the XVth Century.* Trans. William George and Emily Waters. New York, 1963.

Boccaccio, Giovanni. *Decameron.* Trans. John Payne. Berkeley, 1982.

———. "The Return of the Muses." In *The Portable Renaissance Reader,* James Bruce Ross, ed. Middlesex, 1953.

Bracciolini, Poggio. "On Avarice." In *The Earthly Republic: Italian Humanists on Government and Society,* trans. Benjamin G. Kohl and Elizabeth B. Welles. Philadelphia, 1978.

———. "On Nobility." In *Humanism and Liberty: Writings on Freedom from Fifteenth-Century Florence,* trans. Renée Neu Watkins. Columbia, 1978.

———. "The Ruins of Rome." In *The Portable Renaissance Reader,* James Bruce Ross, ed. Middlesex, 1953.

Bruni, Leonardo. *History of the Florentine People.* Trans. James Hankins. Cambridge, 2001.

———. *Panegyric to the City of Florence.* In *The Earthly Republic: Italian Humanists on Government and Society,* trans. Benjamin G. Kohl. Philadelphia, 1978.

Castiglione, Baldassare. *The Book of the Courtier.* Trans. George Bull. London, 1967.

Cavalcanti, Giovanni. *Istorie Fiorentine.* Ed. G. Di Pino. Florence, 1838–39.

———. *The "Trattato politico-morale" of Giovanni Cavalcanti (1381–1451).* Ed. Marcella T. Grendler. Geneva, 1973.

Chambers, D. S., ed. and trans. *Patrons and Artists in the Italian Renaissance.* Columbia, 1971.

Chronicles of the Tumult of the Ciompi. Trans. and ed. Rosemary Kantor and Louis Green. Victoria, 1990.

Commines, Philip de. *The Memoirs of Philip de Commines, Lord of Argenton.* Trans. Andrew R. Scoble. London, 1855–56.

Compagni, Dino. *Dino Compagni's Chronicle of Florence.* Trans. Daniel E. Bornstein, Philadelphia, 1986.

Condivi, Ascanio. *The Life of Michelangelo.* Trans. Alice Sedgwick Wohl. Ed. Hellmut Wohl. Baton Rouge, 1976.

Confessione di Francesco Neroni. Reproduced in Nicolai Rubinestein, "La Confessione di Francesco Neroni e la Congiura Antimedicea del 1466," in Archivio Storico Italiano 126, 1968.

Confessione di Giovanbattista da Montesecco, Appendix xv. In William Roscoe, *The Life of Lorenzo de' Medici, Called the Magnificent,* 10th ed. London, 1898.

Consulte della Repubblica Fiorentina, November–December 1465. Reproduced in Guuido Pampaloni, "Fermenti di riforme democratiche nella Firenze medicea del Quattrocento," in *Archivio Storico Italiano* 119 (1961): 242–80.

Dati, Gregorio, and Buonacorso Pitti. *Two Memoirs of Renaissance Florence; the Diaries of Buonacorso Pitti and Gregorio Dati.* Trans. Julia Martines. Ed. Gene Brucker. New York, 1967.

Dei, Benedetto. *La Cronica dall'Anno 1400 all' anno 1500.* Ed. Roberto Barducci. Florence, 1985.

Federico da Montefeltro. "Federico da Montefeltro a Agostino Staccoli e Pietro Felici, Urbino," February 14, 1478. In Marcello Simonetta, "Federico da Montefeltro contro Firenze. Retroscena Inediti della Congiura dei Pazzi," in Archivio Storico Italiano 596, a. CLXI, 2003 II.

Ficino, Marsilio. *Commentary on Plato's Symposium on Love.* Trans. Sears Jayne. Dallas, 1985.

———. *The Letters of Marsilio Ficino.* Trans. members of the Language Department of the School of Economic Science. New York, 1985.

———. "The Soul of Man." In *The Portable Renaissance Reader,* James Bruce Ross ed. Middlesex, 1953.

Filarete (Antonio Averlino). *Treatise on Architecture.* 2 vols. Trans. John R. Spencer. New Haven and London, 1965.

Guicciardini, Francesco. *Dialogue on the Government of Florence.* Trans. Alison Brown. Cambridge, 1994.

———. *The History of Florence.* Trans. Mario Domandi. New York, 1970.

———. *The History of Italy.* Trans. Sidney Alexander. Princeton, 1984.

Guicciardini, Piero. "On the Scrutiny of 1484." In Nicolai Rubinstein, *The Government of Florence Under the Medici,* 2nd ed. Appendix XI. Oxford, 1997.

Landino, Cristoforo. *Disputationes Camaldulenses.* Ed. Peter Lohe. Florence, 1980.

Landucci, Luca. *A Florentine Diary from 1450 to 1516 by Luca Landucci, Continued by an Anonymous Writer till 1542 with Notes by Iodoco del Badia.* Trans. Alice de Rosen Jervis. London, 1927.

Machiavelli, Niccolò. *The Art of War.* Trans. Ellis Farneworth. New York, 1990.

———. *Florentine Histories.* Trans. Laura F. Banfield and Harvey C. Mansfield, Jr. Princeton, 1988.

———. *The Letters of Machiavelli: A Selection.* Trans. Allan Gilbert. Chicago, 1988.

———. *The Prince.* Trans. George Bull. New York, 1981.

Medici, Lorenzo de'. *Commento de Miei Sonetti.* In James Wyatt Cook, *The Autobiography of Lorenzo de' Medici The Magnificent.* Tempe, 2000.

———. *Giacoppo.* Trans. Murtha Baca. In *An Italian Renaissance Sextet,* Lauro Martines ed. New York, 1994.

———. *Lettere.* 7 vols. Ed. Nicolai Rubinstein. Florence, 1977–2004.

———. *Lorenzo de' Medici: Selected Poems and Prose.* Trans. Jon Thiem and others. ed. Jon Thiem. University Park, 1991.

———. *Opere Scelte.* Novara, 1969.

———. *Selected Writings, edited, with an English Translation of the Rappresentazione di San Giovanni e Paolo.* Ed. Corinna Salvadori. Dublin, 1992.

Parenti, Marco. *Lettere.* Ed. Maria Marrese. Florence, 1996.

———. *Ricordi Storici, 1464–1467.* Ed. Manuela Doni Garfagnini. Rome, 2001.

Pico della Mirandola, Giovanni. "On the Dignity of Man." Trans. Charles Glenn Wallis. Indianapolis, 1965.

Pius II. *Memoirs of a Renaissance Pope, the Commentaries of Pius II, an Abridgement.* Trans. Florence A. Gragg. New York, 1962.

Platina, Bartolomeo. "The Restoration of Rome." In *The Portable Renaissance Reader,* James Bruce Ross, ed. Middlesex, 1953.

Poliziano, Angelo. *Letters.* Trans. Shane Butler. Cambridge 2006.

———. "The Pazzi Conspiracy." In *Humanism and Liberty: Writings on Freedom from Fifteenth-Century Florence,* trans. Renée Neu Watkins. Columbia, 1978.

———. *Stanze per la Giostra di Giuliano de' Medici.* In *The Stanze of Angelo Poliziano.* Trans. David Quint, Amherst, 1979.

Pulci, Luigi. *La Giostra di Lorenzo de' Medici.* In *Morgante e Opere Minori.* Ed., Aulo Greco. Torino, 1997.

———. *Lettere di Luigi Pulci a Lorenzo e ad Altri.* Lucca, 1886.

"Report of the Milanese Ambassadors in Florence Regarding the Conspiracy of the Pazzi." In Ludwig Pastor, *The History of the Popes from the Close of the Middle Ages,* Appendix, no. 57. St. Louis, 1898.

Rinuccini, Alemanno. "Dialogue on Liberty." In *Humanism and Liberty: Writings on Freedom from Fifteenth-Century Florence,* trans. Renée Neu Watkins. Columbia, 1978.

———. *Ricordi Storici di Filippo di Cino Rinuccini dal 1282 al 1460 colla Continuazione di Alamanno e Neri, Suoi Figli Fino al 1506.* Florence, 1840.

Ross, Janet, trans. *Lives of the Early Medici, as Told in Their Correspondence.* Boston, 1911.

Savonarola, Girolamo. *Lettere e Scritti Apolegetici.* Ed. Angelo Belardetti. Rome, 1984.

———. *Liberty and Tyranny in the Government of Men.* Trans. C. M. Flumiani. Albuqerque, 1976.

———. *Treatise on the Constitution and the Government of the City of Florence.* In *Humanism and Liberty: Writings on Freedom from Fifteenth-Century Florence.* Trans. Renée Neu Watkins. Columbia, 1978.

Strozzi, Alessandra (Macinghi). *Selected Letters of Alessandra Strozzi.* Trans. Heather Gregory. Berkeley, 1997.

———. *Tempo di Affetti e di Mercanti: Lettere ai Figli Esuli.* Milan, 1987.

Strozzi, Filippo. "Account of the Pazzi Conspiracy." Reproduced in Janet Ross, *Florentine Palaces and Their Stories.* London. 1905, 372–74.

Tornabuoni, Lucrezia (de' Medici). *Sacred Narratives.* Ed. and trans. Jane Tylus. Chicago, 2001.

Valori, Niccolò. *Vita di Lorenzo il Magnifico.* Palermo, 1992.

Vasari, Giorgio. *Lives of the Painters, Sculptors, and Architects.* 2 vols. Trans. Gaston du C. de Vere. New York, 1927.

Villani, Giovanni. *Nuova Cronica.* 3 vols. Ed. Giovanni Porta. Parma, 1991.

SECONDARY SOURCES

Acidini Luchinat, Cristina. *Benozzo Gozzoli.* New York, 1994.

Acidini Luchinat, Cristina, et al. *The Medici, Michelangelo, and the Art of Late Renaissance Florence.* New Haven, 2002.

Acidini Luchinat, Cristina, ed. *The Chapel of the Magi: Benozzo Gozzoli's Frescoes in the Palazzo Medici-Riccardi Florence.* Trans. Eleanor Daunt. London, 1994.

———. *Renaissance Florence: The Age of Lorenzo de' Medici, 1449–1492.* Milan, 1993.

———. *Treasures of Florence: The Medici Collection, 1400–1700.* Trans. Eve Leckey. Munich, 1997.

Ackerman, James S. *The Villa: Form and Ideology of Country Houses.* Princeton, 1990.

Acton, Harold. *The Pazzi Conspiracy: The Plot Against the Medici.* London, 1979.

Ady, Cecilia M. *Lorenzo dei Medici and Renaissance Italy.* London, 1970.

Altomonte, Antonio. *Il Magnifico: Vita di Lorenzo de' Medici.* Milan, 1982.

Armstrong, Edward. *Lorenzo de' Medici and Florence in the Fifteenth Century.* New York, 1896.

Balestracci, Duccio. *The Renaissance in the Fields: Family Memoirs of a Fifteenth-Century Tuscan Peasant.* Trans. Paolo Squatriti. University Park, 1999.

Baron, Hans. *The Crisis of the Early Italian Renaissance: Civic Humanism and Republican Liberty.* Princeton, 1955.

Battera, Francesca. "Le *Pistole* di Luca Pulci e la Formazione Culturale del Giovane Lorenzo." In *Lorenzo the Magnificent: Culture and Politics,* Michael Mallet and Nicholas Mann, eds. London, 1996, 177–90.

Baxandall, Michael. *Painting and Experience in Fifteenth-Century Italy.* Oxford, 1972.

Beck, James. "Lorenzo il Magnifico and His Cultural Possessions." In *Lorenzo de Medici: New Perspectives,* Bernard Toscani, ed. New York, 1992, 131–43.

Bessi, Rossella. "Lo Spettacolo e la Scrittura." In *Le Tems Revient, 'L Tempo si Rinuova: Feste e Spettacoli nella Firenze di Lorenzo il Magnifico,* Paola Ventrone, ed. Florence, 1992.

Beyer, Andreas, and Bruce Boucher, eds. *Piero de' Medici, "il Gottoso" (1416–1469).* Berlin, 1993.

Black, Robert. "Lorenzo and Arezzo." In *Lorenzo the Magnificent Culture and Politics,* Michael Mallet and Nicholas Mann, eds. London, 1996, 217–34.

Bottari, Stefano. *The Cathedral of Florence.* Florence, 1965.

Branca, Vittore. "Il Periodo Conclusivo dei Rapporti Fra Lorenzo e Poliziano." In *Lorenzo de Medici: New Perspectives,* Bernard Toscani, ed. New York, 1992, 49–61.

Breisach, Ernst. *Caterina Sforza: A Renaissance Virago.* Chicago, 1967.

Brown, Alison. *Bartolomeo Scala, 1430–1497, Chancellor of Florence: The Humanist as Bureaucrat.* Princeton, 1979.

———. "Lorenzo and Guicciardini." In *Lorenzo the Magnificent Culture and Politics,* Michael Mallet and Nicholas Mann, eds. London, 1996, 281–96.

———. "Piero's Infirmity and Political Power." In *Piero de' Medici, "il Gottoso" (1416–1469),* Andreas Beyer and Bruce Boucher, eds. Berlin, 1993.

Brown, David Alan. *Leonardo da Vinci: Origins of a Genius.* New Haven, 1998.

Brucker, Gene. "The Ciompi Revolution." In *Florentine Studies: Politics and Society in Renaissance Florence,* Nicolai Rubinstein, ed. Evanston, 1968, 314–57.

———. *The Civic World of Renaissance Florence.* Princeton, 1977.

———. *Florence: The Golden Age, 1138–1737.* Berkeley, 1998.

———. "The Florentine *Popolo Minuto* and Its Political Role, 1340–1450." In *Violence and Civil Disorders in Italian Cities, 1200–1500,* Lauro Martines, ed. Los Angeles, 1972.

———. *Giovanni and Lusanna: Love and Marriage in Renaissance Florence.* Berkeley and Los Angeles, 1986.

———. *Renaissance Florence.* New York, 1969.

Brucker, Gene, ed. *The Society of Renaissance Florence: A Documentary Study.* New York, 1971.

Bullard, Melissa. "The Language of Diplomacy in the Renaissance." In *Lorenzo de Medici: New Perspectives,* Bernard Toscani, ed. New York, 1992, 263–79.

———. "Lorenzo and Patterns of Diplomatic Discourse in the Late Fifteenth Century." In *Lorenzo the Magnificent: Culture and Politics,* Michael Mallet and Nicholas Mann, eds. London, 1996, 263–74.

————. *Lorenzo il Magnifico: Image and Anxiety, Politics and Finance.* Florence, 1994.

Burckhardt, Jacob. *The Civilization of the Renaissance in Italy.* 2 vols. Trans. S. G. C. Middlemore. New York, 1958.

Burke, Jill. *Changing Patrons: Social Identity and the Visual Arts in Renaissance Florence.* University Park, 2004.

Butters, Humfrey. "Lorenzo and Machiavelli." In *Lorenzo the Magnificent: Culture and Politics,* Michael Mallet and Nicholas Mann, eds. London, 1996, 275–80.

Cardini, Franco. "Le insegne Laurenziane." In *Le Tems Revient, 'L Tempo si Rinuova: Feste e Spettacoli nella Firenze di Lorenzo il Magnifico,* Paola Ventrone, ed. Florence, 1992.

Carrai, Stefano. "Lorenzo e l'umanesimo volgare dei fratelli Pulci." In *Lorenzo de Medici: New Perspectives,* Bernard Toscani, ed. New York, 1992, 1–23.

Castagnola, Raffaella. "Lorenzo Classico: Considerazioni sulle 'Stanze.'" In *Lorenzo de Medici: New Perspectives,* Bernard Toscani, ed. New York, 1992, 61–85.

Chamberlin, E. R. *Everyday Life in Renaissance Times.* London, 1966.

————. *The World of the Italian Renaissance.* London, 1982.

Chambers, D. S. *Patrons and Artists in the Italian Renaissance.* Columbia, 1971.

————. "Spas in the Italian Renaissance" in Mario di Cesare, *Reconsidering the Renaissance,* Binghamton, 1992.

Cheetham, Sir Nicolas. *Keepers of the Keys: A History of Popes from St. Peter to John Paul II.* New York, 1983.

Cheney, Liana. *Botticelli's Neoplatonic Images: Quattrocento Neoplatonism and Medici Humanism in Botticelli's Mythological Paintings.* Lanham, 1985.

Clark, Kenneth. "The Young Michelangelo." In *The Penguin Book of the Renaissance.* Middlesex, 1961, 99–118.

Clarke, Paula C. "A Sienese Note on 1466." In *Florence and Italy: Renaissance Studies in Honor of Nicolai Rubinstein,* Peter Denley and Caroline Elam, eds. London, 1988.

————. *The Soderini and the Medici: Power and Patronage in Fifteenth Century Florence.* Oxford, 1991.

Cloulas, Ivan. *Lorenzo il Magnifico.* Trans. Cesare Scarton. Rome, 1986.

Cook, James Wyatt. *Autobiography of Lorenzo de Medici: A Commentary on My Sonnets Together with the Text of "Il commento" in the Critical Edition of Tiziano Zanato.* Binghamton, 1995.

Courtney, Louise. *The Trumpet of the Truth: An Analysis of Benedetto Dei's Cronica.* Victoria, 1986.

Crabb, Ann Morton. *The Strozzi of Florence: Widowhood and Family Solidarity.* Ann Arbor, 2000.

Davie, Mark. *Half-Serious Rhymes: The Narrative Poetry of Luigi Pulci.* Dublin, 1998.

————. "Luigi Pulci's 'Stanze per la Giostra di Lorenzo de' Medici.'" *IS* 44 (1989): 41–58.

Davies, John Kenyon. *Democracy and Classical Greece.* Cambridge, 1993.

Davies, Norman. *Europe: A History.* New York, 1996.

Deimling, Barbara. *Botticelli.* Cologne, 2000.

Dempsey, Charles. "Portraits and Mask in the Art of Lorenzo de' Medici, Botticelli, and Politian's 'Stanze Per La Giostra.'" *RQ* 52 (Spring 1999).

Denley, Peter, and Caroline Elam, eds. *Florence and Italy: Renaissance Studies in Honor of Nicolai Rubinstein.* London, 1988.

de Roover, Raymond. *The Rise and Decline of the Medici Bank, 1397–1494.* Washington, 1963.

Donne, Giovanni Delle. *Lorenzo il Magnifico e il Suo Tempo.* Rome, 2003.

Draper, James David. *Bertoldo di Giovanni, Sculptor of the Medici Household.* Columbia, 1992.

Eisenbichler, Konrad, and Olga Zorzi Pugliese, eds. *Ficino and Renaissance Neoplatonism.* Ottowa, 1986.

Elam, Caroline. "Lorenzo de' Medici and the Urban Development of Renaissance Florence." *AH* I,1 (March 1978).

———. "Lorenzo de' Medici's Sculpture Garden." *MKIF* 36 (1992): 41–84

Field, Arthur. *The Origins of the Platonic Academy of Florence.* Princeton, 1988.

Findlen, Paula, ed. *The Italian Renaissance.* Malden, 2002.

Foster, Philip Ellis. *A Study of Lorenzo de' Medici's Villa at Poggio a Caiano.* New York, 1979.

Frick, Carole Collier. *Dressing Renaissance Florence: Families, Fortunes and Fine Clothing.* Baltimore, 2002.

Frieda, Leonie. *Catherine de Medici: Renaissance Queen of France.* New York, 2003.

Fryde, E. B. "Lorenzo's Greek Manuscripts, and in Particular His Own Commissions." In *Lorenzo the Magnificent: Culture and Politics,* Michael Mallet and Nicholas Mann, eds. London, 1996, 93–104.

Fubini, Riccardo. "La Congiura dei Pazzi: Radici Politico-Sociali e Ragioni di un Fallimento." In *Lorenzo de Medici: New Perspectives,* Bernard Toscani, ed. New York, 1992, 219–49.

———. "Ficino e i Medici all'Avvento di Lorenzo Il Magnifico." *Rinascimento* 24, (1984): 3–51.

Gage, John. *Life in Italy at the Time of the Medici.* New York, 1970.

Ganz, Margery A. "Donato Acciaiuoli and the Medici: A Strategy for Survival in 1400 Florence." *Rinascimento* 2nd ser., 22 (1982): 33–73.

Gentile, Sebastiano. "Ficino e il Platonismo di Lorenzo." In *Lorenzo de Medici: New Perspectives,* Bernard Toscani, ed. New York, 1992, 23–49.

Gilbert, Felix. *Machiavelli and Guicciardini: Politics and History in Sixteenth-Century Florence.* New York, 1984.

———. "The Venetian Constitution in Florentine Political Thought." In *Florentine Studies: Politics and Society in Renaissance Florence,* N. Rubinstein, ed. London, 1968, 463–500.

Goldthwaite, Richard A. *The Building of Renaissance Florence: An Economic and Social History.* Baltimore, 1980.

———. *Private Wealth in Renaissance Florence: A Study of 4 Families.* Princeton, 1968.

Gombrich, E. H. "The Early Medici as Patrons of Art." In *Norm and Form: Studies in the Art of the Renaissance, 1.* London and New York, 1966.

———. "The Renaissance Conception of Artistic Progress." In *Norm and Form: Studies in the Art of the Renaissance, 1.* London and New York, 1966.

Grafton, Anthony. *Leon Battista Alberti: Master Builder of the Italian Renaissance.* New York, 2000.

Hale, John R. *Florence and the Medici: The Pattern of Control.* London, 1977.

———. "Violence in the Late Middle Ages: A Background." In *Violence and Civil Disorders in Italian Cities, 1200–1500,* Lauro Martines, ed. Los Angeles, 1972.

Hankins, James. "Lorenzo de' Medici as a Patron of Philosophy." *Rinascimento* 2nd ser., 34 (1994): 15–53.

———. "The Myth of the Platonic Academy. *RQ* 44 (Autumn, 1991): 429–75.

Hatfield, Rab. "The Compagnia de' Magi." *JWCI* 33 (1970): 107–61.

———. "Some Unknown Descriptions of the Medici Palace in 1459." *AB* 52 (1970).

Herlihy, David. "Some Psychological and Social Roots of Violence in the Tuscan Cities." In *Violence and Civil Disorders in Italian Cities, 1200–1500,* Lauro Martines, ed. Los Angeles, 1972.

Hibbert, Christopher. *Florence: The Biography of a City.* New York, 1993.

———. *The House of the Medici: Its Rise and Fall.* New York, 1975.

———. *The Popes.* Chicago, 1982.

Hole, Robert. "Lorenzo and Giuliano, Citizens of Florence." *HR* (March 1999).

Holmes, George. *Florence, Rome and the Origins of the Renaissance.* Oxford, 1986.

———. *The Florentine Enlightenment, 1400–1450.* London, 1969.

———. "How the Medici Became the Pope's Bankers." In *Florentine Studies: Politics and Society in Renaissance Florence,* N. Rubinstein, ed. London, 1968, 357–80.

Holmes, George ed. *Art and Politics in Renaissance Italy.* Oxford, 1993.

Hook, Judith. *Lorenzo de' Medici: An Historical Biography.* London, 1984.

Ilardi, Vincent. "The Assassination of Galeazzo Maria Sforza and the Reaction of Italian Diplomancy." In *Violence and Civil Disorders in Italian Cities, 1200–1500,* Lauro Martines, ed. Los Angeles, 1972.

Jayne, Emily. "A Choreography by Lorenzo in Botticelli's Primavera." In *Lorenzo de Medici: New Perspectives,* Bernard Toscani, ed. New York, 1992, 163–79.

Jurdjevig, Mark. "Civic Humanism and the Rise of the Medici." *RQ* 52 (Winter 1999): 494–517.

Kent, Dale. *Cosimo de' Medici and the Florentine Renaissance: The Patron's Oeuvre.* New Haven, 2000.

———. "The Florentine *Reggimento* in the Fifteenth Century." *RQ* 28 (1975): 575–638.

———. *The Rise of the Medici Faction in Florence, 1426–1434.* Oxford, 1978.

Kent, D. V., and F. W. Kent. *Neighbours and Neighbourhood in Renaissance Florence: The District of the Red Lion in the Fifteenth Century.* Locust Valley, 1982.

———. "Two Vignettes of Florentine Society in the Fifteenth Century." *Rinascimento* 23 (1983): 237–60.

Kent, F. W. "Gardens, Villas and Social Life in Renaissance Florence." In *Renaissance Gardens—Italy.* Victoria, 2001.

———. *Household and Lineage in Renaissance Florence: The Family Life of the Capponi, Ginori, and Rucellai.* Princeton, 1977.

———. "Lorenzo de' Medici's Acquisition of Poggio a Caiano in 1474 and an Early Reference to His Architectural Expertise." *JWCI* (1979): 250–57.

———. *Lorenzo de' Medici and the Art of Magnificence.* Baltimore, 2004.

———. "Patron-Client Networks in Renaissance Florence and the Emergence of Lorenzo as 'Maestro della Bottega.'" In *Lorenzo de' Medici: New Perspectives,* Bernard Toscani, ed. New York, 1994, 279–314.

———. "The Young Lorenzo, 1449–1469." In *Lorenzo the Magnificent: Culture and Politics,* Michael Mallet and Nicholas Mann, eds. London, 1996, 1–22.

King, Ross. *Machiavelli.* New York, 2007.

Kohl, Benjamin, and Ronald Witt, ed. and trans. *The Earthly Republic: Italian Humanists on Government and Society.* Philadelphia, 1978.

Kraye, Jill. "Lorenzo and the Philosophers." In *Lorenzo the Magnificent Culture and Politics,* Michael Mallet and Nicholas Mann, eds. London, 1996, 151–66.

Kristeller, Paul. *Eight Renaissance Philosophers.* Stanford, 1964.

———. *The Philosophy of Marsilio Ficino.* Trans. Virginia Conant. New York, 1943.

———. *Renaissance Thought and Its Sources.* New York, 1979.

Lang, Jack. *Il Magnifico: Vita di Lorenzo de' Medici.* Trans. Alessandra Benabbi. Milan, 2002.

Larner, John. "Order and Disorder in Romagna, 1450–1500." In *Violence and Civil Disorders in Italian Cities, 1200–1500,* ed. Lauro Martines. Los Angeles, 1972.

Lee, Felicia R. "1478 Assassination Solved. The Humanist Did It." *NYT,* March 6, 2004.

Levey, Michael. *Florence, A Portrait.* Cambridge, 1996.

Lightbown, Ronald. *Sandro Botticelli: Life and Work.* New York, 1989.

Lowe, Katherine J. P. "A Matter of Piety or of Family Tradition and Custom," in *Piero de' Medici, "Il Gotloso" (1416–1469).* Berlin, 1993.

Lubkin, Gregory. *A Renaissance Court: Milan Under Galeazzo Maria Sforza.* Berkeley, 1994.

Lucas-Dubreton, J. *Daily Life in Florence in the Time of the Medici.* Trans. Lytton Sells. New York, 1961.

Maguire, Yvonne. *The Women of the Medici.* London, 1927.

Mallett, Michael. "Diplomacy and War in Later Fifteenth-Century Italy." In *Art and Politics in Renaissance Italy.* Oxford, 1993.

———. "Horse-Racing and Politics in Lorenzo's Florence." In *Lorenzo the Magnificent: Culture and Politics,* Michael Mallet and Nicholas Mann, eds. London, 1996, 253–62.

———. "Lorenzo de' Medici and the War of Ferrara." In *Lorenzo de Medici: New Perspectives,* Bernard Toscani, ed. New York, 1992, 249–63.

———. "Pisa and Florence in the Fifteenth Century: Aspects of the Period of the First Florentine Domination." In *Florentine Studies: Politics and Society in Renaissance Florence,* Nicolai Rubinstein, ed. Evanston, 1968, 403–42.

Mallett, Michael, and Nicholas Mann, eds. *Lorenzo the Magnificent: Culture and Politics.* London, 1996.

Manchester, William. *A World Lit Only by Fire: The Medieval Mind and the Renaissance: Portrait of an Age.* Boston, 1992.

Martelli, Mario. "La Cultura Letteraria nell età di Lorenzo." *In Lorenzo the Magnificent: Culture and Politics,* Michael Mallet and Nicholas Mann, eds. London, 1996, 167–76.

———. "Il 'Giacoppo' di Lorenzo." *Interpres* 7 (1987): 103–24.

Martines, Lauro. *April Blood: Florence and the Plot Against the Medici.* Oxford, 2003.

———. *Fire in the City: Savonarola and the Struggle for the Soul of Renaissance Florence.* Oxford, 2006.

———. *An Italian Renaissance Sextet: Six Tales in Historical Context.* Trans. Murtha Baca. Toronto, 2004.

———. *Power and Imagination; City-States in Renaissance Italy.* Baltimore, 1988.

———. *The Social World of the Florentine Humanists, 1390–1460.* Princeton, 1963.

————. *Strong Words: Writing and Social Strain in the Italian Renaissance.* Baltimore, 2001.

Martines, Lauro, ed. *Violence and Civil Disorders in Italian Cities, 1200–1500.* Berkeley, 1972.

Mattingly, Garrett. *Renaissance Diplomacy.* New York, 1970.

Milner, Stephen. "Lorenzo and Pistoia: Peacemaker or Partisan?" In *Lorenzo the Magnificent: Culture and Politics,* Michael Mallet and Nicholas Mann, eds. London, 1996, 235–52.

Newbigin, Nerida. "Politics in the *Sacre Rappresentazioni* of Lorenzo's Florence." In *Lorenzo the Magnificent: Culture and Politics,* Michael Mallet and Nicholas Mann, eds. London, 1996, 117–30.

Pacciani, Riccardo. "Immagini, Arti e Architetture nelle Feste di età Laurenziana." In *Le Tems Revient, 'L Tempo si Rinuova: Feste e Spettacoli nella Firenze di Lorenzo il Magnifico,* Paola Ventrone, ed. Florence, 1992.

Palmarocchi, Roberto. "Lorenzo de' Medici e la Nomina Cardinalizia di Giovanni." *ASI* 398, (1952): 38ff.

Pampaloni, G. "Fermenti di Riforme Democratiche nella Firenze Medicea del Quattrocento." *ASI* 119 (1961): 11ff.

Parks, Tim. *Medici Money: Banking, Metaphysics, and Art in Fifteenth-Century Florence.* New York, 2005.

Partner, Peter. "Florence and the Papacy in the Earlier Fifteenth Century." In *Florentine Studies: Politics and Society in Renaissance Florence,* Nicolai Rubinstein, ed. Evanston, 1968, 381–403.

————. *Renaissance Rome: 1500–1559*

Pastor, Ludwig. *The History of the Popes from the Close of the Middle Ages.* St. Louis, 1898.

Pastori, Paolo. "La 'Leggenda Laurenziana.' Momenti di un Mito Politico fra XVI e XIX Secolo." In *Lorenzo dopo Lorenzo: La Fortuna Storica di Lorenzo il Magnifico,* Paola Pirolo, ed. Florence, 1992.

Pernis, Maria Grazia. "The Young Michelangelo and Lorenzo de' Medici's Circle." In *Lorenzo de Medici: New Perspectives.* Bernard Toscani, ed. New York, 1992, 143–63.

Pernis, Maria Grazia, and Laurie Schneider Adams. *Federico da Montefeltro and Sigismonod Malatesta: The Eagle and the Elephant.* New York, 2003.

Phillips, Mark. *The Memoir of Marco Parenti: A Life in Medici Florence.* Princeton, 1987.

Pirolo, Paola. "Su Alcuni Aspetti della Formazione della Legenda Medicea: Da Cosimo a Lorenzo." In *Lorenzo dopo Lorenzo: La Fortuna Storica di Lorenzo il Magnifico,* Paola Pirolo, ed. Florence, 1992.

Pirolo, Paola, ed. *Lorenzo dopo Lorenzo: La Fortuna Storica di Lorenzo il Magnifico.* Florence, 1992.

Plebani, Eleonora. *Lorenzo e Giuliano de' Medici: Tra Potere e Legame di Sangue.* Rome, 1993.

Plumb, J. H. "Milan: City of Strife." In *The Penguin Book of the Renaissance.* Middlesex, 1961, 155–69.

————. "Rome: Splendour and the Papacy." In *The Penguin Book of the Renaissance.* Middlesex, 1961, 189–208.

Plumb, J. H., ed. *The Penguin Book of the Renaissance.* Middlesex, 1961.

Polizzotto, Lorenzo. "Lorenzo il Magnifico, Savonarola and Medicean Dynasticism." In *Lorenzo de Medici: New Perspectives,* Bernard Toscani, ed. New York, 1992, 331–55.

Rendina, Claudio. *The Popes: Histories and Secrets.* Trans. Paul D. McCusker. Santa Ana, 2002.

Reumont, Alfred von. *Lorenzo de' Medici the Magnificent.* 2 vols. Trans. Robert Harrison. London, 1876.

Rochon, Andre. *La Jeunesse de Laurent de Medicis (1449–1478).* Paris, 1963.

Rocke, Michael. *Forbidden Friendships: Homosexuality and Male Culture in Renaissance Florence.* New York, 1996.

Roeder, Ralph. "Lorenzo de' Medici." In *The Penguin Book of the Renaissance.* Middlesex, 1961.

———. *The Man of the Renaissance. Four Lawgivers: Savonarola, Machiavelli, Castiglione, Aretino.* New York, 1933.

Roscoe, William. *The Life and Pontificate of Leo X.* 2 vols. London, 1893.

———. *The Life of Lorenzo de Medici, Called the Magnificent.* London, 1889.

Ross, James, and Mary Martin McLaughlin. *The Portable Renaissance Reader.* New York, 1953.

Ross, Janet. *Florentine Palaces and Their Stories.* London, 1905.

———. *Lives of the Early Medici.* Boston, 1911. London, 1910.

Ross Williamson, Hugh. *Lorenzo the Magnificent.* New York, 1974.

Rubin, Patricia Lee, and Alison Wright. *Renaissance Florence: The Art of the 1470s.* London, 1999.

Rubinstein, Nicolai. "La Confessione di Francesco Neroni e la Congiura Anti-Medicea del 1466." *ASI* 126 (1968): 373ff.

———. "Florentine Constitutionalism and Medici Ascendancy in the Fifteenth Century." In *Florentine Studies: Politics and Society in Renaissance Florence,* Nicolai Rubinstein, ed. Evanston, 1968, 442–63.

———. *The Government of Florence Under the Medici.* Oxford, 1997.

———. "Lorenzo's Image in Europe." In *Lorenzo the Magnificent: Culture and Politics,* Michael Mallet and Nicholas Mann, eds. London, 1996, 297–312.

———. *The Palazzo Vecchio, 1298–1532: Government, Architecture, and Imagery in the Civic Palace of the Florentine Republic.* Oxford, 1995.

Rubinstein, Nicolai, et al. *The Age of the Renainssance.* London, 1967.

Rubinstein, Nicolai, ed. *Florentine Studies: Politics and Society in Renaissance Florence.* Evanston, 1968.

Ruggiers, Paul G. *Florence in the Age of Dante.* Norman, 1964.

Scalini, Mario. "Il 'Ludus' Equestre nell'età Laurenziana." In *Le Tems Revient, 'L Tempo si Rinuova: Feste e Spettacoli nella Firenze di Lorenzo il Magnifico,* Paola Ventrone, ed. Florence, 1992.

Schevill, Ferdinand. *History of Florence, from the Founding of the City Through the Renaissance.* New York, 1961.

———. *The Medici.* New York, 1949.

Simonetta, Marcello. "Federico da Montefeltro Contro Firenze: Retroscena Inediti della Congiura dei Pazzi." *ASI* 596 (2003): 261ff.

Smith, Dennis Mack. "Federigo da Montefeltro." In *The Penguin Book of the Renaissance.* Middlesex, 1961, 279–94.

Soranzo, Giovanni. "Lorenzo il Magnifico alla Morte del Padre e il Suo Promo Balzo Verso la *Signoria.*" *ASI* 400 (1953): 42ff.

Toscani, Bernard. "Lorenzo, the Religious Poet." In *Lorenzo de Medici: New Perspectives,* Bernard Toscani, ed. New York, 1992, 85–107.

Toscani, Bernard, ed. *Lorenzo de Medici: New Perspectives.* New York, 1992.

Trachtenberg, Marvin. "Found the Palazzo Vecchio in 1299: The Corso Donati Paradox." *RQ* 52, (1999): 967ff.

Trexler, Richard. "Lorenzo de' Medici and Savonarola: Martyrs for Florence." *RQ* 31 (1978): 293–308.

———. *Public Life in Renaissance Florence.* Ithaca, 1991.

Van Passen, Pierre. *A Crown of Fire: The Life and Times of Girolamo Savonarola.* London, 1961.

Ventrone, Paola. "Feste e Spetacoli nella Firenze di Lorenzo il Magnifico." In *Le Tems Revient, 'L Tempo si Rinuova: Feste e Spettacoli nella Firenze di Lorenzo il Magnifico.* Florence, 1992.

———. "Lorenzo's *Politica festiva.*" In *Lorenzo the Magnificent Culture and Politics,* Michael Mallet and Nicholas Mann, eds. London, 1996, 105–16.

Ventrone, Paola, ed. *Le Tems Revient, 'L Tempo si Rinuova: Feste e Spettacoli nella Firenze di Lorenzo il Magnifico.* Florence, 1992.

Villari, Pasquale. *The Life and Times of Girolamo Savonarola.* 2 vols. Trans. Linda Villari. London, 1888.

———. *The Life and Times of Niccolò Machiavelli.* 2 vols. Trans Linda Villari. London, 1898.

Viroli, Maurizio. *Niccolò's Smile: A Biography of Machiavelli.* Trans. Antony Shugaar. New York, 2000.

Viti, Paolo. "Il Mito di Lorenzo nell'umanesimo fiorentino." In *Lorenzo dopo Lorenzo: La Fortuna Storica di Lorenzo il Magnifico,* Paola Pirolo, ed. Florence, 1992.

Waley, Daniel Philip. *The Italian City-Republics.* New York, 1969.

Watkins, Renée Neu, ed. *Humanism and Liberty: Writings on Freedom from Fifteenth Century Florence.* Columbia, 1978.

Weinstein, Donald. "The Myth of Florence." In *Florentine Studies: Politics and Society in Renaissance Florence,* Nicolai Rubinstein, ed. Evanston, 1968.

Weissman, Ronald F. E. "Lorenzo de' Medici and the Confraternity of San Paolo." In *Lorenzo de Medici: New Perspectives,* Bernard Toscani, ed. New York, 1992, 315–31.

Wright, Alison. "A Portrait for the Visit of Galeazzo Maria Sforza to Florence in 1471." In *Lorenzo the Magnificent: Culture and Politics,* Michael Mallet and Nicholas Mann, eds. London, 1996, 65–92.

Young, G. F. *The Medici.* New York, 1933.

INDEX

Page numbers in *italics* refer to illustrations.